Strategic
Management

FIFTH EDITION

Strategic Management

Frank T. Rothaermel

Georgia Institute of Technology

STRATEGIC MANAGEMENT

1 2 3 4 5 6 7 8 9 LWI 24 23 22 21 20

ISBN 978-1-260-57123-3
MHID 1-260-57123-8

Cover Image: (Earth): *skegbydave/Getty Images;* (Spheres): *Ilin Sergey/Shutterstock*

mheducation.com/highered

DEDICATION

To my eternal family for their love, support, and sacrifice: Kelleyn, Harris, Winston, Roman, Adelaide, Avery, and Ivy.

—Frank T. Rothaermel

CONTENTS IN BRIEF

MINI**CASES** & FULL-LENGTH **CASES**

MINI**CASES** /

FULL-LENGTH **CASES** /

The twelve cases included in Connect are noted below. All cases are available through McGraw-Hill Create: www.mcgrawhillcreate.com/rothaermel

* NEW TO FIFTH EDITION, >> REVISED AND UPDATED FOR THE FIFTH EDITION, + THIRD-PARTY CASE

CHAPTERCASES & STRATEGY HIGHLIGHTS

CONTENTS

ABOUT THE AUTHOR

Frank T. Rothaermel
Georgia Institute of Technology

Frank T. Rothaermel, PhD, a Professor of Strategy & Innovation, holds the Russell and Nancy McDonough Chair in the Scheller College of Business at the Georgia Institute of Technology (GT) and is an Alfred P. Sloan Industry Studies Fellow. He received a National Science Foundation (NSF) CAREER award, which "offers the National Science Foundation's most prestigious awards in support of ... those teacher-scholars who most effectively integrate research and education" (NSF CAREER Award description).

©Kelleyn Rothaermel

Frank's research interests lie in the areas of strategy, innovation, and entrepreneurship. Frank has published over 35 articles in leading academic journals such as the *Strategic Management Journal, Organization Science, Academy of Management Journal, Academy of Management Review,* and elsewhere. Based on having published papers in the top 1 percent based on citations, *Thomson Reuters* identified Frank as one of the "world's most influential scientific minds." He is listed among the top-100 scholars based on impact over more than a decade in both economics and business. *Bloomberg Businessweek* named Frank one of Georgia Tech's Prominent Faculty in its national survey of business schools. The Kauffman Foundation views Frank as one of the world's 75 thought leaders in entrepreneurship and innovation.

Frank has received several recognitions for his research, including the Sloan Industry Studies Best Paper Award, the Academy of Management Newman Award, the Strategic Management Society Conference Best Paper Prize, the DRUID Conference Best Paper Award, the Israel Strategy Conference Best Paper Prize, and he is the inaugural recipient of the Byars Faculty Excellence Award. Frank currently serves or has served on the editorial boards of the *Strategic Management Journal, Organization Science, Academy of Management Journal, Academy of Management Review,* and *Strategic Organization.*

Frank regularly translates his research findings for wider audiences in articles in the *MIT Sloan Management Review, The Wall Street Journal, Forbes,* and elsewhere. To inform his research Frank has conducted extensive fieldwork and executive training with leading corporations such as Amgen, Daimler, Eli Lilly, Equifax, GE Energy, GE Healthcare, Hyundai Heavy Industries (South Korea), Kimberly-Clark, Microsoft, McKesson, NCR, Turner (TBS), UPS, among others.

Frank has a wide range of executive education experience, including teaching in programs at GE Management Development Institute (Crotonville, New York), Georgia Institute of Technology, Georgetown University, ICN Business School (France), Politecnico di Milano (Italy), St. Gallen University (Switzerland), and the University of Washington. He received numerous teaching awards for excellence in the classroom including the GT-wide Georgia Power Professor of Excellence award.

When launched in 2012, Frank's *Strategic Management* text received the McGraw-Hill 1st Edition of the Year Award in Business & Economics. In 2018, the 4th edition of the text received McGraw-Hill's Product of the Year Award in Business & Economics. Frank's *Strategic Management* text has been translated into Greek, Korean, Mandarin, and Spanish. Sixteen of his case studies are Most Popular among the cases distributed by Harvard Business Publishing.

Frank held visiting professorships at EBS University of Business and Law (Germany), Singapore Management University (Tommie Goh Professorship), and the University of St. Gallen (Switzerland). He is a member of the American Economic Association, Academy of Management, and the Strategic Management Society.

Frank holds a PhD degree in strategic management from the University of Washington; an MBA from the Marriott School of Management at Brigham Young University; and is Diplom-Volkswirt (M.Sc. equivalent) in economics from the University of Duisburg-Essen, Germany. Frank completed training in the case teaching method at the Harvard Business School.

PREFACE

The market for strategy texts can be broadly separated into two overarching categories: traditional application-based and research-based. Traditional application-based strategy books represent the first-generation texts with first editions published in the 1980s. The research-based strategy books represent the second-generation texts with first editions published in the 1990s. I wrote this text to address a needed new category—a third generation of strategy content that *combines* into one the student-accessible, application-oriented frameworks of the first-generation texts with the research-based frameworks of the second-generation texts. The market response to this unique approach to teaching and studying strategy continues to be overwhelmingly enthusiastic.

To facilitate an enjoyable and refreshing reading experience that enhances student learning and retention, I *synthesize* and *integrate* strategy frameworks, empirical research, and practical applications with current real-world examples. This approach and emphasis on real-world examples offers students a learning experience that uniquely combines rigor and relevance. As John Media of the University of Washington's School of Medicine and life-long researcher on how the mind organizes information explains:

> How does one communicate meaning in such a fashion that learning is improved? A simple trick involves the liberal use of relevant real-world examples, thus peppering main learning points with meaningful experiences. . . . Numerous studies show this works. . . . The greater the number of examples . . . the more likely the students were to remember the information. It's best to use real-world situations familiar to the learner. . . . Examples work because they take advantage of the brain's natural predilection for pattern matching. Information is more readily processed if it can be immediately associated with information already present in the brain. We compare the two inputs, looking for similarities and differences as we encode the new information. Providing examples is the cognitive equivalent of adding more handles to the door. [The more handles one creates at the moment of learning, the more likely the information can be accessed at a later date.] Providing examples makes the information more elaborative, more complex, better encoded, and therefore better learned.*

Strategic Management brings conceptual frameworks to life via examples that cover products and services from companies with which students are familiar, such as Facebook, Amazon, Google, Tesla, Starbucks, Apple, McDonald's, Nike, Disney, Airbnb, and Uber. Liberal use of such examples aids in making strategy relevant to students' lives and helps them internalize strategy concepts and frameworks. Integrating current examples with modern strategy thinking, I prepare students with the foundation they need to understand how companies gain and sustain competitive advantage. I also develop students' skills to become successful leaders capable of making well-reasoned strategic decisions in a turbulent 21st century.

I'm pleased to introduce the new 5th edition of *Strategic Management*. My distinctive approach to teaching strategy not only offers students a unique learning experience that combines theory and practice, but also provides tight linkages between concepts and cases. In this new 5th edition, I build upon the unique strengths of this product, and continue to add improvements based upon hundreds of insightful reviews and important feedback from professors, students, and working professionals. The hallmark features of this text continue to be:

- *Student engagement* via practical and relevant application of strategy concepts using a holistic **Analysis, Formulation, and Implementation (AFI) Strategy Framework**.

- *Synthesis and integration* of empirical research and practical applications combined with relevant strategy material to focus on "*What is important?*" for the student and "*Why is it important?*"

*Medina, J. (2014), *Brain Rules: 12 Principles for Surviving and Thriving at Work, Home, and School.* (Seattle: Pear Press), 139–140.

- *Strong emphasis on diversity and inclusion* by featuring a wide range of strategic leaders from different backgrounds and fields, not just in business, but also in entertainment, professional sports, and so forth.
- *Coverage of a wide array of organizations,* including for-profit public (Fortune 100) companies, private firms (including startups), as well as nonprofit organizations. All of them need a good strategy!
- *Global perspective,* with a focus on competing around the world, featuring many leading companies from Asia, Europe, and Latin America, as well as North America. I was fortunate to study, live, and work across the globe, and I attempt to bring this cosmopolitan perspective to bear in this text.
- *Direct personal applications* of strategy concepts to careers and lives to help internalize the content (including the popular **myStrategy** modules at the end of each chapter).
- *Industry-leading digital delivery option* (Create), *adaptive learning system* (SmartBook), and *online assignment and assessment system* (Connect).
- Standalone module on **How to Conduct a Case Analysis**.
- *High-quality* **Cases,** well integrated with text chapters and standardized, *high-quality and detailed teaching notes;* there are three types of cases that come with this text:
  - **12 ChapterCases** begin and end each chapter, framing the chapter topic and content.
  - **12 MiniCases** in Part 4 of the book, with one MiniCase tailored specifically to each chapter with accompanying discussion questions. All of the cases are based on original research, provide dynamic opportunities for students to apply strategy concepts by assigning them in conjunction with specific chapters, and can be used in a variety of ways (as individual assignments, group work, and in class).
  - **22 full-length Cases,** authored or co-authored by Frank T. Rothaermel specifically to accompany this text; 12 of these cases are included complimentary in **5e Connect.**

I have taken great pride in authoring all the case materials that accompany this text. This additional touch is a differentiating feature from other offerings on the market and allows for strict quality control and seamless integration with chapter content. All case materials come with sets of questions to stimulate class discussion and provide guidance for written assignments. High-quality case teaching notes that more fully integrate content and cases are available to instructors in the **Connect Library**.

In addition to these in-text cases, McGraw-Hill's custom-publishing Create program offers all of the cases and teaching notes accompanying the current as well as prior editions (www.mcgrawhillcreate.com/rothaermel).

What's New in the Fifth Edition?

I have revised and updated the new edition in the following ways, many of which were inspired by conversations and feedback from the many users and reviewers of the prior editions.

OVERVIEW OF MAJOR CHANGES IN 5E

- Section "Stakeholder Strategy and Competitive Advantage" now in Chapter 1.
- Section "Vision, Mission, and Values" now in Chapter 2.
- New section "Strategic Decision Making" in Chapter 2.
- New section "From External to Internal Analysis" in Chapter 4.

- Three new **ChapterCases:** Five Guys (Chapter 4), Alphabet and Google (Chapter 11), and Theranos (Chapter 12); all other ChapterCases revised and updated.
- All new or updated and revised **Strategy Highlights** (two per chapter).
- Revised and updated module on **How to Conduct a Case Analysis**.
- Five new **MiniCases** (Uber, PayPal, JCPenney, GE, and BlackBerry), featuring not only success stories but also failures; all other MiniCases revised and updated. One MiniCase per chapter, tightly integrated with learning objectives. Detailed and high-quality teaching notes are available in the Connect Library.
- Three new **full-length Cases** (Airbnb, Nike, and The Vanguard Group); all other cases including most popular ones such as Amazon, Apple, Best Buy, Facebook, McDonald's, and Tesla, among others, are revised and updated. Detailed and updated case teaching notes, as well as financial data for these cases, are available in the Connect Library.

IN DETAIL
CHAPTER 1

- Revised and updated ChapterCase: "Tesla's Secret Strategy"
- New Strategy Highlight: "Does Twitter have a Strategy?"
- New Strategy Highlight: "Merck's Stakeholder Strategy"
- Improved chapter flow through moving the updated section "Stakeholder Strategy and Competitive Advantage" into Chapter 1 (from Chapter 2)

CHAPTER 2

- Revised and updated ChapterCase: "Leadership Crisis at Facebook?"
- New section: "Strategic Decision Making"
- New exhibit: "Two Distinct Modes of Decision Making"
- New exhibit: "How to Use a Devil's Advocate to Improve Strategic Decision Making"
- New Strategy Highlight: "Teach for America: How Wendy Kopp Inspires Future Leaders"
- Improved chapter flow through moving the updated section "Vision, Mission, and Values" into Chapter 2 (from Chapter 1)

CHAPTER 3

- Revised and updated ChapterCase: "Airbnb: Disrupting the Hotel Industry"
- New Strategy Highlight: "Blockbuster's Bust"
- New Strategy Highlight: "From League of Legends to Fortnite: The Rise of e-Sports"

CHAPTER 4

- New ChapterCase: "Five Guys' Core Competency: 'Make the Best Burger, Don't Worry about Cost'"
- New section: "From External to Internal Analysis"
- New Strategy Highlight: "Dr. Dre's Core Competency: Coolness Factor"

CHAPTER 5

- Revised and updated ChapterCase: "The Quest for Competitive Advantage: Apple vs. Microsoft"
- New Strategy Highlight: "PepsiCo's Indra Nooyi: Performance with a Purpose"

CHAPTER 6

- Revised and updated ChapterCase: "JetBlue Airways: En Route to a New Blue Ocean?"
- New Strategy Highlight: "Cirque du Soleil: Finding a New Blue Ocean?"

CHAPTER 7

- Revised and updated ChapterCase: "Netflix: Disrupting the TV Industry"
- New Strategy Highlight: "Wikipedia: Disrupting the Encyclopedia Business"

CHAPTER 8

- Revised and updated ChapterCase: "Amazon's Corporate Strategy"
- New Strategy Highlight: "P&G Diversification Strategy: Turning the Tide?"

CHAPTER 9

- Revised and updated ChapterCase: "Little Lyft Gets Big Alliance Partners and Beats Uber in Going Public"

CHAPTER 10

- Revised and updated ChapterCase: "IKEA: The World's Most Profitable Retailer"
- New Strategy Highlight "Does GM's future lie in China?"

CHAPTER 11

- New ChapterCase: "'A' is for Alphabet and 'G' is for Google"
- New exhibit: "Formal and Informal Building Blocks of Organizational Design"
- New Strategy Highlight: "Zappos: Of Happiness and Holacracy"

CHAPTER 12

- New ChapterCase: "Theranos: Bad Blood"
- New Strategy Highlight: "HP's Board Room Drama and Divorce"
- New Strategy Highlight: "VW's Dieselgate: School of Hard NOx"

MINICASES

- 12 MiniCases, one for each chapter; each MiniCase is closely tied to the chapter's learning objectives and includes discussion questions and detailed teaching notes.
- Five new MiniCases: Uber, PayPal, JCPenney, GE, and BlackBerry
- The most popular MiniCases from the prior editions have been updated and revised.

FULL-LENGTH CASES

- Three new full-length cases (Airbnb, Nike, and The Vanguard Group); all other cases, including most popular ones such as Amazon, Apple, Best Buy, Facebook, McDonald's, and Tesla, are updated and revised.
- Detailed and updated case teaching notes as well as financial data for these cases are available for instructors in the Connect Library.

CONNECT

- **12 full-length Cases are now included—complimentary—for students in 5e Connect.** Detailed case teaching notes are available in the Connect Library. All full-length cases included in 5e Connect were authored by Frank T. Rothaermel.

Connect, McGraw-Hill's online assignment and assessment system, offers a wealth of content for both students and instructors. Assignable activities include the following:

- **SmartBook**, one of the first fully adaptive and individualized study tools, provides students with a personalized learning experience, giving them the opportunity to practice and challenge their understanding of core strategy concepts. It allows the instructor to set up all assignments prior to the semester, to have them auto-released on preset dates, and to receive auto-graded progress reports for each student and the entire class. Students love SmartBook because they learn at their own pace, and it helps them to study more efficiently by delivering an interactive reading experience through adaptive highlighting and review.
- **Application Exercises** (such as Whiteboard Animation video cases, MiniCase case analyses, click-and-drag activities, and new case exercises for all 12 full-length cases that are available in Connect) require students to apply key concepts, thereby closing the knowing and doing gap, while providing instant feedback for the student and progress tracking for the instructor.

INSTRUCTOR RESOURCES

The **Instructor Resources** located in **Connect** provide the following teaching tools, all of which have been tested and updated with this edition:

- The **Teacher's Resource Manual (TRM)** includes thorough coverage of each chapter, as well as guidance for integrating **Connect**—all in a single resource. Included in this newly combined TRM, which retains favorite features of the previous edition's Instructor's Manual, is the appropriate level of theory, framework, recent application, additional company examples not found in the textbook, teaching tips, PowerPoint references, critical discussion topics, and answers to end-of-chapter exercises.
- The **PowerPoint (PPT)** slide decks, available in an accessible version for individuals with visual impairment, provide comprehensive lecture notes, video links, and additional company examples not found in the textbook. Options include instructor media-enhanced slides as well as notes with outside application examples. All slides can be edited by individual instructors to suit their needs.
- The **Test Bank** includes 100 to 150 questions per chapter, in a range of formats and with a greater-than-usual number of comprehension, critical-thinking, and application or scenario-based questions. Each question is tagged to learning objectives, Bloom's Taxonomy levels, and AACSB compliance requirements. Many questions are new and written especially for this new edition.

- The **Video Guide** includes video links that relate to concepts from chapters. The video links include sources such as Big Think, Stanford University's Entrepreneurship Corner, The McKinsey Quarterly, ABC, BBC, CBS, CNN, ITN/Reuters, MSNBC, NBC, PBS, and YouTube.

CREATE

- **Create**, McGraw-Hill's custom-publishing tool, is where you access additional full-length cases (and Teaching Notes) beyond those included complimentary in Connect that accompany *Strategic Management* (http://www.mcgrawhillcreate.com/Rothaermel). You can create customized course packages in print and/or digital form at a competitive price point.
- Through Create, you will be able to select from all author-written cases as well instructor-written cases that match specifically with the new 5th edition. Create also contains cases from Harvard, Ivey Darden, NACRA, and much more! You can assemble your own course, selecting the chapters, cases (multiple formats), and readings that will work best for you, or choose from several ready-to-go, author-recommended complete course solutions, which include chapters, cases, and readings, preloaded in Create. Among the preloaded solutions, you'll find options for undergraduate, MBA, accelerated, and other strategy courses.

ACKNOWLEDGMENTS

Any list of acknowledgments will always be incomplete, but I would like to thank some special people without whom this product would not have been possible. First and foremost, my wife, Kelleyn, and our children: Harris, Winston, Roman, Adelaide, Avery, and Ivy. Over the last few years, I have worked longer hours than when I was a graduate student to conduct the research and writing necessary for this text and accompanying case studies and other materials. I sincerely appreciate the sacrifice this has meant for my family.

The Georgia Institute of Technology provides a conducive, intellectual environment and superb institutional support to make this project possible. I thank Russell and Nancy McDonough for generously funding the endowed chair that I am honored to hold. I'm grateful for Dean Maryam Alavi and Senior Associate Deans Saby Mitra and Peter Thompson for providing the exceptional leadership that allows faculty to focus on research, teaching, and service. I like to thank my colleagues at Georgia Tech—all of whom are not only great scholars but also fine individuals whom I'm fortunate to have as friends: Marco Ceccagnoli, Annamaria Conti, Anne Fuller, Jonathan Giuliano, Stuart Graham, Matt Higgins, David Ku, John McIntyre, Alex Oettl, Pian Shu, Eunhee Sohn, and Laurina Zhang.

I'm also fortunate to work with a great team at McGraw-Hill: Michael Ablassmeir (director), Terri Schiesl (managing director), Anne Ehrenworth (senior product developer), Haley Burmeister (product developer), Debbie Clare (executive marketing manager), Mary Powers and Keri Johnson (content project managers), and Matt Diamond (senior designer). Lai T. Moy contributed as a superb content development editor on the fifth edition manuscript; and I'm grateful for excellent research assistance provided by Laura Zhang.

I'm more than grateful for the contributions of great colleagues on various resources that accompany this new edition of *Strategic Management*:

- John Burr (Purdue University) on the *Video Guide.*

- Carla Flores (Ball State University) on the revision of Connect, including the *Interactive Exercises*, *MiniCase Exercises*, and *Case Exercises.*

- Melissa Francisco (University of Central Florida) on the accessible *PowerPoint* slide decks.

- Anne Fuller (Georgia Institute of Technology) on *Teacher Resource Manual, Discussion Questions,* and *myStrategy* boxes.

- Gita Mathur (San Jose State University) on *MiniCase Teaching Notes*.

- Chandran Mylvaganam (Northwood University) on selected *Case Abstracts* and *Case Teaching Notes.*

Last, but certainly not least, I wish to thank the reviewers and focus group attendees who shared their expertise with us, from the very beginning when we developed the prospectus to the new teaching and learning package that you hold in your hands. The reviewers have given us the greatest gift of all—the gift of time! These very special people are listed starting on page xxi.

Frank T. Rothaermel
Georgia Institute of Technology

Web: ftrStrategy.com
Email: frank@ftrStrategy.com

THANK YOU . . .

This book has gone through McGraw-Hill Education's thorough development process. Over the course of several years, the project has benefited from numerous developmental focus groups, hundreds of reviews from instructors across the country, and beta-testing of the first-edition manuscript as well as market reviews of subsequent editions on a variety of campuses. The author and McGraw-Hill wish to thank the following people who shared their insights, constructive criticisms, and valuable suggestions throughout the development of this project. Your contributions have greatly improved this product:

Joshua R. Aaron
East Carolina University

Moses Acquaah
University of North Carolina, Greensboro

Garry Adams
Auburn University

M. David Albritton
Northern Arizona University

Benjamin N. Alexander
California Polytechnic State University

Brent B. Allred
The College of William & Mary

Semiramis Amirpour
University of Texas, El Paso

Cory J. Angert
University of Houston-Downtown

Melissa Appleyard
Portland State University

Jorge A. Arevalo
William Paterson University

Asli Arikan
Kent State University

Marne Arthaud-Day
Kansas State University

Bindu Arya
University of Missouri, St. Louis

Seung Bach
California State University, Sacramento

Jeffery Bailey
University of Idaho

David Baker
Kent State University

LaKami T. Baker
Auburn University

Dennis R. Balch
University of North Alabama

Edward R. Balotsky
Saint Joseph's University

Kevin Banning
Auburn University, Montgomery

Jeff Barden
Oregon State University

James W. Barrow
Suffolk University

Patricia Beckenholdt
University of Maryland University College

Geoff Bell
University of Minnesota, Duluth

Bruce W. Bellner
The Ohio State University

Heidi Bertels
City University of New York, Staten Island

Lorenzo Bizzi
California State University, Fullerton

Audrey M. Blume, D.B.A.
Wilmington University

Tim Blumentritt
Kennesaw State University

William C. Bogner
Georgia State University

David S. Boss
Ohio University

Michael Bowen
University of South Florida

Nathan A. Bragaw
Louisiana State University

Dorothy Brawley
Kennesaw State University

Wm. David Brice
California State University, Dominguez Hills

Michael G. Brizek
South Carolina State University

James W. Bronson
University of Wisconsin, Whitewater

Jill A. Brown
Bentley University

Barry Bunn
Valencia College

Richard A. L. Caldarola
Troy University

Marco Ceccagnoli
Georgia Institute of Technology

Janice F. Cerveny
Florida Atlantic University

Clint Chadwick
University of Alabama, Huntsville

Kenneth H. Chadwick
Nicholls State University

Jay P. Chandran
Northwood University

Jianhong Chen
University of New Hampshire

Tianxu Chen
Oakland University

Yi-Yu Chen
New Jersey City University

Mike Cheng
Golden Gate University

Steve Childers
Radford University

Sanjib Chowdhury
Eastern Michigan University

Valerie L. Christian
Sacred Heart University

Brent Clark
University of South Dakota

Timothy S. Clark
Northern Arizona University

John Clarry
Rutgers University

Betty S. Coffey
Appalachian State University

Anne N. Cohen
University of Minnesota

Jamie Collins
University of Canterbury

Brian Connelly
Auburn University

W. J. Conwell
University of Texas at El Paso

Rick Corum
Liberty University

Eva Lynn Cowell
University of Tennessee

Cynthia S. Cycyota
United States Air Force Academy

Derrick E. D'Souza
University of North Texas

Joshua J. Daspit
Texas State University

Parthiban David
American University

Samuel DeMarie
Iowa State University

Irem Demirkan
Northeastern University

Geoffrey Desa
San Francisco State University

Edward Desmarais
Salem State University

Steven S. Dionne
Georgia State University

Michael E. Dobbs
Eastern Illinois University

Mark Dobeck
Cleveland State University

Darla Domke-Damonte
Coastal Carolina University

Stephen A. Drew
Florida Gulf Coast University

Mohinder Dugal
Western Connecticut State University

Arthur J. Duhaime III
Nichols College

David Duhon
University of Southern Mississippi

Danielle Dunne
Fordham University

Supradeep Dutta
State University of New York, Buffalo

Loretta S. Duus
Midlands Technical College

Jason Scott Earl
Brigham Young University, Hawaii

Andrew G. Earle
University of New Hampshire

Helen Eckmann
Brandman University

Linda F. Edelman
Bentley University

Alan Ellstrand
University of Arkansas, Fayetteville

David Epstein
University of Houston Downtown

Michael M. Fathi
Georgia Southwestern State University

Kevin Fertig
University of Illinois at Urbana, Champaign

James Fiet
University of Louisville

Robert S. Fleming
Rowan University

Carla C. Flores
Ball State University

Daniel Forbes
University of Minnesota

Isaac Fox
University of Minnesota

Susan Fox-Wolfgramm
Hawaii Pacific University

William Foxx
Troy University

Charla S. Fraley
Columbus State Community College

W.A. Franke
Northern Arizona University

Steven A. Frankforter
Winthrop University

Anne W. Fuller
Georgia Institute of Technology

Venessa Funches
Auburn University, Montgomery

Jeffrey Furman
Boston University

Nolan Gaffney
University of North Texas

Scott Gallagher
James Madison University

David L. Gartenberg
Seattle University

John E. Gentner
University of Dayton

Jim Glasgow
Villanova University

Eric Glymph
Virginia Commonwealth University

Devi R. Gnyawali
Virginia Tech

Sanjay Goel
University of Minnesota, Duluth

Steve Gove
University of Vermont

Patrick Greek
Macomb Community College

Shirley A. Green
Indian River State College

Regina A. Greenwood
Nova Southeastern University

Christin Van Wyk Greiman
Northwood University

Robert D. Gulbro
Athens State University

Michael Gunderson
University of Florida

Craig Gustin
American InterContinental University

Stephen F. Hallam
University of Akron

Marcia McLure Hardy
Northwestern State University, Louisiana

Darel Hargrove
Central Michigan University

Ahma Hassan
Morehead State University

Scott D. Hayward
Elon University / Appalachian State University

Jon Timothy Heames
West Virginia University

Richard A. Heiens
University of South Carolina, Aiken

Duane Helleloid
University of North Dakota

Kurt A. Heppard
United States Air Force Academy

Theodore T. Herbert
Rollins College

Kurt Herrmann
Brigham Young University

Ken Hess
Metropolitan State University

Scott Hicks
Liberty University

Glenn Hoetker
The University of Melbourne

Phyllis Holland
Valdosta State University

R. Michael Holmes, Jr.
Florida State University

Stephen V. Horner
Arkansas State University

George Hruby
Cleveland State University

Tammy Huffman
Utah Valley University

Tobias M. Huning
University of North Florida

Tammy G. Hunt
University of North Carolina Wilmington

Ana Elisa Iglesias
University of Wisconsin, La Crosse

Syeda Noorein Inamdar
The Chinese University of Hong Kong

John G. Irwin
Troy University

Carol K. Jacobson
Purdue University

Sean Jasso
University of California, Riverside

Scott Johnson
Oklahoma State University

Mahesh P. Joshi
George Mason University

Jon Kalinowski
Minnesota State University, Mankato

Necmi Karagozoglu
California State University, Sacramento

Joy Karriker
East Carolina University

J. Kay Keels
Coastal Carolina University

Franz Kellermanns
University of North Carolina, Charlotte

Theodore A. Khoury
Portland State University

David King
Iowa State University

Brent Kinghorn
Missouri State University

Jerry Kopf
Radford University

Donald J. Kopka, Jr.
Towson University

Frank Kozak
Bowling Green State University

Mario Krenn
Louisiana State University

Bruce C. Kusch
Brigham Young University, Idaho

Melody Waller LaPreze
Missouri State University

K. Blaine Lawlor
University of West Florida

Marty Lawlor
Rochester Institute of Technology

John Lawrence
University of Idaho

Mariana J. Lebrn
Towson University

Hun Lee
George Mason University

Jay Lee
California State University Sacramento

Mina Lee
Xavier University

Mingxiang Lee
Florida Atlantic University

Charles J. F. Leflar
University of Arkansas, Fayetteville

Jon Lehman
Vanderbilt University

David Leibsohn
California State University, Fullerton

Aristotle T. Lekacos
Stony Brook University

Jun Lin
State University of New York, New Paltz

Eduardo V. Lopez, Ph.D.
Belmont University

Joseph Mahoney
University of Illinois at Urbana-Champaign

David Major
University of Miami

Paul Mallette
Colorado State University

Tatiana S. Manolova
Bentley University

Daniel B. Marin
Louisiana State University

Sarah Marsh
Northern Illinois University

Louis Martinette
University of Mary Washington

Anthony U. Martinez
San Francisco State University

Blake Mathias
Louisiana State University

Gita Mathur
San Jose State University

Patricia Matuszek
Troy University, Montgomery

David McCalman
University of Central Arkansas

Jeffrey E. McGee
The University of Texas, Arlington

Jean McGuire
Louisiana State University

Rick McPherson
University of Washington

Michael Merenda
University of New Hampshire

John M. Mezias
University of Miami

Grant Miles
University of North Texas

Douglas R. Miller
University of North Carolina, Wilmington

Michael Miller
University of Illinois, Chicago

Elouise Mintz
Saint Louis University

Raza Mir
William Paterson University

Kelly Mollica
University of Memphis

Mike Montalbano
Bentley University

Debra L. Moody
Virginia Commonwealth University

Gwen Moore
University of Missouri, St. Louis

James P. Morgan
Webster University, Fort Leonard Wood

Richard T. Mpoyi
Middle Tennessee State University

John Mullane
Middle Tennessee State University

Canan C. Mutlu
Kennesaw State University

Chandran Mylvaganam
Northwood University

Louise Nemanich
Arizona State University

Don O. Neubaum
Oregon State University

Kent Neupert
Boise State University

Charles Newman
University of Maryland University College

Kuei-Hsien Niu
California State University, Sacramento

Jill Novak
Indian River State College

Frank Novakowski
Davenport University

Jeffrey R. Nystrom
University of Colorado Denver

Kevin J. O'Mara
Elon University

Kenny (Kyeungrae) Oh
University of Missouri, St. Louis

Don Okhomina
Fayetteville State University

Eren Ozgen
Troy University-Dothan

Chris Papenhausen
University of Massachusetts, Dartmouth

James M. Pappas
Oklahoma State University

Audrey Parajon
Wilmington University

Ronaldo Parente
Florida International University

Srikanth Paruchuri
Pennsylvania State University

Christine Cope Pence
University of California, Riverside

Luis A. Perez-Batres
Central Michigan University

Clifford R. Perry
Florida International University

Keith Perry
San Jose State University

Antoaneta Petkova
San Francisco State University

JoDee Phillips
Kaplan University

Michael W. Pitts
Virginia Commonwealth University

Erin Pleggenkuhle-Miles
University of Nebraska-Omaha

Robert Porter
University of Central Florida

Richard A. Quinn
University of Central Florida

Vasudevan Ramanujam
Case Western Reserve University

Krishnan Ramaya
Pacific University

Annette L. Ranft
Auburn University

Christopher R. Reutzel
Sam Houston State University

Gary B. Roberts
Kennesaw State University

Simon Rodan
San Jose State University

Donald Roomes
Florida International University

Jessica R. Salmon
Rutgers University

Yassir M. Samra
Manhattan College

Carol Sánchez
Grand Valley State University

Michael D. Santoro
Lehigh University

Tim Schoenecker
Southern Illinois University, Edwardsville

Elton Scifres
Stephen F. Austin State University

Gary Scudder
Vanderbilt University

Wendell Seaborne
Franklin University

Deborah Searcy
Florida Atlantic University

Russell Seidle
Suffolk University, Boston

Jim Sena
California Polytechnic State University, San Luis Obispo

Anju Seth
Virginia Tech

Deepak Sethi
Old Dominion University

Jennifer Sexton
West Virginia University

Ali Shahzad
James Madison University

Mark Sharfman
University of Oklahoma

Thomas Shirley
San Jose State University

Eugene S. Simko
Monmouth University

Faye A. Sisk
Mercer University, Atlanta

Lise Anne D. Slatten
University of Louisiana, Lafayette

Alan D. Smith
Kent State University/Robert Morris University

Garry D. Smith
Mississippi State University

Ned Smith
University of Michigan

James D. Spina
University of Maryland

Peter A. Stanwick
Auburn University

Mark Starik
San Francisco State University

Warren Stone
University of Arkansas, Little Rock

Mohan Subramaniam
Boston College

Ram Subramanian
Montclair State University

James Anthony Swaim
Kennesaw State University

Timothy Syfert
Grand Valley State University

Jing'an Tang
Sacred Heart University

Linda F. Tegarden
Virginia Tech

Robert Thompson
University of Texas, San Antonio

Paul W. Thurston, Jr.
Siena College

Thuhang Tran
Middle Tennessee State University

Kim K. J. Tullis
University of Central Oklahoma

Rashada Houston Turner
Florida A&M University

Beverly B. Tyler
North Carolina State University

Isaiah O. Ugboro
North Carolina A&T State University

Tolga Ulusemre
Hawaii Pacific University

Barry VanderKelen
California Polytechnic State University, San Luis Obispo

Jorge Walter
The George Washington University

Bruce Walters
Louisiana Tech University

Jia Wang
California State University, Fresno

David B. Wangrow
Marquette University

Andrew Ward
Lehigh University

Vincent Weaver
Greenville Technical College

Joel West
Claremont Graduate University

Laura Whitcomb
California State University, Los Angeles

George O. White III
University of Michigan, Flint

Margaret White
Oklahoma State University

Marta Szabo White
Georgia State University

Carolyn Wiethoff
Indiana University

Scott Williams
Wright State University

James Winters
Portland State University

Ross A. Wirth
Franklin University

Cathy Coleman Wood
University of Tennessee

Robert Chapman Wood
San Jose State University

Beth Woodard
Belmont University

Chuanyin Xie
The University of Tampa

George Young
Liberty University

John Yudelson
California State University Northridge

Michael J. Zhang
Sacred Heart University

Zhe Zhang
Eastern Kentucky University

Xia Zhao
California State University, Dominguez Hills

Yanfeng Zheng
The University of Hong Kong

Arvids A. Ziedonis
KU Leuven

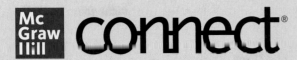

You're in the driver's seat.

Want to build your own course? No problem. Prefer to use our turnkey, prebuilt course? Easy. Want to make changes throughout the semester? Sure. And you'll save time with Connect's auto-grading too.

65%
Less Time Grading

Laptop: McGraw-Hill; Woman/dog: George Doyle/Getty Images

They'll thank you for it.

Adaptive study resources like SmartBook® 2.0 help your students be better prepared in less time. You can transform your class time from dull definitions to dynamic debates. Find out more about the powerful personalized learning experience available in SmartBook 2.0 at **www.mheducation.com/highered/ connect/smartbook**

Make it simple, make it affordable.

Connect makes it easy with seamless integration using any of the major Learning Management Systems— Blackboard®, Canvas, and D2L, among others—to let you organize your course in one convenient location. Give your students access to digital materials at a discount with our inclusive access program. Ask your McGraw-Hill representative for more information.

Padlock: Jobalou/Getty Images

Solutions for your challenges.

A product isn't a solution. Real solutions are affordable, reliable, and come with training and ongoing support when you need it and how you want it. Our Customer Experience Group can also help you troubleshoot tech problems— although Connect's 99% uptime means you might not need to call them. See for yourself at **status. mheducation.com**

Checkmark: Jobalou/Getty Images

SUPPORT AT *every step*

FOR STUDENTS

Effective, efficient studying.

Connect helps you be more productive with your study time and get better grades using tools like SmartBook 2.0, which highlights key concepts and creates a personalized study plan. Connect sets you up for success, so you walk into class with confidence and walk out with better grades.

Study anytime, anywhere.

Download the free ReadAnywhere app and access your online eBook or SmartBook 2.0 assignments when it's convenient, even if you're offline. And since the app automatically syncs with your eBook and SmartBook 2.0 assignments in Connect, all of your work is available every time you open it. Find out more at **www.mheducation.com/readanywhere**

"I really liked this app—it made it easy to study when you don't have your text-book in front of you."

- Jordan Cunningham,
Eastern Washington University

Calendar: owattaphotos/Getty Images

No surprises.

The Connect Calendar and Reports tools keep you on track with the work you need to get done and your assignment scores. Life gets busy; Connect tools help you keep learning through it all.

Learning for everyone.

McGraw-Hill works directly with Accessibility Services Departments and faculty to meet the learning needs of all students. Please contact your Accessibility Services office and ask them to email accessibility@mheducation.com, or visit **www.mheducation.com/about/accessibility** for more information.

Top: Jenner Images/Getty Images, Left: Hero Images/Getty Images, Right: Hero Images/Getty Images

PART

1

Analysis

The AFI Strategy Framework

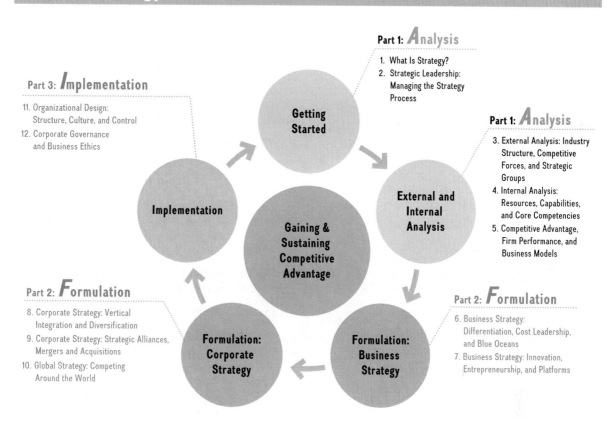

Getting
Started

External and
Internal
Analysis

Implementation

Gaining &
Sustaining
Competitive
Advantage

Formulation:
Corporate
Strategy

Formulation:
Business
Strategy

What Is Strategy?

Chapter Outline

Learning Objectives

After studying this chapter, you should be able to:

LO 1-1 Explain the role of strategy in a firm's quest for competitive advantage.

LO 1-2 Define competitive advantage, sustainable competitive advantage, competitive disadvantage, and competitive parity.

LO 1-3 Assess the relationship between stakeholder strategy and sustainable competitive advantage.

LO 1-4 Conduct a stakeholder impact analysis.

LO 1-5 Explain the Analysis, Formulation, Implementation (AFI) Strategy Framework.

Tesla's Secret Strategy

TESLA INC., an American manufacturer of all-electric cars—boasted a market capitalization[1] of some $60 billion (in early 2019), an appreciation of more than 1,400 percent over its initial public offering price in 2010. How can a California startup achieve a market valuation that exceeds that of GM, one of the largest car manufacturers in the world, making some 10 million vehicles a year? The answer: Tesla's secret strategy. In a summer 2006 blog entry on Tesla's website, Elon Musk, Tesla's co-founder and CEO, explained the startup's master plan:[2]

1. Build sports car.

2. Use that money to build an affordable car.

3. Use *that* money to build an even more affordable car.

4. While doing above, also provide zero-emission electric power generation options.

5. Don't tell anyone.[2]

Let's see if Tesla stuck to its strategy. In 2008, Tesla introduced its first car: the Roadster, a $110,000 sports coupe with faster acceleration than a Porsche or a Ferrari. Tesla's first vehicle served as a prototype to demonstrate that electric vehicles can be more than mere golf carts. Tesla thus successfully completed Step 1 of the master plan.

In Step 2, after selling some 2,500 Roadsters, Tesla discontinued its production in 2012 to focus on its next car: the Model S, a four-door family sedan, with an initial base price of $73,500. The line appeals to a somewhat larger market and thus allows for larger production runs to drive down unit costs. The Model S received an outstanding market reception. It was awarded not only the 2013 Motor Trend Car of the Year, but also received the highest score of any car ever tested by Consumer Reports (99/100). Tesla manufactures the Model S in the Fremont, California, factory that it purchased from Toyota. By the end of 2018, it had sold more than 250,000 of the Model S worldwide.

Hoping for an even broader customer appeal, Tesla also introduced the Model X, a crossover between an SUV and a family van with futuristic falcon-wing doors for convenient access to second- and third-row seating. The $100,000 starting sticker price of the Model X is quite steep, thus limiting its mass-market appeal. Technical difficulties with its innovative doors delayed its launch until the fall of 2015. By the end of 2018, however, Tesla had sold more than 100,000 of the Model X globally.

Tesla also completed Step 3 of its master plan. In 2016, the electric car maker unveiled the Model 3, an all-electric compact luxury sedan, with a starting price of $35,000. Many want-to-be Tesla owners stood in line overnight, eagerly waiting for Tesla stores to open so they could put down their $1,000 deposits to secure a spot on the waiting list for the Model 3—a car they had not even seen, let alone taken for a test drive. As a result of this consumer enthusiasm, Tesla received more than 500,000 preorders before the first delivery, and thus $500 million in interest-free loans. Despite initial difficulties in scaling up production, deliveries of the Model 3 began in the fall of 2017. By the end of 2018, Tesla had delivered more than 100,000 of the Model 3 globally. To meet the strong demand for the lower priced Model 3, Tesla hopes to increase its annual production to 1 million vehicles by 2020.

In the spring of 2019, Tesla launched the Model Y, a compact SUV that is a smaller and much lower priced version of the Model X. Elon Musk plans to start deliveries of the new Model Y between the fall of 2020 and spring 2021, with the entry version starting at $39,000 (and 230 miles range) and the high-end performance version starting at $60,000 (and 280 miles range).

Step 4 of Musk's master plan for Tesla aims to provide zero-emission electric power generation options. To achieve

The Tesla Roadster 2 set new records for a vehicle to be driven on public roads: It goes from 0–60 mph in 1.9 seconds and from 0–100 mph in 4.2 seconds, with top speeds of well above 250 mph. The base price of this newest Tesla, scheduled to launch in 2020, is $200,000.

KYDPL KYODO/AP Images

this goal, Tesla acquired SolarCity, a solar energy company, for more than $2 billion in the fall of 2016. This successful integration of Tesla and SolarCity, which resulted in the first fully integrated clean-tech energy company that combines solar power, power storage, and transportation, marks the completion of Step 4 in Tesla's master plan.

Step 5: "Don't tell anyone"—a humorous statement added by Elon Musk—thus the ChapterCase title "Tesla's Secret Strategy."[3]

NOTE: By summer 2019, Tesla's market cap stood at about $45 billion.

Part II of this ChapterCase appears in Section 1.4.

WHY IS TESLA SO SUCCESSFUL? In contrast to Tesla's success, the big-three U.S. automakers—Ford, GM, and Chrysler—struggled during the first decade of the 21st century, with both GM and Chrysler filing for bankruptcy protection.

If once-great firms can fail, why is any company successful? What enables some firms to gain and then sustain their competitive advantage over time? How can you as a strategic leader influence firm performance? These are the big questions that define strategic management. Answering these questions requires integrating the knowledge you've obtained in your studies of various business disciplines to understand what leads to superior performance, and how you can help your organization achieve it.

Strategic management is the integrative management field that combines *analysis, formulation,* and *implementation* in the quest for competitive advantage. Mastery of strategic management enables you to view an organization such as a firm or a nonprofit outfit in its entirety. It also enables you to think like a general manager to help position your organization for superior performance. The *AFI Strategy Framework* embodies this view of strategic management. It will guide our exploration of strategic management through the course of your study.

In this chapter, we lay the groundwork for the study of strategic management. We'll introduce foundational ideas about strategy and competitive advantage. We also move beyond an understanding of competitive advantage solely as superior financial performance, and introduce the concept of stakeholder strategy. This allows us to appreciate the role of business in society more broadly. Next, we take a closer look at the components of the AFI framework and provide an overview of the entire strategic management process. We conclude this introductory chapter, as we do with all others in this text, with a section titled *Implications for Strategic Leaders.* Here we provide practical applications and considerations of the material developed in the chapter. Let's begin the exciting journey to understand strategic management and competitive advantage.

1.1 What Strategy Is: Gaining and Sustaining Competitive Advantage

Strategy is a set of goal-directed actions a firm takes to gain and sustain superior performance *relative* to competitors.[4] To achieve superior performance, companies compete for resources: New ventures compete for financial and human capital, existing companies compete for profitable growth, charities compete for donations, universities compete for the best students and professors, sports teams compete for championships, while celebrities compete for endorsements.

As highlighted in the ChapterCase, Tesla, a new entrant in the automotive industry, is competing for customers with established U.S. companies such as GM, Ford, and Chrysler and also with foreign automakers Toyota, Honda, Nissan, Hyundai, VW, Audi, Porsche,

Mercedes, and BMW, among others. In any competitive situation, a **good strategy** enables a firm to achieve superior performance and sustainable competitive advantage relative to its competitors. A good strategy is based on a strategic management process that consists of three key elements:

1. A *diagnosis* of the competitive challenge. This element is accomplished through *analysis* of the firm's external and internal environments (Part 1 of the AFI framework).
2. A *guiding policy* to address the competitive challenge. This element is accomplished through strategy *formulation,* resulting in the firm's corporate, business, and functional strategies (Part 2 of the AFI framework).
3. A *set of coherent actions* to implement the firm's guiding policy. This element is accomplished through strategy *implementation* (Part 3 of the AFI framework).

good strategy Enables a firm to achieve superior performance and sustainable competitive advantage relative to its competitors. It is based on a strategic management process that consists of three elements: (1) a diagnosis of the competitive challenge; (2) a guiding policy to address the competitive challenge; and (3) a set of coherent actions to implement a firm's guiding policy.

CRAFTING A GOOD STRATEGY AT TESLA

Let's revisit ChapterCase 1 to see whether Tesla is pursuing a good strategy. Tesla appears to be performing quite well when considering indicators such as stock appreciation, where it outperforms its competitors. The appreciation of Tesla stock since its initial public offering (IPO) points to investors' expectations of future growth. By other measures, such as generating profits, Tesla underperforms compared to established car companies. Losses are common for startups early on, especially if the business requires large upfront investments such as building new and retooling existing factories, which Tesla was required to do. What we can say at this point is that Tesla seems to be starting with a promising strategy and is in the process of achieving superior performance relative to its competitors. But can Tesla sustain this superior performance over time? Let's use the three elements of good strategy to explore this question.

THE COMPETITIVE CHALLENGE. A good strategy needs to start with a clear and critical diagnosis of the competitive challenge. Musk, Tesla's co-founder and CEO, describes himself as an "engineer and entrepreneur who builds and operates companies to solve environmental, social, and economic challenges."[5] Tesla was founded with the vision to "accelerate the world's transition to sustainable transport."[6]

To accomplish this mission, Tesla must build zero-emission electric vehicles that are attractive and affordable. Beyond achieving a competitive advantage for Tesla, Musk is working to set a new standard in automotive technology. He hopes that zero-emission electric vehicles will one day replace gasoline-powered cars.

Tesla's competitive challenge is sizable: To succeed it must manufacture attractive and affordable vehicles using its new technology, which will compete with traditional cars running on gasoline. It also needs the required infrastructure for electric vehicles, including a network of charging stations to overcome "range anxiety"[7] by consumers; many mass-market electric vehicles cannot drive as far on one charge as gasoline-powered cars can with a full tank of gas. Gas stations can be found pretty much on any corner in cities and every couple of miles on highways.[8]

A GUIDING POLICY. After the diagnosis of the competitive challenge, the firm needs to formulate an effective guiding policy in response. The formulated strategy needs to be consistent, often backed up with *strategic commitments* such as sizable investments or changes to an organization's incentive and reward system—big changes that cannot be easily reversed. Without consistency in a firm's guiding policy, employees become confused and cannot make effective day-to-day decisions that support the overall strategy. Moreover, without consistency in strategy, other stakeholders, including investors, also become frustrated.

To address the competitive challenge, Tesla's current guiding policy is to build a cost-competitive mass-market vehicle such as the Model 3 (this is also Step 3 in Tesla's "Secret Strategy," as discussed in the ChapterCase). Tesla's formulated strategy is consistent with its mission and the competitive challenge identified. It also requires significant strategic commitments, as demonstrated by Tesla's $5 billion investment in a new lithium-ion battery plant in Nevada, the so-called Gigafactory. Batteries are the most critical component for electric vehicles, so to accomplish this major undertaking, Tesla partnered with Panasonic of Japan, a world leader in battery technology. To achieve its massive scale-up in Model 3 production, Tesla invested over $2 billion in a new manufacturing facility.

In 2019, Tesla followed up with another multibillion investment by breaking ground for a factory in Shanghai, China. This factory is huge, combining the size of the Tesla car manufacturing facility in Fremont, California, with its Gigafactory in Nevada. The goal is to produce batteries and cars not only at large scale, but also in the same location. This will help lower the price of the Model 3 further to service the Chinese market, which is already the largest electric vehicle market globally by a wide margin. Although such large, up-front investments frequently lead to early-year losses, they also represent strong and credible commitments to becoming a viable competitor in the mass automobile market.

COHERENT ACTIONS. A clear guiding policy needs to be implemented with a set of coherent actions. Tesla appears to implement its formulated strategy with actions consistent with its diagnosis of the competitive challenge. To accomplish building a cost-competitive mass-market vehicle, Tesla must benefit from *economies of scale,* which are decreases in cost per vehicle as output increases. To reap these critical cost reductions, Tesla must ramp up its production volume. This is a huge challenge: Tesla aims to increase its production output by some 20 times, from 50,000 cars built in 2015 to 1 million cars by 2020. Tesla's retooling of its manufacturing facility in Fremont, California, to rely more heavily on cutting-edge robotics as well as its multibillion-dollar investment to secure an uninterrupted supply of lithium-ion batteries exemplify actions coherent with Tesla's formulated strategy.

After production of the Model 3 began in mid-2017, major problems in operations limited the number of Model 3s produced to a mere 2,500 for the year. However, by the end of 2018, Tesla's huge investments in both its highly automated car manufacturing facility and in its battery plant started to pay off—production of the Model 3 increased to 1,000 units *a day*. Thus, Tesla plans to produce more than 350,000 Model 3s (by end of 2019), a number it needs to achieve if it is to sustain its cash flow and meet pent-up product demand. At the same time, Tesla is expanding its network of charging stations across North America, Europe, and China. To fund this initiative and to avoid bottlenecks, it announced it will no longer provide new Tesla owners free use of the company's charging network.

To accomplish the lofty goal of making zero-emission electric motors the new standard in automotive technology rather than internal combustion engines, Tesla decided to make some of its proprietary technology available to the public. Musk's hope is that sharing Tesla's patents will expand the overall market size for electric vehicles as other manufacturers can employ Tesla's technology.

In review, to craft a good strategy, three steps are crucial in the strategic management process: First, a good strategy defines the competitive challenges facing an organization through a critical and honest assessment of the status quo. Second, a good strategy provides an overarching approach on how to deal with the competitive challenges identified. The approach needs to be communicated in policies that provide clear guidance for employees. Last, a good strategy requires effective implementation through a coherent set of actions. Strategy Highlight 1.1 takes a closer look at Twitter, and asks whether the social media news service has a strategy.

Strategy Highlight **1.1**

Does Twitter Have a Strategy?

Twitter is not flying high! Shortly after its successful initial public offering in 2014, its market capitalization[9] has fallen by 50 percent—from $40 billion to $20 billion in late 2018. Twitter's user growth has stagnated, while core Tweeters are tweeting less and less. In 2015, co-founder Jack Dorsey returned as CEO but could not reverse Twitter's decline. In comparison, during the same time period, Facebook's market cap quadrupled from some $100 billion to $400 billion. The question thus arises: Does Twitter have a strategy?

Twitter is not flying high! Between 2014 and 2018, it lost $20 billion in market capitalization.
x9626/Shutterstock

Launched in 2006, Twitter is an online news and social networking site that allows its Tweeters to send short messages ("tweets") of up to 280 characters or less (and can include images or videos) to all followers. People who follow each other on Twitter can see each others' status updates in their feeds. Users with the most followers include Katy Perry, American singer-songwriter and actress, with more than 107 million; Justin Bieber, Canadian singer-songwriter, with 105 million; and former President Barack Obama with 104 million.

While popular for its scannable content, Twitter's social significance resulted from its pivotal role during the Arab Spring (2010–2012), in the Black Lives Matter movement (founded in 2013), and for its real-time coverage of such breaking news as the raid on Osama bin Laden's compound in Pakistan (2011). Many of the most powerful politicians in the world such as President Donald Trump and India Prime Minister Narendra Modi use Twitter to communicate directly with the public, allowing them to bypass traditional media outlets.

To answer the question of whether Twitter has a strategy, let's apply the three critical elements of a good strategy and the three critical tasks of a good strategic management process: *diagnose the competitive challenge, derive a guiding policy,* and *implement a coherent set of actions.*

THE COMPETITIVE CHALLENGE   Twitter's business model is to grow its user base and then charge advertisers for promoting goods and services to that user base. While individual users pay nothing, their tweets give Twitter free user-generated content to drive more traffic to its site. Companies pay for "promoted tweets" that are directly inserted into a user's news stream. But compare Twitter's 330 million monthly users to Facebook's over 2 billion users—this tells us that Facebook's user base is almost seven times the size of Twitter's. Given its much smaller user base, advertisers view Twitter as a niche application and thus will direct the bulk of their digital ad dollars to larger sites such as Facebook, Google, and Amazon.

Compared to Facebook, Twitter suffers in ways other than sheer scale. For instance, it has allowed competitors such as Snapchat, WhatsApp, and Instagram (all owned by Facebook) to move into the space it originally created. In addition, Facebook allows advertisers to target their online ads more precisely by using the demographic data Facebook collects, including birth year, university affiliation, network of friends, interests, and so forth. (This data collection has created a whole different set of problems for Facebook, which is discussed further in ChapterCase 2). Clearly, Twitter needs a larger user base to attract more online advertisers and better monetize its social media service.

A GUIDING POLICY   Here is where Twitter's problems begin. While its leaders have accurately identified and diagnosed Twitter's competitive challenge (to grow its user base), they still lack a clear guiding policy for how to address this challenge. One way would be to simplify the sign-up process. Another would be to better explain the sometimes idiosyncratic conventions of Twitter use to a broader audience. Yet another would be to root out offensive content, fake accounts, and misinformation, and to be more aggressive about blocking cyber trolls. Perhaps even more important, Twitter needs to find a way to take

(Continued)

back the social media space that's now being dominated by Snapchat, WhatsApp, and Instagram.

COHERENT ACTIONS Changing the goalpost of which users (core, noncore, or passive viewers that see tweets on other media) to target not only confused management, but it also limited functional guidance for employees in day-to-day operations. Consequences of confusing directions for strategy implementation followed, including increased frustration among managers and engineers, which led to the turnover of key personnel. As Twitter attempts to be more attractive to different types of users, it encounters trade-offs that are hard if not impossible to reconcile. Consider the search or mobile functionality of an application, for example: The needs of core users are very different from that of casual visitors or passive viewers.

Internal turmoil was further stoked by several management demotions as well as promotions of close personal friends of the CEO. From its inception, Twitter's culture has been hampered by infighting and public intrigues among co-founders and other early leaders.

To reduce the gap with Facebook's enormous scale and global reach, Twitter has attempted to be everything to everybody, without considering the strategic trade-offs. This has resulted in not only low employee morale, but also inferior performance. Declaring that Twitter's "ambition is to have the largest audience in the world"[10] is not a good strategy; it is no strategy at all. Rather it is a mere statement of desire. With Twitter's continuing decline in its market cap, it is likely to end up a takeover target.[11]

LO 1-2

Define competitive advantage, sustainable competitive advantage, competitive disadvantage, and competitive parity.

competitive advantage Superior performance relative to other competitors in the same industry or the industry average.

sustainable competitive advantage Outperforming competitors or the industry average over a prolonged period of time.

competitive disadvantage Underperformance relative to other competitors in the same industry or the industry average.

competitive parity Performance of two or more firms at the same level.

WHAT IS COMPETITIVE ADVANTAGE?

A firm that achieves superior performance relative to other competitors in the same industry or the industry average has a **competitive advantage**.[12] Competitive advantage is always *relative,* not absolute. To assess competitive advantage, we compare firm performance to a *benchmark*—that is, either the performance of other firms in the same industry or an industry average. In terms of stock market valuation, Tesla has appreciated much more in recent years than GM, Ford, or Chrysler, and thus appears to have a competitive advantage, at least on this dimension.

A firm that is able to outperform its competitors or the industry average over a prolonged period has a **sustainable competitive advantage**. Apple, for example, has enjoyed a sustainable competitive advantage over Samsung in the smartphone industry for over a decade since its introduction of the iPhone in 2007. Other phone makers such as Microsoft (which purchased Nokia) and BlackBerry have all but exited the smartphone market, while new entrants such as Huawei and Xiaomi of China are trying to gain traction.

If a firm underperforms its rivals or the industry average, it has a **competitive disadvantage**. For example, a 15 percent return on invested capital may sound like superior firm performance. In the consulting industry, though, where the average return on invested capital is often above 20 percent, such a return puts a firm at a competitive disadvantage. In contrast, if a firm's return on invested capital is 2 percent in a declining industry, like newspaper publishing, where the industry average has been negative (–5 percent) for the past few years, then the firm has a competitive advantage. Should two or more firms perform at the same level, they have **competitive parity**. In Chapter 5, we'll discuss in greater depth how to evaluate and assess competitive advantage and firm performance.

To gain a competitive advantage, a firm needs to provide either goods or services consumers value more highly than those of its competitors, or goods or services similar to the competitors' at lower cost. The rewards of superior value creation and capture are profitability and market share. Elon Musk is particularly motivated to address global warming, and thus formed Tesla to build electric vehicles with zero emissions. Sara Blakely, the founder and CEO of Spanx, the global leader in the shapewear industry, is motivated to change women's lives. Sam Walton was driven by offering acceptable value at lower cost than his competitors when creating Walmart, the world's largest (brick-and-mortar) retailer. For Musk, Blakely, Walton, and numerous other entrepreneurs and businesspeople, creating shareholder value and making money is the *consequence* of filling a need and providing a product, service, or experience consumers wanted, at a price they could afford while still making a profit.

Spanx founder and CEO Sara Blakely, a graduate of Florida State University and former salesperson of fax machines, was America's richest self-made woman in 2018, according to *Forbes*. Marla Aufmuth/Getty Images

The important point here is that strategy is about delivering superior value, while containing the cost to create it, or by offering similar value at lower cost. Managers achieve these combinations of value and cost through *strategic positioning*. That is, they stake out a unique position within an industry that allows the firm to provide value to customers, while controlling costs. The greater the difference between value creation and cost, the greater the firm's *economic contribution* and the more likely it will gain competitive advantage.

Strategic positioning requires *trade-offs,* however. As a low-cost retailer, Walmart has a clear strategic profile and serves a specific market segment. Upscale retailer Nordstrom has also built a clear strategic profile by providing superior customer service to a higher end, luxury market segment. Although these companies are in the same industry, their customer segments overlap very little, and they are not direct competitors. Walmart and Nordstrom have each chosen a distinct but different strategic position. The managers make conscious trade-offs that enable each company to strive for competitive advantage in the retail industry, using different competitive strategies: cost leadership versus differentiation. In regard to the customer service dimension, Walmart provides acceptable service by low-skill employees in a big-box retail outlet offering "everyday low prices," while Nordstrom provides a superior customer experience by professional salespeople in a luxury setting.

A clear strategic profile—in terms of product differentiation, cost, and customer service—allows each retailer to meet specific customer needs. Competition focuses on creating value for customers (through lower prices or better service and selection, in this example) rather than destroying rivals. Even though Walmart and Nordstrom compete in the same industry, both can win if they achieve a clear strategic position through a well-executed competitive strategy. Strategy, therefore, is not a zero-sum game.

The key to successful strategy is to combine a set of activities to stake out a *unique strategic position* within an industry. Competitive advantage has to come from performing different activities or performing the same activities differently than rivals are doing. Ideally, these activities reinforce one another rather than create trade-offs. For instance, Walmart's strategic activities strengthen its position as cost leader: Big retail stores in rural locations, extremely high purchasing power, sophisticated IT systems, regional distribution centers, low corporate overhead, and low base wages and salaries combined with employee profit sharing reinforce each other, to maintain the company's cost leadership.

Since clear strategic positioning requires trade-offs, strategy is as much about deciding what *not* to do, as it is about deciding what to do.[13] Because resources are limited, managers must carefully consider their strategic choices in the quest for competitive advantage. Trying to be everything to everybody will likely result in inferior performance.

As a striking example, the department store chain Sears was founded in 1886 and long hailed as an innovator. Sears pioneered its iconic mail-order catalog shortly after its founding, which allowed customers in rural and remote areas of the United States to shop like city dwellers (a similar service to what Amazon provides today, albeit relying on a much smaller selection and slower deliveries). Yet, as time progressed and Sears failed to adapt to new competitive challenges, it lost its competitive advantage. More recently, Sears did not have a clear strategic position but tried to be too many things for too many types of customers. As a consequence, after more than 130 years in business, Sears filed for bankruptcy in 2018.

It is also important to note that operational effectiveness, marketing skills, and other functional expertise all strengthen a unique strategic position. Those capabilities, though, do not substitute for competitive strategy. Competing to be similar but just a bit better than your competitor is likely to be a recipe for cut-throat competition and low profit potential. Let's take this idea to its extreme in a quick thought experiment: If all firms in the same industry pursued a low-cost position through application of competitive benchmarking, all firms would have identical cost structures. None could gain a competitive advantage. Everyone would be running faster, but nothing would change in terms of relative strategic positions. There would be little if any value creation for customers because companies would have no resources to invest in product and process improvements. Moreover, the least-efficient firms would be driven out, further reducing customer choice.

To gain a deeper understanding of what strategy is, it may be helpful to think about what strategy is *not*.[14] Be on the lookout for the following major hallmarks of what strategy is *not*:

GRANDIOSE STATEMENTS ARE NOT STRATEGY. You may have heard firms say things like, "Our strategy is to win" or "We will be No. 1." Twitter, for example, declared its "ambition is to have the largest audience in the world."[15] Such statements of desire, on their own, are not strategy. They provide little managerial guidance and often lead to goal conflict and confusion. Moreover, such wishful thinking frequently fails to address economic fundamentals. As we will discuss in the next section, an effective vision and mission *can* lay the foundation upon which to craft a good strategy. This foundation must be backed up, however, by strategic actions that allow the firm to address a competitive challenge with clear consideration of economic fundamentals, in particular, value creation and costs.

A FAILURE TO FACE A COMPETITIVE CHALLENGE IS NOT STRATEGY. If a firm does not define a clear competitive challenge, employees have no way of assessing whether they are making progress in addressing it. Strategic leaders at the now-defunct video rental chain Blockbuster, for example, failed to address the competitive challenges posed by new players Netflix, Redbox, Amazon Prime, and Hulu.

OPERATIONAL EFFECTIVENESS, COMPETITIVE BENCHMARKING, OR OTHER TACTICAL TOOLS ARE NOT STRATEGY. People casually refer to a host of different policies and initiatives as some sort of strategy: pricing strategy, internet strategy, alliance strategy, operations strategy, IT strategy, brand strategy, marketing strategy, HR strategy, China strategy, and so on. All these elements may be a *necessary* part of a firm's functional and global initiatives to support its competitive strategy, but these elements are *not sufficient* to achieve competitive advantage. In this text, we will reserve the term *strategy* for describing the firm's overall efforts to *gain and sustain competitive advantage*.

1.2 Stakeholder Strategy and Competitive Advantage

VALUE CREATION

Companies with a good strategy generate value for society. When firms compete in their own self-interest while obeying the law and acting ethically, they ultimately create value. **Value creation** occurs because companies with a good strategy are able to provide products or services to consumers at a price point that they can afford while keeping their costs in check, thus making a profit at the same time. Both parties benefit from this trade as each captures a part of the value created. In so doing, they leave society better off.[16]

Value creation in turn lays the foundation for the benefits that successful economies can provide: education, infrastructure, public safety, health care, clean water and air, among others. Superior performance allows a firm to reinvest some of its profits and to grow, which in turn provides more opportunities for employment and fulfilling careers. Although Google (a division of Alphabet) started as a research project in graduate school by Larry Page and Sergey Brin in the late 1990s, some 20 years later it had become one of the most valuable companies in the world with over $800 billion in market capitalization and 100,000 employees, not to mention the billions of people across the world who rely on it for information gathering and decision making, which is free for the end user.[17]

Strategic failure, in contrast, can be expensive. Once a leading technology company, Hewlett-Packard was known for innovation, resulting in superior products. The "HP way of management" included lifetime employment, generous benefits, work/life balance, and freedom to explore ideas, among other perks.[18] However, HP has not been able to address the competitive challenges of mobile computing or business IT services effectively. As a result, HP's stakeholders suffered. Shareholder value was destroyed. The company also had to lay off tens of thousands of employees. Its customers no longer received the innovative products and services that made HP famous.

The contrasting examples of Alphabet and HP illustrate the relationship between individual firms, competitive advantage, and society at large. Successful firms ultimately create value for society. In the first decade of the new millennium, this relationship received more critical scrutiny due to major shocks to free market capitalism.[19] In particular, the implicit trust relationship between the corporate world and society at large has deteriorated because of several notable crises. One of the first crises of the 21st century occurred when the accounting scandals at Enron, Arthur Andersen, WorldCom, Tyco, Adelphia, and others, came to light. Those events led to bankruptcies, large-scale job loss, and the destruction of billions of dollars in shareholder value. As a result, the public's trust in business and free market capitalism began to erode.

Another major event occurred in the fall of 2008 with the global financial crisis, which shook the entire free market system to its core.[20] A real estate bubble had developed in the United States, fueled by cheap credit and the availability of subprime mortgages. When that bubble burst, many entities faced financial duress or bankruptcy—those who had unsustainable mortgages, investors holding securities based on those mortgages, and the financial institutions that had sold the securities. Some went under, and others were sold at fire-sale prices. Home foreclosures skyrocketed as a large number of borrowers defaulted on their mortgages. House prices in the United States plummeted by roughly 30 percent. The United States plunged into a deep recession. In the process, the Dow Jones Industrial Average (DJIA) lost about half its market value.

The impact was worldwide. The freezing of capital markets during the global financial crisis triggered a debt crisis in Europe. Some European governments (notably Greece) defaulted on government debt; other countries were able to repay their debts only through the assistance of other, more solvent European countries. This severe financial crisis not only put Europe's common currency, the euro, at risk, but also led to a prolonged and deep recession in Europe. Disenchanted with the European Union, the United Kingdom voted in 2016 to leave the alliance in wake of the Brexit movement (short for British exit). In the United States, the Occupy Wall Street protest movement was born out of dissatisfaction with the capitalist system. Issues of income disparity, corporate ethics, corporate influence on governments, and ecological sustainability were key drivers.

Although these major events in the business world differed in their specifics, two common features are pertinent to our study of strategic management.[21] First, these events demonstrate that managerial actions can affect the economic well-being of large numbers of people around the globe. Most of the events resulted from executive actions within a few organizations, or compounded across a specific industry or government. The second pertinent feature relates to **stakeholders**—organizations, groups, and individuals that can affect or be affected by a firm's actions.[22] This leads us to *stakeholder strategy,* which we discuss next.

stakeholders Organizations, groups, and individuals that can affect or are affected by a firm's actions.

STAKEHOLDER STRATEGY

Stakeholders have a vested claim or interest in the performance and continued survival of the firm. Stakeholders can be grouped by whether they are internal or external to a firm. As shown in Exhibit 1.1, *internal stakeholders* include employees (executives, managers, and workers), stockholders, and board members. *External stakeholders* include customers, suppliers, alliance partners, creditors, unions, communities, governments at various levels, and the media.

All stakeholders make specific contributions to a firm, which in turn provides different types of benefits to different stakeholders. Employees contribute their time and talents to the firm, receiving wages and salaries in exchange. Shareholders contribute capital with the expectation that the stock will rise and the firm will pay dividends. Communities provide real estate, infrastructure, and public safety. In return, they expect that companies will pay

EXHIBIT 1.1 Internal and External Stakeholders in an Exchange Relationship with the Firm

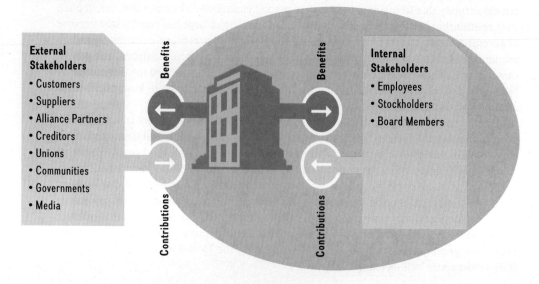

taxes, provide employment, and not pollute the environment. The firm, therefore, is embedded in a multifaceted *exchange relationship* with a number of diverse internal and external stakeholders. If any stakeholder withholds participation in the firm's exchange relationships, it can negatively affect firm performance. The aerospace company Boeing, for example, has a long history of acrimonious labor relations, leading to walk-outs and strikes. This in turn has not only delayed production of airplanes but also raised costs.

Stakeholder strategy is an integrative approach to managing a diverse set of stakeholders effectively in order to gain and sustain competitive advantage.[23] The unit of analysis is the web of exchange relationships a firm has with its stakeholders (see Exhibit 1.1). Stakeholder strategy allows firms to analyze and manage how various external and internal stakeholders interact to jointly create and trade value.[24] A core tenet of stakeholder strategy is that a single-minded focus on shareholders alone exposes a firm to undue risks. Simply putting shareholder interest above all else can undermine economic performance and even threaten the very survival of the enterprise. A strategic leader, therefore, must understand the complex web of exchange relationships among different stakeholders. With that understanding, the firm can proactively shape the various relationships to maximize the joint value created and manage the distribution of this larger pie in a fair and transparent manner. Effective stakeholder management exemplifies how strategic leaders can act to improve firm performance, thereby enhancing the firm's competitive advantage and the likelihood of its continued survival.[25]

Taken together, strategy scholars have provided several arguments as to why effective stakeholder management can benefit firm performance:[26]

- Satisfied stakeholders are more cooperative and thus more likely to reveal information that can further increase the firm's value creation or lower its costs.
- Increased trust lowers the costs for firms' business transactions.
- Effective management of the complex web of stakeholders can lead to greater organizational adaptability and flexibility.
- The likelihood of negative outcomes can be reduced, creating more predictable and stable returns.
- Firms can build strong reputations that are rewarded in the marketplace by business partners, employees, and customers. Most managers do care about public perception of the firm and frequently celebrate and publicize high-profile rankings such as the "World's Most Admired Companies" published annually by *Fortune*.[27] In 2018, the top five companies in this ranking were Apple, Amazon, Alphabet, Berkshire Hathaway (the conglomerate led by Warren Buffett), and Starbucks. Because of its continued innovation in products, services, and delivery, Apple has been ranked as the world's most admired company for the past several years by *Fortune*.

STAKEHOLDER IMPACT ANALYSIS

The key challenge of stakeholder strategy is to effectively balance the needs of various stakeholders. The firm needs to ensure that its primary stakeholders—the firm's shareholders and other investors—achieve their objectives. At the same time, the firm needs to recognize and address the concerns of other stakeholders—employees, suppliers, and customers—in an ethical and fair manner, so that they too are satisfied. This all sounds good in theory, but how can strategic leaders go about this in practice?

Stakeholder impact analysis provides a decision tool with which strategic leaders can recognize, prioritize, and address the needs of different stakeholders. This tool helps the firm achieve a competitive advantage while acting as a good corporate citizen. Stakeholder

stakeholder strategy
An integrative approach to managing a diverse set of stakeholders effectively in order to gain and sustain competitive advantage.

LO 1-4

Conduct a stakeholder impact analysis.

stakeholder impact analysis A decision tool with which managers can recognize, prioritize, and address the needs of different stakeholders, enabling the firm to achieve competitive advantage while acting as a good corporate citizen.

impact analysis takes strategic leaders through a five-step process of recognizing stakeholders' claims. In each step, they must pay particular attention to three important stakeholder attributes: *power, legitimacy,* and *urgency.*[28]

- A stakeholder has *power* over a company when it can get the company to do something that it would not otherwise do.
- A stakeholder has a *legitimate claim* when it is perceived to be legally valid or otherwise appropriate.
- A stakeholder has an *urgent claim* when it requires a company's immediate attention and response.

Exhibit 1.2 depicts the five steps in stakeholder impact analysis and the key questions to be asked. Let's look at each step in detail.

STEP 1: IDENTIFY STAKEHOLDERS. In Step 1, strategic leaders ask, "Who are our stakeholders?" In this step, the strategic leaders focus on stakeholders that currently have, or potentially can have, a material effect on a company. This prioritization identifies the most powerful internal and external stakeholders as well as their needs. For public-stock companies, key stakeholders are the shareholders and other providers of capital. If shareholders are not satisfied with returns to investment, they will sell the company's stock, leading to a fall in the firm's market value. If this process continues, it can make the company a takeover target, or launch a vicious cycle of continued decline.

A second group of stakeholders includes customers, suppliers, and unions. Local communities and the media are also powerful stakeholders that can affect the smooth operation of the firm. Any of these groups, if their needs are not met, can materially affect the company's operations.

For example, Boeing opened an airplane factory in South Carolina to move production away from its traditional plant near Seattle, Washington. South Carolina is one of 28 states in the United States that operates under a right-to-work law in which employees in unionized workplaces are allowed to work without being required to join the union. In contrast to its work force in Washington state, the South Carolina plant is nonunionized, which should

EXHIBIT 1.2 Stakeholder Impact Analysis

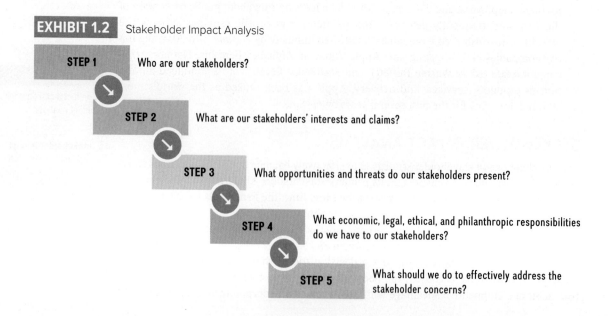

STEP 1 — Who are our stakeholders?

STEP 2 — What are our stakeholders' interests and claims?

STEP 3 — What opportunities and threats do our stakeholders present?

STEP 4 — What economic, legal, ethical, and philanthropic responsibilities do we have to our stakeholders?

STEP 5 — What should we do to effectively address the stakeholder concerns?

lead to fewer work interruptions due to strikes and Boeing hopes to higher productivity and improvements along other performance dimensions (like on-time delivery of new airplanes). Boeing decided to build its new 787 Dreamliner jet exclusively in its nonunionized South Carolina factory.[29]

STEP 2: IDENTIFY STAKEHOLDERS' INTERESTS. In Step 2, strategic leaders ask, "What are our stakeholders' interests and claims?" They need to specify and assess the interests and claims of the pertinent stakeholders using the power, legitimacy, and urgency criteria introduced earlier. As the legal owners, shareholders have the most legitimate claim on a company's profits. However, the wall separating the claims of ownership (by shareholders) and of management (by employees) has been eroding. Many companies incentivize top executives by paying part of their overall compensation with stock options. They also turn employees into shareholders through *employee stock ownership plans (ESOPs).* These plans allow employees to purchase stock at a discounted rate or use company stock as an investment vehicle for retirement savings. For example, Alphabet, Coca-Cola, Facebook, Microsoft, Southwest Airlines, Starbucks, and Walmart all offer ESOPs. Clearly, the claims and interests of stakeholders who are employed by the company, and who depend on the company for salary and other benefits, will be somewhat different from those of stakeholders who merely own stock. The latter are investors who are primarily interested in the increased value of their stock holdings through appreciation and dividend payments. Executives, managers, and workers tend to be more interested in career opportunities, job security, employer-provided health care, paid vacation time, and other perks.

Even within stakeholder groups there can be significant variation in the power a stakeholder may exert on the firm. For example, public companies pay much more attention to large investors than to the millions of smaller, individual investors. *Shareholder activists,* such as Bill Ackman, Carl Icahn, or Daniel Loeb, tend to buy equity stakes in a corporation that they believe is underperforming to put public pressure on a company to change its strategy. Examples include the takeover battle at Dell Computer (which founder Michael Dell subsequently took private, before going public again a few years later), the pressure on PepsiCo to spin off its Frito-Lay brand, or on Yahoo to sell itself to Verizon, which it did. Even top-performing companies are not immune to pressure by shareholder activists.[30] As a result of a sustained competitive advantage over the last decade, Apple had not only become the first company to be valued above $1 trillion but also amassed some $200 billion in cash in the process. Apple CEO Tim Cook faced significant pressure from Carl Icahn, who held roughly $4 billion worth of Apple stock, to buy back more of its shares and thus to further raise Apple's share price. Cook obliged, and Apple bought back a significant amount of stock, using its cash to buttress its share price.

Although both individual and activist investors may claim the same legitimacy as stockholders, shareholder activists have much more power over a firm. They can buy and sell a large number of shares at once or exercise block-voting rights in the *corporate governance process* (which we'll discuss in detail in Chapter 12). Shareholder activists frequently also demand seats on the company's board to more directly influence its corporate governance, and with it exert more pressure to change a company's strategy. These abilities make activist investors powerful stakeholders, with urgent and legitimate claims.

STEP 3: IDENTIFY OPPORTUNITIES AND THREATS. In Step 3, strategic leaders ask, "What opportunities and threats do our stakeholders present?" Since stakeholders have a claim on the company, opportunities and threats are two sides of the same coin. Consumer boycotts, for example, can be a credible threat to a company's behavior. Some consumers boycotted BP for its role in the 2010 Gulf of Mexico oil spill and resulting environmental damages; Nestlé products were boycotted when the firm promoted infant formula over breast milk in developing countries. PETA[31] called for a boycott of McDonald's due to alleged animal-rights abuses.

In the best-case scenario, managers transform such threats into opportunities. Sony Corp. of Japan, for example, was able to do just that.[32] During one holiday season, the Dutch government blocked Sony's entire holiday season shipment of PlayStation game systems, valued at roughly $500 million, into the European Union because of a small but legally unacceptable amount of toxic cadmium discovered in one of the system's cables. This incident led to an 18-month investigation in which Sony inspected over 6,000 supplier factories around the world to track down the source of the problem. The findings allowed Sony to redesign and develop a cutting-edge supplier management system that now adheres to a stringent extended value chain responsibility.

STEP 4: IDENTIFY SOCIAL RESPONSIBILITIES. In Step 4, strategic leaders ask, "What economic, legal, ethical, and philanthropic responsibilities do we have to our stakeholders?" To identify these responsibilities more effectively, scholars have advanced the notion of **corporate social responsibility (CSR).** This framework helps firms recognize and address the economic, legal, ethical, and philanthropic expectations that society has of the business enterprise at a given point in time.[33] According to the CSR perspective, strategic leaders need to realize that society grants shareholders the right and privilege to create a publicly traded stock company. Therefore, the firm owes something to society.[34] CSR provides strategic leaders with a conceptual model that more completely describes a society's expectations and can guide strategic decision making more effectively. In particular, CSR has four components:

> **corporate social responsibility (CSR)** A framework that helps firms recognize and address the economic, legal, social, and philanthropic expectations that society has of the business enterprise at a given point in time.

- Economic responsibilities
- Legal responsibilities
- Ethical responsibilities
- Philanthropic responsibilities[35]

Economic Responsibilities. The business enterprise is first and foremost an economic institution. Investors expect an adequate return for their risk capital. Creditors expect the firm to repay its debts. Consumers expect safe products and services at appropriate prices and quality. Suppliers expect to be paid in full and on time. Governments expect the firm to pay taxes and to manage natural resources such as air and water under a decent stewardship. To accomplish all this, firms must obey the law and act ethically in their quest to gain and sustain competitive advantage.

Nobel laureate Milton Friedman views the economic responsibility of the firm as its primary objective, as captured in his famous quote: "There is one and only one social responsibility of business—to use its resources and engage in activities designed to increase its profits so long as it stays within the rules of the game, which is to say, engages in open and free competition without deception or fraud."[36]

Legal Responsibilities. Laws and regulations are a society's codified ethics, embodying notions of right and wrong. They also establish the rules of the game. For example, business as an institution can function because property rights exist and contracts can be enforced in courts of law. Strategic leaders must ensure that their firms obey all the laws and regulations, including but not limited to labor, consumer protection, and environmental laws.

One far-reaching piece of U.S. legislation in terms of business impact, for example, is the Patient Protection and Affordable Care Act (PPACA), more commonly known as the

Affordable Care Act (ACA) or Obamacare. Key provisions of this federal law include, among others, that firms with 50 or more full-time employees must offer affordable health insurance to their employees and dependents, or pay a fine for each worker. This makes it harder for entrepreneurs to grow their ventures above this threshold. One reaction of many small businesses has been to reduce the number of full-time workers to 49 employees and add part-time employees only, which do not fall under this provision. Another reaction of employers is to offer lower wages to compensate for higher health care costs. Moreover, health insurance providers are no longer allowed to deny coverage based on preexisting medical conditions. As a consequence, health care premiums have been rising as the overall risk pool of insurers is less healthy.[37]

Ethical Responsibilities. Legal responsibilities, however, often define only the minimum acceptable standards of firm behavior. Frequently, strategic leaders are called upon to go beyond what is required by law. The letter of the law cannot address or anticipate all possible business situations and newly emerging concerns such as internet privacy or advances in artificial intelligence, DNA testing, genetic engineering, and stem-cell research. A firm's ethical responsibilities, therefore, go beyond its legal responsibilities. They embody the full scope of expectations, norms, and values of its stakeholders. Strategic leaders are called upon to do what society deems just and fair.

In the spring of 2018, Starbucks received harsh criticism from multiple stakeholders.[38] Calls to #BoycottStarbucks went viral on social media. What caused the firestorm? Two African-American men were arrested at one of its Philadelphia locations. Reports indicated that the two men had entered the Starbucks store and asked one of the employees to use the restroom. The employee refused permission because the men had not (yet) purchased anything. They proceeded to sit down, stating they were meeting an associate for a business meeting and that they would order upon his arrival. Shortly thereafter the two men were asked to leave the store. The store manager eventually called the police who arrested them for alleged trespassing. A patron videotaped the entire scene and then posted it to Twitter; it has since been viewed more than 11 million times and retweeted more than 150,000 times. In the video, we see police officers handcuffing the two men while a perplexed and upset bystander repeatedly asks the police, "But what did they do? What did they do? Someone tell me what they did."[39]

In response to the public outcry over the store's actions and the grave concerns expressed by stakeholders, Starbucks CEO Kevin Johnson issued a formal apology in which he expressed regret over the situation's "reprehensible outcome" and stated that the actions of the employees were "not representative of ... Starbucks' mission and values."[40] A few weeks after the incident, Starbucks, at a significant cost, closed its more than 8,000 stores across the United States for a full day and dedicated the day to racial bias and diversity training for all employees. This was not an action the firm was legally required to do, but one it felt ethically obligated to do to avoid a repeat of such incidents.[41]

Philanthropic Responsibilities. Philanthropic responsibilities are often subsumed under the idea of *corporate citizenship,* reflecting the notion of voluntarily giving back to society. Over the years, Microsoft's corporate philanthropy program has donated more than $3 billion in cash and software to people who can't afford computer technology.[42]

The pyramid in Exhibit 1.3 summarizes the four components of corporate social responsibility.[43] Economic responsibilities are the foundational building block, followed by legal, ethical, and philanthropic responsibilities. Note that society and shareholders *require* economic and legal responsibilities. Ethical and philanthropic responsibilities result from a society's expectations toward business. The pyramid symbolizes the need for firms to

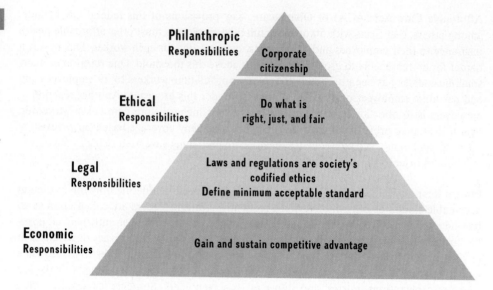

EXHIBIT 1.3

The Pyramid of
Corporate Social
Responsibility

Adapted from A. B.
(Carroll, 1991, July–
August), "The pyramid of
corporate social
responsibility: Toward the
moral management of
organizational
stakeholders," *Business
Horizons*: 42.

Philanthropic
Responsibilities

Corporate
citizenship

Ethical
Responsibilities

Do what is
right, just, and fair

Legal
Responsibilities

Laws and regulations are society's
codified ethics
Define minimum acceptable standard

Economic
Responsibilities

Gain and sustain competitive advantage

carefully balance their social responsibilities. Doing so ensures not only effective strategy
implementation, but also long-term viability.

STEP 5: ADDRESS STAKEHOLDER CONCERNS. Finally, in Step 5, the firm asks, "What
should we do to effectively address any stakeholder concerns?" In the last step in stakeholder impact analysis, strategic leaders need to decide the appropriate course of action
for the firm, given all of the preceding factors. Thinking about the attributes of power,
legitimacy, and urgency helps to prioritize the legitimate claims and to address them
accordingly.

Strategy Highlight 1.2 describes Merck's stakeholder strategy anchored in ethical core
values. It showcases how Merck considered and addressed various claims from a wide variety
of stakeholders, among them the most disadvantaged patients that can't afford to pay for
medications.

Strategy Highlight **1.2**

Merck's Stakeholder Strategy

Merck's vision is to *preserve and improve human life.* The
words of founder George W. Merck still form the basis of
the company's values today: *We try to never forget that
medicine is for the people. It is not for profits. The profits
follow, and if we have remembered that, they have never
failed to appear.*[44]

ENDING RIVER BLINDNESS Ray Vagelos, a former
Merck scientist turned CEO, announced (in 1987) that the
company would donate its recently discovered drug Mectizan, without charge, to treat river blindness. For centuries,

river blindness—a parasitic disease that leads to loss of eye-
sight—plagued remote communities in Africa and other parts
of the world. Merck's executives formed a novel private-
public partnership, the Mectizan Donation Program (MDP), to
distribute the drug in remote areas, where health services
are often not available.

After more than 25 years, more than 1 billion treatments, and some 120,000 communities served, the disease had effectively been eradicated. Merck's current
CEO, Kenneth Frazier, announced himself "humbled" by
the result of the company's value-driven actions.[45]

WITHDRAWING VIOXX In the case of another drug, though, Merck's stakeholder strategy was questioned. Vioxx was a painkiller developed to produce fewer gastrointestinal side effects than aspirin or ibuprofen. Once the Food and Drug Administration (FDA) approved the new drug in 1999, Merck engaged in typical big pharma promotional practices:

- Heavy direct-to-consumer advertising via TV and other media.
- Luxury doctor inducements, including consulting contracts and free retreats at exotic resorts.

Merck's new drug was a blockbuster, generating revenues of $2.5 billion a year by 2002 and growing fast.

Kenneth Frazier, CEO of Merck.
Stephanie Keith/Getty Images

Allegations began to appear, however, that Vioxx caused heart attacks and strokes. Critics alleged that Merck had suppressed evidence about Vioxx's dangerous side effects from early clinical trials. In 2004, Merck voluntarily recalled the drug. Merck's CEO at the time, Raymond Gilmartin, framed the situation in terms of knowledge learned *after* the initial release. He said he received a phone call from the head of research. "He told me that our long-term safety study of Vioxx was showing an increased risk of cardiovascular events compared to placebo, and the trial was being discontinued.... After analyzing the data further and consulting with outside experts, the Merck scientists recommended that we voluntarily withdraw the drug."[46]

Regardless of what Merck knew when, the voluntary withdrawal reconfirmed in a costly way its core value that patients come before profits. Merck's reputation damaged, its stock fell almost 30 percent, eradicating $27 billion in market value almost overnight—an amount much greater than the estimated net present value of the profits that Merck would have obtained from continued sales of Vioxx. Merck has been hit by lawsuits ever since; legal liabilities have cost the company up to $30 billion thus far.

Some corporate social responsibility experts argue that Merck should have never put Vioxx on the market in the first place, or that it should have at least provided up front, clear assessments of the risks associated with Vioxx.[47]

1.3 The Analysis, Formulation, Implementation (AFI) Strategy Framework

LO 1-5

Explain the Analysis, Formulation, Implementation (AFI) Strategy Framework.

How do leaders craft and execute a strategy that enhances their chances of achieving superior performance? A successful strategy details a set of actions that managers take to gain and sustain competitive advantage. Effectively managing the strategy process is the result of

1. Analysis (A)
2. Formulation (F)
3. Implementation (I)

These three tasks are the pillars of research and knowledge of strategic management. Although we will study these tasks one at a time, they are highly interdependent and frequently occur simultaneously. Effective managers do not formulate strategy without thinking about how to implement it, for instance. Likewise, while managers implement strategy, they also analyze the need to adjust to changing circumstances.

EXHIBIT 1.4   The Analysis, Formulation, Implementation (AFI) Strategy Framework

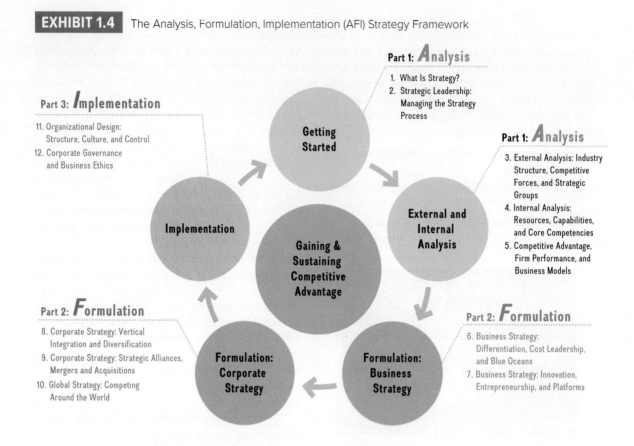

Part 1: *A*nalysis
1. What Is Strategy?
2. Strategic Leadership: Managing the Strategy Process

Part 1: *A*nalysis
3. External Analysis: Industry Structure, Competitive Forces, and Strategic Groups
4. Internal Analysis: Resources, Capabilities, and Core Competencies
5. Competitive Advantage, Firm Performance, and Business Models

Part 2: *F*ormulation
6. Business Strategy: Differentiation, Cost Leadership, and Blue Oceans
7. Business Strategy: Innovation, Entrepreneurship, and Platforms

Part 2: *F*ormulation
8. Corporate Strategy: Vertical Integration and Diversification
9. Corporate Strategy: Strategic Alliances, Mergers and Acquisitions
10. Global Strategy: Competing Around the World

Part 3: *I*mplementation
11. Organizational Design: Structure, Culture, and Control
12. Corporate Governance and Business Ethics

(Circle diagram labels: Getting Started; External and Internal Analysis; Formulation: Business Strategy; Formulation: Corporate Strategy; Implementation; center: Gaining & Sustaining Competitive Advantage)

Analysis, Formulation, Implementation (AFI) Strategy Framework
A model that links three interdependent strategic management tasks—analyze, formulate, and implement—that, together, help managers plan and implement a strategy that can improve performance and result in competitive advantage.

We've captured these interdependent relationships in the **Analysis, Formulation, Implementation (AFI) Strategy Framework** shown in Exhibit 1.4. This framework

1. Explains and predicts differences in firm performance.
2. Helps leaders formulate and implement a strategy that can result in superior performance.

Each broad strategy task raises specific *topics and questions* that managers must address. These questions and topics are listed below. They are also addressed in the specific chapters listed in Exhibit 1.4: chapters 1 to 5 address questions related to analysis; chapters 6 to 10 cover formulation; and chapters 11 to 12 cover implementation.

KEY TOPICS AND QUESTIONS OF THE AFI STRATEGY FRAMEWORK

Analysis (A)

- **Strategic Leadership and the Strategy Process.** *What roles do strategic leaders play, and how do they help shape a firm's vision, mission, and values? How does strategy come about, and what process for creating strategy should strategic leaders put in place?* (Chapter 2)
- **External Analysis.** *What effects do forces in the external environment have on the firm's potential to gain and sustain a competitive advantage? How should the firm deal with them?* (Chapter 3)

- **Internal Analysis.** *What effects do internal resources, capabilities, and core competencies have on the firm's potential to gain and sustain a competitive advantage? How should the firm leverage them for competitive advantage?* (Chapter 4)
- **Competitive Advantage, Firm Performance, and Business Models.** *How does the firm make money? How can one assess and measure competitive advantage? What is the relationship between competitive advantage and firm performance?* (Chapter 5)

Formulation (F)

- **Business Strategy.** *How should the firm compete: cost leadership, differentiation, or value innovation?* (Chapters 6 and 7)
- **Corporate Strategy.** *Where should the firm compete: industry, markets, and geography?* (Chapters 8 and 9)
- **Global Strategy.** *How and where should the firm compete: local, regional, national, or international?* (Chapter 10)

Implementation (I)

- **Organizational Design.** *How should the firm organize to turn the formulated strategy into action?* (Chapter 11)
- **Corporate Governance and Business Ethics.** *What type of corporate governance is most effective? How does the firm anchor strategic decisions in business ethics?* (Chapter 12)

The AFI Strategy Framework shown in Exhibit 1.4 is repeated at the beginning of each part of this text to help contextualize where we are in our study of the firm's quest to gain and sustain competitive advantage. In addition, the *AFI Strategic Management Process Map,* presented at the end of Chapter 1, illustrates the steps in the AFI framework in more detail. This strategic management process map highlights the key strategy concepts and frameworks we'll cover in each chapter. It also serves as a checklist for when you conduct a strategic management analysis.

We next turn to the *Implications for Strategic Leaders* section to provide practical applications and considerations of the material discussed in this chapter.

1.4 Implications for Strategic Leaders

Strategy is the art and science of success and failure. The difference between success and failure lies in an organization's strategy. A good strategy is grounded in a strategic management process that defines the competitive challenge, provides a guiding policy, and is implemented by coherent actions. A good strategy enhances the chances of achieving competitive advantage and superior performance. Moreover, strategic leaders appreciate the fact that competition is *everywhere.* Thus, you need a good strategy to deal with competition.

Strategic leaders are also mindful of the organization's internal and external *stakeholders,* because they have a vested claim or interest in the performance and continued survival of the firm. Using a *stakeholder strategy approach* enables strategic leaders to manage a diverse set of stakeholders effectively in order to gain and sustain competitive advantage.

The strategic leader also realizes that the principles of strategic management can be applied universally to all organizations. Strategy determines performance whether in organizations large or small, multinational Fortune 100 companies, for-profit or nonprofit organizations; in the private or the public sector; and in developed as well as emerging economies.

A good strategy is more likely to result when strategic leaders apply the three key tasks of the AFI Strategy Framework:

1. **A**nalysis of the external and internal environments.
2. **F**ormulation of an appropriate business and corporate strategy.
3. **I**mplementation of the formulated strategy through structure, culture, and controls.

Keep in mind that strategic leaders are making decisions under conditions of uncertainty and complexity. They must carefully monitor and evaluate the progress toward key strategic objectives and make adjustments by fine-tuning any strategy as necessary. We discuss how this is done in the next chapter where we focus on *strategic leaders* and *the strategic management process.*

CHAPTER**CASE 1** Part II

IN 2016, 10 years after Tesla's initial "secret strategy," Elon Musk unveiled the second part of his master plan for the company ("Master Plan, Part Deux") to continue the pursuit of its vision "to accelerate the advent of sustainable energy." Again, CEO Musk detailed a set of stretch goals:

1. Create stunning solar roofs with seamlessly integrated battery storage.
2. Expand the electric vehicle product line to address all major segments.
3. Develop a self-driving capability that is 10 times safer than manual via massive fleet learning.
4. Enable your car to make money for you when you aren't using it.[48]

Tesla's new solar roof, with a Tesla car and Powerwall in the garage.
Tesla/Newscom

In the updated strategy, Step 1 leverages the integration of SolarCity. The new Tesla company is now a fully integrated sustainable energy company, combining energy generation with energy storage from SolarCity. It provides energy generation via beautiful new solar roofs that look like regular shingles, but cost less, all things considered, and last longer. Tesla also offers its Powerwall to residential consumers, which allows customers to store the solar energy captured on their roofs for later use. Energy generation, therefore, becomes decentralized. This implies that consumers are able to generate and use energy without being dependent on any utility, and are able to sell back excess energy to utilities. Indeed, consumers will generate not only energy for the use of their Tesla cars but also enough to cover the energy needs of the entire house.

In Step 2, Tesla is planning to expand the lineup of its electric vehicles to address all major segments. Elon Musk excels in product development, and Tesla has several new vehicles including a compact SUV, a pickup truck, a bus, and a heavy-duty semi in development. In the spring of 2019, Tesla launched the Model Y, a compact SUV that is a smaller and much lower priced version of the Model X, starting at $39,000 (and a 230-mile range) with deliveries in spring 2021 and a higher-priced version starting at $47,000 to be available in the fall of 2020.

In Step 3, Tesla is aiming to further develop the self-driving capabilities of its vehicles. The goal is to make self-driving vehicles 10 times safer than manual driving, and thus being able to offer fully autonomous vehicles. Many industry observers expect that commercial trucks will be some of the first vehicles to drive fully autonomous, especially on interstate highways. In this fashion, the large trucks can drive 24-7, and need to stop only to recharge their batteries.

Fully autonomous driving capabilities are required for Tesla to fulfill Step 4 of the new master plan: Turn your car into an income-generating asset. The idea is to offer an Uber-like service made up of Tesla vehicles, but without any drivers. On average, cars are used less than three hours during a day.

The idea is that your autonomous-driving Tesla will be part of a shared vehicle fleet when you are not using your car. This will drastically reduce the total cost of ownership of a Tesla vehicle, and it will also allow pretty much anyone to ride in a Tesla as a result of the sharing economy.[49]

Questions

1. Do you agree with the assessment that Elon Musk and Tesla successfully fulfilled the first master plan published in 2006? Why or why not? To answer this question, apply the three-step process for crafting a *good strategy* explained in Section 1.1 (*diagnose the competitive challenge, derive a guiding policy,* and *implement a set of coherent actions*).

2. Does Tesla have a *good strategy*? Why or why not? How do you know? Consider: By summer 2019, Tesla's market cap had fallen by 30 percent to $45 billion, down from $65 billion a year earlier. Many wondered: Is Tesla in trouble?

3. Describe the rationale behind Tesla's new master plan. How does this new strategy help Tesla fulfill its vision? To view Tesla's "Master Plan, Part Deux" in its entirety, see Tesla's blog: www.tesla.com/blog/master-plan-part-deux.

4. Apply again the three-step process for crafting a *good strategy* (see Section 1.1), this time to each element of the new master plan. On which steps of the new master plan has Tesla made the most progress? Explain. Also, what recommendations would you offer Elon Musk? Support your arguments and recommendations with examples and observations from the ChapterCase.

mySTRATEGY

Who are your stakeholders?

How do you think about accomplishing your goals? One way to strategize your success is to use a version of the stakeholder impact analysis. On a personal level, your internal stakeholders might be immediate family members and close personal friends. External stakeholders could be neighbors, peers, funding sources, and managers.

A key aspect presented in this chapter is to consider the point of view of a variety of stakeholders in meeting the goals of the firm. The same logic applies to many of your own personal or career goals as well. For instance, let's say you are close to graduating from a university. How do your stakeholders view your job and career prospects? Do they want you to stay close to home? Do they encourage you to start a new business?

As noted in the chapter, stakeholders will have different points of view and also different levels of impact upon your successes or failures.

1. List your personal goals. Which stakeholders are supportive of these goals? Which are likely to try to block these goals?

2. Develop a plan to address key stakeholder concerns from each perspective. Can you find a pathway in the stakeholder analysis to build support for your key goals?

3. What would it take to implement your ideas/plans to move forward with these goals?

TAKE-AWAY CONCEPTS

This chapter introduced the concept of s*trategy* and the key role it plays in the success or failure of an organization. We learned that a *good strategy* results from a strategic management process that defines the competitive challenge, provides a guiding policy, and is implemented by coherent actions. A good strategy enhances the chances of achieving competitive advantage and superior performance. It also examines the relationship between *stakeholder strategy* and s*ustainable competitive advantage.* Finally, this chapter set the stage for further study of strategic management by introducing the *AFI Strategy Framework.*

LO 1-1 / Explain the role of strategy in a firm's quest for competitive advantage.

- Strategy is the set of goal-directed actions a firm takes to gain and sustain superior performance relative to competitors.
- A good strategy enables a firm to achieve superior performance. It consists of three elements:
  1. A diagnosis of the competitive challenge.
  2. A guiding policy to address the competitive challenge.
  3. A set of coherent actions to implement the firm's guiding policy.
- A successful strategy requires three integrative management tasks—analysis, formulation, and implementation.

LO 1-2 / Define competitive advantage, sustainable competitive advantage, competitive disadvantage, and competitive parity.

- Competitive advantage is always judged relative to other competitors or the industry average.
- To obtain a competitive advantage, a firm must either create more value for customers while keeping its cost comparable to competitors, or it must provide the value equivalent to competitors but at a lower cost.
- A firm able to outperform competitors for prolonged periods of time has a sustained competitive advantage.
- A firm that continuously underperforms its rivals or the industry average has a competitive disadvantage.
- Two or more firms that perform at the same level have competitive parity.
- An effective strategy requires that strategic trade-offs be recognized and addressed—for example, between value creation and the costs to create the value.

LO 1-3 / Assess the relationship between stakeholder strategy and sustainable competitive advantage.

- *Stakeholders* are individuals or groups that have a claim or interest in the performance and continued survival of the firm. They make specific contributions for which they expect rewards in return.
- *Internal stakeholders* include stockholders, employees (for instance, executives, managers, and workers), and board members.
- *External stakeholders* include customers, suppliers, alliance partners, creditors, unions, communities, governments at various levels, and the media.
- The effective management of stakeholders is necessary to ensure the continued survival of the firm and to sustain any competitive advantage. This is achieved through *stakeholder strategy.*

LO 1-4 / Conduct a stakeholder impact analysis.

- Stakeholder impact analysis considers the needs of different stakeholders, which enables the firm to perform optimally and to live up to the expectations of good citizenship.
- In a stakeholder impact analysis, managers pay particular attention to three important stakeholder attributes: power, legitimacy, and urgency.
- Stakeholder impact analysis is a five-step process that answers the following questions for the firm:
  1. Who are our stakeholders?
  2. What are our stakeholders' interests and claims?
  3. What opportunities and threats do our stakeholders present?
  4. What economic, legal, ethical, and philanthropic responsibilities do we have to our stakeholders?
  5. What should we do to effectively address the stakeholder concerns?

LO 1-5 / Explain the Analysis, Formulation, Implementation (AFI) Strategy Framework.

- The Analysis, Formulation, Implementation (AFI) Strategy Framework (1) explains and predicts differences in firm performance, and (2) helps managers formulate and implement a strategy that can result in superior performance.
- Effectively managing the strategy process is the result of
  1. *Analysis (A)*
  2. *Formulation (F)*
  3. *Implementation (I)*

KEY TERMS

Analysis, Formulation, Implementation (AFI) Strategy Framework *(p. 22)*

Competitive advantage *(p. 10)*

Competitive disadvantage *(p. 10)*

Competitive parity *(p. 10)*

Corporate social responsibility (CSR) *(p. 18)*

Good strategy *(p. 7)*

Stakeholder impact analysis *(p. 15)*

Stakeholder strategy *(p. 15)*

Stakeholders *(p. 14)*

Strategic management *(p. 6)*

Strategy *(p. 6)*

Sustainable competitive advantage *(p. 10)*

Value creation *(p. 13)*

DISCUSSION QUESTIONS

1. The text discusses strategic trade-offs that are different between Walmart and Nordstrom even though they are in the same industry. Think of another industry that you know fairly well and select two firms there that also have made very different choices for these trade-offs. Describe some of the differences between these firms. What type of trade-off decisions have these firms made?

2. Corporate social responsibility has four components. Do you agree that public firms should address all four elements? Why or why not? If not, where should the firm "draw the line"? Please provide an example to explain your logic.

3. In the discussion about Merck (Strategy Highlight 1.2), the firm faces difficult situations about life-saving drugs. What is your assessment of Merck's consideration of various stakeholders in the two situations described?

ENDNOTES

1. Market capitalization (or, market cap) = Share price × Number of outstanding shares.

2. Musk, E. (2006, Aug. 2), "The secret Tesla Motors Master Plan (just between you and me)," Tesla website, http://bit.ly/29Y1c3m.

3. This ChapterCase is based on: Hoang, H., and F. T. Rothaermel (2016), "How to manage alliances strategically," *MIT Sloan Management Review,* Fall, 58(1): 69–76; Ramsey, M., Jacobides, M. G., J. P. MacDuffie, and C. J. Tae (2016), "Agency, structure, and the dominance of OEMs: Change and stability in the automotive sector," *Strategic Management Journal,* 37(9): 1942– 1967; Perkins, G., and J. P. Murmann (2018), "What does the success of Tesla mean for the future dynamics in the global automobile sector?" *Management and Organization Review* (14) 3: 471–480; Ramsey, M., (2016, March 30), "A lot riding on Tesla's Model 3 unveiling," *The Wall Street Journal;* Ramsey, M., and C. Sweet (2016, Aug. 1), "Tesla and SolarCity agree to $2.6 billion deal," *The Wall Street Journal;* Pulliam, S., M. Ramsey, and I. J. Dugan (2016, Aug. 15), "Elon Musk sets ambitious goals at Tesla—and often falls short," *The Wall Street Journal;* "The

Falcon Heavy's creator is trying to change more worlds than one," *The Economist,* Feb. 10, 2018; and Tesla Inc. Annual Reports (various years).

4. This section draws on: McGrath, R.G. (2013), *The End of Competitive Advantage: How to Keep Your Strategy Moving as Fast as Your Business* (Boston: Harvard Business Review Press); Rumelt, R. (2011), *Good Strategy, Bad Strategy: The Difference and Why It Matters* (New York: Crown Business); Porter, M.E. (2008, January), "The five competitive forces that shape strategy," *Harvard Business Review:* 78–93; Porter, M.E. (1996, November–December), "What is strategy?" *Harvard Business Review:* 61–78; and Porter, M.E. (1980), *Competitive Strategy: Techniques for Analyzing Competitors* (New York: The Free Press).

5. As quoted in: Rothaermel, F. T. (2017), "Tesla, Inc.," *McGraw-Hill Education Case Study MHE-FTR-032.*

6. Tesla's mission statement. Tesla, Inc.

7. Range anxiety denotes the concern that an electric vehicle has insufficient range to reach

its destination on a single charge. Tesla's cars can go some 250 miles per charge. The lower cost Nissan Leaf (~$30k) can go some 85 miles per charge, while GM's Chevy Bolt can drive some 200 miles per charge, based on EPA estimates. The average American drives about 40 miles per day. http://www.fueleconomy.gov/

8. The discussion of Tesla throughout this chapter is based on Rothaermel, F.T., and D. King (2015), Tesla Motors, Inc., *McGraw-Hill Education Case Study MHE-FTR-032;* Hoang, H., and F. T. Rothaermel (2016, Fall), "How to manage alliances strategically," *MIT Sloan Management Review,* 58(1): 69–76; Ramsey, M. (2016, March 30), "A lot riding on Tesla's Model 3 unveiling," *The Wall Street Journal;* Ramsey, M., and C. Sweet (2016, Aug. 1), "Tesla and SolarCity agree to $2.6 billion deal," *The Wall Street Journal;* Pulliam, S., M. Ramsey, and I.J. Dugan (2016, Aug. 15), "Elon Musk sets ambitious goals at Tesla—and often falls short," *The Wall Street Journal;* and Ramsey, M. (2014, June 12), "Tesla Motors offers open licenses to its patents," *The Wall Street Journal.*

9. Market capitalization (or, market cap) = Share price × Number of outstanding shares.

10. "Twitter's future: How high can it fly?" *The Economist* (2014, Nov. 7), https://www. economist.com/business/2014/11/07/how-high-can-it-fly.

11. This Strategy Highlight is based on the following sources: Bilton, N. (2013), *Hatching Twitter: A True Story of Money, Power, Friendship, and Betrayal* (London, UK: Sceptre); "Twitter in retweet," *The Economist* (2016, Sept. 17); "New models for new media," *The Economist* (2017, Feb. 16); Conger, K. (2018, Oct. 25), "Twitter posts another profit as user numbers drop," *The New York Times*; and Twitter annual reports (various years).

12. This section draws on Porter, M.E. (2008, January) "The five competitive forces that shape strategy," *Harvard Business Review*; Porter, M.E. (1996, November–December), "What is strategy?" *Harvard Business Review*; and Porter, M.E. (1989), *Competitive Strategy* (New York: Free Press).

13. Rumelt, R.P. (2011), *Good Strategy, Bad Strategy: The Difference and Why It Matters* (New York: Crown); and Porter, M.E. (1996, November–December), "What is strategy?" *Harvard Business Review*.

14. Rumelt, R.P. (2011), *Good Strategy, Bad Strategy: The Difference and Why It Matters* (New York: Crown); and Porter, M.E. (1996, November–December), "What is strategy?" *Harvard Business Review*.

15. Koh, Y., and K. Grind (2014, Nov. 6), "Twitter CEO Dick Costolo struggles to define vision," *The Wall Street Journal*.

16. Smith, A. (1776), *An Inquiry into the Nature and Causes of the Wealth of Nations,* 5th ed. (published 1904) (London: Methuen and Co.).

17. Levy, S. (2011), *In the Plex: How Google Thinks, Works, and Shapes Our Lives* (New York: Simon & Schuster); and www.wolframalpha.com/input/?i=google.

18. "The HP Way," see www.hpalumni.org/hp_way.htm; and Packard, D. (1995), *HP Way: How Bill Hewlett and I Built Our Company* (New York: HarperCollins).

19. This discussion draws on: Carroll, A.B., and A.K. Buchholtz (2012), *Business & Society: Ethics, Sustainability, and Stakeholder Management* (Mason, OH: South-Western Cengage); Porter, M.E., and M.R. Kramer (2011, January–February), "Creating shared value: How to reinvent capitalism—and unleash innovation and growth," *Harvard Business Review*; Parmar, B.L., R.E. Freeman, J.S. Harrison, A.C. Wicks, L. Purnell, and S. De Colle (2010), "Stakeholder theory: The state of the art," *Academy of Management Annals* 4:

403–445; and Porter, M.E., and M.R. Kramer (2006, December), "Strategy and society: The link between competitive advantage and corporate social responsibility," *Harvard Business Review*: 80–92.

20. See the discussion by Lowenstein, R. (2010), *The End of Wall Street* (New York: Penguin Press); Paulson, H.M. (2010), *On the Brink: Inside the Race to Stop the Collapse of the Global Financial System* (New York: Business Plus); and Wessel, D. (2010), *In FED We Trust: Ben Bernanke's War on the Great Panic* (New York: Crown Business).

21. Parmar, B.L., R.E. Freeman, J.S. Harrison, A.C. Wicks, L. Purnell, and S. De Colle (2010), "Stakeholder theory: The state of the art," *Academy of Management Annals* 4: 403–445.

22. Phillips, R. (2003), *Stakeholder Theory and Organizational Ethics* (San Francisco: Berrett-Koehler); Freeman, E.R., and J. McVea (2001), "A stakeholder approach to strategic management," in Hitt, M.A., E.R. Freeman, and J.S. Harrison (eds.), *The Blackwell Handbook of Strategic Management* (Oxford, UK: Blackwell), 189–207; and Freeman, E.R. (1984), *Strategic Management: A Stakeholder Approach* (Boston, MA: Pitman).

23. To acknowledge the increasing importance of *stakeholder strategy,* the Strategic Management Society (SMS)—the leading association for academics, business executives, and consultants interested in strategic management—has recently created a *stakeholder strategy* division; see http://strategicmanagement.net/. Also see Anderson, R.C. (2009), *Confessions of a Radical Industrialist: Profits, People, Purpose—Doing Business by Respecting the Earth* (New York: St. Martin's Press); Sisodia, R.S., D.B. Wolfe, and J.N. Sheth (2007), *Firms of Endearment: How World-Class Companies Profit from Passion and Purpose* (Upper Saddle River, NJ: Prentice-Hall Pearson); and Svendsen, A. (1998), *The Stakeholder Strategy: Profiting from Collaborative Business Relationships* (San Francisco: Berrett-Koehler).

24. Parmar, B.L., R.E. Freeman, J.S. Harrison, A.C. Wicks, L. Purnell, and S. De Colle (2010), "Stakeholder theory: The state of the art," *Academy of Management Annals* 4: 406.

25. Parmar, B.L., R.E. Freeman, J.S. Harrison, A.C. Wicks, L. Purnell, and S. De Colle (2010), "Stakeholder theory: The state of the art," *Academy of Management Annals* 4: 406.

26. Parmar, B.L., R.E. Freeman, J.S. Harrison, A.C. Wicks, L. Purnell, and S. De Colle (2010), "Stakeholder theory: The state of the art," *Academy of Management Annals* 4: 406.

27. "The World's Most Admired Companies," *Fortune* (2018), http://fortune.com/worlds-most-admired-companies.

28. Eesley, C., and M.J. Lenox (2006), "Firm responses to secondary stakeholder action," *Strategic Management Journal* 27: 765–781; and Mitchell, R.K., B.R. Agle, and D.J. Wood (1997), "Toward a theory of stakeholder identification and salience," *Academy of Management Review* 22: 853–886.

29. Ostrower, J. (2014, July 30), "Boeing to build stretched 787-10 in South Carolina," *The Wall Street Journal*.

30. Benoit, D. (2014, Feb. 10), "Icahn ends Apple push with hefty profit," *The Wall Street Journal*.

31. People for the Ethical Treatment of Animals (PETA) is an animal-rights organization.

32. This example is drawn from: Esty, D.C., and A.S. Winston (2006), *Green to Gold: How Smart Companies Use Environmental Strategy to Innovate, Create Value, and Build Competitive Advantage* (Hoboken, NJ: Wiley).

33. This discussion draws on: Carroll, A.B., and A.K. Buchholtz (2012), *Business & Society: Ethics, Sustainability, and Stakeholder Management* (Mason, OH: South-Western Cengage); Carroll, A.B. (1991, July–August), "The pyramid of corporate social responsibility: Toward the moral management of organizational stakeholders," *Business Horizons*: 39–48; and Carroll, A.B. (1979), "A three-dimensional, conceptual model of corporate social performance," *Academy of Management Review* 4: 497–505.

34. For an insightful but critical treatment of this topic, see the 2003 Canadian documentary film *The Corporation*.

35. For recent empirical findings concerning the relationship between corporate social responsibility and firm performance, see Barnett, M.L., and R.M. Salomon (2012), "Does it pay to be really good? Addressing the shape of the relationship between social and financial performance," *Strategic Management Journal* 33: 1304–1320; Wang, T., and P. Bansal (2012), "Social responsibility in new ventures: Profiting from a long-term orientation,"*Strategic Management Journal* 33: 1135–1153; and Jayachandran, S., K. Kalaignanam, and M. Eilert (2013), "Product and environmental social performance: Varying effect on firm performance,"*Strategic Management Journal* 34: 1255–1264.

36. Friedman, M. (1970, Sept. 13), "The social responsibility of business is to increase its profits," *The New York Times Magazine*.

37. Armour, S. (2015, Oct. 25), "ACA premiums jump 25%; administration acknowledges extended enrollment," *The Wall Street Journal*.

38. Gasparro, A. and T. D. Hobbs (2018, April 15), "Starbucks faces backlash over arrest of black men," *The Wall Street Journal*.

39. The video of the arrest can be viewed at https://bit.ly/2HzKhTH.

40. Stevens, M. (2018, April 17), "Starbucks CEO apologizes after arrests of 2 black men," *The New York Times*.

41. Jargon, J., and L. Weber (2018, April 17), "Starbucks to shut stores for antibias training," *The Wall Street Journal*; and Meyer, D. (2018, May 29), "Starbucks is closing today for its company-wide unconscious bias training: Here's what you need to know," *Fortune*.

42. Gates, B. (2008, Aug. 11), "How to help those left behind," *Time*.

43. Carroll, A.B. (1991, July–August), "The pyramid of corporate social responsibility: Toward the moral management of organizational stakeholders," *Business Horizons*: 39–48.

44. As quoted in: Collins, J. (2009), *How the Mighty Fall. And Why Some Companies Never Give In* (New York: HarperCollins), 53.

45. http://www.merck.com/about/featured-stories/mectizan1.html.

46. Gilmartin, R.V. (2011, Oct. 6), "The Vioxx recall tested our leadership," *Harvard Business Review Blog Network*.

47. The Merck river blindness case and the quote by CEO Kenneth Frazier draw from: http://www.merck.com/about/featured-stories/mectizan1.html. The Vioxx example draws from "Jury finds Merck liable in Vioxx death and awards $253 million," *The New York Times,* August 19, 2005; Heal, G. (2008), *When Principles Pay: Corporate Social Responsibility and the Bottom Line* (New York: Columbia Business School); Collins, J. (2009), *How the Mighty Fall. And Why Some Companies Never Give In* (New York: HarperCollins); and Wang, T., and P. Bansal (2012), "Social responsibility in new ventures: profiting from a long-term orientation," *Strategic Management Journal* 33: 1135–1153.

48. Musk, E. (2016, Jul. 20), "Master Plan, Part Deux," http://bit.ly/2aa5LHv.

49. Ramsey, M. (2016, Jul. 21), "Elon Musk unveils plans for new Tesla vehicle types," *The Wall Street Journal;* Musk, E. (2019, Mar. 14), "Tesla Y Launch Event," www.youtube.com/watch?v=lIkm6xhror4&t=4s [33:53 min].

The Strategic Management Process Map

ANALYSIS

CHAPTER 1
What Is Strategy?

- Gaining and Sustaining Competitive Advantage
- Stakeholder Strategy
- Stakeholder Impact Analysis
- Analysis, Formulation, Implementation (AFI) Framework

CHAPTER 2
Strategic Leadership: Managing the Strategy Process

- Corporate, Business, and Functional Strategy
- Vision, Mission, Values
- Top-Down Strategic Planning
- Scenario Planning
- Strategy as Planned Emergence
- Strategic Decision Making

CHAPTER 3
External Analysis: Industry Structure, Competitive Forces, and Strategic Groups

- PESTEL Framework
- Porter's Five Forces Model
- Strategic Complements
- Entry Choices
- Industry Dynamics
- Strategic Groups

CHAPTER 4
Internal Analysis: Resources, Capabilities, and Core Competencies

- Core Competencies
- Resource-Based View (RBV)
- VRIO Framework
- Dynamic Capabilities Perspective
- Value Chain Analysis
- Strategic Activity Systems
- SWOT Analysis: Integrating External & Internal Analyses

CHAPTER 5
Competitive Advantage, Firm Performance, and Business Models

- Accounting Profitability
- Shareholder Value Creation
- Economic Value Creation
- Balanced Scorecard
- Triple Bottom Line
- Business Models

CHAPTER 6
Business Strategy: Differentiation, Cost Leadership, and Blue Oceans

- Generic Business Strategies
- Value Drivers and Differentiation Strategy
- Cost Drivers and Cost-Leadership Strategy
- Value Drivers, Cost Drivers, and Blue Ocean Strategy
- "Stuck in the Middle"

FORMULATION

CHAPTER 7
Business Strategy: Innovation, Entrepreneurship, and Platforms

- The 4 I's: Idea, Invention, Innovation, & Imitation
- Strategic and Social Entrepreneurship
- Innovation and the Industry Life Cycle
- Crossing the Chasm
- Technology and Markets: Types of Innovation
- Platform vs. Pipeline Business Models
- Platform Ecosystem

CHAPTER 8
Corporate Strategy: Vertical Integration and Diversification

- Boundaries of the Firm
- Vertical Integration along the Industry Value Chain
- Types of Corporate Diversification
- Core Competence-Market Matrix
- BCG Growth-Share Matrix

CHAPTER 9
Corporate Strategy: Strategic Alliances, and Mergers & Acquisitions

- Build-Borrow-Buy Framework
- Strategic Alliances
- Alliance Management Capability
- Mergers and Acquisitions (M&A)
- Horizontal Integration

CHAPTER 10
Global Strategy: Competing Around the World

- Globalization
- Going Global: Why?, Where?, and How?
- The CAGE Distance Framework
- The Integration-Responsiveness Framework
- Porter's Diamond Framework

IMPLEMENTATION

CHAPTER 11
Organizational Design: Structure, Culture, and Control

- Simple Structure
- Functional Structure
- Multidivisional Structure
- Matrix Structure
- Open vs. Closed Innovation
- Organizational Culture
- Control and Reward Systems

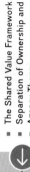

CHAPTER 12
Corporate Governance and Business Ethics

- The Shared Value Framework
- Separation of Ownership and Control
- Agency Theory
- Board of Directors
- Other Governance Mechanisms
- Business Ethics and Sustainable Competitive Advantage

Strategic Leadership: Managing the Strategy Process

Chapter Outline

Learning Objectives

After studying this chapter, you should be able to:

LO 2-1 Explain the role of strategic leaders and what they do.

LO 2-2 Outline how you can become a strategic leader.

LO 2-3 Compare and contrast the roles of corporate, business, and functional managers in strategy formulation and implementation.

LO 2-4 Describe the roles of vision, mission, and values in a firm's strategy.

LO 2-5 Evaluate the strategic implications of product-oriented and customer-oriented vision statements.

LO 2-6 Justify why anchoring a firm in ethical core values is essential for long-term success.

LO 2-7 Evaluate top-down strategic planning, scenario planning, and strategy as planned emergence.

LO 2-8 Describe and evaluate the two distinct modes of decision making.

LO 2-9 Compare and contrast devil's advocacy and dialectic inquiry as frameworks to improve strategic decision making.

Leadership Crisis at Facebook?

WITHIN A MERE SIX MONTHS, in the latter half of 2018, Facebook's share price dropped by more than 30 percent, wiping out over $200 billion in shareholder value. Making matters worse was a seeming crisis of leadership swirling around Facebook's two top executives: founder and Chief Executive Officer Mark Zuckerberg and Chief Operating Officer Sheryl Sandberg. After a decade of exponential growth and unabated success, the global social network with its more than 2 billion monthly active users found itself in serious trouble.

FACEBOOK'S LEADERSHIP DUO

As depicted in the Hollywood movie *The Social Network* (2010), Facebook began as a startup in 2004 in the Harvard dorm room of then 19-year-old Mark Zuckerberg with the support of three college pals. At the time, Myspace was the leading social networking site, and in 2005, it was acquired by News Corp. for close to $600 million. For several years, Facebook lagged behind Myspace in both investments and users, but it stayed alive thanks to cash injections from Microsoft, Yahoo, and a Russian investment group.

In 2008 Mark Zuckerberg made a genius move: He persuaded Sheryl Sandberg, at the time the vice president of global online sales and operations at Google, to leave Google and join Facebook as the new second in command. Zuckerberg was a computer hacker at heart. He opted to spend his energy on fulfilling his vision of Facebook—to turn it into a tool that would "make a more open and connected world."[1] He preferred coding to business deals and freely admitted that he did not have the skills to run a business successfully. Sandberg did. She brought with her all the business skills that Zuckerberg lacked. She had demonstrated her superb leadership capabilities at Google and was recognized for her sales, business development, public policy, and communications prowess. Put simply, and partially, Zuckerberg saw his role as bringing in the users; he saw Sandberg's role as bringing in the money.

Facebook's dynamite leadership duo: CEO Mark Zuckerberg and COO Sheryl Sandberg
(left): David Ramos/Getty Images, (right): Justin Sullivan/Getty Images.

The Zuckerberg–Sandberg leadership duo would turn out to be pure dynamite. It led to exponential growth—from 100 million users in 2008 to 1 billion users in 2012—a feat that no other firm has ever accomplished. Just five years later, in 2017, Facebook crossed the 2 billion users mark. By the summer of 2018, Facebook's market capitalization stood at more than $600 billion, up over 630 percent since its initial public offering (IPO) in 2012—a mere six years earlier.

THE END OF THE ZUCKERBERG–SANDBERG ERA?

By 2019, Facebook found itself caught in a perfect storm, and many were demanding that Zuckerberg and Sandberg step down. What had happened? Due to its lenient privacy controls, third parties were able to siphon off the personal data of tens of millions of Facebook users; lax data oversight also led to other alleged misdeeds, including the enabling of foreign interference during the 2016 U.S. presidential elections. Critics assert that because of its single-minded pursuit of exponential growth, Facebook's leadership failed to consider the potentiality and gravity of negative side effects on the firm, its stakeholders, and its reputation.

Facebook's exclusive focus on user growth began in 2012 shortly before its IPO. In a fateful meeting of top executives and lead product developers, Sandberg showed that Facebook's revenues were flat and user growth was slowing considerably. For a social media company to grow, she said, it must pursue a business model that provides free services to the end user but that charges advertisers for placing online ads. Sandberg admonished the lead product developers, saying "things had to change" and "we have to do something."[2] This meant, as one of the software engineers present at the meeting recalls, that "we needed to pull out all of the stops and to experiment way more aggressively with user engagement with the goal to make money."[3] The marching orders were clear: Drive exponential growth and user engagement, while keeping costs down. Very quickly, software engineers and product developers learned that four features could serve as the keys to increasing user engagement and driving future growth: News Feed, Likes, polarizing news, and microtargeting.

Facebook's News Feed is akin to a personalized newspaper and gossip page. A proprietary algorithm identifies the content that will be most interesting to each unique user and accordingly compiles a customized News Feed for that user. Meanwhile, the Like button, internally described as a "social lubricant and social flywheel by which users [feel] they [are] heard,"[4] has helped Facebook to better understand its users. Product developers noticed that polarizing news and messages were often the most liked. Note that Facebook's algorithm doesn't know which content is good or bad, polarizing or non-polarizing, fake or real. It only knows to which content users most respond. About two-thirds of all Americans get their news from social media sites such as Facebook, and over time, hyped-up and outrageous content increasingly made its way into users' personal News Feeds, creating a much more polarized and tribal user base. Further compounding this situation is the fact that Facebook does not engage in any editorial review of the content that surfaces on its site. Rather, it relies on its algorithm, fine-tuned to maximize user engagement, to serve as its editor. On top of the data breaches and privacy issues, this polarization of Facebook's users has only exacerbated matters for the firm.

Facebook and Google have captured most of the astronomical growth in online advertising spending over the past few years, reaching $100 billion in 2018.[5] A massive base of more than 2 billion users, combined with high user engagement, has enabled Facebook to place and sell ads with extreme accuracy—what is known as microtargeting. For microtargeting to work effectively, it relies on accurate user profiles. Now that Facebook owns the photo-sharing app Instagram and the messaging service WhatsApp, it has additional data sources at its disposal to help it to create even more accurate user profiles. All these data are combined with a user's "shadow profile," which enables Facebook to not only track each of its user's activities, but the activities of his or her friends as well, even as they move across the web visiting other non-Facebook sites. As a result, Facebook can offer the most detailed, accurate, and targeted data to advertisers.

Part II of this ChapterCase appears in Section 2.5.

HOW DO STRATEGIC LEADERS like Sheryl Sandberg guide their companies to gain and sustain a competitive advantage? How do they make strategic decisions? How do strategic leaders formulate and implement their companies' strategies? How do they lead and motivate employees?

In Chapter 2, we move from thinking about *why* strategy is important to what role strategic leaders play, specifically *how* strategic leaders select, guide, and manage the strategy process across different levels in the organization. One of the first things a strategic leader must do is to shape an organization's vision, mission, and values, as each of these plays an important role in anchoring a winning strategy. We then explore some of the frameworks strategic leaders use to develop strategy and maintain an effective strategic management process. Next we delve deeper into strategic decision making, in particular how biases, even those that strategic leaders and groups may not be consciously aware of, can impact the ability to make rational decisions. Lastly, we summarize some of the most important practical insights in our *Implications for Strategic Leaders*.

2.1 Strategic Leadership

Executives whose vision and decisions enable their organizations to achieve competitive advantage demonstrate strategic leadership.[6] **Strategic leadership** pertains to executives' use of power and influence to direct the activities of others when pursuing an organization's goals.[7] *Power* is defined as the strategic leader's ability to influence the behavior of other organizational members to do things, including things they would not do otherwise.[8] Strategic leaders can draw on position power as vested in their authority, for example as chief executive officer (CEO), as well as informal power, such as persuasion to influence others when implementing strategy.

In leading Facebook to become the most successful social network and one of the most valuable companies worldwide, Sheryl Sandberg has clearly demonstrated effective strategic leadership. As chief operating officer (COO), Sandberg has tremendous position power because she is the second in command at Facebook and reports only to CEO Mark Zuckerberg. Sandberg's business development skills are legendary: She transformed a money-losing outfit into a titan of online advertising, with over $65 billion in annual revenues. She designed and implemented Facebook's business model (how it makes money). In particular, Sandberg attracted high-profile advertisers by demonstrating how Facebook can place precisely targeted and timed ads when it matches what it knows about each user, based on that person's social network, with the advertisers' targets. Less quantifiable, but perhaps an even more valuable contribution, Sandberg provides "adult supervision and a professional face" for a firm populated by socially awkward computer geeks.[9]

Indra Nooyi, PepsiCo CEO, 2006–2018. Nooyi is a transformational strategic leader who guided PepsiCo with a powerful vision of "performance with purpose." Under Nooyi's leadership, PepsiCo transformed itself into a company offering more healthy snack and beverage choices, while its revenues grew by 80 percent. Moreover, Nooyi's 12-year tenure as CEO is more than double the length of the average Fortune 500 CEO.

Alex Goodlett/Getty Images

While the effect of strategic leaders may vary, they clearly matter to firm performance.[10] Think of great business founders and their impact on the companies they built—Mark Zuckerberg at Facebook, Phil Knight at Nike, Elon Musk at Tesla and SpaceX, Jack Ma at Alibaba, Oprah Winfrey with her media empire, and Jeff Bezos at Amazon. Many strategic leaders also have shaped and revitalized existing businesses. In addition to Sheryl Sandberg at Facebook, we have Angela Ahrendts at Apple (left in 2019), Sundar Pichai at Google, Mary Barra at GM, Indra Nooyi at PepsiCo (left in 2018), Howard Schultz at Starbucks, and Satya Nadella at Microsoft.[11]

At the other end of the spectrum, some CEOs have massively destroyed shareholder value: Ken Lay at Enron, John Sculley at Apple, Bernard Ebbers at WorldCom, Charles Prince at Citigroup, Richard Fuld at Lehman Brothers, Richard Wagoner at GM, Robert Nardelli at The Home Depot and later Chrysler, Martin Winterkorn at VW, and Ron Johnson at JCPenney, among many others.

Why do some leaders create great companies or manage them to greatness, while others lead them into decline and sometimes even demise? To answer that question, let's first consider what strategic leaders actually do.

WHAT DO STRATEGIC LEADERS DO?

What do strategic leaders do that makes some more effective than others? In a study of more than 350 CEOs, strategy scholars found that they spend, on average, roughly two-thirds of their time in meetings, 13 percent working alone, 7 percent on e-mail, 6 percent on phone calls, 5 percent on business meals, and 2 percent on public events such as ribbon-cutting for a new factory (see Exhibit 2.1).[12] Other studies have also found that most managers prefer oral communication: CEOs spend most of their time "interacting—talking, cajoling, soothing, selling, listening, and nodding—with a wide array of parties inside and outside the organization."[13] Surprisingly given the advances in information technology, CEOs today spend most of their time in face-to-face meetings. They consider face-to-face meetings most effective in getting their message across and obtaining the information they need. Not only do meetings present data through presentations and verbal communications, but they also enable CEOs to pick up on rich nonverbal cues such as facial expressions, body language, and mood, that are not apparent to them if they use e-mail or even Skype, for example.[14]

HOW DO YOU BECOME A STRATEGIC LEADER?

Is becoming an ethical and effective strategic leader innate? Can it be learned? According to the **upper-echelons theory**, organizational outcomes including strategic choices and performance levels reflect the values of the top management team.[15] These are the individuals at

LO 2-2

Outline how you can become a strategic leader.

upper-echelons theory A conceptual framework that views organizational outcomes—strategic choices and performance levels—as reflections of the values of the members of the top management team.

EXHIBIT 2.1   How CEOs Spend Their Days

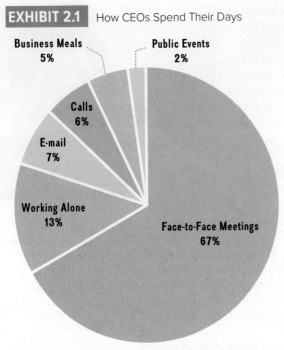

Business Meals
5%

Public Events
2%

Calls
6%

E-mail
7%

Working Alone
13%

Face-to-Face Meetings
67%

Source: Data from O. Bandiera, A. Prat, and R. Sadun (2012), "Management capital at the top: Evidence from the time use of CEOs," *London School of Economics and Harvard Business School Working Paper.*

Level-5 leadership pyramid A conceptual framework of leadership progression with five distinct, sequential levels.

the upper levels of an organization. The theory states that strategic leaders interpret situations through the lens of their unique perspectives, shaped by personal circumstances, values, and experiences. Their leadership actions reflect characteristics of age, education, and career experiences, filtered through personal interpretations of the situations they face. The upper-echelons theory favors the idea that effective strategic leadership is the result of both innate abilities *and* learning.

In the bestseller *Good to Great,* Jim Collins explored over 1,000 *good* companies to find 11 *great* ones. He identified *great companies* as those that transitioned from average performance to sustained competitive advantage. He measured that transition as "cumulative stock returns of almost seven times the general market in the 15 years following their transition points."[16] A lot has happened since the book was published almost two decades ago. Today only a few of the original 11 stayed all that great, including Kimberly-Clark and Walgreens. Some fell back to mediocrity; a few no longer exist in their earlier form. Anyone remember Circuit City or Fannie Mae? Let's agree that competitive advantage is hard to achieve and even harder to sustain. But his study remains valuable for its thought-provoking observations. Studying these large corporations, Collins found consistent patterns of leadership among the top companies, as pictured in the **Level-5 leadership pyramid** in Exhibit 2.2. The pyramid is a conceptual framework that shows leadership progression through five distinct, sequential levels. Collins found that all the companies he identified as *great* were led by Level-5 executives. So if you are interested in becoming an ethical and effective strategic leader, the leadership pyramid suggests the areas of growth required.

According to the Level-5 leadership pyramid, effective strategic leaders go through a natural progression of five levels. Each level builds upon the previous one; the individual can move on to the next level of leadership only when the current level has been mastered. On the left in Exhibit 2.2 are the capabilities associated with each level. But not all companies are Fortune 500 behemoths. On the right-hand side we suggest that the model is also valuable to the individual looking to develop the capacity for greater professional success.

At Level 1, we find the highly capable individual who makes productive contributions through her motivation, talent, knowledge, and skills. These traits are a necessary but not sufficient condition to move on to Level 2, where the individual attains the next level of strategic leadership by becoming an effective team player. As a contributing team member, she works effectively with others to achieve common objectives. In Level 3, the team player with a high individual skill set turns into an effective manager who is able to organize the resources necessary to accomplish the organization's goals. Once these three levels are mastered, in Level 4, the effective professional has learned to do the right things, meaning she does not only command a high individual skill set and is an effective team player and manager, but she also knows what actions are the right ones in any given situation to pursue an organization's strategy. Combining all four prior levels, at Level 5, the strategic leader builds enduring greatness by combining willpower and humility. This

EXHIBIT 2.2 Strategic Leaders: The Level-5 Pyramid

Adapted to compare corporations and entrepreneurs

Capabilities   **Corporation**   **Entrepreneur**

Builds enduring greatness through a combination of
willpower and humility.
                                    Level 5:
                                    Executive

Presents compelling vision and mission to
guide groups toward superior performance.   **Level 4:**
Does the right things.   **Effective Leader**

Is efficient and effective in organizing
resources to accomplish stated goals   **Level 3:**
and objectives. Does things right.   **Competent Manager**

Uses high level of individual
capability to work effectively   **Level 2:**
with others in order to   **Contributing Team Member**
achieve team objectives.

Makes productive
contributions through   **Level 1:**
motivation, talent,   **Highly Capable Individual**
knowledge, and skills.

Distinct positions within corporate structure

Personal growth in response to business needs

Source: Adapted from J. Collins (2001), *Good to Great: Why Some Companies Make the Leap . . . And Others Don't* (New York: HarperCollins), 20.

implies that a Level-5 executive works to help the organization succeed and others to reach their full potential.

As detailed in the ChapterCase, Facebook CEO Mark Zuckerberg highly values COO Sheryl Sandberg. Here he says why: "She could go be the CEO of any company that she wanted, but I think the fact that she really wants to get her hands dirty and work, and doesn't need to be the front person all the time, is the amazing thing about her. It's that low-ego element, where you can help the people around you and not need to be the face of all the stuff."[17] Clearly, Sandberg appears to be a Level-5 executive: She built enduring greatness at Facebook through a combination of skill, willpower, and humility. After a highly successful decade, however, by early 2019 many critics questioned Sandberg and Zuckerberg's leadership skills (see the ChapterCase at the beginning of this chapter).

THE STRATEGY PROCESS ACROSS LEVELS: CORPORATE, BUSINESS, AND FUNCTIONAL MANAGERS

According to the upper-echelons theory, strategic leaders primarily determine a firm's ability to gain and sustain a competitive advantage through the strategies they pursue. Given the importance of such strategies, we need to gain a deeper understanding of how they are created. The *strategy process* consists of two parts: *strategy formulation* (which results from strategy analysis) and *strategy implementation*.

LO 2-3

Compare and contrast the roles of corporate, business, and functional managers in strategy formulation and implementation.

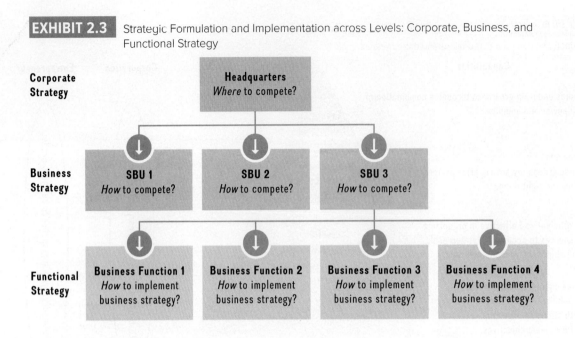

strategy formulation
The part of the strategic management process that concerns the choice of strategy in terms of where and how to compete.

Strategy formulation concerns the choice of strategy in terms of *where and how to compete.* In contrast, **strategy implementation** concerns the organization, coordination, and integration of *how work gets done.* In short, it concerns the *execution of strategy.* It is helpful to break down strategy formulation and implementation into three distinct areas—corporate, business, and functional.

- *Corporate strategy* concerns questions relating to where to compete as to industry, markets, and geography.
- *Business strategy* concerns the question of how to compete. Three generic business strategies are available: cost leadership, differentiation, or value innovation.
- *Functional strategy* concerns the question of how to implement a chosen business strategy. Different corporate and business strategies will require different activities across the various functions.

strategy implementation The part of the strategic management process that concerns the organization, coordination, and integration of how work gets done, or strategy execution.

Exhibit 2.3 shows the three areas of strategy formulation and implementation.

Although we generally speak of the firm in an abstract form, individual employees make strategic decisions—whether at the corporate, business, or functional levels. *Corporate executives* at headquarters formulate corporate strategy, such as Sheryl Sandberg (Facebook), Mukesh Ambani (Reliance Industries), Rosalind Brewer (Starbucks), Mary Barra (GM), Larry Page (Alphabet), or Marillyn Hewson (Lockheed Martin). Corporate executives need to decide in which industries, markets, and geographies their companies should compete. They need to formulate a strategy that can create synergies across business units that may be quite different, and determine the boundaries of the firm by deciding whether to enter certain industries and markets and whether to sell certain divisions. They are responsible for setting overarching strategic objectives and allocating scarce resources among different business divisions, monitoring performance, and making adjustments to the overall portfolio of businesses as needed. The objective of corporate-level strategy is to increase overall corporate value so that it is higher than the sum of the individual business units.

Business strategy occurs within **strategic business units (SBUs)**, the standalone divisions of a larger conglomerate, each with its own profit-and-loss responsibility. General managers in SBUs must answer business strategy questions relating to how to compete in order to achieve superior performance. Within the guidelines received from corporate headquarters, they formulate an appropriate generic business strategy, including cost leadership, differentiation, or value innovation, in their quest for competitive advantage.

Rosalind Brewer, while president and CEO of Sam's Club, pursued a somewhat different business strategy from that of parent company Walmart. By offering higher-quality products and brand names with bulk offerings and by prescreening customers via required Sam's Club memberships to establish creditworthiness, Brewer achieved annual revenues of roughly $60 billion. This would place Sam's Club in the top 50 in the Fortune 500 list. Although as CEO of Sam's Club, Brewer was responsible for the performance of this strategic business unit, she reported to Walmart's CEO, Doug McMillon, who as corporate executive oversees Walmart's entire operations, with over $500 billion in annual revenues and 12,000 stores globally.[18]

Rosalind Brewer is chief operating officer of Starbucks and thus second in command, reporting directly to CEO Kevin Johnson. Previously, Brewer served as Sam's Club president and CEO (2012–2017).
Phelan M. Ebenhack/ AP Images

In 2017, Brewer was appointed COO of Starbucks, the leading coffeehouse chain globally with $25 billion in annual revenues and some 300,000 employees. Brewer is in charge of all Starbucks operations in the Americas (Canada, the United States, and Latin America) as well as the company's global supply chain, product innovation, and store development, which includes 15,000 stores globally. As second in command at Starbucks, Brewer reports directly (and only) to Kevin Johnson, Starbucks CEO. Many observers believe that Brewer is being groomed to become the next CEO of Starbucks.

Within each strategic business unit are various business *functions:* accounting, finance, human resources, product development, operations, manufacturing, marketing, and customer service. Each *functional manager* is responsible for decisions and actions within a single functional area. These decisions aid in the implementation of the business-level strategy, made at the level above (see Exhibit 2.3).

Returning to our ChapterCase, COO Sheryl Sandberg determines Facebook's corporate strategy jointly with CEO Mark Zuckerberg. Facebook, with some 35,000 employees, is a far-flung internet firm—its various services are available in more than 100 languages and it has offices in more than 30 countries.[19] Together, they are responsible for the performance of the entire organization, and decide

> **strategic business units (SBUs)** Standalone divisions of a larger conglomerate, each with their own profit-and-loss responsibility.

- What types of products and services to offer.
- Which industries to compete in.
- Where in the world to compete.

One example of Sandberg's effective strategic leadership is Facebook's turnaround beginning in 2013 when it did not have much of a mobile presence. Part of the problem was the inferior quality of the mobile app; Zuckerberg had initially built Facebook for the desktop personal computer, not for mobile devices. Sandberg initiated a company-wide "mobile first" initiative focusing its engineers and marketers on mobile. The success of this turnaround strategy is stunning: Today Facebook is a mobile advertising powerhouse, generating over 80 percent of its revenues of more than $65 billion annually from mobile advertising.[20]

2.2 Vision, Mission, and Values

he first step in the strategic management process is to define an organization's vision, mis-
n, and values by asking the following questions:

- **Vision.** What do we want to accomplish ultimately?
- **Mission.** How do we accomplish our goals?
- **Values.** What commitments do we make, and what safe guards do we put in place, to act both legally and ethically as we pursue our vision and mission?

The *vision* is the first principle that needs to be defined because it succinctly identifies the primary long-term objective of the organization. Strategic leaders need to begin with the end in mind.[21] In other words, strategic success begins when a vision is formulated; that success continues when that vision is implemented. This process of creating and implementing a vision begins with the formulation of (both business and corporate) strategies that enhance the chances of gaining and sustaining competitive advantage. It ends with the creation of a strategy that enables a firm to implement its vision. This is an iterative process that can be compared to designing and building a house. You need an approved blueprint in place before construction can even begin. The same holds for strategic success; it is first created through strategy formulation based on careful analysis before any actions are taken. Let's look at this process in more detail.

VISION

vision A statement about what an organization ultimately wants to accomplish; it captures the company's aspiration.

A **vision** captures an organization's aspiration and spells out what it ultimately wants to accomplish. An effective vision pervades the organization with a sense of winning and motivates employees at all levels to aim for the same target, while leaving room for individual and team contributions.

Tesla's vision is *to accelerate the world's transition to sustainable transport.* The goal is to provide affordable zero-emission mass-market cars that are the best in class. SpaceX is a spacecraft manufacturer and space transport services company, also founded by Elon Musk, whose inspirational vision is *to make human life multi planetary.* To achieve this goal, SpaceX aims to make human travel to Mars not only possible but also affordable. Moreover, SpaceX also sees a role in helping establish a self-sustainable human colony on Mars.[22]

Employees in visionary companies tend to feel part of something bigger than themselves. An inspiring vision helps employees find meaning in their work and value beyond monetary rewards. It gives them a greater sense of purpose. People have an intrinsic motivation to make the world a better place through their work activities.[23] In turn, this motivation, which inspires individual purpose, can lead to higher organizational performance.[24] Using the vision as its foundation, a firm will build the necessary resources and capabilities to translate a stretch goal or **strategic intent** into a reality, usually through continuous organizational learning, including learning from failure.[25]

strategic intent A stretch goal that pervades the organization with a sense of winning, which it aims to achieve by building the necessary resources and capabilities through continuous learning.

A firm's vision is expressed as a statement, and this statement should be forward-looking and inspiring to ensure it provides meaning for employees in pursuit of the organization's ultimate goals. Strategy Highlight 2.1 shows how at the heart of Teach for America's (TFA) vision statement is an inspiring vision. This statement effectively and clearly communicates TFA's stretch goal, as well as what it ultimately seeks to accomplish.

Strategy Highlight **2.1**

Teach for America: How Wendy Kopp Inspires Future Leaders

Teach for America (TFA) is a nonprofit organization of future leaders that works to ensure that underprivileged youth get an excellent education. TFA corp members spend two years teaching in economically disadvantaged communities across the United States. Although TFA initially targeted college seniors, today it recruits both graduates and professionals to help achieve the following TFA vision: *One day, all children in this nation will have the opportunity to attain an excellent education.*

TFA began as a college senior thesis written in 1989 by a then-21-year-old Wendy Kopp. Kopp was convinced that young people generally sought for meaning in their lives, and that they could create meaning by making a positive contribution to society. Kopp's genius was that she flipped on its head the social perception of teaching—she turned a seemingly unattractive, low-status job into a high-prestige, professional opportunity.

In the first four months after creating TFA, Kopp received more than 2,500 applicants. She marketed the idea by passing out and posting flyers in college dorms. During its first academic year (1990–91), TFA served five states and changed the lives of 36,000 students. By 2018, TFA had some 60,000 corps members and alumni, more than 2,500 school partnerships, and impacted millions of students.

To be chosen for TFA is considered an honor. Of the total number of applicants that TFA receives annually, approximately 15 percent are accepted; this is roughly equivalent to the admission rate of highly selective universities such as Northwestern, Cornell, and University of California, Berkeley. Compared to the national average of people of color in teaching positions (20 percent), 50 percent of TFA corps members are people of color—a more accurate reflection of the population they teach. TFA corps members receive the same pay as other first-year teachers in their respective local school districts.

In an effort to eliminate educational inequity, Kopp deliberately enlists the nation's most promising future leaders; this conscious decision to recruit only the best has

Wendy Kopp, Teach for America founder.
Astrid Stawiarz/Getty Images

had a hugely positive impact on students. Approximately 95 percent of all school principals working with TFA members say they have made significant strides with their students. Furthermore, a study commissioned by the U.S. Department of Education found that students being taught by TFA corps members showed significantly higher achievement, especially in math and science.

TFA CEO Elisa Villanueva Beard was inspired to sign up for TFA when she was a college student at DePauw University. She recalls that what inspired her most was Wendy Kopp's "audacity to believe young people could make a profound difference in the face of intractable problems standing between the ideals of a nation I loved and a starkly disappointing reality; who were bound by a fierce belief that all children, from American Indian reservations in South Dakota to Oakland to the Rio Grande Valley to the Bronx, should have the opportunity to write their own stories and fulfill their true potential."[26]

Yet, despite all its remarkable success, TFA finds itself wrestling with several challenges. For instance, applications in the last few years have dropped (an estimated 35 percent over three years), causing TFA to fail to meet its recruiting target. Second, the short but intensive five-week summer boot camp intended to ready new recruits for teaching in some of the toughest schools in United States is increasingly criticized as insufficient.[27]

That vision statements can inspire and motivate employees in the nonprofit sector comes as no surprise. Who wouldn't find wanting *to help children attain an excellent education*, the vision of TFA, meaningful? Likewise, who wouldn't be moved by the promise *to always be there in times of need*, the vision of the American Red Cross? But can for-profit firms inspire and motivate just as well? The answer is yes; a truly meaningful and inspiring vision—no matter if of a nonprofit or for-profit firm—makes employees feel they are part of something bigger, which can be highly motivating. When employees are highly motivated, firm financial performance can also improve. For example, visionary for-profit companies such as 3M and Walmart provide aspirational ideas that are not exclusively financial; as such, they tend to outperform their competitors over the long run. Tracking the stock market performance of companies over several decades, strategy scholars found that visionary companies outperformed their peers by a wide margin.[28]

However, as the ChapterCase on Facebook warns, single-mindedly pursuing a vision can also be detrimental, even if that vision inspires and motivates. When followed too strictly, it can generate unexpected challenges that can be difficult to overcome. Critics assert that Facebook's leadership failed to consider the potential for serious negative side-effects, such as the mass-manipulation of users by nefarious actors, or the large-scale breach of user privacy that resulted in the siphoning off of personal data by mal-intent third parties.

VISION STATEMENTS AND COMPETITIVE ADVANTAGE. Do vision statements help firms gain and sustain competitive advantage? It depends. The effectiveness of vision statements differs by type. *Customer-oriented* vision statements allow companies to adapt to changing environments. *Product-oriented* vision statements often constrain this ability. This is because customer-oriented vision statements focus employees to think about how best to solve a problem for a consumer.[29]

Clayton Christensen shares how a customer focus let him help a fast food chain increase sales of milkshakes. The company approached Christensen after it had made several changes to its milkshake offerings based on extensive customer feedback but sales failed to improve. Rather than asking customers what kind of milkshake they wanted, he thought of the problem in a different way. He observed customer behavior and then asked customers, "What job were you trying to do that caused you to hire that milkshake?"[30] He wanted to know what problem the customers were trying to solve. Surprisingly he found that roughly half of the shakes were purchased in the mornings, because customers wanted an easy breakfast to eat in the car and a diversion on long commutes. Based on the insights gained from this problem-solving perspective, the company expanded its shake offerings to include healthier options with fruit chunks and provided a prepaid dispensing machine to speed up the drive-through, and thus improve customers' morning commute. A customer focus made finding a solution much easier.

You could say that the restaurant company had a product orientation that prevented its executives from seeing unmet customer needs. Product-oriented vision statements focus employees on improving existing products and services without consideration of underlying customer problems to be solved. Our environments are ever-changing and sometimes seem chaotic. The increased strategic flexibility afforded by customer-oriented vision statements can provide a basis on which companies can build competitive advantage.[31] Let's look at both types of vision statements in more detail.

PRODUCT-ORIENTED VISION STATEMENTS. A *product-oriented vision* defines a business in terms of a good or service provided. Product-oriented visions tend to force managers to take a more myopic view of the competitive landscape. Consider the strategic decisions of U.S. railroad companies. Railroads are in the business of moving goods and people from point A to point B by rail. When they started in the 1850s, their short-distance competition was the horse or horse-drawn carriage. There was little long-distance competition (e.g., ship canals or good roads) to cover the United States from coast to coast. Because of their monopoly, especially in long-distance travel, these companies were initially extremely profitable. Not surprisingly, the early U.S. railroad companies saw their vision as being in the railroad business, clearly a product-based definition.

However, the railroad companies' monopoly did not last. Technological innovations changed the transportation industry dramatically. After the introduction of the automobile in the early 1900s and the commercial jet in the 1950s, consumers had a wider range of choices to meet their long-distance transportation needs. Rail companies were slow to respond; they failed to redefine their business in terms of services provided to the consumer. Had they envisioned themselves as serving the full range of transportation and logistics needs of people and businesses across America (a customer-oriented vision), they might have become successful forerunners of modern logistics companies such as FedEx or UPS.

Recently, the railroad companies seem to be learning some lessons: CSX Railroad is now redefining itself as a green-transportation alternative. It claims it can move one ton of freight 423 miles on one gallon of fuel. However, its vision remains product-oriented: *to be the safest, most progressive North American railroad.*

CUSTOMER-ORIENTED VISION STATEMENTS. *A customer-oriented vision* defines a business in terms of providing solutions to customer needs. For example, "We provide solutions to professional communication needs." Companies with customer-oriented visions can more easily adapt to changing environments. Exhibit 2.4 provides additional examples of companies with customer-oriented vision statements. In contrast, companies that define themselves based on product-oriented statements (e.g., "We are in the typewriter business") tend to be less flexible and thus more likely to fail. The lack of an inspiring needs-based vision can cause the long-range problem of failing to adapt to a changing environment.

Customer-oriented visions identify a critical need but leave open the means of how to meet that need. Customer needs may change, and the *means* of meeting those needs may change with it. The future is unknowable, and innovation is likely to provide new ways to meet needs that we cannot fathom today.[32] For example, consider the need to transmit information over long distances. Communication needs have persisted throughout the millennia,

EXHIBIT 2.4

Companies with Customer-Oriented Vision Statements

Alibaba: To make it easy to do business anywhere.

Amazon: To be Earth's most customer-centric company, where customers can find and discover anything they might want to buy online.

Better World Books: To harness the power of capitalism to bring literacy and opportunity to people around the world.

Facebook: To make the world more open and connected.

GE: To move, cure, build, and power the world.

Google: To organize the world's information and make it universally accessible and useful.

Nike: To bring inspiration and innovation to every athlete in the world.

SpaceX: To make human life multi planetary.

Tesla: To accelerate the world's transition to sustainable energy.

Walmart: To be the best retailer in the hearts and minds of consumers and employees.

Warby Parker: To offer designer eyewear at a revolutionary price, while leading the way for socially conscious businesses.

but the technology to solve this problem has changed drastically over time.[33] During the reign of Julius Caesar, moving information over long distances required papyrus, ink, a chariot, a horse, and a driver. During Abraham Lincoln's time, the telegraph was used for short messages while railroads handled larger documents, and an airplane transported letters when Franklin Delano Roosevelt was president. Today, we use connected mobile devices to move information over long distances at the speed of light. The problem to be solved—moving information over long distance—has remained the same, but the technology employed to do this job has changed quite drastically. Christensen recommends that strategic leaders think hard about how the means of getting a job done have changed over time and ask themselves, "Is there an even better way to get this job done?"

It is critical that an organization's vision should be flexible to allow for change and adaptation. Consider how Ford Motor Co. has addressed the problem of personal mobility over the past 100 years. Before Ford entered the market in the early 1900s, people traveled long distances by horse-drawn buggy, horseback, boat, or train. But Henry Ford had a different idea. In fact, he famously said, "If I had listened to my customers, I would have built a better horse and buggy."[34] Instead, Henry Ford's original vision was *to make the automobile accessible to every American.* He succeeded, and the automobile dramatically changed how mobility was achieved.

Fast-forward to today: Ford Motor Co.'s vision is *to provide personal mobility for people around the world.* Note that it does not even mention the automobile. By focusing on the consumer need for personal mobility, Ford is leaving the door open for exactly how it will fulfill that need. Today, it's mostly with traditional cars and trucks propelled by gas-powered internal combustion engines, with some hybrid electric vehicles in its lineup. In the near future, Ford is likely to provide vehicles powered by alternative energy sources such as electric power or hydrogen. Moreover, vehicles will be driven autonomously, and thus a human driver is no longer needed. With this expected shift to arrive in the near future, automobiles will unlikely be owned personally but rather rides will be provided on demand by ride hailing services such as Uber or Lyft. In the far-reaching future, perhaps Ford will get into the business of individual flying devices. Throughout all of this, its vision would still be relevant and compel its managers to engage in future markets. In contrast, a product-oriented vision would greatly constrain Ford's degree of strategic flexibility.

MOVING FROM PRODUCT-ORIENTED TO CUSTOMER-ORIENTED VISION STATEMENTS. In some cases, product-oriented vision statements do not interfere with the firm's success in achieving superior performance and competitive advantage. Consider Intel Corp., one of the world's leading silicon innovators. Intel's early vision was *to be the preeminent building-block supplier of the PC industry.* Intel designed the first commercial microprocessor chip in 1971 and set the standard for microprocessors in 1978. During the personal computer (PC) revolution in the 1980s, microprocessors became Intel's main line of business. Intel's customers were original equipment manufacturers that produced consumer end-products, such as computer manufacturers HP, IBM, Dell, and Compaq.

In the internet age, though, the standalone PC as the end-product has become less important. Customers want to stream video and share selfies and other pictures online. These activities consume a tremendous amount of computing power. To reflect this shift, Intel in 1999 changed its vision to focus on being *the preeminent building-block supplier to the internet economy.* Although its product-oriented vision statements did not impede performance or competitive advantage, in 2008 Intel fully made the shift to a customer-oriented vision: *to delight our customers, employees, and shareholders by relentlessly delivering the platform and technology advancements that become essential to the way we work and live.* Part of this shift was reflected by the hugely successful "Intel Inside" advertising campaign in the 1990s that made Intel a household name worldwide. Yet, even more than a decade later, this is still Intel's vision statement.

Intel accomplished superior firm performance over decades through continuous adaptations to changing market realities. Its formal vision statement lagged behind the firm's strategic transformations. Intel regularly changed its vision statement *after* it had accomplished each successful transformation.[35] In such a case, vision statements and firm performance are clearly not related to one another.

It is also interesting to note that customer-oriented visions also frequently change over time. When Tesla was founded in 2003, its vision was *to accelerate the world's transition to sustainable transport.* Over the last decade or so, Tesla completed several steps of its initial master plan (as detailed in ChapterCase 1), including providing zero-emission electric power generation options (Step 4), through the acquisition of the SolarCity. Tesla, therefore, no longer views itself as a car company but as a fully integrated clean-tech company. To capture this ambition more accurately Tesla changed its vision: *to accelerate the world's transition to sustainable energy.* To reposition Tesla as an integrated clean-tech energy company, in 2017 Tesla changed its official name from Tesla Motors to simply Tesla, Inc.

Taken together, empirical research shows that sometimes vision statements and firm performance are *associated* with one another. A positive relationship between vision statements and firm performance is more likely to exist under certain circumstances:

- The visions are customer-oriented.
- Internal stakeholders are invested in defining the vision.
- Organizational structures such as compensation systems align with the firm's vision statement.[36]

The upshot is that an effective vision statement can lay the foundation upon which to craft a strategy that creates competitive advantage.

MISSION

Building on the vision, organizations establish a **mission**, which describes what an organization actually does—that is, the products and services it plans to provide, and the markets in which it will compete. People sometimes use the terms *vision* and *mission* interchangeably, but in the strategy process they differ.

- A vision defines what an organization wants *to be*, and what it wants to accomplish ultimately. A vision begins with the infinitive form of a verb (starting with *to*). As discussed in Strategy Highlight 2.1, TFA's vision is *to attain an excellent education for all children.*
- A mission describes what an organization does and *how* it proposes to accomplish its vision. The mission is often introduced with the preposition *by*. Thus, we can cast a mission statement for TFA that reads: *To attain an excellent education for all children by enlisting, developing, and mobilizing as many as possible of our nation's most promising future leaders to grow and strengthen the movement for educational equity and excellence.*

mission Description of what an organization actually does—the products and services it plans to provide, and the markets in which it will compete.

To be effective, firms need to back up their visions and missions with *strategic commitments*, in which the enterprise undertakes credible actions. Such commitments are costly, long-term oriented, and difficult to reverse.[37] However noble the mission statement, to achieve competitive advantage companies need to make strategic commitments informed by economic fundamentals of value creation.

As mentioned in ChapterCase 1, Tesla is investing billions of dollars to equip its car factory in California with cutting-edge robotics and to build the Gigafactory producing lithium-ion batteries in Nevada. These investments by Tesla are examples of strategic commitments because they are costly, long-term, and difficult to reverse. They are clearly supporting Tesla's vision *to accelerate the world's transition to sustainable transport.* Tesla hopes to translate this vision into reality *by providing affordable zero-emission mass-market cars that are the best in class,* which captures Tesla's mission.

VALUES

core values statement Statement of principles to guide an organization as it works to achieve its vision and fulfill its mission, for both internal conduct and external interactions; it often includes explicit ethical considerations.

organizational core values Ethical standards and norms that govern the behavior of individuals within a firm or organization.

While many companies have powerful vision and mission statements, they are not enough. An organization's values also need to be clearly articulated in the strategy process. A **core values statement** matters because it provides touchstones for employees to understand the company culture. It offers bedrock principles that employees at all levels can use to manage complexity and to resolve conflict. Such statements can help provide the organization's employees with a moral compass.

Consider that much of unethical behavior, while repugnant, may not be illegal. Often we read the defensive comment from a company under investigation or fighting a civil suit that "we have broken no laws." However, any firm that fails to establish extra-legal, ethical standards will be more prone to behaviors that can threaten its very existence. A company whose culture is silent on moral lapses breeds further moral lapses. Over time such a culture could result in a preponderance of behaviors that cause the company to ruin its reputation, at the least, or slide into outright legal violations with resultant penalties and punishment, at the worst.

Organizational core values are the ethical standards and norms that govern the behavior of individuals within a firm or organization. Strong ethical values have two important functions. First, ethical standards and norms underlay the vision statement and provide stability to the strategy, thus laying the groundwork for long-term success. Second, once the company is pursuing its vision and mission in its quest for competitive advantage, they serve as guardrails to keep the company on track.

The values espoused by a company provide answers to the question, *how do we accomplish our goals?* They help individuals make choices that are both ethical and effective in advancing the company's goals. For instance, Teach for America (TFA) has a set of core values that focus on transformational change through team-based leadership, diversity, respect, and humility. These values guide TFA corp members in their day-to-day decision making. It aids each corp member in making ethical and value-based decisions in teaching environments that can often be quite stressful.

One last point about organizational values: Without commitment and involvement from top managers, any statement of values remains merely a public relations exercise. Employees tend to follow values practiced by strategic leaders. They observe the day-to-day decisions of top managers and quickly decide whether managers are merely paying lip service to the company's stated values. Organizational core values must be lived with integrity, especially by the top management team. Unethical behavior by top managers is like a virus that spreads quickly throughout an entire organization.

Take, for example, Volkswagen (VW), the largest carmaker by volume worldwide. Although one of its long-time marketing slogans was *Truth in Engineering,* this did not prevent the forced resignation of VW CEO Martin Winterkorn in the fall of 2015—a consequence of an emissions cheating scandal dubbed Dieselgate. Moreover, in 2018, Winterkorn was indicted on fraud and conspiracy charges. What had happened? VW had illegally installed so-called "defeat devices" in some 11 million vehicles. When programmed and installed, the software for these devices enabled emissions controls when the vehicle was on a test stand. However, the device disabled emissions controls when the vehicle was in daily driving mode on public roads. These defeat devices helped VW diesel cars pass stringent emissions tests, even though in reality they were emitting up to 40 times the allowed level of pollutants. In the end, Volkswagen paid more than $22 billion in fines and damaged its stellar reputation. Ironically, the fines alone were much higher than the cost of equipping the diesel engines with the appropriate pollution controls.[38]

As the VW example demonstrates, it is imperative that strategic leaders set the example of ethical behavior by living their firm's core values. Strategic leaders have a strong influence in setting their organization's vision, mission, and values—the first step of the *strategic management process*, which we turn to next.

2.3 The Strategic Management Process

An effective **strategic management process** lays the foundation for sustainable competitive advantage. Strategic leaders design a process to formulate and implement strategy. In the Strategic Leadership section, we gained insight into the corporate, business, and functional levels of strategy. Here we turn to the process or method by which strategic leaders formulate and implement strategy. When setting the strategy process, strategic leaders rely on three approaches:

1. Strategic planning.
2. Scenario planning.
3. Strategy as planned emergence.

This order also reflects the sequence of development of these approaches: We begin with strategic planning, followed by scenario planning, and then strategy as planned emergence. The first two are relatively formal, top-down planning approaches. The third begins with a strategic plan but offers a less formal and less stylized approach. Each approach has its strengths and weaknesses, depending on the circumstances under which it is employed.

LO 2-7

Evaluate top-down strategic planning, scenario planning, and strategy as planned emergence.

strategic management process Method put in place by strategic leaders to formulate and implement a strategy, which can lay the foundation for a sustainable competitive advantage.

top-down strategic planning A rational, data-driven strategy process through which top management attempts to program future success.

TOP-DOWN STRATEGIC PLANNING

The prosperous decades after World War II resulted in tremendous growth of corporations. As company executives needed a way to manage ever more complex firms more effectively, they began to use strategic planning.[39] **Top-down strategic planning**, derived from military strategy, is a rational process through which executives attempt to program future success.[40] In this approach, all strategic intelligence and decision-making responsibilities are concentrated in the office of the CEO. The CEO, much like a military general, leads the company strategically through competitive battles.

Exhibit 2.5 shows the three steps of strategic management: analysis, formulation, and implementation in a traditional top-down strategic planning process. Strategic planners provide detailed analyses of internal and external data and apply them to all quantifiable areas: prices, costs, margins, market demand, head count, and production runs. Five-year plans,

EXHIBIT 2.5 Top-Down Strategic Planning in the AFI Strategy Framework

Analysis
- Vision, Mission, and Values
- External Analysis
- Internal Analysis

Formulation
- Corporate Strategy
- Business Strategy
- Functional Strategy

Implementation
- Structure, Culture, & Control
- Corporate Governance & Business Ethics

revisited regularly, predict future sales based on anticipated growth. Top executives tie the allocation of the annual corporate budget to the strategic plan and monitor ongoing performance accordingly. Based on a careful analysis of these data, top managers reconfirm or adjust the company's vision, mission, and values before formulating corporate, business, and functional strategies. Appropriate organizational structures and controls as well as governance mechanisms aid in effective implementation.

Top-down strategic planning more often rests on the assumption that we can predict the future from the past. The approach works reasonably well when the environment does not change much. One major shortcoming of the top-down strategic planning approach is that the formulation of strategy is separate from implementation, and thinking about strategy is separate from doing it. Information flows one way only: from the top down. Another shortcoming of the strategic planning approach is that we simply cannot know the future. There are no data. Unforeseen events can make even the most scientifically developed and formalized plans obsolete. Moreover, strategic leaders' visions of the future can be downright wrong, save for a few notable exceptions.

At times, strategic leaders impose their visions onto a company's strategy, structure, and culture from the top down to create and enact a desired future state. Under its co-founder and long-time CEO Steve Jobs, Apple was one of the few successful tech companies using a top-down strategic planning process.[41] Jobs felt that he knew best what the next big thing should be. Under his top-down, autocratic leadership, Apple did not engage in market research because Jobs firmly believed that "people don't know what they want until you show it to them."[42] In his well-researched, 700-page biography on Steve Jobs, Walter Isaacson presents to readers Jobs' lessons in strategic leadership in 14 memorable aphorisms, including *push for perfection*, *tolerate only "A" players*, and *bend reality*, among others.[43]

The traditional top-down strategy process served Apple well in its journey to becoming the world's first company to be valued above $1 trillion. Under Tim Cook, Jobs' successor as CEO, Apple's strategy process has become more flexible. The company is now trying to incorporate the possibilities of different future scenarios and bottom-up strategic initiatives.[44]

SCENARIO PLANNING

Given that the only constant is change, should managers even try to strategically plan for the future? The answer is yes—but they also need to expect that unpredictable events will happen. Strategic planning in a fast-changing environment happens in a fashion similar to the way a fire department plans for a fire.[45] There is no way to know in advance where and when the next emergency will arise; neither we can know in advance its magnitude. Nonetheless, fire chiefs always consider the "what-if" scenarios; they put contingency plans in place that address a wide range of emergencies and their different dimensions.

scenario planning
Strategy planning activity in which top management envisions different what-if scenarios to anticipate plausible futures in order to derive strategic responses.

When **scenario planning,** managers also ask those what-if questions. Similar to top-down strategic planning, scenario planning also starts with a top-down approach to the strategy process. In addition, in scenario planning, top management envisions different scenarios, to anticipate plausible futures in order to derive strategic responses. For example, new laws might restrict carbon emissions or expand employee health care. Demographic shifts may alter the ethnic diversity of a nation; changing tastes or economic conditions will affect consumer behavior. Technological advances may provide completely new products, processes, and services. How would any of these changes affect a firm, and how should it respond? Scenario planning takes place at both the corporate and business levels of strategy.

Typical scenario planning addresses both optimistic and pessimistic futures. For instance, strategy executives at UPS identified a number of issues as critical to shaping its future

EXHIBIT 2.6

Scenario Planning
within the AFI
Strategy Framework

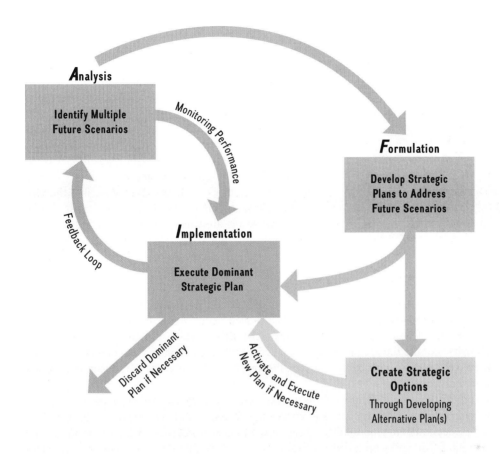

competitive scenarios: (1) big data analytics; (2) being the target of a terrorist attack, or having a security breach or IT system disruption; (3) large swings in energy prices, including gasoline, diesel and jet fuel, and interruptions in supplies of these commodities; (4) fluctuations in exchange rates or interest rates; and (5) climate change.[46] Managers then formulate strategic plans they could activate and implement should the envisioned optimistic or pessimistic scenarios begin to appear.

To model the scenario-planning approach, place the elements in the Analysis, Formulation, Implementation (AFI) strategy framework in a continuous feedback loop, where analysis leads to formulation to implementation and back to analysis. Exhibit 2.6 elaborates on this simple feedback loop to show the dynamic and iterative method of scenario planning.

The goal is to create a number of detailed and executable strategic plans. This allows the strategic management process to be more flexible and more effective than the more static strategic planning approach with one master plan. In the *analysis stage,* managers brainstorm to identify possible future scenarios. Input from several levels within the organization and from different functional areas such as R&D, manufacturing, and marketing and sales is critical. UPS executives considered, for example, how they would compete if the price of a barrel of oil was $35, or $100, or even $200. Strategic leaders may also attach probabilities (highly likely versus unlikely, or 85 percent likely versus 2 percent likely) to different future states.

Although strategic leaders often tend to overlook pessimistic future scenarios, it is imperative to consider negative scenarios carefully. Exporters such as Boeing, Harley-Davidson, or John Deere would want to analyze the impact of shifts in exchange rates on profit

Bernd Wolter/
Shutterstock

black swan events
Incidents that describe
highly improbable but
high-impact events.

margins. They might go through an exercise to derive different strategic plans based on large exchange rate fluctuations of the U.S. dollar against major foreign currencies such as the euro, Japanese yen, or Chinese yuan. What if the euro depreciated to below $1 per euro, or the Chinese yuan depreciated rather than appreciated? How would Disney compete if the dollar were to appreciate so much as to make visits by foreign tourists to its California and Florida theme parks prohibitively expensive? Or, they might consider the implications of tariffs being levied in the trade war between the U.S. and China.

The metaphor of a black swan, therefore, describes the *high impact of a highly improbable event.* In the past, most people assumed that all swans are white, so when they first encountered swans that were black, they were surprised.[47] Strategic leaders need also consider how **black swan events** might affect their strategic planning. In the UPS scenario planning exercise, a terrorist attack or a complete security breach of its IT system are examples of possible black swan events. Looking at highly improbable but high-impact events allows UPS executives to be less surprised and more prepared should they indeed occur. Other examples of black swan events include the 9/11 terrorist attacks, the British exit from the European Union (Brexit), and the European refugee and migrant crisis. Such black swan events are considered to be highly improbable and thus unexpected, but when they do occur, each has a profound impact.

For instance, the BP oil spill was a black swan for many businesses on the Gulf Coast, including the tourism, fishing, and energy industries. In 2010, an explosion occurred on BP's Deepwater Horizon oil drilling rig off the Louisiana coastline, killing 11 workers. The subsequent oil spill continued unabated for over three months. It released an estimated 5 million barrels of crude oil into the Gulf of Mexico, causing the largest environmental disaster in U.S. history. Two BP employees even faced manslaughter charges. The cleanup alone cost BP $14 billion. Because of the company's haphazard handling of the crisis, Tony Hayward, BP's CEO at the time, was fired.

In the aftermath of the oil spill, BP faced thousands of claims by many small-business owners in the tourism and seafood industries. These business owners were not powerful individually, and pursuing valid legal claims meant facing protracted and expensive court proceedings. As a collective organized in a class-action lawsuit, however, they were powerful. Moreover, their claims were backed by the U.S. government, which has the power to withdraw BP's business license or cancel current permits and withhold future ones. Collectively, the small-business owners along the Gulf Coast became powerful BP stakeholders, with a legitimate and urgent claim that needed to be addressed. In response, BP agreed to pay over $25 billion to settle their claims and cover other litigation costs.

Even so, this was not the end of the story for BP. The oil company was found to have committed "gross negligence" (reckless and extreme behavior) by a federal court. Additional fines and other environmental costs added another $8.5 billion. BP's total tab for the Gulf of Mexico disaster was $56 billion! BP CEO Bob Dudley sold about $40 billion in assets, turning BP into a smaller company that aims to become more profitable.

What should strategy leaders do about possible future black swan and other unexpected circumstances? In the *formulation stage* in scenario planning, management teams develop different strategic plans to address possible future scenarios. This kind of what-if exercise forces managers to develop detailed contingency plans before events occur. Each plan relies on an entire set of analytical tools, which we will introduce in upcoming chapters.

They capture the firm's internal and external environments when answering several key questions:

- What resources and capabilities do we need to compete successfully in each future scenario?
- What strategic initiatives should we put in place to respond to each respective scenario?
- How can we shape our expected future environment?

By formulating responses to the varying scenarios, managers build a portfolio of future options. They then continue to integrate additional information over time, which in turn influences future decisions. Finally, managers transform the most viable options into full-fledged, detailed strategic plans that can be activated and executed as needed. The scenarios and planned responses promote strategic flexibility for the organization. If a new scenario should emerge, the company won't lose any time coming up with a new strategic plan. It can activate a better suited plan quickly based on careful scenario analysis done earlier.

In the *implementation stage,* managers execute the **dominant strategic plan,** the option that top managers decide most closely matches the current reality. If the situation changes, managers can quickly retrieve and implement any of the alternate plans developed in the formulation stage. The firm's subsequent performance in the marketplace gives managers real-time feedback about the effectiveness of the dominant strategic plan. If performance feedback is positive, managers continue to pursue the dominant strategic plan, fine-tuning it in the process. If performance feedback is negative, or if reality changes, managers consider whether to modify further the dominant strategic plan in order to enhance firm performance or to activate an alternative strategic plan.

> **dominant strategic plan** The strategic option that top managers decide most closely matches the current reality and which is then executed.

The circular nature of the scenario-planning model in Exhibit 2.6 highlights the continuous interaction among analysis, formulation, and implementation. Through this interactive process, managers can adjust and modify their actions as new realities emerge. The interdependence among analysis, formulation, and implementation also enhances organizational learning and flexibility.

STRATEGY AS PLANNED EMERGENCE: TOP-DOWN *AND* BOTTOM-UP

Critics of top-down and scenario planning argue that *strategic planning* is not the same as *strategic thinking.*[48]

In fact, they argue that strategic planning processes are often too regimented and confining. As such, they lack the flexibility needed for quick and effective response. Managers engaged in a more formalized approach to the strategy process may also fall prey to an *illusion of control,* which describes an inclination by managers to overestimate their ability to control events.[49] Hard numbers in a strategic plan can convey a false sense of security. According to critics of strategic planning, to be successful, a strategy should be based on an inspiring vision and not on hard data alone. They advise that strategic leaders should focus on all types of information sources, including soft sources that can generate new insights, such as personal experience, deep domain expertise, or the insights of front-line employees. The important work, according to this viewpoint, is to synthesize all available input from different internal and external sources into an overall strategic vision. An inspiring vision in turn should then guide the firm's strategy (as discussed in the previous section).

In today's complex and uncertain world, the future cannot be predicted from the past with any degree of certainty. Black swan events can profoundly disrupt businesses and society. Moreover, the other two approaches to planning just discussed do not account sufficiently for the role employees at all levels of the organization may play. This is because lower-level employees not only implement the given strategy, but they also frequently come up with initiatives on their own that may alter a firm's strategy. In many instances, front-line employees have unique insights based on constant and unfiltered customer feedback that may elude the more removed executives. Moreover, hugely successful strategic initiatives are occasionally the result of *serendipity,* or unexpected but pleasant surprises.

In 1990, for example, online retailing was nonexistent. Today, almost all internet users have purchased goods and services online. As a total of all sales, online retailing was about 15 percent in 2018 and is expected to double by 2030.[50] Given the success of Amazon as the world's leading online retailer, brick-and-mortar companies such as Best Buy, The Home Depot, JCPenney, and even Walmart have all been forced to respond and adjust their strategies. Others such as Kmart, Radio Shack, and even the venerable Sears filed for Chapter 11 bankruptcy (a provision of the U.S. bankruptcy code, which allows reorganization and restructuring of debts owed), while Circuit City, Borders, and others went out of business altogether (liquidation bankruptcy). Given the more or less instant global presence of online retailers,[51] Alibaba is emerging as the leading internet-based wholesaler connecting manufacturers in China to retailers in the West, as well as a direct online retailer. In a similar fashion, the ride-hailing services Uber, Lyft, Didi Chuxing, and Grab are disrupting the existing taxi and limousine businesses in many metropolitan areas around the world. Having been protected by decades of regulations, existing taxi and limo services scramble to deal with the unforeseen competition. Many try through the courts or legislative system to block the new entrants, alleging the ride-sharing services violate safety and other regulations. Another new *sharing economy* venture, Airbnb, is facing a similar situation. Airbnb is an online platform that allows users to list or rent lodging of residential properties.

The critics of more formalized approaches to strategic planning, most notably Henry Mintzberg, propose a third approach to the strategic management process. In contrast to the two top-down strategy processes discussed above, this one is a less formal and less stylized approach to the development of strategy. To reflect the reality that strategy can be planned *or* emerge from the bottom up, Exhibit 2.7 shows a more integrative approach to

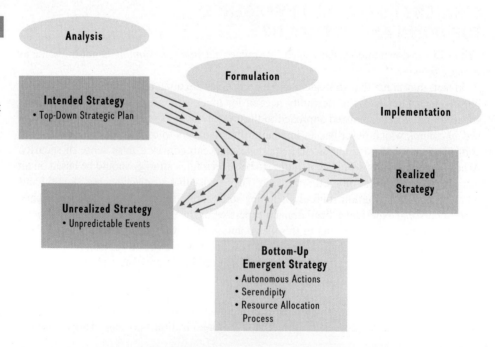

EXHIBIT 2.7

Realized Strategy Is a Combination of Top-Down Intended Strategy and Bottom-Up Emergent Strategy

managing the strategy process. Please note that even in strategy as planned emergence, the overall strategy process still unfolds along the AFI framework of analysis, formulation, and implementation.

According to this more holistic model, the strategy process also begins with a top-down strategic plan based on analysis of external and internal environments. Top-level executives then design an **intended strategy**—the outcome of a rational and structured, top-down strategic plan. Exhibit 2.7 illustrates how parts of a firm's *intended strategy* are likely to fall by the wayside because of unpredictable events and turn into *unrealized strategy.*

A firm's **realized strategy** is generally formulated through a combination of its top-down strategic intentions and bottom-up emergent strategy. An **emergent strategy** describes any unplanned strategic initiative bubbling up from deep within the organization. If successful, emergent strategies have the potential to influence and shape a firm's overall strategy.

The strategic initiative is a key feature in the strategy as a planned emergence model. A **strategic initiative** is any activity a firm pursues to explore and develop new products and processes, new markets, or new ventures. Strategic initiatives can come from anywhere. They could emerge as a response to external trends or come from internal sources. As such, strategic initiatives can be the result of top-down planning by executives, or they can also emerge through a *bottom-up process.* Many high-tech companies employ the planned emergence approach to formulate strategy. For example, the delivery-by-drone project at Amazon was conceived of and invented by a lower-level engineer. Even relatively junior employees can come up with strategic initiatives that can make major contributions if the strategy process is sufficiently open and flexible.[52]

The arrows in Exhibit 2.7 represent different strategic initiatives. In particular, strategic initiatives can bubble up from deep within a firm through

- Autonomous actions.
- Serendipity.
- Resource-allocation process (RAP).[53]

AUTONOMOUS ACTIONS. **Autonomous actions** are strategic initiatives undertaken by lower-level employees on their own volition and often in response to unexpected situations. Strategy Highlight 2.2 illustrates that successful emergent strategies are sometimes the result of *autonomous actions* by lower-level employees.

Functional managers such as Diana, the Starbucks store manager featured in Strategy Highlight 2.2 , are much closer to the final products, services, and customers than are the more removed corporate- or business-level managers. They also receive much more direct customer feedback. As a result, functional managers may start strategic initiatives based on autonomous actions that can influence the direction of the company. To be successful, however, top-level executives need to support emergent strategies that they believe fit with the firm's vision and mission. Diana's autonomous actions might not have succeeded or might have got her in trouble if she did not garner the support of a senior Starbucks executive. This

Amazon Prime Air is a future service that will deliver packages up to five pounds in 30 minutes or less using small drones. This strategic initiative was conceived of and invented by a lower-level engineer. Johannes Schmitt-Tegge/dpa/Alamy Stock Photo

intended strategy The outcome of a rational and structured top-down strategic plan.

realized strategy Combination of intended and emergent strategy.

emergent strategy Any unplanned strategic initiative bubbling up from the bottom of the organization.

strategic initiative Any activity a firm pursues to explore and develop new products and processes, new markets, or new ventures.

autonomous actions Strategic initiatives undertaken by lower-level employees on their own volition and often in response to unexpected situations.

Strategy Highlight 2.2

Starbucks CEO: "It's Not What We Do"

Diana, a Starbucks store manager in Southern California, received several requests a day for an iced beverage offered by a local competitor. After receiving more than 30 requests one day, she tried the beverage herself. Thinking it might be a good idea for Starbucks to offer a similar iced beverage, she requested that headquarters consider adding it to the product lineup. Diana had an internal champion in Howard Behar, then a top Starbucks executive. Behar presented this strategic initiative to the Starbucks executive committee. The committee voted down the idea in a 7:1 vote. Starbucks CEO Howard Schultz commented, "We do coffee; we don't do iced drinks."

Diana, however, was undeterred. She experimented until she created the iced drink, and then she began to offer it in her store. When Behar visited Diana's store, he was shocked to see this new drink on the menu—all

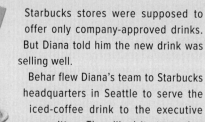

M. Unal Ozmen/Shutterstock

Starbucks stores were supposed to offer only company-approved drinks. But Diana told him the new drink was selling well.

Behar flew Diana's team to Starbucks headquarters in Seattle to serve the iced-coffee drink to the executive committee. They liked its taste, but still said no. Then Behar pulled out the sales numbers that Diana had carefully kept. The drink was selling like crazy: 40 drinks a day the first week, 50 drinks a day the next week, and then 70 drinks a day in the third week after introduction. They had never seen such growth numbers. These results persuaded the executive team to give reluctant approval to introduce the drink in all Starbucks stores.

You've probably guessed by now that we're talking about Starbucks Frappuccino. Frappuccino is now a multibillion-dollar business for Starbucks. At one point, this iced drink brought in more than 20 percent of Starbucks's total revenues, which were over $26 billion in 2019.[54]

executive championed her initiative and helped persuade other top executives. *Internal champions,* therefore, are often needed for autonomous actions to be successful.

Although emergent strategies can arise in the most unusual circumstances, it is important to emphasize the role that top management teams play in this type of strategy process. In the strategy-as-planned-emergence approach, executives need to decide which of the bottom-up initiatives to pursue and which to shut down. This critical decision is made on the basis of whether the strategic initiative fits with the company's vision and mission, and whether it provides an opportunity worth exploiting. Executives, therefore, continue to play a critical role in the potential success or failure of emergent strategies because they determine how limited resources are allocated. After initial resistance, as detailed in Strategy Highlight 2.2, the Starbucks executive team around CEO Howard Schultz fully supported the Frappuccino strategic initiative, providing the resources and personnel to help it succeed.

serendipity Any random events, pleasant surprises, and accidental happenstances that can have a profound impact on a firm's strategic initiatives.

SERENDIPITY. **Serendipity** describes random events, pleasant surprises, and accidental happenstances that can have a profound impact on a firm's strategic initiatives.

There are dozens of examples where serendipity had a crucial influence on the course of business and entire industries. The discovery of 3M's Post-it Notes or Pfizer's Viagra, first intended as a drug to treat hypertension, are well known. Less well known is the discovery of potato chips.[55] The story goes that in the summer of 1853, George Crum was working as a cook at the Moon Lake Lodge resort in Saratoga Springs, New York. A grumpy patron ordered Moon resort's signature fried potatoes. These potatoes were served in thick slices and eaten with a fork as was in the French tradition. When the patron received the fries, he immediately returned them to the kitchen, asking for them to be cut thinner. Crum prepared a second plate in order to please the patron, but this attempt was returned as well. The third plate was prepared by an annoyed Crum who, trying to mock the patron, sliced the potatoes sidewise as thin as he could and fried them. Instead of being offended, the patron was ecstatic with the new fries and suddenly other patrons wanted to try them as well. Crum later opened his own restaurant and offered the famous "Saratoga Chips," which he set up in a box and some customers simply took home as a snack to be eaten later. Today, PepsiCo's line of Frito-Lay's chips are a multibillion-dollar business.

How do strategic leaders create a work environment in which autonomous actions and seren-dipity can flourish? One approach is to provide time and resources for employees to pursue other interests. Google, the online search and advertising subsidiary of Alphabet, for exam-ple, organizes the work of its engineers according to a 70-20-10 rule. The majority of the engineers' work time (70 percent) is focused on its main business (search and ads).[56] Google also allows its engineers to spend one day a week (20 percent) on ideas of their own choosing, and the remainder (10 percent) on total wild cards such as Project Loon, which places high-altitude balloons into the stratosphere to create a high-speed wireless network with global coverage. Google reports that half of its new products and services came from the 20 percent rule, including Gmail, Google Maps, Google News, and Orkut.[57] With the restructuring of Google into a corporation with multiple strategic business units, engineers spending their 10 percent time on total wild cards do so within Google X, its research and development unit.[58]

RESOURCE-ALLOCATION PROCESS. A firm's **resource-allocation process (RAP)** deter-mines the way it allocates its resources and can be critical in shaping its realized strategy.[59] Emergent strategies can result from a firm's resource-allocation process (RAP).[60] Intel Corp. illustrates this concept.[61] Intel was created to produce DRAM (dynamic random-access memory) chips. From the start, producing these chips was the firm's top-down stra-tegic plan, and initially it worked well. In the 1980s, Japanese competitors brought better-quality chips to the market at lower cost, threatening Intel's position and obsoleting its top-down strategic plan. However, Intel was able to pursue a strategic transformation because of the way it set up its resource-allocation process. In a sense, Intel was using functional-level managers to drive business and corporate strategy in a bottom-up fashion. In particular, during this time Intel had only a few fabrication plants (called "fabs") to pro-duce silicon-based products. It would have taken several years and billions of dollars to build additional capacity by bringing new fabs online.

With constrained capacity, Intel had implemented the production-decision rule *to maxi-mize margin-per-wafer-start.* Each time functional managers initiated a new production run, they were to consider the profit margins for DRAM chips and for microprocessors, the "brains" of personal computers. The operations managers then could produce *whichever product* delivered the higher margin. By following this simple rule, front-line managers shifted Intel's production capacity away from the lower-margin DRAM business to the higher-margin microprocessors business. The firm's focus on microprocessors emerged from the bottom up, based on resource allocation. Indeed, by the time top management finally approved the de facto strategic switch, the company's market share in DRAM had dwindled to less than 3 percent.[62]

> **resource-allocation process (RAP)** The way a firm allocates its resources based on predetermined policies, which can be critical in shaping its realized strategy.

Taken together, a firm's realized strategy is frequently a combination of top-down strategic intent and bottom-up emergent strategies, as Exhibit 2.7 shows. This type of strategy process is called **planned emergence**. In that process, organizational structure and systems allow bottom-up strategic initiatives to emerge and be evaluated and coordinated by top management.[63] These bottom-up strategic initiatives can be the result of autonomous actions, serendipity, or the resource allocation process.

Exhibit 2.8 compares and contrasts the three different approaches to the strategic management process: top-down strategic planning, scenario planning, and strategy as planned emergence.

EXHIBIT 2.8   Comparing and Contrasting Top-Down Strategic Planning, Scenario Planning, and Strategy as Planned Emergence

Strategy Process	Description	Pros	Cons	Where Best Used
Top-Down Strategic Planning	A rational strategy process through which top management attempts to program future success; typically concentrates strategic intelligence and decision-making responsibilities in the office of the CEO.	• Provides a clear strategy process and lines of communication. • Affords coordination and control of various business activities. • Readily accepted and understood as process is well established and widely used. • Works relatively well in stable environments.	• Fairly rigid and inhibits flexibility. • Top-down, one-way communication limits feedback. • Assumes that the future can usually be predicted based on past data. • Separates elements of AFI framework so that top management (analysis & formulation) are removed from line employees (implementation).	• Highly regulated and stable industries such as utilities, e.g., Georgia Power in Southeast United States or Framatome, state-owned nuclear operator in France. • Government • Military
Scenario Planning	Strategy-planning activity in which top management envisions different what-if scenarios to anticipate plausible futures in order to plan optimal strategic responses.	• Provides a clear strategy process and lines of communication. • Affords coordination and control of various business activities. • Readily accepted and understood as process is well established and widely used. • Provides some strategic flexibility.	• Top-down, one-way communication limits feedback. • Separates elements of AFI framework so that top management (analysis & formulation) are removed from line employees (implementation). • As the future is unknown, responses to all possible events cannot be planned. • Leaders tend to avoid planning for pessimistic scenarios.	• Fairly stable industries, often characterized by some degree of regulation such as airlines, logistics, or medical devices, e.g., American Airlines, Delta Air Lines, and United Airlines; FedEx and UPS; Medtronic. • Larger firms in industries with a small number of other large competitors (oligopoly).

Strategy Process	Description	Pros	Cons	Where Best Used
Strategy as Planned Emergence	Blended strategy process in which organizational structure and systems allow both top-down vision and bottom-up strategic initiatives to emerge for evaluation and coordination by top management.	• Combines all elements of the AFI framework in a holistic and flexible fashion. • Provides provisional direction through intended strategy. • Accounts for unrealized strategy (not all strategic initiatives can be implemented). • Accounts for emergent strategy (good ideas for strategic initiatives can bubble up from lower levels of hierarchy through autonomous actions, serendipity, and RAP). • The firm's realized strategy is a combination of intended and emergent strategy. • Highest degree of strategic flexibility and buy-in by employees.	• Unclear strategy process and lines of communication can lead to employee confusion and lack of focus. • Many ideas that bubble up from the bottom may not be worth pursuing. • Firms may lack a clear process of how to evaluate emergent strategy, increasing the chances of missing mega opportunities or pursuing dead ends; may also contribute to employee frustration and lower morale.	• New ventures and smaller firms. • High-velocity industries such as technology ventures. • Internet companies; e.g., Airbnb, Alibaba, Alphabet (parent company of Google), Amazon, Facebook, Twitter, and Uber. • Biotech companies; e.g., Amgen, Biogen, Gilead Sciences, Genentech, and Genzyme.

2.4 Strategic Decision Making

LO 2-8

Describe and evaluate the two distinct modes of decision making.

Although we like to believe that we make rational decisions, especially in business, informed by data and facts, the truth is that as fallible human beings, our decision making is fraught with cognitive limitations and biases. Herbert Simon, a Nobel Laureate in economics, developed the **theory of bounded rationality**, the core tenet of which posits that rather than to optimize when faced with decisions, we tend to "satisfice"— a portmanteau of the two words *satisfy* and *suffice*.[64]

Cognitive limitations tend to lead us to choose the "good enough option" that satisfies our immediate needs, rather than to search for an optimal solution. One argument that supports this tendency suggests that we do not have all the information we need to arrive at an optimal decision. However, another argument suggests that online search engines, such as Google, and AI assistants, such as Apple's Siri and Amazon's Alexa, now give us access to a wealth of information—perhaps too much. Simon asserts that cognitive limitations are what prevent us from appropriately processing and evaluating each piece of information that we encounter (a concept known as *information overload*), especially when faced with constraints such as time.

Today, managers are generally faced with an issue of not *too little*, but rather that of *too much* information. The lack of available time and attention also hinder their ability to make optimal decisions. This combination of conditions results in *a wealth of information, but scarcity of attention*. Indeed, one of the strengths of strategy frameworks is that they allow managers to cut through a lot of the "noise" and to focus on the "signal," that is, the most important pieces of information.

Strategic decisions are frequently made using simple heuristics and rules of thumb rather than entirely based on rational thinking, in other words, using tacit (or implicit)

theory of bounded rationality When individuals face decisions, their rationality is confined by cognitive limitations and the time available to make a decision. Thus, individuals tend to "satisfice" rather than to optimize.

cognitive limitations Constraints such as time or the brain's inability to process large amounts of data that prevent us from appropriately processing and evaluating each piece of information we encounter.

knowledge rather than on explicit knowledge. Thus, through professional experience and by viewing the complex and uncertain information world through the lens of theory and frameworks, managers can become better equipped and faster at making sound strategic decision making.

TWO DISTINCT MODES OF DECISION MAKING

In his popular book, *Thinking, Fast and Slow,* Daniel Kahneman, a Nobel Laureate in economics, describes the research in **behavioral economics** that he and his collaborator Amos Tversky spent decades conducting.[65] They posit that our decision making is governed by two different systems. **System 1** is the brain's default mode. It is the gut reaction we experience when we see something beautiful, for instance. It is that confidence we feel while driving down a stretch of highway that we've driven along a thousand times before. So familiar it is, we feel as though we can drive it on autopilot. We like System 1 and use it most of the time because it is fast (giving way to "snap judgments"[66]), efficient, and automatic, and therefore requires little, if any, attentional energy. In contrast, **System 2** is logical, analytical, and deliberate. Because logical and analytical thinking consume much more of our brain's energy, this system of decision making tends to be slower. This is a challenge when the brain is already energy hungry. While it comprises only 2 percent of our body weight, it consumes over 20 percent of our energy. Exhibit 2.9 offers a comparative view of some of the key characteristics of System 1 and System 2.

We tend to rely on System 1 when we are tired or aggravated. For example, let's assume your goal is to lose 15 pounds. It is the end of a long day and you are exhausted and hungry. You stop off at the market to pick up a few healthy items for dinner. Instead, you find yourself wandering to the frozen food aisle and reaching for a pint of Haagen-Dazs ice cream. In this situation, you are activating System 1 precisely because you're exhausted. The brain energy required to keep System 1 in check, and to activate System 2, has already been spent as you moved throughout the course of your day working, studying, or both. Had System 2 been in charge, you would have opted for a salad, perhaps, instead of a pint of ice cream.

| EXHIBIT 2.9 | Two Distinct Modes of Decision Making |

System 1	System 2
Fast	Slow
Unconscious	Conscious
Automatic	Effortful
Everyday, Snap Decisions	Complex, Analytical Decisions
Error Prone, Higher Likelihood of Biases	Reliable, Lower Likelihood of Biases

Source: Author's creation based on D. Kahneman (2011), *Thinking, Fast and Slow* (New York: Farrar, Straus and Giroux).

COGNITIVE BIASES AND DECISION MAKING

Along with cognitive limitations, human beings are also prone to **cognitive biases,** which lead to systematic errors in our decision making and interfere with our

behavioral economics A field of study that blends research findings from psychology with economics to provide valuable insights showing when and why individuals do not act like rational decision makers, as assumed in neoclassical economics.

System 1 One of two distinct modes of thinking used in decision making. It is our default mode because it is automatic, fast, and efficient, requiring little energy or attention. System 1 is prone to cognitive biases that can lead to systematic errors in our decision making.

System 2 One of two distinct modes of thinking used in decision making that applies rationality and relies on analytical and logical reasoning. Thus, it is an effortful, slow, and deliberate way of thinking.

cognitive biases Obstacles in thinking that lead to systematic errors in our decision making and interfere with our rational thinking.

rational thinking. Many of our cognitive biases result from System 1–governed thinking. Research in behavioral economics has identified a host of cognitive biases that can lead to systematic errors in decision making.[67] We highlight the most common ones that can affect managers in the sections that follow. Creating awareness of the sources behind the systematic errors that can negatively impact strategic decision making allows managers to put some safeguards in place for overcoming them and, thus, make better, more rational decisions.

ILLUSION OF CONTROL. One of the more common biases (mentioned briefly in the section covering strategy as planned emergence) is the **illusion of control,** which describes the tendency to overestimate our ability to control events.[68] Put simply, the illusion of control describes the belief that you control things that you do not. Successful individuals such as CEOs and other top-level executives are highly prone to the illusion of control because they tend to attribute their success to their own abilities, including the mistaken belief that they can fully control their circumstances.

illusion of control
A cognitive bias that highlights people's tendency to overestimate their ability to control events.

An example of the illusion of control may be seen in the relationship between air traffic controllers and pilots.[69] Some air traffic controllers observed that after complimenting pilots with phrases such as "nice landing," the next time these same pilots landed an aircraft in the same airport, the landings were not as good. Conversely, when air traffic controllers expressed that the landings were not good (e.g., "you really missed the mark on that one"), the next set of landings would be better. From this, the air traffic controllers formed the mistaken belief that their comments influenced the quality of the landings. They hypothesized that complimenting pilots for good landings would result in pilot complacency and therefore lead to subsequent poor landings. They also hypothesized that criticizing seemingly complacent pilots for sloppy landings would result in pilot improvement and therefore lead to subsequent better landings.

Although this reasoning made perfect sense to the air traffic controllers and resulted in mostly negative feedback, a more likely explanation is simply that a *regression to the mean* is taking place. If we assume a normal (bell-shaped) distribution and the landing under consideration was perfect (thus in the far-right tail of the distribution), then the probability that the pilots' next landing will not be as perfect is nearly 100 percent. Conversely, if the pilot team put down a sloppy landing (far left tail of distribution), then the likelihood that the next landing will be better is close to 100 percent also. In sum, the air traffic controllers were under the illusion that they could directly influence from their towers the quality of the landings the pilots put down. In truth, what they were really observing was the regression of the mean phenomenon.

In "The Strategic Management Process" section, we highlighted that managers that implement a formalized, top-down strategy process frequently fall prey to the illusion of control; this is because such strategic leaders tend to rely on hard data from the past to forecast the future success of their organization. Such thinking is often flawed, however, because we all know that the past often does not predict the future. The only constant is change.

escalating commitment
A cognitive bias in which an individual or a group faces increasingly negative feedback regarding the likely outcome from a decision, but nevertheless continues to invest resources and time in that decision, often exceeding the earlier commitments.

ESCALATING COMMITMENT. An **escalating commitment** is another common cognitive bias. It occurs when decision makers continue to support and invest in a project despite having received feedback that it is likely not going to succeed; typically, a significant amount of time and financial resources have already been committed to the project.[70] Rather than ignoring the prior resources already spent, which are the *sunk costs,* and shut the project down, which would be the rational decision, the strategic decision makers commit more and more resources to a failing course of action ("doubling down"). In other words, past investments, like spilled milk or money spent on salaries, are *sunk costs* because you can't recover them. Thus, the most rational approach would be to ignore the past sunk costs and consider any future decisions with a clean-slate approach. Although this seems a bit counterintuitive, it is the most rational approach when making strategic decisions. Yet, such rational decisions are hard to implement because of *loss aversion;* strategic leaders feel that they need to "recover" the investments already made. An *escalating commitment to a failing course of action* is often observed in R&D projects.

For example, Motorola spent billions of dollars and many years engineering its Iridium project in the hopes that it would eventually be successful.[71] Iridium was an ill-fated, satellite-based telephone system that Motorola attempted to commercialize in the 1990s. Despite clear evidence that an earth-based cellular telephone network was going to be much more successful because it was less expensive to deploy and thus more affordable for the end consumer, Motorola continued investing billions of dollars in its Iridium project for more than a decade. For the project to work, several dozen satellites needed to be launched into space—an exorbitant expense. And even though executives at Motorola knew early on that satellite-based telephone systems would not work in either buildings or cars, something that most businesspeople need to rely on, Motorola kept on spending. Clearly, Motorola's strategic decision makers fell prey to escalating commitment; although apparent that the project was failing commercially, executives persisted in "throwing good money after bad," meaning, they wasted money that could have been put to use much more effectively elsewhere.

confirmation bias A cognitive bias in which individuals tend to search for and interpret information in a way that supports their prior beliefs. Regardless of facts and data presented, individuals will stick with their prior hypothesis.

CONFIRMATION BIAS.   **Confirmation bias,** also called *prior hypothesis bias,* is the tendency of individuals to search for information that confirms their existing beliefs. When confronted with evidence that contradicts these beliefs, they either ignore the evidence or interpret it such that it supports their beliefs. People tend to cling, in particular, to their prior beliefs about a relationship between two variables (e.g., market share is the key to profitability) or how the world works in general.

Confirmation bias often occurs when earlier experience appears to support a prior hypothesis. For example, strategic decision makers at Intel might believe that the key to continued success is to develop yet another faster chip for personal computers (PCs) using the same x86 architecture as in the past. This prior hypothesis is based on the observation that this incremental innovation strategy was successful for 30 years (e.g., starting with the 8086 chip in 1978 to the Intel Atom chip in 2008). In the meantime, while the strategic managers at Intel clung to their prior hypothesis of how to sustain a competitive advantage, the external environment shifted away from personal computing to mobile computing—a change for which Intel was ill-prepared. Consequently, it lost out to ARM, Nvidia, and other mobile chip makers and is now playing catch-up.

reason by analogy A cognitive bias in which individuals use simple analogies to make sense out of complex problems.

REASON BY ANALOGY.   **Reason by analogy** is the tendency to use simple analogies to make sense out of complex problems. Analogies allow us to examine and compare a complex problem to something familiar, even though the two objects or ideas might actually be very different from each other. In essence, this is the primary drawback of reason by analogy: What appears to be similar on the surface may actually be very different on a deeper level. For example, Walmart executives might have fallen prey to reason by analogy when they first entered the Canadian market in 1994. The firm attempted to use the same cost-leadership strategy that garnered it success in the United States (opening large supercenters in rural areas, implementing sophisticated IT systems, and hiring minimum-wage employees, for instance). Walmart looked at Canada and saw opportunity in the country's rural areas, believing the regions strongly resembled the rural areas in the United States. Moreover, they saw English being spoken in both countries and Canada being one of the closest U.S. trading partners as advantages. Yet, despite these similarities and advantages, Walmart struggled in the Canadian market and lost money. What Walmart executives discovered the hard way is that the Canadian market is quite different from the U.S. market in such key areas as customers, preferences, and culture.

REPRESENTATIVENESS. **Representativeness** refers to the cognitive bias of drawing conclusions based on small samples, or even from one memorable case or anecdote. Relying on this simple heuristic violates the *law of large numbers*, which states that a large enough sample is needed so that a calculated value is close enough to the expected value that would be observed across all possible observations.

> **representativeness** A cognitive bias in which conclusions are based on small samples, or even from one memorable case or anecdote.

In the 1990s, many internet entrepreneurs and venture capitalists fell prey to representativeness bias. They saw the early success of Amazon, eBay, and Yahoo and decided that they, too, could build a successful online business. Most of these entrepreneurial ventures failed in the dot-com crash of 2001, taking with it billions in venture capital investments. A similar phenomenon is being observed today in the app economy, where most young entrepreneurs are currently directing their energies. Their reasoning based on representativeness bias goes as follows: "We will be the Uber of X, where X is any other category than ride hailing" or "We will be the Airbnb of Y, where Y is any other category than hospitality services."

GROUPTHINK. While the cognitive limitations discussed so far tend to afflict individuals, one important cognitive bias that can affect entire teams is called **groupthink,** a situation in which opinions coalesce around a leader without individuals critically evaluating and challenging that leader's opinions and assumptions.[72] We have seen this occur in military history. For instance, in 1812, Napoleon Bonaparte's commanders endorsed his idea to invade Russia, convinced that his strategy was a well-thought-out one. The commanders' unquestioned conformity around Napoleon's beliefs led to disastrous consequences. Their groupthink, combined with Napoleon's hubris, led to one of the most devastating military defeats in history.[73] Napoleon began his campaign with almost 700,000 soldiers (the largest army ever amassed at that point in history), but only about 20,000 lived to return home.

> **groupthink** A situation in which opinions coalesce around a leader without individuals critically evaluating and challenging that leader's opinions and assumptions.

In business, strong leaders tend to set the culture of their organizations. This process is reinforced by leaders' strong preference to recruit, retain, and promote employees that subscribe to the same values, which, in turn, attracts more people with similar values to that organization.[74] Although this process strengthens an organization's culture and makes it more distinct, it also creates a more homogeneous organization, leaving its employees vulnerable to groupthink.

Groupthink frequently comes into play when executives consider major strategic decisions such as takeovers. In 2015, for example, General Electric (GE) paid close to $20 billion to acquire Alstom, a French industrial conglomerate.[75] Then CEO Jeffrey Immelt and this team of hand-selected lieutenants were certain that acquiring Alstom was needed to transform the flagging U.S. conglomerate. They further convinced themselves that they could integrate Alstom into GE and manage the combined entity successfully. Their thinking went along these lines: Since GE produced the best business leaders in the world that could manage any situation, who other than GE could pull this off?

Despite many red flags, such as the apparent overpayment for the target and massive regulatory pushback, as well as subsequent deep concessions by GE, Immelt pushed the acquisition through. Just three years later, GE had to write off more than $20 billion in assets from its Power Division, most of it caused by the failed Alstom acquisition. After a 16-year tenure as CEO, Jeffrey Immelt was replaced. His successor, John Flannery (another GE insider), lasted 14 months on the job, before he too was fired. GE, once the most valuable company in the United States with some $600 billion in market capitalization in mid-2000, had lost 90 percent of its market value or $540 billion by the end of 2018.[76]

In sum, cohesive, nondiverse groups are highly susceptible to groupthink, which in turn can lead to flawed decision making with potentially disastrous consequences.

LO 2-9

Compare and contrast devil's advocacy and dialectic inquiry as frameworks to improve strategic decision making.

HOW TO IMPROVE STRATEGIC DECISION MAKING

What can strategic leaders do to ensure that they base their decisions on relevant and critical information, while overcoming groupthink and the cognitive biases that can affect all of us? Two techniques have proven effective at improving strategic decision making: *devil's advocacy* and *dialectic inquiry*.[77]

Devil's Advocacy. The **devil's advocacy** decision framework begins with one team generating a detailed course of action. Next, a second team plays devil's advocate and challenges the proposal generated by Team 1. Team 2 questions the underlying assumptions made in the proposal and highlights anything that might go wrong in the proposed course of action, thus illuminating potential downsides. In a third step, Team 1 then revises its initial proposal based on input and suggestions received from the devil's advocate (that is, Team 2). This process is then repeated one more time. In a final step, both teams agree upon a course of action. The entire process frequently takes place under the supervision of a higher-level executive or executive team.

Amazon, for example, uses the devil's advocacy approach when making strategic decisions. Founder and CEO Jeff Bezos banned all PowerPoint presentations and requires each manager to write a "narrative memo" no longer than six pages to which others are expected to respond as devil's advocates. These written exchanges become the documents referenced when Amazon's management teams meet to make decisions.[78] Exhibit 2.10 shows the devil's advocacy framework to enhance strategic decision making.

devil's advocacy
Technique that can help to improve strategic decision making; a key element is that of a separate team or individual carefully scrutinizing a proposed course of action by questioning and critiquing underlying assumptions and highlighting potential downsides.

EXHIBIT 2.10

How to Use a Devil's Advocate to Improve Strategic Decision Making

Source: Author's own creation.

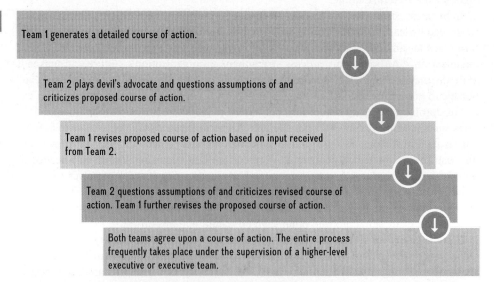

Team 1 generates a detailed course of action.

Team 2 plays devil's advocate and questions assumptions of and criticizes proposed course of action.

Team 1 revises proposed course of action based on input received from Team 2.

Team 2 questions assumptions of and criticizes revised course of action. Team 1 further revises the proposed course of action.

Both teams agree upon a course of action. The entire process frequently takes place under the supervision of a higher-level executive or executive team.

Dialectic Inquiry. In contrast to the devil's advocacy decision framework, which begins with a team generating one detailed course of action, in the **dialectic inquiry** framework, two teams each generate a detailed course of action. In Step 1, Team 1 generates a detailed course of action (*thesis*) and Team 2 responds to Team 1 by generating a second, but alternate detailed course of action (*antithesis*). In Step 2, a debate in front of higher-level executives takes place where both *thesis* and *antithesis* are presented and discussed. In the final step, the executive team synthesizes both proposals into a compromise plan of action and decides whether to adopt either proposal or neither of them. Exhibit 2.11 shows the dialectic inquiry framework as another option to enhance strategic decision making.

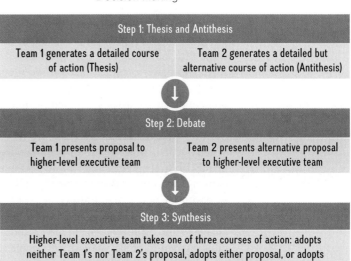

EXHIBIT 2.11 How to Use Dialectic Inquiry to Improve Strategic Decision Making

Step 1: Thesis and Antithesis

Team 1 generates a detailed course of action (Thesis) | Team 2 generates a detailed but alternative course of action (Antithesis)

Step 2: Debate

Team 1 presents proposal to higher-level executive team | Team 2 presents alternative proposal to higher-level executive team

Step 3: Synthesis

Higher-level executive team takes one of three courses of action: adopts neither Team 1's nor Team 2's proposal, adopts either proposal, or adopts a synthesis (some combination of both proposals)

Source: Author's own creation.

2.5 Implications for Strategic Leaders

Executives whose vision and decisions enable their organizations to achieve competitive advantage demonstrate *strategic leadership.* Effective strategic leaders use position as well as informal power and influence to direct the activities of others when implementing the organization's strategy. To gain and sustain a competitive advantage, strategic leaders need to put an effective *strategic management process* in place. An important first step in crafting an effective strategic management process is to articulate an inspiring vision and mission backed up by ethical core values. Customer-oriented or problem-defining vision statements are often correlated with firm success over long periods of time. This is because they allow firms strategic flexibility to change in order to meet changing customer needs and exploit external opportunities.

Another important implication of our discussion is that all employees should feel invested in and inspired by the firm's vision and mission. Companies use different tactics to achieve such commitment; some firms annually invite all employees to review and revise the statement of firm values; others ask employees to rank themselves, their departments, and management on success relative to the vision and mission. Belief in a company's vision and mission motivates its employees.

Strategic leaders, moreover, need to design a process that supports strategy formulation and implementation. In particular, strategic leaders have three options in their strategic toolkit: top-down strategic planning, scenario planning, and strategy as planned emergence. Each of the three strategy processes has its strengths and weaknesses (see Exhibit 2.8). Strategic leaders also need to consider the rate of change and firm size, two factors that affect the effectiveness of a chosen strategy process. The rate of change, internally and externally, can suggest the more useful planning approach. In a slow-moving and stable environment, top-down strategic planning might be the most effective. In a fast-moving and changeable environment, strategy as planned emergence might be the most effective. As to firm size, larger firms tend to use either a top-down strategic planning process or scenario

dialectic inquiry
Technique that can help to improve strategic decision making; key element is that two teams each generate a detailed but alternate plan of action (thesis and anti-thesis). The goal, if feasible, is to achieve a synthesis between the two plans.

planning. Smaller firms may find it easier to implement strategy as planned emergence when feedback loops are short and the ability to respond quickly is keen.

For instance, a nuclear power provider such as Framatome in France, providing over 75 percent of the country's energy and with the long-term backing of the state, might do well using a top-down strategy approach. Take the issue of disaster planning. Nuclear accidents, while rare, have tremendous impact as witnessed in Chernobyl, Russia, and Fukushima, Japan, so power providers need to be prepared. Nuclear accidents are considered *black swans,* low-probability events with high impact. Framatome might use scenario planning to prepare for such a black swan event. Contrast this with fast-moving environments. Internet-based companies, such as Airbnb, Alibaba, Alphabet, Amazon, Facebook, or Uber, tend to use strategy as planned emergence. In this process, every employee plays a strategic role. When a firm is using top-down planning or scenario planning, lower-level employees focus mainly on strategy implementation. As the examples in this chapter have shown, however, *any employee,* even at the entry level, can have great ideas that might become *strategic initiatives* with the potential to transform companies.

Even the most well-designed strategic management process will fail if strategic leaders are unable to use the information at their disposal; our *rationality is bounded*—that is, while many of us attempt to be rational, we are unable to process a vast amount of information in real time. Individuals are not (yet) cyborgs, after all. Furthermore, every individual, including the most astute strategic leaders, are susceptible to a host of *cognitive biases* that lead to systematic errors in our decision making. Thus, it is imperative that strategic leaders put in place safeguards, such as *devil's advocacy* and *dialectic inquiry,* to improve strategic decision making.

The conclusion of our discussion of the strategic management process marks the end of the "getting started" portion of the Analysis, Formulation, Implementation (AFI) strategy framework (see Exhibit 1.4). The next three chapters cover the *analysis* part of the framework, where we begin by studying external and internal analyses before taking a closer look at competitive advantage, firm performance, and business models.

CHAPTER**CASE 2** Part II

DURING THE PAST DECADE, the Zuckerberg-Sandberg leadership duo has created the most successful social network ever. When Sheryl Sandberg joined Facebook in 2008, her main priority was to develop a sustainable business model from which Facebook could make money. In short, her task was to build a big advertising business. Sandberg used the same playbook that she had used so successfully at Google: first, build a large user base—in this area, Mark Zuckerberg and his team of developers excelled.

Second, gather as much personal data as possible from Facebook's users, their friends, and all their activities on the open web. Not only did Facebook excel in this area as well, it also purchased additional personal data from data brokers (such as Acxiom and Epsilon) and consumer credit reporting companies (such as Experian, Equifax, and TransUnion) about each American. From these data, Facebook gathered a wide range of personal information: what each American buys, where each lives, where each works, how much money each makes, each person's traffic patterns, family activities, likes and dislikes, movies watched, restaurants dined at, and much more. Most consumers are unaware that so much personal data are being collected, which has led some critics to accuse Facebook of being a "surveillance machine."

Third, place micro-targeted ads using a proprietary algorithm. Facebook managed to collect a breadth of fine-grained and high-quality consumer data, the best in the industry, which it then used to develop unique profiles for each user. Advertisers then relied on these profiles to place their micro-targeted ads. It was precisely for this capability of accurate individual profiling that advertisers (ranging from consumer product companies to presidential campaigns) were willing to pay a premium. Facebook's business model—offering free

Given the ongoing crises at Facebook around alleged violation of user privacy, foreign meddling in U.S. elections, and the company's continued abdication of taking responsibility for the content published on its site, Facebook CEO Mark Zuckerberg and COO Sheryl Sandberg were both compelled to testify on several occasions in front of Congress in 2018.

(left): Andrew Harnik/AP Images, (right): Ron Sachs/CNP/AdMedia/Newscom

services to end users while allowing advertisers to place finely targeted ads for a premium price—turned out to be highly profitable. It would serve as the foundation for Facebook's decade-long competitive advantage.

Now, however, Facebook appears to be in a deep crisis and is struggling to maintain its reputation. It has lost users' trust as well as legitimacy among many other stakeholders including the media, politicians, and regulators both in the United States and Europe. The demands to regulate its platform more closely are gathering steam. User engagement has fallen, and the company's valuation had dropped by $200 billion during the last six months of 2018 alone.

What led to this crisis? First and foremost, user privacy became a growing concern. Facebook has long been criticized for alleged lax handling of user information and an opaque privacy policy that changed frequently. In the spring of 2018, however, things came to a head when it was revealed that Cambridge Analytica, a political consulting firm, used Facebook data from millions of users (and their friends) without their consent to create micro-targeted political advertising campaigns during the 2016 presidential election in the United States. This privacy scandal compelled Zuckerberg to testify before Senate committees, where he declared that Facebook users "have complete control" over which data they share. This turned out not to be true. As was reported in the fall of 2018, Facebook had allowed a number of tech companies, including Netflix, Microsoft, Yahoo, Amazon, Pandora, and Spotify, access to user data and private messages.

Second, Facebook has been criticized for becoming a news organization rather than a social network, which has become a serious issue in the era of fake news. Roughly two-thirds of Americans of all ages (and a higher percentage of youth) get their political news from social media sites. Critics, therefore, want Facebook to demonstrate a higher degree of editorial oversight, similar to the oversight demonstrated by traditional publishers. Facebook maintains that it is agnostic on news content and points to existing U.S. law (Section 230 of the Communications Decency Act), which states that internet firms are not liable for the content that is published on their platform.

Third, critics and even early investors of Facebook allege that Zuckerberg and Sandberg responded too slowly to the various crises they were facing: Russian meddling in U.S. elections, abuse of personal data by third parties such as Cambridge Analytica, and Facebook's abdication of any responsibilities for the content posted on its website.

Lastly, Facebook's leaders have been criticized for prioritizing exponential growth above anything else and that it failed to consider the potential downsides of creating an information platform for more than 2 billion people. Many have equated the network to "a digital nation-state."[79]

Questions

1. What challenges (as detailed in this ChapterCase) is Facebook facing? How should Mark Zuckerberg and Sheryl Sandberg deal with each of them? List each of the challenges, and make specific recommendations on how to address them.

2. Compare and contrast the strategic leadership of Mark Zuckerberg and Sheryl Sandberg. Which qualities for each strategic leader stand out to you, and why? Where would you place each individual on the Level-5 pyramid for strategic leaders (see Exhibit 2.2), and why? Is either of them an effective strategic leader? Explain your answers.

3. Given the apparent leadership crisis at Facebook should Mark Zuckerberg and/or Sheryl Sandberg be replaced? Why, or why not? Explain your answers.

mySTRATEGY

How Much Are Your Values Worth to You?

How much are you willing to pay for the job you want? This may sound like a strange question, since your employer will pay you to work, but think again. Consider how much you value a specific type of work, or how much you would want to work for a specific organization because of its values.

A study shows scientists who want to continue engaging in research will accept some $14,000 less in annual salary to work at an organization that permits them to publish their findings in academic journals, implying that some scientists will "pay to be scientists." This finding appears to hold in the general business world too. In a survey, 97 percent of Stanford MBA students indicated they would forgo some 14 percent of their expected salary, or about $11,480 a year, to work for a company that matches their own values with concern for stakeholders and sustainability. According to Monster.com, an online career service, about 92 percent of all undergraduates want to work for a "green" company. These diverse examples demonstrate that people put a real dollar amount on pursuing careers in sync with their values.

On the other hand, certain high-powered jobs such as management consulting or investment banking pay very well, but their high salaries come with strings attached. Professionals in these jobs work very long hours, including weekends, and often take little or no vacation time. These workers "pay for pay" in that they are often unable to form stable relationships, have little or no leisure time, and sometimes even sacrifice their health. People "pay for"—make certain sacrifices for—what they value, because strategic decisions require important trade-offs.[80]

1. Identify your personal values. How do you expect these values to affect your work life or your career choice?

2. How much less salary would (did) you accept to find employment with a company that is aligned with your values?

3. How much are you willing to "pay for pay" if your dream job is in management consulting or investment banking?

TAKE-AWAY CONCEPTS

This chapter examined the role strategic leaders play, delineated different processes to create strategy, and outlined the different cognitive biases that can negatively impact strategic decision making and what managers can do to improve decision making. We summarize the discussion in the following learning objectives and related take-away concepts.

LO 2-1 / Explain the role of strategic leaders and what they do.

- Executives whose vision and decisions enable their organizations to achieve competitive advantage demonstrate strategic leadership.

- Strategic leaders use formal and informal power to influence the behavior of other organizational members to do things, including things they would not do otherwise.

- Strategic leaders can have a strong (positive or negative) performance impact on the organizations they lead.

LO 2-2 / Outline how you can become a strategic leader.

- To become an effective strategic leader, you need to develop skills to move sequentially through five leadership levels: highly capable individual, contributing team member, competent manager, effective leader, and executive (see Exhibit 2.2).

- The Level-5 strategic leadership pyramid applies to both distinct corporate positions and personal growth.

LO 2-3 / **Compare and contrast the roles of corporate, business, and functional managers in strategy formulation and implementation.**

- *Corporate executives* must provide answers to the question of *where to compete,* whether in industries, markets, or geographies, and *how to create synergies* among different business units.

- *General managers* in strategic business units must answer the strategic question of *how to compete* in order to achieve superior performance. They must manage and align the firm's different functional areas for competitive advantage.

- *Functional managers* are responsible for *implementing business strategy* within a single functional area.

LO 2-4 / **Describe the roles of vision, mission, and values in a firm's strategy.**

- A vision captures an organization's aspirations. An effective vision inspires and motivates members of the organization.

- A mission statement describes what an organization actually does—what its business is—and why and how it does it.

- Core values define the ethical standards and norms that should govern the behavior of individuals within the firm.

LO 2-5 / **Evaluate the strategic implications of product-oriented and customer-oriented vision statements.**

- Product-oriented vision statements define a business in terms of a good or service provided.

- Customer-oriented vision statements define business in terms of providing solutions to customer needs.

- Customer-oriented vision statements provide managers with more strategic flexibility than product-oriented missions.

- To be effective, visions and missions need to be backed up by hard-to-reverse strategic commitments and tied to economic fundamentals.

LO 2-6 / **Justify why anchoring a firm in ethical core values is essential for long-term success.**

- Ethical core values underlay the vision statement to ensure the stability of the strategy, and thus lay the groundwork for long-term success.

- Ethical core values are the guardrails that help keep the company on track when pursuing its mission and its quest for competitive advantage.

LO 2-7 / **Evaluate top-down strategic planning, scenario planning, and strategy as planned emergence.**

- Top-down strategic planning is a sequential, linear process that works reasonably well when the environment does not change much.

- In scenario planning, managers envision what-if scenarios and prepare contingency plans that can be called upon when necessary.

- Strategic initiatives can be the result of top-down planning or can emerge through a bottom-up process from deep within the organization. They have the potential to shape a firm's strategy.

- A firm's realized strategy is generally a combination of its top-down intended strategy and bottom-up emergent strategy, resulting in planned emergence.

LO 2-8 / **Describe and evaluate the two distinct modes of decision making.**

- When faced with decisions, individuals tend to satisfice rather than to optimize due to cognitive limitations.

- Our decision making is governed by two distinct ways of thinking: System 1 and System 2.

- System 1 is our default mode of thinking because it is automatic, fast, and efficient, requiring little energy or attention. System 1 is prone to cognitive biases that can lead to systematic errors in decision making.

- System 2 is based on attempting to apply rationality to our decision making by relying on analytical and logical reasoning. It is an effortful, slow, and deliberate way of thinking.

- Along with cognitive limitations, as humans we are prone to a host of cognitive biases, which leads to systematic errors in our decision making when compared to a more rational decision.

LO 2-9 / **Compare and contrast devil's advocacy and dialectic inquiry as frameworks to improve strategic decision making.**

- Devil's advocacy and dialectic inquiry are two techniques to improve strategic decision making.

- Devil's advocacy is a technique that can help to improve strategic decision making; a key element is that of a separate team or individual carefully scrutinizing a proposed course of action by questioning and critiquing underlying assumptions and highlighting potential downsides.

- Dialectic inquiry is a technique that can help to improve strategic decision making; the key element is that two teams generate detailed but alternate plans of action (thesis and antithesis). The goal, if feasible, is to achieve a synthesis between the two plans.

KEY TERMS

Autonomous actions *(p. 53)*

Behavioral economics *(p. 58)*

Black swan events *(p. 50)*

Cognitive biases *(p. 58)*

Cognitive limitations *(p. 57)*

Confirmation bias *(p. 60)*

Core values statement *(p. 46)*

Devil's advocacy *(p. 62)*

Dialectic inquiry *(p. 63)*

Dominant strategic plan *(p. 51)*

Emergent strategy *(p. 53)*

Escalating commitment *(p. 59)*

Groupthink *(p. 61)*

Illusion of control *(p. 59)*

Intended strategy *(p. 53)*

Level-5 leadership pyramid *(p. 36)*

Mission *(p. 45)*

Organizational core values *(p. 46)*

Planned emergence *(p. 56)*

Realized strategy *(p. 53)*

Reason by analogy *(p. 60)*

Representativeness *(p. 61)*

Resource-allocation process (RAP) *(p. 55)*

Scenario planning *(p. 48)*

Serendipity *(p. 54)*

Strategic business unit (SBU) *(p. 39)*

Strategic initiative *(p. 53)*

Strategic intent *(p. 40)*

Strategic leadership *(p. 34)*

Strategic management process *(p. 47)*

Strategy formulation *(p. 38)*

Strategy implementation *(p. 38)*

System 1 *(p. 58)*

System 2 *(p. 58)*

Theory of bounded rationality *(p. 57)*

Top-down strategic planning *(p. 47)*

Upper-echelons theory *(p. 35)*

Vision *(p. 40)*

DISCUSSION QUESTIONS

1. The chapter discusses several strategic leadership issues at Facebook. Several other firms are also noted in the chapter with some positive and some negative leadership results. Choose a firm mentioned in the chapter and discuss current controversial issues it faces. How should strategic leaders address the major issues you identified? In what situations is top-down planning likely to be superior to bottom-up emergent strategy development?

2. This chapter introduces three levels appropriate for strategic considerations (see Exhibit 2.3). In what situations would some of these levels be more important than others? For example, what issues might be considered by the corporate level? How should the organization ensure the proper attention to each level of strategy as needed?

3. The "job to do" approach discussed with the Clayton Christensen milkshake example can be useful in a variety of settings. Even when we are the customers ourselves, sometimes we don't look for better solutions because we get into routines and habits. Think about a situation you sometimes find frustrating in your own life or one you hear others complaining about frequently. Instead of focusing on the annoyance, can you take a step back and look for the real job that needed doing when the frustration occurred? What other options can be developed to "do the job" that may lead to less irritation in these situations?

4. In what situations is top-down planning likely to be superior to bottom-up emergent strategy development? Please provide an example.

5. Several elements of strategic decision making are highlighted in this chapter. Think of an important decision a firm has recently faced and choose either devil's advocacy or dialectic inquiry to lay out some of the key factors the firm likely considered in making its decisions.

ENDNOTES

1. *Frontline* (2018, Oct. 29 and Oct. 30), "The Facebook dilemma," PBS, www.pbs.org/wgbh/frontline/film/facebook-dilemma/.

2. Frontline (2018, Oct. 29 and Oct. 30), "The Facebook dilemma," www.pbs.org/wgbh/frontline/film/facebook-dilemma.

3. Quotes from *Frontline* (2018, Oct. 29 and Oct. 30), "The Facebook dilemma," www.pbs.org/wgbh/frontline/film/facebook-dilemma/.

4. The Facebook Dilemma (Part One and Two)," Frontline PBS Documentary, aired on October 29 and 30, 2018, https://www.pbs.org/wgbh/frontline/film/facebook-dilemma

5. This ChapterCase is based on: Sandberg, S. (2010), "Why we have too few women leaders," TED talk, http://bit.ly/1czSD6n; Auletta, K. (2011, Jul. 11), "A woman's place," *The New Yorker*; Holms, A. (2013, Mar. 4), "Maybe you should read the book: The Sheryl Sandberg backlash," *The New Yorker*; Sandberg, S. (2013), *Lean In: Women, Work, and the Will to Lead* (New York: Knopf); Parker, G.G., M.W. Van Alstyne, and S.P. Choudary (2016), *Platform Revolution: How Networked Markets Are Transforming the Economy–And How to Make Them Work for You* (New York: Norton); "The Facebook scandal could change politics as well as the internet," *The Economist* (2018, March 22); "Facebook faces a reputational meltdown," *The Economist* (2018, March 22); Frenkel, S., N. Confessore, C. Kang, M. Rosenberg, and J. Nicas (2018, Nov. 14), "Delay, deny and deflect: How Facebook's leaders fought through crisis," *The New York Times;* Halpern, S. (2018, Dec. 5), "Facebook's very bad month just got worse," *The New Yorker;* and Facebook, Inc. (various annual reports).

6. Finkelstein, S., D.C. Hambrick, and A.A. Cannella (2008), *Strategic Leadership: Theory and Research on Executives, Top Management Teams, and Boards* (Oxford, UK: Oxford University Press), 4.

7. Finkelstein, S., D.C. Hambrick, and A.A. Cannella (2008), *Strategic Leadership: Theory and Research on Executives, Top Management Teams, and Boards* (Oxford, UK: Oxford University Press); and Yulk, G. (1998), *Leadership in Organizations,* 4th ed. (Englewood Cliffs, NJ: Prentice Hall).

8. Pfeffer, J. (1994), *Managing with Power: Politics and Influence in Organizations* (Boston: Harvard Business School Press).

9. "The acceptable face of Facebook," *The Economist* (2011, Jul. 21).

10. Hambrick, D.C., and E. Abrahamson (1995), "Assessing managerial discretion across industries: A multimethod approach,"

Academy of Management Journal 38: 1427–1441.

11. "The 100 best performing CEOs in the World," *Harvard Business Review* (2016, November).

12. Bandiera, O., A. Prat, and R. Sadun (2012), "Managerial capital at the top: Evidence from the time use of CEOs," *London School of Economics and Harvard Business School Working Paper*; and "In defense of the CEO," *The Wall Street Journal* (2013, Jan. 15). The patterns of how CEOs spend their time have held in a number of different studies across the world.

13. Finkelstein, S., D.C. Hambrick, and A.A. Cannella (2008), *Strategic Leadership: Theory and Research on Executives, Top Management Teams, and Boards* (Oxford, UK: Oxford University Press), 17.

14. Bandiera, O., A. Prat, and R. Sadun (2012), "Managerial capital at the top: Evidence from the time use of CEOs," *London School of Economics and Harvard Business School Working Paper*; and "In defense of the CEO," *The Wall Street Journal* (2013, Jan. 15).

15. Hambrick, D.C. (2007), "Upper echelons theory: An update," *Academy of Management Review* 32: 334–343; and Hambrick, D.C., and P.A. Mason (1984), "Upper echelons: The organization as a reflection of its top managers," *Academy of Management Review* 9: 193–206.

16. Collins, J.C. (2001), *Good to Great: Why Some Companies Make the Leap . . . And Others Don't* (New York: HarperBusiness).

17. As quoted in Auletta, K. (2011, July 11), "A woman's place," *The New Yorker*.

18. 2016 Walmart Annual Report at http://bit.ly/1r2LXuV; see also Bowman, J. (2015, May 12), "The largest retailer in history: How Walmart sales reached $500 billion," *Motley Fool.*

19. 2018 Facebook Annual Report.

20. 2018 Facebook Annual Report; and Seetharaman, D. (2016, Apr. 28), "Facebook revenue soars on ad growth," *The Wall Street Journal.*

21. Covey, S.R. (1989), *The 7 Habits of Highly Effective People: Powerful Lessons in Personal Change* (New York: Simon & Schuster).

22. Musk, E. (2011, Sept. 29), "SpaceX vision and mission statement," presentation to The National Press Club, Washington, DC, http://bit.ly/2frJx4f.

23. Frankl, V.E. (1984), *Man's Search for Meaning* (New York: Simon & Schuster).

24. Pink, D.H. (2011), *The Surprising Truth about What Motivates Us* (New York: Riverhead Books).

25. Hamel, G., and C.K. Prahalad (1989, May–June), "Strategic intent," *Harvard Business Review*: 64–65; Hamel, G., and C.K. Prahalad (1994), *Competing for the Future* (Boston: Harvard Business School Press); and Collins, J.C., and J.I. Porras (1994), *Built to Last: Successful Habits of Visionary Companies* (New York: HarperCollins).

26. Villanueva Beard, Elisa. 2016. Teach for America annual report, Teach For America, Inc.

27. Teach for America press kit (www.teachforamerica.org/press); Simon, S. (2013, Sept. 10), "New study finds Teach for America recruits boost student achievement in math," *Politico*; Kopp, W. (2011), *A Chance to Make History: What Works and What Doesn't in Providing an Excellent Education for All* (Philadelphia, PA: Public Affairs); Xu, Z., J. Hannaway, and C. Taylor (2008, Mar. 27), "Making a difference? The effect of Teach for America on student performance in high school," *Urban Institute*; "Wendy Kopp Explains Teach for America," http://bit.ly/2gy1iTy (video 4.05 min); and Kopp, W. (2001), *One Day, All Children. . .: The Unlikely Triumph of Teach for America and What I Learned Along the Way* (Cambridge, MA: Perseus Book Group); Strauss, V. (2016, Mar. 22), "Big trouble at Teach For America?" *The Washington Post*; and Brown, E. (2016, Apr. 12), "Teach for America applications fall again, diving 35 percent in three years," *The Washington Post.*

28. Collins, J.C., and J.I. Porras (1994), *Built to Last: Successful Habits of Visionary Companies* (New York: HarperCollins); Collins, J.C. (2001), *Good to Great: Why Some Companies Make the Leap . . . And Others Don't* (New York: HarperBusiness).

29. For academic work on using a problem-solving perspective as the basis for understanding the firm, see Nickerson, J., and T. Zenger (2004), "A knowledge-based theory of the firm–the problem-solving perspective," *Organization Science* 15: 617–632.

30. This example is drawn from Clayton Christensen's work as described in Kane, Y.I. (2014), *Haunted Empire: Apple after Steve Jobs* (New York: HarperCollins), 191.

31. Germain, R., and M.B. Cooper (1990), "How a customer mission statement affects company performance," *Industrial Marketing Management* 19(2): 47–54; Bart, C.K. (1997),

"Industrial firms and the power of mission," *Industrial Marketing Management* 26(4): 371-383; and Bart, C.K. (2001), "Measuring the mission effect in human intellectual capital," *Journal of Intellectual Capital* 2(3): 320-330.

32. Christensen, C. (1997), *The Innovator's Dilemma* (New York: HarperCollins).

33. Kane, Y.I. (2014), *Haunted Empire: Apple After Steve Jobs* (New York: HarperCollins), 191.

34. "The three habits . . . of highly irritating management gurus," *The Economist* (2009, Oct. 22).

35. Burgelman, R.A., and A.S. Grove (1996), "Strategic dissonance," *California Management Review* 38: 8-28; and Grove, A.S. (1996), *Only the Paranoid Survive: How to Exploit the Crisis Points that Challenge Every Company* (New York: Currency Doubleday).

36. Bart, C.K., and M.C. Baetz (1998), "The relationship between mission statements and firm performance: An exploratory study," *Journal of Management Studies* 35: 823-853.

37. Dixit, A., and B. Nalebuff (1991), *Thinking Strategically: The Competitive Edge in Business, Politics, and Everyday Life* (New York: Norton); and Brandenburger, A.M., and B.J. Nalebuff (1996), *Co-opetition* (New York: Currency Doubleday).

38. Ewing, J. (2017, May 6), "Inside VW's campaign of trickery," *The New York Times*.

39. For a superb treatise of the history of strategy, see: Freedman, L. (2013), *Strategy: A History* (New York: Oxford University Press).

40. This discussion is based on: Mintzberg, H. (1993), *The Rise and Fall of Strategic Planning: Reconceiving Roles for Planning, Plans, and Planners* (New York: Simon & Schuster); and Mintzberg, H. (1994, January–February), "The fall and rise of strategic planning," *Harvard Business Review*: 107-114.

41. Isaacson, W. (2011), *Steve Jobs* (New York: Simon & Schuster). See also: Isaacson, W. (2012, April), "The real leadership lessons of Steve Jobs," *Harvard Business Review*.

42. Jobs, S. (1998, May 25) "There is sanity returning," *BusinessWeek*.

43. Isaacson, W. (2011), *Steve Jobs* (New York: Simon & Schuster). See also: Isaacson, W. (2012, April), "The real leadership lessons of Steve Jobs," *Harvard Business Review.*

44. "CEO Tim Cook pushes employee-friendly benefits long shunned by Steve Jobs," *The Wall Street Journal* (2012, Nov. 12).

45. Grove, A.S. (1996), *Only the Paranoid Survive: How to Exploit the Crisis Points that Challenge Every Company* (New York: Currency Doubleday).

46. UPS 2014 Investor Conference Presentations (2014, Nov. 13); and UPS 2013 Annual Report.

47. Talib, N.N. (2007), *The Black Swan: The Impact of the Highly Improbable* (New York: Random House).

48. Mintzberg, H. (1993), *The Rise and Fall of Strategic Planning: Reconceiving Roles for Planning, Plans, and Planners* (New York: Simon & Schuster); and Mintzberg, H. (1994, January–February), "The fall and rise of strategic planning," *Harvard Business Review*: 107-114.

49. Thompson, S.C. (1999), "Illusions of control: How we overestimate our personal influence," *Current Directions in Psychological Science* 8: 187-190.

50. "FTI Consulting projects U.S. online retail sales to reach $525 billion in 2018," *Global Newswire* (2018, Sept. 11), https://bit.ly/2EvFO5I.

51. Kotha, S., V. Rindova, and F.T. Rothaermel (2001), "Assets and actions: Firm-specific factors in the internationalization of U.S. internet firms,"*Journal of International Business Studies* 32(4): 769-791; and Rothaermel, F.T., S. Kotha, and H.K. Steensma (2006), "International market entry by U.S. internet firms: An empirical analysis of country risk, national culture, and market size," *Journal of Management* 32(1): 56-82.

52. Kantor, J., and D. Streitfeld (2015, Aug. 15), "Inside Amazon: Wrestling big ideas in a bruising workplace," *The New York Times*.

53. Arthur, B.W. (1989), "Competing technologies, increasing returns, and lock-in by historical events," *Economic Journal* 99: 116-131; and Brown, S.L., and K.M. Eisenhardt (1998), *Competing on the Edge: Strategy as Structured Chaos* (Boston, MA: Harvard Business School Press); Bower, J.L. (1970), *Managing the Resource Allocation Process* (Boston: Harvard Business School Press); and Bower, J.L., and C.G. Gilbert (2005), *From Resource Allocation to Strategy* (Oxford, UK: Oxford University Press); Burgelman, R.A. (1983), "A model of the interaction of strategic behavior, corporate context, and the concept of strategy," *Academy of Management Review* 8: 61-71; and Burgelman, R.A. (1983), "A process model of internal corporate venturing in a major diversified firm," *Administrative Science Quarterly* 28: 223-244.

54. Based on: Howard Behar, retired president, Starbucks North America and Starbucks International, (2009), Impact Speaker Series Presentation, College of Management, Georgia Institute of Technology, October 14. See also Behar, H. (2007), *It's Not About the Coffee: Leadership Principles from a Life at Starbucks* (New York: Portfolio).

55. This example is drawn from: "Crispy 'Saratoga chips' potato chips invented in Saratoga," at www.saratoga.com/news/saratoga-chips.cfm; and "George Crum," at http://lemelson.mit.edu/resources/george-crum.

56. Levy, S. (2011), *In the Plex: How Google Thinks, Works, and Shapes Our Lives* (New York: Simon & Schuster).

57. Mayer, M. (2006, May 11), "Nine lessons learned about creativity at Google," presentation at Stanford Technology Ventures Program.

58. Barr, A., and R. Winkler (2015, Aug. 10), "Google creates parent company called Alphabet in restructuring," *The Wall Street Journal*.

59. Bower, J.L., and C.G. Gilbert (2005), *From Resource Allocation to Strategy* (Oxford, UK: Oxford University Press).

60. Bower, J.L. (1970), *Managing the Resource Allocation Process* (Boston: Harvard Business School Press); Bower, J.L., and C.G. Gilbert (2005), *From Resource Allocation to Strategy* (Oxford, UK: Oxford University Press); Burgelman, R.A. (1983), "A model of the interaction of strategic behavior, corporate context, and the concept of strategy," *Academy of Management Review* 8: 61-71; and Burgelman, R.A. (1983), "A process model of internal corporate venturing in a major diversified firm," *Administrative Science Quarterly* 28: 223-244.

61. Burgelman, R.A. (1994), "Fading memories: A process theory of strategic business exit in dynamic environments," *Administrative Science Quarterly* 39: 24-56.

62. Burgelman, R.A., and A.S. Grove (1996), "Strategic dissonance," California Management Review 38: 8-28.

63. Grant, R.M. (2003), "Strategic planning in a turbulent environment: Evidence from the oil majors," *Strategic Management Journal* 24: 491-517; Brown, S.L., and K.M. Eisenhardt (1997), "The art of continuous change: Linking complexity theory and time-based evolution in relentlessly shifting organizations," *Administrative Science Quarterly* 42: 1-34; Farjourn, M. (2002), "Towards an organic perspective on strategy," *Strategic Management Journal* 23: 561-594; Mahoney, J. (2005), *Economic Foundation of Strategy* (Thousand Oaks, CA: Sage); and Burgelman, R.A., and A.S. Grove (2007), "Let chaos reign, then rein in chaos—repeatedly: Managing strategic dynamics for corporate longevity," *Strategic Management Journal* 28(10): 965-979.

64. Simon, H.A. (1956). "Rational choice and the structure of the environment." *Psychological Review,* 63(2): 129-138. Section 2.4 draws on Kahneman, D. (2011), *Thinking, Fast and Slow* (New York: Farrar, Straus and Giroux). See also: Thaler, R.H., and C.R. Sunstein (2008), *Nudge: Improving Decisions About Health, Wealth, and Happiness* (New Haven, CT: Yale University Press).

65. Kahneman, D. (2011), *Thinking, Fast and Slow* (New York: Farrar, Straus and Giroux). See also: Thaler, R.H., and C.R. Sunstein (2008), *Nudge: Improving Decisions About Health, Wealth, and Happiness* (New Haven, CT: Yale University Press).

66. The idea of snap judgments was popularized in: Gladwell, M. (2005), *Blink: The Power of Thinking Without Thinking (*New York: Hachette Group).

67. Kahneman, D. (2003). "Maps of bounded rationality: Psychology for behavioral economics." *American Economic Review* 93 (5): 1449–1475; Kahneman, D. (2011), *Thinking, Fast and Slow* (New York: Farrar, Straus and Giroux). See also: Thaler, R.H., and C.R. Sunstein (2008), *Nudge: Improving Decisions About Health, Wealth, and Happiness* (New Haven, CT: Yale University Press).

68. Thompson, S.C. (1999), "Illusions of control: How we overestimate our personal influence," *Current Directions in Psychological Science* 8: 187–190.

69. I'm deeply indebted to Professor Joseph T. Mahoney, the Caterpillar Chair of Business at the University of Illinois at Urbana-Champaign, for not only encouraging me to include a section on strategic decision making in this text but also for sharing some excellent examples of cognitive biases with me that I'm gratefully including in this section.

70. Staw, B.M. (1981). "The escalation of commitment to a course of action." *Academy of Management Journal* 6: 577–587.

71. The Iridium example is drawn from: Finkelstein, S. (2003)*, Why Smart Executives Fail: And What You Can Learn from Their Mistakes* (New York: Portfolio). We discuss the Iridium case in much more detail in Chapter 7, "Business Strategy: Innovation, Entrepreneurship, and Platforms."

72. Janis, I.L. (1972). *Victims of Groupthink: A Psychological Study of Foreign-Policy Decisions and Fiascoes* (Oxford, England: Houghton Mifflin).

73. Kioll, M.J., L.A. Toombs, and P. Wright (2000), "Napoleon's tragic march home from Moscow: Lessons in hubris," *Academy of Management Executive* 14(1): 117–128.

74. Schneider, B., H.W. Goldstein, and D.B. Smith (1995), "The ASA framework: An update," *Personnel Psychology* 48: 747–773.

75. See a detailed and insightful description of GE's decline over time in: Gryta, T., and T. Mann (2018, Dec. 14). "GE powered the American century—then it burned out," *The Wall Street Journal.*

76. Gryta, T., and T. Mann (2018, Dec. 14). "GE powered the American century—then it burned out." *The Wall Street Journal.*

77. Schweiger, D.M., W.R. Sandberg, and J.W. Ragan (1986). "Group approaches for improving strategic decision making: A comparative analysis of dialectical inquiry, devil's advocacy, and consensus." *Academy of Management Journal*, 29(1): 51–71.

78. Gallo, C. (2018, April 25). "Jeff Bezos banned PowerPoint in meetings. His replacement is brilliant." *Inc. Magazine*, www.inc.com/carmine-gallo/jeff-bezos-bans-powerpoint-in-meetings-his-replacement-is-brilliant.html.

79. Sources: "The Facebook scandal could change politics as well as the internet," *The Economist* (2018, Mar. 22); "Facebook faces a reputational meltdown," *The Economist* (2018, Mar. 22); Frenkel, S., N. Confessore, C. Kang, M. Rosenberg, and J. Nicas (2018, Nov. 14), "Delay, deny and deflect: How Facebook's leaders fought through crisis," *The New York Times*; Dance, G.J.X., M. LaForgia, and N. Confessore (2018, Dec. 18), "As Facebook raised a privacy wall, it carved an opening for tech giants," *The New York Times*; Lapowsky, I. (2018, Dec. 20), "The 21 (and counting) biggest Facebook scandals of 2018," *Wired*; Confessore, N., M. LaForgia, and G.J.X. Dance (2018, Dec. 18), "Facebook's data sharing and privacy rules: 5 takeaways from our Investigation," *The New York Times*; and LaForgia, M., N. Confessore, and G.J.X. Dance (2018, Dec. 19), "Facebook rebuked for failing to disclose data-sharing deals," *The New York Times.*

80. Based on: Stern, S. (2004), "Do scientists pay to be scientists?" *Management Science* 50(6): 835–853; and Esty, D.C., and A.S. Winston (2009), *Green to Gold: How Smart Companies Use Environmental Strategy to Innovate, Create Value, and Build Competitive Advantage,* revised and updated (Hoboken, NJ: John Wiley).

External Analysis: Industry Structure, Competitive Forces, and Strategic Groups

Chapter Outline

Learning Objectives

After studying this chapter, you should be able to:

LO 3-1 Generate a PESTEL analysis to evaluate the impact of external factors on the firm.

LO 3-2 Differentiate the roles of firm effects and industry effects in determining firm performance.

LO 3-3 Apply Porter's five competitive forces to explain the profit potential of different industries.

LO 3-4 Examine how competitive industry structure shapes rivalry among competitors.

LO 3-5 Describe the strategic role of complements in creating positive-sum co-opetition.

LO 3-6 Explain the five choices required for market entry.

LO 3-7 Appraise the role of industry dynamics and industry convergence in shaping the firm's external environment.

LO 3-8 Generate a strategic group model to reveal performance differences between clusters of firms in the same industry.

Airbnb: Disrupting the Hotel Industry

IN 2019, AIRBNB had 5 million listings in over 81,000 cities in some 190 countries, ranging from spare rooms to entire islands. With its "asset-light approach" based on its platform strategy, Airbnb is able to offer more accommodations than the three biggest hotel chains combined: Marriott, Hilton, and Intercontinental. And just like global hotel chains, Airbnb uses sophisticated pricing and reservation systems for guests to find, reserve, and pay for rooms to meet their travel needs. In this sense, Airbnb is a new entrant that competes in the global hotel industry.

Brian Chesky and Joe Gebbia, Airbnb founders, were roommates in San Francisco a little more

Nathan Blecharczyk, Joe Gebbia, and Brian Chesky founded Airbnb on a shoestring budget in 2008. Today, Airbnb is the largest hospitality platform globally.

Stefanie Keenan/Getty Images

than a decade earlier. Both were industrial designers, people who shape the form and function of everything from coffee cups to office furniture to airplane interiors. But since work opportunities were hit-and-miss, they found themselves struggling to make their rent payments. On a whim, they decided to e-mail everyone on the distribution list for an upcoming industrial design conference in their hometown: "If you're heading out to the [industrial design conference] in San Francisco next week and have yet to make accommodations, well, consider networking in your jam-jams. That's right. For an affordable alternative to hotels in the city, imagine yourself in a fellow design industry person's home, fresh awake from a snooze on the ol' air mattress, chatting about the day's upcoming events over Pop Tarts and OJ."[1]

Three people took up the offer, and the two roommates made some money to subsidize their rent payments. But more importantly, Chesky and Gebbia felt that they had stumbled upon a new business idea: Help people rent out their spare rooms. They then brought on computer scientist Nathan Blecharczyk, one of Gebbia's former roommates, to create a website where hosts and guests could meet and transact, naming their site AirBedandBreakfast.com (later

shortened to Airbnb). The three entrepreneurs tested their new site at the 2008 South by Southwest (SXSW), an annual music, film, and interactive media conference. SXSW also serves as an informal launch pad for new ventures; for example, Twitter was unveiled at SXSW just a year earlier to great fanfare. Airbnb's launch at SXSW flopped, however, because the conference organizers had exclusive contracts with local hotels (which Airbnb founders learned about later), and so conference organizers didn't drive any traffic to Airbnb's site.

Not to be discouraged, Airbnb decided to take advantage of the anticipated shortage of hotel rooms in Denver, Colorado, the site of the Democratic National Convention (DNC) in the summer of 2008. After all hotels were booked, the founders prepared media releases with titles such as "Grassroots Housing for Grassroots Campaign," which Obama supporters loved. As luck would have it, Airbnb was covered in both *The New York Times* and *The Wall Street Journal*. And the newly designed Airbnb site worked! It facilitated about 100 rentals during the DNC. Soon after the event, however, website traffic to Airbnb's site fell back to zero. To keep going, Chesky and Gebbia decided to become cereal entrepreneurs, creating "Obama-O's: The breakfast of change" and "Cap'n McCains: A maverick in every bite," with illustrated images of the 2008 presidential candidates on 1,000 cereal boxes. After sending samples to their press contacts and subsequent coverage in the media, the limited edition cereal sold out quickly, providing enough cash to keep going with Airbnb a bit longer.

The fledgling venture's breakthrough came in 2009 when it was accepted into a program run by Y Combinator, a start-up accelerator that has spawned famous tech companies such as Dropbox, Stripe, and Twitch.tv. In exchange for equity in the new venture, these start-up accelerators provide office space, mentoring, and networking opportunities, including with venture capitalists looking to fund the next "big thing." In 2010, Airbnb received funding from Sequoia Capital, one of the most prestigious venture capital firms in

Silicon Valley, having provided early-stage capital to companies such as Apple, Google, Oracle, PayPal, YouTube, and WhatsApp. Although not a first mover in the peer-to-peer rental space, Airbnb, with support of Y Combinator, was the first one to figure out that a sleek website design comprising professional photos of available rentals made all the difference. In addition, Airbnb developed a seamless transaction experience between hosts and guests and was able to earn a little over 10 percent on each transaction conducted on its site. Timing was now much more fortuitous; with the global financial crisis in full swing, people were looking for low-cost accommodations while hosts were trying to pay rent or mortgages to keep their homes.

In 2019, Airbnb was valued at a whopping $31 billion. This makes Airbnb the fourth most valuable private startup on the planet, just after Didi Chuxing, China's version of Uber ($56 billion), WeWork ($47 billion), and JUUL ($38 billion). Even more stunning, Airbnb's valuation approaches that of Marriott ($39 billion in 2019), the world's largest hotel chain with over $20 billion in annual revenues.[2]

Part II of this ChapterCase appears in Section 3.5.

HOW CAN AN INTERNET startup based on the idea of home sharing disrupt the global hotel industry, long dominated by corporate giants such as Marriott, Hilton, and Intercontinental? One reason is that Airbnb, now the world's largest accommodation provider, owns no real estate. Instead, it uses a business model innovation to circumvent traditional entry barriers into the hotel industry. Just like Uber, Facebook, or Amazon, Airbnb provides an online platform for sellers (hosts) and buyers (renters) to connect and transact (we'll take a closer look at "Platform Strategy" in Chapter 7). While traditional hotel chains need years and millions of dollars in real estate investments to add additional capacity (finding properties, building hotels, staffing and running them, etc.), Airbnb's inventory is basically unlimited as long as it can sign up users with spare rooms to rent. Even more importantly, Airbnb does not need to deploy millions of dollars in capital to acquire and manage physical assets or manage a large cadre of employees. For example, Marriott has almost 250,000 employees, while Airbnb's headcount is approximately 2,500 employees (only 1 percent of Marriott's). Thus, Airbnb can grow much faster and respond much more quickly to local circumstances affecting the demand and supply of accommodations. The competitive intensity in the hotel industry is likely to increase, especially in high-traffic metropolitan cities such as New York, Paris, Dubai, and Seoul.

In this chapter, we present a set of frameworks to analyze the firm's *external environment*—that is, the industry in which the firm operates, and the competitive forces that surround the firm from the outside. We move from a more macro perspective to a more micro understanding of how the external environment affects a firm's quest for competitive advantage. We begin with the PESTEL framework, which allows us to scan, monitor, and evaluate changes and trends in the firm's macroenvironment. Next, we study Porter's five forces model of competition, which helps us to determine an industry's profit potential. Depending on the firm's strategic position, these forces can affect its performance for good or ill. We also take a closer look at the choices firms must make when considering entry into an industry. We then move from a static analysis of a firm's industry environment to a dynamic understanding of how industries and competition change over time. We also discuss how to think through entry choices once an attractive industry has been identified. Next we introduce the strategic group model for understanding performance differences among clusters of firms in the same industry. Finally, we offer practical *Implications for Strategic Leaders.*

3.1 The PESTEL Framework

A firm's external environment consists of all factors outside the firm that can affect its potential to gain and sustain a competitive advantage. By analyzing the factors in the firm's external environment, strategic leaders can mitigate threats and leverage opportunities. One

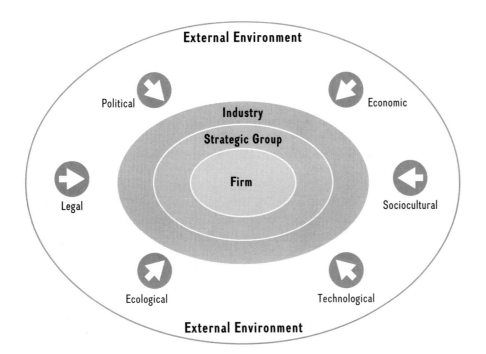

EXHIBIT 3.1

The Firm within Its
External Environment,
Industry, and
Strategic Group,
Subject to PESTEL
Factors

common approach to understanding how external factors impinge upon a firm is to consider the source or proximity of these factors. For example, external factors in the firm's *general environment* are ones that strategic leaders have little direct influence over, such as macroeconomic factors (e.g., interest or currency exchange rates). In contrast, external factors in the firm's *task environment* are ones that strategic leaders do have some influence over, such as the composition of their strategic groups (a set of close rivals) or the structure of the industry. We will now look at each of these environmental layers in detail, moving from a firm's general environment to its task environment. Following along in Exhibit 3.1, we will be working from the outer ring to the inner ring.

The **PESTEL model** groups the factors in the firm's general environment into six segments:

- Political
- Economic
- Sociocultural
- Technological
- Ecological
- Legal

> **PESTEL model** A framework that categorizes and analyzes an important set of external factors (political, economic, sociocultural, technological, ecological, and legal) that might impinge upon a firm. These factors can create both opportunities and threats for the firm.

Together these form the acronym PESTEL. The PESTEL model provides a relatively straightforward way to *scan, monitor,* and *evaluate* the important external factors and trends that might impinge upon a firm. Such factors create both opportunities and threats.

POLITICAL FACTORS

Political factors result from the processes and actions of government bodies that can influence the decisions and behavior of firms.[3]

Although political factors are located in the firm's general environment, where firms traditionally wield little influence, companies nevertheless increasingly work to shape and influence this realm. They do so by applying by pursuing a *nonmarket strategy*—that is, through lobbying, public relations, contributions, litigation, and so on—in ways that are favorable to the firm.[4] For example, hotel chains and resort owners have challenged Airbnb in courts and lobbied local governments, some of which passed regulations to limit or prohibit short-term rentals. Local residents in New York, San Francisco, Berlin, Paris, and many other cities are also pressuring local governments to enact more aggressive rules banning short-term rentals because they argue that companies such as Airbnb contribute to a shortage of affordable housing by turning entire apartment complexes into hotels or transforming quiet family neighborhoods into all-night, every-night party hot spots.

Political and legal factors are closely related, as political pressure often results in changes in legislation and regulation (we discuss legal factors later in this chapter). For example, macro effects of the U.S.-China trade war (since 2016) have direct implications for a number of businesses. U.S. exporters, such as soybean farmers, face higher tariffs in China, so their products are more expensive. Chinese electronics companies, such as Huawei, ZTE, and others, are considered a threat to U.S. national security, so are more or less banned from doing business in the United States.

ECONOMIC FACTORS

Economic factors in a firm's external environment are largely macroeconomic, affecting economy-wide phenomena. Strategic leaders need to consider how the following five macroeconomic factors can affect firm strategy:

- Growth rates.
- Levels of employment.
- Interest rates.
- Price stability (inflation and deflation).
- Currency exchange rates.

GROWTH RATES. The overall economic *growth rate* is a measure of the change in the amount of goods and services produced by a nation's economy. Strategic leaders look to the *real growth rate,* which adjusts for inflation. This real growth rate indicates the current business cycle of the economy—that is, whether business activity is expanding or contracting. In periods of economic expansion, consumer and business demands are rising, and competition among firms frequently decreases. During economic booms, businesses expand operations to satisfy demand and are more likely to be profitable. The reverse is generally true for recessionary periods, although certain companies that focus on low-cost solutions may benefit from economic contractions because demand for their products or services rises in such times. For customers, expenditures on luxury products are often the first to be cut during recessionary periods. For instance, you might switch from a $5 venti latte at Starbucks to a $1 alternative from McDonald's.

Occasionally, boom periods can overheat and lead to speculative asset bubbles. In the early 2000s, the United States experienced an asset bubble in real estate.[5] Easy credit, made possible by the availability of subprime mortgages and other financial innovations, fueled an unprecedented demand in housing. Real estate, rather than stocks, became the investment vehicle of choice for many Americans, propelled by the common belief that house prices could only go up. When the housing bubble burst, the deep economic recession of 2008–2009 began, impacting in some way nearly all businesses in the United States and worldwide.

LEVELS OF EMPLOYMENT. Growth rates directly affect the *level of employment.* In boom times, unemployment tends to be low, and skilled human capital becomes a scarce and more expensive resource. As the price of labor rises, firms have an incentive to invest more into capital goods such as cutting-edge equipment or artificial intelligence (AI).[6] In economic downturns, unemployment rises. As more people search for employment, skilled human capital is more abundant and wages usually fall.

INTEREST RATES. Another key macroeconomic variable for strategic leaders to track is real *interest rates*—the amount that creditors are paid for use of their money and the amount that debtors pay for that use, adjusted for inflation. The economic boom during the early years in the 21st century, for example, was fueled by cheap credit. Low real interest rates have a direct bearing on consumer demand. When credit is cheap because interest rates are low, consumers buy homes, condos, automobiles, computers, smartphones, and vacations on credit; in turn, all of this demand fuels economic growth. During periods of low real interest rates, firms can easily borrow money to finance growth. Borrowing at lower real rates reduces the cost of capital and enhances a firm's competitiveness. These effects reverse, however, when real interest rates are rising. Consumer demand slows, credit is harder to come by, and firms find it more difficult to borrow money to support operations, possibly deferring investments.

PRICE STABILITY. *Price stability*—the lack of change in price levels of goods and services—is rare. Therefore, companies will often have to deal with changing price levels, which is a function of the amount of money in any economy. When there is too much money in an economy, we tend to see rising prices—*inflation.* Indeed, a popular economic definition of inflation is *too much money chasing too few goods and services.*[7] Inflation tends to go with lower economic growth. Countries such as Argentina, Brazil, Mexico, Poland, and Venezuela experienced periods of hyperinflation in the recent past.

Deflation describes a decrease in the overall price level. A sudden and pronounced drop in demand generally causes deflation, which in turn forces sellers to lower prices to motivate buyers. Because many people automatically think of lower prices from the buyer's point of view, a decreasing price level seems at first glance to be attractive. However, deflation is actually a serious threat to economic growth because it distorts expectations about the future.[8] For example, once price levels start falling, companies will not invest in new production capacity or innovation because they expect a further decline in prices. In recent decades, the Japanese economy has been plagued with deflation.

CURRENCY EXCHANGE RATES. The *currency exchange rate* determines how many dollars one must pay for a unit of foreign currency. It is a critical variable for any company that buys or sells products and services across national borders. For example, if the U.S. dollar appreciates against the euro, and so increases in real value, firms need more euros to buy one dollar. This in turn makes U.S. exports such as Boeing aircraft, Intel chips, John Deere tractors, or American soybeans more expensive for European buyers and reduces demand for U.S. exports overall. This process reverses when the dollar depreciates (decreases in real value) against the euro. In this scenario it would take more dollars to buy one euro, and European imports such as LVMH luxury accessories or Porsche automobiles become more expensive for U.S. buyers.

In a similar fashion, if the Chinese yuan appreciates in value, Chinese goods imported into the United States become relatively more expensive. At the same time, Chinese purchasing power increases, which in turn allows their businesses to purchase more U.S. capital goods such as sophisticated machinery and other cutting-edge technologies. The reverse holds true if the Chinese yuan depreciates in value.

In summary, economic factors affecting businesses are ever-present and rarely static. Strategic leaders need to fully appreciate the power of these factors, in both domestic and global markets, to assess their effects on firm performance.

SOCIOCULTURAL FACTORS

Sociocultural factors capture a society's cultures, norms, and values. Because sociocultural factors not only are constantly in flux but also differ across groups, strategic leaders need to closely monitor such trends and consider the implications for firm strategy. In recent years, for example, a growing number of U.S. consumers have become more health-conscious about what they eat. This trend led to a boom for businesses such as Chipotle, Subway, and Whole Foods. At the same time, traditional fast food companies McDonald's and Burger King, along with grocery chains such as Albertsons and Kroger, have all had to scramble to provide healthier choices in their product offerings.

Demographic trends are also important sociocultural factors. These trends capture population characteristics related to age, gender, family size, ethnicity, sexual orientation, religion, and socioeconomic class. Like other sociocultural factors, demographic trends present opportunities but can also pose threats. Recent U.S. census data reveals that 59 million Americans (18.1 percent of the total population) are Hispanic. It is now the largest minority group in the United States and growing fast. On average, Hispanics are also younger and their incomes are climbing quickly. This trend is not lost on companies trying to benefit from this opportunity. For example, MundoFox and ESPN Deportes (specializing in soccer) have joined Univision and NBC's Telemundo in the Spanish-language television market. In the United States, Univision is now the fifth most popular network overall, just behind the four major English-language networks (ABC, NBC, CBS, and Fox). Likewise, advertisers are pouring dollars into the Spanish-language networks to promote their products and services.[9]

TECHNOLOGICAL FACTORS

Technological factors capture the application of knowledge to create new processes and products. Major innovations in process technology include lean manufacturing, Six Sigma quality, and biotechnology. The nanotechnology revolution, which is just beginning, promises significant upheaval for a vast array of industries ranging from tiny medical devices to new-age materials for earthquake-resistant buildings.[10] Recent product innovations include the smartphone, wearable devices such as smart watches, and high-performing electric cars such as the Tesla Model S.

Continued advances in artificial intelligence (AI) and machine learning promise to fundamentally alter the way we work and live.[11] While we are familiar with early AI applications such Amazon's Alexa, Apple's Siri, and Google's Assistant, the future will bring much more significant changes, including autonomous driving as well as the internet of things. The transportation industry is seeing early signs of disruption with autonomous vehicles and trucks, which can drive themselves from coast to coast, 24/7, with no breaks for the driver needed (other than recharging or exchanging battery packs). Our cities will be filled with autonomous taxis, which are already on the road in some places in the United States. The internet of things will connect all sorts of devices such as vehicles, airplanes, home appliances, computers, manufacturing facilities, power grids, and so forth to exchange data and to manage systems in a more holistic and smarter fashion to reduce, for example, energy consumption or letting the user know when a system is in need of maintenance long before it breaks down.

As discussed in the ChapterCase, Airbnb launched a process innovation of offering and renting rooms based on a business model leveraging the sharing economy. If one thing seems certain, technological progress is relentless and seems to be picking up speed.[12] Not surprisingly, changes in the technological environment bring both opportunities and threats for companies. Given the importance of a firm's innovation strategy to competitive advantage, we discuss the effect of technological factors in greater detail in Chapter 7.

Strategy Highlight 3.1 details how the once mighty video rental chain Blockbuster fell when it failed to pay sufficient attention to the PESTEL factors.

Strategy Highlight **3.1**

Blockbuster's Bust

Blockbuster was not only a pioneer in the video rental business, but it was also the undisputed industry leader from the mid-1980s to the early 2000s. At its peak, Blockbuster opened a new store every 17 hours, for a total of 9,000 stores across the United States, and earned $6 billion in annual revenue. As such, Blockbuster was a mainstay of American culture and an essential element of family movie night. But in 2010, the once mighty Blockbuster filed for bankruptcy. What went wrong?

Blockbuster was unable to respond effectively to technological changes in the industry. A first wave of disruption hit the TV industry in the 1980s and 1990s when cable networks started offering hundreds of channels, challenging the cozy oligopoly of the three old-line broadcast networks ABC, CBS, and NBC. With the arrival of the cable networks, Blockbuster's fortunes began to dim as reflected in a double-digit decline in its market valuation. Unable to address the technological challenge posed by cable network content as a substitute to video rentals, Blockbuster's creator and owner, Wayne Huizenga, sold the company to the media conglomerate Viacom in 1994.

By the late 1990s and early 2000s, Blockbuster was also challenged more directly by low-cost substitutes such as Netflix's mail-order DVD service and Redbox's automated DVD rental kiosks. In 1997, annoyed for having to pay more than $40 in late fees for a Blockbuster video, Reed Hastings decided to start Netflix—a subscription-based business model that offered consumers DVD rentals online. When the dot-com bubble burst in 2000, however, Netflix reached near bankruptcy. Hastings approached Blockbuster and proposed selling Netflix to it for a mere $50 million and rebranding the chain Blockbuster.com. The idea was that Netflix would become Blockbuster's online branch. Thinking that it would be a small niche business at best, Blockbuster turned Netflix down.

Netflix managed to stay afloat. Its low-cost option for at-home viewing via higher-quality DVD technology (compared to lower-quality VHS tapes) attracted more and more subscribers; this allowed the firm to weather the dot-com crash. To fund future growth, Netflix went public in 2002 at a valuation of $310 million. Just a year later, Netflix surpassed 1 million subscribers. After seeing Netflix's success, Blockbuster began to mimic its online subscription model. Unlike Netflix, however, which did not charge late fees given Reed Hastings' aversion to penalizing customers, Blockbuster continued to do so. The firm relied on late fees because fees were, unfortunately, one of the most profitable aspects of its business model.

Technological progress continued at a rapid clip. The next wave of technological disruption hit the home media industry in the mid-2000s. The ability to stream content directly onto a host of devices, such as laptops, tablets, smartphones, and newer internet-based TVs, turned basically any screen into a personal media conduit. Prevalence of high-speed internet connections combined with advances in mobile devices, changed the way people consumed entertainment. The days where people needed to go to a brick-and-mortar store to rent a videotape or DVD were gone. With on-demand video streaming, consumers could choose from a near unlimited inventory of movies while sitting on their couch in the living room. In the end, Blockbuster's attempts to change were too little, too late. In 2010, the once mighty Blockbuster filed for bankruptcy. And in 2019, Netflix was valued at close to $160 billion.[13]

ECOLOGICAL FACTORS

Ecological factors involve broad environmental issues such as the natural environment, global warming, and sustainable economic growth. Organizations and the natural environment coexist in an interdependent relationship. Managing these relationships in a responsible and sustainable way directly influences the continued existence of human societies and the organizations we create. Strategic leaders can no longer separate the natural and the business worlds; they are inextricably linked.[14]

Unfortunately, many business organizations have contributed to the pollution of air, water, and land, as well as the depletion of the world's natural resources. One infamous example that comes readily to mind is the 2010 BP oil spill in the Gulf of Mexico. The spill destroyed fauna and flora along the U.S. shoreline from Texas to Florida. It led to a drop in fish and wildlife populations, triggered a decline in the fishery and tourism industries, and threatened the livelihood of thousands of people. It also cost BP more than $50 billion and one-half of its market value.

The relationship between organizations and the natural environment need not be adversarial, however. Ecological factors can also provide business opportunities. As we saw in ChapterCase 1, Tesla is addressing environmental concerns regarding the carbon emissions of gasoline-powered cars by building zero-emission battery-powered vehicles. To generate the needed energy to charge the batteries in a sustainable way, Tesla acquired SolarCity to provide integrated, clean-tech energy services for its customers, including decentralized solar power generation and storage via its Powerwall.

LEGAL FACTORS

Legal factors include the official outcomes of political processes as manifested in laws, mandates, regulations, and court decisions—all of which can have a direct bearing on a firm's profit potential. In fact, regulatory changes tend to affect entire industries at once. Many industries in the United States have been deregulated over the past few decades, including airlines, telecom, energy, and trucking, among others.

As noted earlier, legal factors often coexist with or result from political will. Governments especially can directly affect firm performance by exerting both political pressure and legal sanctions, including court rulings and industry regulations. Consider how several European countries and the European Union (EU) apply political and legal pressure on U.S. tech companies. European targets include Apple, Amazon, Facebook, Google, and Microsoft—the five largest U.S. tech companies—but also startups such as Uber. Europe's policy makers seek to retain control over important industries, including transportation and the internet, to ensure that profits earned in Europe by Silicon Valley firms are taxed locally. The European Parliament even proposed legislation to break up "digital monopolies" such as Google. This proposal would require Google to offer search services independently as a standalone company from its other online services, including Google Drive, a cloud-based file storage and synchronization service.

But the EU's wariness extends beyond tax revenue: It has much stronger legal requirements and cultural expectations concerning data privacy. In 2018, for instance, the EU implemented the General Data Protection Regulation (GDPR), which gives individuals wide-reaching control over their personal data as well as secured protection of these data. Personal data comprise any information related to a person such as a name, home address, e-mail address, phone number, location details, photos, videos, social media postings, computer IP addresses, and so forth. GDPR grants all EU residents far-reaching rights concerning their personal data, including the right to access, the right to be forgotten, the right to data portability across providers, the right to be notified, and so forth. All U.S. companies such as Google and Facebook had to change their policies to comply with the GDPR and thus be permitted to continue doing business in Europe. The data protection and privacy regulations that internet companies face in the EU are currently much more stringent than those in the United States, an aspect that came to the fore during the Facebook crisis regarding alleged foreign interference in U.S. elections and the siphoning off of private data for an unauthorized use by third parties (see ChapterCase 2).

Taken together, political/legal factors, along with other PESTEL factors, can have a direct bearing on a firm's performance—consider the implementation of autonomous vehicles for commercial and private use. Companies such as Uber, Waymo (a unit of Alphabet, the parent company of Google), and Tesla are ready to deploy autonomous vehicles, but political and legal factors are providing serious challenges and are delaying their widespread use.

The Waymo autonomous vehicle marks another step in an effort to revolutionize the way people get around. Instead of driving themselves, people will be chauffeured in self-driving cars if Waymo, Tesla, and ride-hailing services such as Uber realize their vision. Traditional automakers such as GM, Ford, and VW also invest tremendous amounts of money into autonomous vehicles. Taken together, the automobile industry is likely to be upended in the next few years, including who the key players will be and if individuals still want to own a car or prefer catching a ride in an autonomous vehicle available for a per-ride usage fee ("pay as you go") rather than requiring fairly large upfront investments when purchasing or leasing a vehicle.
Sundry Photography/
Shutterstock

3.2 Industry Structure and Firm Strategy: The Five Forces Model

INDUSTRY VS. FIRM EFFECTS IN DETERMINING FIRM PERFORMANCE

Firm performance is determined primarily by two factors: industry and firm effects. **Industry effects** describe the underlying economic structure of the industry. They attribute firm performance to the industry in which the firm competes. The structure of an industry is determined by elements common to all industries, such as entry and exit barriers, number and size of companies, and types of products and services offered. **Firm effects** attribute firm performance directly to the actions strategic leaders take.

In a series of empirical studies, academic researchers show that industry effects explain roughly 20 percent of overall firm performance, while firm effects (i.e., specific managerial actions) explain about 55 percent. In Chapter 4, we look inside the firm to understand why firms within the same industry differ and how differences among firms can lead to competitive advantage. For now, the important point is that external and internal factors combined explain roughly 75 percent of overall firm performance. The remaining 25 percent relates partly to business cycles and other effects.[15] Exhibit 3.2 shows these findings.

To better understand how external factors affect firm strategy and performance, and what strategic leaders can do about it, we take a closer look in this chapter at an industry's underlying structure. As such, we now move one step closer to the firm (in the center of Exhibit 3.1) and come to the industry in which it competes.

An **industry** is a group of incumbent firms facing more or less the same set of suppliers and buyers. Firms competing in the same industry tend to offer similar products or services

LO 3-2

Differentiate the roles of firm effects and industry effects in determining firm performance.

Industry effects Firm performance attributed to the structure of the industry in which the firm competes.

Firm effects Firm performance attributed to the actions strategic leaders take.

industry A group of incumbent companies that face more or less the same set of suppliers and buyers.

EXHIBIT 3.2 Industry, Firm, and Other Effects Explaining Firm Performance

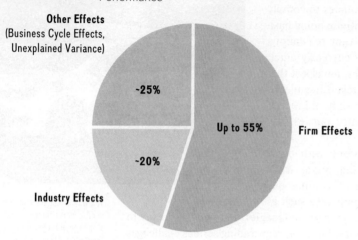

Other Effects
(Business Cycle Effects,
Unexplained Variance)

~25%

Up to 55% — **Firm Effects**

~20%

Industry Effects

to meet specific customer needs. Although the PESTEL framework allows us to scan, monitor, and evaluate the external environment to identify opportunities and threats, **industry analysis** provides a more rigorous basis not only to identify an industry's profit potential—the level of profitability that can be expected for the *average* firm—but also to derive implications for one firm's strategic position within an industry. A firm's **strategic position** relates to its ability to create value for customers (V) while containing the cost to do so (C). Competitive advantage flows to the firm that is able to create as large a gap as possible between the value the firm's product or service generates and the cost required to produce it ($V - C$).

COMPETITION IN THE FIVE FORCES MODEL

LO 3-3

Apply Porter's five competitive forces to explain the profit potential of different industries.

Michael Porter developed the highly influential **five forces model** to help strategic leaders understand the profit potential of different industries and how they can position their respective firms to gain and sustain competitive advantage.[16] By combining theory from industrial organization economics with detailed case studies, Porter derived two key insights that form the basis of his seminal five forces model:

1. *Competition is viewed more broadly in the five forces model.* Rather than defining competition narrowly as the firm's closest competitors to explain and predict a firm's performance, competition must be viewed more broadly to also encompass the other forces in an industry: buyers, suppliers, potential new entry of other firms, and the threat of substitutes.

2. *Profit potential is a function of the five competitive forces.* The profit potential of an industry is neither random nor entirely determined by industry-specific factors. Rather, it is a function of the five forces that shape competition: *threat of entry, power of suppliers, power of buyers, threat of substitutes,* and *rivalry among existing firms.*

COMPETITION BROADLY DEFINED. We start with the concept of competition, which, in Porter's model, is more broadly defined to include other industry forces: buyers, suppliers, potential new entry of other firms, and the threat of substitutes. Strategy addresses the question of how to deal with competition. In the five forces model, any of those forces is viewed as a potential competitor attempting to extract value from the industry. In particular, competition describes the struggle among these forces to capture as much of the economic value created in an industry as possible. A firm's strategic leaders, therefore, must be concerned not only with the intensity of rivalry among direct competitors (e.g., Nike versus Under

---

industry analysis A method to (1) identify an industry's profit potential and (2) derive implications for a firm's strategic position within an industry.

strategic position A firm's strategic profile based on the difference between value creation and cost ($V - C$).

five forces model A framework that identifies five forces that determine the profit potential of an industry and shape a firm's competitive strategy.

Armour, The Home Depot versus Lowe's, Merck versus Pfizer, and so on), but also with the strength of the other competitive forces that are attempting to extract part or all of the economic value that the firm creates.

Recall that firms create economic value by expanding as much as possible the gap between the perceived value (V) the firm's product or service generates and the cost (C) to produce it. *Economic value* thus equals ($V - C$). To succeed, creating value is not enough. Firms must also be able to *capture* a significant share of the value created to gain and sustain a competitive advantage. When faced with competition in this broader sense, strategy explains how a firm should position itself to enhance the chances of achieving superior performance.

PROFIT POTENTIAL. The five forces model enables strategic leaders to not only understand the firm's industry environment but also to shape firm strategy. As a rule of thumb, *the stronger the five forces, the lower the industry's profit potential*—making the industry less attractive for competitors. The reverse is also true: *the weaker the five forces, the greater the industry's profit potential*—making the industry more attractive. Therefore, from the perspective of a strategic leader of an existing firm competing for advantage in an established industry, the company should be positioned in a way that relaxes the constraints of strong forces and leverages weak forces. The goal of crafting a strategic position is of course to improve the firm's ability to achieve and sustain a competitive advantage.

As Exhibit 3.3 shows, Porter's model identifies five key competitive forces that strategic leaders need to consider when analyzing the industry environment and formulating competitive strategy:

1. Threat of entry.
2. Power of suppliers.
3. Power of buyers.
4. Threat of substitutes.
5. Rivalry among existing competitors.

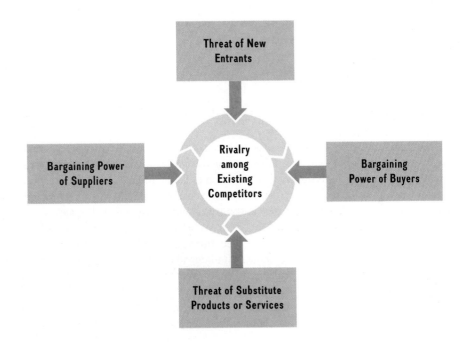

EXHIBIT 3.3

Porter's Five Forces Model

Source: M. E. Porter (2008, January). "The five competitive forces that shape strategy," *Harvard Business Review.*

THE THREAT OF ENTRY

The **threat of entry** describes the risk of potential competitors entering the industry. Potential new entry depresses industry profit potential in two major ways:

1. *Reduces the industry's overall profit potential.* With the threat of additional capacity coming into an industry, incumbent firms may lower prices to make the entry appear less attractive to the potential new competitors, which in turn would reduce the industry's overall profit potential, especially in industries with slow or no overall growth in demand. Consider the market for new microwaves. Demand consists of the replacement rate for older models and the creation of new households. Since this market grows slowly, if at all, any additional entry would likely lead to excess capacity and lower prices overall.

2. *Increases spending among incumbent firms.* The threat of entry by additional competitors may force incumbent firms to spend more to satisfy their existing customers. This spending reduces an industry's profit potential, especially if firms can't raise prices. Consider how Starbucks has chosen to constantly upgrade and refresh its stores and service offerings. Starbucks has over 14,000 U.S. stores and more than 28,000 global locations. By raising the value of its offering in the eyes of consumers, it slows others from entering the industry or from rapidly expanding. This allows Starbucks to keep at bay both smaller regional competitors, such as Peet's Coffee & Tea with fewer than 200 stores mostly on the West Coast, and smaller national chains, such as Caribou Coffee, with 415 stores nationally. Starbucks is willing to accept a lower profit margin to maintain its market share.

Of course, the more profitable an industry, the more attractive it is for new competitors to enter. However, a number of important barriers exist that can reduce that threat. **Entry barriers**, which are advantageous for incumbent firms, are obstacles that determine how easily a firm can enter an industry. Incumbent firms can benefit from several important sources of entry barriers:

entry barriers Obstacles that determine how easily a firm can enter an industry and often significantly predict industry profit potential.

- Economies of scale.
- Network effects.
- Customer switching costs.
- Capital requirements.
- Advantages independent of size.
- Government policy.
- Credible threat of retaliation.

ECONOMIES OF SCALE. *Economies of scale* are cost advantages that accrue to firms with larger output because they can spread fixed costs over more units, employ technology more efficiently, benefit from a more specialized division of labor, and demand better terms from their suppliers. These factors in turn drive down the cost per unit, allowing large incumbent firms to enjoy a cost advantage over new entrants that cannot muster such scale.

We saw the important relationship between scale and production cost with Tesla in ChapterCase 1. Usually entrants into the broad automobile industry need large-scale production to be efficient. Tesla leveraged new technology to circumvent this entry barrier. Yet, reaching sufficient manufacturing scale to be cost-competitive is critical for Tesla as it moves more into the mass market.

To benefit from economies of scale, Tesla gradually introduced new vehicles to appeal more to the mass market. Its first vehicle, the Roadster (priced at over $110,000) was more or less a prototype to prove the viability of an all-electric car that can outperform high-performance traditional sports cars. For consumers, it created a new mind-set of what electric cars can do. Tesla ended production of the Roadster to focus more fully on its next model: the family sedan Model S (with a baseline price of $70,000). With this model, Tesla's manufacturing scale increased more than 50-fold, from 2,500 Roadsters to 125,000 Model S's. Tesla is now hoping for an even broader customer appeal with its Model 3, a smaller and lower-priced vehicle (starting at $35,000) that will allow the company to break into the mass market and manufacture many more cars. Tesla's product introductions over time are motivated by an attempt to capture benefits that accrue to economies of scale. To capture benefits from economies of scale, including lower unit cost, Elon Musk hopes Tesla can increase its production volume to 1 million vehicles a year by 2020 (an increase by a factor of 20, from the 50,000 vehicles Tesla produced in 2015).

NETWORK EFFECTS. **Network effects** describe the positive effect that one user of a product or service has on the value of that product or service for other users. When network effects are present, the value of the product or service increases with the number of users. This is an example of a *positive externality.* The threat of potential entry is reduced when network effects are present.

> **network effects** The value of a product or service for an individual user increases with the number of total users.

For example, Facebook, with over 2 billion active users worldwide, enjoys tremendous network effects, making it difficult for such other social media entrants such as Twitter or Snap to compete effectively. Likewise, Brian Chesky, CEO of Airbnb, argues that Airbnb is able to benefit from global network effects because of listings in 81,000 cities around the globe at all different price points, combined with an inventory of 5 million homes and apartments. This global network effect only grows stronger as more and more guests use the service and become hosts themselves. Given their importance in the *digital economy,* we will discuss network effects in much more detail in Chapter 7.

CUSTOMER SWITCHING COSTS. *Switching costs* are incurred by moving from one supplier to another. Changing vendors may require the buyer to alter product specifications, retrain employees, and/or modify existing processes. Switching costs are onetime sunk costs, which can be quite significant and a formidable barrier to entry. For example, a firm that has used enterprise resource planning (ERP) software from SAP for many years will incur significant switching costs when implementing a new ERP system from Oracle.

Facebook CEO Mark Zuckerberg speaks about Graph Search, a key component in finding information from within a user's network of friends. With over 2 billion active monthly users, Facebook benefits from winner-take-all network effects and thus is often described as a digital monopoly.
Jeff Chiu/AP Images

CAPITAL REQUIREMENTS. *Capital requirements* describe the "price of the entry ticket" into a new industry. How much capital is required to compete in this industry, and which companies are willing and able to make such investments? Frequently related to economies of scale, capital requirements may encompass investments to set up plants with dedicated machinery, run a production process, and cover start-up losses.

Tesla made a sizable capital investment of roughly $150 million when it purchased from Toyota its Fremont, California, manufacturing plant, which it then upgraded with an automated production process that uses robots to produce high-quality cars at large scale.[17] It then invested another $5 billion in a battery gigafactory in Nevada.[18] With this new factory, Tesla is not only able to secure supplies of lithium-ion batteries, the most critical and expensive component of an all-electric car, but it also now has the capability to build as many as 1 million vehicles a year.[19] Any potential new entrant, however, must carefully weigh the required capital investments, the cost of capital, and the expected return on investment.

Taken together, the threat of entry is high when capital requirements are low in comparison to the expected returns. If an industry is attractive enough, efficient capital markets are likely to provide the necessary funding to enter an industry. Capital, unlike proprietary technology and industry-specific know-how, is a *fungible* resource that can be relatively easily acquired in the face of attractive returns.

ADVANTAGES INDEPENDENT OF SIZE. Incumbent firms often possess cost and quality advantages that are independent of size. These advantages can be based on brand loyalty, proprietary technology, preferential access to raw materials and distribution channels, favorable geographic locations, and cumulative learning and experience effects.

Brand Loyalty. Tesla's loyal customers strengthen the firm's competitive position and reduce the threat of entry into the all-electric car segment, at least by other start-up companies.[20] Unlike GM or Ford, which spend billions each year on advertising, Tesla doesn't have a large marketing budget. Rather, it relies on word of mouth. Like Apple in its early days, Tesla has its own "cool factor," as evidenced by its beautifully designed, top-notch quality cars. In fact, when *Consumer Reports* tested the Model S, the usually understated magazine concluded: "The Tesla Model S is the best car we ever tested."[21] In addition, many Tesla owners feel an emotional connection to the company because they deeply believe in the company's vision "to accelerate the world's transition to sustainable energy."

Preferential Access. Preferential access to raw materials and key components can bestow absolute cost advantages. For example, the lithium-ion batteries that are so critical to all-electric vehicles are not only the most expensive component, but they are also in short supply. With its new battery gigafactory, however, Tesla can afford independence from the few worldwide suppliers (such as Panasonic) and also enjoy an absolute cost advantage.[22] This should further reduce the threat of new entry in the all-electric vehicle segment, assuming no radical technological changes are to be expected in battery-cell technology in the next few years.

Favorable Locations. Favorable locations, such as Silicon Valley for Tesla, often present advantages that other locales cannot match easily, including access to human and venture capital, and world-class research and engineering institutions.

Cumulative Learning and Experience. Finally, incumbent firms often benefit from cumulative learning and experience effects accrued over long periods of time. Tesla now has more than a dozen years of experience in designing and building high-performance all-electric vehicles of superior quality and design. Attempting to obtain such deep knowledge within a shorter time frame is often costly, if not impossible due to *time compression diseconomies,* which in turn constitutes a formidable barrier to entry.

GOVERNMENT POLICY. Frequently government policies restrict or prevent new entrants. Until recently, India did not allow foreign retailers such as Walmart or IKEA to own stores and compete with domestic companies in order to protect the country's millions of small vendors and wholesalers. China frequently requires foreign companies to enter joint ventures with domestic ones and to share technology.

In contrast, deregulation in industries such as airlines, telecommunications, and trucking have generated significant new entries. Therefore, the threat of entry is high when restrictive government policies do not exist or when industries become deregulated.

CREDIBLE THREAT OF RETALIATION. Potential new entrants must also anticipate how incumbent firms will react. A credible threat of retaliation by incumbent firms often deters entry. Should entry still occur, however, incumbents are able to retaliate quickly, through initiating a price war, for example. The industry profit potential can in this case easily fall below the cost of capital. Incumbents with deeper pockets than new entrants are able to withstand price competition for a longer time and wait for the new entrants to exit the industry—then raise prices again. Other weapons of retaliation include increased product and service innovation, advertising, sales promotions, and litigation.

Potential new entrants should expect a strong and vigorous response beyond price competition by incumbent firms in several scenarios. If the current competitors have deep pockets, unused excess capacity, reputational clout with industry suppliers and buyers, a history of vigorous retaliation during earlier entry attempts, or heavy investments in resources specific to the core industry and ill-suited for adaptive use, then they are likely to press these advantages. Moreover, if industry growth is slow or stagnant, incumbents are more likely to retaliate against new entrants to protect their market share, often initiating a price war with the goal of driving out these new entrants.

For example, in the southeastern United States, TV cable company Comcast has entered the market for residential and commercial telephone services and internet connectivity (as an ISP, internet service provider), emerging as a direct competitor for AT&T. Comcast also acquired NBC Universal, combining delivery and content. AT&T responded to Comcast's threat by introducing U-verse, a product combining high-speed internet access with cable TV and telephone service, all provided over its fast fiber-optic network. To combine media content with delivery capabilities, AT&T acquired TimeWarner in 2018, bringing in-house content providers such as Warner Bros., HBO, and Turner to compete more effectively against Comcast and others.

In contrast, the threat of entry is high when new entrants expect that incumbents will not or cannot retaliate.

THE POWER OF SUPPLIERS

The bargaining power of suppliers captures pressures that industry suppliers can exert on an industry's profit potential. This force reduces a firm's ability to obtain superior performance for two reasons:

1. Powerful suppliers can raise the cost of production by demanding higher prices for their inputs or by reducing the quality of the input factor or service level delivered.
2. Powerful suppliers are a threat to firms because they reduce the industry's profit potential by capturing part of the economic value created.

To compete effectively, companies generally need a wide variety of inputs into the production process, including raw materials and components, labor (via individuals or labor unions, when the industry faces collective bargaining), and services. The relative bargaining power of suppliers is high when

- The supplier's industry is more concentrated than the industry it sells to.
- Suppliers do not depend heavily on the industry for a large portion of their revenues.
- Incumbent firms face significant switching costs when changing suppliers.
- Suppliers offer products that are differentiated.
- There are no readily available substitutes for the products or services that the suppliers offer.
- Suppliers can credibly threaten to forward-integrate into the industry.

THE POWER OF BUYERS

In many ways, the bargaining power of buyers is the flip side of the bargaining power of suppliers. Buyers are the customers of an industry. The power of buyers relates to the pressure an industry's customers can put on the producers' margins by demanding a lower price or higher product quality. When buyers successfully obtain price discounts, it reduces a firm's top line (revenue). When buyers demand higher quality and more service, it generally raises production costs. Strong buyers can therefore reduce industry profit potential and a firm's profitability. Powerful buyers are a threat to the producing firms because they reduce the industry's profit potential by capturing part of the economic value created.

As with suppliers, an industry may face many different types of buyers. The buyers of an industry's product or service may be individual consumers—like you or me when we decide which provider we want to use for our wireless devices. In many areas, you can choose between several providers such as AT&T, Verizon, and T-Mobile (which merged with Sprint in a $26 billion deal). Although we might be able to find a good deal when carefully comparing their individual service plans, as individual consumers, we generally do not have significant buyer power. On the other hand, large institutions such as businesses or universities have significant buyer power when deciding which provider to use for their wireless services; this is because they are able to sign up or move several thousand employees at once.

FACTORS THAT INCREASE BUYER POWER. The power of buyers is high when

- There are a few buyers and each buyer purchases large quantities relative to the size of a single seller.
- The industry's products are standardized or undifferentiated commodities.
- Buyers face low or no switching costs.
- Buyers can credibly threaten to backwardly integrate into the industry.

Niloo138/123RF

The retail giant Walmart provides perhaps the most potent example of tremendous buyer power. Walmart is not only the largest retailer worldwide (with 12,000 stores and over 2 million employees), but it is also one of the largest companies in the world (with $530 billion in revenues in 2019). Walmart is one of the few large big-box global retail chains and frequently purchases large quantities from its suppliers. Walmart leverages its buyer power by exerting tremendous pressure on its suppliers to lower prices and to increase quality or risk losing access to shelf space at the largest retailer in the world. Walmart's buyer power is so strong that many suppliers co-locate offices next to Walmart's headquarters in Bentonville, Arkansas, because such proximity enables Walmart's strategic leaders to test the suppliers' latest products and negotiate prices.

The bargaining power of buyers also increases when their switching costs are low. Having multiple suppliers of a product category located close to its headquarters allows Walmart to demand further price cuts and quality improvements because it can easily switch from one supplier to the next. This threat is even more pronounced if the products are non-differentiated commodities from the consumer's perspective. For example, Walmart can easily switch from Rubbermaid plastic containers to Sterlite containers by offering more shelf space to the producer that offers the greatest price cut or quality improvement.

Buyers are also powerful when they can credibly threaten backward integration. Backward integration occurs when a buyer moves upstream in the industry value chain, into the seller's business. Walmart has exercised the threat to backward-integrate by producing a number of products as private-label brands such as Equate health and beauty items, Ol'Roy dog food, and Parent's Choice baby products.

Powerful buyers have the ability to extract a significant amount of the value created in the industry, leaving little or nothing for producers. In addition, strategic leaders need to be aware of situations when buyers are especially price sensitive. This is the case when

- The buyer's purchase represents a significant fraction of its cost structure or procurement budget.
- Buyers earn low profits or are strapped for cash.
- The quality (cost) of the buyers' products and services is not affected much by the quality (cost) of their inputs.

CONTEXT-DEPENDENCIES ON BUYER POWER. With regards to any of the five forces that shape competition, it is important to note that their relative strengths are context-dependent. For example, the Mexican multinational CEMEX, one of the world's leading cement producers, faces very different buyer power in the United States than domestically. In the United States, cement buyers consist of a few large and powerful construction companies that account for a significant percentage of CEMEX's output. The result? Razor-thin margins. In contrast, the vast majority of CEMEX customers in its Mexican home market are numerous, small, individual customers facing a few large suppliers, with CEMEX being the biggest. CEMEX earns high profit margins in its home market. With the same undifferentiated product, CEMEX competes in two different industry scenarios in terms of buyer strength.

THE THREAT OF SUBSTITUTES

Substitutes meet the same basic customer needs as the industry's product but in a different way. The threat of substitutes is the idea that products or services available from *outside the given industry* will come close to meeting the needs of current customers.[23] For example, many software products are substitutes to professional services, at least at the lower end. Tax preparation software such as Intuit's TurboTax is a substitute for professional services offered by H&R Block and others. LegalZoom, an online legal documentation service, is a threat to professional law firms. Other examples of substitutes are energy drinks versus coffee, videoconferencing versus business travel, e-mail versus express mail, gasoline versus biofuel, and wireless telephone services versus internet-enabled voice and video apps such as Skype, FaceTime (Apple), WhatsApp (Facebook), and WeChat (Tencent).

A high threat of substitutes reduces industry profit potential by limiting the price the industry's competitors can charge for their products and services. The threat of substitutes is high when

- The substitute offers an attractive price-performance trade-off.
- The buyers cost of switching to the substitute is low.

PRICE-PERFORMANCE TRADE-OFF. The movie rental company Redbox, which uses over 40,000 kiosks in the United States to make movie rentals available for just $2, is a substitute for buying movie DVDs. For buyers, video rental via Redbox offers an attractive price-performance trade-off with low switching costs in comparison to DVD ownership. Moreover, for customers that view only a few movies a month, Redbox is also a substitute for Netflix's basic on-demand internet movie streaming service, which costs $8.99 a month. Rather than a substitute, however, Redbox is a direct competitor to Netflix's DVD rental business, where plans cost $7.99 a month (for one DVD out at a time).

LOW-SWITCHING COSTS. In addition to a lower price, substitutes may also become more attractive by offering a higher value proposition.[24] In Spain, some 6 million people travel annually between Madrid and Barcelona, roughly 400 miles apart. The trip by car or train takes most of the day, and 90 percent of travelers would choose to fly, creating a highly profitable business for local airlines. This all changed when the Alta Velocidad Española (AVE), an ultramodern high-speed train, was completed in 2008. Taking into account total time involved, high-speed trains are faster than short-haul flights. Passengers travel in greater comfort than airline passengers and commute from one city center to the next, with only a short walk or cab ride to their final destinations.

The AVE example highlights the two fundamental insights provided by Porter's five forces framework. First, *competition must be defined more broadly to go beyond direct industry competitors.* In this case, rather than defining competition narrowly as the firm's closest competitors, airline executives in Spain must look beyond other airlines and consider substitute offerings such as high-speed trains. Second, *any of the five forces on its own, if sufficiently strong, can extract industry profitability.* In the AVE example, the threat of substitutes is limiting the airline industry's profit potential. With the arrival of the AVE, the airlines' monopoly on fast transportation between Madrid and Barcelona vanished, and with it the airlines' high profits. The strong threat of substitutes in this case increased the rivalry among existing competitors in the Spanish air transportation industry.

RIVALRY AMONG EXISTING COMPETITORS

LO 3-4

Examine how competitive industry structure shapes rivalry among competitors.

Rivalry among existing competitors describes the intensity with which companies within the same industry jockey for market share and profitability. It can range from genteel to cut-throat. The other four forces—threat of entry, the power of buyers and suppliers, and the threat of substitutes—all exert pressure upon this rivalry, as indicated by the arrows pointing toward the center in Exhibit 3.3. *The stronger the forces, the stronger the expected competitive intensity, which in turn limits the industry's profit potential.*

Competitors can lower prices to attract customers from rivals. When intense rivalry among existing competitors brings about price discounting, industry profitability erodes. Alternatively, competitors can use non-price competition to create more value in terms of product features and design, quality, promotional spending, and after-sales service and support. When non-price competition is the primary basis of competition, costs increase, which can also have a negative impact on industry profitability. However, when these moves create unique products with features tailored closely to meet customer needs and willingness to pay, then average industry profitability tends to increase because producers are able to raise prices and thus increase revenues and profit margins.

The intensity of rivalry among existing competitors is determined largely by the following factors:

- Competitive industry structure.
- Industry growth.
- Strategic commitments.
- Exit barriers.

competitive industry structure Elements and features common to all industries, including the number and size of competitors, the firms' degree of pricing power, the type of product or service offered, and the height of entry barriers.

COMPETITIVE INDUSTRY STRUCTURE. The **competitive industry structure** refers to elements and features common to all industries. The structure of an industry is largely captured by

- The number and size of its competitors.
- The firm's degree of pricing power.

EXHIBIT 3.4 Industry Competitive Structures along the Continuum from Fragmented to Consolidated

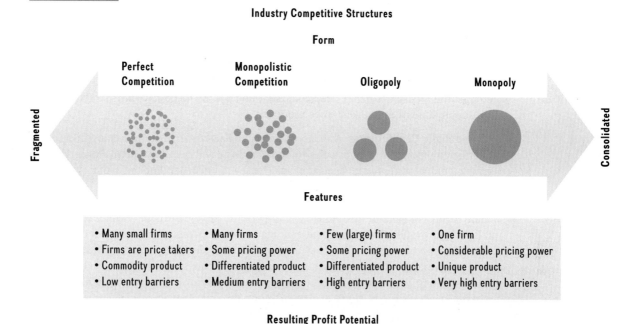

- The type of product or service (commodity or differentiated product).
- The height of entry barriers.[25]

Exhibit 3.4 shows different industry types along a continuum from fragmented to consolidated structures. At one extreme, a *fragmented industry* consists of many small firms and tends to generate low profitability. At the other end of the continuum, a *consolidated industry* is dominated by a few firms, or even just one firm, and has the potential to be highly profitable. The four main competitive industry structures are

1. Perfect competition
2. Monopolistic competition
3. Oligopoly
4. Monopoly

Perfect Competition. A *perfectly competitive* industry is fragmented and has many small firms, a commodity product, ease of entry, and little or no ability for each individual firm to raise its prices. The firms competing in this type of industry are approximately similar in size and resources. Consumers make purchasing decisions solely on price, because the commodity product offerings are more or less identical. The resulting performance of the industry shows low profitability. Under these conditions, firms in perfect competition have difficulty achieving even a temporary competitive advantage and can achieve only competitive parity. Although perfect competition is a rare industry structure in its pure form, markets for commodities such as natural gas, copper, and iron tend to approach this structure.

Modern high-tech industries are also not immune to the perils of perfect competition. Many internet entrepreneurs learned the hard way that it is difficult to beat the forces of perfect competition. Fueled by eager venture capitalists, about 100 online pet supply stores such as *pets.com, petopia.com,* and *pet-store.com* had sprung up by 1999, at the height of the internet bubble.[26] Cut-throat competition ensued, with online retailers selling products below cost. When many small firms are offering a commodity product in an industry that is easy to enter, no one is able to increase prices and generate profits. To make matters worse, at the same time, category-killers such as PetSmart and PetCo were expanding rapidly, opening some 2,000 brick-and-mortar stores in the United States and Canada. The ensuing price competition led to an industry shakeout, leaving online retailers in the dust. Looking at the competitive industry structures depicted in Exhibit 3.4, we might have predicted that online pet supply stores were unlikely to be profitable.

Monopolistic Competition. A *monopolistically competitive* industry has many firms, a differentiated product, some obstacles to entry, and the ability to raise prices for a relatively unique product while retaining customers. The key to understanding this industry structure is that the firms now offer products or services with unique features.

The computer hardware industry provides one example of monopolistic competition. Many firms compete in this industry, and even the largest of them (Apple, ASUS, Dell, HP, or Lenovo) have less than 20 percent market share. Moreover, while products between competitors tend to be similar, they are by no means identical. As a consequence, firms selling a product with unique features tend to have some ability to raise prices. When a firm is able to differentiate its product or service offerings, it carves out a niche in the market in which it has some degree of monopoly power over pricing, thus the name "monopolistic competition." Firms frequently communicate the degree of product differentiation through advertising.

Oligopoly. An *oligopolistic* industry is consolidated with a few large firms, differentiated products, high barriers to entry, and some degree of pricing power. The degree of pricing power depends, just as in monopolistic competition, on the degree of product differentiation.

A key feature of an oligopoly is that the competing firms are *interdependent*. With only a few competitors in the mix, the actions of one firm influence the behaviors of the others. Each competitor in an oligopoly, therefore, must consider the strategic actions of the other competitors. This type of industry structure is often analyzed using *game theory,* which attempts to predict strategic behaviors by assuming that the moves and reactions of competitors can be anticipated.[27] Due to their strategic interdependence, companies in oligopolies have an incentive to coordinate their strategic actions to maximize joint performance. Although explicit coordination such as price fixing is illegal in the United States, tacit coordination such as "an unspoken understanding" is not.

The express-delivery industry is an example of an oligopoly. The main competitors in this space are FedEx and UPS. Any strategic decision made by FedEx (e.g., to expand delivery services to ground delivery of larger-size packages) directly affects UPS; likewise, any decision made by UPS (e.g., to guarantee next-day delivery before 8:00 a.m.) directly affects FedEx. Other examples of oligopolies include the soft drink industry (Coca-Cola versus Pepsi), airframe manufacturing business (Boeing versus Airbus), home-improvement retailing (The Home Depot versus Lowe's), toys and games (Hasbro versus Mattel), and detergents (P&G versus Unilever).[28]

Companies in an oligopoly tend to have some pricing power if they are able to differentiate their product or service offerings from those of their competitors. *Non-price competition*, therefore, is the preferred mode of competition. This means competing by offering unique product features or services rather than competing based on price alone. When one firm in an oligopoly cuts prices to gain market share from its competitor, the competitor typically will respond in kind and also cut prices. This process initiates a price war, which can be especially detrimental to firm performance if the products are close rivals.

In the early years of the soft drink industry, for example, whenever PepsiCo lowered prices, Coca-Cola followed suit. These actions only resulted in reduced profitability for both companies. In recent decades, both Coca-Cola and PepsiCo have repeatedly demonstrated that they have learned this lesson. They shifted the basis of competition from price-cutting to new product introductions and lifestyle advertising. Any price adjustments are merely short-term promotions. By leveraging innovation and advertising, Coca-Cola and PepsiCo have moved to non-price competition, which in turn allows them to charge higher prices and to improve industry and company profitability.[29]

Monopoly. An industry is a *monopoly* when there is only one, often large firm supplying the market. The firm may offer a unique product, and the challenges to moving into the industry tend to be high. The monopolist has considerable pricing power. As a consequence, firm and thus industry profit tends to be high. The one firm is the industry.

In some instances, the government will grant one firm the right to be the sole supplier of a product or service. This is often done to incentivize a company to engage in a venture that would not be profitable if there was more than one supplier. For instance, public utilities incur huge fixed costs to build plants and to supply a certain geographic area. Public utilities supplying water, gas, and electricity to businesses and homes are frequently monopolists. Georgia Power is the only supplier of electricity for some 2.5 million customers in the southeastern United States. Philadelphia Gas Works is the only supplier of natural gas in the city of Philadelphia, serving some 500,000 customers. These are so-called *natural monopolies.* Without them, the governments involved believe the market would not supply these products or services. In the past few decades, however, more and more of these natural monopolies have been deregulated in the United States, including airlines, telecommunications, railroads, trucking, and ocean transportation. This deregulation has allowed competition to emerge, which frequently leads to lower prices, better service, and more innovation.

While natural monopolies appear to be disappearing from the competitive landscape, so-called *near monopolies* are of much greater interest to strategists. These are firms that have accrued significant market power, for example, by owning valuable patents or proprietary technology. In the process, they are changing the industry structure in their favor, generally from monopolistic competition or oligopolies to near monopolies. These near monopolies are firms that have accomplished product differentiation to such a degree that they are in a class by themselves, just like a monopolist. The European Union, for example, views Google with its 90 percent market share in online search as a *digital monopoly.*[30] This is an enviable position in terms of the ability to extract profits by leveraging its data to provide targeted online advertising and other customized services, so long as Google can steer clear of monopolistic behavior, which may attract antitrust regulators and lead to legal repercussions.

INDUSTRY GROWTH. Industry growth directly affects the intensity of rivalry among competitors. In periods of high growth, consumer demand rises, and price competition among firms frequently decreases. Because the pie is expanding, rivals are focused on capturing part of that larger pie rather than taking market share and profitability away from one another.

The demand for knee replacements, for example, is a fast-growing segment in the medical products industry. In the United States, robust demand is driven by the need for knee replacements for an aging population as well as for an increasingly obese population. The leading competitors are Zimmer Biomet, DePuy, and Stryker, with a significant share held by Smith & Nephew. Competition is primarily based on innovative design, improved implant materials, and differentiated products such as gender solutions and a range of high-flex knees. With improvements to materials and procedures, younger patients are also increasingly choosing early surgical intervention. Competitors are able to avoid price competition and, instead, focus on differentiation that allows premium pricing.

In contrast, rivalry among competitors becomes fierce during slow or even negative industry growth. Price discounts, frequent new product releases with minor modifications, intense promotional campaigns, and fast retaliation by rivals are all tactics indicative of an industry with slow or negative growth. Competition is fierce because rivals can gain only at the expense of others; therefore, companies are focused on taking business away from one another. Demand for traditional fast food providers such as McDonald's, Burger King, and Wendy's has been declining in recent years. Consumers have become more health-conscious and demand has shifted to alternative restaurants such as Subway, Chick-fil-A, and Chipotle. Attempts by McDonald's, Burger King, and Wendy's to steal customers from one another include frequent discounting tactics such as dollar menus. Such competitive tactics are indicative of cut-throat competition and a low profit potential in the traditional hamburger fast food industry.

Competitive rivalry based solely on cutting prices is especially destructive to profitability because it transfers most, if not all, of the value created in the industry to the customers—leaving little, if anything, for the firms in the industry. While this may appear attractive to customers, firms that are not profitable are not able to make the investments necessary to upgrade their product offerings or services to provide higher value, and they eventually leave the industry. Destructive price competition can lead to limited choices, lower product quality, and higher prices for consumers in the long run if only a few large firms survive.

STRATEGIC COMMITMENTS. If firms make strategic commitments to compete in an industry, rivalry among competitors is likely to be more intense. **Strategic commitments** are firm actions that are costly, long-term oriented, and difficult to reverse. Strategic commitments to a specific industry can stem from large, fixed cost requirements, but also from noneconomic considerations.[31]

> **strategic commitments** Firm actions that are costly, long-term oriented, and difficult to reverse.

EXIT BARRIERS. The rivalry among existing competitors is also a function of an industry's **exit barriers**, the obstacles that determine how easily a firm can leave that industry. Exit barriers comprise both economic and social factors. They include fixed costs that must be paid regardless of whether the company is operating in the industry or not. A company exiting an industry may still have contractual obligations to suppliers, such as employee health care, retirement benefits, and severance pay. Social factors include elements such as emotional attachments to certain geographic locations. In Michigan, entire communities still depend on GM, Ford, and Chrysler. If any of those carmakers were to exit the industry, communities would suffer. Other social and economic factors include ripple effects through the supply chain. When one major player in an industry shuts down, its suppliers are adversely impacted as well.

> **exit barriers** Obstacles that determine how easily a firm can leave an industry.

An industry with low exit barriers is more attractive because it allows underperforming firms to exit more easily. Such exits reduce competitive pressure on the remaining firms because excess capacity is removed. In contrast, an industry with high exit barriers reduces its profit potential because excess capacity still remains.

To summarize our discussion of the five forces model, Exhibit 3.5 provides a checklist that you can apply to any industry when assessing the underlying competitive forces that shape strategy. The key take-away from the five forces model is that the stronger the forces, the lower the industry's ability to earn above-average profits, and correspondingly, the lower the firm's ability to gain and sustain a competitive advantage. Conversely, the weaker the forces, the greater the industry's ability to earn above-average profits, and correspondingly,

The threat of entry is high when

✓ The minimum efficient scale to compete in an industry is low.

✓ Network effects are not present.

✓ Customer switching costs are low.

✓ Capital requirements are low.

✓ Incumbents do not possess:
  o Brand loyalty.
  o Proprietary technology.
  o Preferential access to raw materials.
  o Preferential access to distribution channels.
  o Favorable geographic locations.
  o Cumulative learning and experience effects.

✓ Restrictive government regulations do not exist.

✓ New entrants expect that incumbents will not or cannot retaliate.

The power of suppliers is high when

✓ Supplier's industry is more concentrated than the industry it sells to.

✓ Suppliers do not depend heavily on the industry for their revenues.

✓ Incumbent firms face significant switching costs when changing suppliers.

✓ Suppliers offer products that are differentiated.

✓ There are no readily available substitutes for the products or services that the suppliers offer.

✓ Suppliers can credibly threaten to forward-integrate into the industry.

The power of buyers is high when

✓ There are a few buyers and each buyer purchases large quantities relative to the size of a single seller.

✓ The industry's products are standardized or undifferentiated commodities.

✓ Buyers face low or no switching costs.

✓ Buyers can credibly threaten to backwardly integrate into the industry.

The threat of substitutes is high when

✓ The substitute offers an attractive price-performance trade-off.

✓ The buyer's cost of switching to the substitute is low.

The rivalry among existing competitors is high when

✓ There are many competitors in the industry.

✓ The competitors are roughly of equal size.

✓ Industry growth is slow, zero, or even negative.

✓ Exit barriers are high.

✓ Incumbent firms are highly committed to the business.

✓ Incumbent firms cannot read or understand each other's strategies well.

✓ Products and services are direct substitutes.

✓ Fixed costs are high and marginal costs are low.

✓ Excess capacity exists in the industry.

✓ The product or service is perishable.

EXHIBIT 3.5

The Five Forces Competitive Analysis Checklist

Source: Adapted from M.E. Porter (2008, January), "The five competitive forces that shape strategy," *Harvard Business Review*.

the greater the firm's ability to gain and sustain competitive advantage. Therefore, strategic leaders need to craft a strategic position for their company that leverages weak forces into opportunities and mitigates strong forces because they are potential threats to the firm's ability to gain and sustain a competitive advantage.

APPLYING THE FIVE FORCES MODEL TO THE U.S. AIRLINE INDUSTRY

Applying the model to the U.S. domestic airline industry provides a neat examination of the five competitive forces that shape strategy.[32]

THREAT OF ENTRY. *Entry barriers* in the airline industry are relatively low, resulting in new airlines popping up occasionally. To enter the industry (on a small scale, serving a few select cities), a prospective new entrant needs only a couple of airplanes, which can be rented; a few pilots and crew members; some routes connecting city pairs; and gate access in airports. Despite notoriously low industry profitability, Virgin America entered the U.S. market in 2007. Virgin America is the brainchild of Sir Richard Branson, founder and chairman of the Virgin Group, a UK conglomerate of hundreds of companies using the Virgin brand, including the international airline Virgin Atlantic. Virgin America's business strategy was to offer low-cost service between major metropolitan cities on the American East and West coasts. In 2016, Alaska Airlines acquired Virgin America for $2.6 billion.

POWER OF SUPPLIERS. In the airline industry, the *supplier power* is also strong. The providers of airframes (e.g., Boeing and Airbus), makers of aircraft engines (e.g., GE and Rolls-Royce), aircraft maintenance companies (e.g., Goodrich), caterers (e.g., Marriott), labor unions, and airports controlling gate access all bargain away the profitability of airlines.

Let's take a closer look at one important supplier group to this industry: Boeing and Airbus, the makers of large commercial jets. Airframe manufacturers are powerful suppliers to airlines because their industry is much more concentrated (only two firms) than the industry it sells to. Compared to two airframe suppliers, there are hundreds of commercial airlines around the world. Given the trend of large airlines merging to create even larger mega-airlines, however, increasing buyer power may eventually balance this out a bit. Nonetheless, the airlines face nontrivial switching costs when changing suppliers because pilots and crew would need to be retrained to fly a new type of aircraft, maintenance capabilities would need to be expanded, and some routes may even need to be reconfigured due to differences in aircraft range and passenger capacity. Moreover, while some aircraft can be used as substitutes, Boeing and Airbus offer differentiated products. This fact becomes clearer when considering some of the more recent models from each company. Boeing introduced the 787 Dreamliner to capture long-distance point-to-point travel (close to an 8,000-mile range, sufficient to fly nonstop from Los Angeles to Sydney), while Airbus introduced the A-380 Superjumbo to focus on high-volume transportation (close to 900 passengers) between major airport hubs (e.g., Tokyo's Haneda Airport and Singapore's Changi Airport).

When considering long-distance travel, there are no readily available substitutes for commercial airliners, a fact that strengthens supplier power. Thus, the supplier power of commercial aircraft manufacturers is quite significant. This puts Boeing and Airbus in a strong position to extract profits from the airline industry, thus reducing the profit potential of the airlines themselves.

Although the supplier power of Boeing and Airbus is strong, several factors further moderate their bargaining positions somewhat. First, the suppliers of commercial airliners depend heavily on the commercial airlines for their revenues. Given the less than expected demand for the A-380, for instance, Airbus announced that it will stop producing the Superjumbo in 2021.[33] Rather, Airbus will focus more on its newer and smaller A-350 model, a versatile and fuel-efficient airplane to be deployed on high-traffic point-to-point routes, and thus a direct competitor to Boeing's 787. As the recent strategic moves by Airbus and Boeing have shown, even a *duopoloy* (a industry with only two suppliers) in the airframe manufacturing business is not immune to changes in customer demand (power of buyers).

Second, Boeing and Airbus are unlikely to threaten forward integration and become commercial airlines themselves. Third, Bombardier of Canada and Embraer of Brazil, both manufacturers of smaller commercial airframes, have begun to increase the size of the jets they offer and thus now compete with some of the smaller planes such as the Boeing 737 and Airbus A-320. Finally, industry structures are not static, but can change over time. Several of the remaining large domestic U.S. airlines have merged (Delta and Northwest, United and Continental, and American and U.S. Airways), which changed the industry structure in their favor. There are now fewer airlines, but they are larger. This fact increases their buyer power, which we turn to next.

POWER OF BUYERS. Large corporate customers contract with airlines to serve all of their employees' travel needs; such *powerful buyers* further reduce profit margins for air carriers. To make matters worse, consumers primarily make decisions based on price as air travel is viewed as a commodity with little or no differentiation across domestic U.S. carriers. In inflation-adjusted dollars, ticket prices have been falling since industry deregulation in 1978. Thanks to internet travel sites such as Orbitz, Travelocity, and Kayak, price comparisons are effortless. Consumers benefit from cut-throat price competition between carriers and capture significant value. Low switching costs and nearly perfect information in real time combine to strengthen buyer power.

THREAT OF SUBSTITUTES. To make matters worse, *substitutes* are also readily available: If prices are seen as too high, customers can drive a car or use the train or bus. For example, the route between Atlanta and Orlando (roughly 400 miles) used to be one of Delta's busiest and most profitable. Given the increasing security requirements at airports and other factors, more people now prefer to drive. Taken together, the competitive forces are quite unfavorable for generating a profit potential in the airline industry: low entry barriers, high supplier power, high buyer power combined with low customer switching costs, and the availability of low-cost substitutes. This type of hostile environment leads to intense rivalry among existing airlines and low overall industry profit potential.

RIVALRY AMONG EXISTING COMPETITORS. As a consequence of the powerful industry forces discussed above, the *nature of rivalry* among airlines has become incredibly intense. Moreover, the required strategic commitments combined with exit barriers further increase the competitive intensity in the U.S. domestic airline industry.

Strategic Commitments. Significant strategic commitments are required to compete in the airline industry when using a hub-and-spoke system to provide not only domestic but also international coverage. U.S.-based airlines Delta, United, and American have large fixed costs to maintain their network of routes that affords global coverage, frequently in conjunction with foreign partner airlines. These fixed costs in terms of aircraft, gate leases, hangars, maintenance facilities, baggage facilities, and ground transportation all accrue before the airlines sell any tickets. High fixed costs create tremendous pressure to fill empty seats. An airline seat on a specific flight, just like an unbooked hotel room, is perishable. Empty airline seats are often filled through price-cutting. Given similar high fixed costs, other airlines respond in kind. Eventually, a vicious cycle of price-cutting ensues, driving average industry profitability to zero, or even negative numbers (where the companies are losing money). To make matters worse, given their strategic commitments, airlines are unlikely to exit an industry. Excess capacity remains, further depressing industry profitability.

In other cases, strategic commitments to a specific industry may be the result of more political than economic considerations. Airbus, for example, was created by a number of European governments through direct subsidies to provide a countervailing power to Boeing. The European Union in turn claims that Boeing is subsidized by the U.S. government indirectly via defense contracts. Given these political considerations and large-scale strategic commitments, neither Airbus nor Boeing is likely to exit the aircraft manufacturing industry even if industry profit potential falls to zero.

Exit Barriers. The U.S. domestic airline industry is characterized by high exit barriers, which further reduces the industry's overall profit potential. All the large U.S. airlines (American, Delta, and United) have filed for bankruptcy at one point. Due to a unique feature of U.S. Chapter 11 bankruptcy law, companies may continue to operate and reorganize while being temporarily shielded from their creditors and other obligations until renegotiated. This implies that excess capacity is not removed from the industry, and by putting pressure on prices further reduces industry profit potential.

CONCLUSION. Although many of the mega-airlines have lost billions of dollars over the past few decades and continue to struggle to generate consistent profitability, other players in the industry have been quite profitable because they were able to extract some of the economic value created. The surprising conclusion, therefore, is that while the mega-airlines themselves frequently struggle to achieve consistent profitability over time, the other players in the industry—such as the suppliers of airframes and aircraft engines, aircraft maintenance companies, IT companies providing reservation and logistics services, caterers, airports, and so on—are quite profitable, all extracting significant value from the air transportation industry. Customers also are better off, as ticket prices have decreased and travel choices increased.

During the mid-2010s, the cash-strapped airlines benefited from a windfall as the price of jet fuel fell from a high of $3.25 per gallon (in the spring of 2011) all the way to $0.80 per gallon (in early 2016), before climbing back to $1.80 (in early 2019). The cost of jet fuel is roughly 50 percent of an airline's total operating costs. Nonetheless, competition remains intense in this industry.

Taking a closer look at the U.S. domestic airline industry shows how the five forces framework is a powerful and versatile tool to analyze industries. The five forces model allows strategic leaders to analyze all players using a wider industry lens, which in turn enables a deeper understanding of an industry's profit potential. Moreover, a five forces analysis provides the basis for how a firm should position itself to gain and sustain a competitive advantage. We will take up the topic of competitive positioning in Chapter 6 when studying business-level strategy in much more detail.

LO 3-5

Describe the strategic role of complements in creating positive-sum co-opetition.

A SIXTH FORCE: THE STRATEGIC ROLE OF COMPLEMENTS

As valuable as the five forces model is for explaining the profit potential and attractiveness of industries, the value of Porter's five forces model can be further enhanced if one also considers the availability of complements.[34]

A **complement** is a product, service, or competency that adds value to the original product offering when the two are used in tandem.[35] Complements increase demand for the primary product, thereby enhancing the profit potential for the industry and the firm. A company is a **complementor** to your company if customers value your product or service offering more when they are able to combine it with the other company's product or service.[36] Firms may choose to provide the complements themselves or work with another company to accomplish this.

CO-OPETITION. For example, in the smartphone industry, Alphabet's Google complements Samsung. The Korean high-tech company's smartphones are more valuable when they come with Google's Android mobile operating system installed. At the same time, Google and Samsung are increasingly becoming competitors. With Google's acquisition of Motorola Mobility, the online search company launched its own line of smartphones and Chromebooks. This development illustrates the process of **co-opetition**, which is cooperation by competitors to achieve a strategic objective. Samsung and Google cooperate as complementors to compete against Apple's strong position in the mobile device industry, while at the same time Samsung and Google are increasingly becoming competitive with one another. While Google retained Motorola's patents to use for development in its future phones and to defend itself against competitors such as Samsung and Apple, Alphabet (Google's parent company) sold the manufacturing arm of Motorola to Lenovo, a Chinese maker of computers and mobile devices.

In 2017, Google acquired HTC's smartphone engineering group for $1.1 billion. The Taiwanese smartphone maker developed the Google Pixel phone. With this acquisition, Google is making a commitment to handset manufacturing, unlike in the Motorola deal, which was more motivated by intellectual property considerations. Integrating HTC's smartphone unit within Google will allow engineers to more tightly integrate hardware and software. This in turn will allow Google to differentiate its high-end Pixel phones from the competition, especially Apple's iPhones and Samsung's Galaxy line of phones.

3.3 Changes over Time: Entry Choices and Industry Dynamics

LO 3-6

Explain the five choices required for market entry.

ENTRY CHOICES

One of the key insights of the five forces model is that the more profitable an industry, the more attractive it becomes to competitors. Let's assume a firm's strategic leaders are aware of potential barriers to entry (discussed earlier), but would nonetheless like to contemplate potential market entry because the industry profitability is high and thus quite attractive. Exhibit 3.6 shows an integrative model that can guide the entry choices firms make. Rather

---

complement A product, service, or competency that adds value to the original product offering when the two are used in tandem.

complementor A company that provides a good or service that leads customers to value your firm's offering more when the two are combined.

co-opetition Cooperation by competitors to achieve a strategic objective.

EXHIBIT 3.6 Entry Choices

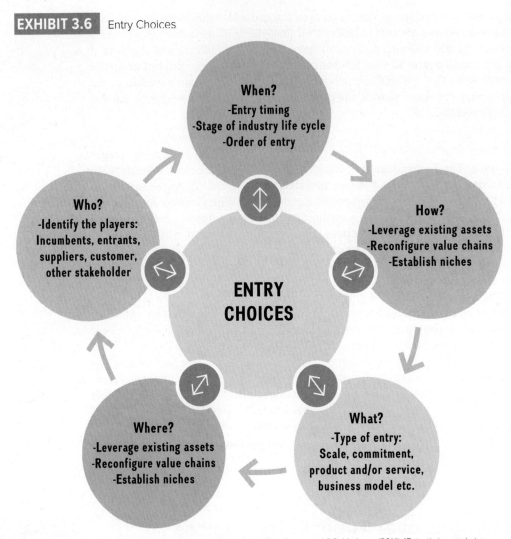

Source: Based on and adapted from M.A., Zachary, P.T. Gianiodis, G. Tyge Payne, and G.D. Markman (2014), "Entry timing: enduring lessons and future directions," *Journal of Management* 41: 1409; and Bryce, D.J., and J.H. Dyer (2007, May), "Strategies to crack well-guarded markets," *Harvard Business Review*: 84–92.

than considering firm entry as a discrete event (i.e., simple yes or no decision), or a discrete event composed of five parts, this model suggests that the entry choices firms make constitute a strategic process unfolding over time.

In particular, to increase the probability of successful entry, strategic leaders need to consider the following five questions:[37]

1. *Who are the players?* Building on Porter's insight that competition must be viewed in a broader sense beyond direct competitors, the *who are the players* question allows strategic leaders to not only identify direct competitors but also focus on other external and internal stakeholders necessary to successfully compete in an industry, such as customers, employees, regulators, and communities (see discussion of stakeholder strategy in Chapter 2).

2. *When to enter?* This question concerns the *timing of entry.* Given that our perspective is that of a firm considering potential entry into an *existing* industry, any first-mover advantages are bygones. Nonetheless, the potential new entrant needs to consider at which stage of the industry life cycle (introduction, growth, shakeout, maturity, or decline) it should enter. We take a deep dive into the industry life cycle and how it unfolds in Chapter 7.

3. *How to enter?* One of the challenges that strategic leaders face is that often the most attractive industries in terms of profitability are also the hardest to break into because they are protected by entry barriers. Thus, the *how to enter* question goes to the heart of this problem.

   ▪ One option is to *leverage existing assets,* that is to think about a new combination of resources and capabilities that firms already possess, and if needed to combine them with partner resources through strategic alliances. Although Circuit City went bankrupt as an electronics retailer, losing out to Best Buy and Amazon, a few years earlier it recombined its existing expertise in big-box retailing including optimization of supply and demand in specific geographic areas to create CarMax, now the largest used-car dealer in the United States and a Fortune 500 company.

   ▪ Another option is to *reconfigure value chains.* This approach allowed Skype to enter the market for long-distance calls by combining value chains differently (offering VoIP rather than relying on more expensive fiber-optic cables), and thus compete with incumbents such as AT&T.

   ▪ The third option is to *establish a niche* in an existing industry, and then use this beachhead to grow further. This is the approach the Austrian maker of Red Bull used when entering the U.S. soft drink market, long dominated by Coca-Cola and PepsiCo. Its energy drink was offered in a small 8.4-ounce (250 ml) can, but priced at multiples compared to Coke or Pepsi. This allowed retailers to stock Red Bull cans in small spaces such as near the checkout counter. In addition, Red Bull initially used many nontraditional outlets as points of sale such as nightclubs and gas stations. This approach created a loyal following from which the energy drink maker could expand its entry into the mainstream carbonated beverage drink in the United States and elsewhere. Indeed, energy drinks are now one of the fastest growing segments in this industry.

4. *What type of entry?* The *what* question of entry refers to the type of entry in terms of product market (e.g., smartphones), value chain activity (e.g., R&D for smartphone chips or manufacturing of smartphones), geography (e.g., domestic and/or international), and type of business model (e.g., subsidizing smartphones when providing services). Depending on the market under consideration for entry, firms may face unique competitive and institutional challenges. For example, discount carrier Spirit Airlines' unbundling of its services by charging customers separately for elements such as checked luggage, assigned seating, carry-on items, and other in-flight perks such as drinks met with considerable backlash in 2007 when introduced. Yet this marked the starting point of Spirit Airlines' strategic positioning as an ultra-low-cost carrier and enabled the company to add many attractive routes, and thus to enter geographic markets it was not able to compete in previously.

5. *Where to enter?* After deciding on the type of entry, the *where* to enter question refers to more fine-tuned aspects of entry such as product positioning (high end versus low end), pricing strategy, potential partners, and so forth.

LO 3-7

Appraise the role of industry dynamics and industry convergence in shaping the firm's external environment.

INDUSTRY DYNAMICS

Although the five forces plus complements model is useful in understanding an industry's profit potential, it provides only a point-in-time snapshot of a moving target. With this model (as with other static models), one cannot determine the changing speed of an industry or the rate of innovation. This drawback implies that strategic leaders must repeat their analysis over time to create a more accurate picture of their industry. It is therefore important that strategic leaders consider industry dynamics.

Industry structures are not stable over time. Rather, they are dynamic. Since a consolidated industry tends to be more profitable than a fragmented one (see Exhibit 3.4), firms have a tendency to change the industry structure in their favor, making it more consolidated through horizontal mergers and acquisitions. Having fewer competitors generally equates to higher industry profitability. Industry incumbents, therefore, have an incentive to reduce the number of competitors in the industry. With fewer but larger competitors, incumbent firms can mitigate more effectively the threat of strong competitive forces such as supplier or buyer power.

The U.S. domestic airline industry has witnessed several large, horizontal mergers between competitors, including Delta and Northwest, United and Continental, Southwest and AirTran, as well as American and U.S. Airways. These moves allow the remaining carriers to enjoy a more benign industry structure. It also allows them to retire some of the excess capacity in the industry as the merged airlines consolidate their networks of routes. The merger activity in the airline industry provides one example of how firms can proactively reshape industry structure in their favor. A more consolidated airline industry is likely to lead to higher ticket prices and fewer choices for customers, but also more profitable airlines.

In contrast, consolidated industry structures may also break up and become more fragmented. This generally happens when there are external shocks to an industry such as deregulation, new legislation, technological innovation, or globalization. For example, the widespread use of the internet moved the stock brokerage business from an oligopoly controlled by full-service firms such as Merrill Lynch and Morgan Stanley to monopolistic competition with many generic online brokers such as Ameritrade, E*Trade, and Scottrade.

industry convergence
A process whereby formerly unrelated industries begin to satisfy the same customer need.

Another dynamic to be considered is **industry convergence**, a process whereby formerly unrelated industries begin to satisfy the same customer need. Industry convergence is often brought on by technological advances. For years, many players in the media industries have been converging due to technological progress in AI, telecommunications, and digital media. Media convergence unites computing, communications, and content, thereby causing significant upheaval across previously distinct industries. Content providers in industries such as newspapers, magazines, TV, movies, radio, and music are all scrambling to adapt. Many standalone print newspapers are closing up shop, while others are trying to figure out how to offer online news content for which consumers are willing to pay.[38] Internet companies such as Google, Facebook, Instagram (acquired by Facebook), LinkedIn (acquired by Microsoft), Snapchat, Pinterest, and Twitter are changing the industry structure by constantly morphing their capabilities and forcing old-line media companies such as News Corp., Time Warner (now part of AT&T), and Disney to adapt. A wide variety of mobile devices, including smartphones, tablets, and e-readers, provide a new form of content delivery that has the potential to make print media obsolete.

Finally, the convergence of different technology can also lead to the emergence of entirely new industries. Strategy Highlight 3.2 documents the recent rise of the e-sports industry.

Strategy Highlight **3.2**

From League of Legends to Fortnite: The Rise of e-Sports

League of Legends (LoL), the popular multiplayer online battle arena (MOBA) game developed and launched in 2009 by Riot Games of Los Angeles, went from being a small niche game to a billion-dollar business, sparking the explosive growth of the e-sports industry. Although online games have been around for a while, Riot Games was the first company to put e-sports on the map and to bring it into the mainstream culture.

Within just two years of its launch, LoL managed to accrue 1.4 million daily players and 3.5 million monthly average users (MAU). Since then, it has garnered 30 million daily players and made more than $7 billion in revenues. For nearly a decade, LoL was the world's most popular video game—until Fortnite took over. The explosive growth and global popularity of LoL did not go unnoticed: In 2011, the Chinese tech company Tencent (also owner of WeChat, the world's largest social media

and mobile payment app with some 1 billion daily users) bought Riot Games for $400 million. Exhibit 3.7 shows the annual revenues of LoL and Fortnite (FN) over time.

League of Legends is free to download and free to play. Game updates released by Riot Games are also free of charge. How has Riot Games been able to make so much money using this "freemium" business model? It relies on four key tactics in its business model: in-game and ancillary transactions, live e-sport events, live-streamed e-sport events, and merchandise sales.

In-game and ancillary transactions are the first source of revenue. Riot Games makes the bulk of its money by selling "champions" (the avatars that fight in the battles; each champion has unique abilities and you unlock more abilities as you go along and win) as well as their "skins" (which change the appearance of the champions) to its extensive user base, offering more than 140 champions with some 800 skins and other accessories, such as

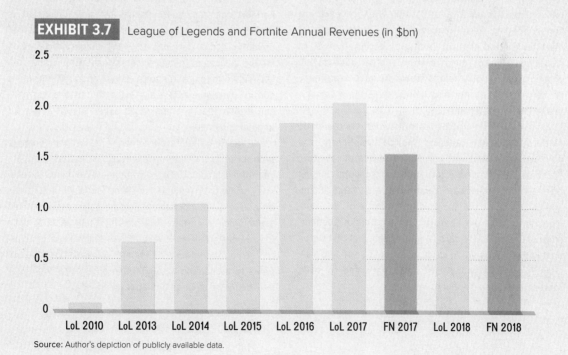

EXHIBIT 3.7   League of Legends and Fortnite Annual Revenues (in $bn)

Source: Author's depiction of publicly available data.

(Continued)

name changes. LoL accepts two types of currency: Blue Essence, which are points that can be earned through playing (accomplishing specific missions in a game, for instance) and Riot Points, which are points that can be purchased with real money using prepaid cards. Since each battle consists of two teams comprising five players, the possible permutations of champions and skins can add up to the billions, and all encounters are unique. Furthermore the LoL in-game store is digital, which means its inventory of items is potentially unlimited. Players also have their own personal stores based on their selected champions and other individual characteristics. Here, players often find items recommended uniquely for them.

Live e-sport events are a second source of revenue. One key differentiator between LoL and previous e-sports games is its competitive focus. Riot Games hosts a League Championship Series (LCS), which attracts vast audiences and significant media and sponsorship attention. It controls all aspects of the LCS: the music, broadcasting, and decisions about where to run LoL tournaments, which are hosted in several global locations. Top professional players can earn millions of dollars a year (in prize money, sponsorship, and streaming fees), while thousands of players have gone professional making more than $100,000 year. These events are hugely popular and fill venues with tens of thousands of attendees, often dressed in cosplay outfits (that is, as characters from LoL, a movie, book, or other video game). These events not only help to create a unique experience for its visitors, but they also help to generate a community of like-minded gamers.

Live-streamed e-sport events delivered via the video platform Twitch.tv (nicknamed "the ESPN of eSports" and now owned by Amazon) are a third source of revenue. These events often have corporate sponsorships ranging from computer hardware companies (e.g., Intel, Razer, and Logitech, etc.) to energy drinks firms (e.g., Red Bull, Monster, and 5-Hour Energy). LoL has a major sponsorship deal with Mastercard, a global financial institution best known for its credit cards. Sales of LoL-specific merchandise, such as hoodies, T-shirts, hats, and so forth, represent the final source of revenue.

Riot Games maintains its revenues even as the game continuously evolves. The constant evolution of the game keeps gamers challenged, creative, and engaged. Many can be found in online chat rooms such as Reddit rethinking and discussing their strategy with other players, and thus further expanding the gaming community and its global reach. Currently, most of the world's ranked players are from the United States, China, South Korea, Germany, France, and Sweden (in rank order). The demographics of the players are highly sought after by advertisers because most players are between the ages of 15 and 35 years old, a notoriously difficult audience to reach. Yet, it is also highly skewed in terms of gender: 85 percent of the players are male. With virtually no barriers to entry, Riot Games managed to build a huge gamer base that continues to grow exponentially and thus created a new industry.

During LoL's rise to success, however, Riot Games found itself contending with competitors such as Minecraft (which Microsoft bought for $2.5 billion in 2014), Dota 2, and others. LoL dominated its competitors until the fall of 2017, when Epic Games (also owned in part by Tencent) released Fortnite. Fortnite is known as a "Battle Royale Game," that is a multiplayer online game that continues until only one survivor is standing. One main reason Fortnite took off so quickly is that the game, unlike LoL, is available on all consoles and mobile devices. LoL is played on laptop and/or desktops only, and cannot be played on mobile devices or game consoles such Xbox. While both LoL and Fortnite are free to download and play, Fortnite is not only available across all devices but also is less difficult to play than LoL, making it especially attractive for beginning gamers.

Within the first few months of its launch, Fortnite brought in $1.5 billion in revenues. In its first complete year of existence (2018), Fortnite had $2.4 billion in revenues, while LoL's revenues declined (see Exhibit 3.7). This drop in revenue indicates that some gamers have moved on from LoL to Fortnite, the next big thing. In sum, while Riot Games created the new billion-dollar e-sports industry, competition never stands still. As such, Fortnite appears to be gaining a competitive advantage, while LoL may be losing its edge and appeal.[39]

3.4 Performance Differences within the Same Industry: Strategic Groups

LO 3-8

Generate a strategic group model to reveal performance differences between clusters of firms in the same industry.

In further analyzing the firm's external environment to explain performance differences, we now move to firms *within the same industry.* As noted earlier in the chapter, a firm occupies a place within a **strategic group**, a set of companies that pursue a similar strategy within a specific industry in their quest for competitive advantage (see Exhibit 3.1).[40] Strategic groups differ from one another along important dimensions such as expenditures on research and development, technology, product differentiation, product and service offerings, market segments, distribution channels, and customer service.

To explain differences in firm performance within the same industry, the **strategic group model** clusters different firms into groups based on a few key strategic dimensions.[41] Even within the same industry, firm performances differ depending on strategic group membership. Some strategic groups tend to be more profitable than others. This difference implies that firm performance is determined not only by the industry to which the firm belongs, but also by its strategic group membership.

The distinct differences across strategic groups reflect the business strategies that firms pursue. Firms in the same strategic group tend to follow a similar strategy. Companies in the same strategic group, therefore, are direct competitors. The rivalry among firms *within* the same strategic group is generally more intense than the rivalry *among* strategic groups: *Intra-group rivalry exceeds inter-group rivalry.* The number of different business strategies pursued within an industry determines the number of strategic groups in that industry. In most industries, strategic groups can be identified along a fairly small number of dimensions. In many instances, two strategic groups are in an industry based on two different business strategies: one that pursues a low-cost strategy and a second that pursues a differentiation strategy (see Exhibit 3.8). We'll discuss each of these generic business strategies in detail in Chapter 6.

strategic group The set of companies that pursue a similar strategy within a specific industry.

strategic group model A framework that explains differences in firm performance within the same industry.

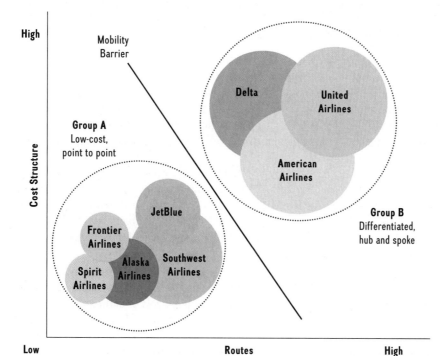

EXHIBIT 3.8

Strategic Groups and Mobility Barrier in U.S. Domestic Airline Industry

THE STRATEGIC GROUP MODEL

To understand competitive behavior and performance within an industry, we can map the industry competitors into strategic groups. We do this by

- Identifying the most important strategic dimensions such as expenditures on research and development, technology, product differentiation, product and service offerings, cost structure, market segments, distribution channels, and customer service. These dimensions are strategic commitments based on managerial actions that are costly and difficult to reverse.

- Choosing two key dimensions for the horizontal and vertical axes, which expose important differences among the competitors.

- Graphing the firms in the strategic group, indicating each firm's market share by the size of the bubble with which it is represented.[42]

The U.S. domestic airline industry provides an illustrative example. Exhibit 3.8 maps companies active in this industry. The two strategic dimensions on the axes are cost structure and routes. As a result of this mapping, two strategic groups become apparent, as indicated by the dashed circles: Group A, low-cost, point-to-point airlines (Alaska Airlines, Frontier Airlines, JetBlue, Southwest Airlines, and Spirit Airlines), and Group B, differentiated airlines using a hub-and-spoke system (American, Delta, and United). The low-cost, point-to-point airlines are clustered in the lower-left corner because they tend to have a lower cost structure but generally serve fewer routes due to their point-to-point operating system.

The differentiated airlines in Group B, offering full services using a hub-and-spoke route system, comprise the so-called legacy carriers. They are clustered in the upper-right corner because of their generally higher cost structures. The legacy carriers usually offer many more routes than the point-to-point low-cost carriers, made possible by use of the hub-and-spoke system, and thus offer many different destinations. For example, Delta's main hub is in Atlanta, Georgia.[43] If you were to fly from Seattle, Washington, to Miami, Florida, you would likely stop to change planes in Delta's Atlanta hub on your way.

The strategic group mapping in Exhibit 3.8 provides additional insights:

- **Competitive rivalry is strongest between firms that are within the same strategic group.** The closer firms are on the strategic group map, the more directly and intensely they are in competition with one another. After a wave of mergers, the remaining mega-airlines—American, Delta, and United—are competing head-to-head, not only in the U.S. domestic market but also globally. They tend to monitor one another's strategic actions closely. While Delta faces secondary competition from low-cost carriers such as Southwest Airlines (SWA) on some domestic routes, its primary competitive rivals remain the other legacy carriers. This is because they compete more on providing seamless global services within their respective airline alliances (SkyTeam for Delta, Oneworld for American, and Star Alliance for United) than on low-cost airfares for particular city pairs in the United States. Nonetheless, when Delta is faced with direct competition from SWA on a particular domestic route (say from Atlanta to Chicago), both tend to offer similar low-cost fares.

- **The external environment affects strategic groups differently.** During times of economic downturn, for example, the low-cost airlines tend to take market share away from the legacy carriers. Moreover, given their generally higher cost structure, the legacy carriers are often unable to stay profitable during recessions, at least on domestic routes. This implies that external factors such as recessions or high oil prices favor the companies in the low-cost strategic group. On the other hand, given a number of governmental restrictions on international air travel, the few airlines that are able to compete globally usually make a tidy profit in this specific industry segment.

▪ **The five competitive forces affect strategic groups differently.** *Barriers to entry,* for example, are higher in the hub-and-spoke (differentiated) airline group than in the point-to-point (low-cost) airline group. Following deregulation, many airlines entered the industry, but all of these new players used the point-to-point system. Since hub-and-spoke airlines can offer worldwide service and are protected from foreign competition by regulation to some extent, they often face weaker *buyer power,* especially from business travelers. While the hub-and-spoke airlines compete head-on with the point-to-point airlines when they are flying the same or similar routes, the *threat of substitutes* is stronger for the point-to-point airlines. This is because they tend to be regionally focused and compete with the viable substitutes of car, train, or bus travel. The threat of *supplier power* tends to be stronger for the airlines in the point-to-point, low-cost strategic group because they are much smaller and thus have weaker negotiation power when acquiring new aircraft, for example. To get around this, these airlines frequently purchase used aircraft from legacy carriers. This brief application of the five forces model leads us to conclude that rivalry among existing competitors in the low-cost, point-to-point strategic group is likely to be more intense than within the differentiated, hub-and-spoke strategic group.

▪ **Some strategic groups are more profitable than others.** Historically, airlines clustered in the lower-left corner tend to be more profitable when considering the U.S. domestic market only. Why? Because they create similar, or even higher, value for their customers in terms of on-time departure and arrival, safety, and fewer bags lost, while keeping their cost structure well below those of the legacy carriers. The point-to-point airlines have generally lower costs than the legacy carriers because they are faster in turning their airplanes around, keep them flying longer, use fewer and older airplane models, focus on high-yield city pairs, and tie pay to company performance, among many other activities that all support their low-cost business model. The point-to-point airlines, therefore, are able to offer their services at a lower cost and a higher perceived value, resulting in more pricing options, and thus creating the basis for a competitive advantage.

MOBILITY BARRIERS

Although some strategic groups tend to be more profitable and therefore more attractive than others, **mobility barriers** restrict movement between groups. These are industry-specific factors that separate one strategic group from another.[44] The dimensions to determine a strategic group are mobility barriers, which are strategic commitments. These are actions that are costly and not easily reversed such as the firm's underlying cost structure because it is based on managerial commitments resulting in hard-to-reverse investments.

mobility barriers
Industry-specific factors that separate one strategic group from another.

The two groups identified in Exhibit 3.8 are separated by the fact that offering international routes necessitates the hub-and-spoke model. Frequently, the international routes tend to be the remaining profitable routes left for the legacy carriers; albeit the Persian Gulf region carriers, in particular Emirates, Etihad Airways, and Qatar Airways, are beginning to threaten this profit sanctuary.[45]

This economic reality implies that if carriers in the lower-left cluster wanted to compete globally, they would likely need to change their point-to-point operating model to a hub-and-spoke model. Or they could select a few profitable international routes and service them with long-range aircrafts such as Boeing 787s or Airbus A-380s. Adding international service to the low-cost model, however, would require managerial commitments resulting in significant capital investments and a likely departure from a well-functioning business model. Additional regulatory hurdles reinforce these mobility barriers, such as the difficulty of securing landing slots at international airports around the world.

Despite using its point-to-point operating system, SWA experienced these and many other challenges when it began offering international flights to selected resort destinations such as Aruba, Cabo San Lucas, Cancun, the Bahamas, and Jamaica: changes to its reservation system, securing passports for crew members, cultural-awareness training, learning instructions in foreign languages, and performing drills in swimming pools on how to evacuate passengers onto life rafts. All of these additional requirements result in a somewhat higher cost for SWA in servicing international routes.[46]

3.5 Implications for Strategic Leaders

At the start of the strategic management process, it is critical for strategic leaders to conduct a thorough analysis of the firm's external environment to identify threats and opportunities. The initial step is to apply a PESTEL analysis to scan, monitor, and evaluate changes and trends in the firm's macroenvironment. This versatile framework allows strategic leaders to track important trends and developments based on the *source* of the external factors: political, economic, sociocultural, technological, ecological, and legal. When applying a PESTEL analysis, the guiding consideration for strategic leaders should be the question of how the external factors identified affect the firm's industry environment.

Exhibit 3.1 delineates external factors based on the *proximity* of these external factors by gradually moving from the general to the task environment. The next layer for strategic leaders to understand is the industry. Applying Porter's five forces model allows strategic leaders to understand the profit potential of an industry and to obtain clues on how to carve out a strategic position that makes gaining and sustaining a competitive advantage more likely. Follow these steps to apply the five forces model:[47]

1. **Define the relevant industry.** In the five forces model, industry boundaries are drawn by identifying a group of incumbent companies that face more or less the same suppliers and buyers. This group of competitors is likely to be an industry if it also has the same entry barriers and a similar threat from substitutes. In this model, therefore, an industry is defined by commonality and overlap in the five competitive forces that shape competition.

2. **Identify the key players in each of the five forces and attempt to group them into different categories.** This step aids in assessing the relative strength of each force. For example, while makers of jet engines (GE, Rolls-Royce, Pratt & Whitney) and local catering services are all suppliers to airlines, their strengths vary widely. Segmenting different players within each force allows you to assess each force at a fine-grained level.

3. **Determine the underlying drivers of each force.** Which forces are strong, and which are weak? And why? Keeping with the airline example, why is the supplier power of jet engine manufacturers strong? Because they are supplying a mission-critical, highly differentiated product for airlines. Moreover, there are only a few suppliers of jet engines worldwide and no viable substitutes.

4. **Assess the overall industry structure.** What is the industry's profit potential? Here you need to identify forces that directly influence industry profit potential, because not all forces are likely to have an equal effect. Focus on the most important forces that drive industry profitability.

The final step in industry analysis is to draw a strategic group map. This exercise allows you to unearth and explain *performance differences within the same industry*. When analyzing a firm's external environment, it is critical to apply the three frameworks introduced in this chapter (PESTEL, Porter's five forces, and strategic group mapping). Taken together, the external environment can determine up to roughly one-half of the performance differences across firms (see Exhibit 3.2).

Although the different models discussed in this chapter are an important step in the strategic management process, they are not without shortcomings. First, all the models presented are *static*. They provide a snapshot of what is actually a moving target and do not allow for consideration of industry dynamics. However, changes in the external environment can appear suddenly, for example, through black swan events. Industries can be revolutionized by innovation. Strategic groups can be made obsolete through deregulation or technological progress. To overcome this important shortcoming, strategic leaders must conduct external analyses at different points in time to gain a sense of the underlying *dynamics*. The frequency with which these tools need to be applied is a function of the rate of change in the industry. The mobile app industry is changing extremely fast, while the railroad industry experiences a less volatile environment.

Second, the models presented in this chapter do not allow strategic leaders to fully understand *why* there are performance differences among firms in the *same* industry or strategic group. To better understand differences in firm performance, we must look *inside the firm* to study its resources, capabilities, and core competencies. We do this in the next chapter by moving from external to internal analysis.

CHAPTERCASE 3 Part II

EVEN THOUGH AIRBNB IS, at $31 billion, one of the most valuable private startups in the world and offers more accommodations than the three largest hotel chains (Marriott, Hilton, and Intercontinental) combined, not all is smooth sailing. In particular, PESTEL factors discussed in this chapter are creating major headwinds for Airbnb. Take regulation, for example.

In 2016, New York state strengthened legislation first passed in 2010 that makes it illegal to rent out entire apartments in residential blocks in New York City for less than 30 days. It remains legal if the renter is living in the apartment at the same time, so "true space sharing" is still possible. Fines start at $1,000 for the first offense and rise to $7,500 for repeat offenders. Paris, Berlin, and Barcelona face similar problems and have passed laws with even stiffer penalties, fining offenders up to $100,000. This legislation creates major problems for Airbnb because New York City is by far its largest market, with more than 50,000 accommodations available for rent. In 2018, the city of New York went a step further and sued residential brokerage firms (as well as some of their employees) for allegedly using Airbnb in an illegal apartment rental scheme that earned them an estimated $20 million.

The issue for Airbnb is that about one-third of its listings in major metropolitan areas such as New York City are from hosts with multiple offerings in the same city. Commercial landlords realized quickly that it is more profitable to convert some apartments into short-term rentals and to offer them via Airbnb than to sign long-term rentals with just one tenant, which often fall under some form of rent control. Although this tactic increases the landlord's return on investment and profits, it creates all kinds of negative externalities. Neighbors complain about noisy tourists partying all night. Some apartments get ransacked or are used for illegal activities such as drug deals and prostitution. New Yorkers expressed their frustration by scrawling on Airbnb posters: "The dumbest person in your building is passing out keys to your front door!"[48]

Hotel chains and resort owners have challenged Airbnb in courts and lobbied local governments to pass regulations to limit or prohibit short-term rentals—some of which already have. Residents in New York City, San Francisco, Berlin, Paris, and many other cities have joined this lobby, arguing that companies like Airbnb contribute to a shortage of affordable housing because they turn entire apartment complexes into hotels and quiet family neighborhoods into daily, all-night party venues. Airbnb is also being criticized for accelerating gentrification in some cities.[49]

1. How was an internet startup able to disrupt the hotel industry, long dominated by giants such as Marriott and Hilton, which took decades to become successful worldwide hospitality chains? Explain.

2. Why is it that PESTEL factors can have such a strong impact on the future of a business? Do you support legislation such as that passed in New York (and elsewhere), or do you think it has more to do with protecting vested interests such as the hotel industry?

3. Citing the Digital Millennium Copyright Act (DMCA), Airbnb is challenging the New York law and others in the United States, arguing that it merely operates a digital marketplace, and thus is not responsible for the content that users place on its site. Do you think Airbnb has a strong argument? Why or why not?

4. Are you concerned that the concept of the sharing economy could be abused by unscrupulous "entrepreneurs" and thus give the entire novel concept a bad reputation? Why or why not? Explain.

mySTRATEGY

Is My New Job Going to Be Around in the Next 10 Years?

When we think about starting a new job, say, as we finish up a college degree, traditionally it is advisable to check out the relevant industry trends first. For instance, raises and promotion opportunities tend to be more abundant in industries that are growing rather than retracting. Overall, professional pay scales are better in industries with higher profit margins (such as financial services and pharmaceuticals) than lower profits (such as retailing). Today though, other technological, global, and environmental factors should be considered. We can see examples of ride-hailing firms upending the taxi and rental car industries and online retailing diminishing brick and mortar stores, but what do these changes portend for the employment market? A full-time taxi driver used to be a pathway to the middle class in the United States and many other countries. Now these jobs are being replaced by "gig economy" workers, who often have it as a second or third job to try to make ends meet.

Autonomous driving could have significant impacts on employment options across the entire transportation sector.

However, far more wide-reaching is the still-developing role of artificial intelligence (AI) on business, governments, and the economy as a whole. There are widely ranging viewpoints on how the inevitable increase of AI will impact the national and global labor markets in the coming years. Thus, there are technological uncertainties for this generation that while not unique, will likely have major effects on employment paths moving forward.

1. Many people approach the job market by thinking about particular firms. What are some advantages of broadening this thought process to consider the industry-level factors of a potential new employer?

2. What industries do you think may offer the best U.S. (or domestic) job opportunities in the future? Which industries do you think may offer the greatest job opportunities in the global market in the future? Use the PESTEL framework and the five forces model to think through a logical set of reasons that some fields will have higher job growth trends than others.

3. Do these types of macroenvironmental and industry trends affect your thinking about selecting a career field after college? Why or why not? Explain.

TAKE-AWAY CONCEPTS

This chapter demonstrated various approaches to analyzing the firm's *external environment,* as summarized by the following learning objectives and related take-away concepts.

LO 3-1 / Generate a PESTEL analysis to evaluate the impact of external factors on the firm.

- A firm's macroenvironment consists of a wide range of political, economic, sociocultural, technological, ecological, and legal (PESTEL) factors that can affect industry and firm performance. These external factors have both domestic and global aspects.
- Political factors describe the influence governmental bodies can have on firms.
- Economic factors to be considered are growth rates, interest rates, levels of employment, price stability (inflation and deflation), and currency exchange rates.
- Sociocultural factors capture a society's cultures, norms, and values.
- Technological factors capture the application of knowledge to create new processes and products.
- Ecological factors concern a firm's regard for environmental issues such as the natural environment, global warming, and sustainable economic growth.
- Legal factors capture the official outcomes of the political processes that manifest themselves in laws, mandates, regulations, and court decisions.

LO 3-2 / Differentiate the roles of firm effects and industry effects in determining firm performance.

- A firm's performance is more closely related to its managers' actions (firm effects) than to the external circumstances surrounding it (industry effects).
- Firm and industry effects, however, are interdependent. Both are relevant in determining firm performance.

LO 3-3 / Apply Porter's five competitive forces to explain the profit potential of different industries.

- The profit potential of an industry is a function of the five forces that shape competition: (1) threat of entry, (2) power of suppliers, (3) power of buyers, (4) threat of substitutes, and (5) rivalry among existing competitors.
- The stronger a competitive force, the greater the threat it represents. The weaker the competitive force, the greater the opportunity it presents.
- A firm can shape an industry's structure in its favor through its strategy.

LO 3-4 / Examine how competitive industry structure shapes rivalry among competitors.

- The competitive structure of an industry is largely captured by the number and size of competitors in an industry, whether the firms possess some degree of pricing power, the type of product or service the industry offers (commodity or differentiated product), and the height of entry barriers.
- A perfectly competitive industry is characterized by many small firms, a commodity product, low entry barriers, and no pricing power for individual firms.
- A monopolistic industry is characterized by many firms, a differentiated product, medium entry barriers, and some pricing power.
- An oligopolistic industry is characterized by few (large) firms, a differentiated product, high entry barriers, and some degree of pricing power.
- A monopoly exists when there is only one (large) firm supplying the market. In such instances, the firm may offer a unique product, the barriers to entry may be high, and the monopolist usually has considerable pricing power.

LO 3-5 / Describe the strategic role of complements in creating positive-sum co-opetition.

- Co-opetition (cooperation among competitors) can create a positive-sum game, resulting in a larger pie for everyone involved.
- Complements increase demand for the primary product, enhancing the profit potential for the industry and the firm.
- Attractive industries for co-opetition are characterized by high entry barriers, low exit barriers, low buyer and supplier power, a low threat of substitutes, and the availability of complements.

LO 3-6 / **Explain the five choices required for market entry.**

- The more profitable an industry, the more attractive it becomes to competitors, who must consider the *who*, *when*, *how*, *what*, and *where* of entry.

- The five choices constitute more than parts of a single decision point; their consideration forms a strategic process unfolding over time. Each choice involves multiple decisions including many dimensions.

- *Who* includes questions about the full range of stakeholders, and not just competitors; *when*, questions about the industry life cycle; *how*, about overcoming barriers to entry; *what*, about options among product market, value chain, geography, and business model; and *where*, about product positioning, pricing strategy, and potential partners.

LO 3-7 / **Appraise the role of industry dynamics and industry convergence in shaping the firm's external environment.**

- Industries are dynamic—they change over time.

- Different conditions prevail in different industries, directly affecting the firms competing in these industries and their profitability.

- In industry convergence, formerly unrelated industries begin to satisfy the same customer need. Such convergence is often brought on by technological advances.

LO 3-8 / **Generate a strategic group model to reveal performance differences between clusters of firms in the same industry.**

- A strategic group is a set of firms within a specific industry that pursue a similar strategy in their quest for competitive advantage.

- Generally, there are two strategic groups in an industry based on two different business strategies: one that pursues a low-cost strategy and a second that pursues a differentiation strategy.

- Rivalry among firms of the same strategic group is more intense than the rivalry between strategic groups: intra-group rivalry exceeds inter-group rivalry.

- Strategic groups are affected differently by the external environment and the five competitive forces.

- Some strategic groups are more profitable than others.

- Movement between strategic groups is restricted by mobility barriers—industry-specific factors that separate one strategic group from another.

KEY TERMS

Competitive industry
   structure *(p. 90)*
Complement *(p. 99)*
Complementor *(p. 99)*
Co-opetition *(p. 99)*
Entry barriers *(p. 84)*
Exit barriers *(p. 94)*
Firm effects *(p. 81)*

Five forces model *(p. 82)*
Industry *(p. 81)*
Industry analysis *(p. 82)*
Industry convergence *(p. 102)*
Industry effects *(p. 81)*
Mobility barriers *(p. 107)*
Network effects *(p. 85)*
Nonmarket strategy *(p. 76)*

PESTEL model *(p. 75)*
Strategic commitments *(p. 94)*
Strategic group *(p. 105)*
Strategic group model *(p. 105)*
Strategic position *(p. 82)*
Threat of entry *(p. 84)*

DISCUSSION QUESTIONS

1. Why is it important for any organization (firms, nonprofits, etc.) to study and understand its external environment?

2. How do the five competitive forces in Porter's model affect the average profitability of an industry? For example, in what way might weak forces

increase industry profits, and in what way do strong forces reduce industry profits? Identify an industry in which many of the competitors seem to be having financial performance problems. Which of the five forces seems to be strongest?

3. This chapter covers the choices firms make in entering new markets. Reflect on ChapterCase 3 and

discuss how Airbnb might have answered these questions in Exhibit 3.6.

4. How do mobility barriers affect the structure of an industry? How do they help us explain differences in firm performance?

ENDNOTES

1. As quoted in Parker, G.G., M.W. Van Alstyne, S.P. Choudary (2016), *Platform Revolution: How Networked Markets Are Transforming the Economy—And How to Make Them Work for You* (New York: Norton).

2. This ChapterCase is based on: "All eyes on the sharing economy," *The Economist* (2013, Mar. 9); "New York deflates Airbnb," *The Economist* (2016, Oct. 27); Austin, S., C. Canipe, and S. Slobin (2015, Feb. 18), "The billion dollar startup club," *The Wall Street Journal* (updated January 2017), http://graphics.wsj.com/billion-dollar-club/; Parker, G.G., M.W. Van Alstyne, S.P. Choudary (2016), *Platform Revolution: How Networked Markets Are Transforming the Economy—And How to Make Them Work for You* (New York: Norton); Pressler, J. (2014, Sept. 23), "The dumbest person in your building is passing out keys to your front door!" *New York*; Stone, B. (2017), *The Upstarts: How Uber, Airbnb, and the Killer Companies of the New Silicon Valley Are Changing the World* (New York: Little, Brown and Co.); Tabarrok, A. (2017, Jan. 30), "How Uber and Airbnb won," *The Wall Street Journal*. "Interview with Brian Chesky, co-founder and CEO Airbnb." (34:24 min) Code 2018. Recode, www.youtube.com/watch?v=nc90n-6dQRo&t=673s.

3. For a detailed treatise on how institutions shape the economic climate and with it firm performance, see: North, D.C. (1990), *Institutions, Institutional Change, and Economic Performance* (New York: Random House).

4. De Figueireo, R.J.P., and G. Edwards (2007), "Does private money buy public policy? Campaign contributions and regulatory outcomes in telecommunications," *Journal of Economics & Management Strategy* 16: 547–576; and Hillman, A.J., G. D. Keim, and D. Schuler (2004), "Corporate political activity: A review and research agenda," *Journal of Management* 30: 837–857.

5. Lowenstein, R. (2010), *The End of Wall Street* (New York: Penguin Press).

6. Brynjolfsson, E., and A. McAfee (2014), *The Second Machine Age: Work, Progress, and Prosperity in a Time of Brilliant Technologies* (New York: Norton).

7. "Professor Emeritus Milton Friedman dies at 94," University of Chicago press release (2006, Nov. 16).

8. Lucas, R. (1972), "Expectations and the neutrality of money," *Journal of Economic Theory* 4: 103–124.

9. U.S. Census Bureau (2017, Jul. 1), "Population estimates," www.census.gov/quickfacts/fact/table/US/PST045217; "Media companies are piling into the Hispanic market. But will it pay off?" *The Economist* (2012, Dec. 15).

10. Woolley, J.L., and R. M. Rottner (2008), "Innovation policy and nanotech entrepreneurship," *Entrepreneurship Theory and Practice* 32: 791–811; and Rothaermel, F.T., and M. Thursby (2007), "The nanotech vs. the biotech revolution: Sources of incumbent productivity in research," *Research Policy* 36: 832–849.

11. See for example: Brynjolfsson, E., and A. McAfee (2014). *The Second Machine Age: Work, Progress, and Prosperity in a Time of Brilliant Technologies* (New York: W. W. Norton & Co.); and McAfee, A., and E. Brynjolfsson (2017). *Machine, Platform, Crowd: Harnessing Our Digital Future* 1st ed., Kindle edition (New York: W. W. Norton & Co.).

12. Afuah, A. (2009), *Strategic Innovation: New Game Strategies for Competitive Advantage* (New York: Routledge); Hill, C.W.L., and F.T. Rothaermel (2003), "The performance of incumbent firms in the face of radical technological innovation," *Academy of Management Review* 28: 257–274; and Bettis, R., and M.A. Hitt (1995), "The new competitive landscape," *Strategic Management Journal* 16 (Special Issue): 7–19.

13. For an in-depth discussion of technological changes in the media industry, see: Rothaermel, F.T., and A. Guenther (2018),

Netflix, Inc., case study MH0043, http://create.mheducation.com; and Sandomirjune, R. (1991, Jun. 9), "Entrepreneurs: Wayne Huizenga's growth complex," *The New York Times Magazine*; "Blockbuster files for bankruptcy," *The Economist* (2010, Sept. 23); Gandel, S. (2010, Oct. 17), "How Blockbuster failed at failing," *Time*; Satel, G. (2014, Sept. 5), "A look back at why Blockbuster really failed and why it didn't have to," *Forbes*; Schmidt, S. (2017, Apr. 26), "Blockbuster has survived in the most curious of places—Alaska," *The Washington Post*.

14. Academy of Management, ONE Division, 2013 domain statement; Anderson, R.C. (2009), *Confessions of a Radical Industrialist: Profits, People, Purpose—Doing Business by Respecting the Earth* (New York: St. Martin's Press); and Esty, D.C., and A.S. Winston (2009), *Green to Gold: How Smart Companies Use Environmental Strategy to Innovate, Create Value, and Build Competitive Advantage,* revised and updated (Hoboken, NJ: John Wiley & Sons).

15. This interesting debate unfolds in the following articles, among others: Misangyi, V.F., H. Elms, T. Greckhamer, and J.A. Lepine (2006), "A new perspective on a fundamental debate: A multilevel approach to industry, corporate, and business unit effects," *Strategic Management Journal* 27: 571–590; Hawawini, G., V. Subramanian, and P. Verdin (2003), "Is performance driven by industry- or firm-specific factors? A new look at the evidence," *Strategic Management Journal* 24: 1–16; McGahan, A.M., and M.E. Porter (1997), "How much does industry matter, really?" *Strategic Management Journal* 18: 15–30; Rumelt, R.P. (1991), "How much does industry matter?" *Strategic Management Journal* 12: 167–185; and Hansen, G.S., and B. Wernerfelt (1989), "Determinants of firm performance: The relative importance of economic and organizational factors," *Strategic Management Journal* 10: 399–411.

16. The discussion in this section is based on: Magretta, J. (2012), *Understanding Michael Porter: The Essential Guide to Competition and Strategy* (Boston: Harvard Business Review Press); Porter, M.E. (2008, January), "The five competitive forces that shape strategy," *Harvard Business Review*; Porter, M.E. (1980), *Competitive Strategy: Techniques for Analyzing Industries and Competitors* (New York: Free Press); and Porter, M.E. (1979, March–April), "How competitive forces shape strategy," *Harvard Business Review*: 137–145.

17. Hull, D. (2014, Jul. 22), "Tesla idles Fremont production line for Model X upgrade," *San Jose Mercury News*; and Vance, A. (2013, Jul. 18), "Why everybody loves Tesla," *Bloomberg Businessweek*.

18. Ramsey, M. (2014, Sept. 3), "Tesla to choose Nevada for battery factory," *The Wall Street Journal*.

19. Ramsey, M. (2014, Feb. 26), "Tesla plans $5 billion battery factory," *The Wall Street Journal*.

20. Walsh, T. (2014, Sept. 2), "The cult of Tesla Motors Inc: Why this automaker has the most loyal customers," *The Motley Fool*.

21. "Tesla Model S road test," *Consumer Reports*, www.consumerreports.org/cro/tesla/model-s/road-test.htm.

22. Wang, U. (2013, Nov. 5), "Tesla considers building the world's biggest lithium-ion battery factory," *Forbes*.

23. Whether a product is a substitute (complement) can be estimated by the cross-elasticity of demand. The cross-elasticity estimates the percentage change in the quantity demanded of good X resulting from a 1 percent change in the price of good Y. If the cross-elasticity of demand is greater (less) than zero, the products are substitutes (complements). For a detailed discussion, see: Allen, W.B., K. Weigelt, N. Doherty, and E. Mansfield (2009), *Managerial Economics Theory, Application, and Cases,* 7th ed. (New York: Norton).

24. This example, as with some others in the section on the five forces, is drawn from: Magretta, J. (2012), *Understanding Michael Porter: The Essential Guide to Competition and Strategy* (Boston: Harvard Business Review Press).

25. Because the threat of entry is one of the five forces explicitly recognized in Porter's model, we discuss barriers to entry when introducing the threat of entry above. The competitive industry structure framework is frequently referred to as the structure-conduct-performance (SCP) model. For a detailed discussion, see: Allen, W.B., K. Weigelt, N. Doherty, and E. Mansfield (2009), *Managerial Economics Theory,*

Application, and Cases, 7th ed. (New York: Norton); Carlton, D.W., and J.M. Perloff (2000), *Modern Industrial Organization,* 3rd ed. (Reading, MA: Addison-Wesley); Scherer, F.M., and D. Ross (1990), *Industrial Market Structure and Economic Performance,* 3rd ed. (Boston: Houghton Mifflin); and Bain, J.S. (1968), *Industrial Organization* (New York: John Wiley & Sons).

26. Besanko, D., E. Dranove, M. Hanley, and S. Schaefer (2010), *The Economics of Strategy,* 5th ed. (Hoboken, NJ: John Wiley & Sons).

27. Dixit, A., S. Skeath, and D.H. Reiley (2009), *Games of Strategy,* 3rd ed. (New York: Norton).

28. When there are only two main competitors, it's called a *duopoly* and is a special case of oligopoly.

29. Yoffie, D.B., and R. Kim (2011, June), "Coca-Cola in 2011: In Search of a New Model," Harvard Business School Case 711-504 (revised August 2012). See also: Yoffie, D.B., and Y. Wang (2002, January), "Cola Wars Continue: Coke and Pepsi in the Twenty-First Century," Harvard Business School Case 702-442 (revised January 2004, et seq).

30. "Trustbusting in the internet age: Should digital monopolies be broken up?" *The Economist* (2014, Nov. 29); and "Internet monopolies: Everybody wants to rule the world," *The Economist* (2014, Nov. 29).

31. See: Chang, S-J., and B. Wu (2013), "Institutional barriers and industry dynamics," *Strategic Management Journal* 35: 1103–1123. Discussion of this new and insightful research offers an opportunity to link the PESTEL analysis to the five forces analysis. The study focuses on the competitive interaction between incumbents and new entrants as a driver of industry evolution. It investigates the impact of institutional characteristics (political, legal, and sociocultural norms in PESTEL analysis) unique to China on productivity and exit hazards of incumbents versus new entrants. China's environment created a divergence between productivity and survival that shaped industry evolution. It also offers an illustration of the role that liability of newness plays in new entrant survival.

32. This example is drawn from: Porter, M.E. (2008), "The five competitive forces that shape strategy," *An Interview with Michael E. Porter: The Five Competitive Forces that Shape Strategy,* Harvard BusinessPublishing video; "Everyone else in the travel business makes money off airlines," *The Economist* (2012, Aug. 25); "How airline ticket prices fell 50% in 30 years (and nobody noticed)," *The Atlantic* (2013, Feb. 28); U.S. gallon of jet fuel prices; author's interviews with Delta Air Lines executives.

33. Wall, R. (2019, Feb. 14), "Airbus to retire the A380, the superjumbo that never quite took off," *The Wall Street Journal*.

34. Brandenburger, A.M., and B. Nalebuff (1996), *Co-opetition* (New York: Currency Doubleday); and Grove, A.S. (1999), *Only the Paranoid Survive* (New York: Time Warner).

35. Milgrom, P., and J. Roberts (1995), "Complementarities and fit strategy, structure, and organizational change in manufacturing," *Journal of Accounting and Economics* 19, no. 2-3: 179–208; and Brandenburger, A.M., and B. Nalebuff (1996), *Co-opetition* (New York: Currency Doubleday).

36. In this recent treatise, Porter also highlights positive-sum competition. See: Porter, M.E. (2008, January), "The five competitive forces that shape strategy," *Harvard Business Review*.

37. This discussion is based on: Zachary, M.A., P.T. Gianiodis, G. Tyge Payne, and G.D. Markman (2014), "Entry timing: Enduring lessons and future directions," *Journal of Management* 41: 1388–1415; and Bryce, D.J., and J.H. Dyer (2007, May), "Strategies to crack well-guarded markets," *Harvard Business Review*: 84-92. I also gratefully acknowledge the additional input received by Professors Zachary, Gianiodis, Tyge Payne, and Markman.

38. "Reading between the lines," *The Economist* (2009, Mar. 26); and "New York Times is near web charges," *The Wall Street Journal* (2010, Jan. 19).

39. Based on: Chokshi, N. (2018, Aug. 27), "What you might not know about e-sports, soon to be a $1 billion industry," *The New York Times*; Grey, A. (2018, July 3), "The explosive growth of eSports," *World Economic Forum*; Fisher, S.D. (2014, January/February), "The rise of eSports: League of Legends article series," white paper, Foster Pepper PLLC; Segal, D. (2014, Oct. 10), "Behind League of Legends, e-sports' main attraction," *The New York Times*; and data drawn from statista.com and "How much money does League of Legends make?" www.youtube.com/watch?v=1ug-YKLwkaA.

40. Porter, M.E. (1980), *Competitive Strategy: Techniques for Analyzing Industries and Competitors* (New York: Free Press); Hatten, K.J., and D.E. Schendel (1977), "Heterogeneity within an industry: Firm conduct in the U.S. brewing industry," *Journal of Industrial Economics* 26: 97–113; and Hunt, M.S. (1972), *Competition in the Major Home Appliance Industry, 1960-1970,* unpublished doctoral dissertation, Harvard University.

41. This discussion is based on: McNamara, G., D.L. Deephouse, and R. Luce (2003),

"Competitive positioning within and across a strategic group structure: The performance of core, secondary, and solitary firms," *Strategic Management Journal* 24: 161–181; Nair, A., and S. Kotha (2001), "Does group membership matter? Evidence from the Japanese steel industry," *Strategic Management Journal* 22: 221–235; Cool, K., and D. Schendel (1988), "Performance differences among strategic group members," *Strategic Management Journal* 9: 207–223; Hunt, M.S. (1972), *Competition in the Major Home Appliance Industry, 1960–1970,* unpublished doctoral dissertation, Harvard University; Hatten, K.J., and D.E. Schendel (1977), "Heterogeneity within an industry: Firm conduct in the U.S. brewing industry," *Journal of Industrial Economics* 26: 97–113; and Porter, M.E. (1980), *Competitive Strategy: Techniques for Analyzing Industries and Competitors* (New York: Free Press), 102.

42. In Exhibit 3.8, United Airlines is the biggest bubble because it merged with Continental in 2010, creating the largest airline in the United States. Delta is the second-biggest airline in the United States after merging with Northwest Airlines in 2008.

43. American's hub is at Dallas-Fort Worth; Continental's is at Newark, New Jersey; United's is at Chicago; and U.S. Airways' is at Charlotte, North Carolina.

44. Caves, R.E., and M.E. Porter (1977), "From entry barriers to mobility barriers," *Quarterly Journal of Economics* 91: 241–262.

45. Carey, S. (2015, Mar. 16.), "U.S. airlines battling gulf carriers cite others' experience," *The Wall Street Journal.*

46. Carey, S. (2014, Oct. 14), "Steep learning curve for Southwest Airlines as it flies overseas," *The Wall Street Journal.*

47. Porter, M.E. (2008, January), "The five competitive forces that shape strategy," *Harvard Business Review;* and Magretta, J. (2012), *Understanding Michael Porter: The Essential Guide to Competition and Strategy* (Boston: Harvard Business Review Press): 56–57.

48. Pressler, J. (2014, Sept. 23), "The dumbest person in your building is passing out keys to your front door!" *New York Magazine.*

49. Greenberg, Z. (2018, Jul. 18), "New York City looks to crack down on Airbnb amid housing crisis," *The New York Times;* and Barbanel, J. (2018, Nov. 11), "New York City raids condo building in crackdown on Airbnb rentals," *The Wall Street Journal.*

Internal Analysis: Resources, Capabilities, and Core Competencies

Chapter Outline

Learning Objectives

After studying this chapter, you should be able to:

LO 4-1 Explain how shifting from an external to internal analysis of a firm can reveal why and how internal firm differences are the root of competitive advantage.

LO 4-2 Differentiate among a firm's core competencies, resources, capabilities, and activities.

LO 4-3 Compare and contrast tangible and intangible resources.

LO 4-4 Evaluate the two critical assumptions about the nature of resources in the resource-based view.

LO 4-5 Apply the VRIO framework to assess the competitive implications of a firm's resources.

LO 4-6 Evaluate different conditions that allow a firm to sustain a competitive advantage.

LO 4-7 Outline how dynamic capabilities can enable a firm to sustain a competitive advantage.

LO 4-8 Apply a value chain analysis to understand which of the firm's activities in the process of transforming inputs into outputs generate differentiation and which drive costs.

LO 4-9 Identify competitive advantage as residing in a network of distinct activities.

LO 4-10 Conduct a SWOT analysis to generate insights from external and internal analysis and derive strategic implications.

Five Guys' Core Competency: "Make the Best Burger, Don't Worry about Cost"

JERRY MURRELL, the founder of Five Guys Burgers and Fries, grew up in northern Michigan. He attended a Catholic high school and did so poorly academically that one of the nuns told him, "If you don't study, you'll be flipping burgers."[1] Little did she know that this prophecy would become reality. Today, Five Guys claims the title of the fastest-growing restaurant chain in the United States, with some 1,500 locations worldwide and revenues of $2 billion. And Jerry Murrell's personal net worth is hundreds of millions of dollars. How did this come about?

In the 1980s, while looking for entrepreneurial opportunities in the Washington, D.C., area, Jerry Murrell was selling insurance. During his leisure time, he and his family would often visit nearby Ocean City, Maryland, where the boardwalk was filled with fast food vendors—many of them selling fries—but only one always had a long line in front of it: Thrashers. One day while reading the text on the potato bags, Murrell noticed the potatoes came from Rick Miles in Rigby, Idaho. The Thrashers encounter brought back memories of Push 'Em Up Tony, a hamburger stand in Murrell's Michigan hometown. Although it offered only hamburgers, people from all over town would drive to Tony's for burgers. Murrell has always loved burgers and fries, so, while observing Thrashers in action and recalling good times at Push 'Em Up Tony, he came up with an idea: Open a stand that offers only hamburgers *and* fries. Keep it simple—this might work.

Murrell excitedly shared his idea with his wife, Janie, but she was not impressed and told him he'd be better off keeping his day job. Her reaction left him undeterred. He went on to seek funding from banks for his new venture, but they all thought he was crazy for wanting to go up against such multinational fast food giants as McDonald's and Burger King. Still determined and with one last option to explore, Murrell asked his two older sons, who were both in high school at the time, whether they wanted to go to college. Both boys said they'd rather do something else. With that, Murrell took their college fund and used it to open the first Five Guys store in Arlington, Virginia, in 1986.

Murrell named the hamburger joint after himself and his four sons at the time (a fifth son would arrive later). From the get-go, they opted not to put a lot of money into the business, to find a place out of the way where the rent was low, and to focus on making the best burgers and fries. They reasoned that if people started buying their product and *kept* buying it, then they would know that their burgers and fries were good. They also decided not to spend any money on marketing, figuring that their customers would be their best salespeople. To their surprise, their little hole-in-the-wall offering takeout-only burgers and fries became instantly popular and profitable.

For the next few years, Five Guys focused on the nuts and bolts of the hamburger business. They obsessed about every detail: store layout and design, the quality of the buns and never-frozen beef, how to fry the potatoes and from where they should be sourced (they eventually settled on Rick Miles in Idaho, the Thrashers supplier). Murrell even had his sons conduct a blind taste test of 16 varieties of mayonnaise to find the perfect one. The winner was the most expensive brand, which was supplied by only one vendor who was notorious for being difficult to deal with, but they went with it, taking to heart their father's instructions: "Make the best burger. Don't worry about cost."

Five Guys burgers are made to order and can be customized with 15 fresh toppings, including grilled mushrooms, green peppers, and jalapenos, all of which can be added at no extra charge. The focus on making the best burgers and fries has resulted in a higher cost structure than that of the fast-casual restaurant segment, which includes Shake Shack and Smashburger. Additionally, Five Guys prices are based on actual ingredient costs plus margin; therefore, the prices are not only several times more than what you would pay for a fast food burger, but they also fluctuate based on the cost of inputs. Not once, however, did the Murrells worry about jeopardizing the quality of their product to keep prices low or even consistent—not even when, in 2005, a hurricane destroyed most of the tomato crop in Florida, causing prices for this ingredient to increase almost threefold.

It took the Murrells 17 years to perfect their recipe for success. During that time, they had only five stores in the Washington, D.C., area, all owned and operated by the family. Despite Jerry Murrell's strong opposition, his boys convinced him to start franchising. He was partly persuaded to

EXHIBIT 4.1   Five Guys' Growth in Number of Stores, 1986–2019

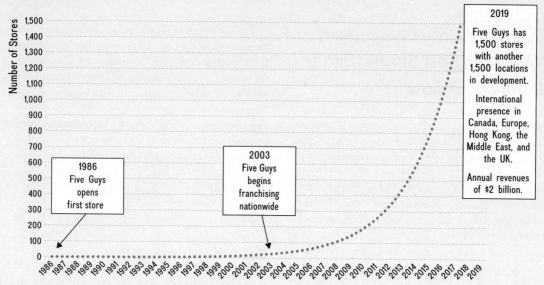

Source: Author's depiction of publicly available data (fitted trend line).

do so after reading *Franchising for Dummies* by Wendy's founder Dave Thomas.

As Exhibit 4.1 shows, by 2003, Five Guys was ready for prime time. Within just 18 months, all regional franchises in the United States were sold out. By 2010, Five Guys started moving beyond the United States, first to Canada and then to the United Kingdom in 2013. During 2015–2018, Five Guys' international expansion picked up speed with store openings in France, Ireland, Kuwait, United Arab Emirates, Saudi Arabia, and Spain. Within the next five years, Five Guys is planning to expand into 20 more countries.

While Jerry and Janie Murrell are now retired, their five sons and now also their grandchildren are involved in leadership positions in the company. Despite now being a global, multibillion-dollar enterprise, Five Guys is still owned and operated by the Murrell family. And the nun who taught Jerry in high school was right: He ended up flipping burgers for the rest of his life.[2]

Part II of this ChapterCase appears in Section 4.6.

ONE OF THE KEY messages of this chapter is that a firm's ability to gain and sustain competitive advantage is partly driven by *core competencies*—unique strengths that are embedded deep within a firm. Core competencies allow a firm to differentiate its products and services from those of its rivals, creating higher value for the customer or offering products and services of comparable value at lower cost.

How was Five Guys so successful in a highly competitive industry dominated by fast food giants like McDonald's and Burger King, as well as direct competitors claiming to be "better burger" joints such as Smashburger, BurgerFi, and Shake Shack? By some estimates, Five Guys captured 50 percent of the market share in the "better burger" segment in the 2010s.[3] How did Five Guys achieve a cult-like following despite having higher menu prices and longer wait times? In short, how did Five Guys gain and sustain a competitive advantage in this highly competitive industry? The answer to all these questions is found in Five Guys' core competency: delivering a customized, made-to-order burger and hand-cut fries using only the highest-quality ingredients available.

To gain a better understanding of why and how differences *within* firms are at the root of competitive advantage, we begin this chapter by shifting the focus from an outward-looking external analysis to an inward-looking internal analysis of the firm. Next, we closely examine a firm's *core competencies.* We then introduce the *resource-based view* of the firm to provide an analytical model that allows us to assess resources, capabilities, and competencies and their potential for creating a sustainable competitive advantage. Subsequently, we discuss the *dynamic capabilities perspective,* a model that emphasizes a firm's ability to modify and leverage its resource base to gain and sustain a competitive advantage in a constantly changing environment. We then turn our attention to the *value chain analysis* to gain a deeper understanding of the internal activities a firm engages in when transforming inputs into outputs. Next, we take a closer look at *strategic activity systems.* Here, a firm's competitive advantages resides in a network of interconnected and reinforcing activities. We conclude with *Implications for Strategic Leaders,* with a particular focus on how to use a *SWOT analysis* to obtain strategic insights from combining external with internal analysis.

4.1 From External to Internal Analysis

LO 4-1

Explain how shifting from an external to internal analysis of a firm can reveal why and how internal firm differences are the root of competitive advantage.

In this chapter, we study analytical tools to explain why differences in firm performance exist even within the *same* industry. For example, why does Five Guys outperform McDonald's, Burger King, In-N-Out Burger, Smashburger, and others in the (hamburger) restaurant industry? Since these companies compete in the same industry and face similar external opportunities and threats, the source for some of the observable performance difference must be found *inside the firm.* In Chapter 3, when discussing industry, firm, and other effects in the context of superior performance, we noted that up to 55 percent of the overall performance differences is explained by firm-specific effects (see Exhibit 3.2). Therefore, looking *inside* the firm to analyze its resources, capabilities, and core competencies allows us to understand the firm's strengths and weaknesses. Linking these insights from a firm's internal analysis to the ones from an external analysis allows managers to determine their strategic options. Ideally, strategic leaders want to leverage their firms' internal strengths to exploit external opportunities, and to mitigate internal weaknesses and external threats.

Exhibit 4.2 depicts how and why we move from the firm's external environment to its internal environment. To formulate and implement a strategy that enhances the firm's chances of gaining and sustaining competitive advantage, the firm must have certain types of resources and capabilities that combine to form core competencies. The best firms conscientiously identify their core competencies, resources, and capabilities to survive and succeed. Firms then determine how to manage and develop internal strengths to respond to the challenges and opportunities in their external environment. In particular, firms conduct the evaluation and development of internal strengths in the context of external PESTEL forces and competition within its industry through application of the five forces model and the strategic group map (see Chapter 3).

The firm's response must be dynamic. Rather than creating a onetime and thus a static fit, the firm's internal strengths need to change with its external environment in a *dynamic* fashion. At each point the goal should be to develop resources, capabilities, and competencies that create a *strategic fit* with the firm's environment. The forward motion and overall

EXHIBIT 4.2

Inside the Firm:
Competitive
Advantage based on
Core Competencies,
Resources, and
Capabilities

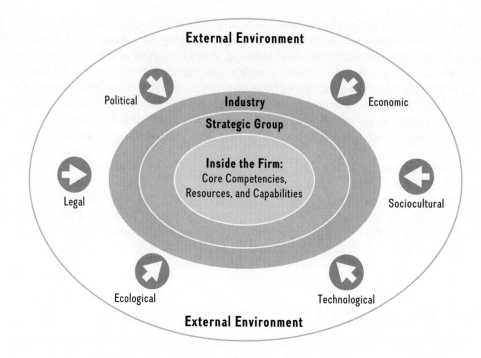

EXHIBIT 4.2

Inside the Firm: Competitive Advantage based on Core Competencies, Resources, and Capabilities

trends of those environmental forces must also be considered. The rest of this chapter will provide a deeper understanding of the *sources* of competitive advantage that reside within a firm.

4.2 Core Competencies

Products and services make up the *visible* side of competition. But residing deep within the firm lies a diverse set of *invisible* elements around which companies also compete; these are the core competencies. **Core competencies** are unique strengths embedded deep within a firm (see Exhibit 4.2). Core competencies allow a firm to differentiate its products and services from those of its rivals, creating higher value for the customer or offering products and services of comparable value at lower cost. Core competencies find their expression in the structures, processes, and routines that strategic leaders put in place. The important point here is that competitive advantage is frequently the result of a firm's core competencies.[4]

Take Five Guys, featured in the ChapterCase, as an example of a company with a clearly defined core competency: A superior ability to deliver fresh, customized hamburgers as well as hand-cut fries using only the highest quality ingredients. By doing things differently than rivals, Five Guys was able to build and hone its core competency over a long period. Strategy is as much about deciding to do things *differently* from rivals, as it is about deciding *not* to do certain things at all. From the start, Five Guys was clear and consistent about what it would do and what it would *not* do.

What did Five Guys decide to do? Five Guys sources only the highest quality ingredients, including fresh, never frozen ground beef for its burgers; freshly baked buns from local bakeries; potatoes from Idaho; tomatoes from Florida; and so forth. Five Guys further differentiates itself from its competitors by offering a wide range of free toppings from classics like ketchup and lettuce to specialties like grilled mushrooms, jalapenos, and green peppers. Some of Five Guys' ingredients cost four times the amount that other chains pay. Its fries are hand-cut from potatoes grown in Idaho north of the 42nd parallel and cooked in pure peanut oil. Five Guys keeps its store designs simple, functional, and consistent: Its iconic red and white tiles are often seen in shopping malls, where many of its stores are located.

What did Five Guys decide NOT to do? It would *not,* for instance, bloat its menu and offer up to 125 items, as McDonald's did over the years. Instead, it kept its menu simple: burgers, fries, and hot dogs. This simplicity allowed each Five Guys team to deliver on its core competency: custom, made-to-order, high-quality burgers for each of its patrons. In fact, it took Five Guys almost *30* years before deciding to add milkshakes to its menu. This new and popular item is available with free mix-in flavors such classic chocolate, vanilla, strawberry, and Oreo, as well as flavors unique to Five Guys such as bacon.

Five Guys does *not* have drive-throughs. Because its food, unlike fast food, is made to order, drive-through wait times would be too long. It does *not* offer food delivery, regardless of who asks for it—not even when an admiral from the Pentagon requested a special lunch delivery for 25 people. Jerry Murrell declined politely. The next day Five Guys hung up a 22-foot-long banner that read "ABSOLUTELY NO DELIVERY." Business from the Pentagon picked up after that. Even former President Barack Obama has been seen waiting in line. As part of its heritage as a takeout only place, Five Guys does not encourage its patrons to linger; for instance, it does *not* offer free WiFi and while the seating is functional, it isn't really that comfortable. Five Guys' focus is to get the customer in and out in an expedient and efficient manner to increase throughput especially during peak lunch hours.

Five Guys also does *not* spend any money on marketing. Murrell believes that happy customers are the best salespeople for the company as they will share their experience with their friends. This word-of-mouth publicity is even more potent now with the prevalence of social media. Over the years local press has provided free publicity as well, showering Five Guys with hundreds of glowing reviews. Many of these reviews can be found framed and hanging on the bathroom walls of its stores. Much of its early fame can also be attributed to Zagat, one of the most important restaurant guides in the United States.

These multiple and varied activities, when combined, reinforce Five Guys' core competency, which enables the hamburger joint to differentiate its product offerings, to create higher perceived value for its customers, and to command premium prices for its products. It is important to note that before expanding geographically, the Murrells spent nearly two decades within just their five northern Virginia stores perfecting the core competency. The initial stores were staffed and operated by family members. But once they started to franchise, Five Guys needed to maintain delivery of the core competency—this time to multiple stores across the United States. Five Guys was able to replicate its unique structure, processes, and routines, including its diverse set of strategic activities, which included a supply chain that sourced only fresh, quality ingredients. Considering that core competencies and their underlying knowledge often do not travel easily across geographic distances, this was no small feat.[5]

Thus, as much as competition is about products and services, it is also about developing, nurturing, honing, and leveraging core competencies. For a closer look of the core competency of Beats by Dr. Dre, see Strategy Highlight 4.1.

Strategy Highlight **4.1**

Dr. Dre's Core Competency: Coolness Factor

In 2014, Andre Young—aka Dr. Dre—was celebrated as the first hip-hop billionaire after Apple acquired Beats Electronics for $3 billion. Dr. Dre has a long track record as a successful music producer, rapper, and entrepreneur. Known for his strong work ethic, he expects nothing less than perfection from the people he works with—similar to some of the personality attributes ascribed to the late Steve Jobs, co-founder and longtime CEO of Apple.

Although Dr. Dre created and subsequently sold several successful music record labels, as an entrepreneur, he is best known as co-founder of Beats Electronics with Jimmy Iovine, also an entrepreneur and record and film producer. Both are considered to be some of the best-connected businesspeople in the music industry, with personal networks spanning hundreds and comprising both famous and up-and-coming artists.

Founded in 2008, Beats Electronics is known globally for its premium consumer headphones, Beats by Dr. Dre, which Dr. Dre claims allows the listeners to hear all the music.[6] Since early 2014, the company has been offering Beats Music, a streaming music subscription service. With this product and service, Beats strives to "bring the energy, emotion, and excitement of playback in the recording studio to the listening experience and introduce an entirely new generation to the possibilities of premium sound entertainment."[7] However, many acoustics experts maintain that playback of digitally compressed MP3 audio files is inferior to high fidelity. Also, the sound quality of Beats headphones is considered poor compared to that of other premium-brand headphones such as Bose, JBL, Sennheiser, and others.

Why then would Apple pay $3 billion to acquire Beats Electronics—its largest acquisition to date? Two main reasons: First, Apple hopes that some of Beats' coolness will spill over to its brand, which has become somewhat stale. The iPhone, for example, is now a standardized commodity given successful imitations by Samsung, Huawei, and Xiaomi. Second, although Apple is the world's largest music vendor boasting 800 million iTunes accounts, the music industry is being disrupted. Content delivery of music and video is shifting from ownership via downloads to streaming on demand (renting). As a consequence, music downloads have declined in the past few years.

BEATS' COOLNESS FACTOR   Beats by Dr. Dre achieved an unprecedented coolness factor with celebrity

Dr. Dre, left, and Jimmy Iovine are co-founders of Beats. Following Apple's acquisition of Beats, Dre and Iovine continue to work together to keep Beats relevant and tied to current artists. In 2018, Iovine left his role at Apple with day-to-day decision authority to work as a consultant to Apple. Kevin Mazur/WireImage/Getty Images.

endorsements not only from music icons but also athletes, actors, and other stars. Before Beats, no musician endorsed audio headphones in the same way as a basketball player such as Michael Jordan endorsed his line of Nike shoes, Air Jordan. Dr. Dre was the first legendary music producer to endorse premium headphones. In addition, he created custom Beats for stars such as Justin Bieber, Lady Gaga, and Nicki Minaj. Other music celebrities including Skrillex, Lil Wayne, and will.i.am endorsed Beats by wearing them in their music videos and at live events and mentioning them on social media. But Beats did not stop at musicians. Famous athletes—basketball superstars LeBron James and Kobe Bryant, tennis champion Serena Williams, and soccer stars Cristiano Ronaldo and Neymar Jr.—wear Beats by Dr. Dre in public and endorse the brand in advertisements.

DISRUPTION IN CONTENT DELIVERY   Online streaming is quickly replacing ownership through downloads. The shift from owning content to renting it on demand is disrupting the content delivery business. This disruption is most visible in movies, as the success of Netflix demonstrates, but is also gaining steam in music.

After disrupting the music download space with iTunes in 2003, Apple found its service being disrupted by leaders in the music streaming industry. Then, in 2013, it created iTunes Radio as an initial attempt at online music streaming. However, that attempt failed to meet with much success until Apple acquired Beats Music, which turned Apple into a dominant player again—this time in the music streaming space. By 2019, Apple Music had surpassed market leader Spotify in paid U.S. subscribers, but it trailed the Swedish rival globally. Coming on strong is Amazon with its Prime Music and Music Unlimited services. In the "coolness space," Apple faces a formidable rival in music streaming service Tidal, founded by rap mogul Jay-Z. Tidal has exclusive release contracts with superstar artists such as Kanye West, Rihanna, and Beyoncé (who is married to Jay-Z). Tidal, however, had only 4.2 million paid subscribers by the end of 2018.

In addition to new strategic initiatives in financial services and online gaming, Apple announced a further major push into the entertainment industry in 2019. The firm is now making its Apple TV app, which will carry original content, available on competitors' devices. Apple TV also will serve as a portal log-on where users can view content from Apple as well as from AT&T's HBO or CBS's Showtime. This strategic initiative marks a stark shift in Apple's focus on a closed ecosystem. With this strategic pivot, Apple is moving into the $100 billion entertainment industry and will compete head-on with other tech companies such as Amazon and Netflix, as well as old-line companies such as Comcast (part-owner of Hulu, a streaming service) and AT&T, which owns WarnerMedia (including HBO).[8]

For an overview of the core competencies of different companies with application examples, see Exhibit 4.3.

EXHIBIT 4.3   Company Examples of Core Competencies and Applications

Company	Core Competencies	Application Examples
Amazon	• Superior IT and AI capabilities. • Superior customer service. • Diversification across different industries. • Establishing an ecosystem, combining hardware with software around its Amazon Echo platform.	• Online retailing: Largest selection of items online. • Full vertical integration in retail, from warehouse to delivery. • Cloud computing: Largest provider through Amazon Web Services (AWS).
Apple	• Superior industrial design in integration of hardware and software. • Superior marketing and retailing experience. • Establishing and maintaining an ecosystem of products and services that reinforce one another in a virtuous fashion.	• Creation of innovative and category-defining mobile devices and software services that take the user's experience to a new level (e.g., iMac, iPod, iTunes, iPhone, iPad, Apple Watch, Apple TV, Apple Pay, and Apple Card).
Beats Electronics	• Superior marketing: creating a perception of coolness. • Establishing an ecosystem, combining hardware (headphones) with software (streaming service).	• Beats by Dr. Dre and Beats Music.
Coca-Cola Co.	• Superior marketing and distribution.	• Leveraging one of the world's most recognized brands (based on its original "secret formula") into a diverse lineup of soft drinks. • Global availability of products.
ExxonMobil	• Superior at discovering and exploring fossil-fuel–based energy sources globally.	• Focus on oil and gas (fossil fuels only, not renewables).
Facebook	• Superior IT and AI capabilities to provide reliable social network services globally on a large scale. • Superior algorithms to offer targeted online ads.	• Connecting over 2 billion social media users worldwide. • News feed, timeline, graph search, and stories.
Five Guys	• Superior ability to deliver fresh, customized hamburgers as well as hand-cut fries using the highest- quality ingredients.	• Hamburgers and fries.

(Continued)

Company	Core Competencies	Application Examples
Google (a subsidiary of Alphabet)	• Superior in creating proprietary algorithms based on large amounts of data collected online. • Superior AI capability.	• Software products and services for the internet and mobile computing, including some mobile devices (Pixel phone, Chromebook). • Online search, Android mobile operating system, Chrome OS, Chrome web browser, Google Play, AdWords, AdSense, Google docs, Gmail, etc.
IKEA	• Superior in designing modern functional home furnishings at low cost. • Superior retail experience.	• Fully furnished room setups, practical tools for all rooms, do-it-yourself.
McKinsey	• Superior in developing practice-relevant knowledge, insights, and frameworks in strategy.	• Management consulting; in particular, strategy consulting provided to company and government leaders.
Netflix	• Superior in creating proprietary algorithms-based individual customer preferences.	• DVD-by-mail rentals, streaming media (including proprietary) content, connection to game consoles.
Tesla	• Superior engineering expertise in designing high-performance battery-powered motors and power trains. • Superior ability to provide complementary assets. • Superior expertise in decentralized power storage and management based on renewable (solar) energy.	• Model S, Model X, Model 3, and Model Y. • Network of proprietary charging stations, spanning entire United States and most of the rest of the world. • Powerwall, solar roof tiles, and complete rooftop solar systems.
Uber	• Superior mobile-app–based transportation and logistics expertise focused on cities, but on global scale.	• Uber, UberX, UberBlack, UberLUX, UberSUV, etc.

RESOURCES AND CAPABILITIES

Because core competencies are critical to gaining and sustaining competitive advantage, it is important to understand how they are created. Companies develop core competencies through the interplay of resources and capabilities. Exhibit 4.4 shows this relationship. **Resources** are any assets such as cash, buildings, machinery, or intellectual property that a firm can draw on when crafting and executing a strategy. Resources can be either tangible or intangible. **Capabilities** are the organizational and managerial skills necessary to orchestrate a diverse set of resources and to deploy them strategically. Capabilities are by nature intangible. They find their expression in a company's structure, routines, and culture.

As shown in Exhibit 4.4, such competencies are demonstrated in the company's activities, which can lead to competitive advantage, resulting in superior firm performance. **Activities** are distinct and fine-grained business processes such as order taking, the physical delivery of products, or invoicing customers. Each distinct activity enables firms to add incremental value by transforming inputs into goods and services. In the interplay of resources and

---

resources Any assets that a firm can draw on when formulating and implementing a strategy.

capabilities Organizational and managerial skills necessary to orchestrate a diverse set of resources and deploy them strategically.

activities Distinct and fine-grained business processes that enable firms to add incremental value by transforming inputs into goods and services.

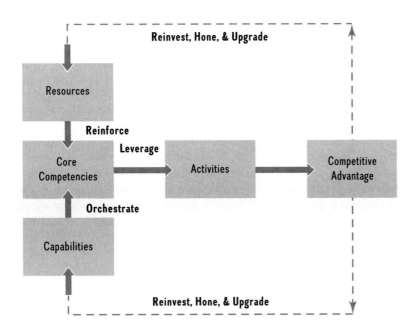

EXHIBIT 4.4

Linking Core
Competencies,
Resources,
Capabilities, and
Activities to
Competitive
Advantage

capabilities, resources reinforce core competencies, while capabilities allow managers to orchestrate their core competencies. Strategic choices find their expression in a set of specific firm activities, which leverage core competencies for competitive advantage. The arrows leading back from competitive advantage to resources and capabilities indicate that superior performance in the marketplace generates profits that to some extent need to be reinvested into the firm (retained earnings) to further hone and upgrade a firm's resources and capabilities in its pursuit of achieving and maintaining a strategic fit within a dynamic environment.

We should make two more observations about Exhibit 4.4 before moving on. First, core competencies that are not continuously nourished will eventually lose their ability to yield a competitive advantage. And second, in analyzing a company's success in the market, it can be too easy to focus on the more *visible* elements or facets of core competencies such as superior products or services. While these are the outward manifestations of core competencies, what is even more important is to understand the *invisible* part of core competencies.

As to the first point, let's consider the consumer electronics industry. For some years, Best Buy outperformed Circuit City based on its strengths in customer-centricity (segmenting customers based on demographic, attitudinal, and value tiers, and configuring stores to serve the needs of the customer segments in that region), employee development, and exclusive branding. Although Best Buy outperformed Circuit City (which filed for bankruptcy in 2009), more recently Best Buy did not hone and upgrade its core competencies sufficiently to compete effectively against Amazon, the world's largest online retailer. Amazon does not have the overhead expenses associated with maintaining buildings or human sales forces; therefore, it has a lower cost structure and thus can undercut in-store retailers on price. When a firm does not invest in continual upgrading or improving core competencies, its competitors are more likely to develop equivalent or superior skills, as Amazon did. This insight will allow us to explain differences between firms in the same industry, as well as competitive dynamics, over time. It will also help us to identify the strategy that firms use to both gain and sustain a competitive advantage, as well as to weather an adverse external environment.

As to the second point, we will soon introduce tools to clarify the more opaque aspects of a firm's core competencies. We start by looking at both tangible and intangible resources.

LO 4-3

Compare and contrast tangible and intangible resources.

4.3 The Resource-Based View

To gain a deeper understanding of how the interplay between resources and capabilities creates core competencies that drive firm activities leading to competitive advantage, we turn to the **resource-based view** of the firm. This model systematically aids in identifying core competencies.[9] As the name suggests, this model sees resources as key to superior firm performance. As Exhibit 4.5 illustrates, resources fall broadly into two categories: tangible and intangible. **Tangible resources** have physical attributes and are visible. Examples of tangible resources are labor, capital, land, buildings, plant, equipment, and supplies. **Intangible resources** have no physical attributes and thus are invisible. Examples of intangible resources are a firm's culture, its knowledge, brand equity, reputation, and intellectual property.

Consider Google (since 2015 a subsidiary of Alphabet, which is a holding company overseeing a diverse set of activities). Alphabet's tangible resources, valued at $59 billion, include its headquarters (The Googleplex)[10] in Mountain View, California, and numerous server farms (clusters of computer servers) across the globe.[11] The Google brand, an intangible resource, is valued at over $300 billion (number one worldwide)—almost seven times higher than the value of Alphabet's tangible assets.[12]

Google's headquarters exemplifies both tangible and intangible resources. The Googleplex is a piece of land on which sits a futuristic building, and thus a tangible resource. However, the *location* of the company in the heart of Silicon Valley is an *intangible* resource in that it provides the company with several benefits. One is access to a valuable network of contacts, which includes a large and computer-savvy work force, as well as graduates and knowledge spillovers from numerous nearby universities; all this adds to Google's technical and managerial capabilities.[13] Another benefit is Google's proximity to Silicon Valley, which contains the highest concentration of venture capital firms in the United States. Venture capitalists tend to prefer local investments because the more local they are, the closer they can be monitored. Thus, their proximity to Google can be viewed as a mutual benefit.[14] In fact, initial funding to Google came from the well-known venture capital firms Kleiner Perkins Caufield & Byers and Sequoia Capital, both located in Silicon Valley.

Competitive advantage is more likely to spring from intangible rather than tangible resources. Tangible assets, such as buildings or computer servers, can be bought on the open market by anyone who has the necessary cash. However, a brand name must be built, often over long periods of time. In fact, it took mainstay firms such

EXHIBIT 4.5 Tangible and Intangible Resources

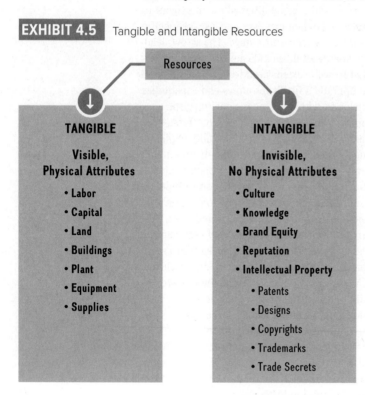

resource-based view A model that sees certain types of resources as key to superior firm performance.

tangible resources Resources that have physical attributes and thus are visible.

intangible resources Resources that do not have physical attributes and thus are invisible.

as Apple, Microsoft, Visa, McDonald's, and AT&T—five of the global top-10 most valuable brands—many years to build their value and to earn brand recognition in the marketplace. Yet, more recent companies such as Google (founded in 1998; brand value of over $300 billion), Amazon (founded in 1994; brand value of over $200 billion), Facebook (founded in 2004; brand value of over $160 billion), and the Chinese technology companies Tencent and Alibaba (founded in 1998 and 1999, respectively, each with brand values of over $110 billion) all accomplished their enormous brand valuations fairly quickly, largely due to their ubiquitous internet presence.[15]

Note that the resource-based view of the firm uses the term **resource** much more broadly than previously defined. In the resource-based view of the firm, a resource includes any assets as well as any capabilities and competencies that a firm can draw upon when formulating and implementing strategy. In addition, the usefulness of the resource-based view to explain and predict competitive advantage rests upon two critical assumptions about the nature of resources, to which we turn next.

RESOURCE HETEROGENEITY AND RESOURCE IMMOBILITY

The two assumptions critical to the resource-based model are: (1) *resource heterogeneity* and (2) *resource immobility*.[16] What does this mean? In the resource-based view, a firm is assumed to be a unique bundle of resources, capabilities, and competencies. The first critical assumption—**resource heterogeneity**—comes from the insight that bundles of resources, capabilities, and competencies differ across firms. This insight requires looking more critically at the resource bundles of firms competing in the *same* industry (or even the same strategic group), because each bundle is unique to some extent. For example, Southwest Airlines (SWA) and Alaska Airlines (AS) both compete in the same strategic group (low-cost, point-to-point airlines, see Exhibit 3.8). But they draw on different resource bundles. SWA's employee productivity tends to be higher than that of AS, because the two companies differ along human and organizational resources. At SWA, job descriptions are informal and employees pitch in to "get the job done." Pilots may help load luggage to ensure an on-time departure; flight attendants clean airplanes to help turn them around at the gate within 15 minutes from arrival to departure. This allows SWA to keep its planes flying for longer and lowers its cost structure, savings that SWA passes on to passengers in lower ticket prices.

The second critical assumption—**resource immobility**—describes the insight that resources tend to be "sticky" and don't move easily from firm to firm. Because of that stickiness, the resource differences that exist between firms are difficult to replicate and, therefore, can last for a long time. For example, SWA has enjoyed a sustained competitive advantage, allowing it to outperform its competitors over several decades. That resource difference is not due to a lack of imitation attempts, though. Continental and Delta both attempted to copy SWA, with Continental Lite and Song airline offerings, respectively. Neither airline, however, was able to successfully imitate the resource bundles and firm capabilities that make SWA unique. Combined, these insights tell us that resource bundles differ across firms, and such differences can persist for long periods. These two assumptions about resources are critical to explaining superior firm performance in the resource-based model.

Note, by the way, that the critical assumptions of the resource-based model are fundamentally different from the way in which a firm is viewed in the perfectly competitive industry structure introduced in Chapter 3. In perfect competition, all firms have access to the *same* resources and capabilities, ensuring that any advantage that one firm has will be short-lived. That is, when resources are freely available and mobile, competitors can move quickly to acquire resources that are utilized by the current market leader. Although some commodity markets approach this situation, most other markets include firms whose resource endowments

resource In the resource-based view of the firm, a resource includes any assets as well as any capabilities and competencies that a firm can draw upon when formulating and implementing strategy.

LO 4-4

Evaluate the two critical assumptions about the nature of resources in the resource-based view.

resource heterogeneity Assumption in the resource-based view that a firm is a bundle of resources and capabilities that differ across firms.

resource immobility Assumption in the resource-based view that a firm has resources that tend to be "sticky" and that do not move easily from firm to firm.

differ. The resource-based view, therefore, delivers useful insights to managers about how to formulate a strategy that will enhance the chances of gaining a competitive advantage.

THE VRIO FRAMEWORK

LO 4-5

Apply the VRIO framework to assess the competitive implications of a firm's resources.

One important tool for evaluating a firm's resource endowments is a framework that answers the question, *What resource attributes underpin competitive advantage?* This framework is implied in the resource-based model, identifying certain *types of resources* as key to superior firm performance.[17] For a resource to be the basis of a competitive advantage, it must be

Valuable,

Rare, and costly to

Imitate. And finally, the firm itself must be

Organized to capture the value of the resource.

VRIO framework
A theoretical framework that explains and predicts firm-level competitive advantage.

Following the lead of Jay Barney, one of the pioneers of the resource-based view of the firm, we call this model the **VRIO framework**.[18] According to this model, a firm can gain and sustain a competitive advantage only when it has resources that satisfy all of the VRIO criteria. Keep in mind that resources in the VRIO framework are broadly defined to include any assets *as well as* any capabilities and competencies that a firm can draw upon when formulating and implementing strategy. So to some degree, this presentation of the VRIO model summarizes all of our discussion in the chapter so far.

Exhibit 4.6 captures the VRIO framework in action. You can use this decision tree to decide if the resource, capability, or competency under consideration fulfills the VRIO requirements. As you study the following discussion of each of the VRIO attributes, you will see that the attributes accumulate. If the answer is "yes" four times to the attributes listed in the decision tree, only then is the resource in question a core competency that underpins a firm's sustainable competitive advantage.

valuable resource
One of the four key criteria in the VRIO framework. A resource is valuable if it helps a firm exploit an external opportunity or offset an external threat.

VALUABLE. A **valuable resource** is one that enables the firm to exploit an external opportunity or offset an external threat. This has a positive effect on a firm's competitive advantage. In particular, a valuable resource enables a firm to increase its economic value creation

EXHIBIT 4.6   Applying the VRIO Framework to Reveal Competitive Advantage

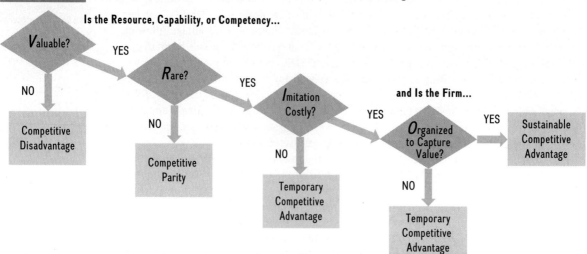

($V - C$). Revenues rise if a firm is able to increase the perceived value of its product or service in the eyes of consumers by offering superior design and adding attractive features (assuming costs are not increasing). Production costs, for example, fall if the firm is able to put an efficient manufacturing process and tight supply chain management in place (assuming perceived value is not decreasing).

Five Guys' superior ability to deliver fresh, customized hamburgers as well as hand-cut fries using the highest-quality ingredients is certainly valuable because it enables the firm to command a premium price due to its perceived higher value creation. Although Five Guys excels at driving up the perceived value of its offerings, it also needs to control costs to ensure that this valuable resource can lay the foundation for a competitive advantage.

RARE. A resource is **rare** if only one or a few firms possess it. If the resource is common, it will result in perfect competition where no firm is able to maintain a competitive advantage (see discussion in Chapter 3). A resource that is valuable but not rare can lead to competitive parity at best. A firm is on the path to competitive *advantage* only if it possesses a valuable resource that is also rare.

When Five Guys was founded in 1986, its superior ability to deliver made-to-order hamburgers from the freshest ingredients and hand-cut fries made from the best potatoes was certainly rare, as was its restaurant concept: It was neither a fast food place nor a traditional sit-down establishment. It offered a limited menu, no drive-through option, and a self-service format. This remains the case and Five Guys has managed to charge premium prices for its product—prices that are multiple times higher than that of its fast food competitors. Today, restaurant models like Five Guys are called fast-casual restaurants, a term that didn't come into the dining vernacular until the 2000s, despite well-known Five Guys' competitors such as Chipotle Mexican Grill (founded in 1993) coming onto the scene much earlier.

To further underscore that Five Guys was rare on multiple fronts is the fact that its more direct competitors (and imitators) in the "better burger" segment—Shake Shack (founded in 2004), Smashburger (founded in 2007), and Burger Fi (founded in 2011)—were not launched until much later. This head start gave Five Guys the ability to perfect its core competencies over a long period of time before it decided to franchise (see Exhibit 4.1). Moreover, because it was so early to the fast-casual dining market, Five Guys was able to enjoy a first-mover advantage, including locking up the best store locations and perhaps more importantly the best suppliers (e.g., Rick Miles of Rigby, Idaho, is Five Guys' sole supplier of potatoes).

COSTLY TO IMITATE. A resource is **costly to imitate** if firms that do not possess the resource are unable to develop or buy the resource at a reasonable price. If the resource in question is valuable, rare, and costly to imitate, then it is an internal strength and a core competency. If the firm's competitors fail to duplicate the strategy based on the valuable, rare, and costly-to-imitate resource, then the firm can achieve a temporary competitive advantage.

For more than 30 years now, Five Guys has delivered fresh, made-to-order premium burgers and fries. In doing so consistently, Five Guys enjoys a cult-like following by its customers. This led to its 50 percent market share in the "better burger" segment during the 2010s. In addition, Five Guys spent almost 20 years refining, honing, upgrading, and eventually perfecting its core competency before franchising nationally. This in turn enabled Five Guys to more easily duplicate its core competency in different geographic areas as it franchised throughout the United States and beyond.

Although it may appear to be a simple business model ("make the best burger"), it is by no means simplistic. Coordinating a multilayered supply chain of a fairly large number of high-quality, fresh ingredients is a complex undertaking. For example, making sure there are no foodborne illnesses requires strict adherence to established food-handling protocols and

rare resource One of the four key criteria in the VRIO framework. A resource is rare if the number of firms that possess it is less than the number of firms it would require to reach a state of perfect competition.

costly-to-imitate resource One of the four key criteria in the VRIO framework. A resource is costly to imitate if firms that do not possess the resource are unable to develop or buy the resource at a comparable cost.

Tiffany & Co. has developed a core competency—elegant jewelry design and craftsmanship delivered through a superior customer experience—that is valuable, rare, and costly for competitors to imitate. The company vigorously protects its trademarks, including its Tiffany Blue Box, but it never trademarked the so-called Tiffany setting for diamond rings, used now by many jewelers. The term has been co-opted for advertising by other retailers (including Costco), which now maintain it is a generic term commonly used in the jewelry industry.
Lucas Oleniuk/Toronto Star/Getty Images

best practices in every one of its 1,500 stores. In addition, much of Five Guys' business was built around Jerry Murrell's gut feeling—something that cannot be imitated. In fact, Murrell himself cannot articulate the many "strategic hunches" he has had over the years.[19]

Unlike Five Guys, imitators such as Shake Shack, Smashburger, and Burger Fi franchised almost immediately after launching. The Five Guys' imitators moved so rapidly because of their relatively late entry in the market, and thus in their attempt to compete nationwide with Five Guys. In doing so, however, the imitators discovered that it is quite costly to imitate Five Guys' core competency. Moreover, given that most of these chains franchised more or less immediately, they were unable to perfect their competency before expanding. Taken together, the combination of the three resource attributes ($V + R + I$) has allowed Five Guys to enjoy a competitive advantage (see Exhibit 4.6).

Direct Imitation. A firm that enjoys a competitive advantage, however, attracts significant attention from its competitors. They will attempt to negate a firm's resource advantage by directly imitating the resource in question (*direct imitation*) or through working around it to provide a comparable product or service (*substitution*).

We usually see direct imitation, as a way to copy or imitate a valuable and rare resource, when firms have difficulty protecting their advantage. (We discuss barriers to imitation shortly.) Direct imitation can be swift if the firm is successful and intellectual property (IP) protection such as patents or trademarks, for example, can be easily circumvented.

Crocs, the maker of the iconic plastic clog, fell victim to direct imitation. Launched in 2002 as a spa shoe at the Fort Lauderdale, Florida, boat show, Crocs experienced explosive growth, selling millions of pairs each year and reaching over $650 million in revenue in 2008. Crocs are worn by people in every age group and across all walks of life, including internet entrepreneur and Google co-founder Sergey Brin, celebrities such as Matt Damon, Heidi Klum, Adam Sandler, and even the Duchess of Cambridge Kate Middleton. To protect its unique shoe design, the firm owns several patents. Given Crocs' explosive growth, however, numerous cheap imitators have sprung up to copy the colorful and comfortable plastic clog. Despite the patents and celebrity endorsements, other firms were able to copy the shoe, taking a big bite into Crocs' profits. Indeed, Crocs' share price plunged from a high of almost $75 to less than $1 in just 13 months.[20]

This example illustrates that competitive advantage cannot be sustained if the underlying capability can easily be replicated and can thus be *directly imitated.* Competitors simply created molds to imitate the shape, look, and feel of the original Crocs shoe. Any competitive advantage in a fashion-driven industry, moreover, is notoriously short-lived if the company fails to continuously innovate or build such brand recognition that imitators won't gain a foothold in the market. Crocs was more or less a "one-trick pony."

The ChapterCase notes that Five Guys' imitators in the "better burger" segment were all founded only after Five Guys started to franchise in 2003. Not only did Five Guys have an almost 20-year lead in perfecting its core competency, but also within 18 months of starting to franchise it sold out of U.S. territory, and its franchisees had locked up most of the best locations. Given the timing of Five Guys' competitors' entry, the success of Five Guys clued them in that the fast-casual burger segment is highly profitable, and thus they set out on a direct imitation attempt. First-mover advantages in combination with a perfected core competency, however, allowed Five Guys to make such direct imitation attempts quite difficult, and thus to sustain its competitive advantage.

Substitution. The second avenue of imitation for a firm's valuable and rare resource is through *substitution.* This is often accomplished through *strategic equivalence.* Take the example of Jeff Bezos launching and developing Amazon.[21] Before Amazon's inception, the retail book industry was dominated by a few large chains and many independent bookstores. As the internet was emerging in the 1990s, Bezos was looking for options in online retail. He zeroed in on books because of their non-differentiated commodity nature and easiness to ship. In purchasing a printed book online, customers knew exactly what they would be shipped, because the products were identical, whether sold online or in a brick-and-mortar store. The only difference was the mode of transacting and delivery. Taking out the uncertainty of online retailing to some extent made potential customers more likely to try this new way of shopping.

The emergence of the internet allowed Bezos to come up with a new distribution system that negated the need for retail stores and thus high real estate costs. Bezos' new business model of ecommerce not only substituted for the traditional fragmented supply chain in book retailing, but also allowed Amazon to offer lower prices due to its lower operating costs. Amazon uses a strategic equivalent substitute to satisfy a customer need previously met by brick-and-mortar retail stores.

Combining Imitation and Substitution. In some instances, firms are able to combine direct imitation and substitution when attempting to mitigate the competitive advantage of a rival. With its Galaxy line of smartphones, Samsung has been able to imitate successfully the look and feel of Apple's iPhones. Samsung's Galaxy smartphones use Google's Android operating system and apps from Google Play as an alternative to Apple's iOS and iTunes Store. Samsung achieved this through a combination of *direct imitation* (look and feel) and *substitution* (using Google's mobile operating system and app store).[22]

More recently Amazon has opened a new chapter in its competitive moves by its acquisition of the brick-and-mortar Whole Foods in 2017. As we will see in ChapterCase 8, Amazon's entry into high-end groceries involves both imitation and substitution.

ORGANIZED TO CAPTURE VALUE. The final criterion of whether a rare, valuable, and costly-to-imitate resource can form the basis of a sustainable competitive advantage depends on the firm's internal structure. To fully exploit the competitive potential of its resources, capabilities, and competencies, a firm must be **organized to capture value**—that is, it must have in place an effective organizational structure and coordinating systems. (We will study organizational design in detail in Chapter 11.)

Before Apple or Microsoft had any significant share of the personal computer market, Xerox's Palo Alto Research Center (PARC) invented and developed an early word-processing application, the graphical user interface (GUI), the Ethernet, the mouse as a pointing device, and even the first personal computer. These technology breakthroughs laid the foundation of the desktop-computing industry.[23] Xerox's invention competency built through a unique combination of resources and capabilities was clearly valuable, rare, and costly to imitate with the potential to create a competitive advantage.

Due to a lack of appropriate organization, however, Xerox failed to appreciate and exploit the many breakthroughs made by PARC in computing software and hardware. Why? Because the innovations did not fit within the Xerox business focus at the time. Under pressure in its core business from Japanese low-cost competitors, Xerox's top management was busy pursuing innovations in the photocopier business. Xerox was not organized to appreciate the competitive potential of the valuable, rare, and inimitable resources generated at PARC, if not in the photocopier field. Such organizational problems were exacerbated by geography: Xerox headquarters is on the East Coast in Norwalk, Connecticut, across the country from PARC on the West Coast in Palo Alto, California.[24] Nor did it help that development engineers at Xerox headquarters had a disdain for the scientists engaging in basic research at PARC. In the meantime, both Apple and Microsoft developed operating systems, graphical user interfaces, and application software.

organized to capture value One of the four key criteria in the VRIO framework. The characteristic of having in place an effective organizational structure, processes, and systems to fully exploit the competitive potential of the firm's resources, capabilities, and competencies.

If a firm is not effectively organized to exploit the competitive potential of a valuable, rare, and costly-to-imitate (VRI) resource, the best-case scenario is a temporary competitive advantage (see Exhibit 4.6). In the case of Xerox, where management was not supportive of the resource, even a temporary competitive advantage would not be realized even though the resource meets the VRI requirements.

In summary, for a firm to gain and sustain a competitive advantage, its resources and capabilities need to interact in such a way as to create unique core competencies (see Exhibit 4.4). Ultimately, though, only a few competencies may turn out to be those *specific* core competencies that fulfill the VRIO requirements.[25] A company cannot do everything equally well and must carve out a unique strategic position for itself, making necessary trade-offs.[26] Strategy Highlight 4.2 demonstrates application of the VRIO framework.

LO 4-6

Evaluate different conditions that allow a firm to sustain a competitive advantage.

ISOLATING MECHANISMS: HOW TO SUSTAIN A COMPETITIVE ADVANTAGE

isolating mechanisms
Barriers to imitation that prevent rivals from competing away the advantage a firm may enjoy.

Although VRIO resources can lay the foundation of a competitive advantage, no competitive advantage can be sustained indefinitely.[27] Several conditions, however, can potentially protect a successful firm by making it more difficult for competitors to imitate the resources, capabilities, and competencies that underlie its competitive advantage. Those conditions include *barriers to imitation,* which are important examples of **isolating mechanisms** that prevent rivals from competing away the advantage a firm may enjoy. They include:[28]

- Better expectations of future resource value.
- Path dependence.
- Causal ambiguity.
- Social complexity.
- Intellectual property (IP) protection.

Each isolating mechanism is directly related to one of the criteria in the resource-based view used to assess the basis of competitive advantage: costly (or difficult) to imitate. If one, or any combination, of these isolating mechanisms is present, a firm may strengthen its basis for competitive advantage, increasing its chance to be sustainable over a longer period of time.

BETTER EXPECTATIONS OF FUTURE RESOURCE VALUE. Sometimes firms can acquire resources at a low cost. This acquisition can lay the foundation for a competitive advantage later, when expectations about the future of the resource turn out to be more accurate than those held by competitors. Better expectations of the future value of a resource allow a firm to gain a competitive advantage. If such better expectations can be systematically repeated over time, then it can help a firm develop a *sustainable* competitive advantage.

Let's see how the concept of better expectations of future resource value works in the case of Jane, a real-estate developer looking to purchase land. Jane must decide when and where to buy land for future development. If she buys a parcel of land for a low cost in an undeveloped rural area 40 miles north of San Antonio, Texas, her firm may gain a competitive advantage—if it anticipates the land will increase in value with shifting demographics. Now, let's assume, several years later, an interstate highway gets built near this land. With the highway, suburban growth explodes. New neighborhoods emerge and several new shopping malls are erected. Jane's firm is now able to further develop the property she purchased. It decides, for instance, to build high-end office and apartment buildings to accommodate the suburban growth. Thus, the value creation resulting from the purchase of the land ends up far exceeding its initial cost. This in turn allows Jane's firm to gain a competitive advantage over other real estate developers in the area.

Strategy Highlight **4.2**

Applying VRIO: The Rise and Fall of Groupon

After graduating with a degree in music from Northwestern University, Andrew Mason spent a couple of years as a web designer. In 2008, the then 27-year-old founded Groupon, a daily-deal website that connects local retailers and other merchants to consumers by offering goods and services at a discount. Groupon creates marketplaces by bringing the brick-and-mortar world of local commerce onto the internet. The company basically offers a "group-coupon." If more than a predetermined number of Groupon users sign up for the offer, the deal is extended to all Groupon users. For example, a local spa may offer a massage for $40 instead of the regular $80. If more than say 10 people sign up, the deal becomes reality. The users prepay $40 for the coupon, which Groupon splits 50-50 with the local merchant. Inspired by how Amazon has become the global leader in ecommerce, Mason's strategic vision for Groupon was *to be the global leader in local commerce.*

Measured by its explosive growth, Groupon became one of the most successful internet startups, with over 260 million subscribers and serving more than 500,000 merchants in the United States and some 50 countries. Indeed, Groupon's success attracted a $6 billion buyout offer by Google in early 2011, which Mason declined. In November 2011, Groupon held a successful initial public offering (IPO), valued at more than $16 billion with a share price of over $26. But a year later, Groupon's share price had fallen 90 percent to just $2.63, resulting in a market cap of less than $1.8 billion. In early 2013, Mason posted a letter for Groupon employees on the web, arguing that it would leak anyway, stating, "After four and a half intense and wonderful years as CEO of Groupon, I've decided that I'd like to spend more time with my family. Just kidding—I was fired today."

Although Groupon is still in business, it is just one competitor among many and not a market leader. What went wrong? The implosion of Groupon's market value can be explained using the VRIO framework. Its competency to drum up more business for local retailers by offering lower prices for its users was certainly *valuable.* Before Groupon, local merchants used online and classified ads, direct mail, yellow pages, and other venues to reach customers. Rather than using one-way communication,

Groupon facilitates the meeting of supply and demand in local markets. When Groupon launched, such local market-making competency was also *rare.* Groupon, with its first-mover advantage, seemed able to use technology in a way so valuable and rare it prompted Google's buyout offer. But was it costly to imitate? Not so much.

The multibillion-dollar Google offer spurred potential competitors to reproduce Groupon's business model. They discovered that Groupon was more of a sales company than a tech venture, despite perceptions to the contrary. To target and fine-tune its local deals, Groupon relies heavily on human labor to do the selling. Barriers to entry in this type of business are nonexistent because Groupon's competency is built more on a tangible resource (labor) than on an intangible one (proprietary technology). Given that Groupon's valuable and rare competency was *not hard to imitate,* hundreds of new ventures (so-called Groupon clones) rushed in to take advantage of this opportunity. Existing online giants such as Google, Amazon (via LivingSocial), and Facebook also moved in. The spurned Google almost immediately created its own daily-deal version with Google Offers.

Also, note that the ability to imitate a rare and valuable resource is directly linked to barriers of entry, which is one of the key elements in Porter's five forces model *(threat of new entrants).* This relationship allows linking internal analysis using the resource-based view to external analysis with the five forces model, which also would have predicted low industry profit potential given low or no barriers to entry.

To make matters worse, these Groupon clones are often able to better serve the needs of local markets and specific population groups. Some daily-deal sites focus only on a specific geographic area. As an example, Conejo Deals meets the needs of customers and retailers in Southern California's Conejo Valley, a cluster of suburban communities. These hyper-local sites tend to have much deeper relationships and expertise with merchants in their specific areas. Since they are mostly matching local customers with local businesses, moreover, they tend to foster more repeat business than the one-off bargain hunters that use Groupon (based in Chicago). In addition, some daily-deal sites often target specific groups. They have greater expertise in matching their users with local retailers (e.g., Daily Pride serving LGBT communities;

(Continued)

Black Biz Hookup serving African-American business owners and operators; Jdeal, a Jewish group-buying site in New York City; and so on).

"Finding your specific group" or "going hyper local" allows these startups to increase the perceived value added for their users over and above what Groupon can offer. Although Groupon aspires to be the *global leader,* there is really no advantage to global scale in serving local markets. This is because daily-deal sites are best suited to market *experience goods,* such as haircuts at a local barber shop or a meal in a specific Thai restaurant. The quality of these goods and services cannot be judged unless they are consumed. Creation of experience goods and their consumption happens in the *same geographic space.*

Once imitated, Groupon's competency to facilitate local commerce using an internet platform was neither valuable nor rare. As an application of the VRIO model would have predicted, Groupon's competitive advantage as a first mover would only be temporary at best (see Exhibit 4.6).[29]

Other developers could have purchased the precise parcel of land that Jane bought. But if they decided to do this only after construction of the highway was announced, then they would have had to pay a much higher price for this land (and the land adjacent to it). Why? Because in order to reflect the new reality of being located next to an interstate, the price of the land would have increased. In other words, the expectations of the future value of the land would have adjusted upwardly. This increase in the price of the land to reflect its future value, in turn, would have negated any potential for competitive advantage.

All these factors together led Jane to develop better expectations of the future value of the resource than her competitors did—in this case, the land she purchased. If Jane is able to repeat these better expectations over time in a more or less systematic fashion, then her firm will likely gain a sustainable competitive advantage. Otherwise, the decision to purchase this particular piece of land may just be considered a stroke of luck. Although luck can play a role in gaining an initial competitive advantage, it is not a basis for sustaining one.

path dependence
A situation in which the options one faces in the current situation are limited by decisions made in the past.

PATH DEPENDENCE. **Path dependence** describes a process in which the options one faces in a current situation are limited by decisions made in the past.[30] Often, early events—sometimes even random ones—have a significant effect on final outcomes.

The U.S. carpet industry provides an example of path dependence.[31] Roughly 85 percent of all carpets sold in the United States and almost one-half of all carpets sold worldwide come from carpet mills located within 65 miles of one city: Dalton, Georgia. While the U.S. manufacturing sector has suffered in recent decades, the carpet industry has flourished. Companies not clustered near Dalton face a disadvantage because they cannot readily access the required know-how, skilled labor, suppliers, low-cost infrastructure, and so on needed to be competitive.

But why Dalton? Two somewhat random events combined. First, the boom after World War II drew many manufacturers to the South to escape restrictions placed upon them in the North, such as higher taxation or the demands of unionized labor. Second, technological progress allowed industrial-scale production of tufted textiles to be used *as substitutes for the more expensive wool.* This innovation emerged in and near Dalton. This historical accident explains why today almost all U.S. carpet mills are located in a relatively small region, including world leaders Shaw Industries Group and Mohawk Industries.

Path dependence also rests on the notion that time cannot be compressed at will. While management can compress resources such as labor and R&D into a shorter period, the push will not be as effective as when a firm spreads out its effort and investments over a longer period. Trying to achieve the same outcome in less time, even with higher investments, tends to lead to inferior results, due to *time compression diseconomies.*[32]

Consider GM's problems in providing a competitive alternative to the highly successful Toyota Prius, a hybrid electric vehicle. Its problems highlight path dependence and time compression issues. The California Air Resource Board (CARB) in 1990 passed a mandate for introducing zero-emissions cars, which stipulated that 10 percent of new vehicles sold by carmakers in the state must have zero emissions by 2003. This mandate not only accelerated research in alternative energy sources for cars, but also led to the development of the first fully electric production car, GM's EV1. GM launched the car in California and Arizona in 1996. Competitive models followed, with the Toyota RAV EV and the Honda EV. In this case, regulations in the legal environment fostered innovation in the automobile industry (see the discussion of PESTEL forces in Chapter 3).

Companies not only feel the nudge of forces in their environment but can also push back. The California mandate on zero emissions, for example, did not stand.[33] Several stakeholders, including the car and oil companies, fought it through lawsuits and other actions. CARB ultimately gave in to the pressure and abandoned its zero-emissions mandate. When the mandate was revoked, GM recalled and destroyed its EV1 electric vehicles and terminated its electric-vehicle program. This decision turned out to be a strategic error that would haunt GM a decade or so later. Although GM was the leader among car companies in electric vehicles in the mid-1990s, it did not have a competitive model to counter the Toyota Prius when its sales took off in the early 2000s. The Chevy Volt (a plug-in hybrid), GM's first major competition to the Prius, was delayed by over a decade because GM had to start its electric-vehicle program basically from scratch. While GM sold about 50,000 Chevy Volts worldwide, Toyota sold some 10 million Prius cars. Moreover, when Nissan introduced its all-electric Leaf in 2010, GM did not have an all-electric vehicle in its lineup. In the meantime, Nissan sold over 400,000 Leafs worldwide.

Not having an adequate product lineup during the early 2000s, GM's U.S. market share dropped below 20 percent in 2009 (from over 50 percent a few decades earlier), the year it filed for bankruptcy. GM subsequently reorganized under Chapter 11 of the U.S. bankruptcy code, and relisted on the New York Stock Exchange in 2010.

Collaborating with LG Corp. of Korea, GM introduced the Chevy Bolt, an all-electric vehicle in 2017.[34] Although some of its features, such as a 230-mile range on a single charge, look attractive, it remains to be seen if the Chevy Bolt will do well in the marketplace. This is because competition did not stand still either. In the meantime, Tesla (featured in Chapter-Case 1) is hoping that its new Model 3 will take the mass market of electric cars by storm, as it is priced at $35,000, much lower than its luxury cars (Model S and Model X).

One important take-away here is that once the train of new capability development has left the station, it is hard to jump back on because of path dependence. Moreover, firms cannot compress time at will; indeed, learning and improvements must take place over time, and existing competencies must constantly be nourished and upgraded.

Strategic decisions generate long-term consequences due to path dependence and time-compression diseconomies; they are not easily reversible. A competitor cannot imitate or create core competencies quickly, nor can one buy a reputation for quality or innovation on the open market. These types of valuable, rare, and costly-to-imitate resources, capabilities, and competencies must be built and organized effectively over time, often through a painstaking process that frequently includes learning from failure.

CAUSAL AMBIGUITY. **Causal ambiguity** describes a situation in which the cause and effect of a phenomenon are not readily apparent. To formulate and implement a strategy that enhances a firm's chances of gaining and sustaining a competitive advantage, managers need to have a hypothesis or theory of how to compete. A hypothesis is simply a specific statement that proposes an explanation of a phenomenon (such as competitive advantage), while a theory is a more generalized explanation of what causes what, and why. This implies that managers need to have some kind of understanding about what causes superior or

causal ambiguity
A situation in which the cause and effect of a phenomenon are not readily apparent.

Marillyn Hewson is CEO of Lockheed Martin, a global player in aerospace, defense, security, and advanced technology. Facing ever more complex challenges, such firms only thrive with an effective organization and a highly skilled CEO like Hewson.
MANDEL NGAN/Contributor/Getty Images

social complexity A situation in which different social and business systems interact with one another.

intellectual property (IP) protection A critical intangible resource that can provide a strong isolating mechanism, and thus help to sustain a competitive advantage.

inferior performance, and why. Comprehending and explaining the underlying reasons of observed phenomena is far from trivial, however.

Everyone can see that Apple has had several hugely successful innovative products such as the iMac, iPod, iPhone, and iPad, combined with its hugely popular iTunes services, leading to a decade of a sustainable competitive advantage. These successes stem from Apple's set of *V, R, I,* and *O* core competencies that supports its ability to continue to offer a variety of innovative products and to create an ecosystem of products and services.

A deep understanding, however, of exactly *why* Apple has been so successful is very difficult. Even Apple's strategic leaders may not be able to clearly pinpoint the sources of their success. Is it the visionary role that the late Steve Jobs played? Is it the rare skills of Apple's uniquely talented design team around Jonathan Ive (who left Apple in 2019)? Is it the timing of the company's product introductions? Is it Apple CEO Tim Cook who adds superior organizational skills and puts all the pieces together when running the day-to-day operations? Or is it a combination of these factors? If the link between cause and effect is ambiguous for Apple's strategic leaders, it is that much more difficult for others seeking to copy a valuable resource, capability, or competency.

SOCIAL COMPLEXITY. **Social complexity** describes situations in which different social and business systems interact. There is frequently no causal ambiguity as to how the *individual* systems such as supply chain management or new product development work in isolation. They are often managed through standardized business processes such as Six Sigma or ISO 9000. Social complexity, however, emerges when two or more such systems are *combined.* Copying the emerging complex social systems is difficult for competitors because neither direct imitation nor substitution is a valid approach. The interactions between different systems create too many possible permutations for a system to be understood with any accuracy. The resulting social complexity makes copying these systems difficult, if not impossible, resulting in a valuable, rare, and costly-to-imitate resource that the firm is organized to exploit.

Look at it this way. A group of three people has three relationships, connecting every person directly with one another. Adding a fourth person to this group *doubles* the number of direct relationships to six. Introducing a fifth person increases the number of relationships to 10.[35] This gives you some idea of how complexity might increase when we combine different systems with many different parts.

In reality, firms may manage thousands of employees from all walks of life. Their interactions within the firm's processes, procedures, and norms make up its culture. Although an observer may conclude that Zappos' culture, with its focus on autonomous teams in a flat hierarchy to provide superior customer service, might be the basis for its competitive advantage, engaging in reverse social engineering to crack Zappos' code of success might be much more difficult. Moreover, an organizational culture that works for online retailer Zappos, led by CEO and chief happiness officer Tony Hsieh, might wreak havoc for an aerospace and defense company such as Lockheed Martin, led by CEO Marillyn Hewson. This implies that one must understand competitive advantage within its organizational and industry context. Looking at individual elements of success without taking social complexity into account is a recipe for inferior performance, or worse.

INTELLECTUAL PROPERTY PROTECTION. **Intellectual property (IP) protection** is a critical intangible resource that can also help sustain a competitive advantage. The five major forms of IP protection are[36]

- Patents
- Designs

- Copyrights
- Trademarks
- Trade secrets

The intent of IP protection is to prevent others from copying legally protected products or services. In many knowledge-intensive industries that are characterized by high research and development (R&D) costs, such as smartphones and pharmaceuticals, IP protection provides not only an incentive to make these risky and often large-scale investments in the first place, but also affords a strong isolating mechanism that is critical to a firm's ability to capture the returns to investment. Although the initial investment to create the first version of a new product or service is quite high in many knowledge-intensive industries, the *marginal cost* (i.e., the cost to produce the next unit) after initial invention is quite low.

For example, Microsoft spends billions of dollars to develop a new version of its Windows operating system; once completed, the cost of the next "copy" is close to zero because it is just software code distributed online in digital form. In a similar fashion, the costs of developing a new prescription drug, a process often taking more than a decade, are estimated to be over $2.5 billion.[37] Rewards to IP-protected products or services, however, can be high. During a little over 14 years on the market, Pfizer's Lipitor, the world's best-selling drug, accumulated over $125 billion in sales.[38]

IP protection can make direct imitation attempts difficult, if not outright illegal. A U.S. court, for example, has found that Samsung infringed in some of its older models on Apple's patents and awarded some $600 million in damages.[39] In a similar fashion, Dr. Dre (featured in Strategy Highlight 4.1) attracted significant attention and support from other artists in the music industry when he sued Napster, an early online music file-sharing service, and helped shut it down in 2001 because of copyright infringements.

IP protection does not last forever, however. Once the protection has expired, the invention can be used by others. Patents, for example, usually expire 20 years after they are filed with the U.S. Patent and Trademark Office. In the next few years, patents protecting roughly $100 billion in sales of proprietary drugs in the pharmaceutical industry are set to expire. Once this happens, producers of generics (drugs that contain the same active ingredients as the original patent-protected formulation) such as Teva Pharmaceutical Industries of Israel enter the market, and prices fall drastically. Pfizer's patent on Lipitor expired in 2011. Just one year later, of the 55 million Lipitor prescriptions, 45 million (or more than 80 percent) were generics.[40] Drug prices fall by 20 to 80 percent once generic formulations become available.[41]

Taken together, each of the five isolating mechanisms discussed here (or combinations thereof) allows a firm to extend its competitive advantage. Although no competitive advantage lasts forever, a firm may be able to protect its competitive advantage (even for long periods) when it has consistently better expectations about the future value of resources, when it has accumulated a resource advantage that can be imitated only over long periods of time, when the source of its competitive advantage is causally ambiguous or socially complex, or when the firm possesses strong intellectual property protection.

4.4 The Dynamic Capabilities Perspective

CORE RIGIDITIES

A firm's external environment is rarely stable (as discussed in Chapter 3). Rather, in many industries, the pace of change is ferocious. Firms that fail to adapt their core competencies to a changing external environment not only lose a competitive advantage but also may go out of business.

We've seen the merciless pace of change in consumer electronics retailing in the United States. Once a market leader, Circuit City's core competencies were in efficient logistics and superior customer service. But the firm neglected to upgrade and hone them over time. As a consequence, Circuit City was outflanked by Best Buy and online retailer Amazon, and the company went bankrupt. Best Buy encountered the same difficulties competing against Amazon just a few years later. Core competencies might form the basis for a competitive advantage at one point, but as the environment changes, the very same core competencies might later turn into *core rigidities,* retarding the firm's ability to change.[42]

> **core rigidity** A former core competency that turned into a liability because the firm failed to hone, refine, and upgrade the competency as the environment changed.

A core competency can turn into a **core rigidity** if a firm relies too long on the competency without honing, refining, and upgrading as the environment changes.[43] Over time, the original core competency is no longer a good fit with the external environment, and it turns from an asset into a liability. The reason reinvesting, honing, and upgrading of resources and capabilities are so crucial to sustaining any competitive advantage is to prevent competencies from turning into core rigidities (see Exhibit 4.4). This ability to hone and upgrade lies at the heart of the dynamic capabilities perspective. We defined *capabilities* as the organizational and managerial skills necessary to orchestrate a diverse set of resources and to deploy them strategically. Capabilities are by nature intangible. They find their expression in a company's structure, routines, and culture.

DYNAMIC CAPABILITIES

> **LO 4-7**
>
> Outline how dynamic capabilities can enable a firm to sustain a competitive advantage.

> **dynamic capabilities** A firm's ability to create, deploy, modify, reconfigure, upgrade, or leverage its resources in its quest for competitive advantage.

The dynamic capabilities perspective adds, as the name suggests, a *dynamic* or time element. In particular, **dynamic capabilities** describe a firm's ability to create, deploy, modify, reconfigure, upgrade, or leverage its resources over time in its quest for competitive advantage.[44] Dynamic capabilities are essential to move beyond a short-lived advantage and create a sustained competitive advantage. For a firm to sustain its advantage, any fit between its internal strengths and the external environment must be dynamic. That is, the firm must be able to change its internal resource base as the external environment changes. The goal should be to develop resources, capabilities, and competencies that create a *strategic fit* with the firm's environment. Rather than creating a static fit, the firm's internal strengths should change with its external environment in a *dynamic* fashion.

> **dynamic capabilities perspective** A model that emphasizes a firm's ability to modify and leverage its resource base in a way that enables it to gain and sustain competitive advantage in a constantly changing environment.

Not only do dynamic capabilities allow firms to adapt to changing market conditions, but they also enable firms to *create market changes* that can strengthen their strategic position. These market changes implemented by proactive firms introduce altered circumstances, to which more reactive rivals might be forced to respond. Apple's dynamic capabilities allowed it to redefine the markets for mobile devices and computing, in particular in music, smartphones, and media content. For the portable music market through its iPod and iTunes store, Apple generated environmental change to which Sony and others had to respond. With its iPhone, Apple redefined the market for smartphones, again creating environmental change to which competitors such as Samsung, BlackBerry, and Nokia needed to respond. Apple's introduction of the iPad redefined the media and tablet computing market, forcing competitors such as Amazon and Microsoft to respond. With the Apple Watch it is attempting to shape the market for computer wearables in its favor. Dynamic capabilities are especially relevant for surviving and competing in markets that shift quickly and constantly, such as the high-tech space in which firms such as Apple, Google, Microsoft, and Amazon compete.

In the **dynamic capabilities perspective**, competitive advantage is the outflow of a firm's capacity to modify and leverage its resource base in a way that enables it to gain and sustain competitive advantage in a constantly changing environment. Given the accelerated pace of technological change, in combination with deregulation, globalization, and demographic shifts, dynamic markets today are the rule rather than the exception. As a response, a firm may create, deploy, modify, reconfigure, or upgrade resources so as to provide value to customers and/or lower costs in a dynamic environment. The essence of this perspective is that competitive advantage is not derived from static resource or market advantages, but from a *dynamic reconfiguration* of a firm's resource base.

RESOURCE STOCKS AND RESOURCE FLOWS

One way to think about developing dynamic capabilities and other intangible resources is to distinguish between resource stocks and resource flows.[45] In this perspective, **resource stocks** are the firm's current level of intangible resources. **Resource flows** are the firm's level of investments to maintain or build a resource. A helpful metaphor to explain the differences between resource stocks and resource flows is a bathtub that is being filled with water (see Exhibit 4.7).[46] The amount of water in the bathtub indicates a company's level of a specific *intangible resource stock*—such as its dynamic capabilities, new product development, engineering expertise, innovation capability, reputation for quality, and so on.[47]

Intangible resource stocks are built through investments over time. In the exhibit, these investments are represented by the four faucets, from which water flows into the tub. Investments in building an innovation capability, for example, differ from investments made in marketing expertise. Each investment flow would be represented by a different faucet. How fast a firm is able to build an intangible resource—how fast the tub fills—depends on how much water comes out of the faucets and how long the faucets are left open. Intangible resources are built through continuous investments and experience over time.

Organizational learning also fosters the increase of intangible resources. Many intangible resources, such as IBM's expertise in cognitive computing, take a long time to build. IBM's

resource stocks The firm's current level of intangible resources.

resource flows The firm's level of investments to maintain or build a resource.

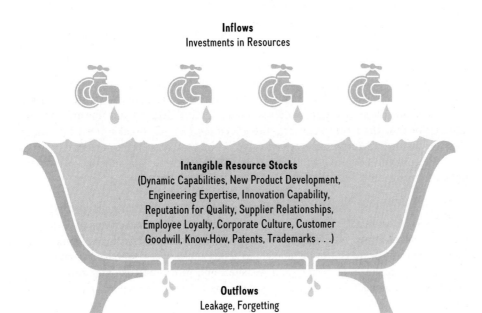

Inflows
Investments in Resources

Intangible Resource Stocks
(Dynamic Capabilities, New Product Development, Engineering Expertise, Innovation Capability, Reputation for Quality, Supplier Relationships, Employee Loyalty, Corporate Culture, Customer Goodwill, Know-How, Patents, Trademarks . . .)

Outflows
Leakage, Forgetting

EXHIBIT 4.7

The Bathtub Metaphor: The Role of Inflows and Outflows in Building Stocks of Intangible Resources

Source: Figure based on metaphor used in I. Dierickx and K. Cool (1989), "Asset stock accumulation and sustainability of competitive advantage," *Management Science* 35: 1504–1513.

quest for cognitive computing began in 1997 after its Deep Blue computer (based on artificial intelligence) beat reigning chess champion Garry Kasparov. It has invested close to $25 billion to build a deep capability in cognitive computing with the goal to take advantage of business opportunities in big data and analytics. Its efforts were publicized when its Watson, a supercomputer capable of answering questions posed in natural language, went up against 74-time *Jeopardy!* quiz-show champion Ken Jennings and won. Watson has demonstrated its skill in many professional areas where deep domain expertise is needed for making decisions in more or less real time: a wealth manager making investments, a doctor working with a cancer patient, an attorney working on a complex case, or even a chef in a five-star restaurant creating a new recipe. Moreover, cognitive computer systems get better over time as they learn from experience.

How fast the bathtub fills, however, also depends on how much water leaks out of the tub. The outflows represent a reduction in the firm's intangible resource stocks. Resource leakage might occur through employee turnover, especially if key employees leave. Significant resource leakage can erode a firm's competitive advantage. A reduction in resource stocks can occur if a firm does not engage in a specific activity for some time and forgets how to do this activity well.

According to the dynamic capabilities perspective, the strategic leaders' task is to decide which investments to make over time (i.e., which faucets to open and how far) in order to best position the firm for competitive advantage in a changing environment. Moreover, strategic leaders also need to monitor the existing intangible resource stocks and their attrition rates due to leakage and forgetting. This perspective provides a dynamic understanding of capability development to allow a firm's continuous adaptation to and superior performance in a changing external environment.

4.5 The Value Chain and Strategic Activity Systems

THE VALUE CHAIN

The **value chain** describes the internal activities a firm engages in when transforming inputs into outputs.[48] Each activity the firm performs along the horizontal chain adds incremental value—raw materials and other inputs are transformed into components that are assembled into finished products or services for the end consumer. Each activity the firm performs along the value chain also adds incremental costs. A careful analysis of the value chain allows strategic leaders to obtain a more detailed and fine-grained understanding of how the firm's *economic value creation* $(V - C)$ breaks down into distinct activities that help determine perceived value (V) and the costs (C) to create it. The value chain concept can be applied to basically any firm—those in manufacturing industries, high-tech, or service.

DISTINCT ACTIVITIES. A firm's core competencies are deployed through its activities (see Exhibit 4.4). A firm's activities, therefore, are one of the key internal drivers of performance differences across firms. Activities are distinct actions that enable firms to add incremental value at each step by transforming inputs into goods and services. Managing a supply chain, running the company's IT system and websites, and providing customer support are all examples of distinct activities. Activities are narrower than functional areas such as marketing because each functional area comprises a set of distinct activities.

Five Guys' core competency is to offer a simple menu of fresh, high-quality burgers and fries and a great customer experience. To command a premium price for these products and service, Five Guys needs to engage in number of distinct activities. Though it may seem simple, the ability to implement diverse sets of distinct activities every day across multiple geographic locations is no small feat.

The activities begin with sourcing ingredients. From the start, the Murrell sons have always selected only the best ingredients *without* knowing their cost. They viewed cost as a distraction from their ability to identify and select only the freshest, tastiest, highest-quality toppings and condiments. For example, the mayonnaise they selected after a blind taste test turned out to be the most expensive brand on the market. It also happened to be sold by a notoriously difficult vendor, but they stuck with him because he offered the best mayonnaise. In addition, sourcing locally is also important to the Five Guys brand. The 15 free toppings that Five Guys offers are locally sourced whenever possible. Likewise, the fresh-baked buns are local as well, in that they come from bakeries that Five Guys built near their stores so they could guarantee their freshness.

In most chain restaurants, fries are a simple side dish; for Five Guys, however, fries are a speciality made with great care. According to founder Jerry Murrell, while fries might look like the easiest item to make, they are actually the hardest. Unlike other fast food chains that dump dehydrated frozen fries into hot oil, Five Guys hand-cuts Idaho potatoes that are only grown north of the 42nd parallel and then soaks them in water to rinse off the starch. Soaking prevents the potatoes from absorbing the pure peanut oil as they are cooked, which gives them their unique Five Guys signature texture and taste.

Obsessing about every detail does not end at the supply chain. The Murrell family also obsesses over how to lay out each store, in particular the cooking area. Unlike other hamburger chains that use the same grill for their meat and buns, Five Guys uses a dedicated grill for its burgers and a separate toaster for buns. Although this approach requires additional equipment, and thus increases cost and operational complexity, it allows for perfectly grilled burgers and perfectly toasted buns. This all contributes to Five Guys' higher perceived value among customers, which then allows the firm to charge premium prices for the products using a simple cost-plus-margin formula.

Each activity that Five Guys engages in is focused on delivering premium burgers and fries. How to maintain this effort if the company were to franchise weighed heavily on Jerry Murrell's mind. He worried that the distinct activities needed to deliver what Five Guys stood for could not be duplicated away from the five original Washington, D.C.-area stores. In particular, he worried that if the activities could not be copied exactly, then they could control neither the quality of the product nor the customer experience. This lack of control could then lead to a diminished brand and risk the loss of Five Guys' hard-earned reputation. It is not surprising, then, that Five Guys waited as long as it did to franchise. It felt it needed to develop the perfect system for its distinct activities before it could expand beyond the home area. When Five Guys opened its store in Richmond, Virginia, a mere 100 miles from its first store in Arlington, Jerry Murrell couldn't sleep for weeks, despite knowing he had a perfect system in place.[49] Today, this set of distinct activities needs to be repeated in each and every locale where Five Guys operates, which is now some 1,500 stores worldwide.

Exhibit 4.8 shows a generic value chain and how the transformation process from inputs to outputs comprises a set of distinct activities. When these activities generate value greater than the costs to create them, the firm obtains a profit margin—this assumes that the market price the firm is able to command also exceeds those costs.

A generic value chain needs to be modified to capture the activities of a specific business. Retail chain American Eagle Outfitters, for example, needs to identify suitable store locations, either build or rent stores, purchase goods and supplies, manage distribution and store inventories, operate stores both in the brick-and-mortar world and online, hire and

EXHIBIT 4.8

A Generic Value
Chain: Primary and
Support Activities

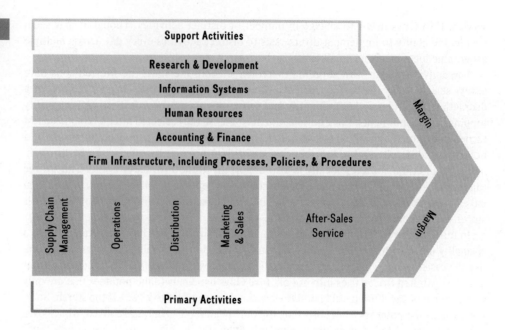

motivate a sales force, create payment and IT systems or partner with vendors, engage in promotions, and ensure after-sales services including returns. A maker of semiconductor chips such as Intel, on the other hand, needs to engage in R&D, design and engineer semiconductor chips and their production processes, purchase silicon and other ingredients, set up and staff chip fabrication plants, control quality and throughput, engage in marketing and sales, and provide after-sales customer support.

PRIMARY AND SUPPORT ACTIVITIES. As Exhibit 4.8 illustrates, the value chain is divided into primary and support activities. The **primary activities** add value directly as the firm transforms inputs into outputs—from raw materials through production phases to sales and marketing and finally customer service, specifically

primary activities
Firm activities that add value directly by transforming inputs into outputs as the firm moves a product or service horizontally along the internal value chain.

- Supply chain management.
- Operations.
- Distribution.
- Marketing and sales.
- After-sales service.

Other activities, called **support activities**, add value indirectly. These activities include

support activities
Firm activities that add value indirectly, but are necessary to sustain primary activities.

- Research and development (R&D).
- Information systems.
- Human resources.
- Accounting and finance.
- Firm infrastructure including processes, policies, and procedures.

To help a firm achieve a competitive advantage, each distinct activity performed needs to either add incremental value to the product or service offering or lower its relative cost. Discrete and specific firm activities are the basic units with which to understand competitive advantage because they are the drivers of the firm's relative costs and level of differentiation the firm can provide to its customers. Although the resource-based view of the firm helps identify the integrated set of resources and capabilities that are the building blocks of core competencies, the value chain perspective enables strategic leaders to see how competitive advantage flows from the firm's distinct set of activities. This is because a firm's core competency is generally found in a network linking different but distinct activities, each contributing to the firm's strategic position as either low-cost leader or differentiator.

STRATEGIC ACTIVITY SYSTEMS

LO 4-9

Identify competitive advantage as residing in a network of distinct activities.

A **strategic activity system** conceives of a firm as a network of interconnected activities that can be the foundation of its competitive advantage.[50] A strategic activity system is socially complex and causally ambiguous. While one can easily observe one or more elements of a strategic activity system, the capabilities necessary to orchestrate and manage a network of distinct activities within the entire system cannot be so easily observed. As such, a strategic activity system is difficult to imitate in its entirety, and this difficulty enhances a firm's possibility of developing a sustainable competitive advantage based on a set of distinct but interconnected activities.

strategic activity system The conceptualization of a firm as a network of interconnected activities.

Let's assume Firm A's strategic activity system, which lays the foundation of its competitive advantage, consists of 25 interconnected activities. Attracted by Firm A's competitive advantage, competitor Firm B closely monitors this activity system and begins to copy it through direct imitation. Turns out, Firm B is very good at copying, managing to achieve a 90 percent accuracy rate. Will Firm B be able to negate Firm A's competitive advantage as a result? Far from it. Recall that Firm A's activity system comprises 25 interconnected activities. Because each of these activities is copied with just 90 percent accuracy, that means Firm B's ability to copy the *entire* system accurately is $0.9 \times 0.9 \times 0.9$ . . ., repeated 25 times, or $0.9^{25} = 0.07$. In other words, Firm B will only be able to imitate Firm A with a total accuracy rate of 7 percent. What this example demonstrates is that using imitation as a path to competitive advantage is extremely difficult because quickly compounding probabilities render copying an entire activity system nearly impossible.

RESPONDING TO CHANGING ENVIRONMENTS. Strategic activity systems need to evolve over time if a firm is to sustain a competitive advantage. In contrast, failure to create a dynamic strategic fit generally leads to a competitive disadvantage, because the external environment changes and also because a firm's competitors get better in developing their own activity systems and capabilities. Strategic leaders, therefore, need to adapt their firm's activity system by upgrading value-creating activities in response to changing environments. To gain and sustain competitive advantage, strategic leaders may add new activities, remove activities that are no longer relevant, and upgrade activities that have become stale or somewhat obsolete. Each of these changes would require changes to the resources and capabilities involved, and as such, would reconfigure the entire strategic activity system.

Let's consider The Vanguard Group, one of the world's largest investment companies.[51] It serves individual investors, financial professionals, and institutional investors such as state retirement funds. Vanguard's mission is to help clients reach their financial goals by being their highest-value provider of investment products and services.[52] Since its founding in 1929, Vanguard has emphasized low-cost investing and quality service for its clients. Vanguard's average expense ratio (fees as a percentage of total net assets paid by investors) is generally the lowest in the industry.[53] The Vanguard Group also is a pioneer in passive index-fund investing. Rather than picking individual stocks and trading frequently as done in traditional money management, a mutual fund tracks the performance of an index (such as the Standard & Poor's 500 or the Dow Jones 30), and discourages active trading and encourages long-term investing.

Despite this innovation in investing, to gain and sustain a competitive advantage, Vanguard's strategic activity system needed to evolve over time as the company grew and market conditions as well as competitors changed. Let's compare how The Vanguard Group's strategic activity developed over more than 20 years, from 1997 to 2019.

EVOLVING A SYSTEM OVER TIME. In 1997, The Vanguard Group had less than $500 million of assets under management. It pursued its mission of being the highest-value provider of investment products and services through its unique set of interconnected activities depicted in Exhibit 4.9. The six larger ovals depict Vanguard's strategic core activities: strict cost control, direct distribution, low expenses with savings passed on to clients, offering of a broad array of mutual funds, efficient investment management approach, and straightforward client communication and education. These six strategic themes were supported by clusters of tightly linked activities (smaller circles), further reinforcing the strategic activity network.

The needs of Vanguard's customers, however, have changed since 1997. Exhibit 4.10 shows Vanguard's strategic activity system in 2019. Some 20 years later, The Vanguard Group had grown more than 10 times in size, from a mere $500 billion (in 1997) to more than $5 trillion (in 2019) of assets under management.[54]

Again, the large ovals in Exhibit 4.10 symbolize Vanguard's strategic core activities that help it realize its strategic position as the low-cost leader in the industry. However, the system evolved over time as Vanguard's strategic leaders added a new core activity—customer segmentation—to the six core activities already in place in 1997 (still valid in 2019). Vanguard's managers put in place the customer-segmentation core activity, along with two new support activities, to address a new customer need that could not be met with its older configuration. Its 1997 activity system

EXHIBIT 4.9

The Vanguard Group's Activity System in 1997

Source: Adapted from N. Siggelkow (2002), "Evolution toward fit," *Administrative Science Quarterly* 47: 146.

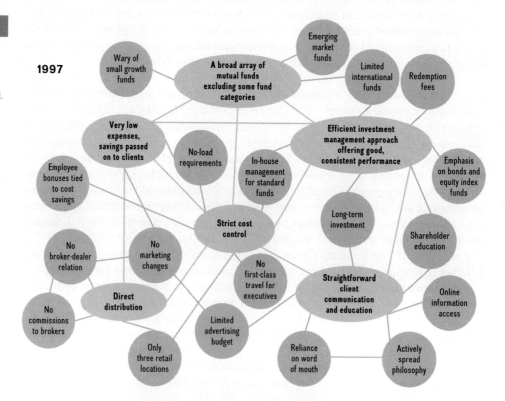

EXHIBIT 4.10

The Vanguard
Group's Activity
System in 2019

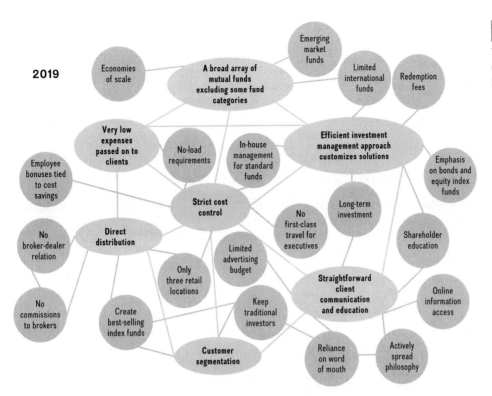

did not allow Vanguard to continue to provide quality service targeted at different customer segments at the lowest possible cost. The 2019 activity-system configuration allows Vanguard to customize its service offerings: It now separates its more traditional customers, who invest for the long term, from more active investors, who trade more often but are attracted to Vanguard funds by the firm's high performance and low cost.

The core activity Vanguard added to its strategic activity system was developed with great care, to ensure that it not only fit well with its existing core activities but also further reinforced its activity network. For example, the new activity of "Create best-selling index funds" also relies on direct distribution; it is consistent with and further reinforces Vanguard's low-cost leadership position. As a result of achieving its "best-selling" goal, Vanguard is now the world's second-largest investment-management company, just behind BlackRock, with over $6 trillion of assets under management. This allows Vanguard to benefit from economies of scale (e.g., cost savings accomplished through a larger number of customers served and a greater amount of assets managed), further driving down cost. In turn, by lowering its cost structure, Vanguard can offer more customized services without raising its overall cost. Despite increased customization, Vanguard still has one of the lowest expense ratios in the industry. Even in a changing environment, the firm continues to pursue its strategy of low-cost investing combined with quality service. If firms add activities that don't fit their strategic positioning (e.g., if Vanguard added local retail offices in shopping malls, thereby increasing operating costs), they create "strategic misfits" that are likely to erode a firm's competitive advantage.

The Vanguard Group's core competency of low-cost investing while providing quality service for its clients is accomplished through a unique set of interconnected primary and support activities including strict cost control, direct distribution, low expenses with savings passed on to clients, a broad array of mutual funds, an efficient investment management approach, and straightforward client communication and education.

In summary, a firm's competitive advantage can result from its unique network of activities. The important point, however, is that a static fit with the current environment is not sufficient; rather, a firm's unique network of activities must evolve over time to take advantage of new opportunities and mitigate emerging threats. Moreover, by using activity-based accounting (which first identifies distinct activities in an organization and then assigns costs to each activity based on estimates of all resources consumed) and by benchmarking the competition, one can identify key activities. In Chapter 5, we look more closely at how to measure and assess competitive advantage.

4.6 Implications for Strategic Leaders

We've now reached a significant point: We can combine external analysis from Chapter 3 with the internal analysis just introduced. Together the two allow you to begin formulating a strategy that matches a firm's internal resources and capabilities to the demands of the external industry environment. Ideally, strategic leaders want to leverage their firm's internal strengths to exploit external opportunities, while mitigating internal weaknesses and external threats. Both types of analysis in tandem allow managers to formulate a strategy that is tailored to their company, creating a unique fit between the company's internal resources and the external environment. A *strategic fit* increases the likelihood that a firm is able to gain a competitive advantage. If a firm achieves a *dynamic* strategic fit, it is likely to be able to *sustain* its advantage over time.

USING SWOT ANALYSIS TO GENERATE INSIGHTS FROM EXTERNAL AND INTERNAL ANALYSIS

We synthesize insights from an internal analysis of the company's *strengths* and *weaknesses* with those from an analysis of external *opportunities* and *threats* using the **SWOT analysis**. Internal strengths (S) and weaknesses (W) concern resources, capabilities, and competencies. Whether they are strengths or weaknesses can be determined by applying the VRIO framework. A resource is a weakness if it is not valuable. In this case, the resource does not allow the firm to exploit an external opportunity or offset an external threat. A resource, however, is a strength and a core competency if it is valuable, rare, costly to imitate, and the firm is organized to capture at least part of the economic value created.

External opportunities (O) and threats (T) are in the firm's general environment and can be captured by PESTEL and Porter's five forces analyses (discussed in the previous chapter). An attractive industry as determined by Porter's five forces, for example, presents an external opportunity for firms not yet active in this industry. On the other hand, stricter regulation for financial institutions, for example, might represent an external threat to banks.

A SWOT analysis allows a strategic leader to evaluate a firm's current situation and future prospects by simultaneously considering internal and external factors. The SWOT analysis encourages strategic leaders to scan the internal and external environments, looking for any relevant factors that might affect the firm's current or future competitive advantage. The focus is on internal and external factors that can affect—in a positive or negative way—the firm's ability to gain and sustain a competitive advantage. To facilitate a SWOT analysis, managers use a set of strategic questions that link the firm's internal environment to its external environment, as shown in Exhibit 4.11, to derive strategic implications. In this SWOT matrix, the horizontal axis is divided into factors that are *external to the firm* (the focus of Chapter 3) and the vertical axis into factors that are *internal to the firm* (the focus of this chapter).

To conduct a SWOT analysis, strategic leaders start by gathering information to link internal factors (*strengths* and *weaknesses*) to external factors (*opportunities* and *threats*).

	External to Firm	
	Opportunities	**Threats**
Strengths	*How can the firm use internal strengths to take advantage of external opportunities?*	*How can the firm use internal strengths to reduce the likelihood and impact of external threats?*
Weaknesses	*How can the firm overcome internal weaknesses that prevent it from taking advantage of external opportunities?*	*How can the firm overcome internal weaknesses that will make external threats a reality?*

(Internal to Firm — row-group label)

EXHIBIT 4.11

Strategic Questions within the SWOT Matrix

Next, they use the SWOT matrix shown in Exhibit 4.11 to develop *strategic alternatives* for the firm. Developing strategic alternatives is a four-step (but not necessarily linear) process:

1. **Focus on the *Strengths–Opportunities* quadrant (top left)** to derive "offensive" alternatives by using an internal strength to exploit an external opportunity.

2. **Focus on the *Weaknesses–Threats* quadrant (bottom right)** to derive "defensive" alternatives by eliminating or minimizing an internal weakness to mitigate an external threat.

3. **Focus on the *Strengths–Threats* quadrant (top right)** to use an internal strength to minimize the effect of an external threat.

4. **Focus on the *Weaknesses–Opportunities* quadrant (bottom left)** to shore up an internal weakness to improve its ability to take advantage of an external opportunity.

Lastly, strategic leaders carefully evaluate the pros and cons of each strategic alternative to select one or more alternatives to implement. They need to carefully explain their decision rationale, including why they rejected the other strategic alternatives.

Although the SWOT analysis is a widely used management framework, a word of caution is in order. A problem with this framework is that a strength can also be a weakness and an opportunity can also simultaneously be a threat. Earlier in this chapter, we discussed the location of Google's headquarters in Silicon Valley and near several universities as a key resource for the firm. Most people would consider this a strength for the firm. However, California has a high cost of living and is routinely ranked among the worst of the states in terms of "ease of doing business." In addition, this area of California is along major earthquake fault lines and is more prone to natural disasters than many other parts of the country. So is the location a strength or a weakness? The answer is "it depends."

In a similar fashion, is global warming an opportunity or threat for car manufacturers? If governments enact higher gasoline taxes and make driving more expensive, it can be a threat. If, however, carmakers respond to government regulations by increased innovation through developing more fuel-efficient cars as well as low- or zero-emission engines such as hybrid or electric vehicles, it may create more demand for new cars and lead to higher sales.

To make the SWOT analysis an effective management tool, strategic leaders must first conduct a thorough external and internal analysis, as laid out in Chapters 3 and 4. This sequential process enables you to ground the analysis in rigorous theoretical frameworks before using SWOT to synthesize the results from the external and internal analyses in order to derive a set of strategic options.

You have now acquired the toolkit with which to conduct a complete strategic analysis of a firm's internal and external environments. In the next chapter, we consider various ways to assess and measure competitive advantage. That chapter will complete Part 1, on strategy analysis, in the AFI framework (see Exhibit 1.4).

CHAPTER**CASE 4** Part II

TO STAND OUT IN A saturated burger market dominated by such giants as McDonald's and Burger King, Five Guys pursues a differentiation strategy that helps it to create a higher perceived value among its customers. One key differentiating feature is its product: Each Five Guys burger is made from never-frozen ground beef nestled atop a toasted, freshly baked bun. Each burger is also made to order and can be customized with any of 15 toppings—all of which can be added free of charge. Its fries are hand-cut and sourced from Idaho potatoes grown north of the 42nd parallel and cooked in pure peanut oil. Another key feature is its streamlined menu: burgers, fries, and hotdogs—no salads, no wraps, no desserts.

High(est) quality and consistency are extremely important to Five Guys. To ensure these standards are regularly met, it conducts two third-party audits in each of its 1,500 stores weekly to ensure the food is always fresh and the stores are always clean. The money that Five Guys does not spend on marketing is, instead, spent on its staff: Bonuses are awarded to the teams that score the highest on these audits. Each week a winning team receives a bonus of about $1,000, which is then split among the team's five or six members. About 200 teams make the cut, receiving the bonus. The way Five Guys motivates its staff also differentiates it from other competitors in the industry, who tend to just pay (minimum) hourly wages.

Although Five Guys' food tastes great and provides emotional comfort to many of its patrons, in recent years, especially with the increased concern about obesity and related health complications, Five Guys has landed on the list of U.S. chain restaurants that offer the most unhealthy meals. A standard bacon cheeseburger has close to 1,000 calories and a large order of fries has about 1,500. As a consequence, Five Guys food offerings have been criticized by watchdogs such as the Center for Science in the Public

Interest. With the new focus on healthy eating, many restaurant chains such as Chipotle have come up with healthier options that include more low-calorie meals and fresh produce.

Five Guys' commitment to the delivery of quality foods using fresh ingredients, simple menus, and classic flavors has allowed it to thrive for more than 30 years in a highly competitive market, with 1,500 stores as of 2019 and another 1,500 locations in development. With all the regional franchises in the United States sold out, the company is focusing on international expansion.[55]

Questions

1. Why is Five Guys so successful? Describe Five Guys' core competency, explain how the company built it, and why it is essential to its success.

2. Five Guys' success led to imitation attempts by more recent entries in the fast-casual "better burger" segment of the restaurant industry such as BurgerFi, Shake Shack, and Smashburger. Do you think these new entrants are competitive threats to Five Guys? Why, or why not? If you think they are competitive threats, what should Five Guys do about it, if anything? Explain.

3. Do you think a trend toward more healthy eating is a threat to Five Guys? If so, what could the company do about it? For example, should the company change its menu to include healthier choices, or should it continue with what made Five Guys so successful? Why, or why not? Use Exhibit 4.11 to discuss your responses.

4. Do you think Five Guys will be as successful outside the United States as it has been in its home market? Why or why not?

mySTRATEGY

Looking Inside Yourself: What Is My Competitive Advantage?

We encourage you to apply what you have learned about competitive advantage to your career. Spend a few minutes looking at yourself to discover *your own* competitive advantage. If you have previous work experience, these questions should be from a work environment perspective. If you do not have any work experience yet, use these questions to evaluate a new workplace or as strategies for presenting yourself to a potential employer.

1. Write down your own strengths and weaknesses. What sort of organization will permit you to really leverage your strengths and keep you highly engaged in your work (person–organization fit)? Do some of your weaknesses need to be mitigated through additional training or mentoring from a more seasoned professional?

2. Personal capabilities also need to be evaluated over time. Are your strengths and weaknesses different today from what they were five years ago? What are you doing to make sure your capabilities are dynamic?

3. Are some of your strengths valuable, rare, and costly to imitate? How can you organize your work to help capture the value of your key strengths (or mitigate your weaknesses)? Are your strengths specific to one or a few employers, or are they more generally valuable in the marketplace? In general, should you be making investments in your human capital in terms of company-specific or market-general skills?

4. As an employee, how could you persuade your boss that you could be a vital source of sustainable competitive advantage? What evidence could you provide to make such an argument?

TAKE-AWAY CONCEPTS

This chapter demonstrated various approaches to analyzing the firm's *internal environment,* as summarized by the following learning objectives and related take-away concepts.

LO 4-1 / Explain how shifting from an external to internal analysis of a firm can reveal why and how internal firm differences are the root of competitive advantage.

- Since companies that compete in the same industry face similar external opportunities and threats, the source of the observable performance difference must be found inside the firm.
- Looking inside a firm to analyze its resources, capabilities, and core competencies allows strategic leaders to understand the firm's strengths and weaknesses.
- Linking the insights from a firm's external analysis to the ones from an internal analysis allows managers to determine their strategic options.

- Strategic leaders want to leverage their firms' internal strengths to exploit external opportunities and to mitigate internal weaknesses and external threats.

LO 4-2 / Differentiate among a firm's core competencies, resources, capabilities, and activities.

- *Core competencies* are unique, deeply embedded, firm-specific strengths that allow companies to differentiate their products and services and thus create more value for customers than their rivals, or offer products and services of acceptable value at lower cost.
- *Resources* are any assets that a company can draw on when crafting and executing strategy.
- *Capabilities* are the organizational and managerial skills necessary to orchestrate a diverse set of resources to deploy them strategically.

- *Activities* are distinct and fine-grained business processes that enable firms to add incremental value by transforming inputs into goods and services.

LO 4-3 / Compare and contrast tangible and intangible resources.

- *Tangible resources* have physical attributes and are visible.
- *Intangible resources* have no physical attributes and are invisible.
- Competitive advantage is more likely to be based on intangible resources.

LO 4-4 / Evaluate the two critical assumptions about the nature of resources in the resource-based view.

- The first critical assumption—*resource heterogeneity*—is that bundles of resources, capabilities, and competencies differ across firms. The resource bundles of firms competing in the same industry (or even the same strategic group) are unique to some extent and thus differ from one another.
- The second critical assumption—*resource immobility*—is that resources tend to be "sticky" and don't move easily from firm to firm. Because of that stickiness, the resource differences that exist between firms are difficult to replicate and, therefore, can last for a long time.

LO 4-5 / Apply the VRIO framework to assess the competitive implications of a firm's resources.

- For a firm's resource to be the basis of a competitive advantage, it must have VRIO attributes: *valuable (V), rare (R),* and *costly to imitate (I).* The firm must also be able to *organize (O) in order to capture the value of the resource.*
- A resource is valuable (V) if it allows the firm to take advantage of an external opportunity and/or neutralize an external threat. A valuable resource enables a firm to increase its economic value creation $(V - C)$.
- A resource is rare (R) if the number of firms that possess it is less than the number of firms it would require to reach a state of perfect competition.
- A resource is costly to imitate (I) if firms that do not possess the resource are unable to develop or buy the resource at a comparable cost.

- The firm is organized (O) to capture the value of the resource if it has an effective organizational structure, processes, and systems in place to fully exploit the competitive potential.

LO 4-6 / Evaluate different conditions that allow a firm to sustain a competitive advantage.

- Several conditions make it costly for competitors to imitate the resources, capabilities, or competencies that underlie a firm's competitive advantage: (1) *better expectations of future resource value,* (2) *path dependence,* (3) *causal ambiguity,* (4) *social complexity,* and (5) *intellectual property (IP) protection.*
- These *barriers to imitation* are isolating mechanisms because they prevent rivals from competing away the advantage a firm may enjoy.

LO 4-7 / Outline how dynamic capabilities can enable a firm to sustain a competitive advantage.

- To sustain a competitive advantage, any fit between a firm's internal strengths and the external environment must be dynamic.
- *Dynamic capabilities* allow a firm to create, deploy, modify, reconfigure, or upgrade its resource base to gain and sustain competitive advantage in a constantly changing environment.

LO 4-8 / Apply a value chain analysis to understand which of the firm's activities in the process of transforming inputs into outputs generate differentiation and which drive costs.

- The value chain describes the internal activities a firm engages in when transforming inputs into outputs.
- Each activity the firm performs along the horizontal chain adds incremental value and incremental costs.
- A careful analysis of the value chain allows managers to obtain a more detailed and fine-grained understanding of how the firm's economic value creation breaks down into a distinct set of activities that helps determine perceived value and the costs to create it.
- When a firm's set of distinct activities is able to generate value greater than the costs to create it, the firm obtains a profit margin (assuming the market price the firm is able to command exceeds the costs of value creation).

LO 4-9 / **Identify competitive advantage as residing in a network of distinct activities.**

- A strategic activity system conceives of a firm as a network of interconnected firm activities.

- A network of primary and supporting firm activities can create a strategic fit that can lead to a competitive advantage.

- To sustain a competitive advantage, firms need to hone, fine-tune, and upgrade their strategic activity systems over time, in response to changes in the external environment and to moves of competitors.

LO 4-10 / **Conduct a SWOT analysis to generate insights from external and internal analysis and derive strategic implications.**

- Formulating a strategy that increases the chances of gaining and sustaining a competitive advantage is based on synthesizing insights obtained from an internal analysis of the company's strengths (S) and weaknesses (W) with those from an analysis of external opportunities (O) and threats (T).

- The strategic implications of a SWOT analysis should help the firm to leverage its internal strengths to exploit external opportunities, while mitigating internal weaknesses and external threats.

KEY TERMS

Activities *(p. 124)*
Capabilities *(p. 124)*
Causal ambiguity *(p. 135)*
Core competencies *(p. 120)*
Core rigidity *(p. 138)*
Costly-to-imitate resource *(p. 129)*
Dynamic capabilities *(p. 138)*
Dynamic capabilities perspective *(p. 138)*
Intangible resources *(p. 126)*
Intellectual property (IP) protection *(p. 136)*

Isolating mechanisms *(p. 132)*
Organized to capture value *(p. 131)*
Path dependence *(p. 134)*
Primary activities *(p. 142)*
Rare resource *(p. 129)*
Resource *(p. 127)*
Resource-based view *(p. 126)*
Resource flows *(p. 139)*
Resource heterogeneity *(p. 127)*
Resource immobility *(p. 127)*

Resource stocks *(p. 139)*
Resources *(p. 124)*
Social complexity *(p. 136)*
Strategic activity system *(p. 143)*
Support activities *(p. 142)*
SWOT analysis *(p. 146)*
Tangible resources *(p. 126)*
Valuable resource *(p. 128)*
Value chain *(p. 140)*
VRIO framework *(p. 128)*

DISCUSSION QUESTIONS

1. Why is it important to study the internal resources, capabilities, and activities of firms? What insights can be gained?

2. Conduct a value chain analysis for Five Guys. What are its primary activities? What are its support activities? Identify the activities that add the most value for the customer. Why? Which activities help Five Guys to build its differentiated brand? Why?

3. The resource-based view of the firm identifies four criteria that managers can use to evaluate whether particular resources and capabilities are core competencies and can, therefore, provide a basis for sustainable competitive advantage. Are these measures independent or interdependent? Explain. If (some of) the measures are interdependent, what implications does that fact have for managers wanting to create and sustain a competitive advantage?

ENDNOTES

1. Raz, G. (2017, Jun. 5), "How I built this," *NPR*, www.npr.org/2017/08/07/531097687/five-guys-jerry-murrell.

2. This ChapterCase was prepared by Frank T. Rothaermel with Laura Zhang, who provided superb research assistance. Sources: Five Guys Media Fact Sheet (2018), www.fiveguys.com/-/media/Public-Site/Files/Media-Fact-Sheet-2018.ashx?la=en; Raz, G. (2017, Jun. 5), "How I built this," *NPR*, www.npr.org/2017/08/07/531097687/five-guys-jerry-murrell; Olmsted, L. (2013, Oct. 10), "Great American bites: Why burger lovers flock to Five Guys," *USA Today*; Egan, T. (2013, Mar. 21), "Burgers, fries and lies," *The New York Times*; Burke, M. (2012, Jul. 18), "Five Guys Burgers: America's fastest growing restaurant chain," *Forbes*; Welch, L. (2010, Apr. 1), "How I did it: Jerry Murrell, Five Guys Burgers and Fries," *Inc. Magazine.*

3. The discussion of Five Guys here and elsewhere in the chapter is based on: Five Guys Media Fact Sheet (2018), www.fiveguys.com/-/media/Public-Site/Files/Media-Fact-Sheet-2018.ashx?la=en; Raz, G. (2017, Jun. 5), "How I built this," *NPR*, www.npr.org/2017/08/07/531097687/five-guys-jerry-murrell; Olmsted, L. (2013, Oct. 10), "Great American bites: Why burger lovers flock to Five Guys," *USA Today*; Egan, T. (2013, Mar. 21), "Burgers, fries and lies," *The New York Times*; Burke, M. (2012, Jul. 18), "Five Guys Burgers: America's fastest growing restaurant chain," *Forbes*; Welch, L. (2010, Apr. 1), "How I did it: Jerry Murrell, Five Guys Burgers and Fries," *Inc. Magazine.*

4. Prahalad, C.K., and G. Hamel (1990, May–June), "The core competence of the corporation," *Harvard Business Review.*

5. For a discussion of core competencies and capabilities as well as their replication and transfer over time and space, see: Dosi, G., R.R. Nelson, and S.G. Winter (2001), Eds., *The Nature and Dynamics of Organizational Capabilities*, rev. ed. (Oxford, UK: Oxford University Press); Helfat, C.E., and M.B. Lieberman (2002), "The birth of capabilities: Market entry and the importance of pre-history," *Industrial and Corporate Change* 11(4): 725–760; and Sorenson, O., and J.B. Sørensen (2001), "Finding the right mix: Franchising, organizational learning, and chain performance," *Strategic Management Journal*, 22(6–7): 713–724.

6. Burrell, I. (2012, Sep. 8), "Dr. Dre: He's all ears with golden Beats," *Independent*, www.independent.co.uk/news/people/profiles/dr-dre-he-s-all-ears-with-golden-beats-8118047.html.

7. "People aren't hearing all the music," *Beats By Dre*, www.beatsbydre.com/aboutus.

8. This Strategy Highlight as well as the discussion of Dr. Dre and Beats Electronics throughout this chapter is based on: www.beatsbydre.com; Hufford, A., and H. Karp (2017, Jan. 23), "Sprint to buy 33% of Jay-Z's Tidal music service," *The Wall Street Journal*; Eels, J. (2014, Nov. 5), "Dr. Dre and Jimmy Iovine's school for innovation," *The Wall Street Journal*; Brownlee, M. (2014, Aug. 30), "The truth about Beats by Dre!" *YouTube*, www.youtube.com/watch?v=ZsxQxS0AdBY; "The sound of music," *The Economist* (2014, Aug. 24); Karp, H. (2014, Jun. 6), "Apple's new beat: What Steve Jobs and Dr. Dre have in common," *The Wall Street Journal*; Cohen, M. (2014, May 29), "Apple buys Beats to regain music mojo," *The Wall Street Journal*; "Can you feel the Beats?" *The Economist* (2014, May 28); Karp, H. (2014, May 9), "Apple-Beats Electronics: The disrupter is disrupted," *The Wall Street Journal*; Karp, H., and D. Wakabayashi (2014, May 9), "Dr. Dre, Jimmy Iovine would both join Apple in Beats deal," *The Wall Street Journal*; "Beats nicked," *The Economist* (2014, May 13); and "The legacy of Napster," *The Economist* (2013, Sep. 13).

9. This discussion is based on: Amit, R., and P.J.H. Schoemaker (1993), "Strategic assets and organizational rent," *Strategic Management Journal* 14: 33–46; Peteraf, M. (1993), "The cornerstones of competitive advantage," *Strategic Management Journal* 14: 179–191; Barney, J. (1991), "Firm resources and sustained competitive advantage," *Journal of Management* 17: 99–120; and Wernerfelt, B. (1984), "A resource-based view of the firm," *Strategic Management Journal* 5: 171–180.

10. Google is working to outdo the existing Googleplex headquarters in Mountain View. The company is building a new 3.4 million-square-foot campus across four pieces of land near the edge of San Francisco Bay. The futuristic site, to be completed in 2020, will be covered by canopy structures that can be rearranged in a flexible manner. See: "Silicon Valley headquarters: Googledome, or temple of doom?" *The Economist* (2015, Mar. 7).

11. Tangible resources are listed under "Property and Equipment" in the Consolidated Balance Sheet, see Alphabet / Google Annual Report, 2018, https://abc.xyz/investor/index.html.

12. "Top 100 most valuable global brands 2018," report by Millward Brown, WPP, www.millwardbrown.com/brandz/rankings-and-reports/top-global-brands/2018.

13. For a discussion on the benefits of being located in a technology cluster, see: Rothaermel, F.T., and D. Ku (2008), "Intercluster innovation differentials: The role of research universities," *IEEE Transactions on Engineering Management*

55: 9–22; and Saxenian, A. L. (1994), *Regional Advantage: Culture and Competition in Silicon Valley and Route 128* (Cambridge, MA: Harvard University Press).

14. Stuart, T., and O. Sorenson (2003), "The geography of opportunity: Spatial heterogeneity in founding rates and the performance of biotechnology firms," *Research Policy* 32: 229–253.

15. "Top 100 most valuable global brands 2018," report by Millward Brown, WPP, www.millwardbrown.com/brandz/rankings-and-reports/top-global-brands/2018.

16. This discussion is based on: Amit, R., and P.J.H. Schoemaker (1993), "Strategic assets and organizational rent," *Strategic Management Journal* 14: 33–46; Barney, J. (1991), "Firm resources and sustained competitive advantage," *Journal of Management* 17: 99–120; Peteraf, M. (1993), "The cornerstones of competitive advantage," *Strategic Management Journal* 14: 179–191; and Wernerfelt, B. (1984), "A resource-based view of the firm," *Strategic Management Journal* 5: 171–180.

17. This discussion is based on: Barney, J., and W. Hesterly (2014), *Strategic Management and Competitive Advantage*, 5th ed. (Upper Saddle River, NJ: Pearson Prentice Hall); Amit, R., and P.J.H. Schoemaker (1993), "Strategic assets and organizational rent," *Strategic Management Journal* 14: 33–46; Barney, J. (1991), "Firm resources and sustained competitive advantage," *Journal of Management* 17: 99–120; Peteraf, M. (1993), "The cornerstones of competitive advantage," *Strategic Management Journal* 14: 179–191; and Wernerfelt, B. (1984), "A resource-based view of the firm," *Strategic Management Journal* 5: 171–180.

18. Barney, J., and W. Hesterly (2014), *Strategic Management and Competitive Advantage*, 5th ed. (Upper Saddle River, NJ: Pearson Prentice Hall); and Barney, J. (1991), "Firm resources and sustained competitive advantage," *Journal of Management* 17: 99–120.

19. Raz, G. (2017, Jun. 5), "How I built this," *NPR*, www.npr.org/2017/08/07/531097687/five-guys-jerry-murrell

20. Crocs' share price hit an all-time high of $74.75 on October 31, 2007. By November 20, 2008, the share price had fallen to $0.94.

21. For a detailed history of the creation and growth of Amazon.com, see: Stone, B. (2013), *The Everything Store: Jeff Bezos and the Age of Amazon* (New York: Little, Brown and Co.).

22. "U.S. judge reduces Apple's patent award in Samsung case," *The Wall Street Journal* (2013, Mar. 1); and "Apple wins big in patent case," *The Wall Street Journal* (2012, Aug. 24).

23. Chesbrough, H. (2006), *Open Innovation: The New Imperative for Creating and Profiting from Technology* (Boston: Harvard Business School Press).

24. In 1968, Xerox moved its headquarters from Rochester, New York, to Norwalk, Connecticut.

25. Prahalad, C.K., and G. Hamel (1990, May–June), "The core competence of the corporation," *Harvard Business Review*.

26. Porter, M.E. (1996, November–December), "What is strategy?" *Harvard Business Review*: 61–78.

27. This discussion is based on: Mahoney, J.T., and J.R. Pandian (1992), "The resource-based view within the conversation of strategic management," *Strategic Management Journal* 13: 363–380; Barney, J. (1991), "Firm resources and sustained competitive advantage," *Journal of Management* 17: 99–120; Dierickx, I., and K. Cool (1989), "Asset stock accumulation and sustainability of competitive advantage," *Management Science* 35: 1504–1513; and Barney, J. (1986), "Strategic factor markets: Expectations, luck, and business strategy," *Management Science* 32: 1231–1241.

28. Lippman, S.A., and R. P. Rumelt (1982), "Uncertain imitability: An analysis of interfirm differences in efficiency under competition," *The Bell Journal of Economics* 13: 418–438.

29. Groupon Annual Report, 2012; Groupon investor deck, March 2013; "Don't weep for Groupon ex-CEO Andrew Mason," *The Wall Street Journal (2013,* Mar. 1); "Groupon CEO fired as daily-deals biz bottoms out," *Wired (2013,* Feb. 28); "Struggling Groupon ousts its quirky CEO," *The Wall Street Journal* (2013, Feb. 28); "Why Groupon is over and Facebook and Twitter should follow," *Forbes* (2012, Aug. 20); "Groupon: Deep discount," *The Economist* (2012, Aug. 14); "The economics of Groupon," *The Economist* (2011, Oct. 22); "In Groupon's $6 billion wake, a fleet of start-ups," *The New York Times* (2011, Mar. 9); and Godin, S. (2008), *Tribes: We Need You to Lead Us* (New York: Portfolio).

30. Arthur, W.B. (1989), "Competing technologies, increasing returns, and lock-in by historical events," *Economics Journal* 99: 116–131; and Dierickx, I., and K. Cool (1989), "Asset stock accumulation and sustainability of competitive advantage," *Management Science* 35: 1504–1513.

31. Krugman, P. (1993), *Geography and Trade* (Cambridge, MA: MIT Press); and Patton, R.L. (2010), "A history of the U.S. carpet industry," *Economic History Association Encyclopedia,* http://eh.net/encyclopedia/article/patton.carpet.

32. Dierickx, I., and K. Cool (1989), "Asset stock accumulation and sustainability of competitive advantage," *Management Science* 35: 1504–1513.

33. For a detailed discussion of how several stakeholders influenced the CARB to withdraw zero-emissions standard, see: Sony Pictures' documentary "Who Killed the Electric Car?" www.whokilledtheelectriccar.com/.

34. Colias, M. (2016, Sep. 16), "GM says Chevy Bolt electric car to get 238-mile range," *The Wall Street Journal*; Sparks, D. (2017, Mar. 7), "Chevy Bolt U.S. deliveries decline in February," *The Motley Fool.*

35. More formally, the number of relationships (r) in a group is a function of its group members (n), with $r = n(n − 1)/2$. The assumption is that two people, A and B, have only one relationship (A ←→ B), rather than two relationships (A → B and A ← B). In the latter case, the number of relationships (r) in a group with n members doubles, where $r = n(n − 1)$.

36. This discussion is based on: Hallenborg, L., M. Ceccagnoli, and M. Clendenin (2008), "Intellectual property protection in the global economy," *Advances in the Study of Entrepreneurship, Innovation, and Economic Growth* 18: 11–34; and Graham, S.J.H. (2008), "Beyond patents: The role of copyrights, trademarks, and trade secrets in technology commercialization," *Advances in the Study of Entrepreneurship, Innovation, and Economic Growth* 18: 149–171. Moreover, for an insightful discussion on trademarks and sourcing innovation, see Bei, X. (2019), "Trademarks, specialized complementary assets, and the external sourcing of innovation," *Research Policy,* 48: forthcoming, DOI: 10.1016/j.respol.2018.11.003.

37. "Cost to develop and win marketing approval for a new drug is $2.6 billion," *Tufts Center for the Study of Drug Development* (2014, November).

38. "Lipitor becomes world's top-selling drug," *Associated Press* (2011, Dec. 28).

39. Sherr, I. (2013, Mar. 1), "U.S. judge reduces Apple's patent award in Samsung case," *The Wall Street Journal*; and Vascellaro, J.E. (2012, Aug. 25), "Apple wins big in patent case," *The Wall Street Journal.*

40. Loftus, P. (2014, Mar. 2), "Lipitor: Pfizer aims to sell over-the-counter version," *The Wall Street Journal.*

41. "Drug prices to plummet in wave of expiring patents," *Drugs.com,* www.drugs.com/news/prices-plummet-wave-expiring-patents-32684.html.

42. Leonard-Barton, D. (1992), "Core capabilities and core rigidities: A paradox in managing new product development," *Strategic Management Journal* 13: 111–125.

43. Leonard-Barton, D. (1995), *Wellsprings of Knowledge: Building and Sustaining the Sources of Innovation* (Boston: Harvard Business School Press).

44. This discussion is based on: Peteraf, M., G. Di Stefano, and G. Verona (2013), "The elephant in the room of dynamic capabilities: Bringing two diverging conversations together," *Strategic Management Journal* 34: 1389–1410; Rothaermel, F.T., and A.M. Hess (2007), "Building dynamic capabilities: Innovation driven by individual-, firm-, and network-level effects," *Organization Science* 18: 898–921; Eisenhardt, K.M., and Martin, J. (2000), "Dynamic capabilities: What are they?" *Strategic Management Journal* 21: 1105–1121; and Teece, D.J., G. Pisano, and A. Shuen (1997), "Dynamic capabilities and strategic management," *Strategic Management Journal* 18: 509–533.

45. Dierickx, I., and K. Cool (1989), "Asset stock accumulation and sustainability of competitive advantage," *Management Science* 35: 1504–1513.

46. Dierickx, I., and K. Cool (1989), "Asset stock accumulation and sustainability of competitive advantage," *Management Science* 35: 1504–1513.

47. Eisenhardt, K.M., and J. Martin (2000), "Dynamic capabilities: What are they?" *Strategic Management Journal* 21: 1105–1121.

48. This discussion is based on: Porter, M.E. (1985), *Competitive Advantage: Creating and Sustaining Superior Performance* (New York: Free Press); Porter, M.E. (1996, November–December), "What is strategy?" *Harvard Business Review*: 61–78; Siggelkow, N. (2001), "Change in the presence of fit: The rise, the fall, and the renaissance of Liz Claiborne," *Academy of Management Journal* 44: 838–857; and Magretta, J. (2012), *Understanding Michael Porter. The Essential Guide to Competition and Strategy* (Boston: Harvard Business School Press).

49. Raz, G. (2017, Jun. 5), "How I Built This," *NPR,* www.npr.org/2017/08/07/531097687/five-guys-jerry-murrell.

50. This discussion draws on: Porter, M.E. (1996, November–December), "What is strategy?" *Harvard Business Review*: 61–78.

51. This discussion draws on: Porter, M.E. (1996, November–December), "What is strategy?" *Harvard Business Review*: 61–78; and Siggelkow, N. (2002), "Evolution toward fit," *Administrative Science Quarterly* 47: 125–159.

52. https://careers.vanguard.com/vgcareers/why_vgi/story/mission.shtml.

53. "Funds: How much you're really paying," *Money* (2005, November); and https://personal.vanguard.com/us/content/Home/WhyVanguard/AboutVanguardWhoWeAreContent.jsp.

54. The Vanguard Group, various annual reports, and "Facts about Vanguard," https://about.vanguard.com/who-we-are/fast-facts/.

55. Sources: Kumer, E. (undated), "This restaurant serves the unhealthiest french fries in America," *Reader's Digest,* www.rd.com/food/fun/unhealthiest-fries-america-five-guys/; and Fryar, C.D., J.P. Hughes, K.A. Herrick, and N. Ahluwalia (2018, October), "Fast food consumption among adults in the United States, 2013-2016," *Centers for Disease Control and Prevention,* www.cdc.gov/nchs/data/databriefs/db322-h.pdf.

5

Competitive Advantage, Firm Performance, and Business Models

Chapter Outline

Learning Objectives

After studying this chapter, you should be able to:

LO 5-1 Conduct a firm profitability analysis using accounting data to assess and evaluate competitive advantage.

LO 5-2 Apply shareholder value creation to assess and evaluate competitive advantage.

LO 5-3 Explain economic value creation and different sources of competitive advantage.

LO 5-4 Apply a balanced scorecard to assess and evaluate competitive advantage.

LO 5-5 Apply a triple bottom line to assess and evaluate competitive advantage.

LO 5-6 Use the why, what, who, and how of business models framework to put strategy into action.

The Quest for Competitive Advantage: Apple vs. Microsoft

BY THE FALL OF 2018, Apple was the first company ever to be valued at more than $1 trillion. However, by the spring of 2019, its market capitalization had fallen by more than 21 percent (approximately $230 billion). From 2009 to 2019, Microsoft's market cap had risen from a low of $145 billion to over $880 billion—an increase of almost 500 percent. How did this happen?

To understand the ups and downs of firm performance and competitive advantage, it is helpful to look at a longer time horizon. Apple and Microsoft have been fierce rivals since they were both founded in the mid-1970s. Although Apple has dominated the market in the decade since the introduction of the iPhone in 2007, in the early decades of the PC revolution, Microsoft was the undisputed leader. It set the standard in the world of personal

Wahavi/Alamy Stock Photo

computers with its Windows operating system, which about 90 percent of all PCs run. Microsoft's business model was to create a large base of users for this operating system and then to make money by selling with it application software such as the ubiquitous Office suite (containing Word, Excel, Power-Point, Outlook, and other software programs).

Microsoft replicated this hugely successful business model with its corporate customers. Once servers became ubiquitous in corporations, Microsoft offered IT departments e-mail systems, databases, and other business applications that tightly integrated with Windows. As a result, 80 percent of Microsoft's total revenues were tied either directly or indirectly to its Windows franchise. Microsoft's strategy of offering bundled discounted software with its operating system, which became an industry standard, allowed it to create a strong strategic position and to extract high profits for many years. It also allowed Microsoft to overtake IBM in 2000 as

the most valuable tech company globally with $510 billion in market capitalization.

In contrast, in 1997, Apple was near bankruptcy and struggling to survive with less than 5 percent market share in the PC market. But in the fall of 2001, when it introduced the iPod, its portable digital music player, Apple's revitalization took off. Eighteen months later, its rise would continue with the opening of its online store, iTunes, which was then quickly followed by the opening of its first brick-and-mortar retail stores; today, these stores earn the highest sales per square foot of any retail outlet, including luxury stores.

Apple didn't stop there. In 2007, the company revolutionized the smartphone market with the introduction of the iPhone. Just three years later, Apple introduced the iPad, reshaping the publishing and media industries. Further, for each of its iPod, iPhone, and iPad lines of business, Apple followed up with incremental product innovations extending each product category. By the fall of 2012, Apple had become the most valuable company in the world with $620 billion market capitalization.

In 2015, the high-tech company introduced Apple Watch, a wearable computer that is fully integrated with its iOS operating system, running basically all the apps available for the iPhone. Not to be stopped, in 2017, Apple introduced its 10th anniversary iPhone to great fanfare. It had a curved screen and was priced at about $1,000. The sticker price increased to $1,100 when, in September 2018, Apple introduced the iPhone XS Max. In looking for the next big thing, in 2019, Apple entered the entertainment industry with Apple TV, among other new strategic initiatives in mobile payment services and online gaming.

The comparison of Microsoft and Apple over time shows that competitive advantage is transitory. Given the rough-and-tumble competition combined with relentless technological progress and innovation, it is hard to gain a competitive advantage in the first place, and it is even harder to sustain it.[1]

Part II of this ChapterCase appears in Section 5.3.

NOTE: A five-year financial ratio review related to this ChapterCase is available in Connect.

GAINING AND SUSTAINING competitive advantage is the defining goal of strategic management. Competitive advantage leads to superior firm performance.

To explain differences in firm performance and to derive strategic implications—including new strategic initiatives—we must understand how to measure and assess competitive advantage. We devote this chapter to studying how to measure and assess firm performance. In particular, we introduce three frameworks to capture the multifaceted nature of competitive advantage. The three traditional frameworks to measure and assess firm performance are

- Accounting profitability.
- Shareholder value creation.
- Economic value creation.

We then will introduce two integrative frameworks, combining quantitative data with qualitative assessments:

- The balanced scorecard.
- The triple bottom line.

Next, we take a closer look at *business models* to understand more deeply how firms put their strategy into action to make money. We conclude the chapter with practical *Implications for Strategic Leaders.*

5.1 Competitive Advantage and Firm Performance

It is easy to compare two firms and identify the better performer as the one with competitive advantage. But such a simple comparison has its limitations. How does it help us to understand how and why a firm has competitive advantage? How can that advantage be measured? And how can we understand it in the context of an entire industry and the ever-changing external environment? What strategic implications for managerial actions can we derive from our assessments? These questions may seem simple, but their answers are not. Strategic management researchers have debated them intensely for the past few decades.[2]

To address these key questions, we will develop a *multidimensional perspective* for assessing competitive advantage. Let's begin by focusing on the three standard performance dimensions:[3]

1. Accounting profitability
2. Shareholder value
3. Economic value

These three performance dimensions generally correlate, particularly over time. Accounting profitability and economic value creation tend to be reflected in the firm's stock price, which in part determines the stock's market valuation.

ACCOUNTING PROFITABILITY

As we discussed in Chapter 1, *strategy* is a set of goal-directed actions a firm takes to gain and sustain competitive advantage. Using accounting data to assess competitive advantage and firm performance is standard managerial practice. When assessing competitive advantage by measuring accounting profitability, we use financial data and ratios derived from publicly available accounting data such as income statements and balance sheets.[4] Since *competitive advantage* is defined as superior performance *relative* to other competitors in the same industry or to the industry average, a firm's strategic leaders must be able to accomplish two critical tasks:

1. Assess the performance of their firm accurately.
2. Compare and benchmark their firm's performance to other competitors in the same industry or against the industry average.

Standardized financial metrics found in publicly available income statements and balance sheets allow a firm to fulfill both these tasks. By law, public companies are required to release these data in compliance with generally accepted accounting principles (GAAP) set by the Financial Accounting Standards Board (FASB), and as audited by certified public accountants. Publicly traded firms are required to file a Form 10-K (or 10-K report) annually with the U.S. Securities and Exchange Commission (SEC), a federal regulatory agency. The 10-K reports are the primary source of companies' accounting data available to the public. The fairly stringent requirements applied to accounting data that are audited and released publicly enhance the data's usefulness for comparative analysis.

Accounting data enable us to conduct direct performance comparisons between different companies. Some of the profitability ratios most commonly used in strategic management are *return on invested capital (ROIC), return on equity (ROE), return on assets (ROA),* and *return on revenue (ROR)*. In the "How to Conduct a Case Analysis" module in Part 4, you will find a complete presentation of accounting measures and financial ratios, how they are calculated, and a brief description of their strategic characteristics.

One of the most commonly used metrics in assessing firm financial performance is *return on invested capital (ROIC),* where *ROIC = Net profits / Invested capital.*[5] ROIC is a popular metric because it is a good proxy for *firm profitability.* In particular, the ratio measures how effectively a company uses its *total invested capital,* which consists of two components: (1) *shareholders' equity* through the selling of shares to the public, and (2) *interest-bearing debt* through borrowing from financial institutions and bondholders.

As a rule of thumb, if a firm's ROIC is greater than its cost of capital, it generates value; if it is less than the cost of capital, the firm destroys value. The *cost of capital* represents a firm's cost of financing operations from both equity through issuing stock and debt through issuing bonds. To be more precise and to be able to derive strategic implications, however, strategic leaders must compare their ROIC to that of other competitors and the industry average.

RETURN ON INVESTED CAPITAL (ROIC): APPLE VS. MICROSOFT. To demonstrate the usefulness of accounting data in assessing competitive advantage and to derive strategic implications, let's revisit the comparison between Apple and Microsoft that we began in ChapterCase 5 and investigate the sources of performance differences in more detail.[6] Exhibit 5.1 shows the ROIC for Apple and Microsoft as of fiscal year 2018.[7] It further breaks down ROIC into its constituent components. This provides important clues for managers on which areas to focus when attempting to improve firm performance relative to their competitors.

Apple's ROIC is 17.3 percent, which is 8.5 percentage points higher than Microsoft's (8.8 percent). This means that for every $1.00 invested in Apple, the company returned $1.17, while for every $1.00 invested in Microsoft, the company returned $1.09. Since Apple was almost twice as efficient as Microsoft at generating

Tim Cook, Apple CEO.
John Gress Media Inc/
Shutterstock

Satya Nadella, Microsoft CEO.
Sean Gallup/Staff/Getty
Images

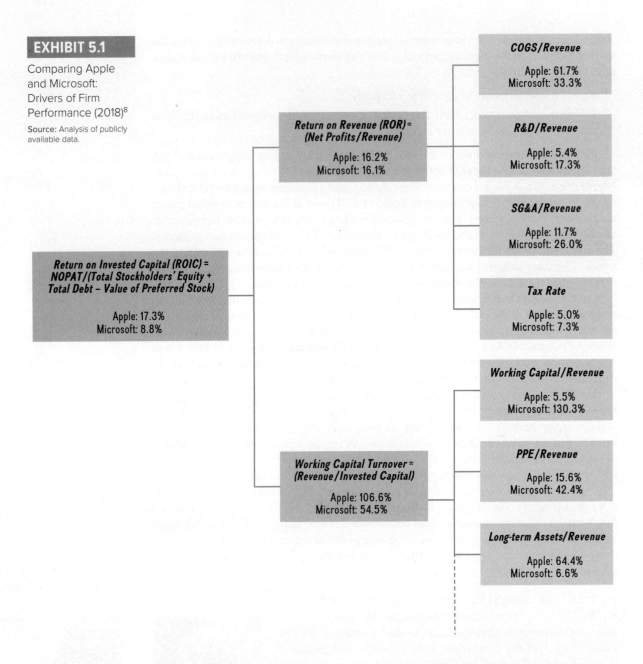

EXHIBIT 5.1

Comparing Apple and Microsoft: Drivers of Firm Performance (2018)[8]

Source: Analysis of publicly available data.

a ROIC, Apple had a clear competitive advantage over Microsoft. Although this is an important piece of information, managers need to know the underlying factors driving differences in firm profitability. Why is the ROIC for these two companies different?

Much like detectives, managers look for clues to solve that mystery: They break down ROIC into its constituents (as shown in Exhibit 5.1)—*return on revenue* and *working capital turnover*—to discover the underlying drivers of the marked difference in firm profitability.

Breaking down Return on Revenue (ROR). We start with the first component of ROIC: *return on revenue (ROR)*. ROR indicates how much of the firm's sales is converted into profits. Apple's ROR was 16.2 percent, while Microsoft's ROR was 16.1 percent. For every $100 in revenue, Apple earns $16.20 in profit, while Microsoft earns $16.10 in profit.

On this metric, Apple and Microsoft do not differ much. Keep in mind, however, that Apple's 2018 revenues were $262 billion, while Microsoft's were $118 billion. Thus, Apple is more than 2.2 times larger than Microsoft in terms of annual sales. As we investigate the differences in ROIC further, we will discover that Microsoft has a higher cost structure than Apple, and that Apple is able to charge a much higher margin for its products and services than Microsoft.

To delve deeper into the drivers of this difference, we need to break down ROR into three additional financial ratios:

- Cost of goods sold (COGS) / Revenue.
- Research & development (R&D) / Revenue.
- Selling, general, & administrative (SG&A) / Revenue.

COGS / Revenue. The first of these three ratios, *COGS / Revenue,* indicates how efficiently a company can produce a good. On this metric, Microsoft turns out to be much more efficient than Apple, with a difference of 28.4 percentage points (see Exhibit 5.1). This is because Microsoft's vast majority of revenues comes from software and online cloud services, with little cost attached to such digitally delivered products and services. In contrast, Apple's revenues were mostly from mobile devices, combining both hardware and software. In particular, the iPhone made up approximately 60 percent (or over $157 billion) of Apple's total revenues in 2018.

R&D / Revenue Even though Apple is more than two times as large as Microsoft in terms of revenues, it spends much less on research and development or on marketing and sales. Both of these help drive down Apple's cost structure. In particular, the next ratio, *R&D / Revenue,* indicates how much of each dollar that the firm earns in sales is invested to conduct research and development. A higher percentage is generally an indicator of a stronger focus on innovation to improve current products and services, and to come up with new ones.

Interestingly, Apple is much less R&D intensive than Microsoft. Apple spent 5.4 percent on R&D for every dollar of revenue, while Microsoft spent more than three times as much (17.3 percent R&D). Even considering the fact that Microsoft's revenues were $118 billion versus Apple's $262 billion, Microsoft spent much more on R&D in absolute dollars than Apple (Microsoft: $20 billion; Apple: $14 billion). For every $100 earned in revenues Microsoft spent $17.30 on R&D, while Apple only spent $5.40. For more than a decade now, Microsoft generally spends the most on R&D in absolute terms among all technology firms.

In contrast, Apple has spent much less on R&D than have other firms in the high-tech industry, in both absolute and relative terms. Apple's co-founder and longtime CEO, the late Steve Jobs, defined Apple's R&D philosophy as follows: "Innovation has nothing to do with how many R&D dollars you have. When Apple came up with the Mac, IBM was spending at least 100 times more on R&D. It's not about money. It's about the people you have, how you're led, and how much you get it."[9]

SG&A / Revenue. The third ratio in breaking down ROR, *SG&A / Revenue,* indicates how much of each dollar that the firm earns in sales is invested in sales, general, and administrative (SG&A) expenses. Generally, this ratio is an indicator of the firm's focus on marketing and sales to promote its products and services. For every $100 earned in revenues Microsoft spent $26.00 on sales and marketing, while Apple spent $11.70. Even though Microsoft SG&A intensity was more than twice as high as Apple, given the significant gap in revenues (Microsoft: $118 billion; Apple: $262 billion), each company spent almost $31 billion in marketing and sales, much more than either company spent on R&D.

Microsoft is spending a significant amount to rebuild its brand, especially on CEO Satya Nadella's strategic initiative of "mobile first, cloud first."[10] This focus on cloud computing on mobile devices marks a significant departure from the Windows-centric strategy for PCs of Nadella's predecessor, Steve Ballmer. Yet, by 2017, the Windows and Office combination still generated about 40 percent of Microsoft's total revenues and 75 percent of its profits. Microsoft is working hard to transition the Office business from the old business model of standalone software licenses ($150 for Office Home & Student) to repeat business via cloud-based subscriptions such as Office 365 Home & Student (which is $70 per year).

We also note, for completeness, that Apple's effective tax rate in 2018 was 5.0 percent (with a net income of $59.4 billion), while that of Microsoft was 7.3 percent (with a net income of $33.5 billion).[11]

Breaking Down Working Capital Turnover. The second component of ROIC is *Working Capital Turnover* (see Exhibit 5.1), which is a measure of how effectively capital is being used to generate revenue. In more general terms, working capital entails the amount of money a company can deploy in the short term, calculated as *current assets* minus *current liabilities.* This is where Apple outperforms Microsoft by a fairly wide margin (106.6 percent vs. 54.5 percent, respectively). For every dollar that Apple puts to work, it realizes $106.60 of sales, whereas Microsoft realizes $54.50 of sales—so a difference of $52.10. This implies that Apple is almost twice as efficient (96 percent) as Microsoft in turning invested capital into revenues.

This significant difference provides an important clue for Microsoft's strategic leaders to dig deeper to find the underlying drivers in working capital turnover. This enables executives to uncover which levers to pull to improve firm financial performance. In a next step, therefore, managers break down working capital turnover into other constituent financial ratios, including *Working Capital / Revenue; Plant, Property, and Equipment (PPE) / Revenue;* and *Long-term Assets / Revenue.* Each of these metrics is a measure of how effective a particular item on the balance sheet is contributing to revenue.

Working Capital / Revenue. The *working capital to revenue* ratio indicates how much of its working capital the firm has tied up in its operations. Apple (with a *working capital to revenue* ratio of 5.5 percent) operates much more efficiently than Microsoft (*working capital to revenue* ratio of 130.3 percent), because it has much less capital tied up in its operations. One reason is that Apple outsources its manufacturing. The vast majority of Apple's manufacturing of its products is done in China by low-cost producer Foxconn, which employs about 1 million people. Moreover, Apple benefits from an effective management of its global supply chain.

Although Apple's installed base of iPhone users globally is about 1 billion, one significant area of future vulnerability for Apple is that about 60 percent of annual revenues are based on sales of a single product—the iPhone, depending on model year. Moreover, China accounts for about 20 percent of Apple's total revenues. But demand in China for the newer high-end iPhones such as the iPhone XS Max has been dropping sharply in the face of local competition from Huawei, Xiaomi, and others. Apple's continued dependence on iPhone sales as well as declining sales in China are pressing issues that Apple CEO Tim Cook needs to address in order to sustain Apple's competitive advantage.

PPE / Revenue. The *PPE over revenue* ratio indicates how much of a firm's revenues are dedicated to cover *plant, property, and equipment,* which are critical assets to a firm's operations but cannot be liquidated easily. One reason Microsoft's *PPE to revenue* ratio (42.4 percent) is significantly higher than that of Apple's (15.6 percent) is the fact that Microsoft invests huge amounts of money on its cloud business, Azure. To do so, it needs to build hundreds of data centers (large groups of networked computer servers used for the remote storage, processing, or distribution of large amounts of data) across the globe, a costly proposition reflected in high *PPE* expenditures on a much lower revenue base than Apple. On the upside, Azure is already reporting some $23 billion in sales (in 2018), second only to Amazon's AWS with $27 billion in sales as the world's largest cloud-computing services provider.

A second area of future growth for Microsoft is likely to be artificial intelligence (AI). For example, algorithms combing through vast amounts of data on professionals and their networks might be able to tell sales staff on which leads to spend most of their time. This explains why Microsoft paid $26 billion in 2016 to acquire LinkedIn, a professional social network with some 250 million monthly active users.

Long-term Assets / Revenue. Finally, the *Long-term assets / Revenue* ratio indicates how much of each dollar a firm earns in revenues is tied up in long-term assets. Such assets include anything that cannot be turned into cash or consumed within one year. In the high-tech industry, long-term assets include not only plant, property, and equipment but also intangible assets. Intangible assets do not have physical attributes (see discussion of intangible resources in Chapter 4), and include a firm's intellectual property (such as patents, copyrights, and trademarks), goodwill, and brand value.

One way to think about this is that intangibles are the missing piece to be added to a firm's physical resource base (that is *plant, property, and equipment* and *current assets*) to make up a company's total (long-term) asset base. With a higher *Long-term assets / Revenue* ratio, Apple (64.4 percent) has much more value tied up in long-term assets than Microsoft (6.6 percent). Because the companies no longer break out their long-term assets into intangible and tangible assets, this figure is a bit harder to interpret. Apple's new campus in Cupertino, California, cost more than $5 billion, making it the most expensive office space ever built.[12] This large investment into long-term assets is one contributing factor why this particular ratio is much higher for Apple than Microsoft.

A deeper understanding of the fundamental drivers for differences in firm profitability allows leaders to develop strategic approaches. For example, CEO Satya Nadella could rework Microsoft's cost structure, in particular, its fairly high R&D and SG&A spending. Perhaps, R&D dollars could be spent more effectively. Apple generates a much higher return on its R&D spending. Microsoft's sales and marketing expenses also seem to be quite high, but may be needed to rebuild Microsoft's brand image with a new focus on mobile and cloud computing.

LIMITATIONS OF ACCOUNTING DATA. Although accounting data tend to be readily available and we can easily transform them into financial ratios to assess and evaluate competitive performance, they also exhibit some important limitations:

- *Accounting data are historical and thus backward-looking.* Accounting profitability ratios show us only the outcomes from past decisions, and the past is no guarantee of future performance. There is also a significant time delay before accounting data become publicly available. Some strategists liken making decisions using accounting data to driving a car by looking in the rearview mirror.[13] While financial strength certainly helps, past performance is no guarantee that a company is prepared for market disruption.

- *Accounting data do not consider off-balance sheet items.* Off-balance sheet items, such as pension obligations (quite large in some U.S. companies) or operating leases in the retail industry, can be significant factors. For example, one retailer may own all its stores, which would properly be included in the firm's assets; a second retailer may lease all its stores, which would *not be* listed as assets. All else being equal, the second retailer's return on assets (ROA) would be higher. Strategists address this shortcoming by adjusting accounting data to obtain an *equivalent* economic capital base, so that they can compare companies with different capital structures.

- *Accounting data focus mainly on tangible assets, which are no longer the most important.*[14] This limitation of accounting data is nicely captured in the adage: *Not everything that can be counted counts. Not everything that counts can be counted.*[15] Although accounting data capture some intangible assets, such as the value of intellectual property (patents, trademarks, and so on) and customer goodwill, many key intangible assets are not captured. Today, the most competitively important assets tend to be intangibles such as innovation, quality, and customer experience, which are not included in a firm's balance sheets. For example, Apple's core competency in designing beautiful and user-friendly mobile devices embedded within a large ecosystem of various services, such as ApplePay, is not a balance sheet item, but nonetheless a critical foundation in its quest for competitive advantage.

INTANGIBLES AND THE VALUE OF FIRMS. Intangible assets that are not captured in accounting data have become much more important in firms' stock market valuations over the last few decades. Exhibit 5.2 shows the firm's book value (accounting data capturing the firm's actual costs of assets minus depreciation) as part of a firm's total stock market valuation (number of outstanding shares times share price). The firm's book value captures the historical cost of a firm's assets, whereas market valuation is based on future expectations for a firm's growth potential and performance. For the firms in the S&P 500 (the 500 largest publicly traded companies by market capitalization in the U.S. stock market, as determined by Standard & Poor's, a rating agency), the importance of a firm's book value has declined dramatically over time. This decline mirrors a commensurate increase in the importance of intangibles that contribute to growth potential and yet are not captured in a firm's accounting data.

In 1980 about 80 percent of a firm's stock market valuation was based on its book value with 20 percent based on the market's expectations concerning the firm's future performance. This almost reversed by 2000 (at the height of the internet bubble), when firm valuations were based only 15 percent on assets captured by accounting data. The important take-away is that intangibles not captured in firms' accounting data have become much more important to a firm's competitive advantage. By 2015, about 75 percent of a firm's market valuation was determined by its intangibles. This trend explains why in 2019, Amazon ($950 billion) is valued almost five times as much as Boeing ($200 billion), or why Alphabet, Google's parent company ($830 billion), is valued over 15 times more than GM ($54 billion).

So what have we learned about accounting profitability? Key financial ratios based on accounting data give us an important tool with which to assess competitive advantage. In particular, they help us measure *relative* profitability, which is

EXHIBIT 5.2 The Declining Importance of Book Value in a Firm's Stock Market Valuation, 1980–2015

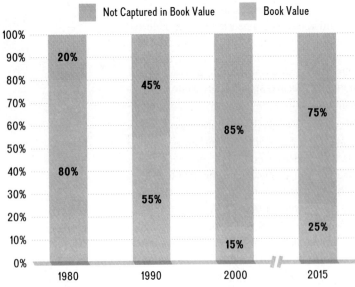

Source: Analysis and depiction of data from Compustat, 1980–2015.

useful when comparing firms of different sizes over time. While not perfect, these ratios are an important starting point when analyzing the competitive performance of firms (and thus are a critical tool for case analysis). Again, see the "How to Conduct a Case Analysis" module in Part 4. We next turn to *shareholder value creation,* a second traditional way to measure and assess competitive advantage, attempting to overcome the shortcomings of a backward-looking internal focus on mostly tangible assets inherent in accounting profitability.

SHAREHOLDER VALUE CREATION

LO 5-2

Apply shareholder value creation to assess and evaluate competitive advantage.

Shareholders—individuals or organizations that own one or more shares of stock in a public company—are the legal owners of public companies. From the shareholders' perspective, the measure of competitive advantage that matters most is the return on their **risk capital**,[16] which is the money they provide in return for an equity share, money that they cannot recover if the firm goes bankrupt. In September 2008, the shareholders of Lehman Brothers, a global financial services firm, lost their entire investment of about $40 billion when the firm declared bankruptcy.

Investors are primarily interested in a company's **total return to shareholders**, which is the return on risk capital, including stock price appreciation plus dividends received over a specific period. Unlike accounting data, total return to shareholders is an *external* and *forward-looking* performance metric. It essentially indicates how the stock market views all available public information about a firm's past, current state, and expected future performance, with most of the weight on future growth expectations.

The idea that all available information about a firm's past, current state, and expected future performance is embedded in the market price of the firm's stock is called the *efficient-market hypothesis.*[17] In this perspective, a firm's share price provides an objective performance indicator. When assessing and evaluating competitive advantage, a comparison of rival firms' share price development or market capitalization provides a helpful yardstick when used over the *long term.* **Market capitalization** (or market cap) captures the total dollar market value of a company's outstanding shares at any given point in time (*Market cap = Number of outstanding shares × Share price*). If a company has 50 million shares outstanding, and each share is traded at $200, the market capitalization is $10 billion (50,000,000 × $200 = $10,000,000,000, or $10 billion).[18]

BENCHMARK METRICS. All public companies in the United States are required to report total return to shareholders annually in the statements they file with the Securities and Exchange Commission (SEC). In addition, companies must also provide benchmarks, usually one comparison to the industry average and another to a broader market index that is relevant for more diversified firms.[19] Since competitive advantage is defined in relative terms, these benchmarks allow us to assess whether a firm has a competitive advantage.

In its annual reports, Microsoft, for example, compares its performance to two stock indices: the NASDAQ computer index and the S&P 500. The computer index includes over 400 high-tech companies traded on the NASDAQ, including Apple, Adobe, Google, Intel, and Oracle. It provides a comparison of Microsoft to the computer industry—broadly

---

shareholders Individuals or organizations that own one or more shares of stock in a public company.	**risk capital** The money provided by shareholders in exchange for an equity share in a company; it cannot be recovered if the firm goes bankrupt.	**total return to shareholders** Return on risk capital that includes stock price appreciation plus dividends received over a specific period.	**market capitalization** A firm performance metric that captures the total dollar market value of a company's total outstanding shares at any given point in time.

defined. The S&P 500 offers a comparison to the wider stock market beyond the computer industry. In its 2018 annual report, Microsoft shows that it *outperformed* the S&P 500 since 2016 and the NASDAQ computer index in 2018.

GROWTH-RATE PREDICTIONS. Effective strategies to grow the business can increase a firm's profitability and thus its stock price.[20] Indeed, investors and Wall Street analysts expect continuous growth. A firm's stock price generally increases only if the firm's rate of growth exceeds investors' expectations. This is because investors discount into the present value of the firm's stock price whatever growth rate they foresee in the future. If a low-growth business like Comcast (in cable TV) is expected to grow 2 percent each year but realizes 4 percent growth, its stock price will appreciate. In contrast, if a fast-growing business like Apple in mobile computing is expected to grow by 10 percent annually but delivers "only" 8 percent growth, its stock price will fall.

Investors also adjust their expectations over time. Since the business in the slow-growth industry surprised them by delivering higher than expected growth, they adjust their expectations upward. The next year, they expect this firm to again deliver 4 percent growth. On the other hand, if the industry average is 10 percent a year in the high-tech business, the firm that delivered 8 percent growth will again be expected to deliver at least the industry average growth rate; otherwise, its stock will be further discounted.

In ChapterCase 5, we noted that Apple was the first company to reach $1 trillion in market cap (in the fall of 2018). By spring 2019, Apple's market cap stood at $995 billion, while Microsoft's market cap was over $1 trillion. Indeed, Microsoft was again the most valuable company worldwide, followed by Apple, Amazon, Alphabet, and Facebook. It is noteworthy that the five most valuable companies globally are all tech companies—underscoring the importance of future growth expectations by investors.

STOCK MARKET VALUATIONS. Considering stock market valuations (*Share price × Number of outstanding shares*) over the long term provides a useful metric to assess competitive advantage. Exhibit 5.3 shows the stock market valuations for Apple and Microsoft from 1990 until 2019. Microsoft was the most valuable company worldwide (in December 1999 with close to $600 billion in market cap), but its market valuation dropped in the following decade. The valuation declined because Microsoft struggled with the transition from desktop to mobile and cloud-based computing. CEO Satya Nadella, however, is moving Microsoft away from its Windows-only business model to compete more effectively in a "mobile first, cloud first world."[21] Nadella's strategic initiative is starting to bear fruit as investors appear to be pleased with how well Microsoft is performing in future growth areas such as cloud computing. As Exhibit 5.3 shows that since Nadella took the helm at Microsoft in 2014, the company's market cap has been increasing at a steep clip, even overtaking Apple at the end of the time period, making Microsoft again the most valuable company globally (see more detail in Part II of ChapterCase 5).

LIMITATIONS OF SHAREHOLDER VALUE CREATION. Although measuring firm performance through total return to shareholders and firm market capitalization has many advantages, just as with accounting profitability, it has its shortcomings:

- *Stock prices can be highly volatile, making it difficult to assess firm performance, particularly in the short term.* This volatility implies that *total return to shareholders* is a better measure of firm performance and competitive advantage over the long term (as shown in Exhibit 5.3), because of the "noise" introduced by market volatility, external factors, and investor sentiment.

EXHIBIT 5.3 Stock Market Valuations of Apple and Microsoft (in $bn), 1990–2019

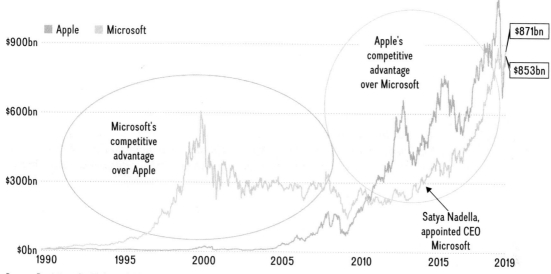

Source: Depiction of publicly available data.

- *Overall macroeconomic factors such as economic growth or contraction, the unemployment rate, and interest and exchange rates all have a direct bearing on stock prices.* It can be difficult to ascertain the extent to which a stock price is influenced more by external macroeconomic factors (as discussed in Chapter 3) than by the firm's strategy (see also Exhibit 3.2 highlighting firm, industry, and other effects in overall firm performance).

- *Stock prices frequently reflect the psychological mood of investors, which can at times be irrational.* Stock prices can overshoot expectations based on economic fundamentals amid periods like the internet boom, during which former Federal Reserve Chairman Alan Greenspan famously described investors' buoyant sentiments as "irrational exuberance."[22] Similarly, stock prices can undershoot expectations during busts like the 2008–2009 global financial crisis, in which investors' sentiment was described as "irrational gloom."[23]

ECONOMIC VALUE CREATION

The relationship between *economic value creation* and competitive advantage is fundamental in strategic management. It provides the foundation upon which to formulate a firm's competitive strategy for cost leadership or differentiation (discussed in detail in Chapter 6). For now, suffice it to say that a firm has a competitive advantage when it creates more *economic value* than rival firms. What does this mean?

Economic value created is the difference between a buyer's willingness to pay for a product or service and the firm's total cost to produce it. Let's say a consumer is considering buying a new laptop and she has a budget of $1,200. She has narrowed her choices down to Model 1 by Firm A and Model 2 by Firm B. Because she has owned a laptop by Firm A before, she is familiar with its models. She values Model 1 at a **reservation price** of $1,000, which is the maximum she is willing to pay for it. Model 1 is comparable to a more or less generic, run-of-the-mill laptop. In contrast, she values Model 2 by Firm B at $1,200 because it has a somewhat higher performance, is more user-friendly, and has a greater "coolness factor." Given that she values Model 2 by Firm B at $200 more than she values Model 1 by Firm A, she purchases Model 2, paying as much as her reservation price allows.

LO 5-3

Explain economic value creation and different sources of competitive advantage.

economic value created Difference between value (V) and cost (C), or ($V - C$).

reservation price The maximum price a consumer is willing to pay for a product or service based on the total perceived consumer benefits.

IMPLICATIONS FOR FIRM-LEVEL COMPETITIVE ADVANTAGE. Let's now move from individual considerations to the overall laptop market in order to derive implications for firm-level competitive advantage. To simplify this illustration, we will recognize Firm A and Firm B as the only firms competing in the laptop market. Assuming that both firms produce their respective models at the same total unit cost ($400), and the market at large has preferences similar to that of our consumer, then Firm B will have a competitive advantage. Why? As Exhibit 5.4 depicts, even though the total unit costs for both firms is the same, Firm B's laptop is perceived as providing more utility than Firm A's laptop, which implies that Firm B creates more economic value ($1,200 − $400 = $800) than Firm A ($1,000 − $400 = $600). Thus, Firm B has a competitive advantage over Firm A because Firm B's *total perceived consumer benefits* are greater than Firm A's, while the firms have the same cost. The amount of *total perceived consumer benefits* equals the *maximum willingness to pay,* or the *reservation price.* In short, Firm B's advantage is based on superior *differentiation* leading to higher perceived value. Further, the competitive advantage can be quantified: It is $200 (or $1,200 − $1,000) per laptop sold for Firm B over Firm A (see Exhibit 5.4).

Exhibit 5.4 shows that Firm B's competitive advantage is based on greater economic value creation because of superior product differentiation. In addition, a firm can achieve competitive advantage through a second avenue. In particular, competitive advantage can also result from a relative *cost advantage* over rivals, assuming both firms can create the same total perceived consumer benefits.

Now let's introduce two new firms to our hypothetical laptop market. Exhibit 5.5 shows how Firm C and Firm D each offer a model that has the same perceived consumer benefits ($1,200). Firm C, however, creates greater economic value ($900, or $1,200 − $300) than does Firm D ($600, or $1,200 − $600). Why? Because Firm C's total unit cost ($300) is lower than Firm D's ($600). Firm C has a relative cost advantage over Firm D, even though both products provide the same total perceived consumer benefits ($1,200). Furthermore, Firm C has a competitive advantage over Firm D in the amount of $300 for each laptop sold. Here, the source of Firm C's competitive advantage is a relative cost advantage over its rival, Firm D, while perceived consumer benefits are the same.

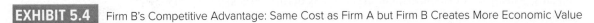

EXHIBIT 5.4 Firm B's Competitive Advantage: Same Cost as Firm A but Firm B Creates More Economic Value

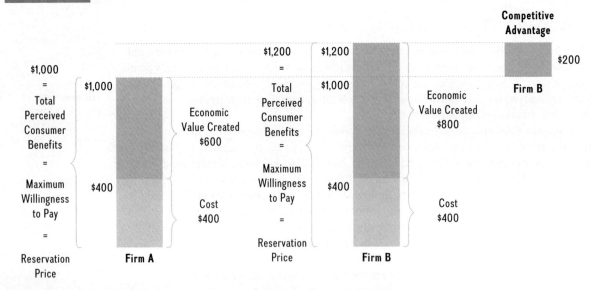

EXHIBIT 5.5 Firm C's Competitive Advantage: Same Total Perceived Consumer Benefits as Firm D but Firm C Creates More Economic Value

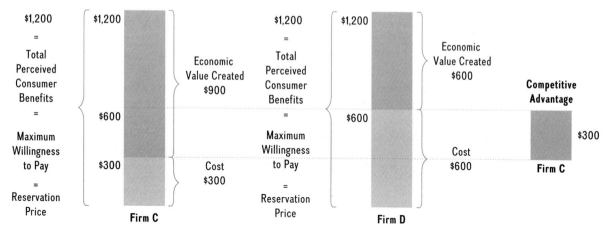

So far we have looked at situations in which products are priced at the maximum that a consumer might be willing to pay. But markets generally don't work like that. More often, the economic value created is shared between the producer and the consumer. That is, most of the time consumers are able to purchase the product at a price point below the maximum they are willing to spend. Both the seller and the buyer benefit.

VALUE, PRICE, AND COST. For ease in calculating competitive advantage, three components are needed. These will help us to further explain *total perceived consumer benefits* and *economic value created* in more detail:

1. Value (*V*)
2. Price (*P*)
3. Cost (*C*)

Value denotes the dollar amount (*V*) a consumer attaches to a good or service. Value captures a consumer's willingness to pay and is determined by the perceived benefits a good or service provides to the buyer. The cost (*C*) to produce the good or service matters little to the consumer, but it matters a great deal to the producer (supplier) of the good or service since it has a direct bearing on the profit margin.

Let's return to our laptop example from Exhibit 5.4, in which Firm A and Firm B sold their laptops at different prices ($1,000 and $1,200, respectively), even though their total unit costs were the same ($400). In each case, the price did not exceed the consumer's maximum willingness to pay for the particular offering. Subtracting the costs, we found that Firm A created an economic value of $600 while Firm B created an economic value of $800, thus achieving a competitive advantage. In most market transactions, however, some of the economic value created benefits the consumer as well.

The Role of Consumer Surplus and Producer Surplus. Again, let's revisit the example depicted in Exhibit 5.4. The consumer's preference was to buy the laptop from Firm B, which she would have done because she preferred this laptop and could afford it given her reservation price. Let's assume Firm B's laptop is actually on sale for $1,000 (everything else remains constant). Assume the consumer again chooses to purchase Firm B's laptop rather than Firm A's (which she considered inferior). In this case, some of the economic

value The dollar amount (*V*) a consumer attaches to a good or service; the consumer's maximum willingness to pay; also called *reservation price*.

value created by Firm B goes to the consumer. On a formula basis, total perceived value of Firm B's laptop ($1,200) splits into *economic value created* ($V - C = \$800$) plus *total unit cost* ($C = \$400$), or: $V = (V - C) + C$.

The difference between the price charged (P) and the cost to produce (C) is the **producer surplus**, or simply **profit**. In the laptop example in Exhibit 5.6, if the price charged is $1,000, the profit is $P - C = \$1,000 - \$400 = \$600$. The firm captures this amount as profit per unit sold. The consumer captures the difference between what she would have been willing to pay (V) and what she actually paid (P), called **consumer surplus**. In our example, the consumer surplus is $V - P = \$1,200 - \$1,000$, or $200. *Economic value creation* therefore equals *consumer surplus* plus *firm profit,* or $(V - C) = (V - P) + (P - C)$. In the laptop example from Exhibit 5.4:

Economic value created ($1,200 − $400) = Consumer surplus ($1,200 − $1,000) + Producer surplus ($1,000 − $400) = $200 + $600 = $800.

The Relationship between Consumer Surplus and Producer Surplus. The relationship between consumer and producer surplus is the reason trade happens: Both transacting parties capture *some* of the overall value created. Note, though, that the distribution of the value created between parties need not be equal to make trade worthwhile. In the example illustrated in Exhibit 5.6, the consumer surplus is $200, while profit per unit sold is $600.

In some cases, where firms offer highly innovative products or services, the relationship can be even more skewed. The entry-level model of the Apple Watch retailed for $349 when it was introduced in 2015; it sold well, selling twice as many watches as iPhones in each device's first year.[24] An analysis by an independent engineering team, however, revealed that the firm's total cost in terms of materials and labor for the Apple Watch was no more than $84.[25] Thus, Apple's profit for each watch sold was an estimated $265, with a profit margin of 315 percent.

EXHIBIT 5.6 The Role of Consumer Surplus and Producer Surplus (Profit)

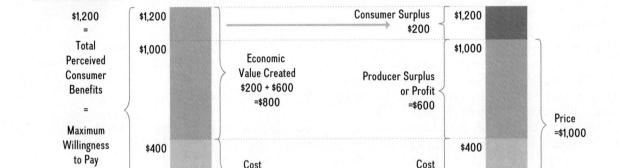

| **producer surplus** Another term for profit, the difference between price charged (P) and the cost to produce (C), or ($P - C$); also called *profit*. | **profit** Difference between price charged (P) and the cost to produce (C), or ($P - C$); also called *producer surplus*. | **consumer surplus** Difference between the value a consumer attaches to a good or service (V) and what he or she paid for it (P), or ($V - P$). |

The economic value creation framework shows that strategy is about

1. Creating economic value.
2. Capturing as much of it as possible.

As a counterexample to Apple, consider Amazon: It is creating a large amount of value for its customers, but it is not capturing much of it (at this point). Amazon has had two decades of negative net income as it attempts to build a stronger position in a variety of businesses. With its online retail business, Amazon is creating significant value for its customers (especially its Prime members) as well as third-party sellers that use its platform, but Amazon is comfortable in taking minor or no profit in doing so. Why? Because at this point, Amazon cares more about the *installed base of its users,* thus Amazon wants to accrue as many customers as possible to benefit from network effects and to lock out competing retail platforms.

Its cloud-computing service, Amazon Web Services (AWS), also is creating tremendous value for the businesses that use it for running their computing needs, including Airbnb, Comcast, Foursquare, NASA, and even the CIA. But Amazon's "profit" margin in online retailing is zero in the United States while it is losing money internationally. In fact, Amazon's comfort level appears to bear on its acquisition of Whole Foods. Even at the high end, the grocery industry has thin margins. Before Amazon acquired it, Whole Foods had been under stockholder pressure to *increase* margins by lowering *costs* for better shareholder returns. Now Whole Foods under Amazon becomes the grocery industry's worst nightmare: It can deliver negative margins and still stockholders applaud. Even if Amazon had no plans to reap synergies between in-store and online tactics, now Whole Foods becomes super competitive with its potential ability to lower prices.[26] Indeed, on its first day after closing the acquisition of Whole Foods, Amazon dropped prices at its new grocery chain by more than 30 percent on some 100 grocery staples.

In this case, Amazon's customers are capturing the value that Amazon is creating. Jeff Bezos, Amazon CEO, however, is focused on long-term performance rather than short-term profitability. Amazon's investors don't seem to mind Bezos' long-term orientation, because Amazon's $1 trillion in market cap (in 2019) makes it one of the most valuable companies on the planet.

Competitive Advantage and Economic Value Created. Exhibit 5.7 illustrates how the components of economic value creation fit together conceptually. On the left side of the exhibit, V represents the total perceived consumer benefits, as captured in the consumer's maximum willingness to pay. In the lower part of the center bar, C is the cost to produce the product or service (the unit cost). It follows that the difference between the consumers' maximum willingness to pay and the firm's cost $(V - C)$ is the economic value created. The price of the product or service (P) is indicated in the dashed line. The economic value created $(V - C)$, as shown in Exhibit 5.7, is split between producer and consumer: $(V - P)$ is the value the consumer captures *(consumer surplus),* and $(P - C)$ is the value the producer captures *(producer surplus,* or *profit).*

Competitive advantage goes to the firm that achieves the largest economic value created, which is the difference between V, the consumer's willingness to pay, and C, the cost to produce the good or service. The reason is that a large difference between V and C gives the firm two distinct pricing options: (1) It can charge higher prices to reflect the higher value and thus increase its profitability, or (2) it can charge the same price as competitors and thus gain market share. Given this, the strategic objective is to maximize $V - C$, or the economic value created.

Applying the notion of *economic value creation* also has direct implications for firm financial performance. Revenues are a function of the value created for consumers and the price

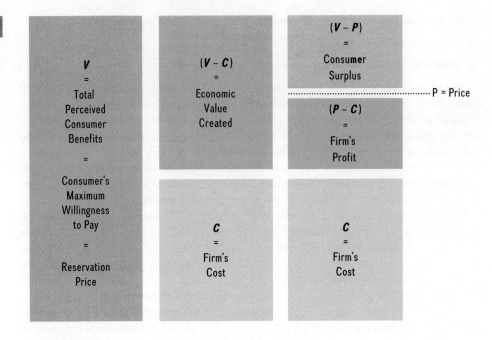

of the good or service, which together determine the volume of goods sold. In this perspective, profit (Π) is defined as total revenues (TR) minus total costs (TC):

$$\Pi = TR - TC, \text{ where } TR = P \times Q, \text{ or } price \text{ times } quantity\ sold$$

Total costs include both fixed and variable costs. *Fixed costs* are independent of consumer demand—for example, the cost of capital to build computer manufacturing plants or an online retail presence to take direct orders. *Variable costs* change with the level of consumer demand—for instance, components such as different types of display screens, microprocessors, hard drives, and keyboards.

Rather than merely relying on historical costs, as done when taking the perspective of *accounting profitability* (introduced earlier), in the *economic value creation* perspective, *all costs,* including *opportunity costs,* must be considered. **Opportunity costs** capture the value of the best forgone alternative use of the resources employed.

An entrepreneur, for example, faces two types of opportunity costs: (1) forgone wages she could be earning if she was employed elsewhere and (2) the cost of capital she invested in her business, which could instead be invested in, say, the stock market or U.S. Treasury bonds.

At the end of the year, the entrepreneur considers her business over the last 12 months. She made an *accounting profit* of $70,000, calculated as total revenues minus expenses, which include all historical costs but not opportunity costs. But she also realizes she has forgone $60,000 in salary she could have earned as an employee at another firm. In addition, she knows she could have earned $15,000 in interest if she had bought U.S. Treasury bills with a 2 percent return instead of investing $750,000 in her business. The opportunity cost of being an entrepreneur was $75,000 ($60,000 + $15,000). Therefore, when considering all costs, including opportunity costs, she actually experienced an economic loss of $5,000 ($75,000 – $70,000). When considering her future options, she should stay in business only if she values her independence as an entrepreneur more than $5,000 per year, or thinks business will be better next year.

opportunity costs The value of the best forgone alternative use of the resources employed.

LIMITATIONS OF ECONOMIC VALUE CREATION. As with any tool to asse advantage, the economic value creation framework also has some limitation

- *Determining the value of a good in the eyes of consumers is not a simple t* tackle this problem is to look at consumers' purchasing habits for thei ences, which indicate how much each consumer is willing to pay for vice. In the earlier example, the value (V) the consumer placed o highest price she was willing to pay, or her reservation price—was $1, able to charge the reservation price ($P = \$1{,}200$), it captures all the e ated ($V - C = \$800$) as producer surplus or profit ($P - C = \$800$).

- *The value of a good in the eyes of consumers changes based on income, preferences, and other factors.* If your income is high, you are likely to place a higher value on some goods (e.g., business-class air travel) and a lower value on other goods (e.g., Greyhound bus travel). In regard to preferences, you may place a higher value on a ticket for a Lady Gaga concert than on one for the New York Philharmonic (or vice versa). As an example of time value, you place a higher value on an airline ticket that will get you to an important business meeting tomorrow than on one for a planned trip to take place eight weeks from now.

- *To measure firm-level competitive advantage, we must estimate the economic value created for all products and services offered by the firm.* This estimation may be a relatively easy task if the firm offers only a few products or services. However, it becomes much more complicated for diversified firms such as General Electric or the Tata Group that may offer hundreds or even thousands of different products and services across many industries and geographies. Although the performance of individual strategic business units (SBUs) can be assessed along the dimensions described here, it becomes more difficult to make this assessment at the corporate level (more on this in our discussion of diversification strategy in Chapter 8).

The economic value creation perspective gives us one useful way to assess competitive advantage. This approach is conceptually quite powerful, and it lies at the center of many strategic management frameworks such as the generic business strategies (which we discuss in the next chapter). However, it falls somewhat short when managers are called upon to operationalize competitive advantage. When the need for "hard numbers" arises, managers and analysts frequently rely on firm financials such as *accounting profitability* or *shareholder value creation* to measure firm performance.

We've now completed our consideration of the three standard dimensions for measuring competitive advantage—accounting profitability, shareholder value, and economic value. Although each provides unique insights for assessing competitive advantage, one drawback is that they are more or less one-dimensional metrics. Focusing on just one performance metric when assessing competitive advantage, however, can lead to significant problems, because each metric has its shortcomings, as listed earlier. We now turn to two more conceptual and qualitative frameworks—the balanced scorecard and the triple bottom line—that attempt to provide a more holistic perspective on firm performance.

THE BALANCED SCORECARD

Just as airplane pilots rely on a number of instruments to provide constant information about key variables—such as altitude, airspeed, fuel, position of other aircraft in the vicinity, and destination—to ensure a safe flight, so should strategic leaders rely on multiple yardsticks to more accurately assess company performance in an integrative way. The **balanced scorecard** is a framework to help managers achieve their strategic objectives more effectively.[27]

LO 5-4

Apply a balanced scorecard to assess and evaluate competitive advantage.

balanced scorecard
Strategy implementation tool that harnesses multiple internal and external performance metrics in order to balance financial and strategic goals.

Balanced-Scorecard Approach to Creating and Sustaining Competitive Advantage

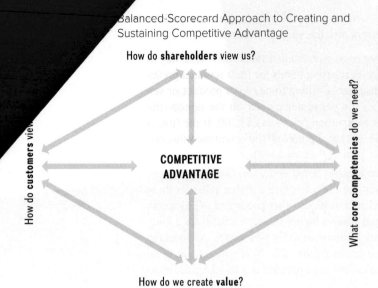

How do **shareholders** view us?

How do **customers** view us?

What **core competencies** do we need?

COMPETITIVE ADVANTAGE

How do we create **value**?

This approach harnesses multiple internal and external performance metrics in order to balance both financial and strategic goals.

Exhibit 5.8 depicts the balanced-scorecard framework. Strategic leaders using the balanced scorecard develop appropriate metrics to assess strategic objectives by answering four key questions.[28] Brainstorming answers to these questions ideally results in measures that give managers a quick but also comprehensive view of the firm's current state. The four key questions are:

1. *How do customers view us?* The customer's perspective concerning the company's products and services links directly to its revenues and profits. Consumers decide their reservation price for a product or service based on how they view it. If the customer views the company's offering favorably, she is willing to pay more for it, enhancing its competitive advantage (assuming production costs are well below the asking price). Managers track customer perception to identify areas to improve, with a focus on speed, quality, service, and cost. In the air-express industry, for example, managers learned from their customers that many don't really need next-day delivery for most of their documents and packages; rather what they really cared about was the ability to track the shipments. This discovery led to the development of steeply discounted second-day delivery by UPS and FedEx, combined with sophisticated real-time tracking tools online.

2. *How do we create value?* Answering this question challenges managers to develop strategic objectives that ensure future competitiveness, innovation, and organizational learning. The answer focuses on the business processes and structures that allow a firm to create economic value. One useful metric is the percentage of revenues obtained from new product introductions. For example, 3M requires that 30 percent of revenues must come from products introduced within the past four years.[29] A second metric, aimed at assessing a firm's external learning and collaboration capability, is to stipulate that a certain percentage of new products must originate from outside the firm's boundaries.[30] Through its Connect + Develop program, the consumer products company Procter & Gamble has raised the percentage of new products that originated (at least partly) from outside P&G to 35 percent, up from 15 percent.[31]

3. *What core competencies do we need?* This question focuses managers internally to identify the core competencies needed to achieve their objectives and the accompanying business processes that support, hone, and leverage those competencies. Honda's core competency is to design and manufacture small but powerful and highly reliable engines. Its business model is to find places to put its engines. Beginning with motorcycles in 1948, Honda nurtured this core competency over many decades and is leveraging it to reach stretch goals in the design, development, and manufacture of small airplanes.

Today, consumers still value reliable, gas-powered engines made by Honda. If consumers start to value electric motors more because of zero emissions, lower maintenance costs, and higher performance metrics, among other possible reasons, the value of Honda's engine competency will decrease. If this happens, then Tesla's core competency in designing and building high-powered battery packs and electric drivetrains will become more valuable. In turn, Tesla (featured in ChapterCase 1) might then be able to leverage this core competency into a strong strategic position in the emerging all-electric car and mobility industry.

4. *How do shareholders view us?* The final perspective in the balanced scorecard is the shareholders' view of financial performance (as discussed in the prior section). Some of the measures in this area rely on accounting data such as cash flow, operating income, ROIC, ROE, and, of course, total returns to shareholders. Understanding the shareholders' view of value creation leads managers to a more future-oriented evaluation.

By relying on both an internal and an external view of the firm, the balanced scorecard combines the strengths provided by the individual approaches to assessing competitive advantage discussed earlier: accounting profitability, shareholder value creation, and economic value creation.

ADVANTAGES OF THE BALANCED SCORECARD. The balanced-scorecard approach is popular in managerial practice because it has several advantages. In particular, the balanced scorecard allows strategic leaders to:

- Communicate and link the strategic vision to responsible parties within the organization.
- Translate the vision into measurable operational goals.
- Design and plan business processes.
- Implement feedback and organizational learning to modify and adapt strategic goals when indicated.

The balanced scorecard can accommodate both short- and long-term performance metrics. It provides a concise report that tracks chosen metrics and measures and compares them to target values. This approach allows strategic leaders to assess past performance, identify areas for improvement, and position the company for future growth. Including a broader perspective than financials allows managers and executives a more balanced view of organizational performance—hence its name. In a sense, the balanced scorecard is a broad diagnostic tool. It complements the common financial metrics with operational measures on customer satisfaction, internal processes, and the company's innovation and improvement activities.

As an example of how to implement the balanced-scorecard approach, let's look at FMC Corp., a chemical manufacturer employing some 5,000 people in different SBUs and earning over $3 billion in annual revenues.[32] To achieve its vision of becoming "the customer's most valued supplier," FMC's strategic leaders initially had focused solely on financial metrics such as return on invested capital (ROIC) as performance measures. FMC is a multibusiness corporation with several standalone profit-and-loss strategic business units; its overall performance was the result of both over- and underperforming units. FMC's managers had tried several approaches to enhance performance, but they turned out to be ineffective. Perhaps even more significant, short-term thinking by general managers was a major obstacle in the attempt to implement an effective business strategy.

Searching for improved performance, FMC's CEO decided to adopt a balanced-scorecard approach. It enabled the managers to view FMC's challenges and shortcomings from a holistic, company perspective, which was especially helpful to the general managers of different business units. In particular, the balanced scorecard allowed general managers to focus on market position, customer service, and product introductions that could generate long-term value. Using the framework depicted in Exhibit 5.7, strategic leaders had to answer tough follow-up questions such as: How do we become the customer's most valued supplier, and how can my division create this value for the customer? How do we become more externally focused? What are my division's core competencies and contributions to the company goals? What are my division's weaknesses?

Implementing a balanced scorecard allowed FMC's managers to align their different perspectives to create a more focused corporation overall. General managers now review progress along the chosen metrics every month, and corporate executives do so on a quarterly basis. Implementing a balanced-scorecard approach is not a onetime effort, but requires continuous tracking of metrics and updating of strategic objectives, if needed. It is a continuous process, feeding performance back into the strategy process to assess its effectiveness (see Chapter 2).

DISADVANTAGES OF THE BALANCED SCORECARD. Though widely implemented by many businesses, the balanced scorecard is not without its critics.[33] It is important to note that the balanced scorecard is a tool for strategy *implementation,* not for strategy *formulation.* It is up to a firm's leaders to formulate a strategy that will enhance the chances of gaining and sustaining a competitive advantage. In addition, the balanced-scorecard approach provides only limited guidance about which metrics to choose. Different situations call for different metrics. All of the three approaches to measuring competitive advantage—accounting profitability, shareholder value creation, and economic value creation—in addition to other quantitative and qualitative measures can be helpful when using a balanced-scorecard approach.

When implementing a balanced scorecard, managers need to be aware that a failure to achieve competitive advantage is not so much a reflection of a poor framework but of a strategic failure. The balanced scorecard is only as good as the skills of the managers who use it: They first must devise a strategy that enhances the odds of achieving competitive advantage. Second, they must accurately translate the strategy into objectives that they can measure and manage within the balanced-scorecard approach.[34]

Once the metrics have been selected, the balanced scorecard tracks chosen metrics and measures and compares them to target values. It does not, however, provide much insight into how metrics that deviate from the set goals can be put back on track.[35]

<table>
<tr><td>**LO 5-5**</td></tr>
<tr><td>Apply a triple bottom line to assess and evaluate competitive advantage.</td></tr>
</table>

THE TRIPLE BOTTOM LINE

Today, strategic leaders are frequently asked to maintain and improve not only the firm's economic performance but also its social and ecological performance. When serving as CEO of PepsiCo, Indra Nooyi responded by declaring the company's vision to be *Performance with Purpose* defined by goals in the social dimension (*human sustainability* to combat obesity by making its products healthier, and the *whole person at work* to achieve work/life balance) and ecological dimension (*environmental sustainability* in regard to clean water, energy, recycling, and so on), in addition to firm financial performance. Strategy Highlight 5.1. discusses Indra Nooyi's triple bottom line initiative in detail.

Being proactive along noneconomic dimensions can make good business sense. In anticipation of coming industry requirements for "extended producer responsibility," which requires the seller of a product to take it back for recycling at the end of its life, the German carmaker BMW was proactive. It not only lined up the leading car-recycling companies but also started to redesign its cars using a modular approach. The modular parts allow for quick car disassembly and reuse of components in the after-sales market

Strategy Highlight 5.1

PepsiCo's Indra Nooyi: Performance with Purpose

"Performance with Purpose is not how we spend the money we make; it's how we make the money," said Indra Nooyi while PepsiCo CEO.[36]

In the 120-year history of PepsiCo, Indra Nooyi was the first, and so far only, female chief executive officer to run the multinational food, snack, and beverage company. As CEO of PepsiCo from 2006 to 2018, Nooyi was one of the world's most powerful business leaders. A native of Chennai, India, Nooyi holds multiple degrees: bachelor's degrees in physics, chemistry, and mathematics from Madras Christian College; an MBA from the Indian Institute of Management; and a master's degree in public and private management from Yale University. Before joining PepsiCo in 1994, Nooyi worked for Johnson & Johnson, Boston Consulting Group, Motorola, and ABB. For the past several years, she has been a regular in *Forbes* Top 20 most powerful women. However, she was not your typical Fortune 500 CEO: She is well known for walking around the office barefoot and singing—a remnant from her days in an all-girls rock band in high school.

It should come as no surprise, therefore, that Nooyi shook things up at PepsiCo, a company with roughly $65 billion in annual revenues in 2018, over $160 billion in stock market valuation, close to 270,000 employees worldwide, and business interests in more than 200 countries. She took the lead role in spinning off Taco Bell, Pizza Hut, and KFC in 1997. Later, she masterminded the acquisitions of Tropicana in 1998 and Quaker Oats, including Gatorade, in 2001. When becoming CEO in 2006, Nooyi declared PepsiCo's vision to be Performance with Purpose:

> Performance with Purpose means delivering sustainable growth by investing in a healthier future for people and our planet.... We will continue to build a portfolio of enjoyable and healthier foods and beverages, find innovative ways to reduce the use of energy, water, and packaging, and provide a great workplace for our associates.... Because a healthier future for all people and our planet means a more successful future for PepsiCo. This is our promise.[37]

In particular, Performance with Purpose has three dimensions:

Indra Nooyi, chief executive officer of PepsiCo from 2006 to 2018, captured her strategic leadership with the mantra "Performance with Purpose." Monica Schipper/Contributor/Getty Images

1. **Human sustainability.** PepsiCo's strategic intent is to make its product portfolio healthier to combat obesity by reducing sugar, sodium, and saturated fat content in certain key brands. It wants to reduce the salt and fat in its "fun foods" such as Frito-Lay and Doritos brands, and to include healthy choices such as Quaker Oats products and Tropicana fruit juices in its lineup. Nooyi was convinced that if food and beverage companies do not make their products healthier, they would face stricter regulation and lawsuits, as tobacco companies did. Nooyi's goal was to increase PepsiCo's revenues for nutritious foods substantially as detailed in her 2025 Performance with Purpose agenda.

2. **Environmental sustainability.** PepsiCo instituted various initiatives to ensure that its operations don't harm the natural environment. The company has programs in place to reduce water and energy use, increase recycling, and promote sustainable agriculture. The goal is to transform PepsiCo into a company with a net-zero impact on the environment. Nooyi believed that young people will not patronize or want to work for a company that does not have a strategy that also addresses ecological sustainability.

3. **The whole person at work.** PepsiCo wants to create a corporate culture in which employees do not "just make a living, but also have a life," Nooyi said.[38] She argued that this type of culture allows employees to unleash both their mental and emotional energies.

PepsiCo's vision of Performance with Purpose acknowledges the importance of the corporate social responsibility

(Continued)

and stakeholder strategy. Nooyi was convinced that companies have a duty to society to "do better by doing better."[39] She subscribed to a triple-bottom-line approach to competitive advantage, which considers not only economic but also social and environmental performance. As CEO, Nooyi declared that the true profits of an enterprise are not just "revenues minus costs" but "revenues minus costs minus costs to society." Problems such as pollution or the increased cost of health care to combat obesity impose costs on society that companies typically do not bear (externalities). As Nooyi saw it, the time when corporations can just pass on their externalities to society is nearing an end.

Although PepsiCo's revenues have remained more or less flat over the past few years, investors see significant future growth potential. Over the five years between 2013 and 2018, PepsiCo under Nooyi outperformed Coca-Cola Co. by a relatively wide margin. During this period, Pepsi-Co's normalized stock appreciation was 66 percent, while Coca-Cola's was 25 percent; thus, PepsiCo outperformed archrival Coca-Cola by 41 percentage points. With better than expected financial results in her last five years as CEO, Nooyi stands vindicated after years of criticism. Despite opposition, she stuck by her strategic mantra for PepsiCo—Performance with Purpose.[40]

triple bottom line
Combination of economic, social, and ecological concerns— *or profits, people, and planet*—that can lead to a sustainable strategy.

sustainable strategy
A strategy along the economic, social, and ecological dimensions that can be pursued over time without detrimental effects on people or the planet.

(so-called refurbished or rebuilt auto parts).[41] Three dimensions—*economic, social, and ecological*—make up the **triple bottom line**, which is fundamental to a sustainable strategy. These three dimensions are also called the three Ps: *profits, people,* and *planet*:

- **Profits.** The *economic dimension* captures the necessity of businesses to be profitable to survive.
- **People.** The *social dimension* emphasizes the people aspect (such as PepsiCo's initiative of the *whole person at work*).
- **Planet.** The *ecological dimension* emphasizes the relationship between business and the natural environment.

As the intersection of the three ovals (*profits, people,* and *planet*) in Exhibit 5.9 suggests, achieving positive results in all three areas can lead to a **sustainable strategy**. Rather than emphasizing sustaining a competitive advantage over time, *sustainable strategy* means a strategy that can be pursued over time without detrimental effects on people or the planet. Using renewable energy sources such as wind or solar power, for example, is sustainable over time. It can also be good for profits, or simply put "green is green," as Jeffrey Immelt when serving as GE's CEO (until 2017). GE's renewable energy business brought in more than $9 billion in revenues in 2016 (up from $3 billion in 2006).[42]

Like the balanced scorecard, the triple bottom line takes a more integrative and holistic view in assessing a company's performance.[43] Using a triple-bottom-line approach, strategic leaders audit their company's fulfillment of its social and ecological obligations to stakeholders such as employees, customers, suppliers, and communities as conscientiously as they track its financial performance.[44] In this sense, the triple-bottom-line framework is related to *stakeholder theory,* an approach to understanding a firm as embedded in a

EXHIBIT 5.9 Sustainable Strategy: A Focus on the Triple Bottom Line

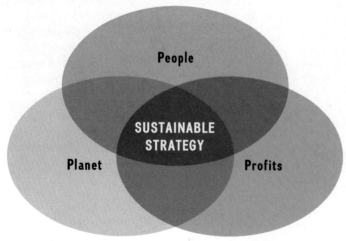

The simultaneous pursuit of performance along social, economic, and ecological dimensions provides a basis for a triple-bottom-line strategy.

network of internal and external constituencies that each make contributions and expect consideration in return (see the discussion in Chapter 1).

5.2 Business Models: Putting Strategy into Action

Strategy is a set of goal-directed actions a firm takes to gain and sustain superior performance relative to competitors or the industry average. The translation of strategy into action takes place in the firm's **business model**, which details the firm's competitive tactics and initiatives. Simply put, the firm's business model explains how the firm intends to make money. In particular, the business model stipulates how the firm conducts its business with its buyers, suppliers, and partners.[45]

How companies do business can sometimes be as important, if not more so, to gaining and sustaining competitive advantage as what they do. Indeed, a slight majority (54 percent) of senior executives responded in a survey stating that they consider business model innovation to be more important than process or product innovation.[46] This is because product and process innovation is often more costly, is higher risk, and takes longer to come up with in the first place and to then implement. Moreover, business model innovation is often an area that is overlooked in a firm's quest for competitive advantage, and thus much value can be unlocked by focusing on business model innovation.

Strategy Highlight 5.2 takes a closer look at how the online startup Threadless uses business model innovation to gain a competitive advantage in the highly competitive apparel industry.

Perhaps most important, a firm's competitive advantage based on product innovation, such as Apple's iPhone, is less likely to be made obsolete if embedded within a business model innovation such as Apple's ecosystem of services that make users less likely to leave Apple for a competing product, even if a competitor's smartphone by itself is a better one. Indeed, Apple has about 1 billion iPhone users embedded within its ecosystem made up of many different products and services including iTunes, iOS, App Store, iCloud, Apple Pay, and so on. Rather than substitutes, business model innovation *complements* product and service innovation, and with it raises the barriers to imitation. This in turn allows a firm that successfully combines product and business model innovation to extend its competitive advantage, as Apple has done since the introduction of the iPod and iTunes business model in 2001. This radical business innovation allowed Apple to link music producers to consumers, and to benefit from each transaction. Apple extended its locus of innovation from mere product innovation to how it conducts its business. That is, Apple provided a two-sided platform for exchange between producers and consumers to take place (see discussion in Chapter 7 on platform strategy for more details).

THE WHY, WHAT, WHO, AND HOW OF BUSINESS MODELS FRAMEWORK

To come up with an effective business model, a firm's leaders need to transform their strategy of how to compete into a blueprint of actions and initiatives that support the overarching goals. Next, managers implement this blueprint through structures, processes, culture, and procedures. The framework shown in Exhibit 5.10 guides strategic leaders through the process of formulating and implementing a business model by asking the important questions of the why, what, who, and how. We illuminate these questions by focusing on Microsoft, also featured in ChapterCase 5.

Strategy Highlight **5.2**

Threadless: Leveraging Crowdsourcing to Design Cool T-Shirts

Threadless, an online design community and apparel store (www.threadless.com), was founded in 2000 by two students with $1,000 as start-up capital. Jake Nickell was then at the Illinois Institute of Art and Jacob DeHart at Purdue University. After Nickell had won an online T-shirt design contest, the two entrepreneurs came up with a business model to leverage user-generated content. The idea is to let consumers "work for you" and turn consumers into *prosumers,* a hybrid between producers and consumers.

Members of the Threadless community, which is some 3 million strong, do most of the work, which they consider fun: They submit T-shirt designs online, and community members vote on which designs they like best. The designs receiving the most votes are put in production, printed, and sold online. Each Monday, Threadless releases 10 new designs and reprints more T-shirts throughout the week as inventory is cleared out. The cost of Threadless T-shirts is a bit higher than that of competitors, about $25.

Threadless leverages *crowdsourcing,* a process in which a group of people voluntarily perform tasks that were traditionally completed by a firm's employees. Rather than doing the work in-house, Threadless outsources its T-shirt design to its website community. The concept of leveraging a firm's own customers via internet-enabled technology to help produce better products is explicitly included in the Threadless business model. In particular, Threadless is leveraging the *wisdom of the crowds,* where the resulting decisions by many participants in the online forum are often better than decisions that could have been made by a single individual. To more effectively leverage this idea, the crowds need to be large and diverse.

At Threadless, the customers play a critical role across the entire value chain, from idea generation to design, marketing, sales forecasting, and distribution. The Threadless business model translates real-time market research and design contests into quick sales. Threadless produces only T-shirts that were approved by its community. Moreover, it has a good understanding of market demand

Two college students started Threadless, which turned into an online company that sells millions of dollars' worth of T-shirts annually (pictured here are models wearing Threadless' T-shirts).
Rene Johnston/Contributor/Getty Images

because it knows the number of people who participated in each design contest. In addition, when scoring each T-shirt design in a contest, Threadless users have the option to check "*I'd buy it.*" These features give the Threadless community a voice in T-shirt design and also coax community members into making a purchasing commitment. Threadless does not make any significant investments until the design and market size are determined, minimizing its downside.

Not surprisingly, Threadless has sold every T-shirt it has printed. Moreover, it has a cult-like following and is outperforming established companies American Eagle, Old Navy, and Urban Outfitters with their more formulaic T-shirt designs. In 2017, revenues for the privately owned Threadless were estimated to be $18 million with a 35 (!) percent profit margin, which equates to some $6.3 million in profits.[47]

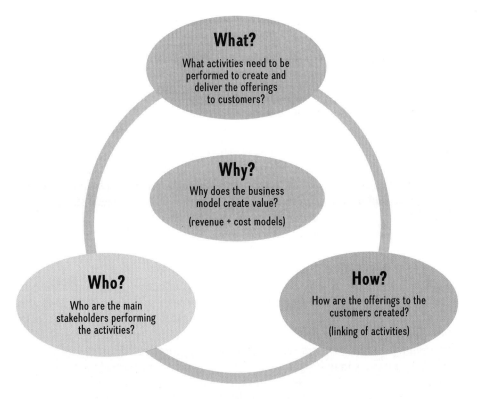

EXHIBIT 5.10

The Why, What, Who, and How of Business Models Framework

Source: Adapted from R. Amit and C. Zott (2012, Spring), "Creating value through business model innovation," *MIT Sloan Management Review*: 41–49.

The Microsoft example lets us see how a firm can readjust its business model responding to business challenges.

1. *Why does the business model create value?* Microsoft's new "mobile first, cloud first" business model creates value for both customers and stockholders. Customers always have the latest software, can access it anywhere, and can collaborate online with other users. Users no longer need to upgrade software or worry about "backward compatibility," meaning the ability to read old (Word) files with new (Word) software. Microsoft enjoys steady revenue that over time provides greater fees than the earlier "perpetual license" model, significantly reduces the problem of software piracy, and balances the cost of ongoing support with the ongoing flow of revenues.

2. *What activities need to be performed to create and deliver the offerings to customers?* To pivot to the new "mobile first, cloud first" business model, Microsoft is making huge investments to create and deliver new offerings to its customers. The Redmond, Washington-based company needed to rewrite much of its software to be functional in a cloud-based environment. CEO Satya Nadella also decided to open the Office suite of applications to competing operating systems including Google's Android, Apple's iOS, and Linux, an open-source operating system. In all these activities, Microsoft's Azure, its cloud-computing service, plays a pivotal role in its new business model.

3. *Who are the main stakeholders performing the activities?* Microsoft continues to focus on both the individual end consumer as well as on more profitable business clients. Microsoft's Azure is particularly attractive to its business customers. For example, Walmart, still the largest retailer globally with some 12,000 stores staffed by over 2 million employees and revenues of some $500 billion, runs its cutting-edge IT logistics on Microsoft's Azure servers, rather than Amazon's AWS service, a major competitor to Walmart.

Likewise, The Home Depot, one of the largest retailers in the United States, also uses Microsoft Azure for its computing needs.

4. *How are the offerings to the customers created?* Microsoft shifted most of its resources, including R&D and customer support, to its cloud-based offerings to not only make them best in class, but also to provide a superior user experience.

To appreciate the value of this change in business model, we should consider for a moment the problems the change allows Microsoft to address.

- Before, with the perpetual license model, Microsoft had revenue spikes on the sale but zero revenues thereafter to support users and produce necessary updates. Now, Microsoft matches revenues to its costs and even comes out further ahead, in that after two years or so, Microsoft makes more money off a software subscription than a standalone software license.

- Before, customers had a financial disincentive to keep their software current. Now, users always have the latest software, can access it anywhere, and can collaborate online with other users without worries about backward compatibility.

- Perhaps most impressively, the new model deals effectively with software piracy. Before, Microsoft suffered tremendous losses through software piracy. This affects consumers too, as the cost of piracy is borne by legal consumers to a large degree. Now, pirating cloud-based software is much more difficult because Microsoft can easily monitor how many users (based on unique internet protocol [IP] addresses) are using the same log-in information at different locations and perhaps even at the same time. Once the provider suspects piracy, it tends to disable the accounts as this goes against the terms of service agreed upon when purchasing the software, not to mention that copyright infringements are illegal. Indeed, the scope of the piracy problem is driven home by the survey-based claim that some 60 percent of computer users confess to pirating software.[48]

POPULAR BUSINESS MODELS

Given their critical importance to achieving competitive advantage, business models are constantly evolving. Below we discuss some of the more popular business models:[49]

- Razor–razor-blades
- Subscription
- Pay-as-you-go
- Freemium
- Wholesale
- Agency
- Bundling

Understanding the more popular business models today will increase the tools in your strategy toolkit.

- **Razor–razor-blades.** The initial product is often sold at a loss or given away to drive demand for complementary goods. The company makes its money on the replacement part needed. As you might guess, it was invented by Gillette, which gave away its razors and sold the replacement cartridges for relatively high prices. The razor–razor-blade model is found in many business applications today. For example, HP charges little for its laser printers but imposes high prices for its replacement toner cartridges.

- **Subscription**. The subscription model has been traditionally used for print magazines and newspapers. Users pay for access to a product or service whether they use the product or service during the payment term or not. Microsoft uses a subscription-based model for its new Office 365 suite of application software. Other industries that use this model presently are cable television, cellular service providers, satellite radio, internet service providers, and health clubs. Netflix also uses a subscription model.

- **Pay-as-you-go**. In the *pay-as-you-go business model,* users pay for only the services they consume. The pay-as-you-go model is most widely used by utilities providing power and water and cell phone service plans, but it is gaining momentum in other areas such as rental cars and cloud computing such as Microsoft's Azure.

- **Freemium.** The *freemium (free + premium) business model* provides the basic features of a product or service *free* of charge, but charges the user for *premium* services such as advanced features or add-ons.[50] For example, companies may provide a minimally supported version of their software as a trial (e.g., business application or video game) to give users the chance to try the product. Users later have the option of purchasing a supported version of software, which includes a full set of product features and product support. Also, news providers such as *The New York Times* and *The Wall Street Journal* use a freemium model. They frequently provide a small number of articles for free per month, but users must pay a fee (often a flat rate) for unlimited access (including a library of past articles).

- **Ultra-low cost.** An ultra low-cost business model is quite similar to freemium: a model in which basic service is provided at a low cost and extra items are sold at a premium. The business pursuing this model has the goal of driving down costs. Examples include Spirit Airlines (in the United States), Ryanair (in Europe), or AirAsia, which provide minimal flight services but allow customers to pay for additional services and upgrades à la carte, often at a premium.

- **Wholesale.** The traditional model in retail is called a *wholesale model*. The book publishing industry is an example. Under the wholesale model, book publishers would sell books to retailers at a fixed price (usually 50 percent below the recommended retail price). Retailers, however, were free to set their own price on any book and profit from the difference between their selling price and the cost to buy the book from the publisher (or wholesaler).

- **Agency.** In this model the producer relies on an agent or retailer to sell the product, at a predetermined percentage commission. Sometimes the producer will also control the retail price. The *agency model* was long used in the entertainment industry, where agents place artists or artistic properties and then take their commission. More recently we see this approach at work in a number of online sales venues, as in Apple's pricing of book products or its app sales. (See further discussion following.)

- **Bundling.** The *bundling* business model sells products or services for which demand is negatively correlated *at a discount.* Demand for two products is negatively correlated if a user values one product more than another. In the Microsoft Office Suite, a user might value Word more than Excel and vice versa. Instead of selling both products for $120 each, Microsoft bundles them in a suite and sells them combined at a discount, say $150. This bundling strategy allowed Microsoft to become the number-one provider of all major application software packages such as word processing, spreadsheets, slideshow presentation, and so on. Before its bundling strategy, Microsoft faced strong competition in each segment. Indeed, Word Perfect was outselling Word, Lotus 1-2-3 was outselling Excel, and Harvard Graphics was outselling PowerPoint. The problem for Microsoft's competitors was that they did not control the operating system (Windows), which made their programs less seamless on this operating system. In addition, the competitor products to Microsoft were offered by three independent companies, so they lacked the option to bundle them at a discount.

DYNAMIC NATURE OF BUSINESS MODELS

Business models evolve dynamically, and we can see many combinations and permutations. Sometimes business models are tweaked to respond to disruptions in the market, efforts that can conflict with fair trade practices and may even prompt government intervention.

COMBINATION. Telecommunications companies such as AT&T or Verizon, to take one industry, combine the *razor-razor-blade* model with the *subscription* model. They frequently provide a basic cell phone at no charge, or significantly subsidize a high-end smartphone, when you sign up for a two-year wireless service plan. Telecom providers recoup the subsidy provided for the smartphone by requiring customers to sign up for lengthy service plans. This is why it is so critical for telecom providers to keep their *churn rate*—the proportion of subscribers that leave, especially before the end of the contractual term—as low as possible.

EVOLUTION. The *freemium* business model can be seen as an evolutionary variation on the *razor-razor-blade* model. The base product is provided free, and the producer finds other ways to monetize the usage. The freemium model is used extensively by open-source software companies (e.g., Red Hat), mobile app companies, and other internet businesses. Many of the free versions of applications include advertisements to make up for the cost of supporting nonpaying users. In addition, the paying premium users subsidize the free users. The freemium model is often used to build a consumer base when the marginal cost of adding another user is low or even zero (such as in software sales). Many online video games, including massive multiplayer online games and app-based mobile games, follow a variation of this model, allowing basic access to the game for free, but charging for power-ups, customizations, special objects, and similar things that enhance the game experience for users.

DISRUPTION. When introducing the *agency* model, we mentioned Apple and book publishing, and you are aware of how severely Amazon disrupted the traditional wholesale model for publishers. Amazon took advantage of the pricing flexibility inherent in the wholesale model and offered many books (especially e-books) below the cost that other retailers had to pay to publishers. In particular, Amazon would offer newly released bestsellers for $9.99 to promote its Kindle e-reader. Publishers and other retailers strongly objected because Amazon's retail price was lower than the wholesale price paid by retailers competing with Amazon. Moreover, the $9.99 e-book offer by Amazon made it untenable for other retailers to continue to charge $28.95 for newly released hardcover books (for which they had to pay $14 to $15 to the publishers). With its aggressive pricing, Amazon not only devalued the printed book, but also lost money on every book it sold. It did this to increase the number of users of its Kindle e-readers and tablets.

RESPONSE TO DISRUPTION. The market is dynamic, and in the above example book publishers looked for another model. Many book publishers worked with Apple on an agency approach, in which the publishers would set the price for Apple and receive 70 percent of the revenue, while Apple received 30 percent. The approach is similar to the Apple App Store pricing model for iOS applications in which developers set a price for applications and Apple retains a percentage of the revenue.

Use of the agency model was intended to give publishers the leverage to raise e-book prices for retailers. Under the agency model, publishers could increase their e-book profits and price e-books more closely to prices of printed books. Publishers inked their deals with Apple, but how could they get Amazon to play ball? For leverage, publishers withheld new releases from Amazon. This forced Amazon to raise prices on newly released e-books in line with the agency model to around $14.95.

LEGAL CONFLICTS. The rapid development of business models, especially in response to disruption, can lead producers to breach existing rules of commerce. In the above example, the publishers' response prompted an antitrust investigation. The Department of Justice determined (in 2012) that Apple and major publishers had conspired to raise prices of e-books. To settle the legal action, each publisher involved negotiated new deals with retailers, including Amazon. A year later, Apple was found guilty of colluding with several major book publishers to fix prices on e-books and had to change its agency model.[51]

5.3 Implications for Strategic Leaders

In this chapter, we discussed how to measure and assess competitive advantage using three traditional approaches: accounting profitability, shareholder value creation, and economic value creation. We then introduced you to two conceptual frameworks to help us understand competitive advantage in a more holistic fashion: the balanced scorecard and the triple bottom line. We then took a closer look at business models, which detail a firm's competitive tactics and initiatives in how it is making money. In particular, a business model stipulates how a firm conducts its business with its buyers, suppliers, and partners.

Exhibit 5.11 summarizes how to measure and assess competitive advantage.

Several implications for strategic leaders emerge from our discussion of competitive advantage and firm performance:

- No *best* strategy exists—only *better* ones (better in comparison with others). We must interpret any performance metric relative to those of competitors and the industry average. True performance can be judged only in comparison to other contenders in the field or the industry average, not on an absolute basis.

- The goal of strategic management is to integrate and align each business function and activity to obtain superior performance at the business unit and corporate levels. Therefore, competitive advantage is best measured by criteria that reflect *overall business unit performance* rather than the performance of specific departments. For example,

EXHIBIT 5.11   How to Measure and Assess Competitive Advantage

Competitive advantage is reflected in superior firm performance.

- Competitive advantage is assessed *relative* to a benchmark, either using competitors or the industry average.
- Competitive advantage is a multifaceted concept.
- Competitive advantage can be measured using accounting profit, shareholder value, or economic value.
- The balanced-scorecard approach harnesses multiple internal and external performance dimensions to balance a firm's financial and strategic goals.
- More recently, competitive advantage has been linked to a firm's triple bottom line, the ability to maintain performance in the economic, social, and ecological contexts (profits, people, planet) to achieve a sustainable strategy.

although the functional managers in the marketing department may (and should) care greatly about the success or failure of their recent ad campaign, the *general* manager cares most about the performance implications of the ad campaign at the business-unit level for which she has profit-and-loss responsibility. Metrics that aggregate upward and reflect overall firm and corporate performance are most useful to assess the effectiveness of a firm's competitive strategy.

- Both *quantitative and qualitative* performance dimensions matter in judging the effectiveness of a firm's strategy. Those who focus on only one metric will risk being blindsided by poor performance on another. Rather, strategic leaders need to rely on a more holistic perspective when assessing firm performance, measuring different dimensions over different time periods.

- A firm's business model is critical to achieving a competitive advantage. How a firm does business is as important as what it does.

This concludes our discussion of competitive advantage, firm performance, and business models, and completes Part 1—strategy analysis—of the AFI framework. In Part 2, we turn our attention to the next steps in the AFI framework—strategy formulation. In Chapters 6 and 7, we focus on business strategy: How should the firm compete (cost leadership, differentiation, or value innovation)? In Chapters 8 and 9, we study corporate strategy: Where should the firm compete (industry, markets, and geography)? Chapter 10 looks at global strategy: How and where (local, regional, national, and international) should the firm compete around the world?

CHAPTER**CASE 5**   Part II

GIVEN MICROSOFT'S lackluster performance in the 2000s, this former tech leader found itself in *turnaround mode.* When a company is in turnaround mode, it has experienced a prolonged period of competitive disadvantage and needs to undertake significant changes in its strategy and/or business model to regain its competitiveness. Over time, Microsoft's competitive advantage turned into a competitive disadvantage, lagging Apple by a wide margin (see Exhibit 5.3). In 2014, Microsoft appointed Satya Nadella as its new CEO. He wasted no time moving Microsoft's strategic focus away from its Windows-only business model to compete more effectively in a "mobile first, cloud first world," the mantra he used in his appointment e-mail as CEO.

Under his leadership, Microsoft made the Office Suite available on Apple iOS and Android mobile devices. Office 365, its cloud-based software offering, is now available as a subscription service. Software applications can be accessed on any device, any time, with online storage, combined with Skype's global calling feature. Nadella still needs to work hard to ensure Microsoft's future viability, however. Although Windows and Office were cash cows for so long, currently still generating

some 40 percent of revenues and 75 percent of profits, both continue to decline. The problem Nadella now faces (due to Microsoft's "monopoly" position) is that the gross margin of "classic" PC-based Office is 90 percent, while the gross margin for Office 365 is only around 50 percent.

Nadella's strongest departure from the Windows-centric strategy is reflected in his attempt to return Microsoft to its early roots as a software firm, providing different yet open platforms for developers and consumers. To accomplish this strategic transformation, Microsoft acquired a string of successful startups including Mojang in 2014 (the maker of Minecraft), LinkedIn in 2016, and GitHub in 2018. (Before Nadella's tenure, Microsoft had also acquired Skype in 2011.) GitHub, which is akin to Facebook for developers, is a space for computer programmers to store and exchange code. This allows software developers to use and

Satya Nadella, Microsoft CEO.

Sean Gallup/Staff/Getty Images

recombine existing code to create new products and services. Microsoft already uses GitHub for its own service development and hopes that GitHub developers in turn now will be more likely to write new software for Azure, Microsoft's cloud computing services. In this space, Microsoft also has already made significant strides. Its Azure cloud business reported $23 billion in sales in 2018, second only to Amazon's AWS with $27 billion in sales.

In five years under Nadella's leadership as CEO, Microsoft has enjoyed a successful turnaround and a stock market valuation that almost tripled from $301 billion in 2014 to $896 billion in 2019, thereby creating $595 billion in shareholder value (see also Exhibit 5.3).[52]

Questions

1. This chapter introduces several approaches to assessing a firm's competitive advantage. Using any one of these approaches, can you ascertain whether Microsoft has a competitive advantage over Apple? Why or why not? From which approach is Microsoft looking the best? Explain.

2. Microsoft CEO Satya Nadella has made drastic changes to Microsoft's strategy. What was Microsoft's strategy before Nadella was appointed CEO in 2014? What is it now under his leadership? Do you agree that Nadella has formulated a promising business model? Why or why not?

3. Looking three to five years into the future, who do you expect will have a competitive advantage: Apple or Microsoft? Explain.

NOTE: A five-year financial ratio analysis related to this ChapterCase is available in Connect.

mySTRATEGY

How Much Is an MBA Worth to You?

The *my*Strategy box at the end of Chapter 2 asked how much you would be willing to pay for the job you want—for a job that reflects your values. Here, we look at a different issue relating to worth: How much is an MBA worth over the course of your career?

Alongside the traditional two-year full-time MBA program, many business schools also offer evening MBAs, online MBAs, and executive MBAs. Let's assume you know you want to pursue an advanced degree, and you need to decide which program format is better for you (or you want to evaluate the choice you already made). You've narrowed your options to either (1) a two-year full-time MBA program, or (2) an executive MBA program at the same institution that is 18 months long with classes every other weekend. Let's also assume the price for tuition, books, and fees is $50,000 for the full-time program and $120,000 for the executive MBA program.

Which MBA program should you choose? Consider in your analysis the value, price, and cost concepts discussed in this chapter. Pay special attention to opportunity costs attached to different MBA program options.

TAKE-AWAY CONCEPTS

This chapter demonstrated three traditional approaches for assessing and measuring firm performance and competitive advantage, as well as two conceptual frameworks designed to provide a more holistic, albeit more qualitative, perspective on firm performance. We also discussed the role of business models in translating a firm's strategy into actions.

LO 5-1 / Conduct a firm profitability analysis using accounting data to assess and evaluate competitive advantage.

- To measure competitive advantage, we must be able to (1) accurately assess firm performance, and (2) compare and benchmark the focal firm's performance to other competitors in the same industry or the industry average.

- To measure accounting profitability, we use standard metrics derived from publicly available accounting data.

- Commonly used profitability metrics in strategic management are *return on assets (ROA), return on equity (ROE), return on invested capital (ROIC),* and *return on revenue (ROR).* See the key financial ratios in five tables in "How to Conduct a Case Analysis."

- Accounting data are historical and thus backward-looking. They focus mainly on tangible assets and do not consider intangibles that are hard or impossible to measure and quantify, such as an innovation competency.

LO 5-2 / Apply shareholder value creation to assess and evaluate competitive advantage.

- Investors are primarily interested in total return to shareholders, which includes stock price appreciation plus dividends received over a specific period.

- Total return to shareholders is an external performance metric; it indicates how the market views all publicly available information about a firm's past, current state, and expected future performance.

- Applying a shareholders' perspective, key metrics to measure and assess competitive advantage are the return on (risk) capital and market capitalization.

- Stock prices can be highly volatile, which makes it difficult to assess firm performance. Overall macroeconomic factors have a direct bearing on stock prices. Also, stock prices frequently reflect the psychological mood of the investors, which can at times be irrational.

- Shareholder value creation is a better measure of competitive advantage over the *long term* due to the "noise" introduced by market volatility, external factors, and investor sentiment.

LO 5-3 / Explain economic value creation and different sources of competitive advantage.

- The relationship between economic value creation and competitive advantage is fundamental in strategic management. It provides the foundation

upon which to formulate a firm's competitive strategy of cost leadership or differentiation.

- Three components are critical to evaluating any good or service: value (V), price (P), and cost (C). In this perspective, cost includes opportunity costs.

- Economic value created is the difference between a buyer's willingness to pay for a good or service and the firm's cost to produce it ($V - C$).

- A firm has a competitive advantage when it is able to create more economic value than its rivals. The source of competitive advantage can stem from higher perceived value creation (assuming equal cost) or lower cost (assuming equal value creation).

LO 5-4 / Apply a balanced scorecard to assess and evaluate competitive advantage.

- The balanced-scorecard approach attempts to provide a more integrative view of competitive advantage.

- Its goal is to harness multiple internal and external performance dimensions to balance financial and strategic goals.

- Managers develop strategic objectives for the balanced scorecard by answering four key questions: (1) How do customers view us? (2) How do we create value? (3) What core competencies do we need? (4) How do shareholders view us?

LO 5-5 / Apply a triple bottom line to assess and evaluate competitive advantage.

- Noneconomic factors can have a significant impact on a firm's financial performance, not to mention its reputation and customer goodwill.

- Managers are frequently asked to maintain and improve not only the firm's economic performance but also its social and ecological performance.

- Three dimensions—economic, social, and ecological, also known as *profits, people,* and *planet*—make up the triple bottom line. Achieving positive results in all three areas can lead to a sustainable strategy—a strategy that can endure over time.

- A sustainable strategy produces not only positive financial results, but also positive results along the social and ecological dimensions.

- Using a triple-bottom-line approach, managers audit their company's fulfillment of its social and ecological obligations to stakeholders such as employees, customers, suppliers, and communities in as serious a way as they track its financial performance.

▪ The triple-bottom-line framework is related to stakeholder theory, an approach to understanding a firm as embedded in a network of internal and external constituencies that each make contributions and expect consideration in return.

LO 5-6 / Use the why, what, who, and how of business models framework to put strategy into action.

▪ The translation of a firm's strategy *(where and how to compete for competitive advantage)* into action

takes place in the firm's business model *(how to make money).*

▪ A business model details how the firm conducts its business with its buyers, suppliers, and partners.

▪ How companies do business is as important to gaining and sustaining competitive advantage as what they do.

▪ The why, what, who, and how framework guides managers through the process of formulating and implementing a business model.

KEY TERMS

Balanced scorecard *(p. 171)*
Business model *(p. 177)*
Consumer surplus *(p. 168)*
Economic value created *(p. 165)*
Market capitalization *(p. 163)*

Opportunity costs *(p. 170)*
Producer surplus *(p. 168)*
Profit *(p. 168)*
Reservation price *(p. 165)*
Risk capital *(p. 163)*

Shareholders *(p. 163)*
Sustainable strategy *(p. 176)*
Total return to shareholders *(p. 163)*
Triple bottom line *(p. 176)*
Value *(p. 167)*

DISCUSSION QUESTIONS

1. How do perspectives on competitive advantage differ when comparing brick-and-mortar stores to online businesses (e.g. Best Buy versus Amazon, Old Navy versus Threadless [noted in Strategy Highlight 5.2]). Make recommendations to a primarily brick-and-mortar retail firm on how to compete more effectively with online firms. Do your suggestions fall mostly into the accounting, shareholder, or economic point of view on competitive advantage?

2. For many people, the shareholder perspective is perhaps the most familiar measure of competitive advantage for publicly traded firms. What are

some of the disadvantages of using shareholder value as the sole point of view for defining competitive advantage?

3. The chapter discusses seven different business models with a brief description of each. Given the changing nature of many industries, choose an industry you have some knowledge of and describe how the business model of a firm in that industry has changed over the last decade. (If you prefer, you can describe how a firm's current business model should be changing in the next few years ahead.)

ENDNOTES

1. This ChapterCase is based on: Apple Inc. and Microsoft Corp. annual reports (various years); "Microsoft at middle age: Opening Windows," *The Economist* (2015, Apr. 4); "What Satya Nadella did at Microsoft," *The Economist* (2017, Mar. 16); and Mochhizuki, T. (2017, Feb. 28), "Apple's next iPhone will have a curved screen," *The Wall Street Journal;* and "Apple succumbs to the smartphone malaise," *The Economist* (2019, Jan. 12).

2. This debate takes place in the following discourses, among others: Misangyi, V.F., H. Elms, T. Greckhamer, and J.A. Lepine (2006), "A new perspective on a fundamental debate: A multilevel approach to industry, corporate, and business unit effects," *Strategic Management Journal* 27: 571–590; McNamara, G., F. Aime, and P. Vaaler (2005), "Is performance driven by industry- or firm-specific factors? A reply to Hawawini, Subramanian, and Verdin," *Strategic*

Management Journal 26: 1075–1081; Hawawini, G., V. Subramanian, and P. Verdin (2005), "Is performance driven by industry- or firm-specific factors? A new look at the evidence: A response to McNamara, Aime, and Vaaler," *Strategic Management Journal* 26: 1083–1086; Rumelt, R.P. (2003), "What in the world is competitive advantage?" *Policy Working Paper 2003-105;* McGahan, A.M., and M.E. Porter (2002), "What do we know about variance in accounting profitability?" *Management Science* 48: 834–851; Hawawini, G., V. Subramanian, and P. Verdin (2003), "Is performance driven by industry- or firm-specific factors? A new look at the evidence," *Strategic Management Journal* 24: 1–16; McGahan, A.M., and M.E. Porter (1997), "How much does industry matter, really?" *Strategic Management Journal* 18: 15–30; Rumelt, R.P. (1991), "How much does industry matter?" *Strategic Management Journal* 12: 167–185; Porter, M.E. (1985), *Competitive Advantage: Creating and Sustaining Superior Performance* (New York: Free Press); and Schmalensee, R. (1985), "Do markets differ much?" *American Economic Review* 75: 341–351;

3. Rumelt, R.P. (2003), "What in the world is competitive advantage?" *Policy Working Paper 2003-105.*

4. For discussion see: McGahan, A.M., and M. E. Porter (2002), "What do we know about variance in accounting profitability?" *Management Science,* 48: 834–851.

5. *(Net profits / Invested capital)* is shorthand for *(Net operating profit after taxes [NOPAT]/ Total stockholders' equity + Total debt − Value of preferred stock).* See discussion of profitability ratios in Table 1, "When and How to Use Financial Measures to Assess Firm Performance," of the "How to Conduct a Case Analysis" guide that introduces Part 4 of the text.

6. The data for this section are drawn from: Apple and Microsoft annual reports (various years); Dou, E. (2017, Feb. 1), "Cheaper rivals eat away at Apple sales in China," *The Wall Street Journal*; "What Satya Nadella did at Microsoft," *The Economist* (2016, Mar. 16); "iPhone, therefore I am," *The Economist* (2016, Jan. 30); "Buying GitHub takes Microsoft back to its roots," *The Economist* (2018, Jun. 9); and "Apple succumbs to the smartphone malaise," *The Economist* (2019, Jan. 12).

7. This example is based on the 2018 SEC 10-K reports for Apple and Microsoft. Connect provides the financial analysis conducted here as an exercise for a five-year time period, 2014–2018. This allows for more dynamic considerations.

8. In 2018, Microsoft took a onetime charge of $13.7 billion due to implementation of the Tax Cuts and Jobs Act, 2017. To allow a comparison across firms and over years, we accounted for this event by adjusting Microsoft's tax provision accordingly. See Microsoft 2018 Annual Report.

9. "The second coming of Apple through a magical fusion of man—Steve Jobs—and company, Apple is becoming itself again: The little anti-company that could," *Fortune* (1998, Nov. 9).

10. "Satya Nadella: Mobile first, cloud first press briefing," Microsoft press release (2014, Mar. 27).

11. In 2018, Microsoft took a onetime charge of $13.7 billion due to implementation of the Tax Cuts and Jobs Act, 2017. To allow a comparison across firms and over years, we accounted for this event by adjusting Microsoft's tax provision accordingly. See Microsoft 2018 Annual Report.

12. "Silicon Valley headquarters," *The Economist* (2015, Mar. 5).

13. Prahalad, C.K., and G. Hamel (1990, May–June), "The core competence of the corporation," *Harvard Business Review.*

14. Baruch, L. (2001), *Intangibles: Management, Measurement, and Reporting* (Washington, DC: Brookings Institution Press).

15. Cameron, W.B. (1967), *Informal Sociology: A Casual Introduction to Sociological Thinking* (New York: Random House).

16. Friedman, M. (2002), *Capitalism and Freedom,* 40th anniversary ed. (Chicago: University of Chicago Press).

17. Beechy, M., D. Gruen, and J. Vickrey (2000), "The efficient market hypothesis: A survey," *Research Discussion Paper,* Federal Reserve Bank of Australia; and Fama, E. (1970), "Efficient capital markets: A review of theory and empirical work," *Journal of Finance* 25: 383–417.

18. The three broad categories of companies by market cap are *large cap* (over $10 billion), *mid cap* ($2 billion to $10 billion), and *small cap* (less than $2 billion).

19. Alexander, J. (2007), *Performance Dashboards and Analysis for Value Creation* (Hoboken, NJ: Wiley-Interscience).

20. This section draws on: Christensen, C.M., and M.E. Raynor (2003), *The Innovator's Solution: Creating and Sustaining Successful Growth* (Boston: Harvard Business School Press).

21. "Satya Nadella: Mobile first, cloud first press briefing," Microsoft press release (2014, Mar. 27).

22. Speech given by Alan Greenspan on Dec. 5, 1996, at the American Enterprise Institute.

23. "Irrational gloom," *The Economist* (2002, Oct. 11).

24. Wakabayashi D. (2016, Apr. 24), "Apple's watch outpaced the iPhone in first year," *The Wall Street Journal.*

25. Olivarez-Giles, N. (2015, Apr. 30), "What makes the Apple Watch tick," *The Wall Street Journal.*

26. For Amazon's acquisition of Whole Foods, see: Stevens, L., and A. Gasparro (2017, Jun. 16), "Amazon to buy Whole Foods for $13.7 billion: Whole Foods would continue to operate stores under its brand," *The Wall Street Journal,* www.wsj.com/articles/amazon-to-buy-whole-foods-for-13-7-billion-1497618446. For industry response, see: La Monica, P.R., and C. Isidore (2017, Jun. 16), "Grocery stocks are getting clobbered after Amazon-Whole Foods deal," *CNN Money,* http://money.cnn.com/2017/06/16/investing/amazon-buying-whole-foods/index.html.

27. Kaplan, R.S., and D.P. Norton (1992, January–February), "The balanced scorecard: Measures that drive performance," *Harvard Business Review*: 71–79.

28. Kaplan, R.S., and D.P. Norton (1992, January–February), "The balanced scorecard: Measures that drive performance," *Harvard Business Review*: 71–79.

29. Govindarajan, V., and J.B. Lang (2002), *3M Corporation,* case study, Tuck School of Business at Dartmouth.

30. Rothaermel, F.T., and A.M. Hess (2010, Spring), "Innovation strategies combined," *MIT Sloan Management Review*: 12–15.

31. Huston, L., and N. Sakkab (2006, March), "Connect & Develop: Inside Procter & Gamble's new model for innovation," *Harvard Business Review*: 58–66.

32. Kaplan, R.S. (1993, September–October), "Implementing the balanced scorecard at FMC Corporation: An interview with Larry D. Brady," *Harvard Business Review*: 143–147.

33. Norreklit, H. (2000), "The balance on the balanced scorecard—A critical analysis of some of its assumptions," *Management Accounting Research* 11: 65–88; Jensen, M.C. (2002), "Value maximization, stakeholder theory, and the corporate objective function," in *Unfolding Stakeholder Thinking,* ed. J. Andriof, et al. (Sheffield, UK: Greenleaf Publishing).

34. Kaplan, R.S., and D.P. Norton (2007, July–August), "Using the balanced scorecard as a strategic management system," *Harvard Business Review*; and Kaplan, R.S., and D.P. Norton (1992, January–February), "The balanced scorecard: Measures that drive performance," *Harvard Business Review*: 71–79.

35. Lawrie, G., and I. Cobbold (2002), "Development of the 3rd generation balanced scorecard: Evolution of the balanced scorecard into an effective strategic performance management tool," *2GC Working Paper* (Berkshire, UK: 2GC Limited).

36. As quoted in: Safian, R. (2014, Oct. 14), "It's got to be a passion, it's gotta be your calling: Indra Nooyi," *Fast Company.*

37. "Performance with a Purpose: 2025 Agenda," www.pepsico.com/docs/album/

sustainability-reporting/pepsico_sustainability_report_2015_and_-2025_agenda.pdf, accessed July 1, 2017.

38. As quoted in: Safian, R. (2017, Jan. 9), "How PepsiCo CEO Indra Nooyi is steering the company toward a purpose-driven future," *Fast Company*.

39. As quoted in: Barnett, M. (2011, Oct. 5), "PepsiCo's Indra Nooyi: Capitalism with a purpose," *Fortune*.

40. This Strategy Highlight is based on: PepsiCo annual reports (various years); "Performance with a Purpose: 2025 Agenda," www.fastcompany.com/3066378/how-pepsico-ceo-indra-nooyi-is-steering-the-company-tow, accessed April 2, 2019; and "Coca-Cola's new boss tries to move beyond its core product," *The Economist* (2017, Mar. 18); Safian, R. (2017, Jan. 9), "How PepsiCo's Indra Nooyi is steering the company toward a purpose-driven future," *Fast Company*; Esterl, M. (2015, Jul. 9), "PepsiCo's outlook for year brightens," *The Wall Street Journal*; Esterl, M. (2015, Mar. 26), "Soft drinks hit 10th year of decline," *The Wall Street Journal*; Esterl, M. (2015, Feb. 27), "Monster beverage shares hit high on strong overseas growth," *The Wall Street Journal*; Safian, K. (2014, Oct. 14), "It's got to be a passion, it's gotta be your calling: Indra Nooyi," *Fast Company*; "As Pepsi struggles to regain market share, Indra Nooyi's job is on the line," *The Economist* (2012, May 17); Barnett, M. (2011, Oct. 5), PepsiCo's Indra Nooyi: Capitalism with a purpose, *Fortune;* "Should Pepsi break up?" *The Economist* (2011,

Oct. 11); "PepsiCo wakes up and smells the cola," *The Wall Street Journal* (2011, Jun. 28); "Pepsi gets a makeover," *The Economist* (2010, Mar. 25); "Keeping cool in hot water," *Bloomberg BusinessWeek* (2007, Jun. 11); "The Pepsi challenge," *The Economist* (2006, Aug. 17); and "PepsiCo shakes it up," *Bloomberg Businessweek* (2006, Aug. 14).

41. Senge, P.M., B. Bryan Smith, N. Kruschwitz, J. Laur, and S. Schley (2010), *The Necessary Revolution: How Individuals and Organizations Are Working Together to Create a Sustainable World* (New York: Crown).

42. GE 2016 Annual Report, www.ge.com/ar2016; Gryta T., J. Lubin, and D. Benoit (2017, Jun. 12), "Jeff Immelt to step down as CEO of GE; John Flannery takes role," *The Wall Street Journal*.

43. Anderson, R.C. (2009), *Confessions of a Radical Industrialist: Profits, People, Purpose—Doing Business by Respecting the Earth* (New York: St. Martin's Press).

44. Norman, W., and C. MacDonald (2004), "Getting to the bottom of 'triple bottom line,'" *Business Ethics Quarterly* 14: 243–262.

45. This discussion is based on: Adner, R. (2012), *The Wide Lens. A New Strategy for Innovation* (New York: Portfolio/Penguin); Amit, R., and C. Zott (2012, Spring), "Creating value through business model innovation," *MIT Sloan Management Review*: 41–49; and Gassmann, O., K. Frankenberger, and M. Csik (2015), *The Business Model Navigator: 55 Models That Will Revolutionise Your Business* (Harlow, UK: FT Press).

46. Amit, R., and C. Zott (2012, Spring), "Creating value through business model in-

novation," *MIT Sloan Management Review*: 41–49.

47. Robey, T.E. (2017, Nov. 6), "What happened to the Internet's favorite T-shirt company?" www.racked.com/2017/11/6/16551468/threadless-t-shirts-ecommerce (accessed May 6, 2019); Nickell, J. (2010), *Threadless: Ten Years of T-shirts from the World's Most Inspiring Online Design Community* (New York: Abrams); Howe, J. (2008), *Crowdsourcing: Why the Power of the Crowd Is Driving the Future of Business* (New York: Crown Business); and Surowiecki, J. (2004), *The Wisdom of Crowds* (New York: Anchor Books).

48. Fitzgerald, B. (2012, Jun. 1), "Software piracy: Study claims 57 percent of the world pirates software," *The Huffington Post*.

49. For a fully dedicated and more in-depth treatment of business models, see: Gassmann, O., K. Frankenberger, and M. Csik (2015), *The Business Model Navigator: 55 Models That Will Revolutionise Your Business* (Harlow, UK: FT Press).

50. Anderson, C. (2009), *Free: The Future of a Radical Price* (New York: Hyperion).

51. Bray, C., J. Palazzolo, and I. Sherr (2013, Jul. 13), "U.S. judge rules Apple colluded on e-books," *The Wall Street Journal*.

52. Sources: Microsoft annual reports (various years); "Microsoft at middle age: Opening Windows," *The Economist* (2015, Apr. 4); "What Satya Nadella did at Microsoft," *The Economist* (2017, Mar. 16); and "Buying GitHub takes Microsoft back to its roots," *The Economist* (2018, Jun. 9).

PART

2

Formulation

The AFI Strategy Framework

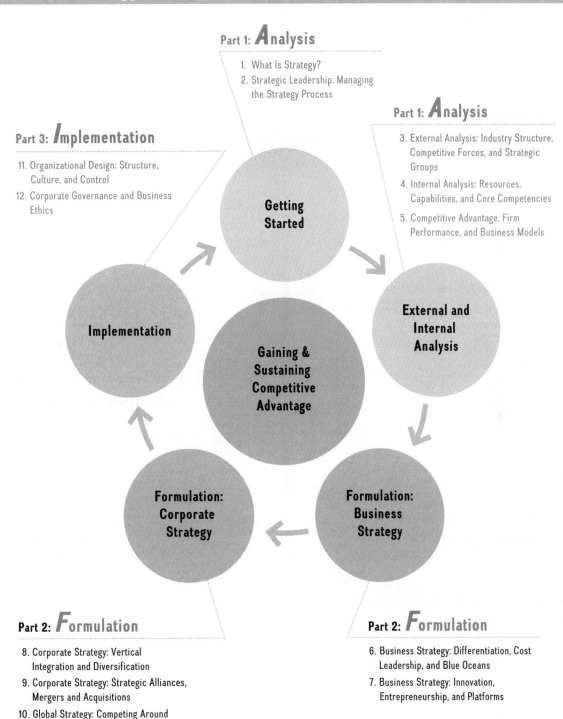

Part 1: **A**nalysis
1. What Is Strategy?
2. Strategic Leadership: Managing the Strategy Process

Part 1: **A**nalysis
3. External Analysis: Industry Structure, Competitive Forces, and Strategic Groups
4. Internal Analysis: Resources, Capabilities, and Core Competencies
5. Competitive Advantage, Firm Performance, and Business Models

Part 3: **I**mplementation
11. Organizational Design: Structure, Culture, and Control
12. Corporate Governance and Business Ethics

Part 2: **F**ormulation
8. Corporate Strategy: Vertical Integration and Diversification
9. Corporate Strategy: Strategic Alliances, Mergers and Acquisitions
10. Global Strategy: Competing Around the World

Part 2: **F**ormulation
6. Business Strategy: Differentiation, Cost Leadership, and Blue Oceans
7. Business Strategy: Innovation, Entrepreneurship, and Platforms

Getting Started

External and Internal Analysis

Gaining & Sustaining Competitive Advantage

Implementation

Formulation: Corporate Strategy

Formulation: Business Strategy

Business Strategy: Differentiation, Cost Leadership, and Blue Oceans

Chapter Outline

Learning Objectives

After studying this chapter, you should be able to:

LO 6-1 Define business-level strategy and describe how it determines a firm's strategic position.

LO 6-2 Examine the relationship between value drivers and differentiation strategy.

LO 6-3 Examine the relationship between cost drivers and cost-leadership strategy.

LO 6-4 Assess the benefits and risks of differentiation and cost-leadership strategies vis-à-vis the five forces that shape competition.

LO 6-5 Evaluate value and cost drivers that may allow a firm to pursue a blue ocean strategy.

LO 6-6 Assess the risks of a blue ocean strategy, and explain why it is difficult to succeed at value innovation.

JetBlue Airways: En Route to a New Blue Ocean?

IN 2019, JETBLUE AIRWAYS became the sixth-largest airline in the United States, following the "big four" (American, Delta, Southwest, and United) and Alaska Airlines, which beat out JetBlue in acquiring Virgin America in 2016. JetBlue offers approximately 1,000 flights daily, employs 22,000 crew members, and services 42 million customers annually.

When JetBlue took to the skies in 2000, founder David Neeleman set out to pursue a blue ocean strategy. This type of competitive strategy combines differentiation and cost-leadership activities. To reconcile the inherent trade-offs in these two distinct strategic positions, it used value innovation. How did Neeleman accomplish this strategy and where did his ideas come from?

At the age of 25, the young entrepreneur co-founded Morris Air, a charter air service that was purchased by Southwest Airlines (SWA) in 1993. Morris Air was a

In an attempt to differentiate its service offering, JetBlue provides its Mint luxury experience, which includes a lie-flat bed up to 6 feet 8 inches long, a high-resolution personal screen, and free in-flight high-speed Wi-Fi, on many domestic U.S. routes. Other U.S. competitors offer such amenities only on a few selected routes.

Carlosyudica/123RF

low-fare airline that pioneered many cost-saving practices that later became standard in the industry, such as e-ticketing. After a stint as an airline executive for SWA, Neeleman went on to launch JetBlue. His strategy was to provide air travel at even lower costs than SWA. At the same time, he wanted to offer service and amenities that were better and more than those offered by such legacy carriers as American, Delta, and United. According to JetBlue's Customer Bill of Rights, its primary mission is to bring humanity back to air travel.

To implement a blue ocean strategy, JetBlue focused on lowering operating costs while driving up perceived customer value in its service offerings. Specifically, it copied and improved upon many of SWA's cost-reducing activities. It used just one type of airplane (the Airbus A-320) to lower the costs of aircraft maintenance and pilot and crew training (but has since expanded its fleet). It also specialized in transcontinental flights connecting the East Coast (from its home base in New York) to the West Coast (e.g., Los Angeles). This model, known as the point-to-point model, focuses on directly connecting fewer but more highly trafficked city pairs, unlike American, Delta, and United's hub-and-spoke system, which connects many different locations via layovers at airport hubs. JetBlue's point-to-point model lowers costs in mainly two ways: flying longer distances and transporting more passengers per flight than SWA, further driving down its costs. As a consequence, JetBlue enjoys one of the lowest cost per available seat-mile (an important performance metric in the airline industry) in the United States.

To enhance its differential appeal, JetBlue drove up its perceived value by implementing its mantra: combining *high-touch*—to enhance the customer experience—and *high-tech*—to drive down costs. JetBlue also had a highly functional website for making reservations and planning other travel-related services. But because research showed that roughly one-third of customers prefer speaking to live reservation agents, it decided to add live agents, all of whom were U.S.-based, work-from-home employees rather than outsourced ones, as per the industry best practice.

To further enhance its value for customers, JetBlue added to its fleet high-end, 100-seat Embraer regional jets—each equipped with leather seats, free movie and television programming via DirecTV, and XM Satellite Radio, and each staffed with friendly and attentive on-board service attendants. Additional amenities included its Mint class, a luxury version of first-class travel featuring small private suites with lie-flat beds of up to 6 feet 8 inches long, a high-resolution personal viewing screen offering a large library of free and on-demand movies, live TV, and free in-flight high-speed Wi-Fi ("Fly-Fi"). JetBlue also offered personal check-in and early boarding, free bag check and priority bag retrieval after flight, and complimentary gourmet food and alcoholic beverages in flight.

In its early years, pursuing a blue ocean strategy by combining a cost-leadership position with a differentiation strategy resulted in a competitive advantage. JetBlue used value innovation to drive up perceived customer value even while lowering operating costs. This approach can work when an airline is small and connecting a few highly profitable city routes. However, it is quite difficult to implement because it involves simultaneous execution of cost-leadership and differentiation activities—two very distinct strategic strategies. Pursuing them simultaneously results in trade-offs that work against each other. For instance, higher perceived customer value (e.g., by providing leather seats and free Wi-Fi throughout the entire aircraft) comes with higher costs. These trade-offs eventually caught up with JetBlue.

Between 2007 and 2015, the airline faced several high-profile mishaps (e.g., emergency landings and erratic pilot and crew behaviors). Following the 2007 "snowmageddon," when JetBlue was forced to cancel about 1,600 flights and passengers were stranded for up to nine hours sitting on the tarmac aboard full airplanes, the board removed founder Neeleman as CEO and replaced him with David Barger, formerly JetBlue's chief operating officer. These public relations

nightmares compounded the fundamental difficulty of resolving the need to limit costs while providing superior customer service and in-flight amenities. Meanwhile, Barger was unable to overcome JetBlue's competitive disadvantage; by 2015, the airline was lagging the Dow Jones U.S. Airline Index by more than 180 percentage points. In that same year, JetBlue's board replaced Barger, appointing Robin Hayes, who had been with British Airways for almost 20 years, as the new CEO.

JetBlue's situation went from bad to worse. In 2017, JetBlue ranked dead last in the annual WSJ survey of U.S. airlines based on objective data such as on-time arrival, tarmac and flight delays, cancelled flights, involuntary bumping of passengers, mishandled bags, and numerous other customer complaints.

So Hayes set out to sharpen JetBlue's strategic profile, doubling down on its blue ocean strategy. He attempted once again to lower operating costs while increasing perceived value creation. To drive down costs, he decided to add more seats to each plane, reducing legroom in coach (now on par with the legacy carriers). He identified other cost-savings opportunities, mainly in aircraft maintenance and crew scheduling. At the same time, Hayes also expanded its Mint class service to many more flights, providing a product that customers loved and some other airlines lacked. JetBlue also added a new airplane, the Airbus A-321, to its fleet, which scores significantly higher in customer satisfaction surveys than the older A-320.[1]

Part II of this ChapterCase appears in Section 6.6.

THE CHAPTERCASE illustrates how JetBlue ran into trouble by pursuing two different business strategies at the same time—a *cost-leadership* strategy, focused on low cost, and a *differentiation* strategy, focused on delivering unique features and service. Although the idea of combining different business strategies seems appealing, it is quite difficult to execute a cost-leadership and differentiation position at the same time. This is because cost leadership and differentiation are distinct strategic positions. Pursuing them simultaneously results in trade-offs that work against each other. Providing higher perceived customer value tends to generate higher costs.

Many firms that attempt to combine cost-leadership and differentiation strategies end up being *stuck in the middle*. In this situation, strategic leaders have failed to carve out a clear *strategic position*. In their attempt to be everything to everybody, these firms end up being neither a low-cost leader nor a differentiator (thus the phrase *stuck in the middle* between the two distinct strategic positions). This common strategic failure contributed to JetBlue's sustained competitive disadvantage from 2007 to 2019. Strategic leaders need to be aware to avoid being *stuck in the middle* between distinct business strategies. A clear strategic position—either as differentiator *or* low-cost leader—is more likely to form the basis for competitive advantage. Although quite attractive at first glance, a *blue ocean strategy* is difficult to implement because of the trade-offs between the two distinct strategic positions (low-cost leadership and differentiation), unless the firm is successful in *value innovation* that allows a reconciliation of these inherent trade-offs (discussed in detail later).

This chapter, the first in Part 2 on strategy *formulation,* takes a close look at business-level strategy, frequently also referred to as *competitive strategy.* It deals with *how* to compete for advantage. Based on the analysis of the external and internal environments (presented in Part 1), the second step in the *AFI Strategy Framework* is to formulate a business strategy that enhances the firm's chances of achieving a competitive advantage.

We begin our discussion of strategy formulation by defining *business-level strategy, strategic position,* and *generic business strategies.* We then look at two key generic business strategies: *differentiation* and *cost leadership.* We pay special attention to value and cost drivers that managers can use to carve out a clear strategic profile. Next, we relate the two business-level strategies to the external environment, in particular, to the five forces, to highlight their respective benefits and risks. We then introduce the notion of *blue ocean strategy*—using *value innovation* to combine a differentiation and cost-leadership strategic position. We also look at changes in competitive positioning over time before concluding with practical *Implications for Strategic Leaders.*

6.1 Business-Level Strategy: How to Compete for Advantage

LO 10-1

Define business-level strategy and describe how it determines a firm's strategic position.

Business-level strategy details the goal-directed actions managers take in their quest for competitive advantage when competing in a single product market.[2] It may involve a single product or a group of similar products that use the same distribution channel. It concerns the broad question, "How should we compete?" To formulate an appropriate business-level strategy, managers must answer the who, what, why, and how questions of competition:

- *Who* are the customer segments we will serve?
- *What* customer needs, wishes, and desires will we satisfy?
- *Why* do we want to satisfy them?
- *How* will we satisfy them?[3]

business-level strategy The goal-directed actions managers take in their quest for competitive advantage when competing in a single product market.

To formulate an effective business strategy, managers need to keep in mind that competitive advantage is determined jointly by *industry* and *firm* effects. As shown in Exhibit 6.1, one route to competitive advantage is shaped by *industry effects,* while a second route is determined by *firm effects.* As discussed in Chapter 3, an industry's profit potential can be assessed using the five forces framework plus the availability of complements. Managers need to be certain that the business strategy is aligned with the five forces that shape competition. They can evaluate performance differences among clusters of firms in the same industry by conducting a strategic-group analysis. The concepts introduced in Chapter 4 are key in understanding firm effects because they allow us to look inside firms and explain why they differ based on their resources, capabilities, and competencies. It is also important to note that industry and firm effects are not independent, but rather they are *interdependent,* as shown by the two-pointed arrow connecting industry effects and firm effects in Exhibit 6.1. At the firm level, performance is determined by value and cost positions *relative* to competitors. This is the firm's *strategic position,* to which we turn next.

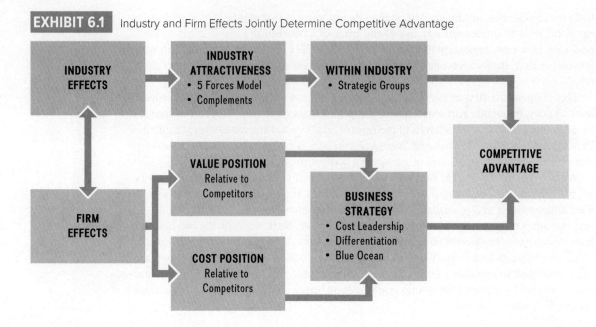

EXHIBIT 6.1 Industry and Firm Effects Jointly Determine Competitive Advantage

STRATEGIC POSITION

We noted in Chapter 5 that competitive advantage is based on the difference between the *perceived value* a firm is able to create for consumers (V), captured by how much consumers are willing to pay for a product or service, and the total cost (C) the firm incurs to create that value. The greater the *economic value created* ($V - C$), the greater is a firm's potential for competitive advantage. To answer the business-level strategy question of how to compete, managers have two primary competitive levers at their disposal: value (V) and cost (C).

A firm's business-level strategy determines its *strategic position*—its strategic profile based on value creation and cost—in a specific product market. A firm attempts to stake out a valuable and unique position that meets customer needs while simultaneously creating as large a gap as possible between the value the firm's product creates and the cost required to produce it. Higher value creation tends to require higher cost. To achieve a desired strategic position, managers must make **strategic trade-offs**—choices between a cost *or* value position. Managers must address the tension between value creation and the pressure to keep cost in check so as not to erode the firm's economic value creation and profit margin.

As shown in the ChapterCase, JetBlue experienced a competitive disadvantage for a number of years because it was unable to effectively address the strategic trade-offs inherent in pursuing a cost-leadership *and* differentiation strategy at the same time. A business strategy is more likely to lead to a competitive advantage if a firm has a clear strategic profile, either as differentiator *or* a low-cost leader. A *blue ocean strategy* is only successful, in contrast, if the firm can implement some type of value innovation that reconciles the inherent trade-off between value creation and underlying costs.

GENERIC BUSINESS STRATEGIES

There are two fundamentally different generic business strategies—*differentiation* and *cost leadership.* A **differentiation strategy** seeks to create higher value for customers than the value that competitors create, by delivering products or services with unique features while

strategic trade-offs Choices between a cost *or* value position. Such choices are necessary because higher value creation tends to generate higher cost.

differentiation strategy Generic business strategy that seeks to create higher value for customers than the value that competitors create, while containing costs.

keeping costs at the same or similar levels, allowing the firm to charge higher prices to its customers. A **cost-leadership strategy**, in contrast, seeks to create the same or similar value for customers by delivering products or services at a lower cost than competitors, enabling the firm to offer lower prices to its customers.

for customers at a lower cost.

These two business strategies are called *generic strategies* because they can be used by any organization—manufacturing or service, large or small, for-profit or nonprofit, public or private, domestic or foreign—in the quest for competitive advantage, independent of industry context. Differentiation and cost leadership require distinct strategic positions, and in turn increase a firm's chances to gain and sustain a competitive advantage.[4] Because value creation and cost tend to be positively correlated, however, important trade-offs exist between value creation and low cost. A business strategy, therefore, is more likely to lead to a competitive advantage if it allows a firm to either *perform similar activities differently* or *perform different activities* than its rivals that result in creating more value or offering similar products or services at lower cost.[5]

When considering different business strategies, strategic leaders also must define the **scope of competition**—whether to pursue a specific, narrow part of the market or go after the broader market.[6] The automobile industry provides an example of the *scope of competition.* Alfred P. Sloan, longtime president and CEO of GM, defined the carmaker's mission as providing a car for every purse and purpose. GM was one of the first to implement a multidivisional structure in order to separate the brands into strategic business units, allowing each brand to create its unique strategic position (with its own profit and loss responsibility) within the broad automotive market. For example, GM's product lineup ranges from the low-cost-positioned Chevy brand to the differentiated Cadillac brand. In this case, Chevy is pursuing a broad cost-leadership strategy, while Cadillac is pursuing a broad differentiation strategy. The two different business strategies are integrated at the corporate level at GM (more on *corporate strategy* in Chapters 8 and 9).

scope of competition
The size—narrow or broad—of the market in which a firm chooses to compete.

On the other hand, Tesla, the maker of all-electric cars (featured in ChapterCase 1), offers a highly differentiated product and pursues only a small market segment. At this point, it uses a *focused differentiation strategy.* In particular, Tesla focuses on environmentally conscious consumers that want to drive a high-performance car and who are willing to pay a premium price. Going forward, Tesla is hoping to broaden its competitive scope with its Model 3, priced at roughly half of the Model S sedan and Model X sport utility crossover. Moreover, Elon Musk hopes the Tesla Model Y (a smaller, compact SUV) will sell even better than the Model 3. Taken together, GM's competitive scope is broad—with a focus on the mass automotive market—while Tesla's competitive scope is narrow—with a focus on all-electric luxury cars.

Now we can combine the dimensions describing a firm's strategic position (*differentiation versus cost*) with the scope of competition (*narrow versus broad*). As shown in Exhibit 6.2, by doing so we get the two major broad business strategies (*cost leadership* and *differentiation*), shown as the top two boxes in the matrix, and the *focused* version of each, shown as the

EXHIBIT 6.2 Strategic Position and Competitive Scope: Generic Business Strategies

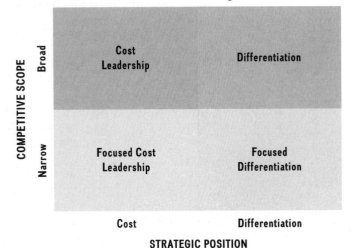

Source: Adapted from M.E. Porter (1980), *Competitive Strategy. Techniques for Analyzing Industries and Competitors* (New York: Free Press).

used cost-leader-ship strategy Same as the cost-leadership strategy except with a narrow focus on a niche market.

focused differentiation strategy Same as the differentiation strategy except with a narrow focus on a niche market.

bottom two boxes in the matrix. The focused versions of the two business strategies—**focused cost-leadership strategy** and **focused differentiation strategy**—are essentially the same as the broad generic strategies *except* that the competitive scope is narrower. For example, the manufacturing company BIC pursues a focused cost-leadership strategy, designing and producing disposable pens and cigarette lighters at a low cost, while Mont Blanc pursues a focused differentiation strategy, offering exquisite pens—what it calls "writing instruments"—frequently priced at several hundred dollars.

As discussed in ChapterCase 6, JetBlue attempts to combine a focused cost-leadership position with a focused differentiation position. Although initially successful, for the last several years, JetBlue has been consistently outperformed by airlines that do not attempt to straddle different strategic positions, but rather have clear strategic profiles as either differentiators or low-cost leaders. For example, Southwest Airlines competes clearly as a broad cost leader (and would be placed squarely in the upper-left quadrant of Exhibit 6.2). The legacy carriers—Delta, American, and United—all compete as broad differentiators (and would be placed in the upper-right quadrant). Regionally, we find smaller airlines that are ultra low cost, such as Allegiant Air, Frontier Airlines, and Spirit Airlines, with very clear strategic positions. These smaller airlines would be placed in the lower-left quadrant of Exhibit 6.2 because they are pursuing a focused cost-leadership strategy. Based on a clear strategic position, these airlines have outperformed JetBlue over many years. JetBlue appears to be stuck between different strategic positions, trying to combine a focused cost-leadership position with focused differentiation. And, as the airline grew, the problems inherent in attempting to combine different strategic positions also grew—and more severe at that because of its attempt to also straddle the (broad) cost-leadership position with the (broad) differentiation position. In essence, JetBlue was trying to be everything to everybody. Being *stuck in the middle* of different strategic positions is a recipe for inferior performance and competitive disadvantage—and this is exactly what JetBlue experienced between 2007 and 2019, when it underperformed the Dow Jones Airlines Index, lagging behind the big four airlines (American, Delta, Southwest, and United) as well as smaller airlines such as Alaska Airlines, Allegiant Air, and Spirit.

LO 6-2

Examine the relationship between value drivers and differentiation strategy.

6.2 Differentiation Strategy: Understanding Value Drivers

The goal of a differentiation strategy is to add unique features that will increase the perceived value of goods and services in the minds of consumers so they are willing to pay a higher price. Ideally, a firm following a differentiation strategy aims to achieve in the minds of consumers a level of value creation that its competitors cannot easily match. The focus of competition in a differentiation strategy tends to be on unique product features, service, and new product launches, or on marketing and promotion rather than price.

Several competitors in the bottled-water industry provide a prime example of pursuing a successful differentiation strategy.[7] As more and more consumers shift from carbonated soft drinks to healthier choices, the industry for bottled water is booming—growing about 10 percent per year. In the United States, the per person consumption of bottled water surpassed that of carbonated soft drinks for the first time in 2016. Such a fast-growing industry provides ample opportunity for differentiation. In particular, the industry is split into two broad segments depending on the sales price. Bottled water with a sticker price of $1.30 or less per 32 ounces (close to one liter) is considered low-end, while those with a higher price tag are seen as luxury items. For example, PepsiCo's Aquafina and Coca-Cola's Dasani are considered low-end products, selling purified tap water at low prices, often in bulk at big-box

retailers such as Walmart. On the premium end, PepsiCo introduced Lifewtr with a splashy ad during Super Bowl LI in 2017,
while Jennifer Aniston markets Smartwater, Coca-Cola's
premium water.

   The idea of selling premium water is not new, however. Evian
(owned by Danone, a French consumer products company) and
S.Pellegrino (owned by Nestlé of Switzerland) have long focused
on differentiating their products by emphasizing the uniqueness
of their respective natural sources (Evian hails from the French
Alps while Pellegrino comes from San Pellegrino Terme in Italy's Lombardy region). Recent entrants into the luxury segment
for bottled water have taken the differentiation of their products
to new heights. Some purveyors, such as Svalbardi, are able to
charge super premium prices. At upscale retailer Harrods in
London, a bottle of Svalbardi costs about $100 for 25 ounces;
the water, sold in a heavy glass bottle, hails from Norwegian ice-
bergs some 4,000 years old. Ordering premium bottled water in

Anythings/Shutterstock

the United States to accompany lunch has become a status symbol. Indeed, many restaurants
now feature water lists besides the more traditional wine selection. "Energy waters" enhanced
with minerals and vitamins are the fastest growing segment. Although flavored waters make
up less than 5 percent of the overall market for bottled water, they rack up 15 percent of total
revenues. And this is nothing to be snuffed at: The market for bottled water globally reached
some $150 billion and continues to grow fast. Although a free substitute can be had from
most taps in industrialized countries, the success of many luxury brands in the bottled-water
industry shows the power of differentiation strategy.

   A company that uses a differentiation strategy can achieve a competitive advantage as long
as its economic value created $(V - C)$ is greater than that of its competitors. Firm A in
Exhibit 6.3 produces a generic commodity. Firm B and Firm C represent two efforts at differentiation. Firm B not only offers greater value than Firm A, but also maintains *cost parity,*
meaning it has the same costs as Firm A. However, even if a firm fails to achieve cost parity
(which is often the case because higher value creation tends to go along with higher costs in
terms of higher-quality raw materials, research and development, employee training to provide
superior customer service, and so on), it can still gain a competitive advantage if its economic
value creation exceeds that of its competitors. Firm C represents just such a competitive advantage. For the approach shown *either* in Firm B or Firm C, economic value creation, $(V - C)_B$ or
$(V - C)_C$, is greater than that of Firm A $(V - C)_A$. Either Firm B or C, therefore, achieves a
competitive advantage because it has a higher value gap over Firm A [$(V - C)_B > (V - C)_A$, or
$(V - C)_C > (V - C)_A$], which allows it to charge a premium price, reflecting its higher value
creation. To complete the relative comparison, although both companies pursue a differentiation strategy, Firm B also has a competitive advantage over Firm C because although both offer
identical value, Firm B has lower costs, thus $(V - C)_B > (V - C)_C$.

   Although increased value creation is a defining feature of a differentiation strategy, managers must also control costs. Rising costs reduce economic value created and erode profit
margins. Indeed, if cost rises too much as the firm attempts to create more perceived value
for customers, its value gap shrinks, negating any differentiation advantage. One reason
JetBlue could not maintain an initial competitive advantage was because it was unable to
keep its costs down sufficiently. JetBlue's current management team put measures in place
to lower the airline's cost structure such as charging fees for checked bags and reducing leg
space to increase passenger capacity on each of its planes. These cost-saving initiatives
should increase its economic value creation.

Differentiation Strategy: Achieving Competitive Advantage

Pursuing a differentiation strategy, firms that successfully differentiate their product can enjoy a competitive advantage, assuming they are able to control costs. Firm A's product is seen as a generic commodity with no unique brand value. Firm B has the same cost structure as Firm A but creates more economic value and thus has a competitive advantage over both Firm A and Firm C because $(V − C)_B > (V − C)_C > (V − C)_A$. Although, Firm C has higher costs than Firm A and B, it still generates a higher economic value than Firm A.

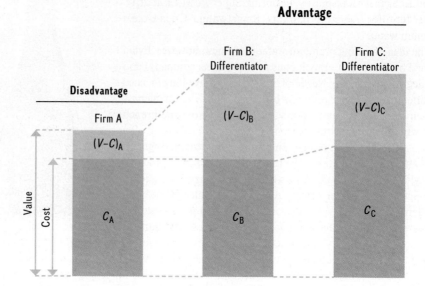

Competitive Position

economies of scope
Savings that come from producing two (or more) outputs at less cost than producing each output individually, despite using the same resources and technology.

Although a differentiation strategy is generally associated with premium pricing, strategic leaders have an important second pricing option. When a firm is able to offer a differentiated product or service and can control its costs at the same time, it is able to gain market share from other firms in the industry by charging a similar price but offering more perceived value. By leveraging its differentiated appeal of superior customer service and quality, for example, Marriott offers a line of different hotels: its flagship Marriott full-service business hotel equipped to host large conferences; Residence Inn for extended stay; Marriott Courtyard for business travelers; and Marriott Fairfield Inn for inexpensive leisure and family travel.[8] Although these hotels are roughly comparable to competitors in price, they generally offer a higher perceived value. With this line of different hotels, Marriott can benefit from economies of scale and scope, and thus keep its cost structure in check. *Economies of scale* denote decreases in cost per unit as output increases (more in the next section when we discuss cost-leadership strategy). **Economies of scope** describe the savings that come from producing two (or more) outputs at less cost than producing each output individually, even though using the same resources and technology. This larger difference between cost and value allows Marriott to achieve greater economic value than its competitors, and thus to gain market share and post superior performance.

Managers can adjust a number of different levers to improve a firm's strategic position. These levers either increase perceived value or decrease costs. Here, we will study the most salient *value drivers* that strategic leaders have at their disposal (we look at cost drivers in the next section).[9] They are

- Product features
- Customer service
- Complements

These value drivers are related to a firm's expertise in, and organization of, different internal value chain activities. Although these are the most important value drivers, no such list can be complete. Applying the concepts introduced in this chapter should allow strategic leaders to identify other important value and cost drivers unique to their business.

When attempting to increase the perceived value of the firm's product or service offerings, managers must remember that the different value drivers contribute to competitive advantage *only if* their increase in value creation (ΔV) exceeds the increase in costs (ΔC). The condition of $\Delta V > \Delta C$ must be fulfilled if a differentiation strategy is to strengthen a firm's strategic position and thus enhance its competitive advantage.

PRODUCT FEATURES

One of the obvious but most important levers that strategic leaders can adjust is product features, thereby increasing the perceived value of the product or service offering. Adding unique product attributes allows firms to turn commodity products into differentiated products commanding a premium price. Strong R&D capabilities are often needed to create superior product features. In the kitchen-utensil industry, OXO follows a differentiation strategy, highlighting product features. By adhering to its philosophy of making products that are easy to use for the largest variety of possible users,[10] OXO differentiates its kitchen utensils through its patent-protected ergonomically designed soft black rubber grips.

CUSTOMER SERVICE

Managers can increase the perceived value of their firms' product or service offerings by focusing on customer service. For example, the online retailer Zappos earned a reputation for superior customer service by offering free shipping both ways: to the customer and for returns.[11] Although several online retailers now offer free shipping both ways, Zappos has done so since its inception in 1999, that is, long before more recent imitators. Perhaps more important, Zappos makes the return process hassle free by providing a link to a prepaid shipping label. All the customer needs to do is drop the box off at the nearby UPS store, all free of charge. Zappos's strategic leaders didn't view free shipping both ways as an additional expense but rather as part of the marketing budget. Moreover, Zappos does not outsource its customer service, and its associates do not use predetermined scripts. They are instead encouraged to build a relationship of trust with each individual customer. Indeed, it is quite fun to interact with Zappos customer service reps. There seemed to be a good return on investment as word spread through the online shopping community. Competitors took notice, too; Amazon bought Zappos for over $1 billion.[12]

COMPLEMENTS

When studying industry analysis in Chapter 3, we identified the availability of complements as an important force determining the profit potential of an industry. Complements add value to a product or service when they are consumed in tandem. Finding complements, therefore, is an important task for strategic leaders in their quest to enhance the value of their offerings.

A prime example of complements is smartphones and cellular services. A

Trader Joe's has some 475 stores, about half of which are in California and the rest in another 43 states plus Washington, D.C. The chain is known for good products, value for money, and great customer service. As just one example, stores stock local products as requested by their communities.[13]

QualityHD/Shutterstock

smartphone without a service plan is much less useful than one with a data plan. Traditionally, the providers of phones such as Apple, Samsung, and others did not provide wireless services. AT&T and Verizon are by far the two largest service providers in the United States, jointly holding some 70 percent of market share. To enhance the attractiveness of their phone and service bundles, phone makers and service providers frequently sign exclusive deals. When first released, for instance, service for the iPhone was exclusively offered by AT&T. Thus, if you wanted an iPhone, you had to sign up for a two-year service contract with AT&T.

Google, a division of Alphabet, decided to offer the important complements of smartphones and wireless services in-house to attract more customers.[14] Google offers high-end phones such as the Pixel 3 with cutting-edge artificial intelligence built in (via its Google Assistant) at competitive prices. It combines this with discounted high-speed wireless services in its Project Fi, a complementary offering. Working in conjunction with smaller wireless service providers such as T-Mobile (which merged with Sprint), Google provides seamless wireless services by stitching together a nationwide network of services based on available free Wi-Fi hotspots (such as at Starbucks) and cellular networks offered by T-Mobile. This not only enables wide coverage, but also reduces data usage significantly because Google phones automatically switch to free Wi-Fi networks wherever available. In addition, rather than to pay for a predetermined amount of data each month, Google Fi charges users for data use "as they go," that is for actual data consumed without throttling services after consuming the data allowance (as do AT&T and Verizon).

Project Fi is intended to drive more demand for Google's phone; sales have been lackluster thus far. Stronger demand for Google's phones locks more users into the Google ecosystem as its wireless services are available only with its own phones. This provides an example where complementary product and service offerings not only reinforce demand for one another, but also create a situation where network externalities can arise. As more users sign up for Project Fi, Google is able to offer faster and more reliable services through investing more into the latest technology, such as 5G, making its network and with it its Google phones more attractive to more users, and so forth.

In summary, by choosing the differentiation strategy as the strategic position for a product, managers focus their attention on adding value to the product through its unique features that respond to customer preferences, customer service during and after the sale, or effective marketing that communicates the value of the product's features. Although this positioning involves increased costs (for example, higher-quality inputs or innovative research and development activities), customers are generally willing to pay a premium price for the product or service that satisfies their needs and preferences. In the next section, we will discuss how strategic leaders formulate a cost-leadership strategy.

6.3 Cost-Leadership Strategy: Understanding Cost Drivers

The goal of a cost-leadership strategy is to reduce the firm's cost below that of its competitors while offering adequate value. The *cost leader,* as the name implies, focuses its attention and resources on reducing the cost to manufacture a product or on lowering the operating cost to deliver a service in order to offer lower prices to its customers. The cost leader attempts to optimize all of its value chain activities to achieve a low-cost position. Although staking out the lowest-cost position in the industry is the overriding strategic objective, a cost leader still needs to offer products and services of acceptable value. As an example, GM and Korean car manufacturer Kia offer some models that compete directly with one another, yet Kia's cars tend to be produced at lower cost, while providing a similar value proposition.

A cost leader can achieve a competitive advantage as long as its economic value created $(V - C)$ is greater than that of its competitors. Firm A in Exhibit 6.4 produces a product with a cost structure vulnerable to competition. Firms B and C show two different approaches to cost leadership. Firm B achieves a competitive advantage over Firm A because Firm B not only has lower cost than Firm A, but also achieves *differentiation parity* (meaning it creates the same value as Firm A). As a result, Firm B's economic value creation, $(V - C)_B$, is greater than that of Firm A, $(V - C)_A$. For example, as the low-cost leader, Walmart took market share from Kmart, which subsequently filed for bankruptcy.

What if a firm fails to create differentiation parity? Such parity is often hard to achieve because value creation tends to go along with higher costs, and Firm B's strategy is aimed at lower costs. A firm can still gain a competitive advantage as long as its economic value creation exceeds that of its competitors. Firm C represents this approach to cost leadership. Even with lower value (no differentiation parity) but lower cost, Firm C's economic value creation, $(V - C)_C$, still is greater than that of Firm A, $(V - C)_A$.

In both approaches to cost leadership in Exhibit 6.4, Firm B's economic value creation is greater than that of Firm A and Firm C. Yet, both firms B and C achieve a competitive advantage over Firm A. Either one can charge prices similar to its competitors and benefit from a greater profit margin per unit, or it can charge lower prices than its competition and gain higher profits from higher volume. Both variations of a cost-leadership strategy can result in competitive advantage. Although Firm B has a competitive advantage over both firms A and C, Firm C has a competitive advantage in comparison to Firm A.

Although companies successful at cost leadership must excel at controlling costs, this doesn't mean that they can neglect value creation. Kia signals the quality of its cars with a five-year, 60,000-mile warranty, one of the more generous warranties in the

EXHIBIT 6.4 Cost-Leadership Strategy: Achieving Competitive Advantage

Pursuing a cost-leadership strategy, firms that can keep their cost at the lowest point in the industry while offering acceptable value are able to gain a competitive advantage. Firm A has not managed to take advantage of possible cost savings and thus experiences a competitive disadvantage. The offering from Firm B has the same perceived value as Firm A but through more effective cost containment creates more economic value (over both Firm A and Firm C because $(V - C)_B > (V - C)_C > (V - C)_A$. The offering from Firm C has a lower perceived value than that of Firm A or B and has the same reduced product cost as with Firm B; as a result, Firm C still generates higher economic value than Firm A.

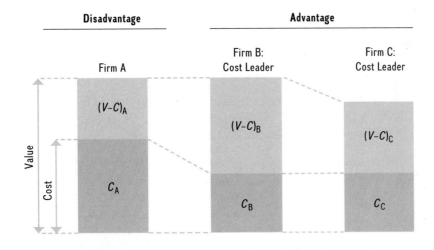

Competitive Position

industry. Walmart offers products of acceptable quality, including many brand-name products.

The most important *cost drivers* that strategic leaders can manipulate to keep their costs low are

- Cost of input factors.
- Economies of scale.
- Learning-curve effects.
- Experience-curve effects.

However, this list is only a starting point; managers may consider other cost drivers, depending on the situation.

COST OF INPUT FACTORS

One of the most basic advantages a firm can have over its rivals is access to lower-cost input factors such as raw materials, capital, labor, and IT services. In the market for international long-distance travel, one of the potent competitive threats facing U.S. legacy carriers—American, Delta, and United—comes from three airlines located in the Persian Gulf states—Emirates, Etihad, and Qatar. These airlines achieve a competitive advantage over their U.S. counterparts thanks to lower-cost inputs—raw materials (access to cheaper fuel), capital (interest-free government loans), labor—and fewer regulations (for example, regarding nighttime take-offs and landings, or in adding new runways and building luxury airports with swimming pools, among other amenities).[15] To benefit from lower-cost IT services, the Gulf carriers also outsource some value chain activities such as booking and online customer service to India. Together, these distinct cost advantages across several key input factors add up to create a greater economic value creation for the Gulf carriers vis-à-vis U.S. competitors, leading to a competitive advantage.

economies of scale Decreases in cost per unit as output increases.

ECONOMIES OF SCALE

Firms with greater market share might be in a position to reap **economies of scale**, decreases in cost per unit as output increases. This relationship between unit cost and output is depicted in the first (left-hand) part of Exhibit 6.5: Cost per unit falls as output increases up

EXHIBIT 6.5

Economies of Scale, Minimum Efficient Scale, and Diseconomies of Scale

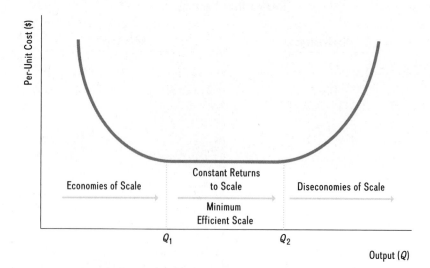

to point Q_1. A firm whose output is closer to Q_1 has a cost advantage over other firms with less output. In this sense, bigger is better.

In the airframe-manufacturing industry, for example, reaping economies of scale and learning is critical for cost-competitiveness. The market for commercial airplanes is often not large enough to allow more than one competitor to reach sufficient scale to drive down unit cost. Boeing chose not to compete with Airbus in the market for superjumbo jets; rather, it decided to focus on a smaller, fuel-efficient airplane (the 787 Dreamliner, priced at roughly $250 million) that allows for long-distance, point-to-point connections. By spring 2019, it had built 800 Dreamliners with more than 600 orders for the new airplane.[16] Boeing can expect to reap significant economies of scale and learning, which will lower per-unit cost. At the same time, Airbus had delivered 290 A-380 superjumbos (sticker price: $450 million) with 64 orders remaining on its books.[17] If both companies would have chosen to compete head-on in each market segment, the resulting per-unit cost for each airplane would have been much higher because neither could have achieved significant economies of scale (overall their market share split is roughly 50-50).

What causes per-unit cost to drop as output increases (up to point Q_1)? Economies of scale allow firms to

- Spread their fixed costs over a larger output.
- Employ specialized systems and equipment.
- Take advantage of certain physical properties.

SPREADING FIXED COSTS OVER LARGER OUTPUT. Larger output allows firms to spread their fixed costs over more units. That is why gains in market share are often critical to drive down per-unit cost. This relationship is even more pronounced in many high-tech industries because most of the cost occurs before a single product or service is sold. Take operating systems software as an example. Microsoft spends over $10 billion a year on research and development (R&D).[18] Between 2011 and 2015, a good part of this was spent on developing Windows 10, its most recent operating system software. This R&D expense was a fixed cost Microsoft had to incur before a single copy of Windows 10 was sold. However, once the initial version of the new software was completed, the marginal cost of each additional copy was basically zero, especially for copies sold in digital form online. Given that Microsoft dominates the operating system market for personal computers (PCs) with more than 90 percent market share, it expects to sell several hundred million copies of Windows 10, thereby spreading its huge fixed cost of development over a large output. Microsoft's huge installed base of Windows operating systems throughout the world allowed it to capture a large profit margin for each copy of Windows sold, after recouping its initial investment. Microsoft's Windows 10 also drives sales for complementary products such as the ubiquitous Microsoft Office Suite made up of Word, Excel, PowerPoint, and Outlook, among other programs (as discussed in ChapterCase 5).

EMPLOYING SPECIALIZED SYSTEMS AND EQUIPMENT. Larger output also allows firms to invest in more specialized systems and equipment, such as enterprise resource planning (ERP) software or manufacturing robots. Tesla's strong demand for its Model 3 sedan allows it to employ cutting-edge robotics in its Fremont, California, manufacturing plant to produce cars of high quality at large scale, and thus driving down costs. Tesla is expecting even more demand for the Model 3 and the newly launched Model Y in China, thus it will employ more specialized systems and equipment in the new and much larger Shanghai, China, factory in its quest for economies of scale.

TAKING ADVANTAGE OF CERTAIN PHYSICAL PROPERTIES. Economies of scale also occur because of certain physical properties. One such property is known as the *cube-square rule:* The volume of a body such as a pipe or a tank increases disproportionately more than its surface. This same principle makes big-box retail stores such as Walmart or The Home Depot cheaper to build and run. They can also stock much more merchandise and handle inventory more efficiently. Their huge size makes it difficult for department stores or small retailers to compete on cost and selection.

Look again at Exhibit 6.5. The output range between Q_1 and Q_2 in the figure is considered the **minimum efficient scale (MES)** to be cost-competitive. Between Q_1 and Q_2, the returns to scale are constant. It is the output range needed to bring the cost per unit down as much as possible, allowing a firm to stake out the lowest-cost position achievable through economies of scale. With more than 10 million Prius cars sold worldwide since its introduction in 1997, Toyota has been able to reach the minimum efficient scale part of the per-unit cost curve. This allows the company to offer the car at a relatively low price and still make a profit.

The concept of minimum efficient scale applies not only to manufacturing processes but also to managerial tasks such as how to organize work. Due to investments in specialized technology and equipment (e.g., electric arc furnaces), Nucor is able to reach MES with much smaller batches of steel than larger, fully vertically integrated steel companies using older technology. Nucor's optimal plant size is about 500 people, which is much smaller than at larger integrated steelmakers such as U.S. Steel which often employ thousands of workers per plant.[19] Of course, minimum efficient scale depends on the specific industry: The average per-unit cost curve, depicted conceptually in Exhibit 6.5, is a reflection of the underlying production function, which is determined by technology and other input factors.

Benefits to scale cannot go on indefinitely, though. Bigger is not always better; in fact, sometimes bigger is worse. Beyond $Q2$ in Exhibit 6.5, firms experience **diseconomies of scale**—increases in cost as output increases. As firms get too big, the complexity of managing and coordinating the production process raises the cost, negating any benefits to scale. Large firms also tend to become overly bureaucratic, with too many layers of hierarchy. They grow inflexible and slow in decision making. To avoid problems associated with diseconomies of scale, Gore Associates, maker of GORE-TEX fabric, Glide dental floss, and many other innovative products, breaks up its company into smaller units. Gore Associates found that employing about 150 people per plant allows it to avoid diseconomies of scale. It uses a simple decision rule:[20] "We put 150 parking spaces in the lot, and when people start parking on the grass, we know it's time to build a new plant."[21]

Finally, there are also physical limits to scale. Airbus is pushing the envelope with its A-380 aircraft, which can hold more than 850 passengers and can fly 9,520 miles (from Newark, New Jersey, to Singapore, for instance). The goal, of course, is to drive down the cost of the average seat-mile flown (CASM, a standard cost metric in the airline industry). It appears, however, that the A-380 superjumbo did not allow airlines to operate at minimum efficient scale, and thus failed to deliver the lowest cost per unit (CASM) possible. Rather, it turned out that the A-380 was simply too large to be efficient, thus causing *diseconomies of scale.* For example, boarding and embarking procedures needed to be completely revamped and streamlined to accommodate more than 850 people in a timely and safe manner. Airports around the world needed to be retrofitted with longer and wider runways to allow the superjumbo to take off and land. To prove the point, Airbus announced in early 2019 that it will cease production of the A-380 in 2021 as demand declined for the superjumbo in recent years.[22]

Scale economies are critical to driving down a firm's cost and strengthening a cost-leadership position. Although strategic leaders need to increase output to operate at a

---

minimum efficient scale (MES) Output range needed to bring down the cost per unit as much as possible, allowing a firm to stake out the lowest-cost position that is achievable through economies of scale.

diseconomies of scale Increases in cost per unit when output increases.

minimum efficient scale (between $Q1$ and $Q2$ in Exhibit 6.5), they also need to be watchful not to drive scale beyond $Q2$, where they would encounter diseconomies. In sum, if the firm's output range is less than Q_1 or more than Q_2, the firm is at a cost disadvantage; reaching an output level between $Q1$ and $Q2$ is optimal in regards to driving down costs. Monitoring the firm's cost structure closely over different output ranges allows managers to fine-tune operations and benefit from economies of scale.

LEARNING CURVE

Do learning curves go up or down? Looking at the challenge of learning, many people tend to see it as an uphill battle, and assume the learning curve goes up. But if we consider our productivity, learning curves go down, as it takes less and less time to produce the same output as we learn how to be more efficient—learning by doing drives down cost. As individuals and teams engage repeatedly in an activity, whether writing computer code, developing new medicines, or building submarines, they learn from their cumulative experience.[23] *Learning curves* were first documented in aircraft manufacturing as the United States ramped up production in the 1930s, before its entry into World War II.[24] Every time production was doubled, the per-unit cost dropped by a predictable and constant rate (approximately 20 percent).[25]

It is not surprising that a learning curve was first observed in aircraft manufacturing. Highly complex, a modern commercial aircraft can contain more than 5 million parts, compared with a few thousand for a car. The more complex the underlying process to manufacture a product or deliver a service, the more learning effects we can expect. As cumulative output increases, managers learn how to optimize the process, and workers improve their performance through repetition and specialization.

TESLA'S LEARNING CURVE. Tesla's production of its Model S vehicle provides a more recent example, depicted in Exhibit 6.6, with the horizontal axis showing cumulative output in units and the vertical axis showing per-unit cost in thousands of dollars.[26]

The California-based designer and manufacturer of all-electric cars made headlines in 2017 when its market capitalization overtook both GM and Ford. This was the first time in U.S. history that the most valuable U.S. car company is not based in Detroit, Michigan, but in Silicon Valley. In 2016, Tesla sold some 80,000 vehicles, while GM sold some 10 million. How can a start-up company that makes less than 1 percent as many vehicles as GM have a higher market valuation? The answer: Future expected growth. Investors bidding up Tesla's share price count on the maker of all-electric cars to sell millions of its newer Model 3 (compact sedan) and Model Y (compact SUV). When the Model 3 was announced in 2016, Tesla garnered some 400,000 preorders from future owners for a car that was not yet produced, let alone test-driven by any potential buyer. The Model Y was announced in 2019 and is expected to be ready for delivery in 2021.

Tesla's learning curve is critical in justifying such lofty stock market valuations, because as production volume increases, production cost per car falls, and the company becomes profitable. Based on a careful analysis of production reports for the Model S between 2012 and 2014[27], Exhibit 6.6 shows how Tesla was able to drive down the unit cost for each car as production volume ramped up. Initially, Tesla lost a significant amount of money on each Model S sold because of high upfront R&D spending to develop the futuristic self-driving car. When producing only 1,000 vehicles, unit cost was $140,000. As production volume of the Model S reached some 12,000 units per year (in 2014), unit cost fell to about $57,000. Although still high, Tesla was able to start making money on each car, because the average selling price for a Model S was about $90,000.

EXHIBIT 6.6

Tesla's Learning
Curve Producing the
Model S

Source: Depiction of
functional relationship
estimated in J. Dyer and H.
Gregersen (2016, Aug. 24),
"Tesla's innovations are
transforming the auto
industry," *Forbes*.

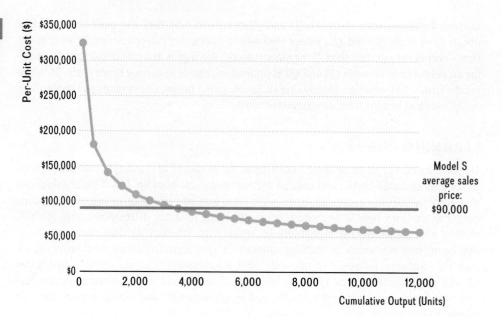

The relationship between production volume and per-unit cost for Tesla (depicted in Exhibit 6.6) suggests that it is an 80 percent learning curve. In an 80 percent learning curve, per-unit cost drops 20 percent every time output is doubled. Assuming a similar relationship holds for the Model 3 production, then per-unit cost would fall to $16,000 per Model 3 with a cumulative production volume of 400,000 (which is the number of preorders Tesla received within one week of announcing this new vehicle). Although the Model 3 base price is pegged at $35,000, the estimated average selling price is more like $50,000 given additional features and eventual expiration of a $7,500 federal tax credit for electric vehicles (when a manufacturer hits 200,000 units). Riding down an 80 percent learning curve, Tesla could make a profit of an estimated $34,000 per Model 3. This would translate to a cumulative profit for Tesla of more than $13.5 billion for the Model 3 preorders alone. As Tesla is reducing the price for the Model 3, the expected profits would decline accordingly. This back-of-the-envelope calculation shows some of the rationale behind Tesla's market capitalization exceeding that of GM and Ford.

Taken together, this example highlights not only the power of the learning curve in driving down per-unit costs, but also how critical cost containment is in gaining a competitive advantage when pursuing a differentiation strategy as Tesla does.

DIFFERENCES IN LEARNING CURVES. Let's now compare different learning curves, and explore their implications for competitive advantage. The steeper the learning curve, the more learning has occurred. As cumulative output increases, firms move down the learning curve, reaching lower per-unit costs. Exhibit 6.7 depicts two different learning curves: a 90 percent and an 80 percent learning curve. In a 90 percent learning curve, per-unit cost drops 10 percent every time output is doubled. The steeper 80 percent learning curve indicates a 20 percent drop every time output is doubled (this was the case in the Tesla example above). It is important to note that the learning-curve effect is driven by increasing cumulative output within the existing technology over time. That implies that the only difference between two points on the same learning curve is the size of the cumulative output. The underlying technology remains the same. The speed of

EXHIBIT 6.7 Gaining Competitive Advantage through Leveraging Learning- and Experience-Curve Effects

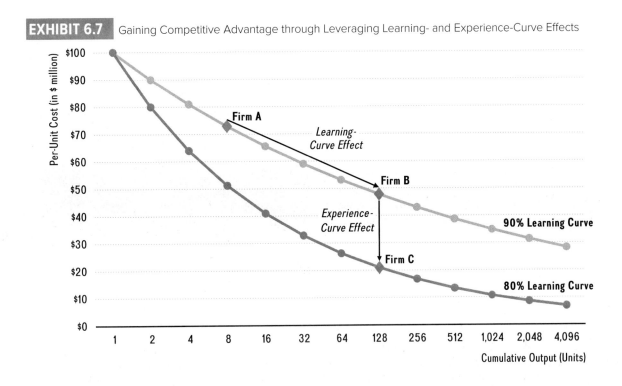

learning determines the slope of the learning curve, or how steep the learning curve is (e.g., 80 percent is steeper than a 90 percent learning curve because costs decrease by 20 percent versus a mere 10 percent each time output doubles). In this perspective, *economies of learning* allow movement down a *given* learning curve based on current production technology.

By moving further down a given learning curve than competitors, a firm can gain a competitive advantage. Exhibit 6.7 shows that Firm B is further down the 90 percent learning curve than Firm A. Firm B leverages *economies of learning* due to larger cumulative output to gain an advantage over Firm A. The only variable that has changed is cumulative output; the technology underlying the 90 percent learning curve remained the same.

Let's continue with the example of manufacturing airframes. To be more precise, as shown in Exhibit 6.7, Firm A produces eight aircraft and reaches a per-unit cost of $73 million per aircraft.[28] Firm B produces 128 aircraft using the same technology as Firm A (because both firms are on the same [90 percent] learning curve), but given a much larger cumulative output, its per unit-cost falls to only $48 million. Thus, Firm B has a clear competitive advantage over Firm A, assuming similar or identical quality in output. We will discuss Firm C when we formally introduce the impact of changes in technology and process innovation.

Learning curves are a robust phenomenon observed in many industries, not only in manufacturing processes but also in alliance management, franchising, and health care.[29] For example, physicians who perform only a small number of cardiac surgeries per year can have a patient mortality rate five times higher than physicians who perform the same surgery more frequently.[30] Strategy Highlight 6.1 features Dr. Devi Shetty of India who reaped huge benefits by applying learning-curve principles to open-heart surgery, driving down cost while improving quality at the same time.

Strategy Highlight **6.1**

Dr. Shetty: "The Henry Ford of Heart Surgery"

Open-heart surgeries are complex medical procedures and loaded with risk. While well-trained surgeons using high-tech equipment are able to reduce mortality rates, costs for cardiac surgeries in the United States have climbed. Difficult heart surgeries can cost $100,000 or more. A heart surgeon in India has driven the costs down to an average of $2,000 per heart surgery, while delivering equal or better outcomes in terms of quality.

Dr. Devi Shetty's goal is to be "the Henry Ford of heart surgery." Just like the American industrialist who applied the learning curve to drive down the cost of an automobile to make it affordable, so Dr. Shetty is reducing the costs of health care and making some of the most complex medical procedures affordable to the world's poorest. A native of Mangalore, India, Dr. Shetty was trained as a heart surgeon at Guy's Hospital in London, one of Europe's best medical facilities. He first came to fame in the 1990s when he successfully conducted an open-heart bypass surgery on Mother Teresa, after she suffered a heart attack.

Dr. Shetty believes that the key to driving down costs in health care is not product innovation, but process innovation. He is able to drive down the cost of complex medical procedures from $100,000 to $2,000 not by doing one big thing, but rather by focusing on doing a thousand small things. Dr. Shetty is applying the concept of the learning curve to make a complex procedure routine and comparatively inexpensive. Part of the Narayana Health group, Dr. Shetty's hospital in Bangalore, India, performs so many cardiac procedures per year that doctors are able to get a great deal of experience quickly, which allows them to specialize in one or two complex procedures. The Narayana surgeons perform two or three procedures a day for six days a week, compared to U.S. surgeons who perform one or two procedures a day for five days a week. The difference adds up. Some of Dr. Shetty's surgeons perform more specialized procedures by the time they are in their 30s than their U.S. counterparts will perform throughout their entire careers. This volume of experienc e allows the cardiac surgeons to move down the learning curve quickly, because the more heart surgeries they perform, the more their skills improve. With this skill level, surgical teams develop robust standard operating procedures and processes, where team members become experts at their specific tasks.

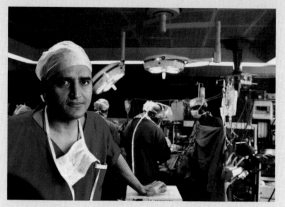

Namas Bhojani

This expertise improves outcomes while the learning-curve effects of performing the same procedures over time also drive down cost (see Exhibit 6.7). Other factors provide additional cost savings. At the same time, Dr. Shetty pays his cardiac surgeons the going rate in India, between $110,000 and $250,000 a year, depending on experience. Their U.S. counterparts earn two to three times the average Indian salary.

Dr. Shetty's health group also reduces costs through economies of scale. By performing thousands of heart surgeries a year, high fixed costs such as the purchase of expensive medical equipment can be spread over a much larger volume. The Narayana hospital in Bangalore has 1,000 beds (many times larger than the average U.S. hospital with 160 beds) and some 20 operating rooms that stay busy pretty much around the clock. This scale allows the Narayana heart clinic to cost-effectively employ specialized high-tech equipment. Given the large size of Dr. Shetty's hospital, it also has significant buying power, driving down the costs of the latest high-tech equipment from vendors such as GE and Siemens. Wherever possible, Dr. Shetty sources lower-cost inputs such as sutures locally, rather than from the more expensive companies such as Johnson & Johnson. Further, the Narayana heart clinic shares common services, such as laboratories and blood bank and more mundane services such as catering, with the 1,400-bed cancer clinic next door. Taken together, all of these small changes result in significant cost savings, and so create a reinforcing system of low-cost value chain activities.

While many worry that high volume compromises quality, the data suggest the opposite: Narayana Health's medical outcomes in terms of mortality rate are equal to or even lower than the best hospitals in the United States. The American College of Cardiology frequently sends surgeons and administrators to visit the Narayana heart clinic. The college concluded that the clinic provides high-tech and high-quality care at low cost. Dr. Shetty now brings top-notch care at low cost to the masses in India.

Narayana Health runs a chain of over 30 hospitals in 20 locations throughout India and performs some 100,000 heart surgeries a year.

Dr. Shetty is also bringing his high-quality, low-cost health care solutions closer to American patients. In 2014, his group opened the doors to Health City Cayman Islands, a fully accredited cardiac and cardiothoracic surgery clinic, a bit over one hour from Miami by air.[31]

Learning effects differ from economies of scale (discussed earlier) as shown:

- **Differences in timing.** Learning effects occur *over time* as output accumulates, while economies of scale are captured at *one point in time* when output increases. The improvements in Tesla's production costs, featured earlier, resulted from some 12,000 units in cumulative output, but it took two years to reach this volume (see Exhibit 6.6). Although learning can decline or flatten (see Exhibit 6.7), there are no *diseconomies to learning* (unlike *diseconomies to scale* in Exhibit 6.5).

- **Differences in complexity.** In some production processes (e.g., the manufacture of steel rods), effects from economies of scale can be quite significant, while learning effects are minimal. In contrast, in some professions (brain surgery or the practice of estate law), learning effects can be substantial, while economies of scale are minimal.

Managers need to understand such differences to calibrate their business-level strategy. If a firm's cost advantage is due to economies of scale, a strategic leader should worry less about employee turnover (and a potential loss in learning) and more about drops in production runs. In contrast, if the firm's low-cost position is based on complex learning, a strategic leader should be much more concerned if a key employee (e.g., a star engineer) was to leave.

EXPERIENCE CURVE

In the *learning curve* just discussed, we assumed the underlying technology remained constant, while only cumulative output increased. In the *experience curve,* in contrast, we now change the underlying technology while holding cumulative output constant.[32]

In general, technology and production processes do not stay constant. *Process innovation*—a new method or technology to produce an existing product—may initiate a new and steeper curve. Assume that Firm C, on the same learning curve as Firm B, implements a new production process (such as lean manufacturing). In doing so, Firm C initiates an entirely new and steeper learning curve. Exhibit 6.7 shows this *experience-curve effect* based on a process innovation. Firm C jumps down to the 80 percent learning curve, reflecting the new and lower-cost production process. Although Firm B and Firm C produce the same cumulative output (each making 128 aircraft), the per-unit cost differs. Firm B's per-unit cost for each airplane, being positioned on the less-steep 90 percent learning curve, is $48 million.[33] In contrast, Firm C's per-unit cost, being positioned on the steeper 80 percent learning curve because of process innovation, is only $21 million per aircraft, and thus less than half that of Firm B. Clearly, Firm C has a competitive advantage over Firm B based on lower cost per unit (assuming similar quality).

Learning by doing allows a firm to lower its per-unit costs by moving down a given learning curve, while experience-curve effects based on process innovation allow a firm to leapfrog to a steeper learning curve, thereby driving down its per-unit costs.

In Strategy Highlight 6.1, we saw how Dr. Shetty leveraged learning-curve effects to save lives while driving down costs. One could argue that his Narayana Health group not only moved down a given learning curve using best industry practice, but it also jumped down to a new and steeper learning curve through process innovation. Dr. Shetty sums up his business strategy based on cost leadership: "Japanese companies reinvented the process of making cars (by introducing lean manufacturing). That's what we're doing in health care. What health care needs is process innovation, not product innovation."[34]

In a cost-leadership strategy, managers must focus on lowering the costs of production while maintaining a level of quality acceptable to the customer. If firms can share the benefits of lower costs with consumers, cost leaders appeal to the bargain-conscious buyer, whose main criterion is price. By looking to reduce costs in each value chain activity, managers aim for the lowest-cost position in the industry. They strive to offer lower prices than competitors and thus to increase sales. Cost leaders such as Walmart ("Every Day Low Prices") can be quite profitable by pursuing this strategic position over time.

6.4 Business-Level Strategy and the Five Forces: Benefits and Risks

The business-level strategies introduced in this chapter allow firms to carve out strong strategic positions that enhance the likelihood of gaining and sustaining competitive advantage. The five forces model introduced in Chapter 3 helps strategic leaders assess the forces—threat of entry, power of suppliers, power of buyers, threat of substitutes, and rivalry among existing competitors—that make some industries more attractive than others. With this understanding of industry dynamics, managers use one of the generic business-level strategies to protect themselves against the forces that drive down profitability.[35] Exhibit 6.8 details the relationship between competitive positioning and the five forces. In particular, it highlights the benefits and risks of differentiation and cost-leadership business strategies, which we discuss next.

DIFFERENTIATION STRATEGY: BENEFITS AND RISKS

A differentiation strategy is defined by establishing a strategic position that creates higher perceived value while controlling costs. The successful differentiator stakes out a unique strategic position, where it can benefit from imperfect competition (as discussed in Chapter 3) and command a premium price. A well-executed differentiation strategy reduces rivalry among competitors.

A successful differentiation strategy is likely to be based on unique or specialized features of the product, on an effective marketing campaign, or on intangible resources such as a reputation for innovation, quality, and customer service. A rival would need to improve the product features as well as build a similar or more effective reputation in order to gain market share. The threat of entry is reduced: Competitors will find such intangible advantages time-consuming and costly, and maybe impossible, to imitate. If the source of the differential appeal is intangible rather than tangible (e.g., reputation rather than observable product and service features), a differentiator is even more likely to sustain its advantage.

Moreover, if the differentiator is able to create a significant difference between perceived value and current market prices, the differentiator will not be so threatened by increases in input prices due to powerful suppliers. Although an increase in input factors could erode margins, a differentiator is likely able to pass on price increases to its customers as long as its value creation exceeds the price charged. Since a successful differentiator creates

EXHIBIT 6.8 Competitive Positioning and the Five Forces: Benefits and Risks of Differentiation and Cost-Leadership Business Strategies

Competitive Force	Differentiation		Cost Leadership	
	Benefits	**Risks**	**Benefits**	**Risks**
Threat of entry	• Protection against entry due to intangible resources such as a reputation for innovation, quality, or customer service	• Erosion of margins • Replacement	• Protection against entry due to economies of scale	• Erosion of margins • Replacement
Power of suppliers	• Protection against increase in input prices, which can be passed on to customers	• Erosion of margins	• Protection against increase in input prices, which can be absorbed	• Erosion of margins
Power of buyers	• Protection against decrease in sales prices, because well-differentiated products or services are not perfect imitations	• Erosion of margins	• Protection against decrease in sales prices, which can be absorbed	• Erosion of margins
Threat of substitutes	• Protection against substitute products due to differential appeal	• Replacement, especially when faced with innovation	• Protection against substitute products through further lowering of prices	• Replacement, especially when faced with innovation
Rivalry among existing competitors	• Protection against competitors if product or service has enough differential appeal to command premium price	• Focus of competition shifts to price • Increasing differentiation of product features that do not create value but raise costs • Increasing differentiation to raise costs above acceptable threshold	• Protection against price wars because lowest-cost firm will win	• Focus of competition shifts to non-price attributes • Lowering costs to drive value creation below acceptable threshold

Source: Based on M.E. Porter (2008, January), "The five competitive forces that shape strategy," *Harvard Business Review*; and M.E. Porter (1980), *Competitive Strategy: Techniques for Analyzing Industries and Competitors* (New York: Free Press).

perceived value in the minds of consumers and builds customer loyalty, powerful buyers demanding price decreases are unlikely to emerge. A strong differentiated position also reduces the threat of substitutes, because the unique features of the product have been created to appeal to customer preferences, keeping them loyal to the product. By providing superior quality beverages and other food items combined with a great customer experience and a global presence, Starbucks has built a strong differentiated appeal. It has cultivated a loyal following of customers who reward it with repeat business.

The viability of a differentiation strategy is severely undermined when the focus of competition shifts to price rather than value-creating features. This can happen when differentiated products become commoditized and an acceptable standard of quality has emerged across rival firms. Although the iPhone was a highly differentiated product when introduced in 2007, touch-based screens and other once-innovative features are now standard in smartphones. Indeed, Android-based smartphones hold some 75 percent market share globally, while Apple's iOS phones hold about 23 percent.[36] Several companies including Google; Samsung and LG, both of South Korea; and low-cost leaders Huawei and Xiaomi of China are attempting to challenge Apple's ability to extract significant profits from the smartphone industry based on its iPhone franchise. A differentiator also needs to be careful not to overshoot its differentiated appeal by adding product features that raise costs but not perceived value in the minds of consumers. For example, any additional increase in screen resolution beyond Apple's retina display cannot be detected by the human eye at a normal viewing distance. Finally, a differentiator needs to be vigilant that its costs of providing uniqueness do not rise above the customer's willingness to pay.

COST-LEADERSHIP STRATEGY: BENEFITS AND RISKS

A cost-leadership strategy is defined by obtaining the lowest-cost position in the industry while offering acceptable value. The cost leader, therefore, is protected from other competitors because of having the lowest cost. If a price war ensues, the low-cost leader will be the last firm standing; all other firms will be driven out as margins evaporate. Since reaping economies of scale is critical to reaching a low-cost position, the cost leader is likely to have a large market share, which in turn reduces the threat of entry.

A cost leader is also fairly well isolated from threats of powerful suppliers to increase input prices, because it is more able to absorb price increases through accepting lower profit margins. Likewise, a cost leader can absorb price reductions more easily when demanded by powerful buyers. Should substitutes emerge, the low-cost leader can try to fend them off by further lowering its prices to reinstall relative value with the substitute. For example, Walmart tends to be fairly isolated from these threats. Walmart's cost structure combined with its large volume allows it to work with suppliers in keeping prices low, to the extent that suppliers are often the party that experiences a profit-margin squeeze.

Although a cost-leadership strategy provides some protection against the five forces, it also carries some risks. If a new entrant with relevant expertise enters the market, the low-cost leader's margins may erode due to loss in market share while it attempts to learn new capabilities. For example, Walmart faces challenges to its cost leadership. Dollar General stores, and other smaller low-cost retail chains, have drawn customers who prefer a smaller format than the big box of Walmart. The risk of replacement is particularly pertinent if a potent substitute emerges due to an innovation. Leveraging ecommerce, Amazon has become a potent substitute and thus a powerful threat to many brick-and-mortar retail outlets including Barnes & Noble, Best Buy, The Home Depot, and even Walmart. Powerful suppliers and buyers may be able to reduce margins so much that the low-cost leader could have difficulty covering the cost of capital and lose the potential for a competitive advantage.

The low-cost leader also needs to stay vigilant to keep its cost the lowest in the industry. Over time, competitors can beat the cost leader by implementing the same business strategy, but more effectively. Although keeping its cost the lowest in the industry is imperative, the cost leader must not forget that it needs to create an acceptable level of value. If continuously lowering costs leads to a value proposition that falls below an acceptable threshold, the low-cost leader's market share will evaporate. Finally, the low-cost leader faces significant difficulties when the focus of competition shifts from price to non-price attributes.

We have seen how useful the five forces model can be in industry analysis. None of the business-level strategies depicted in Exhibit 6.2 (cost leadership, differentiation, and focused variations thereof) is inherently superior. The success of each depends on context and relies on two factors:

- How well the strategy leverages the firm's internal strengths while mitigating its weaknesses.
- How well it helps the firm exploit external opportunities while avoiding external threats.

There is no single correct business strategy for a specific industry. The deciding factor is that the chosen business strategy provides a strong position that attempts to maximize economic value creation and is effectively implemented.

6.5 Blue Ocean Strategy: Combining Differentiation and Cost Leadership

So far we've seen that firms can create more economic value and the likelihood of gaining and sustaining competitive advantage in one of two ways—either increasing perceived consumer value (while containing costs) or lowering costs (while offering acceptable value). Should strategic leaders try to do both at the same time? In general the answer is *no*. To accomplish this, they would need to integrate two different strategic positions: differentiation *and* low cost.[37] Managers should not pursue this complex strategy because of the inherent trade-offs in different strategic positions, unless they are able to reconcile the conflicting requirements of each generic strategy.

blue ocean strategy Business-level strategy that successfully combines differentiation and cost-leadership activities using value innovation to reconcile the inherent trade-offs.

To meet this challenge, strategy scholars Kim and Mauborgne advanced the notion of a **blue ocean strategy**, which is a business-level strategy that successfully combines differentiation and cost-leadership activities using value innovation to reconcile the inherent trade-offs in those two distinct strategic positions.[38] They use the metaphor of an ocean to denote market spaces. *Blue oceans* represent untapped market space, the creation of additional demand, and the resulting opportunities for highly profitable growth. In contrast, *red oceans* are the known market space of existing industries. In *red oceans* the rivalry among existing firms is cut-throat because the market space is crowded and competition is a zero-sum game. Products become commodities, and competition is focused mainly on price. Any market share gain comes at the expense of other competitors in the same industry, turning the oceans bloody red.

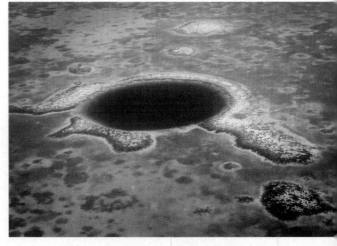

Strategic leaders may use value innovation to move to blue oceans, that is, to new and uncontested market spaces. Shown here is the famous "blue hole" just off Belize. Mlenny/Getty Images

A blue ocean strategy allows a firm to offer a differentiated product or service at low cost. As one example of a blue ocean strategy, consider the grocery chain Trader Joe's. Trader Joe's had much lower costs than Whole Foods (prior to its 2017 acquisition by Amazon) for the same market of patrons desiring high value and health-conscious foods, and Trader Joe's scores exceptionally well in customer service and other areas. When a blue ocean strategy is successfully formulated and implemented, investments in differentiation and low cost are not substitutes but are

complements, providing important positive spill-over effects. A successfully implemented blue ocean strategy allows firms two pricing options: First, the firm can charge
a higher price than the cost leader, reflecting its higher value creation and thus generating greater profit margins. Second, the firm can lower its price below that of the
differentiator because of its lower-cost structure. If the firm offers lower prices than
the differentiator, it can gain market share and make up the loss in margin through
increased sales.

LO 6-5

Evaluate value and cost
drivers that may allow a
firm to pursue a blue
ocean strategy.

VALUE INNOVATION

For a blue ocean strategy to succeed, managers must resolve trade-offs between the two
generic strategic positions—low cost and differentiation.[39] This is done through **value innovation**, aligning innovation with total perceived consumer benefits, price, and cost (also see
the discussion in Chapter 5 on *economic value creation*). Instead of attempting to out-compete rivals by offering better features or lower costs, successful value innovation makes competition irrelevant by providing a leap in value creation, thereby opening new and
uncontested market spaces.

Successful value innovation requires that a firm's strategic moves lower its costs
and also increase the perceived value for buyers (see Exhibit 6.9). Lowering a firm's
costs is primarily achieved by eliminating and reducing the taken-for-granted factors
that the firm's industry rivals compete on. Perceived buyer value is increased by raising existing key success factors and by creating new elements that the industry has not
offered previously. To initiate a strategic move that allows a firm to open a new and
uncontested market space through value innovation, strategic leaders must answer the
four key questions below when formulating a blue ocean business strategy.[40] In terms
of achieving successful value innovation, note that the first two questions focus on
lowering costs, while the second two questions focus on increasing perceived consumer benefits.

value innovation The
simultaneous pursuit of
differentiation and
low cost in a way that
creates a leap in
value for both the firm
and the consumers;
considered a corner-
stone of blue ocean
strategy.

EXHIBIT 6.9 Value Innovation Accomplished
through Simultaneously
Pursuing Differentiation ($V \uparrow$)
and Low Cost ($C \downarrow$)

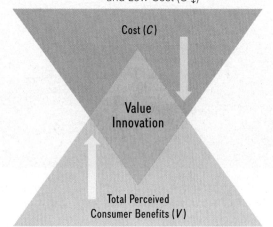

Cost (C)

Value
Innovation

Total Perceived
Consumer Benefits (V)

Source: Adapted from C.W. Kim and R. Mauborgne (2005), *Blue
Ocean Strategy: How to Create Uncontested Market Space and
Make Competition Irrelevant* (Boston: Harvard Business School
Publishing).

Value Innovation—Lower Costs

1. *Eliminate.* Which of the factors that the industry takes for
   granted should be eliminated?
2. *Reduce.* Which of the factors should be reduced well below
   the industry's standard?

Value Innovation—Increase Perceived Consumer Benefits

1. *Raise.* Which of the factors should be raised well above the
   industry's standard?
2. *Create.* Which factors should be created that the industry
   has never offered?

The international furniture retailer IKEA, for example, has
used value innovation based on the *eliminate-reduce-raise-create*
framework to initiate its own blue ocean and to achieve a sustainable competitive advantage.[41]

ELIMINATE (TO LOWER COSTS). IKEA eliminated several
taken-for-granted competitive elements: salespeople, expensive but small retail outlets in prime urban locations and

shopping malls, long wait after ordering furniture, after-sales service, and other factors. In contrast, IKEA displays its products in a warehouse-like setting, thus reducing inventory cost. Customers serve themselves and then transport the furniture to their homes in IKEA's signature flat-packs for assembly. IKEA also uses the big-box concept of locating supersized stores near major metropolitan areas (please refer to the discussion of "Taking Advantage of Certain Physical Properties" under "Economies of Scale" in Section 6.3).

Each IKEA store has a large self-service warehouse section, further driving down its cost.
Tooykrub/Shutterstock

REDUCE (TO LOWER COSTS). Because of its do-it-yourself business model regarding furniture selection, delivery, and assembly, IKEA drastically reduced the need for staff in its mega-stores. Strolling through an IKEA store, you encounter few employees. IKEA also reduced several other taken-for-granted competitive elements: 25-year warranties on high-end custom furniture, high degree of customization in selection of options such as different fabrics and patterns, and use of expensive materials such as leather or hardwoods, among other elements.

RAISE (TO INCREASE PERCEIVED CONSUMER BENEFITS). IKEA raised several competitive elements: It offers tens of thousands of home furnishing items in each of its big-box stores (some 300,000 square feet, roughly five football fields), versus a few hundred at best in traditional furniture stores; it also offers more than furniture, including a range of accessories such as place mats, laptop stands, and much more; each store has hundreds of rooms fully decorated with all sorts of IKEA items, each with a detailed tag explaining the item. Moreover, rather than sourcing its furniture from wholesalers or other furniture makers, IKEA manufactures all of its furniture at fully dedicated suppliers, thus tightly controlling the design, quality, functionality, and cost of each product.

IKEA also raised the customer experience by laying out its stores in such a way that customers see and can touch basically all of IKEA's products, including dishware, bedding, and furniture.

CREATE (TO INCREASE CONSUMER BENEFITS). IKEA created a new way for people to shop for furniture. Customers stroll along a predetermined path winding through the fully furnished showrooms. They can compare, test, and touch all the things in the showroom. The price tag on each item contains other important information: type of material, weight, and so on. Once an item is selected, the customer notes the item number (the store provides a pencil and paper). The tag also indicates the location in the warehouse where the customer can pick up the item in IKEA's signature flat-packs. After paying, the customer transports the products and assembles the furniture. The customer has 90 days to return items for a full refund.

In traditional furniture shopping, customers visit a small retail outlet where salespeople swarm them. After a purchase, the customer has to wait generally a few weeks before the furniture is shipped because many furniture makers do not produce items, such as expensive leather sofas, until they are paid for in advance. Finely crafted couches and chairs cost thousands of dollars (while IKEA's fabric couches retail for $399). When shopping at a traditional furniture store, the customer also pays for delivery of the furniture.

IKEA also created a new approach to pricing its products. Rather than using a "cost plus margin approach" like traditional furniture stores when pricing items, IKEA begins with the retail price first. For example, it sets the price for an office chair at $150, and IKEA's designers figure out how to meet this goal, which includes a profit margin. They need to consider the chair from start to finish, including not only design but also raw materials and the way the product will be displayed and transported. Only then will products go into production.

IKEA also created several other new competitive elements that allow it to offer more value to its customers: Stores provide on-site child care, house a cafeteria serving delicious food options including Swedish delicatessen such as smoked salmon at low prices, and offer convenient and ample parking, often in garages under the store, where escalators bring customers directly into the showrooms.

By implementing these key steps to achieving value innovation—eliminate, reduce, raise, and create—IKEA orchestrates different internal value chain activities to reconcile the tension between differentiation and cost leadership to create a unique market space. IKEA uses innovation in multiple dimensions—in furniture design, engineering, and store design—to solve the trade-offs between value creation and production cost. An IKEA executive highlights the difficulty of achieving value innovation as follows: "Designing beautiful-but-expensive products is easy. Designing beautiful products that are inexpensive and functional is a huge challenge."[42] IKEA leverages its deep design and engineering expertise to offer furniture that is stylish and functional and that can be easily assembled by the consumer. In this way, IKEA can pursue a blue ocean strategy based on value innovation to increase the perceived value of its products, while simultaneously lowering its cost and offering competitive prices. It opened a new market serving a younger demographic than traditional furniture stores. When young people the world over move into their own apartment or house, they frequently furnish it from IKEA.

LO 6-6

Assess the risks of a blue ocean strategy, and explain why it is difficult to succeed at value innovation.

BLUE OCEAN STRATEGY GONE BAD: "STUCK IN THE MIDDLE"

Although appealing in a theoretical sense, a blue ocean strategy can be quite difficult to translate into reality. Differentiation and cost leadership are distinct strategic positions that require important trade-offs.[43] A blue ocean strategy is difficult to implement because it requires the reconciliation of fundamentally different strategic positions—differentiation and low cost—which in turn require distinct internal value chain activities (see Chapter 4) so the firm can increase value *and* lower cost at the same time.

Exhibit 6.10 suggests how a successfully formulated blue ocean strategy based on *value innovation* combines both a differentiation and low-cost position. It also shows the consequence of a blue ocean strategy gone bad—the firm ends up being *stuck in the middle*, meaning the firm has neither a clear differentiation nor a clear cost-leadership profile. Being *stuck in the middle* leads to inferior performance and a resulting competitive disadvantage. Strategy Highlight 6.2 shows how Cirque du Soleil is searching for a new blue ocean to avoid being stuck in the middle.

EXHIBIT 6.10 Value Innovation vs. *Stuck in the Middle*

Strategy Highlight **6.2**

Cirque du Soleil: Finding a New Blue Ocean?

Most of the 11 million people that bought tickets for a Cirque du Soleil show in 2018 were dazzled by its high-quality artistic performances. Founded in 1984 by two street performers, Guy Laliberté and Gilles Ste-Croix, in an inner-city area of Montreal, Canada, Cirque du Soleil today is the largest theatrical producer in the world. With its spectacularly sophisticated shows, Cirque's mission is to "evoke the imagination, invoke the senses, and provoke the emotions of people around the world."[44] Employing more than 5,000 people (with one-third of them performers) and with annual revenues of over $1 billion, Cirque is not only the largest live entertainment businesses in the world but also quite successful. How did Cirque become so successful while most circuses have either shut down or barely survived?

CIRQUE'S BLUE OCEAN STRATEGY AND VALUE INNOVATION Using a *blue ocean strategy* based on *value innovation*, Cirque du Soleil created a new and thus uncontested market space in the live entertainment industry. Let's take a closer look at how Cirque used the *eliminate-reduce-raise-create framework* to reinvent the circus and to create a blue ocean of uncontested market space where competition is less of a concern.

Eliminate. In redefining the circus, Cirque du Soleil eliminated several traditional circus elements. First, it did away with all animal shows, partly because of the public's growing concern in recent years about the humane treatment of animals, but also because their care, transportation, medical attention, insurance, and food consumption (a grown male lion can devour 90 pounds of meat a day) were the most expensive items to maintain. Second, Cirque did away with star performers, who were also expensive; name recognition of star performers in the circus industry is trivial compared to that of sports celebrities (e.g., LeBron James) or movie stars (e.g., Scarlett Johansson). Third, it abolished the standard three-ring stages. These were expensive to upkeep, but they also frequently created anxiety among audience members. Since different acts were being performed on all three stages at the same time, viewers felt forced to switch their attention rapidly from stage to stage. Finally, it did away with aisle concession sales. These annoyed most visitors not only because they frequently interrupted and interfered with the viewing experience, but also because audience members felt like they were being taken advantage of by the vendors' prices.

Cirque du Soleil, the largest live entertainment company globally, dazzles spectators with its high-quality artistic shows. Using a blue ocean strategy allowed Cirque to gain a competitive advantage by creating a new, uncontested market space. The question Cirque's strategic leaders now face is how to sustain its competitive advantage.
Xinhua/Alamy Stock Photo

Reduce. Cirque kept the clowns, but reduced their importance in the shows. It also reduced the amount of slapstick and low-brow clown humor, shifting instead to a more sophisticated and intellectually stimulating style.

Raise. Cirque significantly raised the quality of the live performance with its signature acrobatic and aerial acts featuring stunts never before seen. It also elevated the circus tent experience. While many other circuses replaced the extravagant circus tents of old with generic, low-cost and rented venues, Cirque, in contrast, revised the tent, turning it into a unique and magical venue. Its magnificent exteriors attracted the attention of the public, and its interiors provided luxurious seating and high-quality amenities. Given that Cirque's consumers were used to paying much higher ticket prices for live theater or ballet performances, Cirque decided to raise its ticket prices as well, starting at $75 up to $200. The fact that Cirque's audiences were primarily adults rather than children, made this possible because there were fewer adults attending shows with groups of children in tow.

Create. Cirque du Soleil created an entirely new entertainment experience: It combined in novel ways the fun and thrill of the traditional circus with the classical and cultivated storytelling of the ballet and musical theater—a sharp contrast to traditional circus productions that typically comprise a series of unrelated acts. All dance and musical performances are thoughtfully choreographed and skillfully orchestrated. Akin to Broadway shows, Cirque also offered multiple productions at all major venues across the world. With its productions generally in high demand and being performed in multiple venues around the globe, an increasing number of people were starting to attend the "circus" more frequently, even at high ticket prices.

A PERFECT STORM   Although the Cirque du Soleil experience remains high end and high brow, the company has fallen on hard times in recent years. A combination of external and internal factors led to a significant decline in performance. Cirque du Soleil was hit hard by the economic downturn resulting from the 2008–2010 global financial crisis. Its management worsened the situation through a series of poor strategic decisions, including offering too many shows that were too little differentiated (at least in the mind of the consumer). Consequently, Cirque lost its rarity appeal, its payroll and costs ballooned, and demand for its European shows declined by as much as 40 percent.

Misfortune continued to strike: Cirque du Soleil experienced its first fatality (in 2013) during its signature show Kà in Las Vegas, where one of its performers (a mother of two) fell 95 feet to her death. The U.S. Occupational Safety and Health Administration (OSHA) issued citations and fines, and conducted an in-depth investiga-tion of safety practices that revealed a high injury rate. One investigation found that Kà alone resulted in 56 injuries per 100 workers, which is four times the injury rate for professional sports teams, according to the Bureau of Labor Statistics. Two more fatalities occurred during live shows in 2016 and 2018. Some Cirque performers claimed that the pressure to perform at high levels made it difficult to raise concerns about acrobat safety.

In 2015, Cirque du Soleil founder Guy Laliberté sold his controlling ownership stake to an investor group led by U.S. private-equity firm TPG. Other investors included Fosun, a Chinese investment firm, and a Canadian pension fund. This deal valued Cirque at $1.5 billion, down from a onetime $3 billion valuation. Once flying high, Cirque du Soleil's valuation had dropped by 50 percent.

In the search for a new blue ocean, Cirque is now pursuing a strategy of diversification. In 2017, it bought Blue Man Productions, the New York performance art company. In 2018, Cirque followed up its earlier acquisition by buying Vstar, a children's live entertainment touring group. Mitch Garber, chairman of Cirque du Soleil, who views the company's core competency as "live entertainment touring and logistics,"[45] argues that the two most recent acquisitions will allow Cirque to renew its core business, reach new audiences, and expand its repertoire of creative capabilities. To increase its appeal to high-growth markets outside North America, it is infusing Russian and Chinese influences as well as improv comedy.[46]

value curve Horizontal connection of the points of each value on the strategy canvas that helps strategic leaders diagnose and determine courses of action.

strategy canvas Graphical depiction of a company's relative performance vis-à-vis its competitors across the industry's key success factors.

THE STRATEGY CANVAS.   The **value curve** is the basic component of the **strategy canvas**. It graphically depicts a company's relative performance across its industry's factors of competition. A strong value curve has focus and divergence, and it can even provide a kind of tagline as to what strategy is being undertaken or should be undertaken.

Exhibit 6.11 plots the strategic profiles or value curves for three kinds of competitors in the U.S. airline industry. On the left-hand side, descending in underlying cost structure, are the legacy carriers (for example, Delta), JetBlue, and finally low-cost airlines such as Southwest Airlines (SWA). We also show the different strategic positions (differentiator, stuck in the middle, and low-cost leader) and trace the value curves as they rank high or low on a variety of parameters. JetBlue is stuck in the middle (as discussed in the ChapterCase). Low-cost airlines follow a cost-leadership strategy. The value curve, therefore, is simply a graphic representation of a firm's relative performance across different competitive factors in an industry.

Legacy carriers tend to score fairly high among most competitive elements in the airline industry, including different seating class choices (such as business class, economy comfort, basic economy, and so on); in-flight amenities such as Wi-Fi, personal video console to view movies or play games, complimentary drinks and meals; coast-to-coast coverage via

EXHIBIT 6.11   Strategy Canvas of JetBlue vs. Low-Cost Airlines and Legacy Carriers

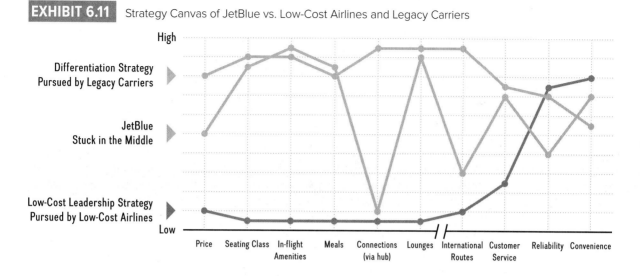

connecting hubs; plush airport lounges; international routes and global coverage; high customer service; and high reliability in terms of safety and on-time departures and arrivals. As
is expected when pursuing a generic differentiation strategy, all these scores along the different competitive elements in an industry go along with a relative higher cost structure.

In contrast, the low-cost airlines tend to hover near the bottom of the strategy canvas,
indicating low scores along a number of competitive factors in the industry, with no assigned
seating, no in-flight amenities, no drinks or meals, no airport lounges, few if any international routes, low to intermediate level of customer service. A relatively lower cost structure
goes along with a generic low-cost leadership strategy.

This strategy canvas also reveals key strategic insights. Look at the few competitive elements where the value curves of the differentiator and low-cost leader diverge. Interestingly,
some cost leaders (e.g., SWA) score much higher than some differentiators (e.g., United
Airlines) in terms of reliability and convenience, offering frequent point-to-point connections to conveniently located airports, often in or near city centers. This key divergence
between the two strategies explains why generic cost leaders have frequently outperformed
generic differentiators in the U.S. airline industry. Overall, both value curves show a consistent pattern representative of a more or less clear strategic profile as either differentiation or
low-cost leader.

Now look at JetBlue's value curve. Rather than being consistent such as the differentiation or low-cost value curves, the JetBlue value curve follows a zigzag pattern. JetBlue
attempts to achieve parity or even out-compete differentiators in the U.S. airline industry
along the competitive factors such as different seating classes (e.g., the high-end Mint offering discussed in the ChapterCase), higher level of in-flight amenities, higher-quality beverages and meals, plush airport lounges, and a large number of international routes (mainly
with global partner airlines). JetBlue, however, looks more like a low-cost leader in terms of
the ability to provide only a few connections via hubs domestically, and it recently has had
a poor record of customer service, mainly because of some high-profile missteps as documented in the ChapterCase. JetBlue's reliability is somewhat mediocre, but it does provide
a larger number of convenient point-to-point flights than a differentiator such as Delta, but
fewer than a low-cost leader such as SWA.

A value curve that zigzags across the strategy canvas indicates a lack of effectiveness
in its strategic profile. The curve visually represents how JetBlue is *stuck in the middle*

and as a consequence experienced inferior performance and thus a sustained competitive disadvantage vis-à-vis airlines with a stronger strategy profile such as SWA and Delta, among others.

6.6 Implications for Strategic Leaders

Formulating a business strategy is never easy, even when, as in achieving competitive advantage, only a handful of strategic options are available (i.e., low cost or differentiation, broad or narrow, or blue ocean). The best strategic leaders work hard to make sure they understand their firm and industry effects, and the opportunities they reveal. They work even harder to fine-tune strategy formulation and execution. When well-formulated and implemented, a business strategy enhances a firm's chances of obtaining superior performance. Strategic positioning requires making important trade-offs (think Walmart versus J. Crew in clothing).

In rare instances, a few exceptional firms might be able to change the competitive landscape by opening previously unknown areas of competition. To do so requires the firm reconcile the significant trade-offs between increasing value and lowering costs by pursuing both business strategies (differentiation and low cost) simultaneously. Such a blue ocean strategy tends to be successful only if a firm is able to rely on a value innovation that allows it to reconcile the trade-offs mentioned. Toyota, for example, initiated a new market space with its introduction of lean manufacturing, delivering cars of higher quality and value at lower cost. This value innovation allowed Toyota a competitive advantage for a decade or more, until this new process technology diffused widely. In a similar fashion, Cirque du Soleil also struggles to sustain competitive advantage based on an initially highly successful blue ocean strategy (see Strategy Highlight 6.2).

CHAPTER**CASE 6**   Part II

Carlosyudica/123RF

IN 2019, THE "BIG FOUR" airlines (American, Delta, SWA, and United) controlled about 70 percent of the U.S. domestic market, so the industry is fairly concentrated. JetBlue had 5.6 percent market share and close to $8 billion in annual revenues.

Early in its history JetBlue Airways achieved a competitive advantage based on *value innovation*. In particular, JetBlue was able to drive up perceived customer value while lowering costs. This allowed it to carve out a strong strategic position and move to a non-contested market space. This implies that no other competitors in the U.S. domestic airline industry were able to provide such value innovation at that point in time. Rather than directly competing with other airlines, JetBlue created a blue ocean.

Although JetBlue was able to create an initial competitive advantage, the airline was unable to sustain it. Because JetBlue failed to reconcile the strategic trade-offs inherent in combining differentiation and cost leadership, it was unable

to continue its blue ocean strategy, despite initial success. Between 2007 and 2019, JetBlue experienced a sustained competitive disadvantage, lagging the Dow Jones U.S. Airlines Index by more than 35 percentage points over the entire time period.

JetBlue's leadership team is attempting to reverse this trend; it made changes to improve the airline's flagging profitability. It is putting strategic initiatives in place to lower costs, while also trying to further increase its value offering. To lower operating costs, JetBlue decided to start charging $25 for the first checked bag and $35 for the second. It also removed the additional legroom JetBlue was famous for in the industry.

To drive up perceived customer value, JetBlue has added to its fleet more than 60 new airplanes (Airbus A-321), which significantly improve in-flight experience and thus customer satisfaction. Although JetBlue already flies internationally by serving destinations in Central and South America as well as the Caribbean, CEO Robin Hayes is considering adding selected flights to Europe. Flying non-stop to cities in Europe such as London is now possible with the new Airbus A-321. Flying longer, non-stop routes drives down costs. International routes, moreover, tend to be much more profitable than domestic routes because of less competition, for the time being.

Questions

1. Despite its initial success, why was JetBlue unable to sustain a blue ocean strategy?

2. JetBlue's chief commercial officer, Marty St. George, was asked by *The Wall Street Journal,* "What is the biggest marketing challenge JetBlue faces?" His response: "We are flying in a space where our competitors are moving toward commoditization. We have taken a position that air travel is not a commodity but a services business. We want to stand out, but it's hard to break through to customers with that message."[47]

    a. Given St. George's statement, which strategic position is JetBlue trying to accomplish: differentiator, cost leader, or blue ocean strategy? Explain why.

    b. Which strategic moves has the team around CEO Hayes put in place, and why? Explain whether they focus on value creation, operating costs, or both simultaneously. Do these moves correspond to St. George's understanding of JetBlue's strategic position? Why or why not? Explain.

3. Consider JetBlue's value curve in Exhibit 6.11. Why is JetBlue experiencing a competitive disadvantage? What recommendations would you offer to JetBlue to strengthen its strategic profile? Be specific.

4. JetBlue CEO Robin Hayes is contemplating adding international routes, connecting the U.S. East Coast to Europe. Would this additional international expansion put more pressure on JetBlue's current business strategy? Or would this international expansion require a shift in JetBlue's strategic profile? Why or why not? And if a strategic repositioning is needed, in which direction should JetBlue pivot? Explain.

mySTRATEGY

Low-Cost and Differentiated Workplaces

We have studied the differences in business-level strategies closely in this chapter, but how might these differences relate directly to you? As you've learned, firms using a differentiation strategy will focus on drivers such as product features and customer service, while firms using a cost-leadership strategy will prioritize cost of inputs and economies of scale. These strategic decisions can have an impact on an employee's experience with the firm's work environment and culture.

Hilton, Publix, and Wegmans Food Markets are companies that routinely end up on *Fortune's* list of "100 Best Places to Work." These companies use a differentiation business strategy. In contrast, Amazon and Walmart use the cost-leadership strategy; and as low-cost leaders, they do not rate nearly as well. According to inputs from the employee review site Glassdoor.com, only 56 percent of the employees working at Walmart would recommend the firm to a friend. Compare this to the over 80 percent who would recommend both Hilton and Wegmans Food Markets.

As you seek options for starting or growing your career, carefully consider the strategy the firm takes in the marketplace. By no means should you avoid low-cost leaders in lieu of strong differentiators (nor should you deem all differentiators as great places to work). Fast-paced organizations that focus on driving tangible results for the organization offer much to learn. For example, Amazon has been a very successful company for the past decade, and many employees have had multiple opportunities to learn enormous amounts in a short period. Amazon employees are encouraged to criticize each other's ideas openly in meetings; they work long days and on weekends; and they strive to meet "unreasonably high" standards. "When you're shooting for the moon, the nature of the work is really challenging. For some people it doesn't work," says Susan Harker, a top recruiter for Amazon. The high standards and relentless pace are a draw for many employees who are motivated to push themselves to learn, grow, and create—perhaps beyond their perceived limits. Many former employees say the nimble and productive environment is great for learning and the Amazon experience has really helped their careers expand. Now consider the following questions.

1. Employees and consultants say the Amazon workplace is the epitome of a "do more for less cost" environment. We recognize this is a hallmark goal of a cost-leadership business strategy. But ask yourself this key question, *Is it the type of high-pressure work environment in which YOU would thrive?*

2. Amazon has surpassed 650,000 employees and is the second publicly traded company in the world to hit $1 trillion market capitalization (just after Apple). The company offers bold new ideas as a retailer and is under an intense pressure to deliver on its goals. The allure from this type of success is compelling and offers tremendous rewards to many employees, shareholders, and customers. What aspects of success are you seeking in your professional career?

3. Before you launch into a new project, job, or firm, or even before you make a change in industry in the effort to move forward in your career, always consider the trade-offs that you would and would not be willing to make.[48]

TAKE-AWAY CONCEPTS

This chapter discussed two generic business-level strategies: *differentiation* and *cost leadership*. Companies can use various tactics to drive one or the other of those strategies, either narrowly or broadly. A *blue ocean strategy* attempts to find a competitive advantage by creating a new competitive area, which it does (when successful) by value innovation, reconciling the trade-offs between the two generic business strategies discussed. These concepts are summarized by the following learning objectives and related take-away concepts.

LO 6-1 / Define business-level strategy and describe how it determines a firm's strategic position.

- Business-level strategy determines a firm's strategic position in its quest for competitive advantage when competing in a single industry or product market.

- Strategic positioning requires that managers address strategic trade-offs that arise between value and cost, because higher value tends to go along with higher cost.

- Differentiation and cost leadership are distinct strategic positions.

- Besides selecting an appropriate strategic position, managers must also define the scope of competition—whether to pursue a specific market niche or go after the broader market.

LO 6-2 / Examine the relationship between value drivers and differentiation strategy.

- The goal of a differentiation strategy is to increase the perceived value of goods and services so that customers will pay a higher price for additional features.

- In a differentiation strategy, the focus of competition is on value-enhancing attributes and features, while controlling costs.

- Some of the unique value drivers managers can manipulate are product features, customer service, customization, and complements.

- Value drivers contribute to competitive advantage only if their increase in value creation (ΔV) exceeds the increase in costs, that is: $(\Delta V) > (\Delta C)$.

LO 6-3 / Examine the relationship between cost drivers and cost-leadership strategy.

- The goal of a cost-leadership strategy is to reduce the firm's cost below that of its competitors.
- In a cost-leadership strategy, the focus of competition is achieving the lowest possible cost position, which allows the firm to offer a lower price than competitors while maintaining acceptable value.
- Some of the unique cost drivers that managers can manipulate are the cost of input factors, economies of scale, and learning- and experience-curve effects.
- No matter how low the price, if there is no acceptable value proposition, the product or service will not sell.

LO 6-4 / Assess the benefits and risks of differentiation and cost-leadership strategies vis-à-vis the five forces that shape competition.

- The five forces model helps managers use generic business strategies to protect themselves against the industry forces that drive down profitability.
- Differentiation and cost-leadership strategies allow firms to carve out strong strategic positions, not only to protect themselves against the five forces, but also to benefit from them in their quest for competitive advantage.
- Exhibit 6.8 details the benefits and risks of each business strategy.

LO 6-5 / Evaluate value and cost drivers that may allow a firm to pursue a blue ocean strategy.

- To address the trade-offs between differentiation and cost leadership at the business level, managers must employ value innovation, a process that will lead them to align the proposed business strategy with total perceived consumer benefits, price, and cost.
- Lowering a firm's costs is primarily achieved by eliminating and reducing the taken-for-granted factors on which the firm's industry rivals compete.
- Increasing perceived buyer value is primarily achieved by raising existing key success factors and by creating new elements that the industry has not yet offered.
- Strategic leaders track their opportunities and risks for lowering a firm's costs and increasing perceived value vis-à-vis their competitors by use of a strategy canvas, which plots industry factors among competitors (see Exhibit 6.11).

LO 6-6 / Assess the risks of a blue ocean strategy, and explain why it is difficult to succeed at value innovation.

- A successful blue ocean strategy requires that trade-offs between differentiation and low cost be reconciled.
- A blue ocean strategy often is difficult because the two distinct strategic positions require internal value chain activities that are fundamentally different from one another.
- When firms fail to resolve strategic trade-offs between differentiation and cost, they end up being "stuck in the middle." They then succeed at neither business strategy, leading to a competitive disadvantage.

KEY TERMS

Blue ocean strategy (p. 215)
Business-level strategy (p. 195)
Cost-leadership strategy (p. 197)
Differentiation strategy (p. 196)
Diseconomies of scale (p. 206)
Economies of scale (p. 204)

Economies of scope (p. 200)
Focused cost-leadership strategy (p. 198)
Focused differentiation strategy (p. 198)
Minimum efficient scale (MES) (p. 206)

Scope of competition (p. 197)
Strategic trade-offs (p. 196)
Strategy canvas (p. 220)
Value curve (p. 220)
Value innovation (p. 216)

DISCUSSION QUESTIONS

1. What are some drawbacks and risks to a broad generic business strategy? To a focused strategy?

2. In Chapter 4, we discussed the internal value chain activities a firm can perform (see Exhibit 4.8). The value chain priorities can be quite different for firms taking different business strategies. Create examples of value chains for three firms: one using cost leadership, another using differentiation, and a third using blue ocean strategy.

3. The chapter notes there are key differences between economies of scale and learning effects. Let us put that into practice with a brief example.

   A company such as Intel has a complex design and manufacturing process. For instance, one fabrication line for semiconductors typically costs more than $1.5 billion to build. Yet the industry also has high human costs for research and development (R&D) departments. Semiconductor firms spend an average of 17 percent of revenues on R&D. For comparison the automobile industry spends under 4 percent of sales on R&D.[49] Thus Intel's management must be concerned with both scale of production and learning curves. When do you think managers should be more concerned with large-scale production runs, and when do you think they should be most concerned with practices that would foster or hinder the hiring, training, and retention of key employees?

ENDNOTES

1. This ChapterCase is based on: McCartney, S. (2019, Jan. 16), "The best and worst U.S. airlines of 2018," *The Wall Street Journal*; McCartney, S. (2018, Jan. 10), "The best and worst U.S. airlines of 2017," *The Wall Street Journal*; McCartney, S. (2017, Mar. 8), "Discount business class? Thank JetBlue," *The Wall Street Journal*; Carey, S. (2016, Dec. 16), "JetBlue unveils cost-cutting plan worth up to $300 million by 2020," *The Wall Street Journal*; Carey, S. (2016, Jul. 26), "JetBlue considers foray into Europe," *The Wall Street Journal*; Carey, S. (2016, Apr. 12), "JetBlue to expand its high-end service, dubbed Mint, to more routes," *The Wall Street Journal*; Nicas, J. (2015, Mar. 27), "Pilot sues JetBlue for allegedly letting him fly while mentally unfit," *The Wall Street Journal*; Mayerowitz, S. (2015, Feb. 16), "JetBlue's CEO vies to please passengers, stocks," *The Associated Press*; Vranica, S. (2015, Feb. 22), "JetBlue's plan to repair its brand," *The Wall Street Journal*; Harris, R.L. (2015, Feb. 11), "On JetBlue, passengers can use ApplePay," *The New York Times*; Rosenbloom, S. (2015, Jan. 22), "Flying deluxe domestic coast-to-coast for around $1,000," *The New York Times*; Nicas, J.

(2014, Nov. 19), "JetBlue to add bag fees, reduce legroom," *The Wall Street Journal*; Gardiner, S. (2010, Aug. 10), "Flight attendant grabs two beers, slides down the emergency chute," *The Wall Street Journal*; Miranda, C.A. (2007, Feb. 21), "Can JetBlue weather the storm?" *Time*; Bailey, J. (2007, Feb. 19), "JetBlue's C.E.O. is 'mortified' after fliers are stranded," *The New York Times*; Zeller, T. (2007, Feb. 16), "Held hostage on the tarmac: Time for a passenger bill of rights?" *The New York Times*; Bryce, D.J., and J.H. Dyer (2007, May), "Strategies to crack well-guarded markets," *Harvard Business Review*; Kim, C.W., and R. Mauborgne (2005), *Blue Ocean Strategy: How to Create Uncontested Market Space and Make Competition Irrelevant* (Boston: Harvard Business School Publishing); Friedman, T. (2005), *The World Is Flat: A Brief History of the Twenty-First Century* (New York: Farrar, Strauss and Giroux); and Neeleman, D. (2003, Apr. 30), "Entrepreneurial thought leaders lecture," *Stanford Technology Ventures Program*.

2. This discussion is based on: Porter, M.E. (2008, January), "The five competitive forces

that shape strategy," *Harvard Business Review*; Porter, M.E. (1996, November–December), "What is strategy?" *Harvard Business Review*; Porter, M.E. (1985), *Competitive Advantage: Creating* and *Sustaining Superior Performance* (New York: Free Press); and Porter, M.E. (1980), *Competitive Strategy: Techniques for Analyzing Industries and Competitors* (New York: Free Press).

3. These questions are based on: Priem, R. (2007), "A consumer perspective on value creation," *Academy of Management Review* 32: 219–235; Abell, D.F. (1980), *Defining the Business: The Starting Point of Strategic Planning* (Englewood Cliffs, NJ: PrenticeHall); and Porter, M.E. (1996, November–December), "What is strategy?" *Harvard Business Review*.

4. The discussion of generic business strategies is based on: Porter, M.E. (1980), *Competitive Strategy: Techniques for Analyzing Industries and Competitors* (New York: Free Press); Porter, M.E. (1985), *Competitive Advantage: Creating* and *Sustaining Superior Performance* (New York: Free Press); Porter, M.E. (1996, November–December), "What is

strategy?" *Harvard Business Review*; and Porter, M.E. (2008, January), "The five competitive forces that shape strategy," *Harvard Business Review*.

5. Porter, M.E. (1996, November–December), "What is strategy?" *Harvard Business Review*.

6. To decide if and how to divide the market, you can apply the market segmentation techniques you have acquired in your marketing and microeconomics classes.

7. This example is drawn from: "Companies are racing to add value to water," *The Economist* (2017, Mar. 25).

8. Christensen, C.M., and M.E. Raynor (2003), *The Innovator's Solution: Creating and Sustaining Successful Growth* (Boston: Harvard Business School Press).

9. The interested reader is referred to the strategy, marketing, and economics literatures. A good start in the strategy literature is the classic work of M.E. Porter: Porter, M.E. (1980), *Competitive Strategy: Techniques for Analyzing Industries and Competitors* (New York: Free Press); Porter, M.E. (1985), *Competitive Advantage: Creating* and *Sustaining Superior Performance* (New York: Free Press); and Porter, M.E. (2008, January), "The five competitive forces that shape strategy," *Harvard Business Review*.

10. www.oxo.com/about.jsp.

11. Hsieh, T. (2010), *Delivering Happiness: A Path to Profits, Passion, and Purpose* (New York: Business Plus).

12. "Amazon opens wallet, buys Zappos," *The Wall Street Journal* (2009, Jul. 23).

13. "Where in the Dickens can you find a Trader Joe's," store listing at www.traderjoes.com/pdf/locations/all-llocations.pdf; "Ten companies with excellent customer service," *Huffington Post* (2014, Aug. 15), www.huffingtonpost.com/2013/08/15/ best-customer-service_n_3720052.html.

14. Olivarez-Giles, N. (2015, Jul. 7), "Project Fi review: Google masters Wi-Fi calling, but needs better phones," *The Wall Street Journal*; Duran M. (2015, Jul. 7), "Google's Project Fi wireless service is crazy cheap. But should you switch?" *Wired*.

15. "Flights of hypocrisy," *The Economist* (2015, Apr. 25).

16. "Boeing 787: Orders and Deliveries (updated monthly)," *The Boeing Co.* (2019, February), www.boeing.com.

17. "Airbus: Orders and deliveries," www.airbus.com/aircraft/market/orders-deliveries.html (accessed March 21, 2019).

18. Microsoft Annual Report (various years).

19. "Nucor's new plant project still on hold," *The Associated Press* (2009, Jul. 23), www.nucor.com.

20. On strategy as simple rules, see: Sull, D., and K.M. Eisenhardt (2015), *Simple Rules: How to Thrive in a Complex World* (New York: Houghton Mifflin Harcourt).

21. Gladwell, Malcolm. *Tipping Point: How Little Things Can Make a Big Difference.* Turtleback Books, 2002, 301.

22. Wall, R. (2019, Feb. 14), "Airbus to retire the A380, the superjumbo that never quite took off," *The Wall Street Journal.*

23. Levitt, B., and J.G. March (1988), "Organizational learning," *Annual Review of Sociology* 14: 319–340.

24. For insightful reviews and syntheses on the learning-curve literature, see: Argote, L., and G. Todorova (2007), "Organizational learning: Review and future directions," *International Review of Industrial and Organizational Psychology* 22: 193–234; and Yelle, L.E. (1979), "The learning curve: Historical review and comprehensive survey," *Decision Sciences* 10: 302–308.

25. Wright, T.P. (1936), "Factors affecting the cost of airplanes," *Journal of Aeronautical Sciences* 3: 122–128.

26. The Tesla example draws on: Dyer, J., and H. Gregersen (2016, Aug. 24),"Tesla's innovations are transforming the auto industry," *Forbes*; Higgins T. (2017, Apr. 10), "How Tesla topped GM as most valuable U.S. automaker," *The Wall Street Journal Tech Talk*; "Tesla increases deliveries of electric cars," *The Economist* (2017, Apr. 6); Tesla Annual Report (various years); and GM Annual Report (various years).

27. Dyer, J., and H. Gregersen (2016, Aug. 24), "Tesla's innovations are transforming the auto industry," *Forbes*. The authors (in conjunction with David Kryscynski of Brigham Young University) estimate that the functional relationship between production volume and production cost for Tesla's Model S between 2012 and 2014 is

$$Y = 1726.5 * (X^{-0.363})$$

Data underlying Exhibit 6.6:

Units	Per-Unit Cost ($)
100	$324,464
500	$180,901
1,000	$140,659
1,500	$121,407
2,000	$109,369
2,500	$100,859
3,000	$94,400
3,500	$89,263
4,000	$85,039
4,500	$81,480
5,000	$78,422
5,500	$75,756
6,000	$73,400
6,500	$71,298
7,000	$69,406
7,500	$67,689
8,000	$66,122
8,500	$64,683
9,000	$63,354
9,500	$62,123
10,000	$60,977
10,500	$59,907
11,000	$58,903
11,500	$57,961
12,000	$57,072

28. The exact data for learning curves depicted in Exhibit 6.7 are depicted below. A simplifying assumption is that the manufacturing of one aircraft costs $100 million, from there the two different learning curves set in. Noteworthy, that while making only one aircraft costs $100 million, when manufacturing over 4,000 aircraft the expected per-unit cost falls to only $28 million (assuming a 90 percent learning curve) and only $7 million (assuming an 80 percent learning curve).

Data underlying Exhibit 6.7

Learning Curves		
	Per-Unit Cost*	
Units	90%	80%
1	$100	$100
2	90	80
4	81	64
8	73	51
16	66	41
32	59	33
64	53	26
128	48	21
256	43	17
512	39	13
1,024	35	11
2,048	31	9
4,096	28	7

* Rounded to full dollar value in millions.

29. This discussion is based on: Gulati, R., D. Lavie, and H. Singh (2009), "The nature of partnering experience and the gain from alliances," *Strategic Management Journal* 30: 1213-1233; Thompson, P. (2001), "How much did the liberty shipbuilders learn? New evidence from an old case study," *Journal of Political Economy* 109: 103-137; Edmondson, A.C., R.M. Bohmer, and G.P. Pisano (2001), "Disrupted routines: Team learning and new technology implementation in hospitals," *Administrative Science Quarterly* 46: 685-716; Pisano, G.P., R.M. Bohmer, and A.C. Edmondson (2001), "Organizational differences in rates of learning: Evidence from the adoption of minimally invasive cardiac surgery," *Management Science* 47: 752-768; Rothaermel, F.T., and D.L. Deeds (2006), "Alliance type, alliance experience and alliance management capability in high-technology ventures," *Journal of Business Venturing* 21: 429-460; Hoang, H., and F.T. Rothaermel (2005), "The effect of general and partner-specific alliance experience on joint R&D project performance," *Academy of Management Journal* 48: 332-345; Zollo, M., J.J. Reuer, and H. Singh (2002), "Interorganizational routines and performance in strategic alliances," *Organization Science* 13: 701-713; King, A.W., and A.L. Ranft (2001), "Capturing knowledge

and knowing through improvisation: What managers can learn from the thoracic surgery board certification process," *Journal of Management* 27: 255-277; and Darr, E.D., L. Argote, and D. Epple (1995), "The acquisition, transfer and depreciation of knowledge in service organizations: Productivity in franchises," *Management Science* 42: 1750-1762.

30. Ramanarayanan, S. (2008), "Does practice make perfect: An empirical analysis of learning-by-doing in cardiac surgery." Available at SSRN: http://ssrn.com/ abstract=1129350.

31. "Coronary artery bypass grafting," (2015), healthcarebluebook.com, doi:10.1016/B978-1-84569-800-3.50011-5; Gokhale, K. (2013, Jul. 29), "Heart surgery in India for $1,583 Costs $106,385 in U.S., *Bloomberg Businessweek*; and Anand, G. (2009, Nov. 25), "The Henry Ford of heart surgery," *The Wall Street Journal*. See also: "Cardiac surgeon salary (United States)," *Payscale.com*, survey updated July 18, 2015; Pearl, R. (2014, Mar. 27), "Offshoring American he alth care: Higher quality at Lower costs?" *Forbes*.

32. Boston Consulting Group (1972), *Perspectives on Experience* (Boston: Boston Consulting Group).

33. See data presented in Endnote 28.

34. Anand, G. (2009, Nov. 25), "The Henry Ford of heart surgery," *The Wall Street Journal*.

35. This discussion is based on: Porter, M.E. (1979, March–April), "How competitive forces shape strategy," *Harvard Business Review*: 137-145; Porter, M.E. (1980), *Competitive Strategy: Techniques for Analyzing Industries and Competitors* (New York: Free Press); and Porter, M.E. (2008, January), "The five competitive forces that shape strategy," *Harvard Business Review*.

36. As of Q1 2019, the exact market share for Google's Android was 74.2 percent and for Apple's iOS was 23.3 percent, thus together they hold 97.5 percent of the entire mobile operating system market globally. Data drawn from http://gs.statcounter.com/os-market-share/mobile/worldwide (accessed March 22, 2019).

37. This discussion is based on: Kim, C.W., and R. Mauborgne (2017), *Blue Ocean Shift: Beyond Competing–Proven Steps to Inspire Confidence and Seize New Growth* (New York: Hachette); Kim, C.W., and R. Mauborgne (2005), *Blue Ocean Strategy: How to Create Uncontested Market Space and Make Competition Irrelevant* (Boston: Harvard Business School Publishing); Miller, A., and G.G. Dess (1993), "Assessing Porter's model

in terms of its generalizability, accuracy, and simplicity," *Journal of Management Studies* 30: 553-585; and Hill, C.W.L. (1988), "Differentiation versus low cost or differentiation and low cost: A contingency framework," *Academy of Management Review* 13: 401-412.

38. Kim, C.W., and R. Mauborgne (2005), *Blue Ocean Strategy: How to Create Uncontested Market Space and Make Competition Irrelevant* (Boston: Harvard Business School Publishing); Miller, A., and G.G. Dess (1993), "Assessing Porter's model in terms of its generalizability, accuracy, and simplicity," *Journal of Management Studies* 30: 553-585; and Hill, C.W.L. (1988), "Differentiation versus low cost or differentiation and low cost: A contingency framework," *Academy of Management Review* 13: 401-412

39. Kim, C.W., and R. Mauborgne (2005), *Blue Ocean Strategy: How to Create Uncontested Market Space and Make Competition Irrelevant* (Boston: Harvard Business School Publishing); Miller, A., and G.G. Dess (1993), "Assessing Porter's model in terms of its generalizability, accuracy, and simplicity," *Journal of Management Studies* 30: 553-585; and Hill, C.W.L. (1988), "Differentiation versus low cost or differentiation and low cost: A contingency framework," *Academy of Management Review* 13: 401-412.

40. Kim, C.W., and R. Mauborgne (2005), *Blue Ocean Strategy: How to Create Uncontested Market Space and Make Competition Irrelevant* (Boston: Harvard Business School Publishing); Miller, A., and G.G. Dess (1993), "Assessing Porter's model in terms of its generalizability, accuracy, and simplicity," *Journal of Management Studies* 30: 553-585; and Hill, C.W.L. (1988), "Differentiation versus low cost or differentiation and low cost: A contingency framework," *Academy of Management Review* 13: 401-412

41. The IKEA example is drawn from: "IKEA: How the Swedish retailer became a global cult brand," *Bloomberg Businessweek* (2005, Nov. 14); Edmonds, M. (2008, Jul. 8), "How IKEA works," http://money. howstuffworks.com/; and www.ikea.com.

42. "IKEA: How the Swedish retailer became a global cult brand," *Bloomberg Businessweek* (2005, Nov. 14).

43. This discussion is based on: Porter, M.E. (1980), *Competitive Strategy: Techniques for Analyzing Industries and Competitors* (New York: Free Press); and Porter, M.E. (1996, November–December), "What is strategy?" *Harvard Business Review*: 61-78.

44. Cirque du Soleil at a Glance, www. cirquedusoleil.com/en/home/about-us/ at-a-glance.aspx.

45. Cirque du Soleil at a Glance, www. cirquedusoleil.com/en/home/about-us/ at-a-glance.aspx.

46. Sources: Ambler, P. (2019, Mar. 21), "Voices of success: Cirque du Soleil chairman's biggest 'ah ha' moment in business," *Forbes* video, www.forbes.com/video/ 6016335943001/#4371b2425fe6; Picker, L. (2017, Jul. 6), "Private equity-backed Cirque du Soleil inks deal for Blue Man Group as it looks to expand beyond circus," *CNBC*; "Son of a Cirque du Soleil founder killed on set," *The Wall Street Journal* / Associated Press (2016, Nov. 30); Berzon, A., and M. Maremont (2015, Apr. 24), "The perils of workers' comp for injured Cirque du Soleil performers," *The Wall Street Journal;* WSJ video on Cirque du Soleil, www.wsj.com/articles/ injuries-put-safety-in-spotlight-at-cirque-du-soleil-1429723558; Berzon, A., and M. Maremont (2015, Apr. 22), "Injuries put safety in spotlight at Cirque du Soleil," *The Wall Street Journal*; King, C. (2015, Apr. 20), "Cirque du Soleil being sold to private-equity group," *The Wall Street Journal*; Berzon, A. (2014, Dec. 1), "Cirque du Soleil's next act: Rebalancing the business," *The Wall Street Journal;* Sylt, C. (2015, Feb. 22), "Cirque du Soleil tour revenue tumbles to £40m," *The Telegraph*; and Kim, W.C., and Mauborgne, R. (2005), *Blue Ocean Strategy: How to Create Uncontested Market Space and Make the Competition Irrelevant* (Boston: Harvard Business Review Press).

47. Vranica S. (2015, Feb. 22), "JetBlue's plan to repair its brand," *The Wall Street Journal.*

48. Sources for this myStrategy include: Kantor, J., and D. Streitfeld (2015, Aug. 15), "Inside Amazon: Wrestling big ideas in a bruising workplace," *The New York Times*; "100 best companies to work for," *Fortune,* 2014, 2015; and www.glassdoor.com.

49. "McKinsey on semiconductors," McKinsey & Co. (2011, Autumn).

Business Strategy: Innovation, Entrepreneurship, and Platforms

Chapter Outline

Learning Objectives

After studying this chapter, you should be able to:

LO 7-1 Outline the four-step innovation process from idea to imitation.

LO 7-2 Apply strategic management concepts to entrepreneurship and innovation.

LO 7-3 Describe the competitive implications of different stages in the industry life cycle.

LO 7-4 Derive strategic implications of the crossing-the-chasm framework.

LO 7-5 Categorize different types of innovations in the markets-and-technology framework.

LO 7-6 Explain why and how platform businesses can outperform pipeline businesses.

Netflix: Disrupting the TV Industry

IN 2019, NETFLIX had 150 million subscribers worldwide, with 61 million in the United States. The revenues for the media services provider were $16 billion, and its market cap was more than $150 billion. Over the past decade, Netflix's stock appreciated by some 2,600 percent, while the tech-heavy NASDAQ-100 index grew by "only" 310 percent in the same period. By continuing to innovate on many dimensions, Netflix was able to not only disrupt the TV industry, but also gain and sustain a competitive advantage. How did Netflix get here?

Netflix started as an obscure online shop renting DVDs delivered through U.S. mail. After being annoyed at having to pay more than $40 in late fees for a Blockbuster video, Reed Hastings started Netflix in 1997 to offer online rentals of DVDs. At the time, the commercial internet was in its infancy; Amazon had just made its IPO in the same year. Streaming content may have been only a distant dream in the era of dial-up internet, but Netflix got a head start by turning from the dwindling VHS format and dealing with DVDs, which were cheaper and easier to mail. An improved business model helped too. In 1999 Netflix rolled out a monthly subscription model, with unlimited rentals for a single monthly rate (and no late fees!). Rental DVDs were sent in distinctive red envelopes, with preprinted return envelopes. New rentals would not be sent until the current rental was returned.

Even with an innovative business model, Netflix got off to a slow start. By 2000, it had only about 300,000 subscribers and was losing money. Hastings approached Blockbuster, at the time the largest brick-and-mortar video rental chain with almost 8,000 stores in the United States. He proposed selling Blockbuster 49 percent of Netflix and rebranding it as Blockbuster.com. Basically the idea was that

The drama *13 Reasons Why* is one of Netflix's most popular original content creations. The series deals with the serious issue of teen suicide committed in a culture of gossip, innuendo, bullying, and sexual assault prevalent in U.S. high schools as well as lack of family and social support for at-risk persons.

Netflix/The Hollywood Archive/PictureLux/Alamy Stock Photo

Netflix would become the online presence for the huge national chain. The dot-com bubble had just burst, and Blockbuster turned Netflix down cold. Netflix, however, survived the dot-com bust, and by 2002, the company was profitable and went public. Blockbuster began online rentals in 2004, but by this time, Netflix already had a subscriber base of almost 4 million and a strong brand identity. Blockbuster lost 75 percent of its market value between 2003 and 2005. From there it went from bad to worse. In 2010, the once mighty Blockbuster filed for bankruptcy.

Netflix was at the forefront of the current wave of disruption in the TV industry as it began streaming content over the internet in 2007. And it stayed at the forefront. It adjusted quickly to the new options consumers had to receive content, making streaming available on a large number of devices including mobile phones, tablets, game consoles, and new devices dedicated to internet content streaming such as Roku, Kindle TV, Google Chromecast, and smart TVs. At the same time, more and more Americans were signing up for high-speed broadband internet connections, making streaming content a much more enjoyable experience. The market for internet-connected, large, high-definition flat-screen TVs also began to take off. Within just two years, Netflix subscriptions (then priced at $7.99 per month) jumped to 12 million.

Old-line media executives continued to dismiss Netflix as a threat. In 2010, Time Warner CEO Jeff Bewkes snubbed Netflix, saying, "It's a little bit like, is the Albanian army going to take over the world? I don't think so."[1] Even Reed Hastings called what Netflix provided "rerun TV." But behind their bravado, the broadcast networks were waking up to the Netflix threat. They stopped distributing content to Netflix and instead made it available through Hulu, an online streaming service jointly owned by Disney and NBCUniversal. In 2011, Hulu began offering original content that was not available on broadcast or cable television.

With its lower-cost structure, the networks saw Hulu's streaming model as a way to test new series ideas with minimal financial risk. In response, Netflix announced a move to create and stream original content online.

But not on the cheap. Since content streaming was Netflix's main business, it devoted significant resources to produce high-quality content. In 2013, Netflix released the political drama *House of Cards,* followed, among others, by the comedy-drama *Orange Is the New Black* and *The Crown,* a biographical series about Queen Elizabeth II. Netflix followed up with the crime drama *Ozark,* the science fiction horror show *Stranger Things,* the teen drama *13 Reasons Why,* and other original content. Some of these shows proved tremendous hits and have received many Emmys and Golden Globes.

In 2019, Netflix spent as much as $15 billion on content, more than any other Hollywood studio and media company. Although this sum is enormous, it is not surprising given that the cost of creating high-quality original content has skyrocketed. For instance, the hugely successful HBO series *Game of Thrones* cost some $10 million per one-hour content.[2]

Part II of this ChapterCase appears in Section 7.6.

INNOVATION—the successful introduction of a new product, process, or business model—is a powerful driver in the competitive process. The ChapterCase provides an example of how innovations in technology and business models in the TV industry can make existing competitors obsolete, and how they allowed Netflix to gain a competitive advantage.

Innovation allows firms to redefine the marketplace in their favor and achieve a competitive advantage.[3] Continued innovation enables a firm to sustain a competitive advantage over time. That's why we focus on innovation and the related topic of entrepreneurship in this chapter—to highlight innovation as a powerful competitive weapon when formulating business strategy. We begin this chapter by detailing how competition is a process driven by continuous innovation. Next we discuss strategic and social entrepreneurship. We then take a deep dive into the industry life cycle. This helps us to formulate a more dynamic business strategy as the industry changes over time. We also introduce the crossing-the-chasm framework, highlighting the difficulties in transitioning through different stages of the industry life cycle. We then move into a detailed discussion of different types of innovation using the markets-and-technology framework. We next present insights on how to compete in two-sided markets when discussing platform strategy. As with every chapter, we conclude with practice-oriented *Implications for Strategic Leaders.*

7.1 Competition Driven by Innovation

Competition is a process driven by the "perennial gale of creative destruction," in the words of famed economist Joseph Schumpeter.[4] Firms must be able to innovate while also fending off competitors' imitation attempts. A successful strategy requires both an effective offense and a hard-to-crack defense.

The continuous waves of market leadership changes in the TV industry demonstrate the potency of innovation as a competitive weapon: It can simultaneously create and destroy value. Many firms have dominated an early wave of innovation only to be challenged and often destroyed by the next wave. The disruption by cable content providers played out in the 1980s and 1990s, upsetting a handful of broadcast networks with cable's dozens and then hundreds of channels. The traditional television networks (ABC, CBS, and NBC) have been struggling to maintain viewers and advertising revenues as cable and satellite providers offered many more channels as wells as innovative programming. Those same cable and satellite providers now are trying hard to hold on to viewers as more and more people "cut the cord," or never sign up for cable TV services in the first place. These consumers prefer customized content online.

The current wave of disruption started in the 2000s, bypassing old-line cable content providers for direct online streaming. Now a multitude of devices—TV, PC, laptop, tablet, smartphone—provides a screen for online streaming. Netflix, riding atop the crest of this wave to industry leadership and competitive advantage, accounts for more than one-third of all downstream internet traffic in the United States during peak hours!

Yet competition does not stand still. To exploit the new opportunities due to technological changes such as streaming video online, Google acquired YouTube, while Comcast, the largest U.S. cable operator, purchased NBCUniversal.[5] Comcast's acquisition helps it integrate delivery services and content, with the goal of establishing itself as a new player in the media industry. Amazon Prime has over 100 million subscribers that enjoy its complimentary streaming services. Thus, both traditional TV and cable networks are currently under threat from content providers that stream via the internet, such as Netflix, YouTube, and Amazon. Other media companies such as Disney have pulled their content from Netflix and now offer their own, stand-alone streaming services. New entrants such as Apple TV have also entered the fray. The competitive intensity in the trillion-dollar media and entertainment industry is surely to heat up.

NETFLIX'S CONTINUED INNOVATION

Innovation can be the basis for gaining a competitive advantage, while continued innovation can lead to a sustainable competitive advantage. As illustrated in the ChapterCase, innovation forms the bedrock of Netflix's business strategy. Using big data analytics, in particular, Netflix introduced a number of early innovations in the video rental business. One of the more ingenious moves by Netflix was to have each user build a queue of movies he or she wanted to watch next. This allowed Netflix to predict future demand for specific movies fairly accurately. Another innovation was to create a "personalized recommendation engine" for each user that would predict what each subscriber might want to watch next based not only on a quick rating survey and the subscriber's viewing history, but also what movies users with a similar profile had watched and enjoyed.

Based on Netflix's proprietary learning algorithm, the recommendations would improve over time as the user's preferences become more clear. This also allowed Netflix to steer users away from hit movies (where wait times for DVD rentals were long because the company only had a limited number in its library) to lesser-known titles in its catalog. The ability to bring in the *long tail* of demand delighted not only viewers, as they enjoyed lesser-known, but often critically acclaimed films, but also movie studios, which could now make additional money on movies that would otherwise not be in demand. The **long tail** is a business model in which companies can obtain a large part of their revenues by selling a small number of units from among almost unlimited choices.[6] Moreover, in contrast to other players in the media industry, Netflix was fast to catch the wave of content streaming via the internet.

THE SPEED OF INNOVATION

As the adage goes, change is the only constant—and the rate of technological change has accelerated dramatically over the past hundred years. Changing technologies spawn new industries, while others die. This makes innovation a powerful strategic weapon to gain and sustain competitive advantage. Exhibit 7.1 shows how many years it took for different technological innovations to reach 50 percent of the U.S. population (either through ownership or usage). For example, it took 84 years for half of the U.S. population to own a car, but only 28 years for half the population to own a TV. The pace of the adoption rate of recent innovations continues to accelerate. It took 19 years for the PC to reach 50 percent ownership, but only 6 years for MP3 players to accomplish the same diffusion rate.

long tail A business model in which companies can obtain a large part of their revenues by selling a small number of units from among almost unlimited choice.

EXHIBIT 7.1

Accelerating Speed
of Technological
Change

Source: Depiction of data
from the U.S. Census Bureau,
the Consumer Electronics
Association, *Forbes,* and the
National Cable and
Telecommunications
Association.

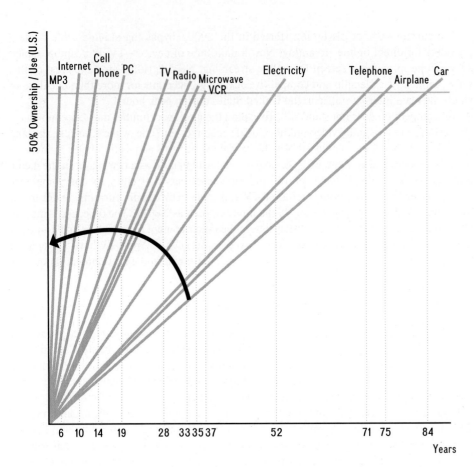

What factors explain increasingly rapid technological diffusion and adoption? One determinant is that initial innovations such as the car, airplane, telephone, and use of electricity provided the necessary infrastructure for newer innovations to diffuse more rapidly. Another reason is the emergence of new business models that make innovations more accessible. For example, Dell's direct-to-consumer distribution system improved access to low-cost PCs, and Walmart's low-price, high-volume model used its sophisticated IT logistics system to fuel explosive growth. In addition, satellite and cable distribution systems facilitated the ability of mass media such as radio and TV to deliver advertising and information to a wider audience. The speed of technology diffusion has accelerated further with the emergence of the internet, social networking sites, and viral messaging. Amazon continues to drive increased convenience, higher efficiency and lower costs in retailing and other services such as cloud computing. The accelerating speed of technological changes has significant implications for the competitive process and firm strategy. We will now look closely at the innovation process unleashed by technological changes.

THE INNOVATION PROCESS

LO 7.1

Outline the four-step
innovation process
from idea to imitation.

Broadly viewed, innovation describes the discovery, development, and transformation of new knowledge in a four-step process captured in the *four I's: idea, invention, innovation,* and *imitation* (see Exhibit 7.2).[7]

EXHIBIT 7.2

The Four I's: Idea, Invention, Innovation, and Imitation

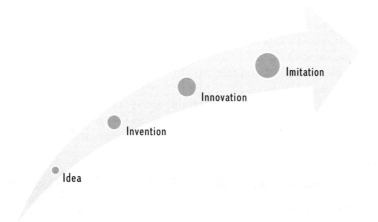

IDEA. The innovation process begins with an *idea*. The idea is often presented in terms of abstract concepts or as findings derived from basic research. Basic research is conducted to discover new knowledge and is often published in academic journals. This may be done to enhance the fundamental understanding of nature, without any commercial application or benefit in mind. In the long run, however, basic research is often transformed into applied research with commercial applications. For example, wireless communication technology today is built upon the fundamental science breakthroughs Albert Einstein accomplished over 100 years ago in his research on the nature of light.[8]

INVENTION. In a next step, **invention** describes the transformation of an idea into a new product or process, or the modification and recombination of existing ones. The practical application of basic knowledge in a particular area frequently results in new technology. If an invention is *useful, novel,* and *non-obvious* as assessed by the U.S. Patent and Trademark Office, it can be patented.[9] A **patent** is a form of *intellectual property* and gives the inventor exclusive rights to benefit from commercializing a technology for a specified time period in exchange for public disclosure of the underlying idea (see also the discussion on *isolating mechanisms* in Chapter 4). In the United States, the time period for the right to exclude others from the use of the technology is 20 years from the filing date of a patent application. Exclusive rights often translate into a *temporary monopoly position* until the patent expires. For instance, many pharmaceutical drugs are patent protected.

Strategically, however, patents are a *double-edged sword.* On the one hand, patents provide a temporary monopoly as they bestow exclusive rights on the patent owner to use a novel technology for a specific time period. Thus, patents may form the basis for a competitive advantage. Because patents require full disclosure of the underlying technology and know-how so that others can use it freely once the patent protection has expired, many firms find it strategically beneficial *not* to patent their technology. Instead they use **trade secrets**, defined as valuable proprietary information that is not in the public domain and where the

---

invention The transformation of an idea into a new product or process, or the modification and recombination of existing ones.

patent A form of *intellectual property* that gives the inventor exclusive rights to benefit from commercializing a technology for a specified time period in exchange for public disclosure of the underlying idea.

trade secret Valuable proprietary information that is not in the public domain and where the firm makes every effort to maintain its secrecy.

firm makes every effort to maintain its secrecy. The most famous example of a trade secret is the Coca-Cola recipe, which has been protected for over a century.[10] The same goes for Ferrero's Nutella, whose secret recipe is said to be known by even fewer than the handful of people who have access to the Coca-Cola recipe.[11]

Avoiding public disclosure and thus making its underlying technology widely known is precisely the reason Netflix does not patent its recommendation algorithm or Google its PageRank algorithm. Netflix has an advantage over competitors because its recommendation algorithm works best; the same goes for Google—its search algorithm is the best available. Disclosing how exactly these algorithms work would nullify their advantage.

> **innovation** The commercialization of any new product or process, or the modification and recombination of existing ones.

INNOVATION. **Innovation** concerns the *commercialization* of an invention.[12] The successful commercialization of a new product or service allows a firm to extract temporary monopoly profits. As detailed in the ChapterCase, Netflix began its life with a business model innovation, offering unlimited DVD rentals via the internet, without any late fees. However, Netflix gained its early lead by applying artificial intelligence to its user preferences to not only predict future demand but also to provide highly personalized viewing recommendations. The success of the latter is evident by the fact that movies that were recommended to viewers scored higher than they were scored previously. To sustain a competitive advantage, however, a firm must continuously innovate—that is, it must produce a string of successful new products or services over time. In this spirit, Netflix further developed its business model innovation, moving from online DVD rentals to directly streaming content via the internet. Moreover, it innovated further in creating proprietary content such as *House of Cards, Orange Is the New Black, The Crown, Ozark,* and *13 Reasons Why.*

> **first-mover advantages** Competitive benefits that accrue to the successful innovator.

Successful innovators can benefit from a number of **first-mover advantages**,[13] including economies of scale as well as experience and learning-curve effects (as discussed in Chapter 6). First movers may also benefit from *network effects* (see the discussion of Netflix and Uber later in this chapter). Moreover, first movers may hold important intellectual property such as critical patents. They may also be able to lock in key suppliers as well as customers through increasing switching costs. For example, users of Microsoft Word might find the switching costs entailed in moving to a different word-processing software prohibitive. Not only would they need to spend many hours learning the new software, but collaborators would also need to have compatible software installed and be familiar with the program to open and revise shared documents.

Google, by offering a free web-based suite of application software that includes word processing (Google Docs), a spreadsheet program (Google Sheets), and a presentation program (Google Slides), is attempting to minimize switching costs by leveraging *cloud computing*—a real-time network of shared computing resources via the internet (Google Drive). Rather than requiring each user to have the appropriate software installed on his or her personal computer, the software is maintained and updated in the cloud. Files are also saved in the cloud, which allows collaboration in real time globally wherever one can access an internet connection. (As discussed in detail in ChapterCase 5, Microsoft has also moved to a cloud-based computing business model).

Innovation need not be high-tech to be a potent competitive weapon, as P&G's history of innovative product launches such as the Swiffer line of cleaning products shows. P&G uses the *razor–razor-blade business model* (introduced in Chapter 5), where the consumer purchases the handle at a low price, but must pay a premium for replacement refills and pads over time. As shown in Exhibit 7.3, an innovation needs to be novel, useful, and successfully implemented to help firms gain and sustain a competitive advantage.

IMITATION. The innovation process ends with *imitation*. If an innovation is successful in the marketplace, competitors will attempt to imitate it. Success attracts attention and with it competition.

Although Netflix has more than 60 million U.S. subscribers, imitators are set to compete its advantage away. Amazon offers its Instant Video service to its estimated 100 million Prime subscribers ($119 a year or roughly $10 a month), with selected titles free. In addition, Prime members receive free two-day shipping on Amazon purchases (with one-day shipping announced in 2019). Hulu Plus ($7.99 a month), a video-on-demand service, has some 25 million subscribers. One advantage Hulu Plus has over Netflix and Amazon is that it typically makes the latest episodes of popular TV shows available the day following broadcast; the shows are often delayed by several months before being offered by Netflix or Amazon. A joint venture of Disney (67 percent ownership, but 100 percent voting rights) and NBCUniversal (33 percent), Hulu Plus uses advertisements along with its subscription fees as revenue sources. Google's YouTube with its more than 1 billion users is evolving into a TV ecosystem, benefiting not only from free content uploaded by its users but also creating original programming. Google's core business is, of course, ad supported. Yet, Google offers its ad-free service YouTube Premium for $12 per month, which allows users to download content such as videos and music for later, off-line use (e.g., while traveling in an airplane). And Apple has over 1 billion devices worldwide such as iPhones and iPads as an *installed base* where users can now enjoy Apple TV and Apple Music. Only time will tell whether Netflix will be able to sustain its competitive advantage given the imitation attempts by a number of potent competitors.

EXHIBIT 7.3 Innovation: A Novel and Useful Idea That Is Successfully Implemented

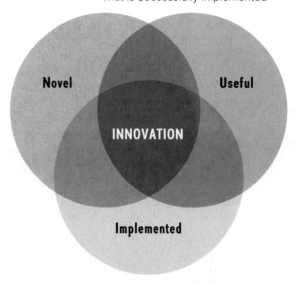

7.2 Strategic and Social Entrepreneurship

LO 7-2

Apply strategic management concepts to entrepreneurship and innovation.

Entrepreneurship describes the process by which change agents (entrepreneurs) undertake economic risk to innovate—to create new products, processes, and sometimes new organizations.[14] Entrepreneurs innovate by commercializing ideas and inventions.[15] They seek or create new business opportunities and then assemble the resources necessary to exploit them.[16] Indeed, innovation is the competitive weapon entrepreneurs use to exploit opportunities created by change, or to create change themselves, in order to commercialize new products, services, or business models.[17] If successful, entrepreneurship not only drives the competitive process, but it also creates value for the individual entrepreneurs and society at large.

Although many new ventures fail, some achieve spectacular success. Examples of successful entrepreneurs are:

entrepreneurship
The process by which people undertake economic risk to innovate—to create new products, processes, and sometimes new organizations.

- **Reed Hastings,** founder of Netflix featured in the ChapterCase. Hastings grew up in Cambridge, Massachusetts. He obtained an undergraduate degree in math from Bowdoin College (in Maine), and then volunteered for the Peace Corps for two years, teaching high school math in Swaziland (Africa). Next, he pursued a master's degree in computer science, which brought him to Silicon Valley. Hastings declared his love affair with writing computer code, but emphasized, "The big thing that Stanford did for me was to turn me on to the entrepreneurial model."[18] His net worth is an estimated $4 billion.

Jeni Bauer, founder and chief creative officer of Jeni's Splendid Ice Creams, started her first venture as a sophomore in college at the Ohio State University.

Brooke LaValley/The Washington Post/Getty Images

- **Jeni Bauer,** founder of and chief creative officer of Jeni's Splendid Ice Creams. Bauer's story begins at Ohio State University, where she was studying art history. Rather than study, however, she spent most of her time on her fragrance-making hobby. One day, Bauer experimented with mixing essential oils with ice cream. Her first creation was a mix of hot pepper oil and chocolate, which became an instant hit among her friends and classmates. (This unique flavor is now a signature ice cream flavor at Jeni's Splendid Ice Creams.) After realizing that ice cream was "the perfect carrier of scent,"[19] Bauer decided to leave college to start her first ice cream stand, Scream Ice Cream, at the North Market in Columbus, Ohio. This first venture failed after a short time. Undeterred, Bauer went on to attend Penn State's acclaimed crash course on ice cream making (covering all topics from "Cow to Cone"), which was also attended by Ben Cohen and Jerry Greenfield of the famous Ben & Jerry's Ice Cream (which shot to fame in the 1980s). Bauer's tenacity paid off because a few years later she secured the necessary funding to start Jeni's Splendid Ice Creams, with her first location again at North Market, coming full circle. What differentiates Jeni's Ice Creams from other brands is her use of direct trade ingredients, milk from grass-pastured cows, and unique combination of flavors. Jeni's Splendid Ice Creams now has over 30 stores across the United States, distributes prepackaged pints to more than 3,000 stores, and surpassed $30 million in annual revenues in 2018. As her secret recipe for success, Bauer reveals that "every year you get tested and you get stronger. You build more resilience. It becomes who you are."[20]

- **Dr. Dre,** featured in Strategy Highlight 4.1, a successful rapper, music and movie producer, and serial entrepreneur. Born in Compton, California, Dr. Dre focused on music and entertainment during high school, working his first job as a DJ. Dr. Dre's major breakthrough as a rapper came with the group N.W.A. One of his first business successes as an entrepreneur was Death Row Records, which he founded in 1991. A year later, Dr. Dre's first solo album, *The Chronic,* was a huge hit. In 1996, Dr. Dre founded Aftermath Entertainment and signed famed rappers such as 50 Cent and Eminem. Dr. Dre, known for his strong work ethic and attention to detail, expects nothing less than perfection from the people with whom he works. Stories abound that Dr. Dre made famous rappers rerecord songs hundreds of times if he was not satisfied with the outcome. In 2014, Dr. Dre became the first hip-hop billionaire after Apple acquired Beats Electronics for $3 billion. In 2015, N.W.A's early success was depicted in the biographical movie *Straight Outta Compton,* focusing on group members Eazy-E, Ice Cube, and Dr. Dre, who coproduced the film, grossing over $200 million at the box office, with a budget of $45 million.[21]

- **Jeff Bezos,** the founder of Amazon (featured in ChapterCase 8), the world's largest online retailer. The stepson of a Cuban immigrant, Bezos graduated with a degree in computer science and electrical engineering, before working as a financial analyst on Wall Street. In 1994, after reading that the internet was growing by 2,000 percent a month, he set out to leverage the internet as a new distribution channel. Listing products that could be sold online, he finally settled on books because that retail market was fairly fragmented, with huge inefficiencies in its distribution system. Perhaps even more important, books are a perfect commodity because they are identical regardless of where a consumer buys them. This reduced uncertainty when introducing online shopping to consumers. From humble beginnings, Amazon has branched out into a wide variety of business endeavors (see ChapterCase 8). In 2019, his personal wealth exceeded $150 billion, making him the wealthiest person in the world.[22]

- **Elon Musk,** an engineer and serial entrepreneur with a deep passion to "solve environmental, social, and economic challenges."[23] He is featured in his role as leader of Tesla in ChapterCase 1. Musk left his native South Africa at age 17. He went to Canada and then to the United States, where he completed a bachelor's degree in economics and physics at the University of Pennsylvania. After only two days in a PhD program in applied physics and material sciences at Stanford University, Musk left graduate school to found Zip2, an online provider of content publishing software for news organizations. Four years later, in 1999, computer maker Compaq acquired Zip2 for $341 million (and was in turn acquired by HP in 2002). Musk moved on to co-found PayPal, an online payment processor. When eBay acquired PayPal for $1.5 billion in 2002, Musk had the financial resources to pursue his passion to use science and engineering to solve social and economic challenges. He is leading multiple new ventures simultaneously: Tesla (electric cars and renewable, decentralized energy) and space exploration with SpaceX.[24]

■ **Jimmy Wales,** the founder of Wikipedia (featured in Strategy Highlight 7.2), typifies *social entrepreneurship.*[25] Raised in Alabama, Wales was educated by his mother and grandmother who ran a nontraditional school. In 1994, he dropped out of a doctoral program in economics at Indiana University to take a job at a stock brokerage firm in Chicago. In the evenings he wrote computer code for fun and built a web browser. During the late 1990s internet boom, Wales was one of the first to grasp the power of an open-source method to provide knowledge on a large scale. What differentiates Wales from other web entrepreneurs is his idealism: Wikipedia is free for the end user and supports itself solely by donations and not, for example, by online advertising. Wikipedia has more than 40 million articles in over 300 languages, including some 6 million items in English. About 500 million people use Wikipedia each month. Wales' idealism is a form of social entrepreneurship: His vision is to make the entire repository of human knowledge available to anyone anywhere for free.

Entrepreneurs are the agents who introduce change into the competitive system. They do this not only by figuring out how to use inventions, but also by introducing new products or services, new production processes, and new forms of organization. Entrepreneurs can introduce change by starting new ventures, such as Reed Hastings with Netflix or Mark Zuckerberg with Facebook. Or they can be found within existing firms, such as A.G. Lafley at Procter & Gamble (P&G), who implemented an *open-innovation model* (which will be discussed in Chapter 11). When innovating within existing companies, change agents are often called *intrapreneurs:* those pursuing *corporate entrepreneurship.*[26]

Entrepreneurs who drive innovation need just as much skill, commitment, and daring as the inventors who are responsible for the process of invention.[27] As an example, the engineer Nikola Tesla invented the alternating-current (AC) electric motor and was granted a patent in 1888 by the U.S. Patent and Trademark Office.[28] Because this breakthrough technology was neglected for much of the 20th century and Nikola Tesla did not receive the recognition he deserved in his lifetime, the entrepreneur Elon Musk is not just commercializing Tesla's invention but also honoring Tesla with the name of his company, Tesla, which was formed to design and manufacture all-electric automobiles. Tesla launched several all-electric vehicles based on Tesla's original invention (see ChapterCase 1).

Strategic entrepreneurship describes the pursuit of innovation using tools and concepts from strategic management.[29] We can leverage innovation for competitive advantage by applying a strategic management lens to entrepreneurship. The fundamental question of strategic entrepreneurship, therefore, is how to combine entrepreneurial actions, creating new opportunities or exploiting existing ones with strategic actions taken in the pursuit of competitive advantage.[30] This can take place within new ventures such as Tesla or within established firms such as Apple.

entrepreneurs The agents that introduce change into the competitive system.

strategic entrepreneurship The pursuit of innovation using tools and concepts from strategic management.

Apple's continued innovation in mobile devices and user experience is an example of strategic entrepreneurship: Apple's leaders use strategic analysis, formulation, and implementation when deciding which new type of mobile device to research and develop, when to launch it, and how to implement the necessary organizational changes to support the product launch. Each new release is an innovation; each is therefore an act of entrepreneurship—planned and executed using strategic management concepts. In 2015, for example, Apple entered the market for computer wearables by introducing the Apple Watch. In 2017, Apple released the 10th-year anniversary model of its original iPhone, introduced in 2007. In 2019, Apple announced a major push into the media and entertainment industry with Apple TV.

Social entrepreneurship describes the pursuit of social goals while creating profitable businesses. Social entrepreneurs evaluate the performance of their ventures not only by financial metrics but also by ecological and social contribution (*profits, planet,* and *people*). They use a *triple-bottom-line* approach to assess performance (discussed in Chapter 5). Examples of social entrepreneurship ventures include Teach For America, TOMS (which gives a pair of shoes to an economically disadvantaged child for every pair of shoes it sells), Better World Books (an online bookstore that uses capitalism to alleviate illiteracy around the world),[31] and Wikipedia, whose mission is to collect and develop educational information, and make it freely available to any person in the world (see Strategy Highlight 7.2)

Since entrepreneurs and the innovations they unleash frequently create entire new industries, we now turn to a discussion of the industry life cycle to derive implications for competitive strategy.

7.3 Innovation and the Industry Life Cycle

Innovations frequently lead to the birth of new industries. Innovative advances in IT and logistics facilitated the creation of the overnight express delivery industry by FedEx and that of big-box retailing by Walmart. The internet set online retailing in motion, with new companies such as Amazon and eBay taking the lead, and it revolutionized the advertising industry first through Yahoo, and later Google and Facebook. Advances in nanotechnology are revolutionizing many different industries, ranging from medical diagnostics and surgery to lighter and stronger airplane components.[32] Advances in AI are reshaping a wide set of industries ranging from call centers, health care, agriculture, and logistics to transportation via autonomous vehicles and trucks.

Industries tend to follow a predictable **industry life cycle**: As an industry evolves over time, we can identify five distinct stages: *introduction, growth, shakeout, maturity,* and *decline.*[33] We illustrate how the type of innovation and resulting strategic implications change at each stage of the life cycle as well as how innovation can initiate and drive a new life cycle.

The number and size of competitors change as the industry life cycle unfolds, and different types of consumers enter the market at each stage. That is, both the supply and demand sides of the market change as the industry ages. Each stage of the industry life cycle requires different competencies for the firm to perform well and to satisfy that stage's unique customer group. We first introduce the life cycle model before discussing different customer groups in more depth when introducing the crossing-the-chasm concept later in this chapter.[34]

Exhibit 7.4 depicts a typical industry life cycle, focusing on the smartphone industry in emerging and developed economies. In a stylized industry life cycle model, the horizontal axis shows time (in years) and the vertical axis market size. In Exhibit 7.4, however, we are taking a snapshot of the global smartphone industry in the year 2020. This implies that we are joining two different life cycles (one for emerging economies and one for developed economies) in the same exhibit at one point in time.

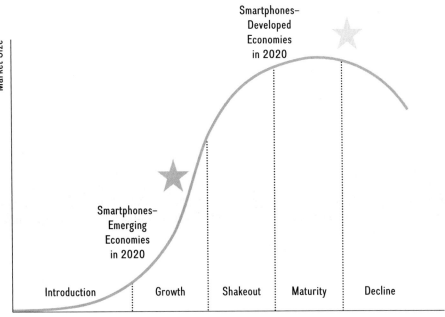

EXHIBIT 7.4

Industry Life Cycle: The Smartphone Industry in Emerging and Developed Economies

The development of most industries follows an S-curve. Initial demand for a new product or service is often slow to take off, then accelerates, before decelerating, and eventually turning to zero, and even becoming negative as a market contracts.

As shown in Exhibit 7.4, in emerging economies such as Argentina, Brazil, China, India, Indonesia, Mexico, and Russia, the smartphone industry is in the growth stage. The market for smartphones in these countries is expected to grow rapidly over the next few years. More and more of the consumers in these countries with large populations are expected to upgrade from a simple mobile phone to a smartphone.

In contrast, the market for smartphones is in the maturity stage in 2020 in developed economies such as Australia, Canada, Germany, Japan, South Korea, the United Kingdom, and the United States. This implies that developed economies moved through the prior three stages of the industry life cycle (introductory, growth, and shakeout) some years earlier. Because the smartphone industry is mature in these markets, little or no growth in market size is expected over the next few years because most consumers own smartphones. This implies that any market share gain by one firm comes at the expense of others, as users replace older smartphones with newer models. In addition, consumers in developed countries are also holding on longer to their existing (and highly priced) smartphones, as improvements in newer models is viewed as too incremental. Going forward, competitive intensity in the smartphone industry in advanced economies is expected to be high.

Each stage of the industry life cycle—introduction, growth, shakeout, maturity, and decline—has different strategic implications for competing firms. We now discuss each stage in detail.

INTRODUCTION STAGE

When an individual inventor or company launches a successful innovation, a new industry may emerge. In this introductory stage, the innovator's core competency is R&D, which is necessary to creating a product category that will attract customers. This is often a capital-intensive process, in which the innovator is investing in designing a unique product, trying new ideas to attract customers, and producing small quantities—all of which contribute to a high cost for the innovator, and frequently resulting in a high price for the consumer when the product is launched. The initial market size is small, and growth is slow.

In this introductory stage, when barriers to entry tend to be high, generally only a few firms are active in the market. In their competitive struggle for market share, they emphasize unique product features and performance rather than price.

Although there are some benefits to being early in the market (as previously discussed), innovators also may encounter *first-mover disadvantages*. They must educate potential customers about the product's intended benefits, find distribution channels and complementary assets, and continue to perfect the fledgling product. Although a core competency in R&D is necessary to create or enter an industry in the introductory stage, some competency in marketing also is helpful in achieving a successful product launch and market acceptance. Competition can be intense, and early winners are well-positioned to stake out a strong position for the future.

The strategic objective during the introductory stage is to achieve market acceptance and seed future growth. One way to accomplish these objectives is to initiate and leverage **network effects**,[35] the positive effect that one user of a product or service has on the value of that product for other users. Network effects occur when the value of a product or service increases, often exponentially, with the number of users. If successful, network effects propel the industry to the next stage of the life cycle, the growth stage (which we discuss next).

> **network effects** The positive effect (externality) that one user of a product or service has on the value of that product for other users.

Apple effectively leveraged the network effects generated by numerous complementary software applications (apps) available via iTunes to create a tightly integrated ecosystem of hardware, software, and services, which competitors find hard to crack. The consequence has been a competitive advantage for over a decade, beginning with the introduction of the iPod in 2001 and iTunes in 2003. Apple launched its enormously successful iPhone in the summer of 2007. A year later, it followed up with the Apple App Store, which boasts that for almost anything you might need, "there's an app for that." Popular apps allow iPhone users to access their business contacts via LinkedIn, hail a ride via Uber, call colleagues overseas via Skype, check delivery of Zappos packages shipped via UPS, get the latest news on Twitter, and engage in customer relationship management using Salesforce.com. You can stream music via Apple Music, post photos using Instagram, stream your favorite shows via Netflix, access Facebook to check on your friends, message others using Snapchat, or post videos on TikTok.

Even more important is the effect that apps have on the value of an iPhone. Arguably, the explosive growth of the iPhone was due to the fact that the Apple App Store offers the largest selection of apps to its users. The App Store offers more than 2 million apps, which had been downloaded some 150 billion times, earning Apple billions of dollars in revenues. Apple argues that users have a better experience because the apps take advantage of the tight integration of hardware and software provided by the iPhone. The availability of apps, in turn, leads to network effects that increase the value of the iPhone for its users. Exhibit 7.5 shows how. Increased value creation, as we know from Chapter 6, is positively related to demand, which in turn increases the installed base, meaning the number of people using an iPhone. As the installed base of iPhone users further increases, this incentivizes software developers to write even more apps. Making apps widely available strengthened Apple's position in the smartphone industry. Based on positive feedback loops, a virtuous cycle emerges where one factor positively reinforces another. Apple's ecosystem based on integrated hardware, software, and services providing a superior user experience is hard to crack for competitors.

GROWTH STAGE

Market growth accelerates in the growth stage of the industry life cycle (see Exhibit 7.4). After the initial innovation has gained some market acceptance, demand increases rapidly as first-time buyers rush to enter the market, convinced by the proof of concept demonstrated in the introductory stage.

As the size of the market expands, a **standard** signals the market's agreement on a common set of engineering features and design choices.[36] Standards can emerge from the bottom up through competition in the marketplace or be imposed from the top down by government or other standard-setting agencies such as the Institute of Electrical and Electronics Engineers (IEEE) that develops and sets industrial standards in a broad range of industries, including energy, electric power, biomedical and health care technology, IT, telecommunications, consumer electronics, aerospace, and nanotechnology. Strategy Highlight 7.1 discusses the unfolding standards battle in the automotive industry.

Since demand is strong during the growth phase, both efficient and inefficient firms thrive; the rising tide lifts all boats. Moreover, production costs begin to fall, often rapidly, as standard business processes are put in place and firms begin to reap economies of scale and learning. Distribution channels are expanded, and complementary assets in the form of products and services become widely available.[37]

After a standard is established in an industry, the basis of competition tends to move away from product innovations toward process innovations.[38] **Product innovations**, as the name suggests, are new or recombined knowledge embodied in new products—the jet airplane, electric vehicle, smartphone, and wearable computer. **Process innovations** are new ways to produce existing products or to deliver existing services. Process innovations are made possible through advances such as artificial intelligence, the internet, lean manufacturing, Six Sigma, biotechnology, nanotechnology, and so on.

Process innovation need not be high-tech to be impactful, however. The invention of the standardized shipping container, for instance, has transformed global trade. Loading goods into uniform containers that could easily be moved among trucks, rail, and ships resulted in significant savings in cost and time. Before containerization was invented about 60 years ago, it cost almost $6 to load a ton of (loose) cargo, and theft was rampant. After containerization, the cost for loading a ton of cargo had plummeted to $0.16 and theft all but disappeared (because containers are sealed at the departing factory). Efficiency gains in terms of labor and time were even more impressive. Before containerization, dock labor could move 1.7 tons per hour onto a cargo ship. After containerization, this number jumped to 30 tons per hour. Ports are now able to accommodate much larger ships, and travel time across the oceans has fallen by half. As a consequence, costs for shipping goods across the globe fell rapidly. Moreover, containerization enabled optimization of global supply chains and set the stage for subsequent process innovations such as *just-in-time (JIT) operations*

EXHIBIT 7.5 Leveraging Network Effects to Drive Demand: Apple's iPhone

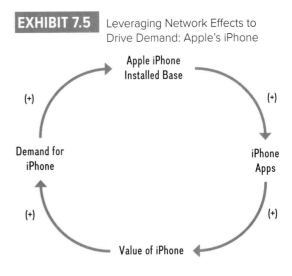

---

standard An agreed-upon solution about a common set of engineering features and design choices.

product innovation New or recombined knowledge embodied in new products.

process innovation New ways to produce existing products or deliver existing services.

Strategy Highlight 7.1

Standards Battle: Which Automotive Technology Will Win?

In the envisioned future transition away from gasoline-powered cars, Nissan firmly believes the next technological paradigm will be electric motors. The Japanese carmaker views hybrids (which combine battery power with internal combustion engines) as a "halfway technology," and suggests they will be a temporary phenomenon at best. A number of start-up companies, including Tesla in the United States as well as BYD, NIO, and others in China, share Nissan's belief in this particular future scenario.

One of the biggest impediments to large-scale adoption of electric vehicles (EVs), however, remains the lack of appropriate infrastructure: There are few stations where drivers can recharge their car batteries when necessary. With the range of most electric vehicles currently limited to approximately 200 miles, many potential consumers suffer from "range anxiety," wherein the lack of recharging stations is considered a serious problem. High-end Tesla vehicles can achieve 300 miles per charge or more, while the lower-priced, first-generation Nissan Leaf (an acronym for Leading, Environmentally friendly, Affordable, Family car) can achieve a maximum range of roughly 85 miles. The second-generation Leaf, which came out in 2017, can run for up to 150 miles before needing to be recharged. Tesla, Nissan, and other independent charging providers such as ChargePoint are working hard to develop a network of charging stations. By early 2019, Tesla had a dense (but proprietary) network of more than 10,000 supercharger stations throughout the United States, allowing for convenient coast-to-coast travel in one of its vehicles.

Moreover, industry experts believe EVs will account for 15 percent of global auto sales by 2025 (up from 2 percent in 2019). In 2019, Swedish carmaker Volvo ceased producing cars equipped with only internal combustion engines. All its new vehicles are now fully electric or hybrid. This is a strong strategic commitment by a traditional car manufacturer. It is also the first of its kind. Similarly, Volkswagen (VW), one of the largest carmakers globally in terms of units, has shifted its strategic focus fully toward electrification of its vehicles. In 2019, VW announced an ambitious plan to invest some $35 billion to develop and

The Nissan Leaf, the world's best-selling electric vehicle, is now in its second generation with a 150-mile range per single battery charge.
Grzegorz Czapski/Shutterstock

launch 70 new fully electric vehicles over the next decade. Similar to Tesla, VW further announced that it plans to build its "gigafactory" to produce and supply its own batteries, rather than rely on an outside vendor such as Panasonic of Japan. In contrast, Toyota remains convinced that gasoline-electric hybrids will play an important role for decades to come. Nonetheless, the Japanese carmaker has also made investments in fuel cell cars and hopes that the prices of fuel cell cars will fall to match those of electric vehicles in the future. Going forward, Toyota also plans to shift more of its resources toward EVs.

These somewhat different predictions have significant influence on how much Nissan, VW, Toyota, and others are willing to invest in new technology and where. For example, Nissan builds its Leaf at a plant in Smyrna, Tennessee. Since the 1990s, it has spent billions developing its electric-car program. Following its debut in December 2010, Nissan's Leaf has become the best-selling electric vehicle, selling approximately 500,000 units. In 2017, GM introduced the all-electric Chevy Bolt, with a range of 250 miles per charge, similar to Tesla's Model 3 and Model Y.

Toyota, on the other hand, has already sold more than 10 million of its popular Prius cars since it was introduced in 1997. Toyota, having expanded its R&D investments in hybrid technology, now offers hybrid technology in most of its vehicles. Eventually, the investments made by Nissan, Tesla, VW, Toyota, and others will yield different returns, depending on which predictions prove more accurate.

An alternative outcome in this standards battle is that neither hybrids nor electric cars will become the next paradigm. Some manufacturers are betting on cars powered by hydrogen fuel cells. In sum, many alternative technologies are competing to become the winner in setting a new standard for propelling cars. This situation is depicted in Exhibit 7.6, where the new technologies represent a swarm of new entries vying for dominance. At this point, it appears that EV technology will be the likely winner, but it is far from clear.[39]

EXHIBIT 7.6 Automotive Technologies Compete for Industry Dominance

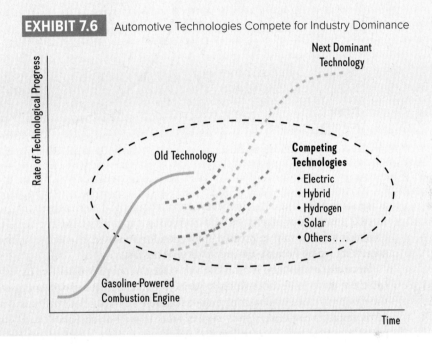

management. A set of research studies estimated that within just five years of adopting this critical process innovation, containerization alone more than tripled international trade.[40]

Exhibit 7.7 shows the level of product and process innovation throughout the entire life cycle.[41] In the introductory stage, the level of *product* innovation is at a maximum because new features increasing perceived consumer value are critical to gaining traction in the market. In contrast, process innovation is at a minimum in the introductory stage because companies produce only a small number of products, often just prototypes or beta versions. The main concern is to commercialize the invention—that is, to demonstrate that the product works and that a market exists.

The relative importance, however, reverses over time. Frequently, a standard emerges during the growth stage of the industry life cycle (see the second column, "Growth," in Exhibit 7.7). At that point, most of the technological and commercial uncertainties about the new product are gone. After the market accepts a new product, and a standard for the new technology has emerged, *process* innovation rapidly becomes more important than product innovation. As market demand increases, economies of scale kick in: Firms establish and optimize standard business processes through applications of AI, lean manufacturing, Six Sigma, and so on. As a consequence, product improvements become incremental, while the level of process innovation rises rapidly.

During the growth stage, process innovation ramps up (at increasing marginal returns) as firms attempt to keep up with rapidly rising demand while attempting to bring down costs

EXHIBIT 7.7

Product and Process
Innovation
throughout an
Industry Life Cycle

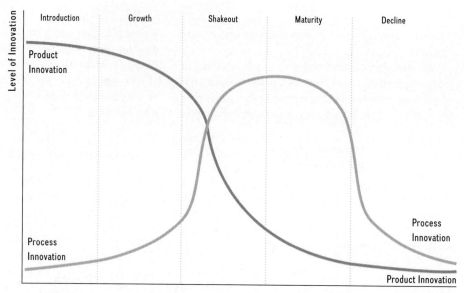

at the same time. The core competencies for competitive advantage in the growth stage tend to shift toward manufacturing and marketing capabilities. At the same time, the R&D emphasis tends to shift to process innovation for improved efficiency. Competitive rivalry is somewhat muted because the market is growing fast.

Since market demand is robust in this stage and more competitors have entered the market, there tends to be more strategic variety: Some competitors will continue to follow a *differentiation* strategy, emphasizing unique features, product functionality, and reliability. Other firms employ a *cost-leadership strategy* in order to offer an acceptable level of value but lower prices to consumers. They realize that lower cost is likely a key success factor in the future, because this will allow the firm to lower prices and attract more consumers into the market.

When introduced in the spring of 2010, for example, Apple's first-generation iPad was priced at $829 for 64GB with a 3G Wi-Fi connection.[42] Just three years later, in spring 2013, the same model was priced at only one-third of the original price, or $275.[43] Access to efficient and large-scale manufacturing operations (such as those offered by Foxconn in China, the company that assembles most of Apple's products) and effective supply chain capabilities are key success factors when market demand increases rapidly. By 2017, Gazelle, an ecommerce company that allows people to sell their electronic devices and to buy used ones, offered a mere $15 for a "flawless" first-generation iPad. By 2019, the first-generation iPad (in "flawless" condition) was no longer available on any ecommerce sites specializing in used mobile devices.

The key objective for firms during the growth phase is to stake out a strong strategic position not easily imitated by rivals. In the fast-growing shapewear industry, start-up company Spanx has staked out a strong position. In 1998, Florida State University graduate Sara Blakely decided to cut the feet off her pantyhose to enhance her looks when wearing pants.[44] Soon after she obtained a patent for her body-shaping undergarments, and Spanx began production and retailing of its shapewear in 2000. Sales grew exponentially after Blakely appeared on *The Oprah Winfrey Show*. Taking the risk paid off for Spanx's founder: After investing an initial $5,000 into her startup, Blakely became the world's then youngest self-made female billionaire (a title now taken by Kylie Jenner, who became the world's youngest self-made billionaire by age 21, beating out Mark Zuckerberg who was 23).

By 2019, Spanx had grown to some 1,000 employees and sold millions of Spanx "power panties," with estimated revenues of some $500 million. To stake out a strong position and to preempt competitors, Spanx now offers hundreds of products ranging from slimming apparel and swimsuits to bras and activewear. It also now designs and manufactures body-shaping undergarments for men ("Spanx for Men—Manx"). Spanx products are now available in over 50 countries via the internet. Moreover, to strengthen its strategic position and brand image in the United States, Spanx is opening retail stores across the country.

The shapewear industry's explosive growth—it is expected to reach $6 billion in annual sales by 2022—has attracted several other players: Flexees by Maidenform, BodyWrap, and Miraclesuit, to name a few. They are all attempting to carve out positions in the new industry. Given Spanx's ability to stake out a strong position during the growth stage of the industry life cycle and the fact that it continues to be a moving target, it might be difficult for competitors to dislodge the company.

SHAKEOUT STAGE

Rapid industry growth and expansion cannot go on indefinitely. As the industry moves into the next stage of the industry life cycle, the rate of growth declines (see Exhibit 7.4). Firms begin to compete directly against one another for market share, rather than trying to capture a share of an increasing pie. As competitive intensity increases, the weaker firms are forced out of the industry. This is the reason this phase of the industry life cycle is called the shakeout stage: Only the strongest competitors survive increasing rivalry as firms begin to cut prices and offer more services, all in an attempt to gain more of a market that grows slowly, if at all. This type of cutthroat competition erodes profitability of all but the most efficient firms in the industry. As a consequence, the industry often consolidates, as the weakest competitors either are acquired by stronger firms or exit through bankruptcy.

The winners in this increasingly competitive environment are often firms that stake out a strong position as cost leaders. Key success factors at this stage are the manufacturing and process engineering capabilities that can be used to drive costs down. The importance of process innovation further increases (albeit at diminishing marginal returns), while the importance of product innovation further declines.

Assuming an acceptable value proposition, price becomes a more important competitive weapon in the shakeout stage because product features and performance requirements tend to be well established. A few firms may be able to implement a blue ocean strategy, combining differentiation and low cost, but given the intensity of competition, many weaker firms are forced to exit. Any firm that does not have a clear strategic profile is likely to not survive the shakeout phase.

MATURITY STAGE

After the shakeout is completed and a few firms remain, the industry enters the maturity stage. During the fourth stage of the industry life cycle, the industry structure morphs into an oligopoly with only a few large firms. Most of the demand was largely satisfied in the shakeout stage. Any additional market demand in the maturity stage is limited. Demand now consists of replacement or repeat purchases. The market has reached its maximum size, and industry growth is likely to be zero or even negative going forward. This decrease in market demand increases competitive intensity within the industry. In the maturity stage, the level of process innovation reaches its maximum as firms attempt to lower cost as much as possible, while the level of incremental product innovation sinks to its minimum (see Exhibit 7.7).

Generally, the firms that survive the shakeout stage tend to be larger and enjoy economies of scale, as the industry consolidated and most excess capacity was removed. The domestic airline industry has been in the maturity stage for a long time. The large number of bankruptcies as well as the wave of mega-mergers, such as those of Delta and Northwest, United and Continental, and American Airlines and US Airways, are a consequence of low or zero growth in a mature market characterized by significant excess capacity.

DECLINE STAGE

Changes in the external environment (such as those discussed in Chapter 3 when presenting the PESTEL framework) often take industries from maturity to decline. In this final stage of the industry life cycle, the size of the market contracts further as demand falls, often rapidly. At this final phase of the industry life cycle, innovation efforts along both product and process dimensions cease (see Exhibit 7.7). If a technological or business model breakthrough emerges that opens up a *new* industry or resets the industry life cycle, however, then this dynamic interplay between product and process innovation starts anew. For instance, with 5G (fifth generation cellular network technology) becoming more prevalent in advanced economies, demand for newer smartphone might increase significantly over and above the replacement rate of existing smartphones using the older 4G technology.

If there is any remaining excess industry capacity in the decline stage, this puts strong pressure on prices and can further increase competitive intensity, especially if the industry has high exit barriers. At this final stage of the industry life cycle, leaders generally have four strategic options: *exit, harvest, maintain,* or *consolidate*.[45]

- **Exit.** Some firms are forced to *exit* the industry by bankruptcy or liquidation. The U.S. textile industry has experienced a large number of exits over the last few decades, mainly due to low-cost foreign competition.

- **Harvest.** In pursuing a *harvest strategy,* the firm reduces investments in product support and allocates only a minimum of human and other resources. While several companies such as IBM, Brother, Olivetti, and Nakajima still offer typewriters, they don't invest much in future innovation. Instead, they are maximizing cash flow from their existing typewriter product line.

- **Maintain.** Philip Morris, on the other hand, is following a *maintain strategy* with its Marlboro brand, continuing to support marketing efforts at a given level despite the fact that U.S. cigarette consumption has been declining.

- **Consolidate.** Although market size shrinks in a declining industry, some firms may choose to *consolidate* the industry by buying rivals. This allows the consolidating firm to stake out a strong position—possibly approaching monopolistic market power, albeit in a declining industry.

  Although chewing tobacco is a declining industry, Swedish Match has pursued a number of acquisitions to consolidate its strategic position in the industry. It acquired, among other firms, the Pinkerton Tobacco Co. of Owensboro, Kentucky, maker of the Red Man brand. Red Man is the leading chewing tobacco brand in the United States. Red Man has carved out a strong strategic position built on a superior reputation for a quality product and by past endorsements of Major League Baseball players since 1904. Despite gory product warnings detailing the health risk of chewing tobacco and a federally mandated prohibition on marketing, the Red Man brand has remained popular and profitable.

The industry life cycle model assumes a more or less smooth transition from one stage to another. This holds true for most continuous innovations that require little or no change in consumer behavior. But not all innovations enjoy such continuity.

CROSSING THE CHASM

In the influential bestseller *Crossing the Chasm*[46] Geoffrey Moore documented that many innovators were unable to successfully transition from one *stage of the industry life cycle* to the next. Based on empirical observations, Moore's core argument is that *each stage of the industry life cycle is dominated by a different customer group.* Different customer groups with distinctly different preferences enter the industry at each stage of the industry life cycle. Each customer group responds differently to a technological innovation. This is due to differences in the psychological, demographic, and social attributes observed in each unique customer segment. Moore's main contribution is that the significant differences between the *early* customer groups—who enter during the introductory stage of the industry life cycle—and *later* customers—who enter during the growth stage—can make for a difficult transition between the different parts of the industry life cycle. Such differences between customer groups lead to a big gulf or *chasm* into which companies and their innovations frequently fall. Only companies that recognize these differences and are able to apply the appropriate competencies at each stage of the industry life cycle will have a chance to transition successfully from stage to stage.

Exhibit 7.8 shows the **crossing-the-chasm framework** and the different customer segments. The industry life cycle model (shown in Exhibit 7.4) follows an S-curve leading up to 100 percent total market potential that can be reached during the maturity stage. In contrast, the *chasm framework* breaks down the 100 percent market potential into different customer segments, highlighting the *incremental* contribution each specific segment can bring into the market. This results in the familiar bell curve. Note the big gulf, or *chasm,* separating the early adopters from the early and late majority that make up the mass market. Social network sites have followed a pattern similar to that illustrated in Exhibit 7.8. Friendster was unable to cross the big chasm. Myspace was successful with the early majority, but only Facebook went on to succeed with the late majority and laggards. Each stage customer segment, moreover, is also separated by smaller chasms. Both the large competitive chasm and the smaller ones have strategic implications.

Both new technology ventures and innovations introduced by established firms have a high failure rate. This can be explained as a failure to successfully cross the chasm from the early users to the mass market because the firm does not recognize that the business strategy needs to be fine-tuned for each customer segment. Formulating a business strategy for each segment guided by the *who, what, why,* and *how* questions of competition (Who to serve? What needs to satisfy? Why and how to satisfy them?), introduced in Chapter 6, strategic leaders will find that the core competencies to satisfy each of the different customer

LO 7-4

Derive strategic implications of the crossing-the-chasm framework.

crossing-the-chasm framework Conceptual model that shows how each stage of the industry life cycle is dominated by a different customer group.

EXHIBIT 7.8

The Crossing-the-Chasm Framework

Source: Adapted from G.A. Moore (1991), *Crossing the Chasm: Marketing and Selling Disruptive Products to Mainstream Customers* (New York: HarperCollins), 17.

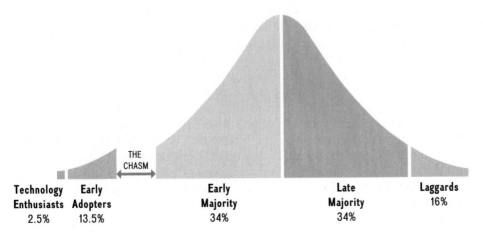

| Technology Enthusiasts 2.5% | Early Adopters 13.5% | THE CHASM | Early Majority 34% | Late Majority 34% | Laggards 16% |

segments are quite different. If not recognized and addressed, this will lead to the demise of the innovation as it crashes into the chasm between life cycle stages.

We first introduce each customer group and map it to the respective stage of the industry life cycle. To illustrate, we then apply the chasm framework to an analysis of the mobile phone industry.

TECHNOLOGY ENTHUSIASTS. The customer segment in the introductory stage of the industry life cycle is called **technology enthusiasts**.[47] The smallest market segment, it makes up some 2.5 percent of total market potential. Technology enthusiasts often have an engineering mind-set and pursue new technology proactively. They frequently seek new products before the products are officially introduced. Technology enthusiasts enjoy using beta versions of products, tinkering with the product's imperfections and providing (free) feedback and suggestions to companies. For example, many software companies such as Google and Microsoft launch beta versions to accumulate customer feedback to work out bugs before the official launch. Moreover, technology enthusiasts will often pay a premium price to have the latest gadget. The endorsement by technology enthusiasts validates the fact that the new product does in fact work.

> **technology enthusiasts** A customer segment in the introductory stage of the industry life cycle. Often have an engineering mind-set and pursue new technology proactively, frequently seeking out new products before they are officially introduced to the market.

An example of an innovation that appealed to technology enthusiasts is Google Glass, a mobile computer that is worn like a pair of regular glasses. Instead of a lens, however, one side displays a small, high-definition computer screen. Google Glass was developed as part of Google's wild-card program. Technology enthusiasts were eager to get ahold of Google Glass when made available in a beta testing program in 2013. Those interested had to compose a Google+ or Twitter message of 50 words or less explaining why they would be a good choice to test the device and include the hashtag #ifihadglass. Approximately 150,000 people applied and 8,000 winners were chosen. They were required to attend a Google Glass event and pay $1,500 for the developer's version of the product.

Although many industry leaders, including Apple CEO Tim Cook, agree that wearable computers such as the Apple Watch or the Fitbit smartwatch are important mobile devices, they suggest that there is a large chasm between the current technology for computerized eyeglasses and a successful product for early adopters let alone the mass market.[48] They seem to be correct, because Alphabet's Google was until now unable to cross the chasm between technology enthusiasts and early adopters, even after spending billions on R&D per year (spread over all of its products and services).[49]

> **early adopters** Customers entering the market in the growth stage of the industry life cycle that are eager to buy early into a new technology or product concept. Their demand is driven by recognizing and appreciating the possibilities the new technology can afford them in their professional and personal lives.

EARLY ADOPTERS. The customers entering the market in the growth stage are **early adopters**. They make up roughly 13.5 percent of the total market potential. Early adopters, as the name suggests, are eager to buy early into a new technology or product concept. Unlike technology enthusiasts, however, their demand is driven by their imagination and creativity rather than solely by the new technology per se. They ask themselves the question, *what can this new product do for me or my business?* Early adopters do recognize and appreciate, however, the possibilities the new technology can afford them in their professional and personal lives. Early adopters' demand is fueled as much by intuition and vision as by technology concerns.

For instance, early adopters are the people that put down thousands of dollars in deposits to reserve a new Tesla Model S or Model X when first introduced, without having been able to test-drive the vehicle or even seen it other than on the internet. They then often needed to wait a significant amount of time before receiving the new vehicle. Since early adopters are influenced by standard technological performance metrics as well as by intuition and imagination, the firm needs to communicate the product's potential applications in a more direct way than when it attracted the initial technology enthusiasts. Attracting the early adopters to the new offering is critical to opening any new high-tech market segment.

EARLY MAJORITY. The customers coming into the market in the shakeout stage are called **early majority**. Their main consideration in deciding whether or not to adopt a new technological innovation is a strong sense of practicality. They are pragmatists and are most concerned with the question of what the new technology can do for them. Before adopting a new product or service, they weigh the benefits and costs carefully. Customers in the early majority are aware that many hyped product introductions will fade away, so they prefer to wait and see how things shake out. They like to observe how early adopters are using the product. Early majority customers rely on endorsements by others. They seek out reputable references such as reviews in prominent trade journals or in magazines such as *Consumer Reports.*

Because the early majority makes up roughly one-third of the entire market potential, winning them over is critical to the commercial success of the innovation. They are on the cusp of the mass market. Bringing the early majority on board is the key to catching the growth wave of the industry life cycle. Once they decide to enter the market, a *herding effect* is frequently observed: The early majority enters in large numbers.[50]

The significant differences in the attitudes toward technology of the early majority when compared to the early adopters signify the wide competitive gulf—*the chasm*—between these two consumer segments (see Exhibit 7.8). Without adequate demand from the early majority, most innovative products wither away.

Fisker Automotive, a California-based designer and manufacturer of premium plug-in hybrid vehicles, fell into the chasm because it was unable to transition to early adopters, let alone the mass market. Between its founding in 2007 and 2012, Fisker sold some 1,800 of its Karma model, a $100,000 sports car, to technology enthusiasts. It was unable, however, to follow up with a lower-cost model to attract the early adopters into the market. In addition, technology and reliability issues for the Karma could not be overcome. By 2013, Fisker had crashed into the first chasm (between technology enthusiasts and early adopters), filing for bankruptcy. The assets of Fisker Automotive were purchased by Wanxiang, a Chinese auto parts maker.[51]

In contrast, Tesla, the maker of all-electric vehicles introduced in ChapterCase 1 and a fierce rival of Fisker at one time, was able to overcome some of the early chasms. The Tesla Roadster was a proof-of-concept car that demonstrated that electric vehicles could achieve an equal or better performance than the best gasoline-engine sports cars. The 2,400 Roadsters that Tesla built between 2008 and 2012 were purchased by technology enthusiasts. Next, Tesla successfully launched the Model S, a family sedan, sold to early adopters. The Tesla

> **early majority** Customers coming into the market in the shakeout stage of the industry life cycle. Pragmatists that are mainly concerned with whether adopting a new technological innovation serves a practical purpose or not.

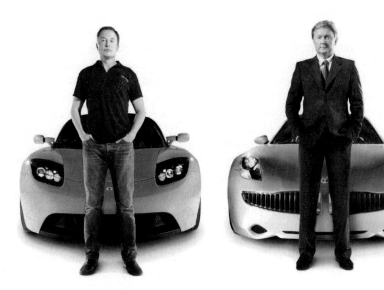

Tesla CEO Elon Musk (left) in front of a Tesla Roadster; Fisker Automotive CEO Henrik Fisker (right) in front of a Fisker Karma.
Misha Gravenor

Model S received a strong endorsement as the 2013 *Motor Trend* Car of the Year and the highest test scores ever awarded by *Consumer Reports*. This may help in crossing the chasm to the early majority, because consumers would now feel more comfortable in considering and purchasing a Tesla vehicle. Tesla is hoping to cross the large competitive chasm between early adopters and early majority with its new, lower-priced models including a smaller sedan (Model 3) and a compact SUV (Model Y).

LATE MAJORITY. The next wave of growth comes from buyers in the **late majority** entering the market in the maturity stage. Like the early majority, they are a large customer segment, making up approximately 34 percent of the total market potential. Combined, the early majority and late majority form the lion's share of the market potential. Demand coming from just two groups—early and late majority—drives most industry growth and firm profitability.

Members of the early and late majority are also quite similar in their attitudes toward new technology. The late majority shares all the concerns of the early majority. But there are also important differences. Although members of the early majority are confident in their ability to master the new technology, the late majority is not. They prefer to wait until standards have emerged and become firmly entrenched, so as to ensure reduction in uncertainty. The late majority also prefers to buy from well-established firms with a strong brand image rather than from unknown new ventures.

LAGGARDS. Finally, **laggards** are the last consumer segment to come into the market, entering in the declining stage of the industry life cycle. These are customers who adopt a new product only if it is absolutely necessary, such as first-time cell phone adopters in the United States today. These customers generally don't want new technology, either for personal or economic reasons. Given their reluctance to adopt new technology, they are generally not considered worth pursuing. Laggards make up no more than 16 percent of the total market potential. Their demand is far too small to compensate for reduced demand from the early and late majority (jointly almost 70 percent of total market demand), who are moving on to different products and services.

CROSSING THE CHASM: APPLICATION TO THE MOBILE PHONE INDUSTRY. Let's apply the crossing-the-chasm framework to one specific industry. In this model, the transition from stage to stage in the industry life cycle is characterized by different competitive chasms that open up because of important differences between customer groups. Although the large chasm between early adopters and the early majority is the main cause of demise for technological innovations, other smaller mini-chasms open between each stage.

Exhibit 7.9 shows the application of the chasm model to the mobile phone industry. The first victim was Motorola's Iridium, an ill-fated satellite-based telephone system.[52] Development began in 1992 after the spouse of a Motorola engineer complained about being unable to get any data or voice access to check on clients while vacationing on a remote island. Motorola's solution was to launch 66 satellites into low orbit to provide global voice and data coverage. In late 1998, Motorola began offering its satellite phone service, charging $5,000 per handset (which was almost too heavy to carry around) and up to $14 per minute for calls.[53] Problems in consumer adoption beyond the few technology enthusiasts became rapidly apparent. The Iridium phone could not be used inside buildings or in cars. Rather, to receive a satellite signal, the phone needed an unobstructed line of sight to a satellite. Iridium crashed into the first chasm, never moving beyond technology enthusiasts (see Exhibit 7.9). For Motorola, it was a billion-dollar blunder. Iridium was soon displaced by cell phones that relied on Earth-based networks of radio towers. The global satellite telephone industry never moved beyond the introductory stage of the industry life cycle.

late majority Customers entering the market in the maturity stage of the industry life cycle that are less confident about their ability to master new technology. Will wait until standards have emerged and become firmly entrenched so as to ensure reduction in uncertainty. Tend to buy from well-established firms with strong brand image.

laggards Customers entering the market in the declining stage of the industry life cycle. Will adopt a new product only if absolutely necessary, generally don't want new technology, and are generally not a customer segment worth pursuing.

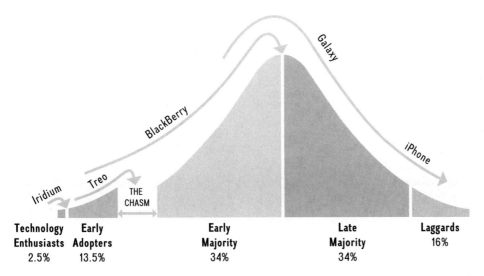

EXHIBIT 7.9

Crossing the Chasm: The Mobile Phone Industry

The first Treo, a fully functioning smartphone combining voice and data capabilities, was released in 2002 by Handspring. The Treo fell into the main chasm that arises between early adopters and the early majority (see Exhibit 7.9). Technical problems, combined with a lack of apps and an overly rigid contract with Sprint as its sole service provider, prevented the Treo from gaining traction in the market beyond early adopters. For these reasons, the Treo was not an attractive product for the early majority, who rejected it. This caused the Treo to plunge into the chasm. Just a year later, Handspring was folded into Palm, which in turn was acquired by HP for $1 billion in 2010.[54] HP shut down Palm in 2011 and wrote off the acquisition.[55]

BlackBerry (formerly known as Research in Motion or RIM)[56] introduced its first fully functioning smartphone in 2000. It was a huge success—especially with two key consumer segments. First, corporate IT managers were early adopters. They became product champions for the BlackBerry smartphone because of its encrypted security software and its reliability in staying connected to a company's network. This allowed users to receive e-mail and other data in real time, anywhere in the world where wireless service was provided. Second, corporate executives were the early majority pulling the BlackBerry smartphone over the chasm because it allowed 24/7 access to data and voice. BlackBerry was able to create a beachhead to cross the chasm between the technology enthusiasts and early adopters on one side and the early majority on the other.[57] BlackBerry's strategic leaders identified the needs of not only early adopters (e.g., IT managers) but also the early majority (e.g., executives), who pulled the BlackBerry over the chasm. By 2005, the BlackBerry had become a corporate executive status symbol. As a consequence of capturing the first three stages of the industry life cycle, between 2002 and 2007, BlackBerry enjoyed no less than 30 percent year-over-year revenue growth as well as double-digit growth in other financial performance metrics such as return on equity. BlackBerry enjoyed a temporary competitive advantage.

In 2007, BlackBerry's dominance over the smartphone market began to erode quickly. The main reason was Apple's introduction of the iPhone. Although technology enthusiasts and early adopters argue that the iPhone is an inferior product to the BlackBerry based on technological criteria, the iPhone enticed not only the early majority, but also the late majority to enter the market. For the late majority, encrypted software security was much less important than having fun with a device that allowed users to surf the web, take pictures, play games, and send and receive e-mail. Moreover, the Apple iTunes Store soon provided thousands of apps for basically any kind of service. While the BlackBerry couldn't cross the gulf between the early and the late majority, Apple's iPhone captured the mass market rapidly. Moreover, consumers began to bring their personal iPhone to work, which forced corporate IT departments to expand their services beyond the BlackBerry. Apple rode the wave of this success to capture each market segment. Likewise, Samsung with its Galaxy line of phones, having successfully imitated the look and feel of an iPhone (as discussed in Chapter 4), is enjoying similar success across the different market segments.

This brief application of the chasm framework to the mobile phone industry shows its usefulness. It provides insightful explanations of why some companies failed, while others succeeded—and thus goes at the core of strategy management.

In summary, Exhibit 7.10 details the features and strategic implications of the entire industry life cycle at each stage.

EXHIBIT 7.10 Features and Strategic Implications of the Industry Life Cycle

	Life Cycle Stages				
	Introduction	**Growth**	**Shakeout**	**Maturity**	**Decline**
Core Competency	R&D, some marketing	R&D, some manufacturing, marketing	Manufacturing, process engineering	Manufacturing, process engineering, marketing	Manufacturing, process engineering, marketing, service
Type and Level of Innovation	Product innovation at a maximum; process innovation at a minimum	Product innovation decreasing; process innovation increasing	After emergence of standard: product innovation decreasing rapidly; process innovation increasing rapidly	Product innovation at a minimum; process innovation at a maximum	Product and process innovation ceased
Market Growth	Slow	High	Moderate and slowing down	None to moderate	Negative
Market Size	Small	Moderate	Large	Largest	Small to moderate
Cost	High	Falling	Moderate	Low	Low to high
Number of Competitors	Few, if any	Many	Fewer	Moderate, but large	Few, if any
Mode of Competition	Non-price competition	Non-price competition	Shifting from non-price to price competition	Price	Price or non-price competition
Type of Buyers	Technology enthusiasts	Early adopters	Early majority	Late majority	Laggards
Business-Level Strategy	Differentiation	Differentiation	Differentiation, or blue ocean strategy	Cost-leadership or blue ocean strategy	Cost-leadership, differentiation, or or blue ocean strategy
Strategic Objective	Achieving market acceptance	Staking out a strong strategic position; generating "deep pockets"	Surviving by drawing on "deep pockets"	Maintaining strong strategic position	Exit, harvest, maintain, or consolidate

A word of caution is in order: Although the industry life cycle is a useful framework to guide strategic choice, industries do not *necessarily evolve* through these stages. Moreover, innovations can emerge at any stage of the industry life cycle, which in turn can initiate a new cycle. Industries can also be rejuvenated, often in the declining stage.

Although the industry life cycle is a practical tool, it does not explain everything about changes in industries. Some industries may never go through the entire life cycle, while others are continually renewed through innovation. Be aware, too, that other external factors that can be captured in the PESTEL framework (introduced in Chapter 3) such as fads in fashion, changes in demographics, or deregulation can affect the dynamics of industry life cycles at any stage.

FAILED INNOVATIONS' SECOND WIND. It is also important to note that innovations that failed initially can sometimes get a second chance in a new industry or for a new application. When introduced in the early 1990s as an early wireless telephone system, Iridium's use never went beyond that by technology enthusiasts. After Motorola's failure, the technology was spun out as a standalone venture called Iridium Communications. Some 25 years later, it looks like Iridium's satellite-based communications system will get another chance of becoming a true breakthrough innovation.[58] Rather than in an application in the end-consumer market, this time Iridium is considered for global deployment by airspace authorities to allow real-time tracking of airplanes wherever they may be. The issue of being able to track airplanes around the globe at all times came to the fore in 2014, when Malaysia Airlines Flight 370 with 239 people on board disappeared without a trace and authorities were unable to locate the airplane.

For the last few decades, air traffic controllers had to rely on ground-based radar to direct planes and to triangulate their positions. A major problem with any ground-based system is that it only works over land or near the shore, but not over oceans, which cover more than 70 percent of the Earth's surface. Moreover, radar does not work in mountain ranges. Oceans and mountain terrain, therefore, are currently dead zones where air traffic controllers are unable to track airplanes.

Iridium's 66-satellite constellation now hosts the Aireon technology used for a space-based flight tracking system. By 2019, Elon Musk's SpaceX had launched the first 10 of these Iridium satellites into space to begin the construction of a space-based air traffic control system. Such a system affords air traffic controllers full visibility of, and real-time flight information from, any airplane over both sea and land. It also allows pilots greater flexibility to change routes as necessary to avoid bad weather and turbulence, thus increasing passenger convenience, saving fuel, and reducing greenhouse-gas emissions. In addition, the Aireon technology would permit planes to fly closer together (15 miles apart instead of the customary 80 miles), allowing for more air traffic on efficient routes. A research study by an independent body predicts that global deployment of Aireon can lead to a substantial improvement in air safety.

Providing the next-generation air traffic control technology and services is a huge business opportunity for Iridium Communications. National air traffic control agencies will be the main customers to deploy the new Aireon technology. This goes to show that a second chance of success for an innovation may arise, even after the timing and application of an initial technology were off.

7.4 Types of Innovation

LO 7-5

Categorize different types of innovations in the markets-and-technology framework.

Because of the importance of innovation in shaping competitive dynamics and as a critical component in formulating business strategy, we now turn to a discussion of different types of innovation and the strategic implications of each. We need to know, in particular, along

EXHIBIT 7.11 Types of Innovation: Combining Markets and Technologies

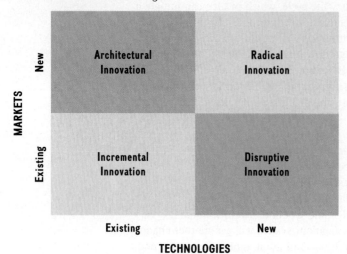

which dimensions we should assess innovations. This will allow us to formulate a business strategy that can leverage innovation for competitive advantage.

One insightful way to categorize innovations is to measure their degree of newness in terms of *technology* and *markets*.[59] Here, *technology* refers to the methods and materials used to achieve a commercial objective.[60] For example, Amazon integrates different types of technologies (hardware, software, artificial intelligence, cloud computing, logistics, and so on) to provide not only the largest selection of retail goods online, but also an array of services and mobile devices (e.g., Alexa, a digital personal assistant; Kindle tablets; Prime; cloud-computing services; and so on). We also want to understand the *market* for an innovation—e.g., whether an innovation is introduced into a new or an existing market—because an invention turns into an innovation only when it is successfully commercialized.[61] Measuring an innovation along these dimensions gives us the **markets-and-technology framework** depicted in Exhibit 7.11. Along the horizontal axis, we ask whether the innovation builds on existing technologies or creates a new one. On the vertical axis, we ask whether the innovation is targeted toward existing or new markets. Four types of innovations emerge: incremental, radical, architectural, and disruptive. As indicated by the color coding in the exhibit, each diagonal forms a pair: incremental versus radical innovation and architectural versus disruptive innovation.

INCREMENTAL VS. RADICAL INNOVATION

Although radical breakthroughs such as smartphones and magnetic resonance imaging (MRI) radiology capture most of our attention, the vast majority of innovations are actually incremental ones. An **incremental innovation** squarely builds on an established knowledge base and steadily improves an existing product or service offering.[62] It targets existing markets using existing technology.

On the other hand, **radical innovation** draws on novel methods or materials, is derived either from an entirely different knowledge base or from a recombination of existing knowledge bases with a new stream of knowledge. It targets new markets by using new technologies.[63] Well-known examples of radical innovations include the introduction of the automobile, the airplane, X-ray technology, and more recently biotechnology breakthroughs such as genetic engineering and the decoding of the human genome.

markets-and-technology framework A conceptual model to categorize innovations along the market (existing/new) and technology (existing/new) dimensions.

incremental innovation An innovation that squarely builds on an established knowledge base and steadily improves an existing product or service.

radical innovation An innovation that draws on novel methods or materials, is derived either from an entirely different knowledge base or from a recombination of the existing knowledge bases with a new stream of knowledge.

Many firms get their start by successfully commercializing radical innovations, some of which, such as the jet-powered airplane, even give birth to new industries. Although the British firm de Havilland first commercialized the jet-powered passenger airplane, Boeing was the company that rode this radical innovation to industry dominance. More recently, Boeing's leadership has been contested by Airbus; each company has approximately half the market. This stalemate is now being challenged by aircraft manufacturers such as Bombardier of Canada and Embraer of Brazil, which are moving up-market by building larger luxury jets that are competing with some of the smaller airplane models offered by Boeing and Airbus.

A predictable pattern of innovation is that firms (often new ventures) use radical innovation to create a temporary competitive advantage. They then follow up with a string of incremental innovations to sustain that initial lead. Gillette is a prime example of this pattern of strategic innovation. In 1903, entrepreneur King C. Gillette invented and began selling the safety razor with a disposable blade. This *radical innovation* launched the Gillette Co. (now a brand of Procter & Gamble). To sustain its competitive advantage, Gillette introduced its *razor-razor-blade business model* (first discussed in Chapter 5), making sure that its razors were not only inexpensive but also widely available to its customers. It also continuously improved its blades. Through a string of *incremental innovations,* Gillette kept adding a blade with each new version of its razor until the total number of blades went from one to six. Though this innovation strategy seemed predictable, it worked. One of Gillette's newest razor, the Fusion ProGlide with Flexball technology, which features a handle with a swiveling ball hinge, costs $11.49 ($12.59 for a battery-operated one) *per* razor![64] Such *overshooting* of consumer demand provided an opening for a new, low-cost entry. Enter Dollar Shave Club (see also MiniCase 5), which is disrupting Gillette's business model with its own incremental innovation, offering razors as low as $1 (thus the name). As a result, Gillette's market share in the $15 billion wet shaving industry has declined from approximately 70 percent (in 2010) to some 50 percent (in 2019).[65]

Despite its decline in market share, the Gillette example shows how radical innovation can create a competitive advantage, and how a company can sustain that advantage through follow-up incremental innovation. Such an outcome is not a foregone conclusion, though. In some instances, the innovator is outcompeted by second movers that quickly introduce a similar incremental innovation to continuously improve their own offerings. For example, although CNN was the pioneer in 24-hour cable news, today Fox News is the most watched cable news network in the United States (note: the entire cable TV industry is in decline as viewers now stream content directly via the internet, as discussed in ChapterCase 7 about Netflix). Once firms have achieved market acceptance of a breakthrough innovation, they tend to follow up with incremental rather than radical innovations. Over time, these companies morph into industry incumbents. Future radical innovations are generally introduced by new entrepreneurial ventures. Why is this so? The reasons concern *economic incentives, organizational inertia,* and the firm's embeddedness in an *innovation ecosystem.*[66]

ECONOMIC INCENTIVES. Economists highlight the role of *incentives* in strategic choice. Once an innovator has become an established incumbent firm (such as Alphabet's Google has today), it has strong incentives to defend its strategic position and market power. An emphasis on incremental innovations strengthens the incumbent firm's position and thus maintains high entry barriers. A focus on incremental innovation is particularly attractive once an industry standard has emerged and technological uncertainty is reduced. Moreover, many markets where network effects are important (such as online search), turn into **winner-take-all markets**, where the market leader captures almost all of the market share. As a near monopolist, the winner in these types of markets is able to extract a significant amount of the value created. In the United States, Google handles some 65 percent of all

winner-take-all markets Markets where the market leader captures almost all of the market share and is able to extract a significant amount of the value created.

online queries, while it handles more than 90 percent in Europe. As a result, the incumbent firm uses incremental innovation to extend the time it can extract profits based on a favorable industry structure (see the discussion in Chapter 3). Any potential radical innovation threatens the incumbent firm's dominant position.

The incentives for entrepreneurial ventures, however, are just the opposite. Successfully commercializing a radical innovation is frequently the only option to enter an industry protected by high entry barriers. One of the first biotech firms, Amgen, used newly discovered drugs based on genetic engineering to overcome entry barriers to the pharmaceutical industry, in which incumbents had enjoyed notoriously high profits for several decades. Because of differential economic incentives, incumbents often push forward with incremental innovations, while new entrants focus on radical innovations.

ORGANIZATIONAL INERTIA. From an organizational perspective, as firms become established and grow, they rely more heavily on formalized business processes and structures. In some cases, the firm may experience *organizational inertia*—resistance to changes in the status quo. Incumbent firms, therefore, tend to favor incremental innovations that reinforce the existing organizational structure and power distribution while avoiding radical innovation that could disturb the existing power distribution. Take, for instance, power distribution between different functional areas, such as R&D and marketing. New entrants, however, do not have formal organizational structures and processes, giving them more freedom to launch an initial breakthrough. We discuss the link between organizational structure and firm strategy in depth in Chapter 11.

innovation ecosystem
A firm's embeddedness in a complex network of suppliers, buyers, and complementors, which requires interdependent strategic decision making.

INNOVATION ECOSYSTEM. A final reason incumbent firms tend to be a source of incremental rather than radical innovations is that they become embedded in an **innovation ecosystem**: a network of suppliers, buyers, complementors, and so on.[67] They no longer make independent decisions but must consider the ramifications on other parties in their innovation ecosystem. Continuous incremental innovations reinforce this network and keep all its members happy, while radical innovations disrupt it. Again, new entrants don't have to worry about preexisting innovation ecosystems, since they will be building theirs around the radical innovation they are bringing to a new market.

ARCHITECTURAL VS. DISRUPTIVE INNOVATION

Firms can also innovate by leveraging *existing technologies* into *new markets.* Doing so generally requires them to reconfigure the components of a technology, meaning they alter the overall *architecture* of the product.[68] An **architectural innovation**, therefore, is a new product in which known components, based on existing technologies, are reconfigured in a novel way to create new markets.

architectural innovation A new product in which known components, based on existing technologies, are reconfigured in a novel way to attack new markets.

As a radical innovator commercializing the xerography invention, Xerox was long the most dominant copier company worldwide.[69] It produced high-volume, high-quality, and high-priced copying machines that it leased to its customers through a service agreement. Although these machines were ideal for the high end of the market such as Fortune 100 companies, Xerox ignored small and medium-sized businesses. By applying an architectural innovation, the Japanese entry Canon was able to redesign the copier so that it didn't need professional service—reliability was built directly into the machine, and the user could replace parts such as the cartridge. This allowed Canon to apply the *razor–razor-blade business model*, charging relatively low prices for its copiers but adding a steep markup to its cartridges. Xerox had not envisioned the possibility that the components of the copying machine could be put together in an altogether different way that was more user-friendly.

More importantly, Canon addressed a need in a specific consumer segment—small and medium-sized businesses and individual departments or offices in large companies—that Xerox neglected.

Finally, a **disruptive innovation** leverages *new technologies* to attack *existing markets.* It invades an existing market from the bottom up, as shown in Exhibit 7.12.[70] The dashed lines represent different market segments, from Segment 1 at the low end to Segment 4 at the high end. Low-end market segments are generally associated with low profit margins, while high-end market segments often have high profit margins. As first demonstrated by Clayton Christensen, the dynamic process of disruptive innovation begins when a firm, frequently a startup, introduces a new product or process based on a new technology to meet existing customer needs. To be a disruptive force, however, this new technology has to have additional characteristics:

1. It begins as a low-cost solution to an existing problem.
2. Initially, its performance is inferior to the existing technology, but its rate of technological improvement over time is faster than the rate of performance increases required by different market segments. In Exhibit 7.12, the solid upward curved line captures the new technology's trajectory, or rate of improvement over time.

The following examples illustrate disruptive innovations:

- Japanese carmakers successfully followed a strategy of disruptive innovation by first introducing small fuel-efficient cars and then leveraging their low-cost and high-quality advantages into high-end luxury segments, captured by brands such as Lexus, Infiniti, and Acura. More recently, the South Korean carmakers Kia and Hyundai have followed a similar strategy. Now, Chinese car manufacturers such as BYD and others are attempting to ride the wave of disruptive innovation with low-cost all-electric vehicles.
- Digital photography improved enough over time to provide higher-definition pictures. As a result, it has been able to replace film photography, even in most professional applications.
- Laptop computers disrupted desktop computers; now tablets and larger-screen smartphones are disrupting laptops.

disruptive innovation
An innovation that leverages new technologies to attack existing markets from the bottom up.

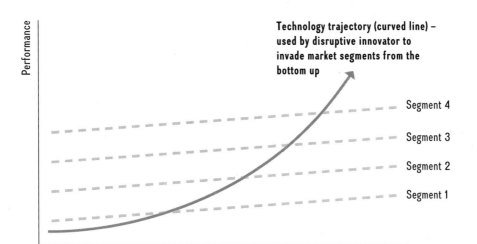

EXHIBIT 7.12

Disruptive Innovation: Riding the Technology Trajectory to Invade Different Market Segments from the Bottom Up

- Educational organizations such as Coursera and Udacity are disrupting traditional universities by offering *massive open online courses* (MOOCs), using the web to provide large-scale, interactive online courses with open access.

One factor favoring the success of disruptive innovation is that it relies on a stealth attack: It invades the market from the bottom up, by first capturing the low end. Many times, incumbent firms fail to defend (and sometimes are even happy to cede) the low end of the market, because it is frequently a low-margin business. Alphabet's Google, for example, is using its mobile operating system, Android, as a beachhead to challenge Microsoft's dominance in the personal computer industry, where 90 percent of machines run Windows.[71] Google's Android, in contrast, is optimized to run on mobile devices, the fastest-growing segment in computing. To appeal to users who spend most of their time on the web accessing e-mail and other online applications, for instance, it is designed to start in a few seconds. Moreover, Google provides Android free of charge.[72] In contrast to Microsoft's proprietary Windows operating system, Android is open-source software, accessible to anyone for further development and refinement. As a consequence, only two mobile operating systems are relevant today: Google's Android holds an 85 percent market share in mobile operating systems, while Apple's iOS has 14 percent.[73]

Another factor favoring the success of disruptive innovation is that incumbent firms often are slow to change. Incumbent firms tend to listen closely to their current customers and respond by continuing to invest in the existing technology and in incremental changes to the existing products. When a newer technology matures and proves to be a better solution, those same customers will switch. At that time, however, the incumbent firm does not yet have a competitive product ready that is based on the disruptive technology. Although customer-oriented visions are more likely to guard against firm obsolescence than product-oriented ones (see Chapter 2), they are no guarantee that a firm can hold out in the face of disruptive innovation. One of the counterintuitive findings that Clayton Christensen unearthed in his studies is that it can hurt incumbents to listen too closely to their existing customers. Apple is famous for not soliciting customer feedback because it believes it knows what customers need before they even realize it.

Netflix, featured in the ChapterCase, disrupted the television industry from the bottom up (as shown in Exhibit 7.12) with its online streaming video-on-demand service. Netflix's streaming service differentiated itself from cable television by making strategic trade-offs. By initially focusing on older "rerun TV" (such as *Breaking Bad*) and not including local content or exorbitant expensive live sport events, Netflix was able to price its subscription service considerably lower than cable bundles. Netflix improved the viewing experience by allowing users to watch shows and movies without commercial breaks and on-demand, thus enhancing perceived consumer value. By switching its focus and investments from DVD-by-post delivery service to online streaming, Netflix was able to ride the upward-sloping technology trajectory (shown in Exhibit 7.12) to invade the media industry from the bottom up, all the way to providing premium original content such as *The Crown*. Netflix's pivot to online streaming was aided by increased technology diffusion (see Exhibit 7.1) as more and more Americans adopted broadband internet connections in the 2000s.

Strategy Highlight 7.2 takes a close look at the waves of innovation in the encyclopedia business, and how Wikipedia disrupted this multibillion dollar industry.

HOW TO RESPOND TO DISRUPTIVE INNOVATION? Many incumbents tend to dismiss the threat by startups that rely on disruptive innovation because initially their product or service offerings are considered low end and too niche-focused. As late as 2010 (the year Blockbuster filed for bankruptcy), the CEO of Time Warner, one of the incumbent media companies to be disrupted by Netflix, did not take it seriously. When asked about the online

Strategy Highlight **7.2**

Wikipedia: Disrupting the Encyclopedia Business

Wikipedia, the free online multi-language encyclopedia, is often the first source that people consult for information about an unfamiliar topic, but this was not always the case. For almost 250 years, *Encyclopaedia Britannica* was the gold standard in authoritative references, delving into more than 65,000 topics with articles written by nearly 4,000 scholars—many of them Nobel laureates. The beautiful leather-bound, multivolume set of books made a decorative item in many homes. In the early 1990s, when annual total sales for encyclopedias were over $1.2 billion, *Encyclopaedia Britannica* stood as the undisputed market leader, holding more than 50 percent market share and earning $650 million in revenues. Not surprisingly, its superior differentiated appeal was highly correlated with cost, as reflected in its steep sticker price of up to $2,000.

The first wave of disruptive innovation was initiated by the introduction of Encarta. Banking on the widespread diffusion of the personal computer, Microsoft launched its electronic encyclopedia Encarta in 1993 at a price of $99. Although some viewed it as merely a CD version of the lower-cost and lower-quality Funk & Wagnalls encyclopedia sold in supermarkets, Encarta still took a big bite out of Britannica's market. Within just three years, the market for printed encyclopedias shrunk by half, along with Britannica's revenues, while Microsoft sold more than $100 million worth of Encarta CDs. This level of disruption was compounded by a later development that overtook both Encarta and printed encyclopedias.

The second wave of disruption was ultimately what drove the *Encyclopaedia Britannica* out of print in 2012. In January 2001, internet entrepreneur Jimmy Wales launched Wikipedia. In Hawaiian, *wiki* means quick, referring to the instant do-it-yourself editing capabilities of the site. Jimmy Wales identifies September 11, 2001, as a "eureka moment" for Wikipedia. Before 9/11, Wikipedia was a small niche site. Immediately following the terrorist attacks, millions of people visited the site to learn more about what they had seen and heard on the news. Massive numbers of queries for search terms such as Al-Qaeda, the World Trade Center, the Pentagon, the different airlines and airports involved, etc., made Wales realize that Wikipedia "could be big."

It has been nearly 20 years since Wikipedia's inception and it has been visited about 200 times a second, or 500 million times a month! It is ranked number five on the list of the world's most visited websites, just behind Google, YouTube (owned by Google/Alphabet), Facebook, and Baidu (the leading Chinese search engine), but before well-known sites such as Amazon, Twitter, Reddit, and Instagram (owned by Facebook). Wikipedia has more than 40 million articles written in over 300 languages, with approximately 6 million entries in English. Roughly 12,000 new pages spring up each day.

The combined effect of these two disruptive innovations (Encarta and Wikipedia) devastated the business of printed encyclopedias. Sales of the beautiful leather-bound *Encyclopaedia Britannica* volumes declined from a peak of 120,000 sets in 1990 to a mere 12,000 sets in 2010. As a consequence, Encyclopaedia Britannica Inc. announced in 2012 that it no longer would print its namesake books. Its content is now accessible via a paid subscription through its website and apps for mobile devices. Encarta, which began the disruptive cycle and had developed its own online models to supplement delivery via CD, also fell. Microsoft ceased all Encarta versions in 2009.

Wikipedia owes its success to being free to all users, open to improvement by all, and easy to use, with no registration requirements and no advertisements to suffer through. It is exclusively financed by donations. The site runs regular calls for donations using slogans such as: "Please help us feed the servers," "We make the Internet not suck. Help us out," and "We are free, our bandwidth isn't!"[74] Calls for donations also come in the form of personal appeals by co-founder Wales. These appeals are effective. In 2017, people from more than 30 countries donated some $90 million, mostly via a large number of small donations (about $15) through its website. When asked why Wales wouldn't want to monetize one of the world's most successful websites by placing targeted ads for example, he responded that running Wikipedia as a charity "just felt right, knowledge should be free for everyone."[75] The question arises whether the donation model is sustainable given not only the increasing demand for Wikipedia's services, but also the emergence of competitors.

Since Wikipedia is open source, any person, expert or novice, can contribute content and edit pages using the

(Continued)

handy "edit this page" button. Although Wikipedia has 70 million registered accounts, and any of these account holders can edit the content, Wikipedia's core is made up of its 100,000 Wikipedians— the volunteer editors and authors that represent the widely diverse views of a global community.

Although Wikipedia's volume of English entries is more than 500 times greater than that of the *Britannica*, the site is not as error-prone as one might think. Wikipedia relies on the *wisdom of the crowds*, which assumes "the many" often know more than "the expert." Moreover, user-generated content needs to be made verifiable by reliable sources such as links to reputable websites. A peer-reviewed study by *Nature* of selected science topics found that the error rates of Wikipedia and Britannica were roughly the same.[76]

Wikipedia's crowdsourcing approach to user-generated content is not without criticism. The most serious criticisms are that the content may be unreliable and not authoritative, that it could exhibit systematic bias, and that group dynamics might prevent objective and factual reporting. Many users approach Wikipedia with caution; ideally, careful researchers go to and review the sources of Wikipedia articles for verification.

Every year or so articles come out questioning the ability of Wikipedia to survive, given its uncertain funding and amorphous (and possibly shrinking) body of active volunteer editors.[77] Others note that with expanding use, the demands on its servers and infrastructure threaten to bring the enterprise down. In the meanwhile, social entrepreneur and founder Jimmy Wales keeps going. In 2017 he proposed a new and parallel effort, Wikitribune, aimed at fixing "broken" journalism.[78] His goal? Evidence-based journalism following a model similar to Wikipedia.[79]

streaming service as a potential competitor, he ridiculed the threat as equivalent to the likelihood of the Albanian army taking over the entire world.[80] It is critical to have an effective response to disruptive innovation.

Although the examples in the previous section show that disruptive innovations are a serious threat for incumbent firms, some have devised strategic initiatives to counter them:

1. *Continue to innovate in order to stay ahead of the competition.* A moving target is much harder to hit than one that is standing still and resting on existing (innovation) laurels. Amazon is an example of a company that has continuously morphed through innovation,[81] from a simple online book retailer to the largest ecommerce company, and now to include stores on the ground in the grocery sector. It also offers a personalized digital assistant (Alexa), consumer electronics (Kindle tablets), cloud computing, and content streaming, among other many other offerings (see ChapterCase 8). Netflix continued to innovate by pivoting to online streaming and away from sending DVDs through the mail.

2. *Guard against disruptive innovation by protecting the low end of the market* (Segment 1 in Exhibit 7.12) by introducing low-cost innovations to preempt stealth competitors. Intel introduced the Celeron chip, a stripped-down, budget version of its Pentium chip, to prevent low-cost entry into its market space. More recently, Intel followed up with the Atom chip, a new processor that is inexpensive and consumes little battery power, to power low-cost mobile devices.[82] Nonetheless, Intel also listened too closely to its existing personal computer customers such as Dell, HP, Lenovo, and so on, and allowed ARM Holdings, a British semiconductor design company (that supplies its technology to Apple, Samsung, HTC, and others), to take the lead in providing high-performing, low-power-consuming processors for smartphones and other mobile devices.

3. *Disrupt yourself, rather than wait for others to disrupt you.* A firm may develop products specifically for emerging markets such as China and India, and then introduce these innovations into developed markets such as the United States, Japan, or the European Union. This process is called **reverse innovation**[83] and allows a firm to disrupt itself.

reverse innovation An innovation that was developed for emerging economies before being introduced in developed economies. Sometimes also called *frugal innovation.*

7.5 Platform Strategy

LO 7-6

Explain why and how platform businesses can outperform pipeline businesses.

Up to this point in our discussion of strategy and competitive advantage, we focused mainly on businesses that operate at one or more stages of the linear value chain (introduced in Chapter 4).

A firm's value chain captures the internal activities a firm engages in, beginning with raw materials and ending with retailing and after-sales service and support. The value chain represents a linear view of a firm's business activities. As such, this traditional system of horizontal business organization has been described as a *pipeline*, because it captures a linear transformation with producers at one end and consumers at the other. Take BlackBerry as an example of a business using a linear pipeline approach based on a step-by-step arrangement for creating and transferring value. This Canadian ex-leader in smartphones conducted internal R&D, designed the phones, then manufactured them (often in company-owned plants), and finally retailed them in partner stores such as AT&T or Verizon, which offered wireless services and after-sales support.

THE PLATFORM VS. PIPELINE BUSINESS MODELS

Read the examples below, and try to figure out how these businesses' operations differ from the traditional pipeline structure described earlier.[84]

- Valued at some $50 billion in 2019 (post IPO), the ride-hailing service Uber was launched just 10 years earlier in a single city, San Francisco. Uber is not only disrupting the traditional taxi and limousine business in hundreds of cities around the globe, but also reshaping the transportation and logistics industries, without owning a single car. In the near future, Uber is planning to deploy a fleet of driverless cars; it is currently testing autonomous vehicles.

- Reaching over 2 billion people (out of a total worldwide population of some 7.5 billion), Facebook is where people get their news, watch videos, listen to music, and share photos. Garnering over $60 billion in annual advertising revenues (in 2019), Facebook has become one of the largest media companies in the world, without producing a single piece of content.

- China-based ecommerce firm Alibaba is the largest web portal that offers online retailing as well as business-to-business services on a scale that dwarfs Amazon and eBay combined. On its Taobao site (similar to eBay), Alibaba offers more than 1 billion products, making it the world's largest retailer without owning a single item of inventory. When going public in 2014 by listing on the New York Stock Exchange (NYSE), Alibaba was the world's largest initial public offering (IPO), valued at $25 billion. In early 2019, Alibaba was valued at some $500 billion (20 times the IPO valuation!), making it one of the most valuable technology companies in the world.

What do Uber, Facebook, and Alibaba have in common? They are *not* organized as traditional linear pipelines, but instead as **platform businesses**. The five most valuable companies globally (Alphabet, Amazon, Apple, Microsoft, and Facebook) all run platform business models. ExxonMobil, which runs a traditional linear business model from raw materials (fossil fuels) to distribution (of refined petroleum products) and long the most valuable company in the world, barely makes it into the top 10 (in 2019).[85] Based on the popular book *Platform Revolution* by Parker, Van Alstyne, and Choudary, platforms can be defined along three dimensions:

1. A platform is a business that enables value-creating interactions between external producers and consumers.

platform business
An enterprise that creates value by matching external producers and consumers in a way that creates value for all participants, and that depends on the infrastructure or platform that the enterprise manages.

2. The platform's overarching purpose is to consummate matches among users and facilitate the exchange of goods, services, or social currency, thereby enabling value creation for all participants.

3. The platform provides an infrastructure for these interactions and sets governance conditions for them.

The business phenomenon of platforms, however, is not a new one. *Platforms*, often also called *multi-sided markets*, have been around for millennia. The town squares in ancient cities were marketplaces where sellers and buyers would meet under a set of governing rules determined by the owner or operator (such as what type of wares could be offered, when the marketplace was open for business, which vendor would get what stand on the square, etc.). The credit card, often hailed has the most important innovation in the financial sector over the last few decades,[86] provides a more recent example of a multi-sided market. Credit cards facilitate more frictionless transactions between vendors and customers because the vendor is guaranteed payment by the bank that issues the credit card, and customers using credit cards can easily transact online without the need to carry cash in the physical world. In addition, credit card users can buy goods or services on credit based on their promise of repaying the bank.

In the digital age, *platforms* are business model innovations that use technology (such as the internet, cloud computing, artificial intelligence, etc.) to connect organizations, resources, information, and people in an interactive ecosystem where value-generating transactions (such as hailing a ride on Uber, catching up on news on Facebook, or connecting a Chinese supplier to a U.S. retailer via Alibaba) can be created and exchanged. Effective use of technology allows platform firms to drastically reduce the barriers of time and space: Information is available in real time across the globe, and market exchanges can take place effectively across vast distances (i.e., China to the United States) or even in small geographic spaces (such as Tinder, a location-based dating service).

platform ecosystem
The market environment in which all players participate relative to the platform.

THE PLATFORM ECOSYSTEM

To formulate an effective platform strategy, a first step is to understand the roles of the players within any **platform ecosystem** (see Exhibit 7.13). From a value chain perspective, *producers*

EXHIBIT 7.13 The Players in a Platform Ecosystem

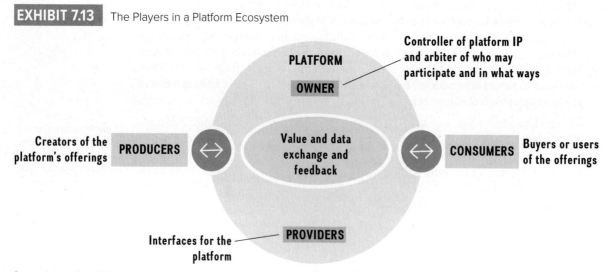

Source: Adapted from M. Van Alstyne, G. G. Parker, and S. P. Choudary (2016, April) "Pipelines, platforms, and the new rules of strategy," *Harvard Business Review.*

create or make available a product or service that *consumers* use. The *owner* of the platform controls the platform IP address and controls who may participate and in what ways. The *providers* offer the interfaces for the platform, enabling its accessibility online.

The players in the ecosystem typically fill one or more of the four roles but may rapidly shift from one role to another. For example, a producer may decide to purchase the platform to become an owner, or an owner may use the platform as a producer. Producer and consumer can also switch, for example, as when a passenger (consumer) who uses Uber for transportation decides to become an Uber driver (producer). This is an example of so-called *side switching.*

ADVANTAGES OF THE PLATFORM BUSINESS MODEL. *Platform businesses* tend to frequently outperform *pipeline businesses,* because of the following advantages:[87]

1. *Platforms scale more efficiently than pipelines by eliminating gatekeepers.* Platform businesses leveraging digital technology can also grow much faster—that is, they scale efficiently—because platforms create value by orchestrating resources that reside in the ecosystem. The platform business does not own or control these resources, facilitating rapid and often exponential growth.

In contrast, pipelines tend to be inefficient in managing the flow of information from producer to consumer. When hiring a professional services firm such as consultants or lawyers, the buyer has to purchase a bundle of services offered by the firm, for example, retaining a consulting team for a specific engagement. This team of consultants contains both senior and junior consultants, as well as administrative support staff. The client is unable to access the services of only one or two senior partners but not the rest of the team, where inexperienced junior associates are also billed at a high rate to the client. Platforms such as Upwork unbundle professional services by making available precisely defined individual services while eliminating the need to purchase a bundle of services as required by gatekeepers in old-line pipelines.

2. *Platforms unlock new sources of value creation and supply.* Consider how upstart Airbnb (featured in ChapterCase 3) disrupted the hotel industry. To grow, traditional competitors such as Marriott or Hilton would need to add additional rooms to their existing stock. To add new hotel room inventory to their chains, they would need to find suitable real estate, develop and build a new hotel, furnish all the rooms, and hire and train staff to run the new hotel. This often takes years, not to mention the multimillion-dollar upfront investments required and the risks involved.

In contrast, Airbnb faces no such constraints because it does not own any real estate, nor does it manage any hotels. Just like Marriott or Hilton, however, it uses sophisticated pricing and booking systems to allow guests to find a large variety of rooms pretty much anywhere in the world to suit their needs. As a digital platform, Airbnb allows any person to offer rooms directly to pretty much any consumer that is looking for accommodation online. Airbnb makes money by taking a cut on every rental through its platform. Given that Airbnb is a mere digital platform, it can grow much faster than old-line pipeline businesses such as Marriott. Airbnb's inventory is basically unlimited as long as it can sign up new users with spare rooms to rent, combined with little if any cost to adding inventory to its existing online offerings. Unlike traditional hotel chains, Airbnb's growth is not limited by capital, hotel staff, or ownership of real estate. In 2019, Airbnb offered over 6 million listings worldwide for rent in over 81,000 cities in some 190 countries. With its asset-light approach based on its platform strategy, Airbnb is able to offer more accommodations than the three biggest hotel chains combined: Marriott, Hilton, and Intercontinental.

3. *Platforms benefit from community feedback.* Feedback loops from consumers back to the producers allow platforms to fine-tune their offerings and to benefit from AI. TripAdvisor, a travel website, derives significant value from the large amount of quality reviews (including

pictures) by its users of hotels, restaurants, and so on. This enables TripAdvisor to consummate more effective matches between hotels and guests via its website, thus creating more value for all participants. It also allows TripAdvisor to capture a percentage of each successful transaction in the process.

Netflix also collects large amounts of data about users' viewing habits and preferences across the world. This allows Netflix to not only make effective recommendations on what to watch next, but also affords a more effective resource allocation process when making content investments. Before even producing a single episode of *House of Cards*, for example, Netflix knew that its audience would watch this series. Netflix has continued following the data, which allows the market to shape new content.

NETWORK EFFECTS. For platform businesses to succeed, however, it is critical to benefit from positive *network effects*. We provided a brief introduction of network effects earlier when discussing how to gain a foothold for an innovation in a newly emerging industry during the introduction stage of the industry life cycle. We now take a closer look at the role of network effects in platforms, including feedback loops that can initiate virtuous growth cycles leading to platform leadership.

Netflix. Consider how the video-streaming service Netflix (featured in the ChapterCase) leverages network effects for competitive advantage. Netflix's business model is to grow its global user base as large as possible and then to monetize it via monthly subscription fees. It does not offer any ads. The established customer base in the old-line DVD rental business gave Netflix a head start when entering into the new business of online streaming. Moreover, the cost to Netflix of establishing a large library of streaming content is more or less fixed, but the per unit cost falls drastically as more users join. Moreover, the marginal cost of streaming content to additional users is also extremely low (it is not quite zero because Netflix pays for some delivery of content either by establishing servers hosting content in geographic proximity of users, or paying online service providers for faster content streaming).

As Netflix acquires additional streaming content, it increases the value of its subscription service to customers, resulting in more people signing up. With more customers, Netflix could then afford to provide more and higher-quality content, further increasing the value of the subscription to its users. This created a virtuous cycle that increased the value of a Netflix subscription as more subscribers signed up (see Exhibit 7.14).

Growing its user base is critical for Netflix to sustain its competitive advantage. Netflix has been hugely successful in attracting new users: In 2019 it had 150 million subscribers worldwide. Yet, while providing a large selection of high-quality streaming content is a necessity of the Netflix business model, this element can and has been easily duplicated by others such as Amazon, Hulu, and premium services on Google's YouTube. To lock in its large installed base of users, however, Netflix has begun producing and distributing original content such as the hugely popular shows *Orange Is the New Black, The Crown, Ozark,* and *13 Reasons Why,* among others. To sustain its competitive advantage going forward, Netflix needs to rely on its core competencies, including its proprietary recommendation engine, data-driven content investments, and network infrastructure management.

EXHIBIT 7.14 Netflix Business Model: Leveraging Network Effects to Drive Demand

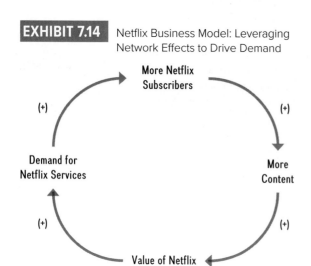

Uber. The feedback loop in network effects becomes even more apparent when taking a closer look at Uber's business model. Like many platforms, Uber performs a classic matching service. In this case, it allows riders to find drivers and drivers to find riders. Uber's deep pockets, thanks to successful rounds of fundraising, allow the startup to lose money on each ride in order to initiate a positive feedback loop. Uber provides incentives for drivers to sign up (such as extending credit so that potential drivers can purchase vehicles) and also charges lower than market rates for its rides. As more and more drivers sign up in each city and thus coverage density rises accordingly, the service becomes more convenient. This drives more demand for its services as more riders choose Uber, which in turn brings in more drivers. This positive feedback loop is shown in Exhibit 7.15.

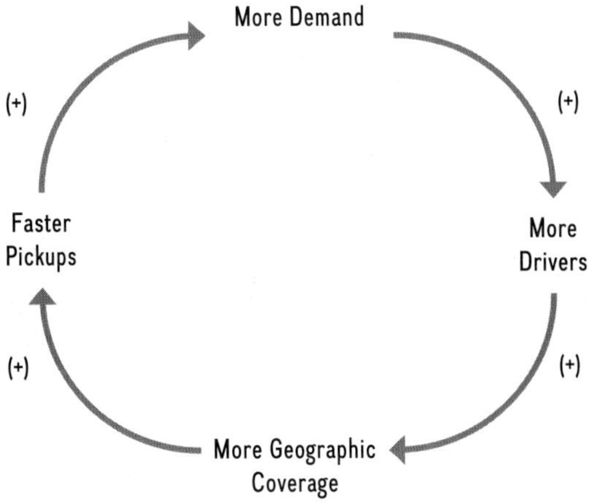

With more and more drivers on the Uber platform, both wait time for rides as well as driver downtime falls. Less downtime implies that a driver can complete more rides in a given time while making the same amount of money, even if Uber should lower its fares. Lower fares and less wait time, in turn, bring in more riders on the platform, and so on. This additional feedback loop is shown in Exhibit 7.16.

This feedback loop also explains the much hated surge pricing that Uber employs. It is based on dynamic pricing for its services depending on demand. For example, during the early hours of each New Year, demand for rides far outstrips supply. To entice more drivers to work during this time, Uber has to pay them more. Higher pay will bring more drivers onto the platform. Some users complain about surge pricing, but it allows Uber to match supply and demand in a dynamic fashion. As surge pricing kicks in, fewer people will demand rides, eventually bringing supply and demand back into an equilibrium (see Exhibit 7.16).

The ability of a platform to evince and manage positive network effects is critical to producing value for each participant, and it allows it to gain and sustain a competitive advantage. In contrast, negative network effects describe the situation where more and more users exit a platform and the value that each remaining user receives from the platform declines. The social network Myspace experienced negative network effects as more and more users

EXHIBIT 7.15 Uber's Business Model: Leveraging Network Effects to Increase Demand

More Demand

(+)   (+)

Faster
Pickups   More
                        Drivers

(+)   (+)

More Geographic
Coverage

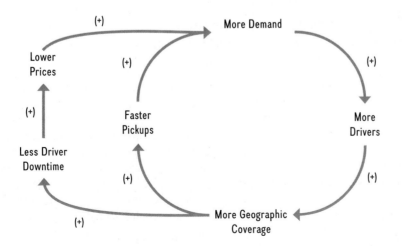

EXHIBIT 7.16

Uber's Network Effects with Feedback Loop

abandoned it for Facebook. One reason was that Myspace attempted to maximize ad revenues per user too early in its existence, while Facebook first focused on building a social media platform that allowed for the best possible user experience before starting to monetize its user base through selling ads.

7.6 Implications for Strategic Leaders

Innovation drives the competitive process. An effective innovation strategy is critical in formulating a business strategy that provides the firm with a competitive advantage. Successful innovation affords firms a temporary monopoly, with corresponding monopoly pricing power. *Fast Company* named as the 2019 most innovative companies Meituan-Dianping (Chinese tech platform and so-called "super app" as it allows and expedites a number of transactions such as food delivery, hotel stays, movie tickets, and so forth), Grab (Singapore-based ride-hailing service and market leader in Southeast Asia), the National Basketball Association (professional basketball league in the United States, which broke attendance records for four straight years), Disney (for making a major push into online streaming and thus competing head-on with Netflix), and Stitch Fix (ecommerce service using AI and supercomputers to improve buying experience).[88] Innovation lays the foundations for their competitive advantage; yet, continuous innovation is needed to sustain a competitive advantage over time.

Entrepreneurs are the agents that introduce change into the competitive system. They do this not only by figuring out how to use inventions, but also by introducing new products or services, new production processes, and new forms of organization. Entrepreneurs frequently start new ventures, but they may also be found in existing firms.

The industry life cycle model and the crossing-the-chasm framework have critical implications for how you manage innovation. To overcome the chasm, you need to formulate a business strategy guided by the who, what, why, and how questions of competition (Chapter 6) to ensure you meet the distinctly different customer needs inherent along the industry life cycle. You also must be mindful that to do so, you need to bring different competencies and capabilities to bear at different stages of the industry life cycle.

It is helpful to categorize innovations along their degree of newness in terms of *technology* and *markets*. Each diagonal pair—incremental versus radical innovation and architectural versus disruptive innovation—has different strategic implications.

Moving from the traditional pipeline business to a platform business model implies three important shifts in strategy focus:[89]

1. From resource control to resource orchestration.
2. From internal optimization to external interactions.
3. From customer value to ecosystem value.

The focus in platform strategy, therefore, shifts from traditional concepts of resource control, industry structure, and firm strategic position to creating and facilitating more or less frictionless market exchanges.

In this and the previous chapter, we discussed how firms can use *business-level strategy*—differentiation, cost leadership, blue ocean, and innovation—to gain and sustain competitive advantage. We now turn our attention to *corporate-level strategy* to help us understand how executives make decisions about *where to compete* (in terms of products and services offered, integration along the value chain, and geography) and how to execute it through strategic alliances as well as mergers and acquisitions. A thorough understanding of business and corporate strategy is necessary to formulate and sustain a winning strategy.

CHAPTER**CASE 7** Part II

ALTHOUGH HUGELY SUCCESSFUL, by 2019 Netflix found itself facing several forces threatening to undermine its ability to sustain a competitive advantage going forward. First, competition in the streaming media business had intensified significantly. Media content companies such as Disney, AT&T (owner of Time Warner, including HBO), and Comcast (owner of NBCUniversal) were forwardly integrating streaming, offering their own proprietary services. In the future, these media companies will be less inclined to continue licensing their content to Netflix.

Tech giants such as Apple and Amazon have increasingly pushed into the content business as well, offering their own fully integrated and proprietary solutions. But developing original content is pricey. HBO, for instance, spent about $10 million per one-hour of content for its hit series *Game of Thrones*. Amazon spends more than $5 billion per year on acquiring content, while Apple TV has also spent billions to build up its library of content. All these companies compete for recurring revenues from tens of millions subscribers in the United States and potentially hundreds of millions overseas. Yet, since each of these proprietary services costs somewhere around $8 to $15 a month, the total number of services a subscriber will pay for is limited. Netflix, for example, now charges $13 per month for its basic streaming service, up from just $8 per month when it was introduced in 2007 (which equates to a more than 60 percent price increase).

Second, and perhaps even more challenging, Netflix's growth in its domestic market has been declining. This implies that the U.S. market is maturing, and that Netflix's future growth must come from overseas. To achieve growth in non-U.S. markets, Netflix needs to develop original content targeted for different languages and cultures, such as its original film *Roma* (2018), a Spanish-language drama set in Mexico City that follows the life of a live-in housekeeper working for a middle-class family. Its director, Alfonso Cuarón, won an Academy Award for best director.[90]

Questions

1. How did Netflix use innovation in its business strategy to gain and sustain a competitive advantage? What role did strategy, technology, and business models play? Explain in detail.

2. Why is competition in internet streaming services heating up? Who is jumping into the fray, and why? How do these companies differ? What do you expect the result of this intensifying competition will be going forward?

3. International expansion appears to be a major growth opportunity for Netflix. Elaborate on the challenges Netflix faces going beyond the U.S. market.

   a. Do you think it is a good idea to rapidly expand to almost 200 countries in one fell swoop, or should Netflix follow a more gradual international expansion?

   b. What are some of the challenges Netflix is likely to encounter internationally? What can Netflix do to address these? Explain.

my**STRATEGY**

Do You Want to Be an Entrepreneur?

Recent years have seen a public debate around whether entrepreneurs are better off skipping college. For reasons noted below, we think this is a false debate, and we'll explain why. But before we're done, we will identify a way in which a higher education can legitimately be seen as limiting one's ability to innovate and start a new business.[91]

Let's start by acknowledging there are complex links between education and entrepreneurship and by explicitly stating our point of view: The right person can become an entrepreneur without the benefit of a college degree. But having a college degree is no impediment to becoming an entrepreneur and can further provide the benefit of formally studying the dynamics of business—just as we are doing in this class.

One volley in the debate was launched by investor Peter Thiel who, for nearly a decade, has offered $100,000 fellowships for a two-year program in lieu of attending college. Thiel argues that higher education is out of step with the business environment. Firms created by Thiel Fellows have a market capitalization of over $8 billion as of 2019.

While the very different entrepreneurs in this chapter were chosen for their business success and innovations, and not their education, they—Jeff Bezos, Sara Blakely, Reed Hastings, Elon Musk, and Jimmy Wales—all have college degrees. Some famous entrepreneurs neglected higher education (Mark Zuckerberg dropped out of Harvard; Steve Jobs dropped out of Reed College). Entrepreneurs, though, are more likely to be better educated than most business owners. Additionally, many entrepreneurs who had some college experience praise the courses, professors, or friends there with providing tremendous help in starting the firm (e.g. Jeni Bauer from Ohio State, as noted in the chapter).

But there is a more likely way in which higher education could be the enemy of entrepreneurship: the impact of large student loans. According to a report, the higher the student loan debt in an area, the lower the net creation of very small businesses. The correlation of those two factors comes with some caveats:

- These effects tend to affect only the smallest businesses, which are more likely to take on debt that's secured by the founder's own personal credit.

- The authors of the report stop short of claiming that heavy debt burdens hamper an individual's attempt.

- An alternate view of the data would be that students with high debt load go directly to higher paying corporate jobs.

1. Thinking about today's business climate, would you say that now is a good time to start a business? Why or why not?

2. Do you see higher education as a benefit or detriment to becoming a successful entrepreneur? Why?

3. Explain how you would apply the strategic management framework to enhance your startup's chances to gain and sustain a competitive advantage.

TAKE-AWAY CONCEPTS

This chapter discussed various aspects of innovation and entrepreneurship as a business-level strategy, as summarized by the following learning objectives and related take-away concepts.

LO 7-1 / Outline the four-step innovation process from idea to imitation.

- Innovation describes the discovery and development of new knowledge in a four-step process captured in the four I's: *idea, invention, innovation,* and *imitation.*
- The innovation process begins with an idea.
- An invention describes the transformation of an idea into a new product or process, or the modification and recombination of existing ones.
- Innovation concerns the commercialization of an invention by entrepreneurs (within existing companies or new ventures).
- If an innovation is successful in the marketplace, competitors will attempt to imitate it.

LO 7-2 / Apply strategic management concepts to entrepreneurship and innovation.

- Entrepreneurship describes the process by which change agents undertake economic risk to innovate—to create new products, processes, and sometimes new organizations.
- Strategic entrepreneurship describes the pursuit of innovation using tools and concepts from strategic management.
- Social entrepreneurship describes the pursuit of social goals by using entrepreneurship. Social entrepreneurs use a triple-bottom-line approach to assess performance.

LO 7-3 / Describe the competitive implications of different stages in the industry life cycle.

- Innovations frequently lead to the birth of new industries.
- Industries generally follow a predictable industry life cycle, with five distinct stages: introduction, growth, shakeout, maturity, and decline.
- Exhibit 7.10 details features and strategic implications of the industry life cycle

LO 7-4 / Derive strategic implications of the crossing-the-chasm framework.

- The core argument of the crossing-the-chasm framework is that each stage of the industry life cycle is dominated by a different customer group, which responds differently to a new technological innovation.

- There exists a significant difference between the customer groups that enter early during the introductory stage of the industry life cycle and customers that enter later during the growth stage.
- This distinct difference between customer groups leads to a big gulf or chasm, which companies and their innovations frequently fall into.
- To overcome the chasm, managers need to formulate a business strategy guided by the who, what, why, and how questions of competition.

LO 7-5 / Categorize different types of innovations in the markets-and-technology framework.

- Four types of innovation emerge when applying the existing versus new dimensions of technology and markets: incremental, radical, architectural, and disruptive innovations (see Exhibit 7.11).
- An incremental innovation squarely builds on an established knowledge base and steadily improves an existing product or service offering (existing market/existing technology).
- A radical innovation draws on novel methods or materials and is derived either from an entirely different knowledge base or from the recombination

of the existing knowledge base with a new stream of knowledge (new market/new technology).

- An architectural innovation is an embodied new product in which known components, based on existing technologies, are reconfigured in a novel way to attack new markets (new market/existing technology).
- A disruptive innovation is an innovation that leverages new technologies to attack existing markets from the bottom up (existing market/new technology).

LO 7-6 / Explain why and how platform businesses can outperform pipeline businesses.

- Platform businesses scale more efficiently than pipeline businesses by eliminating gatekeepers and leveraging digital technology. Pipeline businesses rely on gatekeepers to manage the flow of value from end to end of the pipeline. Platform businesses leverage technology to provide real-time feedback.
- Platforms unlock new sources of value creation and supply. Thus they escape the limits faced by a pipeline company working within an existing industry based on physical assets.
- Platforms benefit from community feedback. Feedback loops from consumers back to the producers allow platforms to fine-tune their offerings and to benefit from big data analytics.

KEY TERMS

Architectural innovation *(p. 258)*

Crossing-the-chasm framework *(p. 249)*

Disruptive innovation *(p. 259)*

Early adopters *(p. 250)*

Early majority *(p. 251)*

Entrepreneurs *(p. 239)*

Entrepreneurship *(p. 237)*

First-mover advantages *(p. 236)*

Incremental innovation *(p. 256)*

Industry life cycle *(p. 240)*

Innovation *(p. 236)*

Innovation ecosystem *(p. 258)*

Invention *(p. 235)*

Laggards *(p. 252)*

Late majority *(p. 252)*

Long tail *(p. 233)*

Markets-and-technology framework *(p. 256)*

Network effects *(p. 242)*

Patent *(p. 235)*

Platform business *(p. 263)*

Platform ecosystem *(p. 264)*

Process innovation *(p. 243)*

Product innovation *(p. 243)*

Radical innovation *(p. 256)*

Reverse innovation *(p. 262)*

Social entrepreneurship *(p. 240)*

Standard *(p. 243)*

Strategic entrepreneurship *(p. 239)*

Technology enthusiasts *(p. 250)*

Trade secret *(p. 235)*

Winner-take-all markets *(p. 257)*

DISCUSSION QUESTIONS

1. Patents are discussed as part of the invention phase of the innovation process in Exhibit 7.2. Describe the trade-offs that a firm makes when deciding to patent its business processes or software. Is this same trade-off applicable to tangible hardware products made by a firm?

2. Select an industry and consider how the industry life cycle affects business strategy for the firms in that industry over time. Detail your answer based on each stage: introduction, growth, shakeout, maturity, and decline.

3. Describe a firm you think has been highly innovative. Which of the four types of innovation—radical, incremental, disruptive, or architectural—did it use? Did the firm use different types over time?

4. While many new firms and industries are using a platform strategy, there are downsides to this approach. Explain two ways in which multi-sided markets may be a disadvantage for firms entering new markets.

ENDNOTES

1. Auletta, K. (2014, Feb. 3), "Outside the box: Netflix and the future of television," *The New Yorker*.

2. This chapter case is based on: Netflix annual reports (various years); Flint, J., and M. Maidenberg (2019, Apr. 16), "Netflix subscriber count rises, but growth slows at Home," *The Wall Street Journal*; Schwartzel, E. (2019, Apr. 10), "Disney's next big remake: Itself to battle Netflix," *The Wall Street Journal*; Lee, E. (2019, Mar. 22), "Why Netflix won't be part of Apple TV," *The New York Times*; "Disney, AT&T and Comcast v Netflix, Amazon and Apple," *The Economist* (2019, Mar. 30); Ramachandran, S., and T. Stynes (2016, Oct. 26), "Netflix CEO Reed Hastings talks with WSJ Financial Editor Dennis K. Berman at the 2016WSJDlive Conference in Laguna Beach, CA,"www.youtube.com/watch?v=pBg3q2vHCLg [25:04 min]; Ramachandran, S., and S. Sharma (2015, Mar. 3), "NBCU plans subscription comedy video service," *The Wall Street Journal*; Vranica, S. (2015, Mar. 10), "Streaming services hammer cable-TV ratings," *The Wall Street Journal*; Lin, L. (2015, May 15), "Netflix in talks to take content to China," *The Wall Street Journal*; Jenkins, H.W. (2015, Mar. 2017), "Netflix is the culprit," The Wall Street Journal; Jakab, S. (2015, Apr. 14), "Don't overlook Netflix's bigger picture," *The Wall Street Journal*; Armental, M., and S. Ramachandran (2015, Apr. 15), "Netflix gains more users than projected," *The Wall Street Journal*; Auletta, K. (2014, Feb. 3), "Outside the box: Netflix and the future of television," *The New Yorker*; "A brief history of the company that revolutionized watching of movies and TV shows," http://netflix.com; "A brief history of Netflix" (2014), CNN.com,www.cnn.com/2014/07/21/showbiz/gallery/netflix-history/; Ramachandran, S. (2014, Feb. 23), "Netflix to pay Comcast for smoother streaming," *The Wall Street Journal*; and Darlin, D. (2005, Aug. 20), "Falling costs of big-screen TVs to keep falling," *The New York Times*.

3. Rothaermel, F.T., and A. Hess (2010, Spring), "Innovation strategies combined," *MIT Sloan Management Review*: 12–15.

4. Schumpeter, J.A. (1942), *Capitalism, Socialism, and Democracy* (New York: Harper & Row); Foster, R., and S. Kaplan (2001), *Creative Destruction: Why Companies That Are Built to Last Underperform the Market—and How to Successfully Transform Them* (New York: Currency).

5. "Comcast, GE strike deal; Vivendi to sell NBC stake," *The Wall Street Journal* (2009, Dec. 4).

6. See: Anderson, C. (2006), *The Long Tail. Why the Future of Business Is Selling Less of More* (New York: Hachette).

7. Rothaermel, F.T., and D.L. Deeds (2004), "Exploration and exploitation alliances in biotechnology: A system of new product development," *Strategic Management Journal* 25: 201–221; Madhavan, R., and R. Grover (1998), "From embedded knowledge to embodied knowledge: New product development as knowledge management," *Journal of Marketing* 62: 1–12; and Stokes, D.E. (1997), *Pasteur's Quadrant: Basic Science and Technological Innovation* (Washington, DC: Brookings Institute Press).

8. Isaacson, W. (2007), *Einstein: His Life and Universe* (New York: Simon & Schuster).

9. A detailed description of patents can be found at the U.S. Patent and Trademark Office's website at www.uspto.gov/.

10. Hallenborg, L., M. Ceccagnoli, and M. Clendenin (2008), "Intellectual property protection in the global economy," *Advances in the Study of Entrepreneurship, Innovation, and Economic Growth* 18: 11–34; and Graham, S.J.H. (2008), "Beyond patents: The role of copyrights, trademarks, and trade secrets in technology commercialization," *Advances in the Study of Entrepreneurship, Innovation, and Economic Growth* 18: 149–171.

11. "Sweet secrets—obituary: Michele Ferrero," *The Economist* (2015, Feb. 21).

12. Schumpeter, J.A. (1942), *Capitalism, Socialism, and Democracy* (New York: Harper & Row). For an updated and insightful discussion, see Foster, R., and S. Kaplan (2001), *Creative Destruction: Why Companies That Are Built to Last Underperform the Market—and How to Successfully Transform Them* (New York: Currency). For a very accessible discussion, see McCraw, T. (2007), *Prophet of Innovation: Joseph Schumpeter and Creative Destruction* (Boston: Harvard University Press).

13. Lieberman, M.B., and D.B. Montgomery (1988), "First-mover advantages," *Strategic Management Journal* 9: 41–58.

14. Schramm, C.J. (2006), *The Entrepreneurial Imperative* (New York: HarperCollins). Dr. Carl Schramm is president of the Kauffman Foundation, the world's leading foundation for entrepreneurship.

15. Schumpeter, J.A. (1942), *Capitalism, Socialism, and Democracy* (New York: Harper

& Row); Foster, R., and S. Kaplan (2001), *Creative Destruction: Why Companies That Are Built to Last Underperform the Market—and How to Successfully Transform Them* (New York: Currency).

16. Shane, S., and S. Venkataraman (2000), "The promise of entrepreneurship as a field of research," *Academy of Management Review* 25: 217–226; Alvarez, S., and J.B. Barney (2007), "Discovery and creation: Alternative theories of entrepreneurial action," *Strategic Entrepreneurship Journal* 1: 11–26.

17. Drucker, P. (1985), *Innovation and Entrepreneurship* (New York: Harper Business), 20.

18. Auletta, K. (2014, Feb. 3), "Outside the box: Netflix and the future of television," *The New Yorker*.

19. Raz, G. (2018, Feb. 28), "How I Built This," *NPR*.

20. This vignette was written by Frank T. Rothaermel with Laura Zhang, who provided excellent research assistance. Sources: Raz, G. (2018, Feb. 28), "How I Built This," *NPR*; Sygiel, J. (2018, Feb. 28), "How the visionary founder behind Jeni's Splendid churned her ice cream dreams into reality," *Forbes*; Jeni's Splendid Ice Creams website, https://jenis.com/about/about-jeni/.

21. Greenburg, Z. O'Malley (2015), "Why Dr. Dre isn't a billionaire yet," *Forbes*, May 5; and "Dr. Dre net worth: $710 million in 2016," *Forbes*, May 5, 2016.

22. Vinton, K. (2016, Oct. 4), "Jeff Bezos becomes second richest person on the Forbes 400," *Forbes*.

23. http://elonmusk.com/.

24. Vance, A. (2015), *Elon Musk: Tesla, SpaceX, and the Quest for a Fantastic Future* (New York: Ecco).

25. This discussion is based on: "How Jimmy Wales' Wikipedia harnessed the web as a force for good," *Wired* (2013, Mar. 19).

26. Burgelman, R.A. (1983), "Corporate entrepreneurship and strategic management: Insights from a process study," *Management Science* 29: 1349–1364; Zahra, S.A., and J.G. Covin (1995), "Contextual influences on the corporate entrepreneurship-performance relationship: A longitudinal analysis," *Journal of Business Venturing* 10: 43–58.

27. Schumpeter, J.A. (1942), *Capitalism, Socialism, and Democracy* (New York: Harper & Row).

28. U.S. Patent 381968, see www.google.com/patents/US381968.

29. Hitt, M.A., R.D. Ireland, S.M. Camp, and D.L. Sexton (2002), "Strategic entrepreneurship: Integrating entrepreneurial and strategic management perspectives," in *Strategic*

Entrepreneurship: Creating a New Mindset, ed. M.A. Hitt, R.D. Ireland, S.M. Camp, and D.L. Sexton (Oxford, UK: Blackwell Publishing); Rothaermel, F.T. (2008, Oct. 12), "Strategic management and strategic entrepreneurship," Presentation at the Strategic Management Society Annual International Conference, Cologne, Germany.

30. Hitt, M.A., R.D. Ireland, S.M. Camp, and D.L. Sexton (2002), "Strategic entrepreneurship: Integrating entrepreneurial and strategic management perspectives," in *Strategic Entrepreneurship: Creating a New Mindset,* ed. M.A. Hitt, R.D. Ireland, S.M. Camp, and D.L. Sexton (Oxford, UK: Blackwell Publishing); Rothaermel, F.T. (2008, Oct. 12), "Strategic management and strategic entrepreneurship," Presentation at the Strategic Management Society Annual International Conference, Cologne, Germany; Bingham, C.B., K.M. Eisenhardt, and N.R. Furr (2007), "What makes a process a capability? Heuristics, strategy, and effective capture of opportunities," *Strategic Entrepreneurship Journal* 1: 27–47.

31. www.betterworldbooks.com/info.aspx?f=corevalues.

32. Rothaermel, F.T., and M. Thursby (2007), "The nanotech vs. the biotech revolution: Sources of incumbent productivity in research," *Research Policy* 36: 832–849; and Woolley, J. (2010), "Technology emergence through entrepreneurship across multiple industries," *Strategic Entrepreneurship Journal* 4: 1–21.

33. This discussion is built on the seminal work by Rogers, E. (1962), *Diffusion of Innovations* (New York: Free Press). For a more recent treatise, see: Baum, J.A.C., and A.M. McGahan (2004), *Business Strategy over the Industry Lifecycle, Advances in Strategic Management,* Vol. 21 (Bingley, United Kingdom: Emerald).

34. Moore, G.A. (1991), *Crossing the Chasm. Marketing and Selling Disruptive Products to Mainstream Customers* (New York: HarperCollins).

35. This discussion is based on: Schilling, M.A. (2002), "Technology success and failure in winner-take-all markets: Testing a model of technological lockout," *Academy of Management Journal* 45: 387–398; Shapiro, C., and H.R. Varian (1998), *Information Rules. A Strategic Guide to the Network Economy* (Boston: Harvard Business School Press); Hill, C.W.L. (1997), "Establishing a standard: Competitive strategy and winner-take-all industries," *Academy of Management Executive* 11: 7–25; and Arthur, W.B. (1989), "Competing technologies, increasing returns, and lock-in by historical events," *Economics Journal* 99: 116–131.

36. This discussion is based on: Schilling, M.A. (1998), "Technological lockout: An integrative model of the economic and strategic factors driving technology success and failure," *Academy of Management Review* 23: 267–284; Utterback, J.M. (1994), *Mastering the Dynamics of Innovation* (Boston: Harvard Business School Press); and Anderson, P., and M. Tushman (1990), "Technological discontinuities and dominant designs: A cyclical model of technological change," *Administrative Science Quarterly* 35: 604–634.

37. This discussion is based on: Ceccagnoli, M., and F.T. Rothaermel (2008), "Appropriating the returns to innovation," *Advances in Study of Entrepreneurship, Innovation, and Economic Growth* 18: 11–34; and Teece, D.J. (1986), "Profiting from technological innovation: Implications for integration, collaboration, licensing and public policy," *Research Policy* 15: 285–305.

38. Benner, M., and M.A. Tushman (2003), "Exploitation, exploration, and process management: The productivity dilemma revisited," *Academy of Management Review* 28: 238–256; and Abernathy, W.J., and J.M. Utterback (1978), "Patterns of innovation in technology," *Technology Review* 80: 40–47.

39. This Strategy Highlight is based on: "Big carmakers are placing vast bets on electric vehicles," *The Economist* (2019, Apr. 17); Boston, W. (2017, Jul. 5), "Volvo plans to go electric, to abandon conventional car engine by 2019," *The Wall Street Journal;* "Tesla unlocks real-time Supercharger occupancy data on vehicle map," *Teslarati* (2017, Feb. 8), www.teslarati.com/tesla-unlocks-real-time-supercharger-occupancy-data-vehicle-map/; "Tesla is now adding new stalls to existing Supercharger stations as a 'top priority,' says CEO Elon Musk,"*Electrek* (2017, Jan. 11), https://electrek.co/2017/01/11/tesla-supercharger-stations-adding-stall-top-priority-elon-musk/; "Propulsion systems: The great powertrain race," *The Economist* (2013, Apr. 20); "Tesla recharges the battery-car market," *The Economist* (2013, May 10), www.teslamotors.com/supercharger; and "Renault-Nissan alliance sells its 250,000th electric vehicle," www.media.blog.alliance-renault-nissan.com/news/24-juin-10-am/#sthash.lwx1fRYG.dpuf.

40. "Containers have been more important for globalization than freer trade," *The Economist* (2013, May 18), presents findings from the following research studies: Hummels, D. (2007), "Transportation costs and international trade in the second era of globalization," *Journal of Economic Perspectives* 21: 131–154; Baldwin, R. (2011), "Trade and industrialization after globalization's 2nd unbundling: How building and joining a supply chain are different and why it matters," *NBER Working Paper*

17716; and Bernhofen, D., Z. El-Sahli, and R. Keller (2013), "Estimating the effects of the container revolution on world trade," Working Paper, Lund University.

41. This discussion is based on: Benner, M., and M.A. Tushman (2003), "Exploitation, exploration, and process management: The productivity dilemma revisited," *Academy of Management Review* 28: 238–256; and Abernathy, W.J., and J.M. Utterback (1978), "Patterns of innovation in technology," *Technology Review* 80: 40–47.

42. www.apple.com/ipad/pricing/.

43. www.geeks.com.

44. O'Connor, C. (2012, Mar. 14), "How Sara Blakely of Spanx turned $5,000 into $1 billion," *Forbes.* The history of Spanx is documented at www.spanx.com.

45. Harrigan, K.R. (1980), *Strategies for Declining Businesses* (Lexington, MA: Heath).

46. Moore, G.A. (1991), *Crossing the Chasm. Marketing and Selling Disruptive Products to Mainstream Customers* (New York: HarperCollins).

47. We follow the customer type category originally introduced by Rogers, E.M. (1962), *Diffusion of Innovations* (New York: Free Press) and also used by Moore, G.A. (1991), *Crossing the Chasm. Marketing and Selling Disruptive Products to Mainstream Customers* (New York: HarperCollins): technology enthusiasts (~2.5%), early adopters (~13.5%), early majority (~34%), late majority (~34%), and laggards (~16%). Rogers' book originally used the term *innovators* rather than *technology enthusiasts* for the first segment. Given the specific definition of innovation as commercialized invention in this chapter, we follow Moore (p. 30) and use the term *technology enthusiasts.*

48. "For wearable computers, future looks blurry," *The Wall Street Journal* (2013, May 30).

49. Barr, A. (2015, Mar. 31), "Google Lab puts a time limit on innovations," *The Wall Street Journal.*

50. Shiller, R. (1995), "Conversation, information, and herd behavior," *American Economic Review* 85: 181–185.

51. Brickley, P. (2014, Jun. 3), "Creditors agree on Chapter 11 plan with former Fisker Automotive," *The Wall Street Journal*; "How the wheels came off for Fisker," *The Wall Street Journal* (2013, Apr. 24); and "A year of few dull moments," *The New York Times* (2012, Dec. 21).

52. The Iridium example is drawn from: Finkelstein, S. (2003), *Why Smart Executives Fail: And What You Can Learn from Their Mistakes* (New York: Portfolio).

53. In inflation-adjusted 2012 U.S. dollars. The original price in 1998 was $3,000 and the cost per minute up to $8.

54. "HP gambles on ailing Palm," *The Wall Street Journal* (2010, Apr. 29).

55. "What's gone wrong with HP?" *The Wall Street Journal* (2012, Nov. 6).

56. In 2013, RIM adopted BlackBerry as its company name.

57. Moore, G.A. (1991), *Crossing the Chasm. Marketing and Selling Disruptive Products to Mainstream Customers* (New York: HarperCollins).

58. Pasztor, A. and S. Carey (2017, Jan. 15), "Space-based flight tracking comes closer with launch of satellites," *The Wall Street Journal.*

59. Shuen, A. (2008), *Web 2.0: A Strategy Guide* (Sebastopol, CA: O'Reilly Media); Thursby, J., and M. Thursby (2006), *Here or There? A Survey in Factors of Multinational R&D Location* (Washington, DC: National Academies Press).

60. Byers, T.H., R.C. Dorf, and A.J. Nelson (2011), *Technology Entrepreneurship: From Idea to Enterprise* (New York: McGraw-Hill).

61. This discussion is based on: Schumpeter, J.A. (1942), *Capitalism, Socialism, and Democracy* (New York: Harper & Row); Freeman, C., and L. Soete (1997), *The Economics of Industrial Innovation* (Cambridge, MA: MIT Press); and Foster, R., and S. Kaplan (2001), *Creative Destruction: Why Companies That Are Built to Last Underperform the Market–and How to Successfully Transform Them* (New York: Currency).

62. The discussion of incremental and radical innovations is based on: Hill, C.W.L., and F.T. Rothaermel (2003), "The performance of incumbent firms in the face of radical technological innovation," *Academy of Management Review* 28: 257–274.

63. The discussion of incremental and radical innovations is based on: Hill, C.W.L., and F.T. Rothaermel (2003), "The performance of incumbent firms in the face of radical technological innovation," *Academy of Management Review* 28: 257–274.

64. Luna, T. (2014, Apr. 29), "The new Gillette Fusion Pro-Glide Flexball razor, to be available in stores June 9," *The Boston Globe*; and "A David and Gillette story," *The Wall Street Journal* (2012, Apr. 12).

65. Tiffany, K. (2018, Dec. 2018). "The absurd quest to make the "best" razor," *Vox,* www.vox.com/the-goods/2018/12/11/18134456/best-razor-gillette-harrys-dollar-shave-club; Chakravorti, B. (2016, July), "Unilever's big strategic bet on the Dollar Shave Club," *Harvard Business Review*; and Terlep, S.

(2016, Dec. 15), "P&G's Gillette swipes at Harry's in new ad campaign," *The Wall Street Journal.*

66. This discussion is based on: Hill, C.W.L., and F.T. Rothaermel (2003), "The performance of incumbent firms in the face of radical technological innovation," *Academy of Management Review* 28: 257–274.

67. Adner, R. (2012), *The Wide Lens. A New Strategy for Innovation* (New York: Portfolio); Brandenburger, A.M., and B.J. Nalebuff (1996), *Co-opetition* (New York: Currency Doubleday); and Christensen, C.M., and J.L. Bower (1996), "Customer power, strategic investment, and the failure of leading firms," *Strategic Management Journal* 17: 197–218.

68. Henderson, R., and K.B. Clark (1990), "Architectural innovation: The reconfiguration of existing technologies and the failure of established firms," *Administrative Science Quarterly* 35: 9–30.

69. This example is drawn from: Chesbrough, H. (2003), *Open Innovation. The New Imperative for Creating and Profiting from Technology* (Boston: Harvard Business School Press).

70. The discussion of disruptive innovation is based on: Christensen, C.M. (1997), *The Innovator's Dilemma: When New Technologies Cause Great Firms to Fail* (Boston: Harvard Business School Press); and Christensen, C.M., and M.E. Raynor (2003), *The Innovator's Solution: Creating and Sustaining Successful Growth* (Boston: Harvard Business School Press).

71. Android here is used to include Chrome OS. "Introducing the Google Chrome OS," *The Official Google Blog* (2009, Jul. 7), http://googleblog.blogspot.com/2009/07/introducing-google-chrome-os.html.

72. See the discussion on business models in Chapter 1. See also: Anderson, C. (2009), *Free. The Future of a Radical Price* (New York: Hyperion).

73. Market share worldwide smartphone shipments by operating system from 2014 to 2022, statista.com.

74. Wikipedia, http://en.wikipedia.org/wiki/Wikipedia:Donation_appeal_ideas

75. "Wikimania," *60 Minutes* (2015, Apr. 5), www.cbsnews.com/news/wikipedia-jimmy-wales-morley-safer-60-minutes/.

76. "Internet encyclopedias go head-to-head," *Nature* (2005, Dec. 15).

77. See, for example: Simonite, T. (2013, Oct. 22), "The decline of Wikipedia," *MIT Technology Review.*

78. See interview by: Smits, L. (2017, Jun. 8), "Wikipedia founder: The future of news," *Finfeed*.

79. Sources: Greenstein, S. (2017), "The reference wars: Encyclopedia Britannica's decline and Encarta's emergence," *Strategic Management Journal* 38: 995–1017; "Wikimania," *60 Minutes* (2015, Apr. 5), www.cbsnews.com/news/wikipedia-jimmy-wales-morley-safer-60-minutes/; "How Jimmy Wales' Wikipedia harnessed the web as a force for good," *Wired* (2013, Mar. 19); Greenstein, S., and F. Zhu (2012), "Is Wikipedia biased?" *American Economic Review* 102: 343–348; "End of era for Encyclopaedia Britannica," *The Wall Street Journal* (2012, Mar. 14); Greenstein, S., and F. Zhu (2012), "Is Wikipedia biased?" *American Economic Review* 102: 343–348; www.encyclopediacenter.com; www.alexa.com/topsites; "Wikipedia's old-fashioned revolution," *The Wall Street Journal* (2009, Apr. 6); Anderson, C. (2009), *Free. The Future of a Radical Price* (New York: Hyperion); "Internet encyclopedias go head-to-head," *Nature* (2005, Dec. 15); Anderson, C. (2006), *The Long Tail. Why the Future of Business Is Selling Less of More* (New York: Hyperion); Surowiecki, J. (2004), *The Wisdom of Crowds* (New York: Bantam Dell); and, of course, various Wikipedia sources.

80. Auletta, K. (2014, Feb. 3), "Outside the box: Netflix and the future of television," *The New Yorker*.

81. Rindova, V., and S. Kotha (2001), "Continuous 'morphing': Competing through dynamic capabilities, form, and function,"

Academy of Management Journal 44: 1263–1280.

82. The new processor not only is inexpensive but also consumes little battery power. Moreover, it marks a departure from the Wintel (Windows and Intel) alliance, because Microsoft did not have a suitable operating system ready for the low-end netbook market. Many of these computers are using free software such as Google's Android operating system and Google Docs for applications.

83. Govindarajan, V., and C. Trimble (2012), *Reverse Innovation: Create Far from Home, Win Everywhere* (Boston: Harvard Business Review Press).

84. This section is based on: Parker G. G., M. W. Van Alstyne and S. P. Choudary (2016), *Platform Revolution: How Networked Markets Are Transforming the Economy—and How to Make Them Work for You* (New York: Norton). Examples are updated and revised by the author or entirely new. Other sources include: Eisenmann, T., G. G. Parker, and M. W. Van Alstyne (2006, October), "Strategies for two-sided markets," *Harvard Business Review*; Gawer, A. (2014), "Bridging differing perspectives on technological platforms: Toward an integrative framework," *Research Policy* 43: 1239–1249; Gawer, A., and M. A. Cusumano (2008, Winter), "How companies become platform leaders," *MIT Sloan Management Review*: 28–35.

85. Publicly available market cap data (as of April 17, 2019).

86. Eisenmann, T., G. G. Parker, and M. W. Van Alstyne (2006, October), "Strategies for two-sided markets," *Harvard Business Review*.

87. Parker, G. G., M. W. Van Alstyne and S. P. Choudary (2016), *Platform Revolution: How Networked Markets Are Transforming the Economy—and How to Make Them Work for You* (New York: Norton), chap. 1.

88. www.fastcompany.com/most-innovative-companies/2019.

89. Parker, G. G., M. W. Van Alstyne and S. P. Choudary (2016), *Platform Revolution: How Networked Markets Are Transforming the Economy—and How to Make Them Work for You* (New York: Norton); and Parker, G. G. (2016, February), "The rise of digital platforms," *The Shard,* www.youtube.com/watch?v=r3pykplgUiw&t=2s [15:44 min].

90. Additional sources for the ChapterCase/Part II include: Flint, J., and M. Maidenberg (2019, Apr. 16), "Netflix subscriber count rises, but growth slows at Home," *The Wall Street Journal;* and Lee, E. (2019, Apr. 16), "As Netflix contends with more rivals, Hulu stands out," *The New York Times*.

91. Sources for this myStrategy include: "Why more MBAs are becoming entrepreneurs straight out of business school," *Business Insider* (2014, Jul. 24); "Top 25 colleges for entrepreneurs," *Entrepreneur* (2014, Sep. 15); "Does college matter for entrepreneurs?" *Entrepreneur* (2011, Sep. 21); "The secret to entrepreneurial success: Forget college," *Forbes* (2013, Jul. 15); "Want to be an entrepreneur: Avoid student debt," *The Wall Street Journal* (2015, May 26); "Full-time MBA programs: Stanford University," *Bloomberg Businessweek* (2008, Nov. 13).

Corporate Strategy: Vertical Integration and Diversification

Chapter Outline

Learning Objectives

After studying this chapter, you should be able to:

LO 8-1 Define corporate strategy and describe the three dimensions along which it is assessed.

LO 8-2 Explain why firms need to grow, and evaluate different growth motives.

LO 8-3 Describe and evaluate different options firms have to organize economic activity.

LO 8-4 Describe the two types of vertical integration along the industry value chain: backward and forward vertical integration.

LO 8-5 Identify and evaluate benefits and risks of vertical integration.

LO 8-6 Describe and examine alternatives to vertical integration.

LO 8-7 Describe and evaluate different types of corporate diversification.

LO 8-8 Apply the core competence–market matrix to derive different diversification strategies.

LO 8-9 Explain when a diversification strategy does create a competitive advantage and when it does not.

Amazon's Corporate Strategy

WHEN JEFF BEZOS founded Amazon, he began by selling books online. He created a makeshift office out of a garage in a Seattle suburb and furnished it with desks made out of discarded wood doors. Twenty-five years later, this fledgling online startup has become one of the world's most valuable companies active in everything from ecommerce, cloud computing, and online advertising to media entertainment, groceries, and, of course, books. In 2019 its market cap reached roughly $1 trillion. In keeping with its door-to-desk roots, strict cost control at Amazon remains paramount to its business operations.

Amazon.com went live in 1995 and became an instant success with booklovers everywhere. In pursuing its mission "to be earth's most customer-centric company," Amazon has focused on providing superior customer service, which is primarily what sets it apart from other internet merchants. Its pioneering one-click shopping, user-generated book and product reviews, and e-mail based order verification and tracking system also contribute to its customer-centric mission.

Although Amazon began as a book and CD e-tailer, it went on to become a global online trading platform. In 2000, it started Marketplace, which allows independent third-party sellers to access Amazon customers globally. In 2005, it launched its Prime membership service. Subscribers initially paid $79 (and then $99 starting in 2014) a year to receive free two-day shipping, as well as access to Amazon's video and music streaming services. By 2019, over 100 million Americans were signed up for Prime membership (which now costs $119 a year). Carrying the moniker "the everything store," Amazon has become the largest online retailer in the United States with some 50 percent market share (which equates to about 5 percent of the total retail market share in the country). In terms of brick-and-mortar stores, only Walmart is larger with about 10 percent market share and over $500 billion in annual revenues.

With its more than 100 distribution centers in the United States, Amazon has become as much a logistics company, competing with the likes of UPS and FedEx, as it has a tech company competing with Microsoft, Google, Facebook, eBay, and others. In 2016, Amazon demonstrated the feasibility of its new Prime Air service, which used drones to deliver its smaller packages. Customers would receive their packages in less than 30 minutes after ordering.

Another innovation (introduced in 2015) is Amazon-Campus, a student-centered program. Amazon runs co-branded university-specific websites (such as purdue.amazon.com) that offer textbooks, paraphernalia such as the ubiquitous logo sweatshirts and baseball hats, and even ramen noodles! As part of this new campus initiative, Amazon offers its Prime membership to students (Prime Student) free for a six-month trial period and then charges a discounted $6.49 a month (or about $78 per year). Prime Student guarantees unlimited next-day delivery of any goods ordered online, besides all the other Prime membership benefits (free streaming of media content, lending one e-book a month for free, discounts on hardware, etc.). To accomplish next-day delivery, Amazon is using fashionable delivery centers on campus, co-branded with the local university, such as "amazon@purdue." Once a package arrives, students receive a text message and can then retrieve it via code-activated lockers or from Amazon employees directly. The on-campus delivery facilities also serve as convenient return centers. Perhaps more important, having a central delivery hub on campus makes addressing the "last-mile problem" (that is delivering a package to a student's dorm room or apartment) moot. In logistics, the last-mile problem is the most expensive part of overall shipping cost; with a central hub, Amazon does not need UPS or FedEx to make the final delivery. All these process innovations allow Amazon to offer Prime Student at low cost and high convenience.

Amazon continues to diversify. Besides offering every imaginable product online, Amazon also sells its own line of consumer products (Amazon Basics) as well as electronics

Jeff Bezos is founder and CEO of Amazon.com, one of the world's most valuable companies.
Mike Kane/Bloomberg/Getty Images

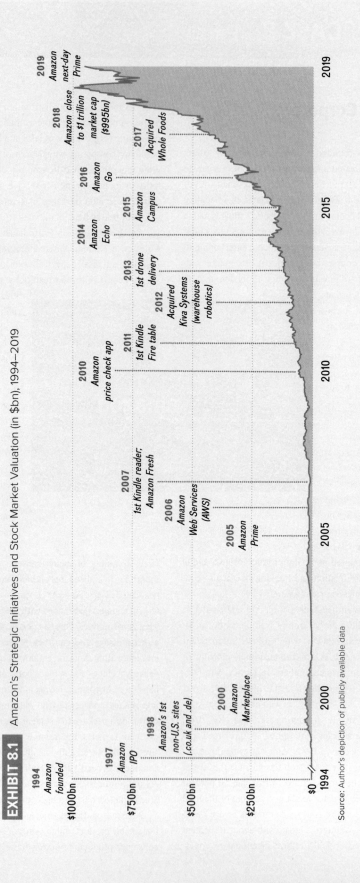

EXHIBIT 8.1 Amazon's Strategic Initiatives and Stock Market Valuation (in $bn), 1994–2019

Source: Author's depiction of publicly available data

such as e-readers, tablets, and voice-enabled wireless devices such as Echo. Among them, the Kindle e-reader (launched in 2007) has transformed the publishing industry. Amazon holds a two-thirds market share in e-books and now sells more e-books than print books. Launched in 2014, Echo is powered by Amazon's Alexa, an AI-based digital assistant that marks Amazon's foray into augmented reality. Based on simple voice commands, Alexa plays any song you request, reads aloud your audiobooks, shares the latest news and weather forecast, controls your home's thermostat and lights, and even turns on the home alarm or the yard's sprinkler system.

In 2016, the Seattle-based tech company debuted AmazonGo, where the purchase of goods, checkout, and payment are automated, thus transactions are being tracked while the consumer is shopping and there is no delay when exiting the store. In 2017, Amazon acquired Whole Foods Market, a U.S.-based organic grocer with some 500 stores nationwide. In 2019, Amazon announced next-day deliveries for its U.S.-based Prime members. Exhibit 8.1 depicts Amazon's key strategic initiatives and stock market valuation over the years.

Today, Amazon operates country-specific sites in more than a dozen countries. Amazon's geographic diversification began nearly at the outset. In 1998, to accommodate its growing popularity in Europe, it added its United Kingdom (amazon.co.uk) and German (amazon.de) sites. In 2000, it debuted its French (amazon.fr) and Japanese (amazon.co.jp) sites. In 2019, however, it withdrew from China, where tech companies Tmall (owned by Alibaba) and NetEase Kaola are the dominant players in the global online market. At the same time, Amazon made additional investments in the Middle East by launching its first Arabic-language site under its own brand (amazon.ae).

In addition to diversifying its products, services, and geography, Amazon also integrated vertically. By developing its own streaming video content with Prime Video, Amazon integrated into media production. To compete more effectively with Netflix and other entertainment companies, Amazon began creating its own original content in 2015. Amazon spent some $6 billion on original content in 2019 while Netflix spent a whopping $15 billion, outspending all media companies by a wide margin.

An example of both vertical integration and diversification is Amazon Web Services (AWS), created in 2006. AWS is a cloud-based computing service that includes software applications, data storage, content delivery, payment and billing systems, and other business applications. AWS is also the world's largest cloud-computing provider, ahead of Microsoft's Azure and Google Cloud.[1]

Part II of this ChapterCase appears in Section 8.5.

Ⓐ **OVER TIME, AMAZON** has morphed from a mere online book retailer into the "everything store."[2] In the process, it transformed into one of the world's largest online retailers. From books, Amazon diversified into consumer electronics, media content, cloud-computing services, and other business endeavors. Jeff Bezos decided to compete in a number of different industries, some related to Amazon's core business of online retailing, some unrelated.

How does a fledgling startup turn from a small online bookseller into one of the world's most valuable companies? The answer lies in Amazon's corporate strategy of vertical integration and diversification. Amazon is now a widely diversified and integrated technology company. *Vertical integration* refers to the firm's ownership of its production of needed inputs or of the channels by which it distributes its outputs. Amazon, for example, now creates its own video content, which it distributes through its streaming services. *Diversification* encompasses the variety of products and services a firm offers or markets and the geographic locations in which it competes. Amazon offers a wide range of products and services. By virtue of being an online business, Amazon has a global presence, reinforced by country-specific investments in specialized sites (such as amazon.de in Germany).

But how does Amazon's founder and CEO Jeff Bezos decide exactly *where to compete?* Answers to this important question—in terms of products and services offered, value chain activities, or geographic markets—are captured in a firm's *corporate strategy,* which we cover in the next three chapters. In this chapter, we define corporate strategy and then look at two fundamental corporate strategy topics: vertical integration and diversification. As with each chapter, we also conclude this one with *Implications for Strategic Leaders.*

LO 8-1

Define corporate strategy and describe the three dimensions along which it is assessed.

8.1 What Is Corporate Strategy?

Strategy formulation centers around the key questions of *where and how* to compete. *Business strategy* concerns the question of *how to compete* in a *single product market.* As discussed in Chapter 6, the two generic business strategies that firms can follow in their quest for competitive advantage are to increase differentiation (while containing cost) *or* lower costs (while maintaining differentiation). If trade-offs can be reconciled, some firms might be able to pursue a blue ocean strategy by increasing differentiation *and* lowering costs. As firms grow, they are frequently expanding their business activities through seeking new markets both by offering new products and services and by competing in different geographies. Strategic leaders must formulate a corporate strategy to guide continued growth. To gain and sustain competitive advantage, therefore, any corporate strategy must align with and strengthen a firm's business strategy, whether it is a differentiation, cost-leadership, or blue ocean strategy.

corporate strategy
The decisions that senior management makes and the goal-directed actions it takes to gain and sustain competitive advantage in several industries and markets simultaneously.

    Corporate strategy comprises the decisions that leaders make and the goal-directed actions they take in the quest for competitive advantage in several industries and markets simultaneously.[3] It provides answers to the key question of *where to compete.* Corporate strategy determines the boundaries of the firm along three dimensions: *vertical integration* along the industry value chain, *diversification* of products and services, and *geographic scope* (regional, national, or global markets). Strategic leaders must determine corporate strategy along these three dimensions and ask three corresponding questions:

1. *Vertical integration:* In what stages of the industry value chain should the company participate? The industry value chain describes the transformation of raw materials into finished goods and services along distinct vertical stages.

2. *Diversification:* What range of products and services should the company offer?

3. *Geographic scope:* Where should the company compete geographically in terms of regional, national, or international markets?

    In most cases, underlying these three questions is an implicit desire for growth. The need for growth is sometimes taken so much for granted that not every manager understands all the reasons behind it. A clear understanding will help strategic leaders to pursue growth for the right reasons and make better decisions for the firm and its stakeholders.

LO 8-2

Explain why firms need to grow, and evaluate different growth motives.

WHY FIRMS NEED TO GROW

Several reasons explain *why firms need to grow.* These can be summarized as follows:

- Increase profitability.
- Lower costs.
- Increase market power.
- Reduce risk.
- Motivate management.

    Let's look at each reason in turn.

INCREASE PROFITABILITY. Profitable growth allows businesses to provide a higher return for their shareholders, or owners, if privately held. For publicly traded companies, the stock market valuation of a firm is determined to some extent by expected future revenue and profit streams. As featured in the ChapterCase, Amazon's high stock market valuation is based to a large extent on expectations of future profitability, because the company invests for the long term and as such has yet to show consistent profitability.

If firms fail to achieve their growth target, their stock price often falls. With a decline in a firm's stock price comes a lower overall market capitalization, exposing the firm to the risk of a hostile takeover. Moreover, with a lower stock price, it is more costly for firms to raise the required capital to fuel future growth by issuing stock.

LOWER COSTS. Firms are also motivated to grow in order to lower their cost. As discussed in detail in Chapter 6, a larger firm may benefit from *economies of scale,* thus driving down average costs as their output increases. Firms need to grow to achieve minimum efficient scale, and thus stake out the lowest-cost position achievable through economies of scale.

INCREASE MARKET POWER. Firms might be motivated to achieve growth to increase their market share and with it their market power. When discussing an industry's structure in Chapter 3, we noted that firms often consolidate industries through horizontal mergers and acquisitions (buying competitors) to change the industry structure in their favor (we'll discuss mergers and acquisitions in detail in Chapter 9). Fewer competitors generally equates to higher industry profitability. Moreover, larger firms have more bargaining power with suppliers and buyers (see the discussion of the five forces in Chapter 3).

REDUCE RISK. Firms might be motivated to grow in order to diversify their product and service portfolio through competing in a number of different industries. The rationale behind these diversification moves is that falling sales and lower performance in one sector (e.g., GE's Power unit) might be compensated by higher performance in another (e.g., GE's Healthcare unit). Such diversified conglomerates attempt to achieve *economies of scope* (as first discussed in Chapter 6).

MOTIVATE MANAGEMENT. Firms need to grow to motivate management. Growing firms afford career opportunities and professional development for employees. Firms that achieve profitable growth can also pay higher salaries and spend more on benefits such as health insurance for its employees and paid parental leave, among other perks.

Research in behavioral economics, moreover, suggests that firms may grow to achieve goals that benefit managers more than stockholders.[4] As we will discuss in detail when presenting the *principal-agent problem* later in the chapter, managers may be more interested in pursuing their own interests such as empire building and job security—plus managerial perks such as corporate jets or executive retreats at expensive resorts—rather than increasing shareholder value. Although there is a weak link between CEO compensation and firm performance, the CEO pay package often correlates more strongly with firm size.[5]

Finally, we should acknowledge that promising businesses can fail because they grow unwisely—usually too fast too soon, and based on shaky assumptions about the future. There is a small movement counter to the need for growth, seen both in small businesses and social activism. Sometimes small-business owners operate a business for convenience, stability, and lifestyle; growth could threaten those goals. In social entrepreneurship, business micro-solutions are often operated outside of capital motives, where the need to solve a social problem outweighs the need of the firm to insure longevity beyond the solution of the problem.

THREE DIMENSIONS OF CORPORATE STRATEGY

All companies must navigate the three dimensions of corporate strategy: vertical integration, diversification, and geographic scope. Although many managers provide input, the responsibility for corporate strategy ultimately rests with the CEO.

In determining the corporate strategy for Amazon, CEO Jeff Bezos asked the three key questions:

Question 1: *In what stages of the industry value chain should Amazon participate*? With its prevalent delivery lockers in large metropolitan areas and now its many brick-and-mortar retail stores (either standalone, as part of Prime Student campus initiative, or within Whole Foods), Amazon moved forward in the industry value chain to be closer to its end customer. With its offering of Amazon-branded electronics and other everyday items, it also moved backward in the industry value chain toward product development and design as well as manufacturing, which it outsources to third-party OEMs (original equipment manufacturers). Similarly, the creation of Amazon Web Services (AWS), now the largest cloud-computing service provider globally, is a backward vertical integration move. AWS provides Amazon with back-end IT services such as website hosting, computing power, data storage and management, etc., which in turn are all critical inputs to its online retail business, but also in high demand from other businesses such as startups as well as large firms.

Question 2: *What range of products and services should Amazon offer (and not offer)?* The ChapterCase discusses Amazon's diversification over time.

Question 3: *Where should Amazon compete geographically?* Bezos decided to customize certain country-specific websites despite the instant global reach of ecommerce firms. With this strategic decision, he was also able to decide where to compete globally beyond the United States. For instance, Bezos decided to invest heavily in India, a growing ecommerce market in which Amazon faces Flipkart, a strong local competitor. Flipkart was bought by Amazon's archrival Walmart in 2018. Amazon's CEO also decides where *not* to compete, as the company's withdrawal from China makes clear.

Where to compete in terms of industry value chain, products and services, and geography are the fundamental corporate strategic decisions. The underlying strategic management concepts that will guide our discussion of vertical integration, diversification, and geographic competition are *core competencies, economies of scale, economies of scope,* and *transaction costs.*

- *Core competencies* are unique strengths embedded deep within a firm (as discussed in Chapter 4). Core competencies allow a firm to differentiate its products and services from those of its rivals, creating higher value for the customer or offering products and services of comparable value at lower cost. According to the *resource-based view of the firm,* a firm's boundaries are delineated by its knowledge bases and core competencies.[6] Activities that draw on what the firm knows how to do well (e.g., Amazon's core competency in developing proprietary recommendation algorithms based on AI) should be done in-house, while noncore activities such as payroll and facility maintenance can be outsourced. In this perspective, the internally held knowledge underlying a core competency determines a firm's boundaries.

- *Economies of scale* occur when a firm's average cost per unit decreases as its output increases (as discussed in Chapter 6). Anheuser-Busch InBev (AB InBev), the largest global brewer (producer of some 225 brands worldwide, including famous ones such as Budweiser, Bud Light, Miller, Stella Artois, and Beck's), reaps significant economies of scale. After AB InBev merged with SABMiller in a more than $100 billion deal in 2016, it now captures some 30 percent of global beer consumption.[7] As a consequence of its huge scale, the beer giant captures some 50 percent of global beer profits. In terms of beer volume, the new AB InBev is also more than double the size of Heineken, the number-two competitor worldwide. Given its tremendous size, AB InBev is able to spread its fixed costs over the millions of gallons of beer it brews each year, in addition to the significant buyer power its large market share affords. Larger market share, therefore, often leads to lower costs.

- *Economies of scope* are the savings that come from producing two (or more) outputs or providing different services at less cost than producing each individually, though using the same resources and technology (as discussed in Chapter 6). Leveraging its online retailing expertise, for example, Amazon benefits from economies of scope: It can offer a large range of different product and service categories at a lower cost than it would take to offer each product line individually. In particular, to offer millions of products to be delivered in two days or less within the United States, Amazon built more than 100 warehouses. Such large-scale investments allow the firm to take advantage of economies of scope.

- *Transaction costs* are all costs associated with an economic exchange. Applying the logic of transaction cost economics enables strategic leaders to answer the question of whether it is cost-effective for their firm to expand its boundaries through vertical integration or diversification. This implies taking on greater ownership of the production of needed inputs or of the channels by which it distributes its outputs, or adding business units that offer new products and services.

We continue our study of corporate strategy by drawing on transaction cost economics to explain vertical integration, meaning the choices a firm makes concerning its boundaries. Later, we will explore managerial decisions relating to diversification, which directly affect the firm's range of products and services in multi-industry competition. The third question of geographic scope will receive attention later, especially in Chapter 10.

8.2 The Boundaries of the Firm

LO 8-3

Describe and evaluate different options firms have to organize economic activity.

Determining the boundaries of the firm so that it is more likely to gain and sustain a competitive advantage is the critical challenge in corporate strategy.[8] **Transaction cost economics** provides useful theoretical guidance to explain and predict the boundaries of the firm. Insights gained from transaction cost economics help strategic leaders decide what activities to do in-house versus what services and products to obtain from the external market. This stream of research was initiated by Nobel Laureate Ronald Coase, who asked a fundamental question: Given the efficiencies of free markets, why do firms even exist? The key insight of transaction cost economics is that different *institutional arrangements*—markets versus firms—have different costs attached.

Transaction costs are all internal and external costs associated with an economic exchange, whether it takes place within the boundaries of a firm or in markets.[9] Exhibit 8.2 visualizes the notion of transaction costs. It shows the respective internal transactions costs within Firm A and Firm B, as well as the external transactions that occur when Firm A and Firm B do business with one another.

The total costs of transacting consist of external and internal transaction costs, as follows:

- When companies transact in the open market, they incur **external transaction costs**: the costs of searching for a firm or an individual with whom to contract, and then negotiating, monitoring, and enforcing the contract.

- Transaction costs can occur within the firm as well. Considered **internal transaction costs** these include costs pertaining to organizing an economic exchange within a firm—for example, the costs of recruiting and retaining employees; paying salaries and benefits;

transaction cost economics A theoretical framework in strategic management to explain and predict the boundaries of the firm, which is central to formulating a corporate strategy that is more likely to lead to competitive advantage.

transaction costs All internal and external costs associated with an economic exchange, whether within a firm or in markets.

external transaction costs Costs of searching for a firm or an individual with whom to contract, and then negotiating, monitoring, and enforcing the contract.

internal transaction costs Costs pertaining to organizing an economic exchange within a hierarchy; also called administrative costs.

EXHIBIT 8.2

Internal and External
Transaction Costs

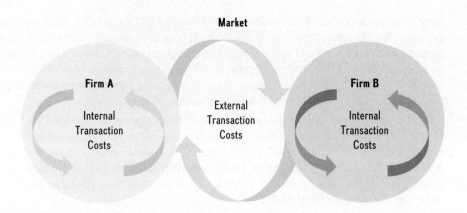

setting up a shop floor; providing office space and computers; and organizing, monitoring, and supervising work. Internal transaction costs also include administrative costs associated with coordinating economic activity between different business units of the same corporation such as transfer pricing for input factors, and between business units and corporate headquarters including important decisions pertaining to resource allocation and capital budgeting, among others. Internal transaction costs tend to increase with organizational size and complexity.

FIRMS VS. MARKETS: MAKE OR BUY?

Predictions derived from transaction cost economics guide strategic leaders in deciding which activities a firm should pursue in-house ("make") versus which goods and services to obtain externally ("buy"). These decisions help determine the boundaries of the firm. In some cases, costs of using the market such as search costs, negotiating and drafting contracts, monitoring work, and enforcing contracts when necessary may be higher than integrating the activity within a single firm and coordinating it through an organizational hierarchy. When the costs of pursuing an activity in-house are less than the costs of transacting for that activity in the market ($C_{\text{in-house}} < C_{\text{market}}$), then the firm should *vertically integrate* by owning production of the needed inputs or the channels for the distribution of outputs. In other words, when *firms* are more efficient in organizing economic activity than are *markets,* which rely on contracts among many independent actors, firms should vertically integrate.[10]

For example, rather than contracting in the open market for individual pieces of software code, Google (a unit of Alphabet) hires programmers to write code in-house. Owning these software development capabilities is valuable to the firm because its costs, such as salaries and employee benefits to in-house computer programmers, are less than what they would be in the open market. More importantly, Google gains economies of scope in software development resources and capabilities and reduces the monitoring costs. Skills acquired in writing software code for its different AI-based service offerings are transferable to new offerings. Programmers working on the original proprietary software code for the Google search engine leveraged these skills in creating a highly profitable online advertising business (AdWords and AdSense).[11] Although some of Google's software products are open source, such as the Android operating system, many of the company's internet services are based on closely guarded and proprietary software code. Google, like many leading high-tech companies such as Amazon, Apple, Facebook, and Microsoft, relies on proprietary software code and algorithms, because using the open market to transact for individual pieces of software would not only be costly, but perhaps more important, the firms would need to disclose the underlying software code to outside developers, thus negating the value-creation potential.

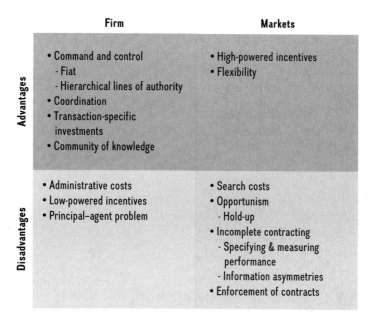

	Firm	Markets

Advantages	• Command and control
	  - Fiat
	  - Hierarchical lines of authority
	• Coordination
	• Transaction-specific
	  investments
	• Community of knowledge
		• High-powered incentives
		• Flexibility

Disadvantages	• Administrative costs
	• Low-powered incentives
	• Principal–agent problem
		• Search costs
		• Opportunism
		  - Hold-up
		• Incomplete contracting
		  - Specifying & measuring
		    performance
		  - Information asymmetries
		• Enforcement of contracts

EXHIBIT 8.3

Organizing Economic Activity: Firms vs. Markets

Firms and markets, as different institutional arrangements for organizing economic activity, have their own distinct advantages and disadvantages, summarized in Exhibit 8.3.

The advantages of firms include:

- The ability to make *command-and-control decisions* by fiat along clear hierarchical lines of authority.

- *Coordination* of highly complex tasks to allow for specialized division of labor.

- *Transaction-specific investments,* such as in AI or specialized robotics equipment that is highly valuable within the firm, but of little or no use in the external market.

- Creation of a *community of knowledge,* meaning employees within firms have ongoing relationships, exchanging ideas and working closely together to solve problems. This facilitates the development of a deep knowledge repertoire and ecosystem within firms. For example, scientists within a biotech company who worked together developing a new cancer drug over an extended time period may have developed group-specific knowledge and routines. These might lay the foundation for innovation, but would be difficult, if not impossible, to purchase on the open market.[12]

The disadvantages of organizing economic activity within firms include:

- *Administrative costs* because of necessary bureaucracy.

- *Low-powered incentives,* such as hourly wages and salaries. These often are less attractive motivators than the entrepreneurial opportunities and rewards that can be obtained in the open market.

- The *principal–agent problem.*

The **principal–agent problem** is a major disadvantage of organizing economic activity within firms, as opposed to within markets. It can arise when an agent such as a manager, performing activities on behalf of the principal (the owner of the firm), pursues his or her own interests.[13] Indeed, the *separation of ownership and control* is one of the hallmarks of a publicly traded company, and so some degree of the principal–agent problem is almost inevitable.[14] For example, a strategic leader may pursue his or her own interests such as job security and managerial

principal–agent problem Situation in which an agent performing activities on behalf of a principal pursues his or her own interests.

perks (e.g., corporate jets and golf outings) that conflict with the principal's goals—in particular, creating shareholder value. One potential way to overcome the principal–agent problem is to give stock options to strategic leaders, thus making them owners. We will revisit the principal–agent problem, with related ideas, in Chapters 11 and 12.

The advantages of markets include:

- *High-powered incentives.* Rather than work as a salaried engineer for an existing firm, for example, an individual can start a new venture offering specialized software. High-powered incentives of the open market include the entrepreneur's ability to capture the venture's profit, to take a new venture through an initial public offering (IPO), or to be acquired by an existing firm. In these so-called *liquidity events,* a successful entrepreneur can make potentially enough money to provide financial security for life.[15]
- *Increased flexibility.* Transacting in markets enables those who wish to purchase goods to compare prices and services among many different providers.

The disadvantages of markets include:

- *Search costs.* On a fundamental level, perhaps the biggest disadvantage of transacting in markets, rather than owning the various production and distribution activities within the firm itself, entails nontrivial *search costs.* In particular, a firm faces search costs when it must scour the market to find reliable suppliers from among the many firms competing to offer similar products and services. Even more difficult can be the search to find suppliers when the specific products and services needed are not offered by firms currently in the market. In this case, production of supplies would require transaction-specific investments, an advantage of firms.
- *Opportunism by other parties. Opportunism* is behavior characterized by self-interest seeking with guile (we'll discuss this in more detail later).
- *Incomplete contracting.* Although market transactions are based on implicit and explicit contracts, all contracts are incomplete to some extent, because not all future contingencies can be anticipated at the time of contracting. It is also difficult to specify expectations (e.g., What stipulates "acceptable quality" in a graphic design project?) or to measure performance and outcomes (e.g., What does "excess wear and tear" mean when returning a leased car?). Another serious hazard inherent in contracting is *information asymmetry* (which we discuss next).
- *Enforcement of contracts.* It often is difficult, costly, and time-consuming to enforce legal contracts. Not only does litigation absorb a significant amount of managerial resources and attention, but also it can easily amount to several million dollars in legal fees. Legal exposure is one of the major hazards in using markets rather than integrating an activity within a firm's hierarchy.

information asymmetry Situation in which one party is more informed than another because of the possession of private information.

Frequently, sellers have better information about products and services than buyers, which creates **information asymmetry**, a situation in which one party is more informed than another because of the possession of private information. When firms transact in the market, such unequal information can lead to a *lemons problem.* Nobel Laureate George Akerlof first described this situation using the market for used cars as an example.[16] Assume only two types of used cars are sold: good cars and bad cars (lemons). Good cars are worth $8,000 and bad ones are worth $4,000. Moreover, only the seller knows whether a car is good or is a lemon. Assuming the market supply is split equally between good and bad cars, the probability of buying a lemon is 50 percent. Buyers are aware of the general possibility of buying a lemon and thus would like to hedge against it. Therefore, they split the difference and offer $6,000 for a used car. This discounting strategy has the perverse effect of crowding out all the good cars because the sellers perceive their value to be above $6,000. Assuming that to be the case, all used cars offered for sale will be lemons.

The important take-away here is *caveat emptor—*buyer beware. Information asymmetries can result in the crowding out of desirable goods and services by inferior ones. This has been shown to be true in many markets, not just for used cars, but also in ecommerce (e.g., eBay), mortgage-backed securities, and even collaborative R&D projects.[17]

Big Pants Production/
Shutterstock

ALTERNATIVES ON THE MAKE-OR-BUY CONTINUUM

The "make" and "buy" choices *anchor each end of a continuum* from markets to firms, as depicted in Exhibit 8.4. Several alternative hybrid arrangements are available between these two extremes.[18] Moving from transacting in the market ("buy") to full integration ("make"), alternatives include short-term contracts as well as various forms of strategic alliances (long-term contracts, equity alliances, and joint ventures) and parent–subsidiary relationships.

SHORT-TERM CONTRACTS. When engaging in *short-term contracting,* a firm sends out *requests for proposals* (*RFPs*) to several companies, which initiates competitive bidding for contracts to be awarded with a short duration, generally less than one year.[19] The benefit to this approach lies in the fact that it allows a somewhat longer planning period than individual market transactions. Moreover, the buying firm can often demand lower prices due to the competitive bidding process. The drawback, however, is that firms responding to the RFP have no incentive to make any transaction-specific investments (e.g., buy new machinery to improve product quality) due to the short duration of the contract. This is exactly what happened in the U.S. automotive industry when GM used short-term contracts for standard car components to reduce costs. When faced with significant cost pressures, suppliers reduced component quality in order to protect their eroding margins. This resulted in lower-quality GM cars, contributing to a competitive advantage vis-à-vis competitors, most notably Toyota but also Ford, which used a more cooperative, longer-term partnering approach with suppliers.[20]

STRATEGIC ALLIANCES. As we move toward greater integration on the make-or-buy continuum, the next organizational forms are strategic alliances. **Strategic alliances** are voluntary

strategic alliances Voluntary arrangements between firms that involve the sharing of knowledge, resources, and capabilities with the intent of developing processes, products, or services.

EXHIBIT 8.4 Alternatives on the Make-or-Buy Continuum

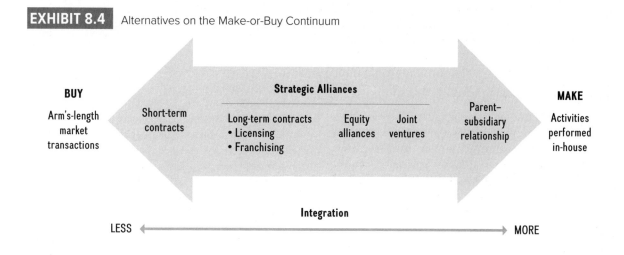

arrangements between firms that involve the sharing of knowledge, resources, and capabilities with the intent of developing processes, products, or services.[21] Alliances have become a ubiquitous phenomenon, especially in high-tech industries. Moreover, strategic alliances can facilitate investments in transaction-specific assets without encountering the internal transaction costs involved in owning firms in various stages of the industry value chain.

Strategic alliances is an umbrella term that denotes different hybrid organizational forms—among them, long-term contracts, equity alliances, and joint ventures. Given their prevalence in today's competitive landscape as a key vehicle to execute a firm's corporate strategy, we take a quick look at strategic alliances here and then study them in more depth in Chapter 9.

Long-Term Contracts. We noted that firms in short-term contracts have no incentive to make transaction-specific investments. *Long-term contracts,* which work much like short-term contracts but with a duration generally greater than one year, help overcome this drawback. Long-term contracts help facilitate transaction-specific investments. **Licensing**, for example, is a form of long-term contracting in the manufacturing sector that enables firms to commercialize intellectual property such as a patent. The first biotechnology drug to reach the market, Humulin (human insulin), was developed by Genentech and commercialized by Eli Lilly based on a licensing agreement.

In service industries, **franchising** is an example of long-term contracting. In these arrangements, a franchisor, such as McDonald's, Burger King, 7-Eleven, H&R Block, or Subway, grants a franchisee (usually an entrepreneur owning no more than a few outlets) the right to use the franchisor's trademark and business processes to offer goods and services that carry the franchisor's brand name. Besides providing the capital to finance the expansion of the chain, the franchisee generally pays an up-front (buy-in) lump sum to the franchisor plus a percentage of revenues.

Equity Alliances. Yet another form of strategic alliance is an *equity alliance*—a partnership in which at least one partner takes partial ownership in the other partner. A partner purchases an ownership share by buying stock or assets (in private companies), and thus making an equity investment. The taking of equity tends to signal greater commitment to the partnership. Strategy Highlight 8.1 describes how soft drink giant Coca-Cola Co. formed an equity alliance with energy-drink maker Monster Beverage Corp.

licensing A form of long-term contracting in the manufacturing sector that enables firms to commercialize intellectual property.

franchising A long-term contract in which a franchisor grants a franchisee the right to use the franchisor's trademark and business processes to offer goods and services that carry the franchisor's brand name.

Strategy Highlight 8.1

The Equity Alliance between Coca-Cola and Monster: A Troubled Engagement?

While Americans are drinking ever more nonalcoholic beverages, the demand for longtime staples such as the regular Coke or Pepsi are in free fall. More health-conscious consumers are moving away from sugary drinks at the expense of Coke and Pepsi, the two archrivals among colas. Unlike in the 1990s, however, Americans are not replacing them with diet sodas, but rather with bottled water and

energy drinks. Indeed, Coca-Cola was slow to catch the trend toward bottled water and other healthier choices such as vitamin water.

Protecting its wholesome image, the conservative Coca-Cola Co. also shunned energy drinks. The makers of energy drinks, such as 5-hour Energy, Red Bull, Monster, Rockstar, and Amp Energy, have faced wrongful death lawsuits. PepsiCo, on the other hand, was much more aggressive early on in moving into the energy-drink business with Amp Energy (owned by PepsiCo) and

Rockstar (distributed by PepsiCo). Indeed, over the past decade, the market for energy drinks in the United States has almost doubled in sales from some $8.7 billion in 2008 to more than $15 billion in 2018. This rapid growth, of course, did not go unnoticed in Coca-Cola's Atlanta headquarters.

Albeit late to the party, Coca-Cola decided to not miss out completely on energy drinks, one of the fastest-growing segments in nonalcoholic beverages. After years of deliberation, in 2015 the Coca-Cola Co. formed an equity alliance with Monster Beverage Corp., spending $2 billion for a nearly 17 percent stake in the edgy energy-drink company. As part of the deal, Coca-Cola is distributing Monster globally and agreed to not distribute any other energy drinks competing directly with Monster. As of 2019, Coca-Cola upped its equity stake, and now owns an 18.5 percent stake in Monster Beverage Corp.

What might have finally persuaded the traditional Coca-Cola Co. to finally make this important strategic decision? Not only was Monster the market leader with 45 percent market share in the energy-drink industry, but the company also had settled a number of wrongful death lawsuits out of court. Meanwhile, however, the U.S. Food and Drug Administration continues to investigate hundreds of "adverse event" reports allegedly linked to the consumption of energy drinks, including over 30 deaths. While the Coca-Cola Co. insists that it completed its due diligence before concluding energy drinks are safe, it hedges its bets with a minority investment in Monster rather than an outright acquisition. The equity alliance with Monster allows the market leader in nonalcoholic beverages to benefit from the explosive growth in energy drinks, while limiting potential exposure of Coca-Cola's wholesome image and brand.

Not all is well, however, with the Coca-Cola and Monster engagement. To better serve consumers who prefer all-natural ingredients in energy drinks, Coca-Cola developed two energy products (Coca-Cola Energy and Coca-Cola Energy No Sugar). Coca-Cola launched the two new energy drinks first in Europe in 2019 before introducing

The Coca-Cola Co. holds an ownership stake through an equity alliance in the Monster Beverage Corp., which sponsors the NASCAR top racing series.
Chris Graythen/Getty Images Sport/Getty Images

the new products in additional countries. Meanwhile, Monster is crying foul by arguing that these new energy drinks violate the noncompete clause in their alliance agreement. The dispute between Monster and Coca-Cola is in arbitration.

Moreover, Monster is battling other threats as well. Its 45 percent market share (some $7 billion in annual sales) has been decreasing in recent years because of new entries into the energy-drink segment, including Bang (owned by Vital Pharmaceuticals Inc.) and Adrenaline Shoc (owned by Keurig Dr Pepper), as well as a consumer push toward more natural ingredients in energy drinks. The early movers in the energy-drink segment—Monster, Red Bull, and 5-hour Energy—can't seem to shake the bad reputation they have for consumer health. Just like Coca-Cola has been slow in addressing the consumer shift away from soft drinks to water and energy drinks, so Monster has been slow to move toward all-natural ingredients. This is the segment where Coca-Cola wants to compete with its two new products, Coca-Cola Energy and Coca-Cola Energy No Sugar. In spring 2019, Monster launched a new line of energy drinks called Reign, which contains a dietary supplement for heart health.[22]

Why did the Coca-Cola Co. form an equity alliance with Monster Beverage Corp. and not just enter a short- or long-term contract, such as a distribution and profit-sharing agreement? One reason is that an equity investment in Monster might give Coca-Cola an inside look into the company. Gaining more information could be helpful if Coca-Cola decides to acquire Monster in the future. Gaining such private information might not be possible with a mere contractual agreement. Buying time is also helpful so Coca-Cola Co. can see how the wrongful death lawsuits play out, and thus limit the potential downside to Coca-Cola's wholesome brand image (as mentioned in Strategy Highlight 8.1). Making an equity investment can be seen as a "try before you buy option."

Moreover, in strategic alliances based on a mere contractual agreement, one transaction partner could attempt to *hold up* the other by demanding lower prices or threatening to walk away from the agreement (with whatever financial penalties might be included in the contract). This might be a real concern for Monster because Coca-Cola, with about $33 billion in annual sales, is about five times larger than Monster with $7 billion in revenues. To assuage Monster's concerns, with its equity investment, Coca-Cola made a **credible commitment**—a long-term strategic decision that is both difficult and costly to reverse. Even with credible commitments, however, equity alliances are no guarantee that strategic differences between partners will not arise (as detailed in Strategy Highlight 8.1).

Joint Ventures. In a **joint venture**, which is another special form of strategic alliance, two or more partners create and jointly own a new organization. Since the partners contribute equity to a joint venture, they make a long-term commitment, which in turn facilitates transaction-specific investments. Dow Corning, initially created and owned jointly by Dow Chemical and Corning, was an example of a long-standing and successful joint venture. Dow Corning focuses on silicone-based technology and employs roughly 10,000 people with $5 billion in annual revenues. That success shows that some joint ventures can be quite large.[23] Since 2017, Dow Corning is now owned by DowDuPont, after Dow Chemical and DuPont merged, creating a chemical-agricultural giant with some $120 billion in annual sales.

> **credible commitment** A long-term strategic decision that is both difficult and costly to reverse.
>
> **joint venture** A stand-alone organization created and jointly owned by two or more parent companies.

Hulu, a subscription video-on-demand service, is also a joint venture, owned by Disney (67 percent ownership, but 100 percent voting rights) and NBCUniversal (33 percent). In the United States, Hulu, with close to 30 million subscribers in 2019, is a smaller competitor to Netflix (61 million) and to Amazon Prime with its 100 million members.[24]

PARENT–SUBSIDIARY RELATIONSHIP. The *parent–subsidiary relationship* describes the most-integrated alternative to performing an activity within one's own firm boundaries (and thus anchors the make-or-buy continuum in Exhibit 8.4 on the "make" side). The corporate parent owns the subsidiary and can direct it via command and control (*fiat*). Transaction costs that arise are frequently due to political turf battles, which may include the capital budgeting process and transfer prices, among other areas. Other areas of potential conflict concern how profitable a strategic business unit is, how centralized or decentralized a subsidiary unit should be run, which type of products should be launched, and technology transfer.

GM CEO Mary Barra divested both Opel and Vauxhall by selling the GM subsidiaries to Peugeot, a French carmaker. Over many years the conflict in the parent–subsidiary relationship between GM and its European units shows that even the most integrated form of corporate relationships can be prone to high transaction costs.
Bill Pugliano/Getty Images News/Getty Images

For example, although GM owned its European carmakers (Opel in Germany and Vauxhall in the United Kingdom), it had problems bringing some of their know-how and design of small fuel-efficient cars back into the United States. This failure put GM at a competitive disadvantage vis-à-vis the Japanese competitors when the Japanese were first entering the U.S. market with more fuel-efficient cars. In addition, the Japanese carmakers were able to improve the quality and design of their vehicles faster, which enabled them to gain a competitive advantage, especially in an environment of rising gas prices. More recently, the Korean car manufacturers used the same playbook when entering the U.S. market.

The GM versus Opel and Vauxhall parent–subsidiary relationship was burdened by political problems because strategic leaders in Detroit did not respect the engineering behind the small, fuel-efficient cars that Opel and Vauxhall made. They were not interested in using

European know-how for the U.S. market and didn't want to pay much or anything for it. Indeed, executives and engineers in Detroit derided the smaller European cars as inferior, small boxes. Moreover, Detroit was tired of subsidizing the losses of Opel and Vauxhall, and felt that its European subsidiaries were manipulating the capital budgeting process.[25] In turn, the Opel and Vauxhall subsidiaries felt resentment toward their parent company: GM had threatened to shut them down as part of its bankruptcy restructuring, whereas they instead hoped to be divested as independent companies.[26]

After many years of acrimonious parent–subsidiary relationships, GM sold Opel and Vauxhall to Peugeot, a French carmaker, for a bit over $2 billion in 2017.[27] This marks GM's exit from the European car market, which has been a notorious money-losing venture for the Detroit automaker. Europe is one of the most competitive automobile markets in the world and home to several strong car brands. The European market also is consistently plagued by excess capacity because of fickle consumer tastes. Rather than focusing on being the world's largest carmaker in terms of volume, GM CEO Mary Barra is now focusing more on profitability. In contrast to Europe, GM is much stronger in its home market and highly profitable, especially in large pickup trucks and SUVs. Divesting its European operations also allows Barra to focus the Detroit-based carmaker more on growth markets in Asia, especially in China, where GM holds a strong position, with Shanghai GM Co., the 50-50 joint venture between GM and SAIC Motor Corp., a Chinese carmaker.

Having laid a strong theoretical foundation by considering transaction cost economics and the boundaries of the firm, we now turn our attention to the firm's position along the vertical industry value chain.

> **vertical integration**
> The firm's ownership of its production of needed inputs or of the channels by which it distributes its outputs.

> **industry value chain** Depiction of the transformation of raw materials into finished goods and services along distinct vertical stages, each of which typically represents a distinct industry in which a number of different firms are competing.

8.3 Vertical Integration along the Industry Value Chain

The first key question when formulating corporate strategy is: In what stages of the industry value chain should the firm participate? Deciding whether to make or buy the various activities in the industry value chain involves the concept of vertical integration. **Vertical integration** is the firm's ownership of its production of needed inputs or of the channels by which it distributes its outputs. Vertical integration can be measured by a firm's value added:

- *What percentage of a firm's sales is generated within the firm's boundaries?*[28] The degree of vertical integration tends to correspond to the number of industry value chain stages in which a firm directly participates.

Exhibit 8.5 depicts a generic **industry value chain**. Industry value chains are also called *vertical value chains* because they depict the transformation of raw materials into finished goods and services along distinct vertical stages. Each stage of the vertical value chain typically represents a distinct *industry* in which a number of different firms are competing. This is also why the expansion of a firm up or down the *vertical* industry value chain is called *vertical* integration.

EXHIBIT 8.5 Backward and Forward Vertical Integration along an Industry Value Chain

UPSTREAM INDUSTRIES

BACKWARD VERTICAL INTEGRATION

FORWARD VERTICAL INTEGRATION

DOWNSTREAM INDUSTRIES

- Stage 1 • Raw Materials
- Stage 2 • Components • Intermediate Goods
- Stage 3 • Final Assembly • Manufacturing
- Stage 4 • Marketing • Sales
- Stage 5 • After-Sales Service & Support

To explain the concept of vertical integration along the different stages of the industry value chain more fully, let's use your cell phone as an example. This ubiquitous device is the result of a globally coordinated industry value chain of different products and services:

- *Stage 1: Raw Materials.* The raw materials to make your cell phone, such as chemicals, ceramics, metals, oil for plastic, and so on, are commodities. In each of these commodity businesses are different companies, such as DuPont (United States), BASF (Germany), Kyocera (Japan), and ExxonMobil (United States).

- *Stage 2: Intermediate Goods and Components.* Elements such as integrated circuits, displays, touchscreens, cameras, and batteries are provided by firms such as ARM Holdings (United Kingdom), Jabil (United States), Intel (United States), LG Display (Korea), Altek (Taiwan), and BYD (China).

- *Stage 3: Final Assembly and Manufacturing.* Original equipment manufacturing firms (OEMs) such as Flextronics (Singapore) or Foxconn (Taiwan) typically assemble cell phones under contract for consumer electronics and telecommunications companies such as Apple (United States), Samsung and LG (both South Korea), Huawei and Oppo Electronics (both China), and others. If you look closely at an iPhone, for example, you'll notice it says, "Designed by Apple in California. Assembled in China."

- *Stages 4 and 5: Marketing, Sales, After-Sales Service, Support.* Finally, to get wireless data and voice service, you pick a service provider such as AT&T, Sprint, T-Mobile, or Verizon in the United States; América Móvil in Mexico; Oi in Brazil; Orange in France; T-Mobile or Vodafone in Germany; NTT Docomo in Japan; Airtel in India; or China Mobile in China, among others. In 2015, Google launched a low-cost wireless service in the United States. Called Google Fi, the wireless service plans offered by Google cost $20 a month for talk and text, including Wi-Fi and international coverage. Each gigabyte of data costs $10 per month. Google's goal is that by providing lower-priced wireless services, more people will connect to the internet, which means more demand for its core online search business and ad-supported YouTube video service. On the downside, initially it is available only with Google phones such as the Pixel.[29]

All of these companies—from the raw-materials suppliers to the service providers—make up the global industry value chain that, as a whole, delivers you a working cell phone. Determined by its corporate strategy, each firm decides where in the industry value chain to participate. This in turn defines the vertical boundaries of the firm.

TYPES OF VERTICAL INTEGRATION

Along the industry value chain, firms pursue varying degrees of vertical integration in their corporate strategy. Some firms participate in only one or a few stages of the industry value chain, while others comprise many if not all stages. In general, fewer firms are fully vertically integrated. Most firms concentrate on only a few stages in the industry value chain, and some firms just focus on one. The following examples illuminate different degrees of vertical integration along the industry value chain.

E&J Gallo Winery is the world's largest family-owned winery. With sales in some 90 countries, it is also the largest exporter of California wines. As a fully vertically integrated producer and distributor, it participates in all stages of the industry value chain. E&J Gallo's corporate strategy and resulting activities along the industry value chain are guided by the mantra "from grape to glass." E&J Gallo owns its own vineyards, bottling plants, distribution and logistics network, and retails via the internet where allowed. (Some states in the United States ban direct-to-consumer sale of alcoholic beverages.)

Being fully vertically integrated allows E&J Gallo to achieve *economies of scale*, resulting in lower cost. Additional operational efficiency is achieved by effective coordination such as scheduling along the industry value chain. E&J Gallo also emphasizes that being fully vertically integrated allows it to control quality better and to provide the end user with a better experience. Offering a house of brands, consisting of many different wines at different price points, also allows E&J Gallo to differentiate its product and to reap economies of scope. E&J Gallo's value added approaches 100 percent. The California winery, therefore, competes in a number of different industries along the entire vertical value chain. As a consequence, it faces different competitors in each stage of the industry value chain, both domestically and internationally.

On the other end of the spectrum are firms that are more or less vertically disintegrated with a low degree of vertical integration. These firms focus on only one or a few stages of the industry value chain. Apple, for example, focuses only on design, marketing, and retailing; all other value chain activities are outsourced.

E&J Gallo, the California winery, is fully vertically integrated, following its corporate strategy mantra "from grape to glass." E&J Gallo is also the largest exporter of California wines.

Sherri Camp/123RF

Be aware that not all industry value chain stages are equally profitable. Apple captures significant value by designing mobile devices through integration of hardware and software in novel ways, but it outsources the manufacturing to generic OEMs. The logic behind these decisions can be explained by applying Porter's five forces model and the **VRIO** model. The many small cell phone OEMs are almost completely interchangeable and are exposed to the perils of perfect competition. However, Apple's competencies in innovation, system integration, and marketing are valuable, rare, and unique (non-imitable) resources, and Apple is organized to capture most of the value it creates. Apple's continued innovation through new products and services provides it with a string of temporary competitive advantages.

Exhibit 8.6 displays part of the industry value chain for smartphones. In this figure, note HTC's transformation from a no-name OEM manufacturer in stage 2 of the vertical value chain to a player in the design, manufacture, and sale of smartphones (stages 1 and 3). It now offers a lineup of innovative and high-performance smartphones under the HTC label.[30]

Firms regularly start out as OEMs and then vertically integrate along the value chain in either a backward and/ or forward direction. With these moves, former contractual partners to brand-name phone makers such as Apple and Samsung then become their competitors. OEMs are able to

EXHIBIT 8.6 HTC's Backward and Forward Integration along the Industry Value Chain in the Smartphone Industry

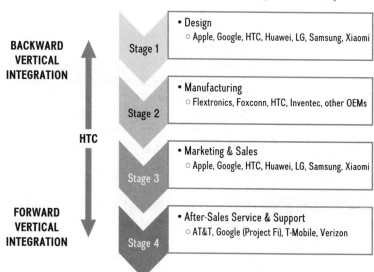

BACKWARD VERTICAL INTEGRATION

Stage 1
- Design
  - Apple, Google, HTC, Huawei, LG, Samsung, Xiaomi

Stage 2
- Manufacturing
  - Flextronics, Foxconn, HTC, Inventec, other OEMs

HTC

Stage 3
- Marketing & Sales
  - Apple, Google, HTC, Huawei, LG, Samsung, Xiaomi

FORWARD VERTICAL INTEGRATION

Stage 4
- After-Sales Service & Support
  - AT&T, Google (Project Fi), T-Mobile, Verizon

vertically integrate because they acquire the skills needed to compete in adjacent industry value chain activities from their alliance partners, which need to share the technology behind their proprietary phone to enable large-scale manufacturing.

Over time, HTC was able to upgrade its capabilities from merely manufacturing smartphones to also designing products.[31] In doing so, HTC engaged in **backward vertical integration**—moving ownership of activities upstream to the originating inputs of the value chain. Moreover, by moving downstream into sales and increasing its branding activities, HTC has also engaged in **forward vertical integration**—moving ownership of activities closer to the end customer. Although HTC has long benefited from *economies of scale* as an OEM, it is now also benefiting from *economies of scope* through participating in different stages of the industry value chain. For instance, it now can share competencies in product design, manufacturing, and sales, while at the same time attempting to reduce transaction costs.

Although, HTC with some 9 percent market share in the smartphone industry in 2011 was the third largest handset maker–just behind Samsung and Apple—the Taiwanese smartphone maker fell on hard times. By 2017, HTC's market share had plummeted to less than 1 percent. New firms from China such as Huawei, Oppo, Vivo, and Xiaomi outperformed HTC. Yet HTC's vertical integration into design as well as manufacturing and sales and marketing of smartphones allowed it build a core competency that Google, a unit of Alphabet, found valuable. Google contracted HTC to design and build its new high-end phone (the Pixel) for the California-based high-tech company. In 2017, Google acquired HTC's smartphone engineering group for $1.1 billion. Integrating HTC's smartphone unit within Google will allow engineers to more tightly integrate hardware and software. This in turn will allow Google to differentiate its high-end Pixel phone more from the competition, especially Apple's new iPhone models and Samsung's Galaxy line of phone. Even though HTC by itself lost out to Samsung, Apple, and a handful of new Chinese firms in the highly competitive smartphone industry, vertical integration along the industry value chain allowed HTC to build a core competency in the design and manufacturing of smartphones for which Google paid over $1 billion, and thus to integrate it more fully with its Android group that develops the software for Google's mobile operating system.

Likewise, Foxconn, Apple's largest OEM, is also vertically integrating along the industry value chain.[32] In 2016, it purchased the struggling Japanese electronics manufacturer Sharp for some $4 billion. Sharp is known for its high-quality display panels (used in smartphones and elsewhere) as well as other innovative consumer electronics such as microwave ovens and air purifiers.

Foxconn hopes to move upmarket by leveraging Sharp's strong brand name and to benefit from the Japanese high-tech company's efforts to produce organic light-emitting diode (OLED) displays. Similarly to HTC, Foxconn is moving backward in the industry value chain into design of consumer electronics and forward into marketing and sales by using the Sharp brand. This shows that OEMs, over time, tend to acquire skills, knowhow, and ambition to move beyond mere manufacturing, where profit margins are often razor thin.

backward vertical integration Changes in an industry value chain that involve moving ownership of activities upstream to the originating (inputs) point of the value chain.

forward vertical integration Changes in an industry value chain that involve moving ownership of activities closer to the end (customer) point of the value chain.

BENEFITS AND RISKS OF VERTICAL INTEGRATION

LO 8-5

Identify and evaluate benefits and risks of vertical integration.

To decide the degree and type of vertical integration to pursue, strategic leaders need to understand the possible benefits and risks of vertical integration. At a minimum, they need to proceed with caution and carefully consider the countervailing risks at the same time they consider the benefits.

BENEFITS OF VERTICAL INTEGRATION. Vertical integration, either backward or forward, can have a number of benefits, including[33]

- Lowering costs.
- Improving quality.
- Facilitating scheduling and planning.
- Facilitating investments in specialized assets.
- Securing critical supplies and distribution channels.

As noted earlier, HTC started as an OEM for brand-name mobile device companies such as Motorola (acquired by Google) and Nokia (acquired by Microsoft) and telecom service providers AT&T and T-Mobile. More recently, HTC has been manufacturing phones for Google (which uses Motorola's patents after its acquisition of Motorola; the handset-making unit of Motorola was sold later by Google to Lenovo, a Chinese computer company). HTC backwardly integrated into smartphone design by acquiring One & Co., a San Francisco-based design firm.[34] The acquisition allowed HTC to secure scarce design talent and capabilities that it leveraged into the design of smartphones with superior quality and features, enhancing the differentiated appeal of its products. Moreover, HTC can now design phones that leverage its low-cost manufacturing capabilities.

Likewise, forward integration into distribution and sales allows companies to more effectively plan for and respond to changes in demand. HTC's forward integration into sales enables it to offer its products directly to wireless providers such as AT&T, Verizon, and T-Mobile. HTC even offers unlocked phones directly to the end consumer via its own website. With ownership and control of more stages of the industry value chain, HTC is now in a much better position to respond if, for example, demand for its latest phone should suddenly pick up.

Vertical integration along the industry value chain can also facilitate *investments in specialized assets.* What does this mean? **Specialized assets** have a high opportunity cost: They have significantly more value in their intended use than in their next-best use.[35] They can come in several forms:[36]

- *Site specificity*—assets required to be co-located, such as the equipment necessary for mining bauxite and aluminum smelting.
- *Physical-asset specificity*—assets whose physical and engineering properties are designed to satisfy a particular customer. Examples include the bottling machinery for E&J Gallo. Given the many brands of wine offered by E&J Gallo, unique equipment, such as molds and a specific production process, is required to produce the different and trademarked bottle shapes.
- *Human-asset specificity*—investments made in human capital to acquire unique knowledge and skills, such as mastering the routines and procedures of a specific organization, which are not transferable to a different employer.

Investments in specialized assets tend to incur high opportunity costs because making the specialized investment opens up the threat of opportunism by one of the partners. *Opportunism* is defined as self-interest seeking with guile.[37] Backward vertical integration is often undertaken to overcome the threat of opportunism and to secure key raw materials.

In an effort to secure supplies and reduce the costs of jet fuel, Delta was the first airline to acquire an oil refinery. It purchased a Pennsylvania-based facility from ConocoPhillips (in 2012). Delta estimates that this backward vertical integration move not only allows it to provide 80 percent of its fuel internally, but also saves it some $300 million in costs annually.

> **specialized assets**
> Unique assets with high opportunity cost: They have significantly more value in their intended use than in their next-best use. They come in three types: site specificity, physical-asset specificity, and human-asset specificity.

Fuel costs are quite significant for airlines; for Delta, they are some 40 percent of its total operating cost.[38]

RISKS OF VERTICAL INTEGRATION. It is important to note that the risks of vertical integration can outweigh the benefits. Depending on the situation, vertical integration has several risks, some of which directly counter the potential benefits, including[39]

- Increasing costs.
- Reducing quality.
- Reducing flexibility.
- Increasing the potential for legal repercussions.

A higher degree of vertical integration can lead to increasing costs for a number of reasons. In-house suppliers tend to have higher cost structures because they are not exposed to market competition. Knowing there will always be a buyer for their products reduces their incentives to lower costs. Also, suppliers in the open market, because they generally serve a larger market, can achieve economies of scale that elude in-house suppliers. Organizational complexity increases with higher levels of vertical integration, thereby increasing administrative costs such as determining the appropriate transfer prices between an in-house supplier and buyer. Administrative costs are part of internal transaction costs and arise from the coordination of multiple divisions, political maneuvering for resources, the consumption of company perks, or simply from employees slacking off.

The knowledge that there will always be a buyer for their products not only reduces the incentives of in-house suppliers to lower costs, but also can reduce the incentive to increase quality or come up with innovative new products. Moreover, given their larger scale and greater exposure to more customers, external suppliers often can reap higher learning and experience effects and so develop unique capabilities or quality improvements.

A higher degree of vertical integration can also reduce a firm's strategic flexibility, especially when faced with changes in the external environment such as fluctuations in demand and technological change.[40] For instance, when technological process innovations enabled significant improvements in steelmaking, mills such as U.S. Steel and Bethlehem Steel were tied to their fully integrated business models and were thus unable to switch technologies, leading to the bankruptcy of many integrated steel mills. Non-vertically integrated mini-mills such as Nucor and Chaparral, on the other hand, invested in the new steelmaking process and grew their business by taking market share away from the less flexible integrated producers.[41]

U.S. regulators such as the Federal Trade Commission (FTC) and the Justice Department (DOJ) tend to allow vertical integration, arguing that it generally makes firms more efficient and lowers costs, which in turn can benefit customers. However, due to monopoly concerns, vertical integration has not gone entirely unchallenged.[42] Before engaging in vertical integration, therefore, strategic leaders need to be aware that this corporate strategy can increase the potential for legal repercussions.

Amazon, featured in the ChapterCase, is facing potential legal repercussions because of its increasing scale and scope. Amazon now accounts for roughly one-half of all internet retail spending in the United States. In addition, with AWS, physical retail stores, and drone deliveries, Amazon is increasingly becoming a fully vertically integrated enterprise. Many argue that Amazon is much like a utility, providing the backbone for internet commerce, both in the business-to-consumer (B2C) as well as in the business-to-business (B2B) space. This paints a future picture in which rivals are depending more and more on Amazon's products and services to conduct their own business. Amazon's tremendous scale and scope can bring it increasingly into conflict with governments. Antitrust enforcers such as the Department of Justice might train their sights on Amazon.

WHEN DOES VERTICAL INTEGRATION MAKE SENSE?

U.S. business saw a number of periods of higher than usual vertical integration, and looking back may reveal useful lessons on how a company can make better decisions around its corporate strategy.[43]

In the early days of automobile manufacturing, Ford Motor Co. was frustrated by shortages of raw materials and the limited delivery of parts suppliers. In response, Henry Ford decided to own the whole supply chain, so his company soon ran mining operations, rubber plantations, freighters, blast furnaces, glassworks, and its own parts manufacturer. In Ford's River Rogue plant, raw materials entered on one end, new cars rolled out the other end. But over time, the costs of vertical integration caught up, both financial costs that undid earlier cost savings and operational costs that hampered the manufacturer's flexibility to respond to changing conditions. Indeed, Ford experienced diseconomies of scale (see Exhibit 6.5) due to its level of vertical integration and the unwieldy size of its huge plants.

In the 1970s, the chipmakers and the manufacturers of electronic products tried to move into each others' business. Texas Instruments went downstream into watches and calculators. Bowmar, which at first led the calculator market, tried to go upstream into chip manufacturing and failed. The latter 2000s saw a resurgence of vertical integration. In 2009, General Motors was trying to reacquire Delphi, a parts supplier that it had sold in 1997. In the 2010s, PepsiCo and Coca-Cola Co., the two major soft drink companies, purchased bottling plants (and later divested them again).

Rita McGrath suggested that the siren call of vertical integration looms large for companies seeking to completely change the customer's experience: "An innovator who can figure out how to eliminate annoyances and poor interfaces in the chain can build an incredible advantage, based on the customers' desire for that unique solution."[44] So what should company executives do as they contemplate a firm's corporate strategy? As far back as the 1990s, the consulting firm McKinsey was counseling clients that firms had to consider carefully *why* they were looking at integrating along their industry value chain. McKinsey identified the main reason to vertically integrate: failure of vertical markets.

Vertical market failure occurs when transactions within the industry value chain are too risky, and alternatives to integration are too costly or difficult to administer. This recommendation corresponds with the one derived from transaction cost economics earlier in this chapter. When discussing research on vertical integration, *The Economist* concluded, "Although reliance on [external] supply chains has risks, owning parts of the supply chain can be riskier—for example, few clothing-makers want to own textile factories, with their pollution risks and slim profits." The findings suggest that when a company vertically integrates two or more steps away from its core competency, it fails two-thirds of the time.[45]

> **vertical market failure**
> When the markets along the industry value chain are too risky, and alternatives too costly in time or money.

The risks of vertical integration and the difficulty of getting it right bring us to look at alternatives that allow companies to gain some of the benefits of vertical integration without the risks of full ownership of the supply chain.

ALTERNATIVES TO VERTICAL INTEGRATION

> **LO 8-6**
> Describe and examine alternatives to vertical integration.

Ideally, one would like to find alternatives to vertical integration that provide similar benefits without the accompanying risks. Taper integration and strategic outsourcing are two such alternatives.

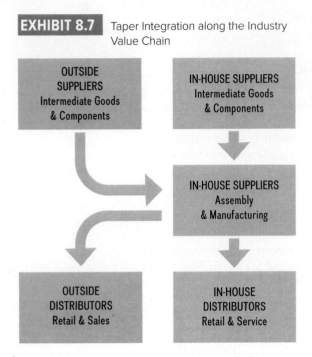

EXHIBIT 8.7 Taper Integration along the Industry Value Chain

TAPER INTEGRATION. One alternative to vertical integration is **taper integration**. It is a way of orchestrating value activities in which a firm is backwardly integrated, but it also relies on outside-market firms for some of its supplies, and/or is forwardly integrated but also relies on outside-market firms for some if its distribution.[46] Exhibit 8.7 illustrates the concept of taper integration along the vertical industry value chain. Here, the firm sources intermediate goods and components from in-house suppliers as well as outside suppliers. In a similar fashion, a firm sells its products through company-owned retail outlets and through independent retailers. Both Apple and Nike, for example, use taper integration: They own retail outlets but also use other retailers, both the brick-and-mortar type and online.

Taper integration has several benefits:[47]

- It exposes in-house suppliers and distributors to market competition so that performance comparisons are possible. Rather than hollowing out its competencies by relying too much on outsourcing, taper integration allows a firm to retain and fine-tune its competencies in upstream and downstream value chain activities.[48]

taper integration A way of orchestrating value activities in which a firm is backwardly integrated but also relies on outside-market firms for some of its supplies and/or is forwardly integrated but also relies on outside-market firms for some of its distribution.

- Taper integration also enhances a firm's flexibility. For example, when adjusting to fluctuations in demand, a firm could cut back on the finished goods it delivers to external retailers while continuing to stock its own stores.

- Using taper integration, firms can combine internal and external knowledge, possibly paving the path for innovation.

Based on a study of 3,500 product introductions in the computer industry, researchers have provided empirical evidence that taper integration can be beneficial.[49] Firms that pursued taper integration achieved superior performance in both innovation and financial performance when compared with firms that relied more on vertical integration or strategic outsourcing.

strategic outsourcing Moving one or more internal value chain activities outside the firm's boundaries to other firms in the industry value chain.

STRATEGIC OUTSOURCING. Another alternative to vertical integration is **strategic outsourcing**, which involves moving one or more internal value chain activities outside the firm's boundaries to other firms in the industry value chain. A firm that engages in strategic outsourcing reduces its level of vertical integration. Rather than developing their own human resource management systems, for instance, firms outsource these noncore activities to companies such as PeopleSoft (owned by Oracle), EDS (owned by HP), or Perot Systems (owned by Dell), which can leverage their deep competencies and produce scale effects.

In the popular media and in everyday conversation, you may hear the term *outsourcing* used to mean sending jobs out of the country. Actually, when outsourced activities take place outside the home country, the correct term is *offshoring* (or *offshore outsourcing*). For example, Infosys, one of the world's largest technology companies and providers of IT services to many Fortune 100 companies, is located in Bangalore, India. The global offshoring market for services peaked at more than $1 trillion in 2015, but has since been declining somewhat.[50] Banking and financial services, IT, and health care are the most active sectors in such offshore outsourcing. U.S. law firms are also offshoring low-end legal work, such as drafting standard contracts and background research, to India.[51] We discuss *global strategy* in detail in Chapter 10.

8.4 Corporate Diversification: Expanding Beyond a Single Market

Early in the chapter, we listed three questions related to corporate strategy and, in particular, the boundaries of the firm. We discussed the first question of defining corporate strategy in detail:

1. *Vertical integration: In what stages of the industry value chain should the firm participate?*

We explored this question primarily in terms of firm boundaries based on the *degree of vertical integration.* We now turn to the second and third questions that determine corporate strategy and the boundaries of the firm.

2. *Product diversification: What range of products and services should the firm offer?*

The second question relates to the firm's *degree of product diversification:* What range of products and services should the firm offer? In particular, why do some companies compete in a single product market, while others compete in several different product markets? Coca-Cola Co., for example, focuses on soft drinks and thus on a *single* product market. Its archrival PepsiCo competes directly with Coca-Cola by selling a wide variety of soft drinks and other beverages, and also offering different types of chips such as Lay's, Doritos, and Cheetos, as well as Quaker Oats products such as oatmeal and granola bars. Although PepsiCo is more diversified than Coca-Cola, it has reduced its level of diversification in recent years.

3. *Geographic diversification: Where should the firm compete in terms of regional, national, or international markets?*

The third and final of the key questions concerns *where to compete* in terms of regional, national, or international markets. This decision determines the firm's *degree of geographic diversification.* For example, why do some firms compete beyond state boundaries, while others are content to focus on the local market? Why do some firms compete beyond their national borders, while others prefer to focus on the domestic market?

Kentucky Fried Chicken (KFC), the world's largest quick-service chicken restaurant chain, operates 20,000 outlets in some 120 countries.[52] Interestingly, KFC has more restaurants in China with over 5,000 outlets than in the United States, its birthplace, with some 4,500 outlets. Of course, China has 1.4 billion people and the United States has a mere 320 million. Former PepsiCo CEO Indra Nooyi was instrumental in spinning out KFC, as well as Pizza Hut and Taco Bell, to reduce PepsiCo's level of diversification. In 1997, the three fast food chains were established as an independent company under the name Yum Brands. In 2014, Yum Brands' annual revenues were $13 billion. In 2016, after being pressured by activist investors, Yum Brands sold a stake in its China operation to Alibaba Group (a Chinese internet conglomerate) and an individual Chinese investor. After spinning out its China operation, the remaining Yum Brands had annual revenues of close to $6 billion in 2018.[53] The activist investors argued that Yum's China operation was really the crown jewel in Yum Brand's portfolio, and that more value for shareholders would be unlocked if the China operation would be managed as a standalone unit, rather than being part of the geographically diversified Yum Brands.[54]

Compare KFC, active in 120 countries, with the privately held Chick-fil-A, the world's second-largest quick-service chicken restaurant.[55] KFC and Chick-fil-A are direct competitors in the United States, both specializing in chicken in the fast food market. But Chick-fil-A operates only in the United States;[56] by 2018 it had over 2,200 locations across

47 states (only Hawaii, Alaska, and Vermont have no Chick-fil-A outlets), and earned than $10 billion in sales.

Why are KFC and Chick-fil-A pursuing different corporate strategies? Although both companies were founded roughly during the same time period (KFC in 1930 and Chick-fil-A in 1946), one big difference between KFC and Chick-fil-A is the ownership structure. KFC is a publicly traded stock company, as part of Yum Brands (stock ticker symbol: YUM) and Yum China (traded under YUMC, also on the New York Stock Exchange). Chick-fil-A, in contrast, is privately owned. Indeed, the privately owned Chick-fil-A is one of the largest family-owned businesses in the United States.

Public companies are often expected by shareholders to achieve profitable growth to result in an appreciation of the stock price and thus an increase in shareholder value (see the discussion in Chapter 5). That is also the reason Yum's China operation was spun off from Yum Brands, because it is performing much better. In addition, investors were concerned that the lower-performing units at Yum Brands (e.g., KFC in the United States) would continue to be subsidized by the higher-performing China unit.

In contrast, private companies generally grow slower than public companies because their growth is mostly financed through retained earnings and debt rather than equity. Before an initial public offering, private companies do not have the option to sell shares (equity) to the public to fuel growth. This is one explanation why KFC focuses on international markets, especially China, where future expected growth continues to be high, while Chick-fil-A focuses on the domestic U.S. market. KFC is geographically diversified, while Chick-fil-A is not.

Answers to questions about the number of markets to compete in and where to compete geographically relate to the broad topic of **diversification**. A firm that engages in diversification increases the variety of products and services it offers or markets and the geographic regions in which it competes. A *non-diversified company* focuses on a single market, whereas a *diversified company* competes in several different markets simultaneously.[57]

There are various general diversification strategies:

- A firm that is active in several different product markets is pursuing a **product diversification strategy**.
- A firm that is active in several different countries is pursuing a **geographic diversification strategy**.
- A company that pursues *both* a product *and* a geographic diversification strategy simultaneously follows a **product–market diversification strategy**.

Because shareholders expect continuous growth from public companies, strategic leaders frequently turn to product and geographic diversification to achieve it. It is therefore not surprising that the vast majority of the Fortune 500 companies are diversified to some degree. Achieving performance gains through diversification, however, is not guaranteed. Some forms of diversification are more likely to lead to performance improvements than others. We now discuss which diversification types are more likely to lead to a competitive advantage, and why.

diversification An increase in the variety of products and services a firm offers or markets and the geographic regions in which it competes.

product diversification strategy Corporate strategy in which a firm is active in several different product markets.

geographic diversification strategy Corporate strategy in which a firm is active in several different countries.

product–market diversification strategy Corporate strategy in which a firm is active in several different product markets and several different countries.

TYPES OF CORPORATE DIVERSIFICATION

LO 8-7

Describe and evaluate different types of corporate diversification.

To understand the different types and degrees of corporate diversification, Richard Rumelt developed a helpful classification scheme that identifies four main types of diversification by identifying two key variables:[58]

- The *percentage of revenue* from the dominant or primary business.
- The *relationship of the core competencies* across the business units.

Note that this classification scheme concerns product markets, and not geographic diversification. Knowing the percentage of revenue of the dominant business (the first variable), lets us identify the first two types of diversification: *single business* and *dominant business.* Asking questions about the relationship of core competencies across business units allows us to identify the other two types: *related diversification* and *unrelated diversification.* Taken together, the four main types of business diversification are

1. Single business.
2. Dominant business.
3. Related diversification.
4. Unrelated diversification: the conglomerate.

Please note that related diversification (type 3) is divided into two subcategories. We discuss each type of diversification below.

SINGLE BUSINESS. A *single-business firm* is characterized by a low level of diversification, if any, because it derives more than 95 percent of its revenues from one business. The remainder of less than 5 percent of revenue is not (yet) significant to the success of the firm.

>95%

Founded in 1774, the German company Birkenstock only makes one product: its namesake contoured cork shoes. Although of a more recent vintage, Facebook is also a single business at this point because it receives almost all of its revenues from online advertising.

DOMINANT BUSINESS. A *dominant-business firm* derives between 70 and 95 percent of its revenues from a single business, but it pursues at least one other business activity that accounts for the remainder of revenue. The dominant business shares competencies in products, services, technology, or distribution. In the schematic figure shown here and those to follow, the remaining revenue (R) is generally obtained in other strategic business units (SBU) within the firm. This remaining revenue is by definition less than that of the primary business. (Note: The areas of the boxes in this and following graphics are not scaled to specific percentages.)

70%-95%

R

Harley-Davidson, the Milwaukee-based manufacturer of the iconic Harley motorcycles, is a dominant-business firm. Of its $6 billion in annual revenues, some 80 percent comes from selling its iconic motorcycles.[59] The remaining 20 percent of revenues come from other business activities such as motorcycle parts and accessories as well as general merchandise, including licensing the Harley logo. The brand has a loyal following overseas as well as in the United States.

RELATED DIVERSIFICATION. A firm follows a **related diversification strategy** when it derives less than 70 percent of its revenues from a single business activity and obtains revenues from other lines of business linked to the primary business activity. The rationale behind related diversification is to benefit from economies of scale and scope: These multi-business firms can pool and share resources as well as leverage competencies across different business lines.

related diversification strategy Corporate strategy in which a firm derives less than 70 percent of its revenues from a single business activity and obtains revenues from other lines of business that are linked to the primary business activity.

The two variations of this type, which we explain next, relate to how much the other lines of business benefit from the core competencies of the primary business activity.

Related-Constrained Diversification   A firm follows a **related-constrained diversification strategy** when it derives less than 70 percent of its revenues from a single business activity and obtains revenues from other lines of business related to the primary business activity. Executives engage in a new business opportunity only when they can leverage their existing competencies and resources. Specifically, the choices of alternative business activities are limited—constrained—by the fact that they need to be related through common resources, capabilities, and competencies.

ExxonMobil's strategic move into natural gas is an example of related diversification. ExxonMobil bought XTO Energy (in 2009), a natural gas company, for $31 billion.[60] XTO Energy is known for its core competency to extract natural gas from unconventional places such as shale rock—the type of deposits currently being exploited in the United States. ExxonMobil hopes to leverage its core competency in the exploration and commercialization of oil into natural gas extraction. The company is producing nearly equal amounts of crude oil and natural gas, making it the world's largest producer of natural gas. The company believes that roughly 50 percent of the world's energy for the next 50 years will continue to come from fossil fuels, and that its diversification into natural gas, the cleanest of the fossil fuels in terms of greenhouse gas emissions, will pay off. ExxonMobil's strategic scenario may be right on the mark. Because of major technological advances in hydraulic fracking to extract oil and natural gas from shale rock by companies such as XTO Energy, the United States has emerged as the world's richest country in natural gas resources and the third-largest producer of crude oil, just behind Saudi Arabia and Russia.[61]

Related-Linked Diversification   If executives consider new business activities that share only a limited number of linkages, the firm is using a **related-linked diversification strategy**.

Amazon, featured in the ChapterCase, began business by selling only one product: books. Over time, it expanded into CDs and later gradually leveraged its online retailing capabilities into a wide array of product offerings. As the world's largest online retailer, and given the need to build huge data centers to service its peak holiday demand, Amazon decided to leverage spare capacity into cloud computing (AWS), again benefiting from economies of scope and scale. Amazon also offers a variety of consumer electronics such as tablets, e-readers, and digital virtual assistants in speakers, as well as proprietary content that can be streamed via the internet and is free for its Prime service. Amazon follows a related-linked diversification strategy.

UNRELATED DIVERSIFICATION: THE CONGLOMERATE.   A firm follows an **unrelated diversification strategy** when less than 70 percent of its revenues comes from a single business and there are few, if any, linkages among its businesses. A company that combines two or more strategic

---

related-constrained diversification strategy   A kind of related diversification strategy in which executives pursue only businesses where they can apply the resources and core competencies already available in the primary business.

related-linked diversification strategy   A kind of related diversification strategy in which executives pursue various businesses opportunities that share only a limited number of linkages.

unrelated diversification strategy   Corporate strategy in which a firm derives less than 70 percent of its revenues from a single business and there are few, if any, linkages among its businesses.

EXHIBIT 8.8 Four Main Types of Diversification

Revenues from Primary Business	Type of Diversification	Competencies (in products, services, technology, or distribution)	Examples	Graphic
>95%	Single business	Single business leverages its competencies.	Birkenstock Coca-Cola Facebook	>95%
70%–95%	Dominant business	Dominant and minor businesses share competencies.	Harley-Davidson Nestlé UPS	70%-95% — R
	Related Diversification			
	Related-constrained	Businesses generally share competencies.	ExxonMobil Johnson & Johnson Nike	<70% R—R
<70%	Related-linked	Some businesses share competencies.	Amazon Disney GE	<70% R—R
	Unrelated diversification (conglomerate)	Businesses share few, if any, competencies.	Samsung Berkshire Hathaway Yamaha	<70% R R

Note: R = Remainder revenue, generally in other strategic business units (SBU) within the firm.

Source: Adapted from R.P. Rumelt (1974), *Strategy, Structure, and Economic Performance* (Boston: Harvard Business School Press).

business units under one overarching corporation and follows an unrelated diversification strategy is called a **conglomerate**.

Some research evidence suggests that an unrelated diversification strategy can be advantageous in emerging economies.[62] Such an arrangement helps firms gain and sustain competitive advantage because it allows the conglomerate to overcome institutional weaknesses in emerging economies, such as a lack of capital markets and well-defined legal systems and property rights. Companies such as Samsung and LG (representing a uniquely South Korean form of organization, the *chaebol*), Warren Buffet's Berkshire Hathaway, the Japanese Yamaha group, and the Tata group of India are all considered conglomerates due to their unrelated diversification strategy.

Exhibit 8.8 summarizes the four main types of diversification—single business, dominant business, related diversification (including its subcategories related-constrained and related-linked diversification), and unrelated diversification.

LEVERAGING CORE COMPETENCIES FOR CORPORATE DIVERSIFICATION

In Chapter 4, when looking inside the firm, we introduced the idea that competitive advantage can be based on core competencies. Core competencies are unique strengths embedded deep

conglomerate A company that combines two or more strategic business units under one overarching corporation; follows an unrelated diversification strategy.

LO 8-8

Apply the core competence–market matrix to derive different diversification strategies.

EXHIBIT 8.9   The Core Competence–Market Matrix

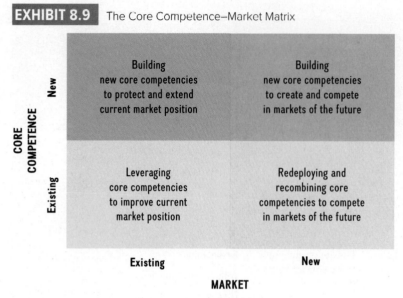

Source: Adapted from G. Hamel and C.K. Prahalad (1994), *Competing for the Future* (Boston: Harvard Business School Press).

within a firm. They allow companies to increase the perceived value of their product and service offerings and/or lower the cost to produce them.[63] Examples of core competencies are

- Walmart's ability to effectively orchestrate a globally distributed supply chain at low cost.
- Infosys's ability to provide high-quality information technology services at a low cost by leveraging its global delivery model. This implies taking work to the location where it makes the best economic sense, based on the available talent and the least amount of acceptable risk and lowest cost.

To survive and prosper, companies need to grow. This mantra holds especially true for publicly owned companies because they create shareholder value through profitable growth. Strategic leaders respond to this relentless growth imperative by leveraging their existing core competencies to find future growth opportunities. Gary Hamel and C.K. Prahalad advanced the **core competence–market matrix**, depicted in Exhibit 8.9, as a way to guide managerial decisions in regard to diversification strategies. The first task for managers is to identify their existing core competencies and understand the firm's current market situation. When applying an existing or new dimension to core competencies and markets, four quadrants emerge, each with distinct strategic implications.

core competence–market matrix A framework to guide corporate diversification strategy by analyzing possible combinations of existing/new core competencies and existing/new markets.

The lower-left quadrant combines existing core competencies with existing markets. Here, strategic leaders must come up with ideas of how to leverage existing core competencies to improve the firm's current market position. Bank of America is one of the largest banks in the United States and has at least one customer in 50 percent of U.S. households.[64] Developed from the Bank of Italy and started in San Francisco, California, in 1904, it became the Bank of America and Italy in 1922. Over the next 60 years it grew in California and then nationally into a major banking powerhouse. And then in 1997, in what was the largest bank acquisition of its time, NationsBank bought Bank of America.

You could say that acquisitions were a NationsBank specialty. While still the North Carolina National Bank (NCNB), one of its unique core competencies was identifying, appraising, and integrating acquisition targets. In particular, it bought smaller banks to supplement its organic growth throughout the 1970s and '80s. From 1989 to 1992, NCNB purchased more than 200 regional community and thrift banks to further improve its market position. It then turned its core competency to national banks, with the goal of becoming the first nationwide bank. Known as NationsBank in the 1990s, it purchased Barnett Bank, BankSouth, FleetBank, LaSalle, CountryWide Mortgages, and its eventual namesake, Bank of America. This example illustrates how NationsBank, rebranded as Bank of America since 1998, honed and deployed its core competency of selecting, acquiring, and integrating other commercial banks to grow dramatically in size and geographic scope and emerge as one of the leading banks in the United States. As a key vehicle of corporate strategy, we study acquisitions in more detail in Chapter 9.

The lower-right quadrant of Exhibit 8.9 combines existing core competencies with new market opportunities. Here, leaders must strategize about how to redeploy and recombine existing core competencies to compete in future markets. During the global financial crisis in 2008, Bank of America bought the investment bank Merrill Lynch for $50 billion.[65] Although many problems ensued for Bank of America following the Merrill Lynch acquisition, it is now the bank's investment and wealth management division. Bank of America's corporate executives applied an existing competency (acquiring and integrating) into a new market (investment and wealth management). The combined entity is now leveraging economies of scope through cross-selling when, for example, consumer banking makes customer referrals for investment bankers to follow up.[66]

Yasiel Puig, a professional baseball player, is one of the celebrity endorsements for BodyArmor, a new sports drink. In 2018, the Coca-Cola Co. took an equity stake in BodyArmor in an attempt to challenge the market leader Gatorade.
Lisa Blumenfeld/ Getty Images

The upper-left quadrant combines new core competencies with existing market opportunities. Here, leaders must come up with strategic initiatives to build new core competencies to protect and extend the company's current market position. For example, in the early 1990s, Gatorade dominated the market for sports drinks, a segment in which it had been the original innovator. Some 25 years earlier, medical researchers at the University of Florida had created the drink to enhance the performance of the Gators, the university's football team, thus the name Gatorade. Stokely-Van Camp commercialized and marketed the drink, and eventually sold it to Quaker Oats. PepsiCo brought Gatorade into its lineup of soft drinks when it acquired Quaker Oats in 2001.

By comparison, Coca-Cola had existing core competencies in marketing, bottling, and distributing soft drinks, but had never attempted to compete in the sports-drink market. Over a 10-year R&D effort, Coca-Cola developed competencies in the development and marketing of its own sports drink, Powerade, which launched in 1990. In 2019, Powerade held 17.5 percent of the sports-drink market, making it a viable competitor to Gatorade, which still holds more than 75 percent of the market. But Coca-Cola is not satisfied with just a small part of the $8 billion market for sports drinks. In 2018, Coca-Cola applied the same playbook as featured in Strategy Highlight 8.1 and made an equity investment in sports-drink company BodyArmor. The new entry made a splash with star endorsements by basketball greats Kobe Bryant and Skylar Diggins-Smith as well as baseball star Mike Trout, among other sports celebrities. In 2019, the upstart BodyArmor held 3 percent market share of the sports-drink market and continued to grow.[67]

Finally, the upper-right quadrant combines new core competencies with new market opportunities. Hamel and Prahalad call this combination *mega-opportunities*—those that hold significant future growth opportunities. It is likely the most challenging diversification strategy because it requires building new core competencies to create and compete in future markets.

Salesforce.com, for example, is a company that employs this diversification strategy well.[68] In recent years, Salesforce experienced tremendous growth, the bulk of it coming from the firm's existing core competency in delivering customer relationship management (CRM) software to its clients. Salesforce's product distinguished itself from the competition by providing software as a service via cloud computing: Clients did not need to install software or manage any servers but could easily access the CRM through a web browser (a business model called *software as a service,* or *SaaS*). Salesforce recognized an emerging market for *platform as a service* (*PaaS*) offerings, which would enable clients to build their own software solutions that are accessed the same way as the Salesforce CRM. Seizing the opportunity, Salesforce developed a new competency in delivering software development and deployment tools that allowed its customers to either extend their existing CRM offering or build completely new types of software. A decade later, Salesforce's Force.com offering is one of the leading providers of PaaS tools and services.

The core competence–market matrix provides guidance to executives on how to diversify to achieve continued growth. Once strategic leaders have a clear understanding of their firm's core competencies (see Chapter 4), they have four options to formulate corporate strategy:

Four Options to Formulate Corporate Strategy via Core Competencies

1. Leverage existing core competencies to improve current market position.
2. Build new core competencies to protect and extend current market position.
3. Redeploy and recombine existing core competencies to compete in markets of the future.
4. Build new core competencies to create and compete in markets of the future.

Strategy Highlight 8.2 illustrates how P&G is remaking its diversification strategy to overcome a decade-long competitive disadvantage.

Strategy Highlight 8.2

P&G's Diversification Strategy: Turning the Tide?

With revenues of more than $65 billion and business in basically every country except North Korea, Procter & Gamble (P&G) is the world's largest consumer products company. Some of its category-defining brands include Ivory soap, Tide detergent, Febreze air freshener, Crest toothpaste, and Pampers diapers. As one of the world's largest conglomerates, P&G comprises more than 20 consumer brands that each bring in over $1 billion in revenues per year. P&G's iconic brands are a result of a clearly formulated and effectively implemented corporate strategy. The company leverages its core competencies for diversification and attempts to create higher perceived value for its customers than its competitors by delivering products with unique features and attributes.

In the past decade, however, P&G's strategic position has weakened considerably. First, it failed to respond to consumers' need to be more frugal following the deep recession of 2008–2009. U.S. consumers moved away from P&G's higher-priced brands to lower-cost alternatives such as those offered by rivals Colgate-Palmolive, Kimberly-Clark, and Unilever. These firms were faster in cutting costs and prices. P&G also fumbled launches of reformulated products such as Tide Pods (detergent sealed in single-use pouches) and the Pantene line of shampoos and conditioners. The resulting decline in U.S. demand hit P&G especially hard because although the domestic mar-

ket delivers about one-third of its sales, it represents almost two-thirds of its profits.

Some of P&G's current problems can also be attributed to its attempt to achieve growth in the 2000s via an aggressive, unrelated diversification strategy. Given the resulting larger P&G revenue base, future incremental revenue growth for the entire company was harder to achieve—as evidenced by P&G's $57 billion acquisition of Gillette in 2005, engineered by then-CEO A.G. Lafley. The value of this acquisition is now being called into question. Although Gillette dominates the $3 billion wet shaving industry, it is losing market share to disruptive online startups such as Dollar Shave Club and Harry's, both of which offer low-cost solutions via monthly online subscription plans. P&G found itself caught off guard by how quickly razor sales moved online.

Finally, by focusing mainly on the U.S. market, P&G missed out on the booming growth years (during the 2000s) of the emerging BRIC economies—Brazil, Russia, India, and China—leaving these markets open to its rivals. For example, nearly 60 percent of Unilever's annual revenue comes from emerging markets, compared with only 40 percent at P&G. As a consequence, Colgate-Palmolive, Kimberly-Clark, and Unilever all outperformed P&G over the last decade (see Exhibit 8.10).

To achieve a turnaround, CEO David Taylor initiated a major shift in corporate strategy that focuses on restructuring and divestitures and on further diversification.

First, P&G has divested most of its underperforming brands, including Duracell batteries, CoverGirl makeup,

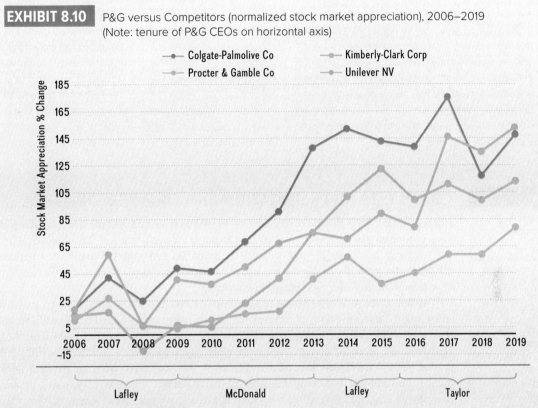

EXHIBIT 8.10   P&G versus Competitors (normalized stock market appreciation), 2006–2019
(Note: tenure of P&G CEOs on horizontal axis)

Source: Author's depiction of publicly available data.

and Iams pet food. Such moves have allowed P&G to consolidate its brands, bringing the total number down from 170 to 65. P&G has also decreased the number of business units from 10 to six. These changes in corporate strategy and structure were done in an effort to refocus the company to leverage its core competencies more fully and to improve its market share in its existing markets. P&G intends for the divestments of its non-core brands to free resources that can then be reallocated to improving its category-leading brands, but also provide a boost to its overall revenue and margins. Moreover, having more manageable business units allows regional centers to have more control, which, in turn, enables them to respond to new market opportunities and changing trends in emerging markets more quickly. P&G has also focused on streamlining its bureaucracy and implementing strict cost-cutting measures by eliminating all spending not directly related to sales. It has also and more closely aligned salaries with company performance. As part of this initiative, P&G eliminated thousands of jobs; in five years, it reduced its workforce by 25 percent. P&G has become a leaner and more agile

organization as a result and now has a lower cost structure—the hope is that these strategic decisions will improve its competitiveness.

The second component of P&G's corporate strategy is better leveraging its existing core competencies for further diversification. In 2018, P&G acquired Merck KGaA, a German consumer-health business, for $4.2 billion. With this acquisition, P&G will be adding vitamins and food supplements to its health care business unit, which includes well-known brands such as Crest toothpaste and Vicks cold medicine. The goal with this diversification move is to combine existing core competencies with new market opportunities in order to increase value and reduce costs. The combined entity is leveraging economies of scope through cross-selling when, for example, consumers are sick with a cold and need extra vitamin supplements to combat the sickness.

P&G also has plans to expand its direct-to-consumer offerings through smaller brand portfolios. Also in 2018, it acquired a trio of startups: Native natural deodorant and two skin care companies, Snowberry and FAB. P&G hopes that these acquisitions will allow it to better compete with

(Continued)

direct-to-consumer upstarts (think Dollar Shave Club, Harry's, etc.), which have disrupted the market space in recent years, capturing significant market share from legacy brands and thus forcing these older brands to rethink their business and corporate strategies. By acquiring a slew of start-up companies, P&G plans not only to tap into each business's respective markets but also to gain key insights into marketing and other business techniques unique to direct-to-consumer upstarts.

Combining the agility of a startup with the scale, expertise, and deep resources of an established brand has allowed P&G to slowly but steadily improve its market performance as demonstrated through rising profits and sales growth in recent years. These corporate strategy initiatives have also helped P&G achieve a better strategic fit with the new environment. Taken together, P&G's CEO Taylor hopes to turn the tide in order to once more gain a competitive advantage.[69]

LO 8-9

Explain when a diversification strategy does create a competitive advantage and when it does not.

CORPORATE DIVERSIFICATION AND FIRM PERFORMANCE

Corporate executives pursue diversification to gain and sustain competitive advantage. But does corporate diversification indeed lead to superior performance? To answer this question, we need to evaluate the performance of diversified companies. The critical question to ask when doing so is *whether the individual businesses are worth more under the company's management than if each were managed individually.*

The diversification-performance relationship is a function of the underlying type of diversification. A cumulative body of research indicates an inverted U-shaped relationship between the type of diversification and overall firm performance, as depicted in Exhibit 8.11.[70] High and low levels of diversification are generally associated with lower overall performance, while moderate levels of diversification are associated with higher firm performance. This implies that companies that focus on a single business, as well as companies that pursue unrelated diversification, often fail to achieve additional value creation. Firms that compete in single markets could potentially benefit from economies of scope by leveraging their core competencies into adjacent markets.

diversification discount Situation in which the stock price of highly diversified firms is valued at less than the sum of their individual business units.

Firms that pursue unrelated diversification are often unable to create additional value. They experience a **diversification discount**: The stock price of such highly diversified firms is valued at less than the sum of their individual business units.[71] For the past decade or so, GE experienced a diversification discount, as its capital unit contributed 50 percent of profits on one-third of the conglomerate's revenues. The presence of the diversification discount in GE's depressed stock price was a major reason GE's then CEO, Jeffrey Immelt, decided to spin out GE Capital (in 2015). On the day of the announcement, GE's stock price jumped 11 percent, adding some $28 billion to GE's market capitalization. This provides some idea of the diversification discount that firms pursuing unrelated diversification may experience.[72]

EXHIBIT 8.11 The Diversification-Performance Relationship

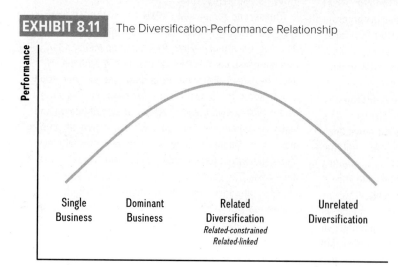

Source: Adapted from L.E. Palich, L.B. Cardinal, and C.C. Miller (2001), "Curvilinearity in the diversification-performance linkage: An examination of over three decades of research," *Strategic Management Journal* 21: 155–174.

As GE's performance continued to tumble, more restructuring and CEO turnover ensued. Immelt was replaced by John Flannery in 2017. Just 14 months later, he was let go and Lawrence Culp, the first outsider in GE's history, was appointed CEO. As GE lost 90(!) percent of its market value (from a high of $600 billion in 2000 to a low of $60 billion in 2018) significant restructuring of the corporate portfolio continues (see MiniCase 8 "GE: Corporate Strategy Gone Wrong" for an in-depth discussion).

The presence of the diversification discount, however, depends on the institutional context. Although it holds in advanced economies with developed capital markets such as the United States, some research suggests an unrelated diversification strategy can be advantageous in emerging economies such as India or some countries in Africa.[73] Here, unrelated diversification may help firms gain and sustain competitive advantage because it allows the conglomerate to overcome institutional weaknesses in emerging economies such as a lack of a functioning capital market, courts of law, and so on.

In contrast, companies that pursue related diversification are more likely to improve their performance. They create a **diversification premium**: On average, the stock price of related-diversification firms is valued at greater than the sum of their individual business units.[74]

Why is this so? At the most basic level, a corporate diversification strategy enhances firm performance when its value creation is greater than the costs it incurs. Exhibit 8.12 lists the sources of value creation and costs for different corporate strategies, for vertical integration as well as related and unrelated diversification. For diversification to enhance firm performance, it must do at least one of the following:

- Provide *economies of scale,* which reduces costs.
- Exploit *economies of scope,* which increases value.
- Reduce costs *and* increase value.

diversification premium
Situation in which the stock price of related-diversification firms is valued at greater than the sum of their individual business units.

Corporate Strategy	Sources of Value Creation (V)	Sources of Costs (C)
Vertical Integration	• Can lower costs • Can improve quality • Can facilitate scheduling and planning ————————————— • Facilitating investments in specialized assets • Securing critical supplies and distribution channels	• Can increase costs • Can reduce quality • Can reduce flexibility ————————————— • Increasing potential for legal repercussions
Related Diversification	• Economies of scope • Economies of scale • Financial economies — Restructuring — Internal capital markets	• Coordination costs • Influence costs
Unrelated Diversification	• Financial economies — Restructuring — Internal capital markets	• Influence costs

EXHIBIT 8.12

Vertical Integration and Diversification: Sources of Value Creation and Costs

We discussed these drivers of competitive advantage—economies of scale, economies of scope, and increase in value and reduction of costs—in depth in Chapter 6 in relation to business strategy. Other potential benefits to firm performance when following a diversification strategy include *financial economies,* resulting from *restructuring* and using *internal capital markets.*

RESTRUCTURING. *Restructuring* describes the process of reorganizing and divesting business units and activities to refocus a company to leverage its core competencies more fully. The Belgium-based Anheuser-Busch InBev sold Busch Entertainment, its theme park unit that owns SeaWorld and Busch Gardens, to a group of private investors for roughly $3 billion. This strategic move allows InBev to focus more fully on its core business of brewing and distributing beer across the world.[75]

Corporate executives can restructure the portfolio of their firm's businesses, much like an investor can change a portfolio of stocks. One helpful tool to guide corporate portfolio planning is the **Boston Consulting Group (BCG) growth–share matrix,** shown in Exhibit 8.13.[76] This matrix locates the firm's individual SBUs in two dimensions:

- Relative market share (horizontal axis).
- Speed of market growth (vertical axis).

The firm plots its SBUs into one of four categories in the matrix: *dog, cash cow, star,* and *question mark.* Each category warrants a different investment strategy. All four categories shape the firm's corporate strategy.

SBUs identified as *dogs* are relatively easy to identify: They are the underperforming businesses. Dogs hold a small market share in a low-growth market; they have low and unstable earnings, combined with neutral or negative cash flows. The strategic recommendations are either to *divest* the business or to *harvest* it. This implies stopping investment in the business and squeezing out as much cash flow as possible before shutting it or selling it.

Cash cows, in contrast, are SBUs that compete in a low-growth market but hold considerable market share. Their earnings and cash flows are high and stable. The strategic recommendation is to invest enough into cash cows to hold their current position and to avoid having them turn into dogs (as indicated by the arrow in Exhibit 8.13). As a general rule, strategic leaders would want to manage their SBU portfolio in a clockwise manner (as indicated by three of the four arrows).

A corporation's *star* SBUs hold a high market share in a fast-growing market. Their earnings are high and either stable or growing. The recommendation for the corporate strategist is to invest sufficient resources to hold the star's position or even increase investments for future growth. As indicated by the arrow, stars may turn into cash cows as the market in which the SBU is situated slows after reaching the maturity stage of the industry life cycle.

Finally, some SBUs are *question marks:* It is not clear whether they will turn into dogs or stars (as indicated by the arrows in Exhibit 8.13). Their earnings are low and unstable, but they might be growing. The cash flow, however, is negative. Ideally, corporate executives want to invest in question marks to increase their relative market share so they turn into stars. If market conditions change, however, or the overall market growth slows, then a question-mark SBU is likely to turn into a dog (as indicated by the arrow). In this case, executives would want to harvest the cash flow or divest the SBU.

INTERNAL CAPITAL MARKETS. *Internal capital markets* can be a source of value creation in a diversification strategy if the conglomerate's headquarters does a more efficient job of allocating capital through its budgeting process than what could be achieved in external capital markets. Based on private information, corporate managers are in a position to discover which of their strategic business units will provide the highest return on invested capital. In addition, internal capital markets may allow the company to access capital at a lower cost.

Until recently, for example, GE Capital brought in close to $70 billion in annual revenues and generated more than half of GE's profits.[77] In combination with GE's triple-A debt rating, having access to such a large finance arm allowed GE to benefit from a lower cost of capital, which in turn was a source of value creation in itself. At the height of the global financial crises (in 2009), GE lost its AAA debt rating. The lower debt rating and the smaller finance unit were likely to result in a higher cost of capital, and thus a potential loss in value creation through internal capital markets. As mentioned above, GE sold its GE Capital business unit in a restructuring of its corporate portfolio (in 2015).

A strategy of related-constrained or related-linked diversification is more likely to enhance corporate performance than either a single or dominant level of diversification or an unrelated level of diversification. The reason is that the sources of value creation include not only restructuring, but also the potential benefits of economies of scope and scale. To create additional value, however, the benefits from these sources of incremental value creation must outweigh their costs. A related-diversification strategy entails two types of costs: coordination and influence costs. *Coordination costs* are a function of the number, size, and types of businesses that are linked. *Influence costs* occur due to political maneuvering by managers to influence capital and resource allocation and the resulting inefficiencies stemming from suboptimal allocation of scarce resources.[78]

8.5 Implications for Strategic Leaders

An effective corporate strategy increases a firm's chances to gain and sustain a competitive advantage. By formulating corporate strategy, strategic leaders make important choices along three dimensions that determine the boundaries of the firm:

- **The degree of vertical integration**—in what stages of the industry value chain to participate.
- **The type of diversification**—what range of products and services to offer.
- **The geographic scope**—where to compete.

Since a firm's external environment never remains constant over time, *corporate strategy needs to be dynamic over time.* As firms grow, they tend to diversify and globalize to capture additional growth opportunities. In the next chapter, we discuss strategic alliances in more depth as well as mergers and acquisitions, both are critical tools in executing corporate strategy. In Chapter 10, we take a closer look at geographic diversification by studying how firms compete for competitive advantage around the world.

CHAPTER**CASE 8**   Part II

Mike Kane/Bloomberg/
Getty Images

AMAZON WEB SERVICES (AWS) is by far Amazon's most profitable business endeavor: Amazon's total revenues stood at some $240 billion in 2018, with retail bringing in $203 billion, AWS $27 billion, and online advertising the remaining $10 billion. Amazon's profits were $12 billion, with AWS bringing in $7 billion and retail just $5 billion. Thus, AWS's profit margin is approximately 26 percent while the online retailing profit margin is a mere 2 percent. Indeed, while Amazon is barely profitable in its online retailing operation in the United States, it is losing money internationally. At the same time, AWS is growing by more than 40 percent a year. Given its hugely successful business, AWS has become Amazon's cash cow, which allows Amazon to undertake various strategic initiatives such as paying $14 billion for Whole Foods Market (in 2017) and funding the money-losing international retail expansion as well as original content development for Prime Video (see Exhibit 8.1 for more examples of recent strategic initiatives).

Despite these efforts, some clouds are gathering on the horizon over Amazon. Although AWS is growing fast, its growth rate has slowed in recent years. Moreover, with Microsoft's Azure, Google's Cloud, as well as IBM's and now Apple's stronger push into cloud computing, competition is heating up. In addition, many competitors such as Netflix—a current customer of AWS—may shift to Azure or another cloud services provider for strategic reasons. Moreover, although offering one-day free shipping for Prime members raises the bar on customer service to which Walmart and others need to respond, it does not come cheap. The investment to make one-day free shipping a reality in the United States alone is estimated be between $800 million and $1 billion. Given that Amazon's retail operation is barely profitable that money must—at this point—come from AWS.

As mentioned, AWS's growth rate is declining. Therefore, Amazon must create another growth engine to finance future improvements to customer service and other diversification experiments. One candidate is online advertising, where

Amazon currently brings in $10 billion a year, and holds some 10 percent market share, far behind Facebook and Google, the dominant players in digital advertising. Yet, Amazon's digital ad business has been growing by 90 percent year over year. Although most searches in the United States are initiated on Google, Amazon is the leader when looking at the more narrow category of product searches. This implies that most U.S. consumers begin an online product search directly on Amazon. As such, Amazon has been described as "a search engine with a warehouse attached to it."[79]

Amazon might be in the best position to take advantage of the future exponential growth in digital advertising because it has the best quality data. While Google knows what people search for in general terms, Amazon knows what each individual views, buys, listens to, watches, and how and when each individual communicates with Alexa. These data will allow Amazon to provide the most fine-grained and targeted ad placements, which will garner a premium from advertisers. And the more data Amazon has, the more it can boost its online sales. Once positive network effects kick in, Amazon might be the winner in the digital ad space—especially in regards to products.

Questions

1. Describe Amazon's diversification strategy using Exhibit 8.8. What type of diversification strategy is Amazon pursuing? Explain.

2. What is Amazon's core business? Is AWS related to Amazon's core business? Why or why not? Some investors are pressuring Jeff Bezos to spin out AWS as a standalone company. Do you agree with this corporate strategy recommendation? Why or why not? Hint: Do you believe AWS would be more valuable within Amazon or as a standalone company?

3. At this point, Google and Facebook are the clear leaders in the digital ad space, which is predicted to continue to grow exponentially (reaching $175 billion in 2021, overtaking traditional advertising with an estimated $100 billion). Although Amazon's market share is a mere 10 percent in 2018, many believe that Amazon is best positioned to be the market leader in the digital ad space in future. Why would people make this argument? Do you agree with this assessment? Why or why not? Buttress your position.

4. Amazon continues to spend billions on seemingly unrelated diversification efforts. Do you believe these efforts contribute to Amazon gaining and sustaining a competitive advantage? Why or why not?

mySTRATEGY

How Diversified Are You?

Corporations diversify by investing time and resources into new areas of business. As individuals, each of us makes choices about how to spend our time and energies. Typically, we could divide our time between school, work, family, sleep, and play. During high-stress work projects, we likely devote more of our time to work; when studying for final exams or a professional board exam (such as the CPA exam), we probably spend more time and effort in the "student learning" mode. This manner of dividing our time can be thought of as "personal diversification." Just as companies can invest in related or unrelated activities, we make similar choices. While we attend college, we may choose to engage in social and leisure activities with campus colleagues, or we may focus on classwork at school and spend our "playtime" with an entirely separate set of people.

Using Exhibit 8.8 as a guide, list each of your major activity areas. Think of each of these as a business. (If you are literally "all work and no play," you are a single-business type of personal diversification.) Instead of revenues, estimate the percentage of *time* you spend per week in each activity. (Most people will be diversified, though some may be dominant perhaps in school or work.) To assess your degree of *relatedness* and *unrelatedness*, consider the subject matter and community involved with each activity. For example, if you are studying ballet and working as an accountant, those would be largely unrelated activities (unless you are an accountant for a ballet company!).

1. What conclusions do you derive based on your personal diversification strategy?

2. Do you need to adjust your portfolio of activities? Explain the reasons for your answer.

3. Let's consider dynamics—has your level of diversification changed over time (say, over the past five years)? Looking toward the future, do you expect your level of diversification to change as you complete your degree? Why or why not?

TAKE-AWAY CONCEPTS

In this chapter, we defined corporate strategy and then looked at two fundamental corporate strategy topics—vertical integration and diversification—as summarized by the following learning objectives and related take-away concepts.

LO 8-1 / Define corporate strategy and describe the three dimensions along which it is assessed.

- Corporate strategy addresses "where to compete." Business strategy addresses "how to compete."

- Corporate strategy concerns the boundaries of the firm along three dimensions: (1) industry value chain, (2) products and services, and (3) geography (regional, national, or global markets).

- To gain and sustain competitive advantage, any corporate strategy must support and strengthen a firm's strategic position, regardless of whether it is a differentiation, cost-leadership, or blue ocean strategy.

LO 8-2 / **Explain why firms need to grow, and evaluate different growth motives.**

- Firm growth is motivated by the following: increasing profits, lowering costs, increasing market power, reducing risk, and managerial motives.

- Not all growth motives are equally valuable.

  - Increasing profits and lowering expenses are clearly related to enhancing a firm's competitive advantage.

  - Increasing market power can also contribute to a greater competitive advantage, but can also result in legal repercussions such as antitrust lawsuits.

  - Growing to reduce risk has fallen out of favor with investors, who argue that they are in a better position to diversify their stock portfolio in comparison to a corporation with a number of unrelated strategic business units.

  - Managerial motives such as increasing company perks and job security are not legitimate reasons a firm needs to grow.

LO 8-3 / **Describe and evaluate different options firms have to organize economic activity.**

- Transaction cost economics help managers decide what activities to do in-house ("make") versus what services and products to obtain from the external market ("buy").

- When the costs to pursue an activity in-house are less than the costs of transacting in the market ($C_{\text{in-house}} < C_{\text{market}}$), then the firm should vertically integrate.

- Principal–agent problems and information asymmetries can lead to market failures, and thus situations where internalizing the activity is preferred.

- A principal–agent problem arises when an agent, performing activities on behalf of a principal, pursues his or her own interests.

- Information asymmetries arise when one party is more informed than another because of the possession of private information.

- Moving from less integrated to more fully integrated forms of transacting, alternatives include short-term contracts, strategic alliances (including long-term contracts, equity alliances, and joint ventures), and parent–subsidiary relationships.

LO 8-4 / **Describe the two types of vertical integration along the industry value chain: backward and forward vertical integration.**

- Vertical integration denotes a firm's addition of value—what percentage of a firm's sales is generated by the firm within its boundaries.

- Industry value chains (vertical value chains) depict the transformation of raw materials into finished goods and services. Each stage typically represents a distinct industry in which a number of different firms compete.

- Backward vertical integration involves moving ownership of activities upstream nearer to the originating (inputs) point of the industry value chain.

- Forward vertical integration involves moving ownership of activities closer to the end (customer) point of the value chain.

LO 8-5 / **Identify and evaluate benefits and risks of vertical integration.**

- Benefits of vertical integration include securing critical supplies and distribution channels, lowering costs, improving quality, facilitating scheduling and planning, and facilitating investments in specialized assets.

- Risks of vertical integration include increasing costs, reducing quality, reducing flexibility, and increasing the potential for legal repercussions.

LO 8-6 / **Describe and examine alternatives to vertical integration.**

- Taper integration is a strategy in which a firm is backwardly integrated but also relies on outside-market firms for some of its supplies, and/or is forwardly integrated but also relies on outside-market firms for some if its distribution.

- Strategic outsourcing involves moving one or more value chain activities outside the firm's boundaries to other firms in the industry value chain. Offshoring is the outsourcing of activities outside the home country.

LO 8-7 / **Describe and evaluate different types of corporate diversification.**

- A single-business firm derives 95 percent or more of its revenues from one business.

- A dominant-business firm derives between 70 and 95 percent of its revenues from a single business, but pursues at least one other business activity.

- A firm follows a related diversification strategy when it derives less than 70 percent of its revenues from a single business activity, but obtains revenues from other lines of business that are linked to the primary business activity. Choices within a related diversification strategy can be related-constrained or related-linked.

- A firm follows an unrelated diversification strategy when less than 70 percent of its revenues come from a single business, and there are few, if any, linkages among its businesses.

LO 8-8 / Apply the core competence–market matrix to derive different diversification strategies.

- When applying an existing/new dimension to core competencies and markets, four quadrants emerge, as depicted in Exhibit 8.9.

- The lower-left quadrant combines existing core competencies with existing markets. Here, managers need to come up with ideas of how to leverage existing core competencies to improve their current market position.

- The lower-right quadrant combines existing core competencies with new market opportunities. Here, managers need to think about how to redeploy and recombine existing core competencies to compete in future markets.

- The upper-left quadrant combines new core competencies with existing market opportunities. Here, managers must come up with strategic initiatives of how to build new core competencies to protect and extend the firm's current market position.

- The upper-right quadrant combines new core competencies with new market opportunities. This is

likely the most challenging diversification strategy because it requires building new core competencies to create and compete in future markets.

LO 8-9 / Explain when a diversification strategy does create a competitive advantage and when it does not.

- The diversification-performance relationship is a function of the underlying type of diversification.

- The relationship between the type of diversification and overall firm performance takes on the shape of an inverted U (see Exhibit 8.11).

- Unrelated diversification often results in a diversification discount: The stock price of such highly diversified firms is valued at less than the sum of their individual business units.

- Related diversification often results in a diversification premium: The stock price of related-diversification firms is valued at greater than the sum of their individual business units.

- In the BCG matrix, the corporation is viewed as a portfolio of businesses, much like a portfolio of stocks in finance (see Exhibit 8.13). The individual SBUs are evaluated according to relative market share and the speed of market growth, and are plotted using one of four categories: dog, cash cow, star, and question mark. Each category warrants a different investment strategy.

- Both low levels and high levels of diversification are generally associated with lower overall performance, while moderate levels of diversification are associated with higher firm performance.

KEY TERMS

Backward vertical integration *(p. 294)*
Boston Consulting Group (BCG) growth–share matrix *(p. 310)*
Conglomerate *(p. 303)*
Core competence–market matrix *(p. 304)*
Corporate strategy *(p. 280)*
Credible commitment *(p. 290)*
Diversification *(p. 300)*

Diversification discount *(p. 308)*
Diversification premium *(p. 309)*
External transaction costs *(p. 283)*
Forward vertical integration *(p. 294)*
Franchising *(p. 288)*
Geographic diversification strategy *(p. 300)*
Industry value chain *(p. 291)*
Information asymmetry *(p. 286)*

Internal transaction costs *(p. 283)*
Joint venture *(p. 290)*
Licensing *(p. 288)*
Principal–agent problem *(p. 285)*
Product diversification strategy *(p. 300)*
Product–market diversification strategy *(p. 300)*
Related-constrained diversification strategy *(p. 302)*

Related diversification
strategy *(p. 301)*

Related-linked diversification
strategy *(p. 302)*

Specialized assets *(p. 295)*

Strategic alliances *(p. 287)*

Strategic outsourcing *(p. 298)*

Taper integration *(p. 298)*

Transaction cost
economics *(p. 283)*

Transaction costs *(p. 283)*

Unrelated diversification
strategy *(p. 302)*

Vertical integration *(p. 291)*

Vertical market failure *(p. 297)*

DISCUSSION QUESTIONS

1. Franchising is widely used in the casual dining and fast food industry, yet Starbucks is quite successful with a large number of company-owned stores. In 2019 Starbucks had more than 8,500 company-owned stores in the United States. How do you explain this difference? Is Starbucks bucking the trend of other food-service stores, or is something else going on?

2. Nike is a large and successful firm in the design of athletic shoes. It could easily decide to forward-integrate and manufacture the shoes it designs. Thus, the firm has a credible threat over its current outsourced manufacturers. If Nike has no intention of actually entering the manufacturing arena, is it ethical for the Nike supply chain management to bring up this credible threat during annual pricing negotiations? What are some reasons Nike may want to consider such a vertical integration more seriously?

3. The chapter notes that some firms choose to outsource their human resource management systems. If a firm has a core value of respecting its employees and rewarding top performance with training, raises, and promotions, does outsourcing HR management show a lack of commitment by the firm? Why or why not?

ENDNOTES

1. This ChapterCase is based on: Jones, R. (2019, May 1), "Amazon targets Middle East with Arabic website," *The Wall Street Journal;* "Amazon's ambitious drive into digital-advertising," *The Economist* (2018, Oct. 27); Galloway, S. (2017, Sep. 22), "Amazon takes over the world," *The Wall Street Journal;* Stevens, L., and A. Gasparro (2017, Jun. 16), "Amazon to buy Whole Foods for $13.7 billion," *The Wall Street Journal;* "Are investors too optimistic about Amazon?" *The Economist* (2017, Mar. 25); "Amazon, the world's most remarkable firm, is just getting started," *The Economist* (2017, Mar. 25); Stone, B. (2014), *The Everything Store: Jeff Bezos and the Age of Amazon* (New York: Back Bay Books); and Amazon.com, Inc., annual reports (various years).

2. Rindova, V.P., and S. Kotha (2001), "Continuous 'morphing': Competing through dynamic capabilities, form, and function," *Academy of Management Journal* 44: 1263–1280.

3. Collis, D.J. (1995), "The scope of the corporation," *Harvard Business School Note,* 9-795-139.

4. For a discussion of behavioral economics in general and executive incentives in particular, see: Kahneman, D. (2011), *Thinking, Fast*

and Slow (New York: Farrar, Straus and Giroux); Ariely, D. (2009), *Predictably Irrational: The Hidden Forces That Shape Our Decisions* (New York: Harper Perennial); Kahneman, D. (2003), "Maps of bounded rationality: Psychology for behavioral economics," *The American Economic Review* 93: 1449–1475; and Thaler, R.H., and C.R. Sunstein (2003), *Nudge: Improving Decisions About Health, Wealth, and Happiness* (New York: Farrar, Straus and Giroux).

5. For a discussion and detailed data on firm performance and CEO pay for some 300 companies, see: Lublin, J.S. (2015, Jun. 25), "How much the best-performing and worst-performing ceos got paid. WSJ ranking shows top performers aren't the highest paid," *The Wall Street Journal*. For a second study that shows a significant difference in the return on investment for higher vs. lower paid CEOs, see: Francis, T. (2016, Jul. 25), "Best-paid CEOs run some of worst-performing companies: Analysis by MSCI calls into question the idea that high CEO pay helps drive better results," *The Wall Street Journal*. The results of this study indicate that $100 invested in the 20 percent of companies with the highest-paid CEOs would have grown to $265 over 10 years. In

contrast, the same amount of money over the same time period invested in companies with the lowest-paid CEOs would have grown to $367.

6. Kogut, B., and U. Zander (1992), "Knowledge of the firm, combinative capabilities, and the replication of technology," *Organization Science* 3: 383–397; O'Connor, G.C., and M. Rice (2001), "Opportunity recognition and breakthrough innovation in large firms," *California Management Review* 43: 95–116; O'Connor, G.C., and R.W. Veryzer (2001), "The nature of market visioning for technology-based radical innovation," *Journal of Product Innovation Management* 18: 231–224.

7. Mickle, T. (2016, Sep. 28), "SABMiller, AB InBev shareholders approve $100 billion-plus merger," *The Wall Street Journal*.

8. The literature on transaction cost economics is rich and expanding. For important theoretical and empirical contributions, see: Folta, T.B. (1998), "Governance and uncertainty: The trade-off between administrative control and commitment," *Strategic Management Journal* 19: 1007–1028; Klein, B., R. Crawford, and A. Alchian (1978), "Vertical integration, appropriable rents, and the competitive contracting process," *Journal of Law and Economics* 21: 297-326; Leiblein, M.J., and D.J. Miller (2003), "An empirical examination of transformation- and firm-level influences on the vertical boundaries of the firm," *Strategic Management Journal* 24: 839-859; Leiblein, M.J., J. J. Reuer, and F. Dalsace (2002), "Do make or buy decisions matter? The influence of organizational governance on technological performance," *Strategic Management Journal* 23: 817-833; Mahoney, J. (1992), "The choice of organizational form: Vertical financial ownership versus other methods of vertical integration," *Strategic Management Journal* 13: 559-584; Mahoney, J.T. (2005), *Economic Foundations of Strategy* (Thousand Oaks, CA: Sage); Tsang, E.W.K. (2006), "Behavioral assumptions and theory development: The case of transaction cost economics," *Strategic Management Journal* 27: 999-1011; Williamson, O.E. (1975), *Markets and Hierarchies* (New York: Free Press); Williamson, O.E. (1981), "The economics of organization: The transaction cost approach," *American Journal of Sociology* 87: 548-577; and Williamson, O.E. (1985), *The Economic Institutions of Capitalism* (New York: Free Press).

9. This draws on: Mahoney, J.T. (2005), *Economic Foundations of Strategy* (Thousand Oaks, CA: Sage); Williamson, O.E. (1975), *Markets and Hierarchies* (New York: Free Press); Williamson, O.E. (1981), "The economics of organization: The transaction cost approach," *American Journal of Sociology* 87: 548-577; Williamson, O.E. (1985), *The Economic Institutions of Capitalism* (New York: Free Press); and Hart, O., and O. Moore (1990), "Property rights and the nature of the firm," *Journal of Political Economy* 98: 1119-1158.

10. Highlighting the relevance of research on transaction costs, both Ronald Coase (1991) and Oliver Williamson (2009), who further developed and refined Coase's initial insight, were each awarded a Nobel Prize in economics in the years shown.

11. Levy, S. (2011), *In the Plex: How Google Thinks, Works, and Shapes Our Lives* (New York: Simon & Schuster).

12. Grigoriou, K., and F.T. Rothaermel (2014), "Structural microfoundations of innovation: The role of relational stars," *Journal of Management* 40: 586-615.

13. This is based on: Fama, E. (1980), "Agency problems and the theory of the firm," *Journal of Political Economy* 88: 375-390; Jensen, M., and W. Meckling (1976), "Theory of the firm: Managerial behavior, agency costs and ownership structure," *Journal of Financial Economics* 3: 305-360; and Berle, A., and G. Means (1932), *The Modern Corporation and Private Property* (New York: Macmillan).

14. Berle, A., and G. Means (1932), *The Modern Corporation and Private Property* (New York: Macmillan).

15. This discussion draws on: Zenger, T.R., and W.S. Hesterly (1997), "The disaggregation of corporations: Selective intervention, high-powered incentives, and molecular units," *Organization Science* 8: 209-222; and Zenger, T.R., and S.G. Lazzarini (2004), "Compensating for innovation: Do small firms offer high-powered incentives that lure talent and motivate effort," *Managerial and Decision Economics* 25: 329-345.

16. This discussion draws on: Akerlof, G.A. (1970), "The market for lemons: Quality uncertainty and the market mechanism," *Quarterly Journal of Economics* 94: 488-500.

17. Pisano, G.P. (1997), "R&D performance, collaborative arrangements, and the market for know-how: A test of the 'lemons' hypothesis in biotechnology," *Working Paper No. 97-105,* Harvard Business School; Lerner, J., and R.P. Merges (1998), "The control of technology alliances: An empirical analysis of the biotechnology industry," *Journal of Industrial Economics* 46: 125-156; Huston, J.H., and R.W. Spencer (2002), "Quality, uncertainty and the Internet: The market for cyber lemons," *The American Economist* 46: 50-60; Rothaermel, F.T., and D.L. Deeds (2004), "Exploration and exploitation alliances in biotechnology: A system of new product development," *Strategic Management Journal* 25: 201-221; Downing, C., D. Jaffee, and N. Walla (2009), "Is the market for mortgage-backed securities a market for lemons?" *Review of Financial Studies* 22: 2457-2494.

18. This discussion draws on: Williamson, O. E. (1991), "Comparative economic organization: The analysis of discrete structural alternatives," *Administrative Science Quarterly* 36: 269-296.

19. Since short-term contracts are unlikely to be of strategic significance, they are not subsumed under the term *strategic alliances,* but rather are considered to be mere contractual arrangements.

20. Dyer, J.H. (1997), "Effective interfirm collaboration: How firms minimize transaction costs and maximize transaction value," *Strategic Management Journal* 18: 535-556.

21. This is based on: Gulati, R. (1998), "Alliances and networks," *Strategic Management Journal* 19: 293-317; Ireland, R.D., M.A. Hitt, and D. Vaidyanath (2002), "Alliance management as a source of competitive advantage," *Journal of Management* 28: 413-446; Hoang, H., and F.T. Rothaermel (2005), "The effect of general and partner-specific alliance experience on joint R&D project performance," *Academy of Management Journal* 48: 332-345; and Lavie, D. (2006), "The competitive advantage of interconnected firms: An extension of the resource-based view," *Academy of Management Review* 31: 638-658.

22. This Strategy Highlight is based on: Maloney, J. (2019, Apr. 17), "Energy-drink upstarts are sapping Monster's strength," *The Wall Street Journal;* Maloney, J. (2018, Nov. 8), "Coke to launch its own energy drinks. Monster cries foul," *The Wall Street Journal;* Mickle, T., and V. Bauerlein (2017, Feb. 21), "Nascar, once a cultural icon, hits the skids," *The Wall Street Journal,* February 21; Esterl, M. (2015, May 26), "Coke says it's ready to let Monster in," *The Wall Street Journal;* Esterl, M. (2015, Mar. 26), "Soft drinks hit 10th year of decline," *The Wall Street Journal;* Esterl, M., and J.S. Lublin (2014, Aug. 15), "Why didn't Coke buy all of Monster?" *The Wall Street Journal;* Esterl, M. (2014, Aug. 14), "Coca-Cola buys stake in Monster Beverage," *The Wall Street Journal;* and McGrath, M. (2014, Aug. 14), "Coca-Cola buys stake in Monster Beverage for $2 Billion," *Forbes.*

23. www.dowcorning.com.

24. Reisinger, D. (2019, Jan. 17), "Amazon Prime has more than 100 million U.S. subscribers," *Fortune.*

25. "Rising from the ashes in Detroit," *The Economist* (2010, Aug. 19).

26. "Small cars, big question," *The Economist* (2010, Jan. 21).

27. Colias, M., and J.D. Stoll (2017, Mar. 6), "GM's Opel exit is rare no-confidence vote in European market," *The Wall Street Journal.*

28. Tucker, I., and R.P. Wilder (1977), "Trends in vertical integration in the U.S. manufacturing sector," *Journal of Industrial Economics* 26: 81-97; Harrigan, K.R. (1984), "Formulating vertical integration strategies," *Academy of Management Review* 9: 638-652; Harrigan, K.R. (1986), "Matching vertical integration strategies to competitive conditions," *Strategic Management Journal* 7: 535-555; Rothaermel, F.T., M.A. Hitt, and L.A. Jobe (2006), "Balancing vertical integration and strategic outsourcing: Effects on product portfolios, new product success, and firm performance," *Strategic Management Journal* 27: 1033-1056.

29. Barr, A., and R. Knutson (2015, Apr. 22), "Google Project Fi wireless service undercuts phone plans," *The Wall Street Journal.*

30. "HTC clones Nexus One, launches 3 new phones," *Wired.com* (2010, Feb. 16).

31. www.htc.com.

32. Mochizuki, T. (2016, Aug. 13), "Taiwan's Foxconn completes acquisition of Sharp," *The Wall Street Journal.*

33. Harrigan, K.R. (1984), "Formulating vertical integration strategies," *Academy of Management Review* 9: 638–652; Harrigan, K.R. (1986), "Matching vertical integration strategies to competitive conditions," *Strategic Management Journal* 7: 535–555.

34. "HTC clones Nexus One, launches 3 new phones," *Wired.com* (2010, Feb. 16).

35. Williamson, O.E. (1975), *Markets and Hierarchies* (New York: Free Press); Williamson, O.E. (1981), "The economics of organization: The transaction cost approach," *American Journal of Sociology* 87: 548–577; Williamson, O.E. (1985), *The Economic Institutions of Capitalism* (New York: Free Press); and Poppo, L., and T. Zenger (1998), "Testing alternative theories of the firm: Transaction cost, knowledge based, and measurement explanations for make or buy decisions in information services," *Strategic Management Journal* 19: 853–878.

36. Williamson, O.E. (1975), *Markets and Hierarchies* (New York: Free Press); Williamson, O.E. (1981), "The economics of organization: The transaction cost approach," *American Journal of Sociology* 87: 548–577; Williamson, O.E. (1985), *The Economic Institutions of Capitalism* (New York: Free Press).

37. Williamson, O.E. (1975), *Markets and Hierarchies* (New York: Free Press).

38. "Delta to buy refinery in effort to lower jet-fuel costs," *The Wall Street Journal* (2012, Apr. 30).

39. Harrigan, K.R. (1984), "Formulating vertical integration strategies," *Academy of Management Review* 9: 638–652; Harrigan, K.R. (1986), "Matching vertical integration strategies to competitive conditions," *Strategic Management Journal* 7: 535–555; Afuah, A. (2001), "Dynamic boundaries of the firm: Are firms better off being vertically integrated in the face of a technological change?" *Academy of Management Journal* 44: 1211–1228; and Rothaermel, F.T., M.A. Hitt, and L.A. Jobe (2006), "Balancing vertical integration and strategic outsourcing: Effects on product portfolios, new product success, and firm performance," *Strategic Management Journal* 27: 1033–1056.

40. Afuah, A. (2001), "Dynamic boundaries of the firm: Are firms better off being vertically integrated in the face of a technological change?" *Academy of Management Journal* 44: 1211–1228.

41. Ghemawat, P. (1993), "Commitment to a process innovation: Nucor, USX, and thin slab casting," *Journal of Economics and Management Strategy* 2: 133–161; Christensen, C.M., and M.E. Raynor (2003), *The*

Innovator's Solution: Creating and Sustaining Successful Growth (Boston: Harvard Business School Press).

42. "Companies more prone to go vertical," *The Wall Street Journal* (2009, Dec. 1).

43. This section is based on: McGrath, R. (2009, December), "Why vertical integration is making a comeback," *Harvard Business Review*; "Vertical integration: Moving on up," *The Economist* (2009, Mar. 7); Stuckey, J., and D. White (1993, August), "When and when not to vertically integrate," *McKinsey Quarterly*; and Buzzell, R.D. (1983, January), "Is vertical integration profitable?" *Harvard Business Review*.

44. McGrath, R. (2009, December), "Why vertical integration is making a comeback," *Harvard Business Review*.

45. "Vertical integration: Moving on up," *The Economist* (2009, Mar. 7).

46. Harrigan, K.R. (1984), "Formulating vertical integration strategies," *Academy of Management Review* 9: 638–652.

47. This is based on: Harrigan, K.R. (1984), "Formulating vertical integration strategies," *Academy of Management Review* 9: 638–652; and Harrigan, K.R. (1986), "Matching vertical integration strategies to competitive conditions," *Strategic Management Journal* 7: 535–555.

48. This is based on the following: Prahalad and Hamel argued that a firm that outsources too many activities risks hollowing out ("unlearning") its core competencies because the firm no longer participates in key adjacent value chain activities. A similar argument has been made by Prahalad, C.K., and G. Hamel (1990, May–June), "The core competence of the corporation," *Harvard Business Review*; and Teece, D.J. (1986), "Profiting from technological innovation: Implications for integration, collaboration, licensing and public policy," *Research Policy* 15: 285–305.

49. Rothaermel, F.T., M.A. Hitt, and L.A. Jobe (2006), "Balancing vertical integration and strategic outsourcing: Effects on product portfolios, new product success, and firm performance," *Strategic Management Journal* 27: 1033–1056.

50. "Global market size of outsourced services from 2000 to 2016 (in billion U.S. dollars)," *statista.com*, www.statista.com/statistics/189788/global-outsourcing-market-size/.

51. "Passage to India," *The Economist* (2010, Jun. 26).

52. Yum Brands Annual Report (various years); and http://www.worldatlas.com/articles/the-world-s-largest-fast-food-restaurant-chains.html.

53. Yum Brands Annual Report (various years).

54. Benoit, D., K. Wu, and R. Crew (2016, Sep. 2), "Yum Brands sells slice of China business ahead of spinoff," *The Wall Street Journa*.

55. Chick-fil-A data drawn from www.chick-fil-a.com/Company/Highlights-Fact-Sheets.

56. Technically speaking, Chick-fil-A also operates in Canada, as it has one restaurant in the Calgary, Alberta, airport, near the departure gate for U.S.-bound flights. See: Robertson, D. (2014, May 29), "U.S. fast-food chain Chick-fil-A opens Canadian franchise, talks down gay marriage controversy," *Calgary Herald*.

57. This section is based on: Rumelt, R.P. (1974), *Strategy, Structure, and Economic Performance* (Boston: Harvard Business School Press); and Montgomery, C.A. (1985), "Product-market diversification and market power," *Academy of Management Review* 28: 789–798.

58. Rumelt, R.P. (1974), *Strategy, Structure, and Economic Performance* (Boston: Harvard Business School Press). More recent research contributions go beyond mere relatedness, for instance: Sakhartov, A.V., and T. B. Folta (2015), "Getting beyond relatedness as a driver of corporate value," *Strategic Management Journal* 36: 1939–1959. The authors present a more complex approach to why some conglomerates are successful and why some related diversification does not add value. They argue that relatedness alone is insufficient as a predictor. They propose that the *redeployability of potentially shared resources* and the *inducement to redeploy resources* created by higher performance in new industries versus existing industries are also important factors.

59. 2018 Harley-Davidson Annual Report.

60. This is based on: ExxonMobil annual reports; "Oil's decline slows Exxon, Chevron profit growth," *The Wall Street Journal* (2009, Jan. 30); "The greening of ExxonMobil," *Forbes*, (2009, Aug. 24); Friedman, T.L. (2008), *Hot, Flat, and Crowded. Why We Need a Green Revolution—And How It Can Renew America* (New York: Farrar, Straus and Giroux); "Exxon to acquire XTO Energy in $31 billion stock deal," *The Wall Street Journal* (2009, Dec. 14); and "ExxonMobil buys XTO Energy," *The Economist* (2009, Dec. 17).

61. "The shale revolution: What could go wrong?" *The Wall Street Journal* (2012, Sep. 6); and "U.S. oil notches record growth," *The Wall Street Journal* (2013, Jun. 12).

62. This is based on: Peng, M.W. (2005), "What determines the scope of the firm over time? A focus on institutional relatedness," *Academy of Management Review* 30: 622–633; Peng, M.W. (2000), *Business Strategies in Transition Economies* (Thousand Oaks, CA: Sage); and Peng, M.W., and P.S. Heath (1996), "The growth of the firm in planned economies in transitions: Institutions, organizations, and strategic choice," *Academy of Management Review* 21: 492–528.

63. Prahalad, C.K., and G. Hamel (1990, May–June), "The core competence of the corporation," *Harvard Business Review.*

64. This discussion is based on: Burt, C., and F.T. Rothaermel (2013), "Bank of America and the new financial landscape," in Rothaermel, F.T., *Strategic Management* (New York: McGraw-Hill), http://mcgrawhillcreate.com/rothaermel.

65. Bank of America had long coveted Merrill Lynch, a premier investment bank. Severely weakened by the global financial crisis, Merrill Lynch became a takeover target, and Bank of America made a bid. In the process, Bank of America learned that Merrill Lynch's exposure to subprime mortgages and other exotic financial instruments was much larger than previously disclosed. Other problems included Merrill Lynch's payments of multimillion-dollar bonuses to many employees, despite the investment bank's having lost billions of dollars in 2008. After learning this new information, Bank of America (under its then-CEO Ken Lewis) attempted to withdraw from the Merrill Lynch takeover. The Federal Reserve Bank, under the leadership of its chairman, Ben Bernanke, insisted that Bank of America fulfill the agreement, noting that the takeover was part of a grand strategy to save the financial system from collapse. Once Bank of America shareholders learned that Lewis had not disclosed the problems at Merrill Lynch, they first stripped him of his chairmanship of the board of directors and later fired him as CEO. For a detailed and insightful discussion on the Merrill Lynch takeover by Bank of America, see: Lowenstein, R. (2010), *The End of Wall Street* (New York: Penguin Press).

66. "Bank of America and Merrill Lynch," *The Economist* (2010, Apr. 14).

67. Maloney, J., and C. Lombardo (2018, Aug. 18), "Coca-Cola invests in BodyArmor as it chases Gatorade," *The Wall Street Journal.*

68. "Oracle vs. salesforce.com," *Harvard Business School Case Study, 9-705-440;* "How to innovate in a downturn," *The Wall Street Journal* (2009, Mar. 18); and Dyer, J., H. Gregersen, and C.M. Christensen (2011). *The Innovator's DNA: Mastering the Five Skills of Disruptive Innovators* (Boston: Harvard Business Review Press).

69. This Strategy Highlight was prepared by Frank T. Rothaermel and Laura Zhang, who provided superb research assistance. Sources: Al-Muslim, A. (2018, Nov. 8), "P&G moves to streamline its structure," *The Wall Street Journal;* Al-Muslim, A. (2018, Oct. 19), "P&G posts strongest sales growth in five years," *The Wall Street Journal;* Terlep, S. (2018, Sep. 29), "Procter & Gamble tries to break a cycle of stagnation," *The Wall Street Journal;* Terlep, S. (2017, Apr. 4), "Gillette, bleeding market share, cuts prices of razors," *The Wall Street Journal;* "By The Numbers: Procter & Gamble is a better buy than its peers,"*Forbes* (2016, Dec. 29); Reuters (2016, Feb. 16), "Why P&G's CEO says the company needs to be more nimble," *Fortune;* Ng, S., J.S. Lublin and E. Byron (2015, Jul. 29), "P&G names David Taylor as CEO," *The Wall Street Journal;* "Here's How P&G's brand consolidation program could backfire and push its valuation below $60," *Forbes* (2015, Jun. 30); Ng, S., and P. Ziobro (2015, Jun. 23), "Razor sales move online, away from Gillette," *The Wall Street Journal;* "Are P&G and Unilever headed in opposite directions?" *Forbes* (2015, Mar. 25); Ziobro, P., J. Mitchell, and T. Francis (2014, Jan. 27), "Strong dollar squeezes U.S. firms," *The Wall Street Journal;* Ng, S. (2014, Aug. 1), "P&G to shed more than half its brands," *The Wall Street Journal;* "P&G's billion-dollar brands: Trusted, valued, recognized," Fact Sheet, www.pg.com; and Lafley, A.G., and R.L. Martin (2013), *Playing to Win: How Strategy Really Works* (Boston: Harvard Business Review Press).

70. Palich, L.E., L.B. Cardinal, and C.C. Miller (2000), "Curvilinearity in the diversification-performance linkage: An examination of over three decades of research," *Strategic Management Journal* 21: 155–174.

71. This is based on: Lang, L.H.P., and R.M. Stulz (1994), "Tobin's *q*, corporate diversification, and firm performance," *Journal of Political Economy* 102: 1248–1280; Martin, J.D., and A. Sayrak (2003), "Corporate diversification and shareholder value: A survey of recent literature," *Journal of Corporate Finance* 9: 37–57; and Rajan, R., H. Servaes, and L. Zingales (2000), "The cost of diversity: The diversification discount and inefficient investment," *Journal of Finance* 55: 35–80.

72. Mann, T., and V. McGrane (2015, Apr. 10), "GE to cash out of banking business," *The Wall Street Journal.*

73. This is based on: Peng, M.W., and P.S. Heath (1996), "The growth of the firm in planned economies in transitions: Institutions, organizations, and strategic choice," *Academy of Management Review* 21: 492–528; Peng, M.W. (2000), *Business Strategies in Transition Economies* (Thousand Oaks, CA: Sage); Peng, M.W. (2005), "What determines the scope of the firm over time? A focus on institutional relatedness," *Academy of Management Review* 30: 622–633.

74. Villalonga, B. (2004), "Diversification discount or premium? New evidence from the business information tracking series," *Journal of Finance* 59: 479–506.

75. This section is based on: "U.S. clears InBev to buy Anheuser," *The Wall Street Journal* (2008, Nov. 15); and "Blackstone nears deal," *The Wall Street Journal* (2009, Oct. 5).

76. Boston Consulting Group (1970), *The Product Portfolio* (Boston: Boston Consulting Group); and Shay, J.P., and F.T. Rothaermel (1999), "Dynamic competitive strategy: Towards a multi-perspective conceptual framework," *Long Range Planning* 32: 559–572; and Kiechel, W. (2010), *The Lords of Strategy: The Secret Intellectual History of the New Corporate World* (Boston: Harvard Business School Press).

77. GE annual reports.

78. Milgrom, P., and J. Roberts (1990), "Bargaining costs, influence costs, and the organization of economic activity," in ed. J. Alt and K. Shepsle, *Perspectives on Positive Political Economy* (Cambridge, UK: Cambridge University Press).

79. Galloway, S. (2017, Sep. 22), "Amazon takes over the world," *The Wall Street Journal.*

Corporate Strategy: Strategic Alliances, Mergers and Acquisitions

Chapter Outline

Learning Objectives

After studying this chapter, you should be able to:

LO 9-1 Apply the build-borrow-or-buy framework to guide corporate strategy.

LO 9-2 Define strategic alliances, and explain why they are important to implement corporate strategy and why firms enter into them.

LO 9-3 Describe three alliance governance mechanisms and evaluate their pros and cons.

LO 9-4 Describe the three phases of alliance management and explain how an alliance management capability can lead to a competitive advantage.

LO 9-5 Differentiate between mergers and acquisitions, and explain why firms would use either to execute corporate strategy.

LO 9-6 Define horizontal integration and evaluate the advantages and disadvantages of this option to execute corporate-level strategy.

LO 9-7 Explain why firms engage in acquisitions.

LO 9-8 Evaluate whether mergers and acquisitions lead to competitive advantage.

Little Lyft Gets Big Alliance Partners and Beats Uber in Going Public

IN THE SPRING OF 2019, Uber's valuation before its initial public offering (IPO) was $82 billion, making it the most valuable privately held company ever. Serving approximately 600 cities in more than 60 countries worldwide and with 100 million monthly users, Uber dominates the global ride-hailing app market. However, Lyft, coming in second, is Uber's closest competitor in the United States and managed to beat this market leader in the IPO race. On March 29, 2019, Lyft became the first U.S.-ride-hailing and sharing service to sell its shares to the public with a valuation of more than $26 billion at the end of its first trading day. In 2017, Lyft was worth less than one-tenth of Uber (some $7.5 billion). Within this brief span of time, Lyft increased the number of its active riders from 6 million to almost 20 million, thereby gaining market share vis-à-vis Uber. How did Lyft beat Uber to an IPO and more than triple its valuation within a mere two years? (Uber had its IPO on May 10, 2019, and was valued at $76 billion at the end of its first trading day).

Smith Collection/Gado/Archive Photos/Getty Images

Lyft is clearly the underdog in the fiercely competitive ride-hailing industry. A shrewd strategy is about "getting more out of a situation than the starting balance of power would suggest."[1] As when dealing with a schoolyard bully, it helps to have strong friends. Lyft's co-founders, Logan Green and John Zimmer, appear to have paid close attention to this idea. To pursue their underdog strategy against Uber, they allied Lyft with some powerful friends.

Strengthen Competitive Position. Strategic alliances with powerful partners enabled Lyft to strengthen its competitive position against Uber. Lyft formed two important alliances: In 2016, it formed an equity alliance with GM (one of the largest car manufacturers globally), which invested $500 million in the startup. A year later, Lyft announced an alliance with Waymo (a subsidiary of Alphabet, the parent company of Google), an autonomous car technology venture. Why did these firms enter strategic alliances with Lyft?

Waymo happens to be a fierce rival of Uber in the development of self-driving car technology. When Lyft announced its alliance with Waymo, Alphabet and Uber were entangled in a lawsuit, wherein Alphabet alleged that Uber stole proprietary technology when acquiring Otto, a self-driving technology company. Otto was founded by a former Waymo engineer that headed its self-driving car efforts. Thus, the alliance with Waymo allowed Lyft to strengthen its competitive position vis-à-vis Uber. Having autonomous vehicle technology succeed is critical for both Uber and Lyft because human drivers are the biggest cost factor in offering rides. Moreover, autonomous-driving technology is also expected to be safer than human driving, resulting in fewer accidents. In addition, since smart traffic guidance can be employed much more easily with self-driving cars that can run 24/7, 365 days a year, traffic congestion is expected to be much less and delays much fewer, if any.

Enter New Markets. GM's alliance with Lyft allowed the firm to tap into the second-largest mobile transportation network in North America. The goal was to deploy GM cars on Lyft's network, ideally as self-driving vehicles. GM's equity alliance with Lyft allowed GM to enter into the mobile transportation and logistics market.

Hedge against Uncertainty. GM's equity investment in Lyft also allowed GM to hedge against uncertainty. With network effects supporting winner-take-all dynamics, it is likely that only one or a few mobile transportation companies will survive in the long run. GM also wants to be in this new market because the age-old private car ownership model is likely to shift in favor of fleet ownership and management. Consumers will rent a car for a specific ride, rather than own a car as a fixed asset. Noteworthy is that private cars in the United States are used only about

5 percent of the time, and sit idle for most of the day. Car owners have the fixed costs of purchasing a car, buying insurance, and maintaining the car. All this goes away with the new business model that is likely to emerge.

Learn New Capabilities. Lyft may need to learn how to manage large fleets of cars—a capability that GM, a key supplier to many large car rental companies, can provide. In addition, Lyft may want to learn some of the self-driving technology that Waymo can provide. In turn, this might motivate Waymo to learn more about how to establish and maintain a large mobile logistics network that it can then leverage into more precise target advertising for its Google partner division, or other new services it might want to offer one day.

Despite its successful IPO, however, Lyft is facing a number of challenges on its road to profitability. First, Lyft continues to lose a lot of money. In 2018, Lyft lost almost $1 billion in subsidizing fares, incentivizing drivers, bringing on new modes of mobility such as scooters and bikes, and paying high insurance costs, among other expenses. This is the largest loss for any U.S. startup in the 12 months preceding its initial public offering. Second, the threat of local regulation is ongoing as many cities in the United States and around the globe are starting to restrict ride-hailing services and require minimum pay for drivers.

Finally, Lyft's archrival Uber, which also went public in 2019, could be better positioned for growth because it offers a more diversified service portfolio with Uber Eats and its long-distance freight service. Lyft remains a ride-hailing service only. Moreover, Lyft is geographically restricted to the United States and Canada at this point, while Uber is global. Thus, many view Uber as the likely victor in the winner-take-all competition among the U.S.-ride-hailing platforms. As a consequence of all these combined threats, Lyft's market cap has fallen from $26 billion (on the day of its IPO) to $16 billion just a few weeks later. By the fall of 2019, Lyft's valuation had fallen further to $13 billion, while Uber's had fallen to $52 billion. Although Lyft was smart in allying with strong partners and to beat Uber to the IPO goal line, the race is far from over.[2]

Part II of this ChapterCase appears in Section 9.4.

LYFT IS USING strategic alliances with GM and Waymo in an attempt to close the gap with Uber, as highlighted in the ChapterCase. Lyft's strategic leaders realized it would be difficult for the much smaller ride-hailing company to catch up with Uber on its own. Tapping into its partners' resources and expertise allowed Lyft to become a much more potent rival to Uber than as a standalone company. Indeed, within a short two years, Lyft's co-founders were able to triple the valuation of the startup and to beat Uber in the race of going public. Lyft, therefore, was able to close the performance gap with Uber considerably. This example shows how strategic alliances can help firms to grow and to possibly outperform much stronger rivals.

In Chapter 8, we discussed *why* firms grow. In this chapter we discuss *how* firms grow. In addition to internal organic growth (achieved through reinvesting profits, see discussion of Exhibit 4.4 in Chapter 4), firms have two critical strategic options to execute corporate strategy: *alliances* and *acquisitions*. For instance, Lyft used strategic alliances with GM and Waymo to grow, and Uber acquired its Middle Eastern rival Careem for $3.1 billion in 2019 to strengthen its global position. We devote this chapter to the study of these fundamental pathways through which firms implement corporate strategy.

We begin this chapter by introducing the *build-borrow-or-buy framework* to guide corporate strategy in deciding whether and when to grow internally (build), use alliances (borrow), or make acquisitions (buy). We then take a close look at strategic alliances before studying mergers and acquisitions. We discuss alliances before acquisitions because alliances are smaller strategic commitments and thus are much more frequent. In some cases, alliances may lead to acquisitions later, offering "try before you buy." For example, before Disney acquired Pixar (for $7.4 billion in 2006), the firms had a long-standing strategic alliance, where Pixar would develop computer-animated films that Disney would market and distribute. We conclude with *Implications for Strategic Leaders,* in which we discuss practical applications.

9.1 How Firms Achieve Growth

After discussing in Chapter 8 why firms need to grow, the next question that arises is: *How do firms grow?* Corporate executives can drive firm growth using one of three corporate strategy options: organic growth through internal development, external growth through alliances, or external growth through acquisitions. Laurence Capron and Will Mitchell developed an insightful step-by-step decision model to guide managers in selecting the most appropriate corporate strategy.[3] Selecting the most suitable option in response to a specific strategic challenge also makes successful implementation more likely.

THE BUILD-BORROW-OR-BUY FRAMEWORK

The **build-borrow-or-buy framework** provides a conceptual model that aids strategic leaders in deciding whether to pursue internal development (*build*), enter a contractual arrangement or strategic alliance (*borrow*), or acquire new resources, capabilities, and competencies (*buy*). Firms that are able to learn how to select the right pathways to obtain new resources are more likely to gain and sustain a competitive advantage. Note that in the build-borrow-or-buy model, the term *resources* is defined broadly to include capabilities and competencies (as in the *VRIO model* discussed in Chapter 4). Exhibit 9.1 shows the *build-borrow-or-buy* decision framework.

Determining which corporate strategy option to use to respond to a strategic challenge begins with the identification of a strategic resource gap that will impede future growth. The resource gap is *strategic* because closing this gap can lead to a competitive advantage. As discussed in Chapter 4, resources with the potential to lead to competitive advantage cannot be simply bought on the open market. Indeed, if any firm could readily buy this type of resource, its availability would negate its potential for competitive advantage. It would no longer be *rare*, a key condition for a resource to form the basis of competitive advantage. Moreover, resources that are *valuable, rare*, and *difficult to imitate* are often

build-borrow-or-buy framework Conceptual model that aids firms in deciding whether to pursue internal development (*build*), enter a contractual arrangement or strategic alliance (*borrow*), or acquire new resources, capabilities, and competencies (*buy*).

EXHIBIT 9.1 Guiding Corporate Strategy: The Build-Borrow-or-Buy Framework

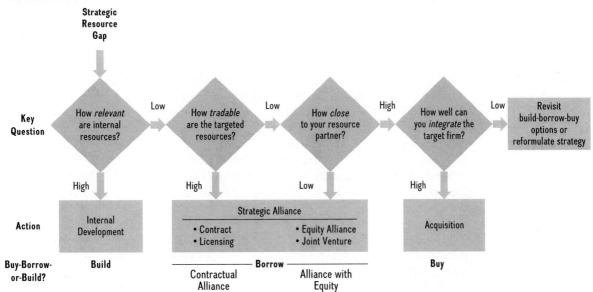

Source: Adapted from L. Capron and W. Mitchell (2012), *Build, Borrow, or Buy: Solving the Growth Dilemma* (Boston: Harvard Business Review Press).

embedded deep within a firm, frequently making up a resource bundle that is hard to unplug whole or in part.

The options to close the strategic resource gap are, therefore, to build, borrow, or buy. *Build* in the build-borrow-buy framework refers to internal development; *borrow* refers to the use of strategic alliances; and *buy* refers to acquiring a firm. When acquiring a firm, you buy an entire "resource bundle," not just a specific resource. This resource bundle, if obeying VRIO principles and successfully integrated, can then form the basis of competitive advantage.

Exhibit 9.1 provides a schematic of the build-borrow-or-buy framework. In this approach strategic leaders must determine the degree to which certain conditions apply, either high or low, by responding to up to four questions sequentially before finding the best course. The questions cover issues of *relevancy, tradability, closeness,* and *integration:*

1. **Relevancy.** How *relevant* are the firm's existing internal resources to solving the resource gap?
2. **Tradability.** How *tradable* are the targeted resources that may be available externally?
3. **Closeness.** How *close* do you need to be to your external resource partner?
4. **Integration.** How well can you *integrate* the targeted firm, should you determine you need to acquire the resource partner?

As shown in Exhibit 9.1, the answers to these questions lead to a recommended action or the next question. We'll review each in more depth.

1. HOW *RELEVANT* ARE THE FIRM'S EXISTING INTERNAL RESOURCES TO SOLVING THE RESOURCE GAP? The firm's strategic leaders start by asking whether the firm's internal resources are high or low in relevance. If the firm's internal resources are highly relevant to closing the identified gap, the firm should itself build the new resources needed through internal development.

But how does a strategic leader know whether the firm's resources are relevant in addressing a new challenge or opportunity? Firms evaluate the relevance of internal resources in two ways: they test whether resources are (1) *similar* to those the firm needs to develop and (2) *superior* to those of competitors in the targeted area.[4] If *both* conditions are met, then the firm's internal resources are relevant and the firm should pursue internal development.

Let's look at both conditions. Strategic leaders are often misled by the first test because things that might appear similar at the surface are actually quite different deep down.[5] Moreover, they tend to focus on the (known) similarities rather than on (unknown) differences. Strategic leaders often don't know how the resources needed for the existing and new business opportunity differ. An executive at a newspaper publisher such as *The New York Times* may conclude that the researching, reporting, writing, and editing activities done for a printed newspaper are similar to those done for an online one. Although the activities may be similar, they are also different because the underlying business model and technology for online publishing are radically different from that of traditional print media. Managing the community interactions of online publishing as well as applying data analytics to understand website traffic and reader engagement are also elements that are entirely new. To make the challenge even greater, online news reporting is required in real time, 24/7, 365 days a year. To make matters worse, old-line news companies are now competing with millions of "citizen journalists" on social media, such as Twitter or Weibo, which often have an edge on breaking news.[6]

The second test, determining whether your internal resources are *superior* to those of competitors in the targeted area, can best be assessed by applying the VRIO framework (see

Exhibit 4.5). In the case of the print publisher, the answer to both questions is likely a "no." This implies that building the new resource through *internal* development is not an option. The firm then needs to consider *external*—borrow or buy—options. This then leads us to the next question.

2. HOW *TRADABLE* ARE THE TARGETED RESOURCES THAT MAY BE AVAILABLE EXTERNALLY? For external options, the firm needs to determine how tradable the targeted resources may be. The term *tradable* implies that the firm is able to source the resource externally through a contract that allows for the transfer of ownership or use of the resource. Short-term as well as long-term contracts, such as licensing or franchising, are a way to *borrow* resources from another company (see discussion in Chapter 8). In the biotech-pharma industry, some producers use licensing agreements to transfer knowledge and technology from the licensor's R&D to the licensee's manufacturing. Eli Lilly, for example, has commercialized several breakthrough biotech drugs using licensing agreements with new ventures. The implication is that if a resource is highly tradable, then the resource should be *borrowed* via a licensing agreement or other contractual agreement. If the resource in question is not easily tradable, then the firm needs to consider either a deeper strategic alliance through an equity alliance or a joint venture, or an outright acquisition.

3. HOW *CLOSE* DO YOU NEED TO BE TO YOUR EXTERNAL RESOURCE PARTNER? Many times, firms are able to obtain the required resources to fill the strategic gap through more integrated strategic alliances such as equity alliances or joint ventures (see Exhibit 8.4) rather than through outright acquisition. Mergers and acquisitions are the most costly, complex, and difficult to reverse strategic option. This implies that only if extreme closeness to the resource partner is necessary to understand and obtain its underlying knowledge should M&A be considered the *buy* option. Regardless, the firm should always first consider *borrowing* the necessary resources through strategic alliances before looking at M&A.

4. HOW WELL CAN YOU *INTEGRATE* THE TARGETED FIRM, SHOULD YOU DETERMINE YOU NEED TO ACQUIRE THE RESOURCE PARTNER? The final decision question using the build-borrow-buy lens is: *Can you integrate the target firm?* The list of post-integration failures, often due to cultural differences, is long. Multibillion-dollar failures resulting include the integration of Bayer and Monsanto, Alcatel and Lucent, Daimler and Chrysler, AOL and Time Warner, HP and Autonomy, and Bank of America and Countrywide. More than cultural differences were involved in Microsoft's decision (in 2015) to write down $7.6 billion in losses (or more than 80 percent) on its $9.4 billion acquisition of Nokia some 15 months earlier. It's now up to Microsoft CEO Satya Nadella to decide whether and how to compete in the mobile device arena after former CEO Steve Ballmer made a desperate gamble on acquiring the Finnish cell phone maker.[7]

Only if the three prior conditions *(low relevancy, low tradability,* and *high need for closeness)* shown in the decision tree in Exhibit 9.1 are met, should the firm's strategic leaders consider M&A: If the firm's internal resources are insufficient to *build, and* the resource needed to fill the strategic gap cannot be *borrowed* through a strategic alliance, *and* closeness to the resource partner is needed, then the final question to consider is whether the integration of the two firms using a merger or acquisition will be successful. In all other cases, the firms should consider finding a less costly *borrow* arrangement when *building* is not an option. Since strategic alliances are the less costly and more common tool to execute corporate strategy, we discuss alliances first before mergers and acquisitions. Per the build-borrow-buy decision framework, strategic alliances *(borrow)* also need to be considered before mergers and acquisitions *(buy)*.

9.2 Strategic Alliances

Firms enter many types of alliances, from small contracts that have no bearing on a firm's competitiveness to multibillion-dollar joint ventures that can make or break the company. An alliance, therefore, qualifies as *strategic* only if it has the potential to affect a firm's competitive advantage.

Strategic alliances are voluntary arrangements between firms that involve the sharing of knowledge, resources, and capabilities with the intent of developing processes, products, or services.[8] The use of strategic alliances to implement corporate strategy has grown significantly in the past few decades, with thousands forming each year. As the speed of technological change and innovation has increased (see discussion in Chapter 7), firms have responded by entering more alliances. Globalization has also contributed to an increase in cross-border strategic alliances (see discussion in Chapter 10).

Strategic alliances are attractive for a number of reasons. They enable firms to achieve goals faster and at lower costs than going it alone. Strategic alliances may join complementary parts of a firm's value chain, such as R&D and marketing, or they may focus on joining the same value chain activities. In contrast to mergers and acquisitions, strategic alliances also allow firms to circumvent potential legal repercussions including potential lawsuits filed by U.S. federal agencies or the European Union.

A strategic alliance has the potential to help a firm gain and sustain a competitive advantage when it joins resources and knowledge in a combination that obeys the VRIO principles (introduced in Chapter 4).[9] The locus of competitive advantage is often not found within the individual firm but within a strategic partnership. According to this **relational view of competitive advantage**, critical resources and capabilities frequently are embedded in strategic alliances that span firm boundaries. Applying the VRIO framework, we know that the basis for competitive advantage is formed when a strategic alliance creates resource combinations that are valuable, rare, and difficult to imitate, and the alliance is organized appropriately to allow for value capture. In support of this perspective, over 80 percent of Fortune 1000 CEOs indicated in a survey that more than one-quarter of their firm's revenues were derived from strategic alliances.[10]

WHY DO FIRMS ENTER STRATEGIC ALLIANCES?

To affect a firm's competitive advantage, an alliance must promise a positive effect on the firm's economic value creation through increasing value and/or lowering costs (see discussion in Chapter 5). This logic is reflected in the common reasons firms enter alliances.[11] They do so to

- Strengthen competitive position.
- Enter new markets.
- Hedge against uncertainty.
- Access critical complementary assets.
- Learn new capabilities.

STRENGTHEN COMPETITIVE POSITION. Firms frequently resort to strategic alliances to strengthen their competitive position, as did Lyft when competing against Uber (see the ChapterCase). Firms can also use strategic alliances to change the industry structure in their favor by reducing competitive rivalry.[12] Moreover, firms frequently use strategic alliances when competing in setting an industry standard (see discussion in Chapter 7).

Strategy Highlight **9.1**

How Tesla Used Alliances Strategically

Since its initial public offering in 2010, the electric-car manufacturer Tesla has had tremendous impact. Indeed, by 2017 it had become the most valuable car company in the United States, ahead of GM and Ford. (Although, by 2019, GM's value once more exceeded Tesla's). One critical factor in the early success of the California startup is the role its alliance strategy played, in particular, its alliances with Daimler and Toyota. The Daimler partnership provided a much-needed cash injection as well as automobile engineering expertise; the Toyota partnership gave Tesla access to a world-class manufacturing facility located near its headquarters in Palo Alto, California.

Initially, Tesla, which began selling its all-electric Roadster model in 2008, had neither a market nor legitimacy. Moreover, it was plagued with both thorny technical problems and cost overruns. Yet it managed to overcome these early challenges, in part by turning prospective rivals into alliance partners. In 2009, the year before its IPO, Tesla allied with Daimler, whose roots in automobile engineering go back to its invention of the internal combustion engine some 130 years ago. The deal provided Tesla with superior engineering expertise and a cash infusion of $50 million, which helped to save the company from potential bankruptcy.

The alliance with Toyota, signed the following year, brought other benefits. It enabled Tesla to buy the former New United Motor Manufacturing Inc. (NUMMI) factory in Fremont, California—created as a joint venture between Toyota and General Motors Corp. in 1984—and to learn large-scale, high-quality manufacturing from a pioneer of lean manufacturing. As it happened, the NUMMI plant was the only remaining large-scale car manufacturing plant in California, and some 25 miles from Tesla's Palo Alto headquarters. Without this factory, Tesla would not have been able to produce nearly 400,000 vehicles in 2019.

In 2014, Tesla signed another strategic alliance—this one with Osaka-based Panasonic, the Japanese consumer electronics company and a world leader in battery technology. As Tesla tries to position itself in the business of sustainable and decentralized energy, the relationship with Panasonic is significant. The two companies are jointly investing in a new $5 billion lithium-ion battery plant in Nevada. Tesla's ability to attract and manage leading companies in the automotive and other key industries as strategic alliance partners is an important part of its formula for success.

The decisions by Tesla to collaborate with Daimler, Toyota, and Panasonic to collaborate highlight the fact that individual companies may not need to own all of the resources, skills, and knowledge necessary to undertake key strategic growth initiatives.[13]

Strategy Highlight 9.1 shows how Tesla used alliances strategically to strengthen its competitive standing and to position itself advantageously in making electric vehicles a serious contender for the future standard in car propulsion, eventually obsoleting internal combustion engines.

ENTER NEW MARKETS. Firms may use strategic alliances to enter new markets, either in terms of products and services or geography.[14]

Using a strategic alliance, HP and DreamWorks Animation SKG created the Halo Collaboration Studio, which makes virtual communication possible around the globe.[15] Halo's conferencing technology gives participants the vivid sense that they are in the same room. The conference rooms of clients match, down to the last detail, giving participants the impression that they are sitting together at the same table. DreamWorks produced several of its computer-animated movies such as the *Shrek* franchise using this new technology for its meetings. People with different creative skills—script writers, computer animators, directors—though dispersed geographically, were able to participate as if in the same room, even seeing the work on each other's laptops. Use of the technology enabled faster decision making, enhanced productivity, reduced (or even eliminated) travel time and expense, and increased job satisfaction. Neither HP nor DreamWorks would have been able to produce this technology breakthrough alone, but moving into the videoconferencing arena together via a strategic alliance allowed both partners to pursue related diversification. Moreover, HP's alliance with DreamWorks Animation SKG enabled HP to compete head on with Cisco's high-end videoconferencing solution, TelePresence.[16] The HP and DreamWorks Animation SKG alliance was motivated by the desire to enter a new market, in terms of products and services offered, that neither could enter alone.

When entering new geographic markets, in some instances, governments such as Saudi Arabia or China may require that foreign firms have a local joint venture partner before doing business in their countries. These cross-border strategic alliances have both benefits and risks. While the foreign firm can benefit from local expertise and contacts, it is exposed to the risk that some of its proprietary know-how may be appropriated by the foreign partner. We will address such issues in Chapter 10 when studying global strategy.

HEDGE AGAINST UNCERTAINTY. In dynamic markets, strategic alliances allow firms to limit their exposure to uncertainty in the market.[17] For instance, in the wake of the biotechnology revolution, incumbent pharmaceutical firms such as Pfizer, Novartis, and Roche entered into hundreds of strategic alliances with biotech startups.[18] These alliances allowed the big pharma firms to make small-scale investments in many of the new biotechnology ventures that were poised to disrupt existing market economics. In some sense, the pharma companies were taking **real options** in these biotechnology experiments, providing them with the right but not the obligation to make further investments when new drugs were introduced from the biotech companies.

A **real-options perspective** to strategic decision making breaks down a larger investment decision (such as whether to enter biotechnology or not) into a set of smaller decisions that are staged sequentially over time. This approach allows the firm to obtain additional information at predetermined stages. At each stage, after new information is revealed, the firm evaluates whether or not to make further investments. In a sense, a real option, which is the right, but not the obligation, to continue making investments, allows the firm to buy time until sufficient information for a go versus no-go decision is revealed. Once the new biotech drugs were a known quantity, the uncertainty was removed, and the incumbent firms could react accordingly.

Early on during the biotechnology revolution, for instance, the Swiss pharma company Roche initially invested $2.1 billion (in 1990) in an equity alliance to purchase a controlling interest (greater than 50 percent) in the biotech startup Genentech. After witnessing the success of Genentech's drug discovery and development projects in subsequent years, Roche spent $47 billion (in 2009) to purchase the remaining minority interest in Genentech, making it a wholly owned subsidiary.[19] Taking a wait-and-see approach by entering strategic alliances allows incumbent firms to buy time and wait for the uncertainty surrounding the market and technology to fade. Many firms in fast-moving markets subscribe to this rationale. Waiting can also be expensive, however. To acquire the remaining less than 50 percent of Genentech some 20 years after its initial investment required a price that was some 24 times higher than the initial investment, as uncertainty settled and the biotech startup turned out to be hugely successful. Besides biotechnology, the use of a *real-options perspective* in making strategic investments has also been documented in nanotechnology, semiconductors, and other dynamic markets.[20]

ACCESS CRITICAL COMPLEMENTARY ASSETS. The successful commercialization of a new product or service often requires complementary assets such as marketing, manufacturing, and after-sale service.[21] In particular, new firms are in need of complementary assets to complete the value chain from upstream innovation to downstream commercialization. This

real options Choices that afford managers the right but not the obligation to make further investments.

real-options perspective Approach to strategic decision making that breaks down a larger investment decision into a set of smaller decisions that are staged sequentially over time.

implies that a new venture that has a core competency in R&D, for example, will need to access distribution channels and marketing expertise to complete the value chain. Building downstream complementary assets such as marketing and regulatory expertise or a sales force is often prohibitively expensive and time-consuming, and thus frequently not an option for new ventures. Strategic alliances allow firms to match complementary skills and resources to complete the value chain. Moreover, licensing agreements of this sort allow the partners to benefit from a division of labor, allowing each to efficiently focus on its core competency.

LEARN NEW CAPABILITIES. Firms also enter strategic alliances because they are motivated by the desire to learn new capabilities from their partners.[22] When the collaborating firms are also competitors, *co-opetition* ensues.[23]

Co-opetition. **Co-opetition** is a portmanteau describing cooperation by competitors. They may cooperate to create a larger pie but then might compete about how the pie should be divided. Such co-opetition can lead to **learning races** in strategic alliances,[24] a situation in which both partners are motivated to form an alliance for learning, but the rate at which the firms learn may vary. The firm that learns faster and accomplishes its goal more quickly has an incentive to exit the alliance or, at a minimum, to reduce its knowledge sharing. Since the cooperating firms are also competitors, learning races can have a positive effect on the winning firm's competitive position vis-à-vis its alliance partner.

NUMMI (New United Motor Manufacturing, Inc.) was the first joint venture in the U.S. automobile industry, formed between GM and Toyota (in 1984). Recall from Chapter 8 that joint ventures are a special type of a strategic alliance in which two partner firms create a third, jointly owned entity. In the NUMMI joint venture, each partner was motivated to learn new capabilities: GM entered the equity-based strategic alliance to learn the lean manufacturing system pioneered by Toyota to produce high-quality, fuel-efficient cars at a profit. Toyota entered the alliance to learn how to implement its lean manufacturing program with an American work force. NUMMI was a test-run for Toyota before building fully owned *greenfield plants* (new manufacturing facilities) in Alabama, Indiana, Kentucky, Mississippi, Texas, and West Virginia. In this 25-year history, GM and Toyota built some 7 million high-quality cars at the NUMMI plant. In fact, NUMMI was transformed from worst performer (under GM ownership before the joint venture) to GM's highest-quality plant in the United States. In the end, as part of GM's bankruptcy reorganization during 2009–2010, it pulled out of the NUMMI joint venture. Toyota later sold the NUMMI plant to Tesla (as mentioned in Strategy Highlight 9.1).

The joint venture between GM and Toyota can be seen as a learning race. Who won? Strategy scholars argue that Toyota was faster in accomplishing its alliance goal—learning how to manage U.S. labor—because of its limited scope.[25] Toyota had already perfected lean manufacturing; all it needed to do was learn how to train U.S. workers in the method and transfer this knowledge to its subsidiary plants in the United States. On the other hand, GM had to learn a completely new production system. GM was successful in transferring lean manufacturing to its newly created Saturn brand (which was discontinued in 2010 as part of GM's reorganization), but it had a hard time implementing lean manufacturing in its *existing* plants. These factors suggest that Toyota won the learning race with GM, which in turn helped Toyota gain and sustain a competitive advantage over GM in the U.S. market.

Also, note that different motivations for forming alliances are not necessarily independent and can be intertwined. For example, firms that collaborate to access critical complementary assets may also want to learn from one another to subsequently pursue vertical integration. In sum, alliance formation is frequently motivated by leveraging economies of scale, scope, specialization, and learning.

co-opetition Cooperation by competitors to achieve a strategic objective.

learning races Situations in which both partners in a strategic alliance are motivated to form an alliance for learning, but the rate at which the firms learn may vary.

LO 9-3

Describe three alliance governance mechanisms and evaluate their pros and cons.

GOVERNING STRATEGIC ALLIANCES

In Chapter 8, we showed that strategic alliances lie in the middle of the make-or-buy continuum (see Exhibit 8.4). Alliances can be governed by the following mechanisms:[26]

- Non-equity alliances
- Equity alliances
- Joint ventures

Exhibit 9.2 provides an overview of the key characteristics of the three alliance types, including their advantages and disadvantages.

EXHIBIT 9.2 Key Characteristics of Different Alliance Types

Alliance Type	Governance Mechanism	Frequency	Type of Knowledge Exchanged	Pros	Cons	Examples
Non-equity (supply, licensing, and distribution agreements)	Contract	Most common	Explicit	• Flexible • Fast • Easy to initiate and terminate	• Weak tie • Lack of trust and commitment	• Genentech-Lilly (exclusive) licensing agreement for Humulin • Microsoft-IBM (nonexclusive) licensing agreement for MS-DOS
Equity (purchase of an equity stake or corporate venture capital investment, or investment in kind such as a plant and equipment)	Equity investment	Less common than non-equity alliances, but more common than joint ventures	Explicit; exchange of tacit knowledge possible	• Stronger tie • Trust and commitment can emerge • Window into new technology (option value)	• Less flexible • Slower • Can entail significant investments	• GM's equity investment in Lyft • Coca-Cola's equity investments in Monster and BodyArmor energy drinks
Joint venture (JV)	Creation of new entity by two or more parent firms	Least common	Both tacit and explicit knowledge exchanged	• Strongest tie • Trust and commitment likely to emerge • May be required by institutional setting	• Can entail long negotiations and significant investments • Long-term solution • JV managers have double reporting lines (2 bosses)	• Hulu, owned by Disney (67%) and Comcast (33%) • The A++ trans-Atlantic joint venture, owned by United Airlines, Lufthansa, and Air Canada

NON-EQUITY ALLIANCES. The most common type of alliance is a **non-equity alliance**, which is based on contracts between firms. The most frequent forms of non-equity alliances are *supply agreements, distribution agreements*, and *licensing agreements*. As suggested by their names, these contractual agreements are vertical strategic alliances, connecting different parts of the industry value chain. In a non-equity alliance, firms tend to share **explicit knowledge**—knowledge that can be codified. Patents, user manuals, fact sheets, and scientific publications are all ways to capture explicit knowledge, which concerns the notion of *knowing about* a certain process or product.

Licensing agreements are contractual alliances in which the participants regularly exchange codified knowledge. The biotech firm Genentech licensed its newly developed drug Humulin (human insulin) to the pharmaceutical firm Eli Lilly for manufacturing, facilitating approval by the Food and Drug Administration (FDA), and distribution. This partnership was an example of a vertical strategic alliance: One partner (Genentech) was positioned upstream in the industry value chain focusing on R&D, while the other partner (Eli Lilly) was positioned downstream focusing on manufacturing and distribution. This type of vertical arrangement is often described as a hand-off from the upstream partner to the downstream partner and is possible because the underlying knowledge is largely explicit and can be easily codified. When Humulin reached the market, it was the first approved genetically engineered human therapeutic drug worldwide.[27] Subsequently, Humulin became a billion-dollar blockbuster drug.

Because of their contractual nature, non-equity alliances are flexible and easy to initiate and terminate. However, because they can be temporary in nature, they also sometimes produce weak ties between the alliance partners, which can result in a lack of trust and commitment.

EQUITY ALLIANCES. In an **equity alliance**, at least one partner takes partial ownership in the other partner. Equity alliances are less common than contractual, non-equity alliances because they often require larger investments. Because they are based on partial ownership rather than contracts, equity alliances are used to signal stronger commitments. Moreover, equity alliances allow for the sharing of **tacit knowledge**—knowledge that cannot be codified.[28] Tacit knowledge concerns *knowing how* to do a certain task. It can be acquired only through actively participating in the process. In an equity alliance, therefore, the partners frequently exchange personnel to make the acquisition of tacit knowledge possible.

Toyota used an equity alliance with Tesla, a designer and maker of electric cars (featured in ChapterCase 1 and Strategy Highlight 9.1), to learn new knowledge and gain a window into new technology. Toyota made a $50 million equity investment in the California startup (in 2010). In the same year, Tesla purchased the NUMMI plant in Fremont, California, where it now manufactures its cars for the U.S. market and overseas (other than Asia, where Tesla has a factory in Shanghai, China). Tesla CEO Elon Musk stated, "The Tesla factory effectively leverages an ideal combination of hard-core Silicon Valley engineering talent, traditional automotive engineering talent, and the proven Toyota production system." Toyota in turn hopes to infuse its company with Tesla's entrepreneurial spirit. Toyota President Akio Toyoda commented, "By partnering with Tesla, my hope is that all Toyota employees will recall that

---

| **non-equity alliance** Partnership based on contracts between firms. | **explicit knowledge** Knowledge that can be codified; concerns knowing about a process or product. | **equity alliance** Partnership in which at least one partner takes partial ownership in the other. | **tacit knowledge** Knowledge that cannot be codified; concerns knowing how to do a certain task and can be acquired only through active participation in that task. |

'venture business spirit' and take on the challenges of the future." Toyoda hoped that a transfer of tacit knowledge would occur, in which Tesla's entrepreneurial spirit would reinvigorate Toyota.[29] This equity-based learning race ended in 2014 when Toyota sold its stake in Tesla.[30]

Another governance mechanism that falls under the broad rubric of equity alliances is **corporate venture capital (CVC)** investments, which are equity investments by established firms in entrepreneurial ventures.[31] The value of CVC investments is estimated to be in the double-digit billion-dollar range each year. Larger firms frequently have dedicated CVC units, such as Google Ventures, Siemens Venture Capital, Kaiser Permanente Ventures, and Johnson & Johnson Development Corp. Rather than hoping primarily for financial gains, as venture capitalists traditionally do, CVC investments create real options in terms of gaining access to new, and potentially disruptive, technologies.[32] Strategy scholars find that CVC investments have a positive impact on value creation for the investing firm, especially in high-tech industries such as semiconductors, computing, and the medical-device sector.[33]

Taken together, equity alliances tend to produce stronger ties and greater trust between partners than non-equity alliances do. They also offer a window into new technology that, like a real option, can be exercised if successful or abandoned if not promising. Equity alliances are frequently stepping-stones toward full integration of the partner firms either through a merger or an acquisition. Essentially, they are often used as a "try before you buy" strategic option.[34] The downside of equity alliances is the amount of investment that can be involved, as well as a possible lack of flexibility and speed in putting together and reaping benefits from the partnership.

JOINT VENTURES. A *joint venture* (JV) is a standalone organization created and jointly owned by two or more parent companies (as discussed in Chapter 8). For example, Hulu (a streaming service) is jointly owned by Disney and Comcast. Since partners contribute equity to a joint venture, they are making a long-term commitment. Exchange of both explicit and tacit knowledge through interaction of personnel is typical. Joint ventures are also frequently used to enter foreign markets where the host country requires such a partnership to gain access to the market in exchange for advanced technology and know-how. In terms of frequency, joint ventures are the least common of the three types of strategic alliances.

The advantages of joint ventures are the strong ties, trust, and commitment that can result between the partners. However, they can entail long negotiations and significant investments. If the alliance doesn't work out as expected, undoing the JV can take some time and involve considerable cost. A further risk is that knowledge shared with the new partner could be misappropriated by opportunistic behavior. Finally, any rewards from the collaboration must be shared between the partners.

ALLIANCE MANAGEMENT CAPABILITY

Strategic alliances create a paradox for managers. Although alliances appear to be necessary to compete in many industries, between 30 and 70 percent of all strategic alliances do not deliver the expected benefits, and are considered failures by at least one alliance partner.[35] Given the high failure rate, effective alliance management is critical to gaining and sustaining a competitive advantage, especially in high-technology industries.[36]

Alliance management capability is a firm's ability to effectively manage three alliance-related tasks concurrently, often across a portfolio of many different alliances (see Exhibit 9.3):[37]

- Partner selection and alliance formation.
- Alliance design and governance.
- Post-formation alliance management.

corporate venture capital (CVC) Equity investments by established firms in entrepreneurial ventures; CVC falls under the broader rubric of equity alliances.

LO 9-4

Describe the three phases of alliance management and explain how an alliance management capability can lead to a competitive advantage.

alliance management capability A firm's ability to effectively manage three alliance-related tasks concurrently: (1) partner selection and alliance formation, (2) alliance design and governance, and (3) post-formation alliance management.

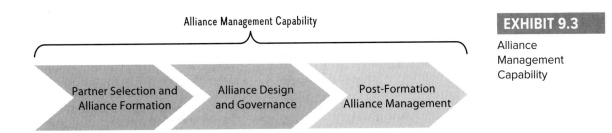

EXHIBIT 9.3

Alliance
Management
Capability

PARTNER SELECTION AND ALLIANCE FORMATION. When making the business case for an alliance, the expected benefits of the alliance must exceed its costs. When one or more of the five reasons for alliance formation are present—to strengthen competitive position, enter new markets, hedge against uncertainty, access critical complementary resources, or learn new capabilities—the firm must select the best possible alliance partner. Partner compatibility and partner commitment are necessary conditions for successful alliance formation.[38] *Partner compatibility* captures aspects of cultural fit between different firms. *Partner commitment* concerns the willingness to make available necessary resources and to accept short-term sacrifices to ensure long-term rewards.

ALLIANCE DESIGN AND GOVERNANCE. Once two or more firms agree to pursue an alliance, managers must then design the alliance and choose an appropriate governance mechanism from among the three options: non-equity contractual agreement, equity alliances, or joint venture. For example, in a study of over 640 alliances, researchers found that the joining of specialized complementary assets increases the likelihood that the alliance is governed hierarchically. This effect is stronger in the presence of uncertainties concerning the alliance partner as well as the envisioned tasks.[39]

In addition to the formal governance mechanisms, *interorganizational trust* is a critical dimension of alliance success.[40] Because all contracts are necessarily incomplete, trust between the alliance partners plays an important role for effective post-formation alliance management. Effective governance, therefore, can be accomplished only by skillfully combining formal and informal mechanisms.

POST-FORMATION ALLIANCE MANAGEMENT. The third phase in a firm's alliance management capability concerns the ongoing management of the alliance. To be a source of competitive advantage, the partnership needs to create resource combinations that obey the VRIO criteria. As shown in Exhibit 9.4, this can most likely be accomplished if the alliance partners *make relation-specific investments, establish knowledge-sharing routines*, and *build interfirm trust*.[41]

Trust is a critical aspect of any alliance. Interfirm trust entails the expectation that each alliance partner will behave in good faith and develop norms of reciprocity and fairness.[42] Such trust helps ensure that the relationship survives and thereby increases the possibility of meeting the intended goals of the alliance. Interfirm trust is also important for fast decision making.[43] Several firms such as Eli Lilly, HP, Procter & Gamble, and IBM compete to obtain trustworthy reputations in order to become the alliance "partner of choice" for small technology ventures, universities, and individual inventors.

Indeed, the systematic differences in firms' alliance management capability can be a source of competitive advantage.[44] But how do firms build alliance management capability? The answer is to build capability through repeated experiences over time, that is *learning by doing*. In support of this idea, several empirical studies have shown that firms move down the learning curve (see Section 6.3) and become better at managing alliances through repeated alliance exposure.[45]

EXHIBIT 9.4

How to Make
Alliances Work

Source: Adapted from J.H.
Dyer and H. Singh (1998),
"The relational view:
Cooperative strategy and the
sources of intraorganizational
advantage," *Academy of
Management Review* 23:
660–679.

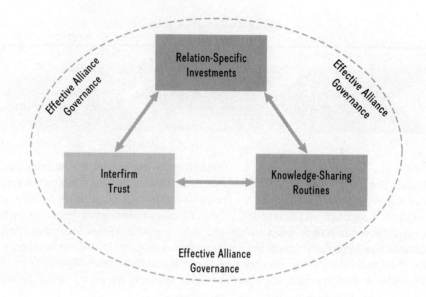

The *learning-by-doing* approach has value for small ventures in which a few key people coordinate most of the firms' activities.[46] However, there are clearly limitations for larger companies. Conglomerates such as ABB, GE, Philips, or Siemens are engaged in hundreds of alliances simultaneously. In fact, if alliances are not managed from a portfolio perspective at the corporate level, serious negative repercussions can emerge.[47] Groupe Danone, a large French food conglomerate, lost its leading position in the highly lucrative and fast-growing Chinese market because its local alliance partner, Hangzhou Wahaha Group, terminated the long-standing alliance.[48] Wahaha accused different Danone business units of subsequently setting up partnerships with other Chinese firms that were a direct competitive threat to Wahaha. This example makes it clear that although alliances are important pathways by which to pursue business-level strategy, they are best managed at the corporate level.

To accomplish effective alliance management, strategy scholars suggest that firms create a *dedicated alliance function*,[49] led by a vice president or director of alliance management and endowed with its own resources and support staff. The dedicated alliance function should be given the tasks of coordinating all alliance-related activity in the entire organization, taking a corporate-level perspective. It should serve as a repository of prior experience and be responsible for creating processes and structures to teach and leverage that experience and related knowledge throughout the rest of the organization across all levels. Research shows that firms with a dedicated alliance function are able to create value from their alliances above and beyond what could be expected based on experience alone.[50]

Pharmaceutical company Eli Lilly is an acknowledged leader in alliance management.[51] Lilly's Office of Alliance Management, led by a director and endowed with several full-time positions, manages its far-flung alliance activity across all hierarchical levels and around the globe. Lilly's process prescribes that each alliance is managed by a three-person team: an alliance champion, alliance leader, and alliance manager.

- The *alliance champion* is a senior, corporate-level executive responsible for high-level support and oversight. This senior manager is also responsible for making sure that the alliance fits within the firm's existing alliance portfolio and corporate-level strategy.

- The *alliance leader* has the technical expertise and knowledge needed for the specific technical area and is responsible for the day-to-day management of the alliance.

- The *alliance manager*, positioned within the Office of Alliance Management, serves as an alliance process resource and business integrator between the two alliance partners and provides alliance training and development, as well as diagnostic tools.

Some companies are also able to leverage the relational capabilities obtained through managing alliance portfolios into a successful acquisition strategy.[52] Eli Lilly has an entire department at the corporate level devoted to managing its alliance portfolio. Following up on an earlier 50/50 joint venture formed with ICOS, maker of the over $2 billion-plus (in annual revenues) erectile-dysfunction drug Cialis, Lilly acquired ICOS in 2007. Just a year later, Eli Lilly outmaneuvered Bristol-Myers Squibb to acquire biotech venture ImClone for $6.5 billion. ImClone discovered and developed the cancer-fighting drug Erbitux, also a $1 billion blockbuster in terms of annual sales. The acquisition of these two smaller biotech ventures allowed Lilly to address its problem of an empty drug pipeline.[53]

9.3 **Mergers and Acquisitions**

A popular vehicle for executing corporate strategy is mergers and acquisitions (M&A). Hundreds of mergers and acquisitions occur each year, with a cumulative value in the trillions of dollars.[54] Although the terms are often used interchangeably, and usually in tandem, mergers and acquisitions are, by definition, distinct from each other. A **merger** describes the joining of two independent companies to form a *combined entity*. Mergers tend to be friendly; in mergers, the two firms agree to join in order to create a combined entity. In the live event-promotion business, for example, Live Nation merged with Ticketmaster.

An **acquisition** describes the purchase or takeover of one company by another. Acquisitions can be friendly or unfriendly. For example, Disney's acquisition of Pixar, for example, was a friendly one, in which both strategic leadership teams believed that joining the two companies was a good idea. When a target firm does not want to be acquired, the acquisition is considered a **hostile takeover**. British telecom company Vodafone's acquisition of Germany-based Mannesmann, a diversified conglomerate with holdings in telephony and internet services, at an estimated value of $150 billion, was a hostile one. It was also the largest takeover in corporate history.

In defining mergers and acquisitions, size can matter as well. The combining of two firms of comparable size is often described as a merger even though it might in fact be an acquisition. For example, the integration of Daimler and Chrysler was pitched as a merger, though in reality Daimler acquired Chrysler and later sold it. After emerging from bankruptcy restructuring, Chrysler is now majority-owned by Fiat, an Italian auto manufacturer.

In contrast, when large, incumbent firms such as GE, Cisco, Alphabet, Facebook, or Microsoft buy start-up companies, the transaction is generally described as an acquisition. Although there is a distinction between mergers and acquisitions, many observers simply use the umbrella term *mergers and acquisitions,* or M&A.

WHY DO FIRMS MERGE WITH COMPETITORS?

In contrast to vertical integration, which concerns the number of activities a firm participates in up and down the industry value chain (as discussed in Chapter 8), **horizontal integration**

| **merger** The joining of two independent companies to form a combined entity. | **acquisition** The purchase or takeover of one company by another; can be friendly or unfriendly. | **hostile takeover** Acquisition in which the target company does not wish to be acquired. | **horizontal integration** The process of merging with competitors, leading to industry consolidation. |

EXHIBIT 9.5	Corporate Strategy	Sources of Value Creation (V)	Sources of Costs (C)
Sources of Value Creation and Costs in Horizontal Integration	Horizontal integration through M&A	• Reduction in competitive intensity • Lower costs • Increased differentiation	• Integration failure • Reduced flexibility • Increased potential for legal repercussions

is the process of merging with a competitor at the same stage of the industry value chain. Horizontal integration is a type of corporate strategy that can improve a firm's strategic position in a single industry. As a rule, firms should go ahead with horizontal integration (i.e., acquiring a competitor) *if the target firm is more valuable inside the acquiring firm than as a continued standalone company.* This implies that the net value creation of a horizontal acquisition must be positive to aid in gaining and sustaining a competitive advantage.

An industry-wide trend toward horizontal integration leads to industry consolidation. In particular, competitors in the same industry such as airlines, automotive, banking, telecommunications, pharmaceuticals, or health insurance frequently merge to respond to changes in their external environment and to change the underlying industry structure in their favor.

There are three main benefits to a horizontal integration strategy:

- Reduction in competitive intensity.
- Lower costs.
- Increased differentiation.

Exhibit 9.5 previews the sources of value creation and costs in horizontal integration, which we discuss next.

REDUCTION IN COMPETITIVE INTENSITY. Looking through the lens of Porter's five forces model with a focus on rivalry among competitors (introduced in Chapter 3), horizontal integration changes the underlying industry structure in favor of the surviving firms. Excess capacity is taken out of the market, and competition tends to decrease as a consequence of horizontal integration, assuming no new entrants. As a whole, the industry structure becomes more consolidated and potentially more profitable. If the surviving firms find themselves in an oligopolistic industry structure and maintain a focus on non-price competition (i.e., focus on R&D spending, customer service, or advertising), the industry can indeed be quite profitable, and rivalry would likely decrease among existing firms. The wave of recent horizontal integration in the U.S. airline industry, for example, provided several benefits to the surviving carriers. By reducing excess capacity, the mergers between Delta and Northwest Airlines, United Airlines and Continental, Southwest and AirTran, and American and US Airways lowered competitive intensity in the industry overall.

Horizontal integration can favorably affect several of Porter's five forces for the surviving firms: strengthening bargaining power vis-à-vis suppliers and buyers, reducing the threat of entry, and reducing rivalry among existing firms. Because of the potential to reduce competitive intensity in an industry, government authorities such as the Federal Trade Commission (FTC) in the United States and/or the European Commission usually must approve any large horizontal integration activity. Industry dynamics, however, are in constant flux as new competitors emerge and others fall by the wayside.

The FTC, for instance, did not approve the proposed merger between Staples and Office Depot in 2005, arguing that the remaining industry would have only two competitors, with Office Max being the other. Staples and Office Depot argued that the market for office supplies needed to be defined more broadly to include large retailers such as Walmart and

Target. The U.S. courts sided with the FTC, which argued that the prices for end consumers would be significantly higher if the market had only two category killers.[55] A few years later, however, the competitive landscape had shifted further as Walmart and Amazon had emerged as ferocious competitors offering rock-bottom prices for office supplies. Subsequently, in 2013, the FTC approved the merger between Staples and Office Max. Just two years later, the FTC also approved the merger between the now much larger Staples and Office Depot.[56]

LOWER COSTS. Firms use horizontal integration to lower costs through economies of scale and to enhance their economic value creation, and in turn their performance.[57] In industries that have high fixed costs, achieving economies of scale through large output is critical in lowering costs. The dominant pharmaceutical companies such as Pfizer, Roche, and Novartis, for example, maintain large sales forces ("detail people") who call on doctors and hospitals to promote their products. These specialized sales forces often number 10,000 or more and thus are a significant fixed cost to the firms, even though part of their compensation is based on commissions. Maintaining such a large and sophisticated sales force (many with MBAs) is costly if the firm has only a few drugs it can show the doctor. As a rule of thumb, if a pharma company does not possess a blockbuster drug that brings in more than $1 billion in annual revenues, it cannot maintain its own sales force.[58] When existing firms such as Pfizer and Wyeth merge, they join their drug pipelines and portfolios of existing drugs. They are likely to have one sales force for the combined portfolio, consequently reducing the size of the sales force and lowering the overall cost of distribution.

INCREASED DIFFERENTIATION. Horizontal integration through M&A can help firms strengthen their competitive positions by increasing the differentiation of their product and service offerings. In particular, horizontal integration can do this by filling gaps in a firm's product offering, allowing the combined entity to offer a complete suite of products and services.

As an example, Disney acquired Marvel for $4 billion (in 2009). This acquisition certainly allowed Disney to further differentiate its product offering as an entire new lineup of superheroes was joining Mickey's family, besides being able to offer Marvel superhero themed-rides and merchandise such as clothing and toys. The Marvel acquisition passed an important test of value creation because Marvel is seen as more valuable inside Disney than outside Disney.[59] Because of economies of scope and economies of scale, Marvel is becoming more valuable inside Disney than as a standalone enterprise. The same argument could be made for other recent Disney acquisitions, including Pixar (acquired for $7.4 billion in 2006), Lucasfilm (acquired for $4 billion in 2012), and 21st Century Fox (acquired for $70 billion in 2019).

WHY DO FIRMS ACQUIRE OTHER FIRMS?

When first defining the terminology at the beginning of the chapter, we noted that an *acquisition* describes the purchase or takeover of one company by another. Why do firms make acquisitions? Three main reasons stand out:

- Access to new markets and distribution channels.
- Access to a new capability or competency.
- Strategic preemption.

ACCESS TO NEW MARKETS AND DISTRIBUTION CHANNELS. Firms may resort to acquisitions when they need to overcome entry barriers into markets they are currently not competing in or to access new distribution channels. Strategy Highlight 9.2 discusses Kraft's history with aggressive acquisitions, both successful and otherwise, in this regard.

LO 9-7

Explain why firms engage in acquisitions.

Strategy Highlight **9.2**

Kraft Heinz: From Hostile Takeovers as Specialty to Eating Humble Pie

One example of a firm that pursues acquisitions aggressively is Kraft, a trait that can be traced through the years. Kraft Foods bought UK-based Cadbury PLC for close to $20 billion in a hostile takeover (in 2010). Unlike the more diversified food-products company Kraft, Cadbury was focused solely on candy and gum. Hailing to 1824, Cadbury established itself in markets across the globe, in concert with the British Empire.

Kraft was attracted to Cadbury due to its strong position in fast-growing countries such as India, Egypt, and Thailand and in many Latin American markets. Cadbury held 70 percent of the market share for chocolate in India, with more than 1 billion people. Children there specifically ask for "Cadbury chocolate" instead of just plain "chocolate." It is difficult for outsiders like Kraft to break into emerging economies because earlier entrants have developed and perfected their distribution systems to meet the needs of millions of small, independent vendors. To secure a strong strategic position in these fast-growing emerging markets, therefore, Kraft felt that horizontal integration with Cadbury was critical. Kraft continues to face formidable competitors in global markets, including Nestlé and Mars, both of which are especially strong in China.

A "Cadbury loyalist" vocally opposing Kraft's acquisition of a company with symbolic value in the United Kingdom.
PAUL ELLIS/AFP/Getty Images

We can see Kraft's approach even through its divisions. To focus its different strategic business units more effectively and to reduce costs, Kraft Foods restructured in 2012. It separated its North American grocery-food business from its global snack-food and candy business (including Oreos and Cadbury chocolate), which is now Mondelez International. In 2015, Kraft Foods merged with Heinz (owned by Warren Buffett's Berkshire Hathaway and 3G Capital, a Brazilian hedge fund) in a $37 billion merger, creating the fifth-largest food company in the world, behind Nestlé, Mondelez, PepsiCo, and Unilever.

In the U.S. market, the Cadbury acquisition allows Mondelez greater access to convenience stores, gives it a new distribution channel, and opens a market for it that is growing fast and tends to have high profit margins. Mondelez, which does not directly compete in the United States, licenses its famous Oreo cookie to its subsidiary Nabisco. Moreover, Mondelez licenses the sale of Cadbury chocolate to The Hershey Co., the largest U.S. chocolate manufacturer.

Hershey's main strategic focus is squarely on its home market. With the U.S. population growing slowly and becoming more health-conscious, however, Hershey decided in 2013 to enter the Chinese market, the world's fastest-growing candy market. Since its founding in 1894, Hershey's entry into China is the company's first product launch outside the United States. Hershey's sales growth in China, however, has been disappointing. Combined with little or no growth in the United States, Hershey had to cut jobs in the recent past.

Inheriting a penchant for hostile takeovers from its parent Kraft Foods, Mondelez saw an opportunity. Spotting a weakness in the Hershey Co., Mondelez made an unsolicited takeover offer to buy the U.S. chocolate maker for some $23 billion in 2016. The goal was to create the world's largest candy-maker. But Hershey's board rebuffed the Mondelez takeover bid unanimously. The Hershey Co. is owned by the Hershey Trust, which was established by Milton Hershey some 125 years ago. The trust's main beneficiary is a school for underprivileged children in Hershey, Pennsylvania, the hometown of the namesake company.

The dominant trait of a preference for hostile takeovers inherited from its progenitor also became apparent in 2017 when Kraft Heinz made a whopping $143 hostile takeover bid for Unilever, a British-Dutch consumer goods company. The intent was to merge the world's two largest packaged-food companies. Unilever then-CEO Paul Polman, however, made it clear that the multinational with a strong focus on corporate social responsibility was not interested in pursuing any merger talks with Kraft Heinz.

Once the aggressive suitor of rivals through unsolicited takeover bids, by 2019, Kraft Heinz itself had fallen on hard times. Critics claim that Kraft Heinz's focus on relentless cost cutting may have prevented the company from recognizing and seizing changing customer preferences. In particular, they point the finger at "zero-based budgeting" as a root cause of Kraft Heinz's problems. In zero-based budgeting, each year managers start off with a clean slate and have to justify all projected expenses and financial results. Providing the executive leadership team of Kraft Heinz, 3G Capital pursues zero-based budgeting with religious fervor. The problem, critics assert, is that with this type of cost control, new innovative projects often don't cross the required financial hurdles and are shut down prematurely. Using a real options approach, that is investing to gain more information about the future potential of projects as time unfolds, is used by many Kraft Heinz competitors such as Unilever, PepsiCo, and Nestlé, which have fared significantly better in the recent past.

As a consequence of these troubles, Kraft Heinz market cap has fallen from a high of $141 billion in 2016 to a mere $31 billion in 2019, losing $110 billion (or almost 80 percent) in its valuation. In recent years, Kraft Heinz has experienced a sustained competitive disadvantage vis-à-vis its competitors. To accomplish a turnaround of the once mighty Kraft Heinz, Miguel Patricio was appointed as new CEO; he comes from AB InBev, the world's largest beer brewer, which is also owned in part by 3G Capital.[60]

ACCESS TO A NEW CAPABILITY OR COMPETENCY. Firms often resort to M&A to obtain new capabilities or competencies. To strengthen its capabilities in server systems and equipment and to gain access to the capability of designing mobile chips for the internet of things, Intel acquired Altera for $17 billion (in 2015).[61]

STRATEGIC PREEMPTION. *Strategic preemption* is related to the reduction in competitive intensity as a motivation to acquire. The difference is while the motivation to reduce competitive intensity concerns the integration of *existing* competitors through mergers, the motivation of strategic preemption—as the name suggests—concerns the integration of *potential* competitors through acquisitions. In strategic preemption, incumbent firms acquire promising startups that have the potential to be a competitive threat before this potential is fully realized. Strategic preemption affords two advantages: (1) the acquiring firm removes a potential competitor, and (2) the acquiring firm preempts existing competitors from buying the startup.

Facebook has been a serial acquirer over the past few years, buying some 80 tech startups.[62] To preempt rivals, Facebook has spent more than $25 billion since 2012 buying promising startups. It acquired, among others, Instagram, a photo- and video-sharing site, for $1 billion in 2012. Facebook then went on to buy the text messaging service startup WhatsApp for $22 billion in 2014, making it one of the largest tech acquisitions ever. In the same year, Facebook paid $2 billion to acquire Oculus, a virtual reality (VR) firm. However, Facebook has recently come under antitrust investigation by the U.S. Federal Trade Commission concerning the acquisition spree to determine if this was an attempt by Facebook to head off startups that could one day pose a competitive threat.

Similarly, Alphabet's Google has also made a string of acquisitions of new ventures to preempt rivals. Google bought YouTube, the video-sharing website, for $1.65 billion (in 2006). Google engaged in a somewhat larger acquisition when it bought Motorola's cell phone unit for $12.5 billion (in 2011). This was done to gain access to Motorola's valuable patent holdings in mobile technology. Google later sold the cell phone unit to Lenovo, while retaining Motorola's patents. Next, Google purchased the Israeli start-up company Waze for $1 billion (in 2013). Google acquired Waze to gain access to a new capability and to prevent rivals from gaining access. Waze's claim to fame is its interactive mobile map app. Google is already the leader in online maps and wanted to extend this capability to mobile devices.

Perhaps even more importantly, Google's intent was to preempt Apple and Facebook from buying Waze. Apple and Facebook are each comparatively weaker than Google in the increasingly important interactive mobile map and information services segment.

Google then purchased the UK-based technology startup DeepMind for $625 million (in 2014) to enhance its competitive position in artificial intelligence. Moreover, this move also prevented others such as Facebook or Amazon from acquiring DeepMind. The company made headlines (in 2016) as its AI-based AlphaGo program beat the reigning Go world champion, the South Korean Lee Sedol.

LO 9-8

Evaluate whether mergers and acquisitions lead to competitive advantage.

M&A AND COMPETITIVE ADVANTAGE

Do mergers and acquisitions create competitive advantage? Despite their popularity, the answer, surprisingly, is that in most cases they do not. In fact, the M&A performance track record is rather mixed. Many mergers destroy shareholder value because the anticipated synergies never materialize.[63] Examples of mergers that destroyed significant shareholder value (as measured one year after the deal closed) include: Bayer-Monsanto (down 47 percent); Bank of America-Countrywide (down 45 percent); Alcatel-Lucent (down 39 percent); AOL-Time Warner (down 37 percent), and Spring-Nextel (down 30 percent).

If shareholder value is created, it generally accrues to the shareholders of the firm that was taken over (the acquiree) because acquirers often pay a premium when buying the target company.[64] Indeed, sometimes companies get involved in a bidding war for an acquisition; the winner may end up with the prize but may have overpaid for the acquisition—thus falling victim to the *winner's curse*.

Given that mergers and acquisitions, *on average*, destroy rather than create shareholder value, why do we see so many mergers? Reasons include

- Principal-agent problems.
- The desire to overcome competitive disadvantage.
- Superior acquisition and integration capability.

PRINCIPAL-AGENT PROBLEMS. When discussing diversification in the previous chapter, we noted that some firms diversify through acquisitions due to principal-agent problems (see Chapter 8 discussion of managerial motives behind firm growth).[65] Managers, as agents, are supposed to act in the best interest of the principals, the shareholders. However, managers may have incentives to grow their firms through acquisitions—not for anticipated shareholder value appreciation, but to build a larger empire, which is positively correlated with prestige, power, and pay. Besides providing higher compensation and more corporate perks, a larger organization may also provide more job security, especially if the company pursues unrelated diversification.

Sometimes the combined value of two companies is less than the value of each company separately.
Oatmeal: BirchTree/Alamy Stock Photo; Snapple: George W. Bailey/Shutterstock

A related problem is **managerial hubris**, a form of self-delusion in which managers convince themselves of their superior skills in the face of clear evidence to the contrary.[66] Managerial hubris comes in two forms:

1. Managers of the acquiring company convince themselves that they are able to manage the business of the target company more effectively and, therefore, create additional shareholder value. This justification is often used for an unrelated diversification strategy.
2. Although most top-level managers are aware that the majority of acquisitions destroy rather than create shareholder value, they see themselves as the exceptions to the rule.

Managerial hubris has led to many ill-fated deals, destroying billions of dollars. For example, Quaker Oats Co. acquired Snapple because its managers thought Snapple was another Gatorade, which was a successful previous acquisition.[67] The difference was that Gatorade had been a standalone company and was easily integrated, but Snapple relied on a decentralized network of independent distributors and retailers that did not want Snapple to be taken over and made it difficult and costly for Quaker Oats to integrate Snapple. The acquisition failed—and Quaker Oats itself was taken over by PepsiCo. Snapple was spun out and eventually ended up being part of the Dr Pepper Snapple Group.

THE DESIRE TO OVERCOME COMPETITIVE DISADVANTAGE. In some instances, mergers are not motivated by gaining competitive advantage, but by the attempt to overcome a competitive disadvantage. For example, to compete more successfully with Nike, the worldwide leader in sports shoes and apparel, Adidas (number two) acquired Reebok (number three) for $3.8 billion (in 2006). This acquisition allowed the now-larger Adidas group to benefit from economies of scale and scope that were unachievable when Adidas and Reebok operated independently. The hope was that this would help in overcoming Adidas' competitive disadvantage vis-à-vis Nike.

SUPERIOR ACQUISITION AND INTEGRATION CAPABILITY. Acquisition and integration capabilities are not equally distributed across firms. Although there is strong evidence that mergers and acquisitions, *on average*, destroy rather than create shareholder value, it does not exclude the possibility that *some* firms are consistently able to identify, acquire, and integrate target companies to strengthen their competitive positions. Since it is valuable, rare, and difficult to imitate, a superior acquisition and integration capability, together with past experience, can lead to competitive advantage.

Disney has shown superior post-merger integration capabilities after acquiring Pixar, Marvel, Lucasfilm, and 21st Century Fox. Disney managed its new subsidiaries more like alliances rather than attempting full integration, which could have destroyed the unique value of the acquisitions. In Pixar's case, Disney kept the entire creative team in place and allowed its members to continue to work in Pixar's headquarters near San Francisco with minimal interference. The hands-off approach paid huge dividends: Although Disney paid a steep $7.4 billion for Pixar, it made some $10 billion on Pixar's *Toy Story 3* franchise revenues alone. As a consequence, Disney has gained a competitive advantage over its rivals such as Sony (with Columbia Pictures), Comcast (with NBCUniversal), and AT&T (with Time Warner) and has also outperformed the Dow Jones Industrial Average over the past few years by a wide margin.

9.4 Implications for Strategic Leaders

The business environment is constantly changing.[68] New opportunities come and go quickly. Firms often need to develop new resources, capabilities, or competencies to take advantage of opportunities. Examples abound. Traditional book publishers must transform themselves

> **managerial hubris** A form of self-delusion in which managers convince themselves of their superior skills in the face of clear evidence to the contrary.

into digital content companies. Old-line banking institutions with expensive networks of branches must now offer seamless online banking services. They must make them work between a set of traditional and nontraditional payment services on a mobile platform. Energy providers are in the process of changing their coal-fired power plants to gas-fired ones in the wake of the shale gas boom. Pharmaceutical companies need to take advantage of advances in biotechnology to drive future growth. Food companies are now expected to offer organic, all natural, and gluten-free products.

The strategic leader also knows that firms need to grow to survive and prosper, especially if they are publicly traded stock companies. A firm's corporate strategy is critical in pursuing growth. To be able to grow as well as gain and sustain a competitive advantage, a firm must not only possess VRIO resources but also be able to leverage existing resources, often in conjunction with partners, and build new ones. The question of how to build new resources, capabilities, and competencies to grow your enterprise lies at the center of corporate strategy. Strategic alliances, mergers, and acquisitions are the key tools that the strategist uses in executing corporate strategy.

Ideally, the tools to execute corporate strategy—strategic alliances and acquisitions—should be centralized and managed at the corporate level, rather than at the level of the strategic business unit. This allows the company to not only assess their effect on the overall company performance, but also to harness spillovers between the different corporate development activities. That is, corporate-level managers should not only coordinate the firm's portfolio of alliances, but also leverage their relationships to successfully engage in mergers and acquisitions.[69] Rather than focusing on developing an alliance management capability in isolation, firms should develop a *relational capability* that allows for the successful management of both strategic alliances *and* mergers and acquisitions. In sum, to ensure a positive effect on competitive advantage, the management of strategic alliances and M&A needs to be placed at the corporate level.

We now have concluded our discussion of corporate strategy. Acquisitions and alliances are key vehicles to execute corporate strategy, each with its distinct advantages and disadvantages. It is also clear from this chapter that strategic alliances, as well as mergers and acquisitions, are a global phenomenon. In the next chapter, we discuss strategy in a global world.

CHAPTER**CASE 9**   Part II

ONE OTHER STRATEGIC reason Lyft entered alliances with GM and Waymo is access to critical complementary assets.

Both Lyft and GM bring critical complementary assets to bear in this alliance. GM has upstream core competencies in manufacturing cost-competitive and reliable cars at a large scale. Lyft, in turn, has downstream competencies as the second-largest mobile transportation network globally, and with it the data that allow Lyft to deploy AI in order to develop proprietary algorithms to have cars at the right time and at the right price.

Alphabet's Waymo, moreover, is an early leader in autonomous vehicle development. Where Waymo lags Tesla in driverless car technology, however, is in miles. In addition to Tesla owners accruing mileage by driving the cars themselves, they also accrue mileage by using Tesla's innovative

autopilot feature—allowing Tesla to rack up billions of miles. As more miles are accrued, more data are collected, which allows the self-driving software to learn and update, making the autopilot feature even better. In addition, Tesla is planning to roll out a fleet of robo-taxis (autonomous-driving Tesla vehicles) by 2021, contingent upon regulatory approval. This rollout will further increase Tesla's wealth of data accrued through the miles driven by its vehicles.

Much like Google's Android mobile operating system for phones, Waymo provides the software that is the brains behind the self-driving car technology, but lacks an opportunity for large-scale deployment, which constrains testing and learning. The alliance with Lyft allows Waymo to deploy its self-driving car technology on a large scale. The goal is to create a fleet of autonomous GM vehicles on Lyft's network, driving with Waymo's autopilot technology.

Questions

1. Describe the reasons Lyft entered strategic alliances with GM and Waymo. Are some reasons more important than others? Why or why not? Explain.

2. GM invested $500 million in Lyft in 2016. What are some possible reasons GM entered an equity alliance with Lyft? Are there any reasons GM would prefer Lyft over Uber as an alliance partner?

3. What are some possible reasons Waymo entered an alliance with Lyft? Are there any reasons Waymo would prefer Lyft over Uber as an alliance partner?

4. Uber is still a much larger and more valuable firm than Lyft. Uber is also more diversified in that it offers services beyond ride-hailing, which is its core service. Do you think the strategic alliances with GM and Waymo could help Lyft to overcome Uber's lead? Can you think of other reasons Lyft could end up as the winner in the mobile transportation network competition? Explain.

mySTRATEGY

What Is Your Network Strategy for Your Career?

Many of us participate in one or more popular social networks online such as Facebook, LinkedIn, Instagram, WeChat, or Twitter. While you may spend countless hours in these social networks, you may not have given a lot of thought to your own network strategy.

Social networks describe the relationships or ties between individuals linked to one another. An important element of social networks is the *different strengths of ties* between individuals. Some ties between two people in a network may be very strong (e.g., soul mates or best friends), while others are weak (mere acquaintances—"I talk to her briefly in the cafeteria at work"). As a member of a social network, you have access to *social capital,* which is derived from the connections within and between social networks. It is a function of whom you know and what advantages you can create through those connections. Social capital is an important concept in business.

Some Facebook users claim to have thousands of "friends." With larger networks, one expects to have greater social capital, right? Though this seems obvious, academic research suggests that humans have the brain capacity to maintain a functional network of only about 150 people. This so-called *Dunbar number* was derived by extrapolating from the brain sizes and social networks of primates.

Sounds far-fetched? Not necessarily. You may have a lot more than 150 friends on Facebook or connections on *LinkedIn, but researchers call that number the social core* of

any network. Why is this the case? Even though it takes only a split second to accept a new request on social media, relationships still need to be groomed. To develop a meaningful relationship, you need to spend some time with this new connection, even in cyberspace.

Social networking sites allow users to broadcast their lives and to passively keep track of more people. They enlarge their social networks, even though many of those ties tend to be weak. It may come as a surprise, however, to learn that research shows new opportunities such as job offers tend to come from weak ties, because it is these weak ties that allow you to access nonredundant and novel information. This phenomenon is called *strength of weak ties.* Consider how to leverage your social capital more fully as part of your career network strategy. Rather than always communicating with the same people, it may be better for you to invest a bit more time in developing your weak ties.[70]

1. Create a list of up to 12 people at your university (or work environment if applicable) with whom you regularly communicate (in person, electronically, or both). Draw your network (place names or initials next to each node), and connect every node where people you communicate with also talk to one another (i.e., indicate friends of friends). Can you identify strong and weak ties in your network?

2. Now compare your actual career-related network using a site such as LinkedIn. Are any of your connections linked? With how many alumni from your university are you linked? These alumni can provide a source of weak ties that may help you get a foot in the door at a potential new employer if you leverage them effectively.

TAKE-AWAY CONCEPTS

This chapter discussed two mechanisms of corporate-level strategy—alliances and acquisitions—as summarized by the following learning objectives and related take-away concepts.

LO 9-1 / Apply the build-borrow-or-buy framework to guide corporate strategy.

- The build-borrow-or-buy framework provides a conceptual model that aids strategists in deciding whether to pursue internal development *(build)*, enter a contract arrangement or strategic alliance *(borrow)*, or acquire new resources, capabilities, and competencies *(buy)*.

- Firms that are able to learn how to select the right pathways to obtain new resources are more likely to gain and sustain a competitive advantage.

LO 9-2 / Define strategic alliances, and explain why they are important to implement corporate strategy and why firms enter into them.

- Strategic alliances have the goal of sharing knowledge, resources, and capabilities to develop processes, products, or services.

- An alliance qualifies as strategic if it has the potential to affect a firm's competitive advantage by increasing value and/or lowering costs.

- The most common reasons firms enter alliances are to (1) strengthen competitive position, (2) enter new markets, (3) hedge against uncertainty, (4) access critical complementary resources, and (5) learn new capabilities.

LO 9-3 / Describe three alliance governance mechanisms and evaluate their pros and cons.

- Alliances can be governed by the following mechanisms: contractual agreements for non-equity alliances, equity alliances, and joint ventures.

- There are pros and cons of each alliance governance mechanism, shown in detail in Exhibit 9.2 with highlights as follows:

  Non-equity alliance's pros: flexible, fast, easy to get in and out; cons: weak ties, lack of trust/commitment.

Equity alliance's pros: stronger ties, potential for trust/commitment, window into new technology (option value); cons: less flexible, slower, can entail significant investment.

Joint venture pros: strongest tie, trust/commitment most likely, may be required by institutional setting; cons: potentially long negotiations and significant investments, long-term solution, managers may have two reporting lines (two bosses).

LO 9-4 / Describe the three phases of alliance management and explain how an alliance management capability can lead to a competitive advantage.

- An alliance management capability consists of a firm's ability to effectively manage alliance-related tasks through three phases: (1) partner selection and alliance formation, (2) alliance design and governance, and (3) post-formation alliance management.

- An alliance management capability can be a source of competitive advantage as better management of alliances leads to more likely superior performance.

- Firms build a superior alliance management capability through "learning by doing" and by establishing a dedicated alliance function.

LO 9-5 / Differentiate between mergers and acquisitions, and explain why firms would use either to execute corporate strategy.

- A merger describes the joining of two independent companies to form a combined entity.

- An acquisition describes the purchase or takeover of one company by another. It can be friendly or hostile.

- Although there is a distinction between mergers and acquisitions, many observers simply use the umbrella term *mergers and acquisitions,* or M&A.

- Firms can use M&A activity for competitive advantage when they possess a superior relational capability, which is often built on superior alliance management capability.

LO 9-6 / **Define horizontal integration and evaluate the advantages and disadvantages of this option to execute corporate-level strategy.**

- Horizontal integration is the process of merging with competitors, leading to industry consolidation.

- As a corporate strategy, firms use horizontal integration to (1) reduce competitive intensity, (2) lower costs, and (3) increase differentiation.

LO 9-7 / **Explain why firms engage in acquisitions.**

- Firms engage in acquisitions (1) to access new markets and distributions channels, (2) to access new capability or competency, and (3) for strategic preemption.

LO 9-8 / **Evaluate whether mergers and acquisitions lead to competitive advantage.**

- Most mergers and acquisitions destroy shareholder value because anticipated synergies never materialize.

- If there is any value creation in M&A, it generally accrues to the shareholders of the firm that is taken over (the acquiree), because acquirers often pay a premium when buying the target company.

- Mergers and acquisitions are a popular vehicle for corporate-level strategy implementation for three reasons: (1) because of principal–agent problems, (2) the desire to overcome competitive disadvantage, and (3) the quest for superior acquisition and integration capability.

KEY TERMS

Acquisition *(p. 335)*

Alliance management capability *(p. 332)*

Build-borrow-or-buy framework *(p. 323)*

Co-opetition *(p. 329)*

Corporate venture capital (CVC) *(p. 332)*

Equity alliance *(p. 331)*

Explicit knowledge *(p. 331)*

Horizontal integration *(p. 335)*

Hostile takeover *(p. 335)*

Learning races *(p. 329)*

Managerial hubris *(p. 341)*

Merger *(p. 335)*

Non-equity alliance *(p. 331)*

Real options *(p. 328)*

Real-options perspective *(p. 328)*

Relational view of competitive advantage *(p. 326)*

Strategic alliances *(p. 326)*

Tacit knowledge *(p. 331)*

DISCUSSION QUESTIONS

1. The chapter identifies three governing mechanisms for strategic alliances: non-equity, equity, and joint venture. List the benefits and downsides for each of these mechanisms.

2. Alliances are often used to pursue business-level goals, but they may be managed at the corporate level. Explain why this portfolio approach to alliance management would make sense.

3. Given the poor track record of M&As, what explains the continuing trend for mergers and acquisitions in many industries? What steps can a firm take to improve the chances of successful M&As?

ENDNOTES

1. Freedman, L. (2013), *Strategy: A History.* Oxford, UK: Oxford University Press.

2. This ChapterCase is based on: MacMillan, D. (2016, Jan. 4), "GM invests $500 million in Lyft, plans system for self-driving cars," *The Wall Street Journal*; Hull, D. (2016, Dec. 20), "The Tesla advantage: 1.3 billion miles of data," *Bloomberg Businessweek*; "Uber is facing the biggest

crisis in its short history," *The Economist* (2017, Mar. 25); "The world's most valuable resource is no longer oil, but data," *The Economist* (2017, May 6); "Data is giving rise to a new economy," *The Economist* (2017, May 6); and Bensinger, G., and J. Nicas (2017, May 15), "Alphabet's Waymo, Lyft to collaborate on self-driving cars," *The Wall Street Journal*.

3. Capron, L., and W. Mitchell (2012), *Build, Borrow, or Buy: Solving the Growth Dilemma* (Boston: Harvard Business Review Press).

4. Capron, L., and W. Mitchell (2012), *Build, Borrow, or Buy: Solving the Growth Dilemma* (Boston: Harvard Business Review Press), 16.

5. Hoang, H., and Rothaermel, F.T. (2010), "Leveraging internal and external experience: Exploration, exploitation, and R&D project performance," *Strategic Management Journal* 31: 734-758; and Gick, M.L., and K.J. Holyoak (1987), "The cognitive basis of knowledge transfer," in ed. S.M. Cormier and J. D. Hagman, *Transfer of Learning* (New York: Academic Press): 9-46.

6. Gilbert, C.G. (2005), "Unbundling the structure of inertia: Resource versus routine rigidity," *Academy of Management Journal* 48: 741-763. For an insightful and in-depth discussion of the challenges faced by old-line media companies in making the transition to the internet, see also: Cozzolino, A. (2015), *Three Essays on Technological Changes and Competitive Advantage: Evidence from the Newspaper Industry* (Milan: Bocconi University); Cozzolino, A., Rothaermel, F.T. 2018. Discontinuities, competition, and cooperation: Coopetitive dynamics between incumbents and entrants. *Strategic Management Journal,* (39) 12: 3053-3085; and Cozzolino, A., Verona, G., Rothaermel, F.T. 2018. Unpacking the disruption process: New technology, business models, and incumbent adaptation. *Journal of Management Studies,* (55) 7: 1166-1202.

7. Ovide, S. (2015, Jul. 8), "Microsoft to cut 7,800 jobs on Nokia woes," *The Wall Street Journal.*

8. Gulati, R. (1998), "Alliances and networks," *Strategic Management Journal* 19: 293-317.

9. This discussion draws on: Dyer, J.H., and H. Singh (1998), "The relational view: Cooperative strategy and the sources of interorganizational advantage," *Academy of Management Review* 23: 660-679.

10. Kale, P., and H. Singh (2009), "Managing strategic alliances: What do we know now, and where do we go from here?" *Academy of Management Perspectives* 23: 45-62.

11. For a review of the alliance literature, see: Kale, P., and H. Singh (2009), "Managing strategic alliances: What do we know now, and where do we go from here?" *Academy of Management Perspectives* 23: 45-62; Lavie, D. (2006), "The competitive advantage of interconnected firms: An extension of the resource-based view," *Academy of Management Review* 31: 638-658; Ireland, R.D., M.A. Hitt, and D. Vaidyanath (2002), "Alliance management as a source of competitive advantage," *Journal of Management* 28: 413-446; Inkpen, A. (2001), "Strategic alliances," in M.A. Hitt, R.E. Freeman, and J.S. Harrison, *Handbook of Strategic Management* (Oxford, UK: Blackwell-Wiley); Gulati, R. (1998), "Alliances and networks," *Strategic Management Journal* 19: 293-317; and Dyer, J.H., and H. Singh (1998), "The relational view: Cooperative strategy and

the sources of interorganizational advantage," *Academy of Management Review* 23: 660-679.

12. Kogut, B. (1991), "Joint ventures and the option to expand and acquire," *Management Science* 37: 19-34.

13. This Strategy Highlight is based on: Hoang, H., and F.T. Rothaermel (2016), "How to manage alliances strategically," *MIT Sloan Management Review* 58(1): 69-76.

14. Markides, C.C., and P.J. Williamsen (1994), "Related diversification, core competences, and performance," *Strategic Management Journal* 15: 149-165; and Kale, P., and H. Singh (2009), "Managing strategic alliances: What do we know now, and where do we go from here?" *Academy of Management Perspectives* 23: 45-62.

15. The author participated in the HP demo; see also: "HP unveils Halo collaboration studio: Life-like communication leaps across geographic boundaries," HP press release (2005, Dec. 12).

16. "Bank of America taps Cisco for TelePresence," *InformationWeek* (2010, Mar. 30).

17. Tripsas, M. (1997), "Unraveling the process of creative destruction: Complementary assets and incumbent survival in the typesetter industry," *Strategic Management Journal* 18: 119-142.

18. Rothaermel, F.T., and C.W.L. Hill (2005), "Technological discontinuities and complementary assets: A longitudinal study of industry and firm performance," *Organization Science* 16: 52-70; Hill, C.W.L., and F.T. Rothaermel (2003), "The performance of incumbent firms in the face of radical technological innovation," *Academy of Management Review* 28: 257-274; Rothaermel, F.T. (2001), "Incumbent's advantage through exploiting complementary assets via interfirm cooperation," *Strategic Management Journal* 22: 687-699; and Rothaermel, F.T. (2001), "Complementary assets, strategic alliances, and the incumbent's advantage: An empirical study of industry and firm effects in the biopharmaceutical industry," *Research Policy* 30: 1235-1251.

19. Arthaud-Day, M.L., F.T. Rothaermel, and W. Zhang (2013), "Genentech: After the acquisition by Roche," case study, http://create.mheducation.com/rothaermel/.

20. Jiang, L., J. Tan, and M. Thursby (2011), "Incumbent firm invention in emerging fields: Evidence from the semiconductor industry," *Strategic Management Journal* 32: 55-75; Rothaermel, F.T., and M. Thursby (2007), "The nanotech vs. the biotech revolution: Sources of incumbent productivity in research," *Research Policy* 36: 832-849.

21. This discussion is based on: Hess, A.M., and F.T. Rothaermel (2011), "When are assets complementary? Star scientists, strategic alliances and innovation in the pharmaceutical industry," *Strategic Management Journal* 32: 895-909; Ceccagnoli, M., and F.T. Rothaermel (2008), "Appropriating the returns to innovation," *Advances in Study of Entrepreneurship, Innovation, and Economic Growth* 18: 11-34; Rothaermel, F.T., and W. Boeker (2008), "Old technology meets new technology: Complementarities, similarities, and alliance formation," *Strategic Management Journal* 29(1): 47-77; Rothaermel, F.T. (2001), "Incumbent's advantage through exploiting complementary assets via interfirm cooperation," *Strategic Management Journal* 22(6-7): 687-699; Tripsas, M. (1997), "Unraveling the process of creative destruction: Complementary assets and incumbent survival in the typesetter industry," *Strategic Management Journal* 18: 51, 119-142; and Teece, D.J. (1986), "Profiting from technological innovation: Implications for integration, collaboration, licensing and public policy," *Research Policy* 15: 285-305.

22. Mowery, D.C., J.E. Oxley, and B.S. Silverman (1996), "Strategic alliances and interfirm knowledge transfer," *Strategic Management Journal* 17: 77-91.

23. See key contributions to the co-opetition literature, including: Dagnino, G.B. (2009), "Coopetition strategy: A new kind of interfirm dynamics for value creation," in G.B. Dagnino and E. Rocco (Eds.), *Co-opetition Strategy: Theory, Experiments and Cases* (New York: Routledge), 45-63; Gnyawali, D., and B. Park (2011), "Co-opetition between giants: Collaboration with competitors for technological innovation," *Research Policy* 40: 650-663; Gnyawali, D., J. He, and R. Madhavan (2008), "Co-opetition: Promises and challenges," in ed. C. Wankel, *21st Century Management: A Reference Handbook* (Thousand Oaks, CA: Sage), 386-398; and Brandenburger, A.M., and B.J. Nalebuff (1996), *Co-opetition* (New York: Currency Doubleday).

24. This discussion is based on: Kale, P., and H. Perlmutter (2000), "Learning and protection of proprietary assets in strategic alliances: Building relational capital," *Strategic Management Journal* 21: 217-237; Khanna, T., R. Gulati, and N. Nohria (1998), "The dynamics of learning alliances: Competition, cooperation, and relative scope," *Strategic Management Journal* 19: 193-210; Larsson, R., L. Bengtsson, K. Henriksson, and J. Sparks (1998), "The interorganizational learning dilemma: Collective knowledge development in strategic alliances," *Organization Science* 9: 285-305; Hamel, G. (1991),

"Competition for competence and interpartner learning within international alliances," *Strategic Management Journal* 12: 83–103; and Hamel, G., Y. Doz, and C.K. Prahalad (1989, January–February), "Collaborate with your competitors–and win," *Harvard Business Review*: 190–196.

25. Nti, K.O., and R. Kumar (2000), "Differential learning in alliances," in ed. D. Faulkner and M. de Rond, *Cooperative Strategy. Economic, Business, and Organizational Issues* (Oxford, UK: University Press), 119–134. For an opposing viewpoint, see: Inkpen, A.C. (2008), "Knowledge transfer and international joint ventures: The case of NUMMI and General Motors," *Strategic Management Journal* 29: 447–453.

26. This discussion is based on: Lavie, D. (2006), "The competitive advantage of interconnected firms: An extension of the resource-based view," *Academy of Management Review* 31: 638–658; Hoang, H., and F.T. Rothaermel (2005), "The effect of general and partner-specific alliance experience on joint R&D project performance," *Academy of Management Journal* 48: 332–345; Ireland, R.D., M.A. Hitt, and D. Vaidyanath (2002), "Alliance management as a source of competitive advantage," *Journal of Management* 28: 413–446; and Gulati, R. (1998), "Alliances and networks," *Strategic Management Journal* 19: 293–317.

27. This discussion is based on: Hoang, H., and F.T. Rothaermel (2010), "Leveraging internal and external experience: Exploration, exploitation, and R&D project performance," *Strategic Management Journal* 31 (7): 734–758; and Pisano, G.P., and P. Mang (1993), "Collaborative product development and the market for know-how: Strategies and structures in the biotechnology industry," in ed. R. Rosenbloom and R. Burgelman, *Research on Technological Innovation, Management, and Policy* (Greenwich, CT: J.A.I. Press): 109–136.

28. The distinction of explicit and tacit knowledge goes back to the seminal work by Polanyi, M. (1966), *The Tacit Dimension* (Chicago: University of Chicago Press). For more recent treatments, see: Spender, J.-C. (1996), "Managing knowledge as the basis of a dynamic theory of the firm," *Strategic Management Journal* 17: 45–62; Spender, J.-C., and R.M. Grant (1996), "Knowledge and the firm," *Strategic Management Journal* 17: 5–9; and Crossan, M. M., H.W. Lane, R.E. White (1999), "An organizational learning framework: From intuition to institution," *Academy of Management Review* 24: 522–537.

29. Direct and indirect quotes above from: "Toyota and Tesla partnering to make electric cars," *The Wall Street Journal* (2010, May 21).

30. White, J.B. (2014, Oct. 24), "Toyota confirms sale of part of Tesla stake," *The Wall Street Journal*.

31. For an insightful treatment of CVC investments, see: Dushnitsky, G., and M.J. Lenox (2005), "When do incumbent firms learn from entrepreneurial ventures? Corporate venture capital and investing firm innovation rates," *Research Policy* 34: 615–639; Dushnitsky, G., and M.J. Lenox (2005), "When do firms undertake R&D by investing in new ventures?" *Strategic Management Journal* 26: 947–965; Dushnitsky, G., and M.J. Lenox (2006), "When does corporate venture capital investment create value?" *Journal of Business Venturing* 21: 753–772; and Wadhwa, A., and S. Kotha (2006), "Knowledge creation through external venturing: Evidence from the telecommunications equipment manufacturing industry," *Academy of Management Journal* 49: 1–17; and Kim, J.Y., H.D. Park (2017), "Two faces of early corporate venture capital funding: Promoting innovation and inhibiting IPOs," *Strategy Science* 2: 161–175.

32. See, for instance: Benson, D., and R.H. Ziedonis (2009), "Corporate venture capital as a wind on new technology for the performance of corporate investors when acquiring startups," *Organization Science* 20: 329–351; Kim, J.Y. and H.K. Steensma, H. K. (2017), Employee mobility, spin-outs, and knowledge spill-in: How incumbent firms can learn from new ventures. *Strategic Management Journal,* 38: 1626–1645; Kim, J.Y., H.K. Steensma, and H.D. Park (2019), The Influence of Technological Links, Social Ties, and Incumbent Firm Opportunistic Propensity on the Formation of Corporate Venture Capital Deals. *Journal of Management,* 45: 1595–1622.

33. Dushnitsky, G., and M.J. Lenox (2006), "When does corporate venture capital investment create value?" *Journal of Business Venturing* 21: 753–772.

34. Higgins, M.J., and D. Rodriguez (2006), "The outsourcing of R&D through acquisition in the pharmaceutical industry," *Journal of Financial Economics* 80: 351–383; and Benson, D., and R.H. Ziedonis (2009), "Corporate venture capital as a window on new technology for the performance of corporate investors when acquiring startups," *Organization Science* 20: 329–351.

35. Reuer, J.J., M. Zollo, and H. Singh (2002), "Post-formation dynamics in strategic alliances," *Strategic Management Journal* 23: 135–151.

36. This discussion is based on: Dyer, J.H., and H. Singh (1998), "The relational view: Cooperative strategy and the sources of interorganizational advantage," *Academy of Management Review* 23: 660–679; Ireland,

R.D., M.A. Hitt, and D. Vaidyanath (2002), "Alliance management as a source of competitive advantage," *Journal of Management* 28: 413–446; and Lavie, D. (2006), "The competitive advantage of interconnected firms: An extension of the resource-based view," *Academy of Management Review* 31: 638–658.

37. For an insightful discussion of alliance management capability and alliance portfolios, see: Schilke, O., and A. Goerzten (2010), "Alliance management capability: An investigation of the construct and its measurement," *Journal of Management* 36: 1192–1219; Schreiner, M., P. Kale, and D. Corsten (2009), "What really is alliance management capability and how does it impact alliance outcomes and success?" *Strategic Management Journal* 30: 1395–1419; Ozcan, P., and K.M. Eisenhardt (2009), "Origin of alliance portfolios: Entrepreneurs, network strategies, and firm performance," *Academy of Management Journal* 52: 246–279; Hoffmann, W. (2007), "Strategies for managing a portfolio of alliances," *Strategic Management Journal* 28: 827–856; and Rothaermel, F.T., and D.L. Deeds (2006), "Alliance type, alliance experience, and alliance management capability in high-technology ventures," *Journal of Business Venturing* 21: 429–460.

38. Kale, P., and H. Singh (2009), "Managing strategic alliances: What do we know now, and where do we go from here?" *Academy of Management Perspectives* 23: 45–62.

39. Santoro, M.D., and J.P. McGill (2005), "The effect of uncertainty and asset cospecialization on governance in biotechnology alliances," *Strategic Management Journal* 26: 1261–1269.

40. This is based on: Gulati, R. (1995), "Does familiarity breed trust? The implications of repeated ties for contractual choice in alliances," *Academy of Management Journal* 38: 85–112; and Poppo, L., and T. Zenger (2002), "Do formal contracts and relational governance function as substitutes or complements?" *Strategic Management Journal* 23: 707–725.

41. Dyer, J.H., and H. Singh (1998), "The relational view: Cooperative strategy and the sources of interorganizational advantage," *Academy of Management Review* 23: 660–679.

42. Zaheer, A., B. McEvily, and V. Perrone (1998), "Does trust matter? Exploring the effects of interorganizational and interpersonal trust on performance," *Organization Science* 8: 141–159.

43. Covey, S.M.R. (2008), *The Speed of Trust: The One Thing That Changes Everything* (New York: Free Press).

44. Dyer, J.H., and H. Singh (1998), "The relational view: Cooperative strategy and the sources of interorganizational advantage," *Academy of Management Review* 23: 660–679; Ireland, R.D., M.A. Hitt, and D. Vaidyanath (2002), "Alliance management as a source of competitive advantage," *Journal of Management* 28: 413–446; and Lavie, D. (2006), "The competitive advantage of interconnected firms: An extension of the resource-based view," *Academy of Management Review* 31: 638–658.

45. This is based on: Anand, B., and T. Khanna (2000), "Do firms learn to create value?" *Strategic Management Journal* 21: 295–315; Sampson, R. (2005), "Experience effects and collaborative returns in R&D alliances," *Strategic Management Journal* 26: 1009–1031; Hoang, H., and F.T. Rothaermel (2005), "The effect of general and partner-specific alliance experience on joint R&D project performance," *Academy of Management Journal* 48: 332–345; and Rothaermel, F.T., and D.L. Deeds (2006), "Alliance type, alliance experience, and alliance management capability in high-technology ventures," *Journal of Business Venturing* 21: 429–460.

46. Rothaermel, F.T., and D.L. Deeds (2006), "Alliance type, alliance experience, and alliance management capability in high-technology ventures," *Journal of Business Venturing* 21: 429–460.

47. Hoffmann, W. (2007), "Strategies for managing a portfolio of alliances," *Strategic Management Journal* 28: 827–856.

48. Wassmer, U., P. Dussage, and M. Planellas (2010, Spring), "How to manage alliances better than one at a time," *MIT Sloan Management Review*: 77–84.

49. Dyer, J. H., P. Kale, and H. Singh (2001, Summer), "How to make strategic alliances work," *MIT Sloan Management Review*: 37–43.

50. Kale, P., J. H. Dyer, and H. Singh (2002), "Alliance capability, stock market response, and long-term alliance success: The role of the alliance function," *Strategic Management Journal* 23: 747–767.

51. Gueth A., N. Sims, and R. Harrison (2001, June), "Managing alliances at Lilly," *In Vivo: The Business & Medicine Report*: 1–9; and Rothaermel, F.T., and D.L. Deeds (2006), "Alliance type, alliance experience, and alliance management capability in high-technology ventures," *Journal of Business Venturing* 21: 429–460.

52. Dyer, J.H., P. Kale, and H. Singh (2004, July–August), "When to ally and when to acquire," *Harvard Business Review*.

53. Rothaermel, F.T., and A. Hess (2010, Spring), "Innovation strategies combined," *MIT Sloan Management Review*: 12–15.

54. Hitt, M.A., R.D. Ireland, and J.S. Harrison (2001), "Mergers and acquisitions: A value creating or value destroying strategy?" in M.A. Hitt, R.E. Freeman, and J.S. Harrison, *Handbook of Strategic Management* (Oxford, UK: Blackwell-Wiley): 384–408. In 2015 alone, M&A deals valued at over $4 trillion were announced, a record high since 2007 before the global financial crisis; see Mattioli, D., and D. Cimilluca (2015, Jun. 26), "Fear of losing out drives deal boom," *The Wall Street Journal*. M&A activity was lower in 2016 and 2017; see: "Global M&A by quarter," in Investment Banking Scorecard, *The Wall Street Journal*, at http://graphics.wsj.com/investment-banking-scorecard/, accessed May 19, 2017.

55. Allen, W.B., N.A. Doherty, K. Weigelt, and E. Mansfield (2005), *Managerial Economics,* 6th ed. (New York: Norton); and Breshnahan, T., and P. Reiss (1991), "Entry and competition in concentrated markets," *Journal of Political Economy* 99: 997–1009.

56. FitzGerald, D., and L. Hoffman (2015, Feb. 4), "Staples inks deal to buy Office Depot for $6.3 billion," *The Wall Street Journal.*

57. Brush, T.H. (1996), "Predicted change in operational synergy and post-acquisition performance of acquired businesses," *Strategic Management Journal* 17: 1–24.

58. Tebbutt, T. (2010, Jan. 29), "An insider's perspective of the pharmaceutical industry," presentation in "Competing in the Health Sciences," Georgia Institute of Technology. Tebbutt is former president of UCB Pharma.

59. Smith, E., and L.A.E. Schuker (2009, Sep. 1), "Disney nabs Marvel heroes," *The Wall Street Journal.*

60. Strategy Highlight 9.2 is based on: Stoll, J.D. (2019, Apr. 23), "What tops Kraft Heinz's menu? Cost cuts or Mac 'n' Cheese?" *The Wall Street Journal;* "Kraft Heinz gets a new boss. Can he save the firm?" *The Economist* (2019, Apr. 27); Kraft Foods annual reports (various years); The Hershey Co. annual reports (various years); Cimilluca, D., D. Mattioli, and C. Dulaney (2015, Mar. 25), "Kraft, Heinz to merge, forming food giant," *The Wall Street Journal;* "Mondelez can slim way to success," *The Wall Street Journal* (2013, May 28); "Analysts bullish on Mondelez ahead of Kraft split," *The Wall Street Journal* (2012, Oct. 1); "Cadbury accepts fresh Kraft offer," *The Wall Street Journal* (2010, Jan. 19); "Kraft wins a reluctant Cadbury with help of clock, hedge funds," *The Wall Street Journal* (2010, Jan. 20); "Cadbury rejects Kraft's $16.73 billion bid," *The Wall Street Journal* (2009, Sep. 7); "Food fight," *The Economist* (2017, Nov. 5); Chaudhuri, S., A. Gasparro, A. Steele (2017, Feb. 17), "Kraft's $143 billion bid for Unilever highlights squeeze in consumer goods," *The Wall Street Journal;* Chaudhuri, S., and A. Gasparro (2017, Feb. 20), "Failed $143 billion deal raises pressure on Unilever, Kraft," *The Wall Street Journal;* Mackintosh, J. (2017, Feb. 21), "Kraft-Unilever deal is off, but Warren Buffett's anomalies live on," *The Wall Street Journal;* and the author's personal communication with Dr. Narayanan Jayaraman, Georgia Institute of Technology.

61. Clark, D., D. Cimilluca, and D. Mattioli (2015, Jun. 1), "Intel agrees to buy Altera for $16.7 billion," *The Wall Street Journal.*

62. Examples are drawn from: Kendall, B., J. McKinnon, and D. Seetharaman (2019, Aug. 1) "FTC antitrust probe of Facebook scrutinizes its acquisitions," *The Wall Street Journal;* Dulaney, C. (2014, Oct. 6), "Facebook completes acquisition of WhatsApp," *The Wall Street Journal;* Albergotti, R., and I. Sherr (2014, Mar. 25), "Facebook to buy virtual reality firm Oculus for $2 billion," *The Wall Street Journal;* "Google buys Waze," *The Economist* (2013, Jun. 15); Rusli, E.M., and D. MacMillan (2013, Nov. 13), "Messaging service Snapchat spurned $3 billion Facebook bid," *The Wall Street Journal;* "Insta-rich: $1 billion for Instagram," *The Wall Street Journal* (2012, Apr. 10); "Google's $12.5 billion gamble," *The Wall Street Journal* (2011; Aug. 16); and "Google in talks to buy YouTube for $1.6 billion," *The Wall Street Journal* (2006, Oct. 7).

63. Capron, L. (1999), "The long-term performance of horizontal acquisitions," *Strategic Management Journal* 20: 987–1018; Capron, L., and J.C. Shen (2007), "Acquisitions of private vs. public firms: Private information, target selection, and acquirer returns," *Strategic Management Journal* 28: 891–911. For M&A data presented here, see Bender, R. (2019, Aug. 28), "How Bayer-Monsanto became one of the worst corporate deals—in 12 charts," *The Wall Street Journal.*

64. Jensen, M.C., and R.S. Ruback (1983), "The market for corporate control: The scientific evidence," *Journal of Financial Economics* 11: 5–50.

65. This discussion is based on: Finkelstein, S. (2003), *Why Smart Executives Fail, and What You Can Learn from Their Mistakes* (New York: Portfolio); Lambert, R.A., D.F. Larcker, and K. Weigelt (1991), "How sensitive is executive compensation to organizational size?" *Strategic Management Journal* 12: 395–402; and Finkelstein, S., and D.C. Hambrick (1989), "Chief executive compensation: A study of the intersection of markets and political processes, *Strategic Management Journal* 10: 121–134.

66. This discussion is based on: Finkelstein. S. (2003), *Why Smart Executives Fail, and What You Can Learn from Their Mistakes* (New York: Portfolio)*;* and Finkelstein, S., J. Whitehead, and A. Campbell (2009), *Think Again: Why Good Leaders Make Bad Decisions and How to Keep It from Happening to You* (Boston: Harvard Business School Press).

67. This discussion is based on: Finkelstein. S. (2003), *Why Smart Executives Fail, and What You Can Learn from Their Mistakes* (New York: Portfolio)*;* and Finkelstein, S., J. Whitehead, and A. Campbell (2009), *Think Again: Why Good Leaders Make Bad Decisions and How to Keep It from Happening to You* (Boston: Harvard Business School Press).

68. This section is based on: Capron, L., and W. Mitchell (2012), *Build, Borrow, or Buy: Solving the Growth Dilemma* (Boston: Harvard Business Review Press).

69. Dyer, J.H., P. Kale, and H. Singh (2004, July–August), "When to ally and when to acquire," *Harvard Business Review*.

70. This myStrategy section is based on: Granovetter, M. (1973), "The strength of weak ties," *American Journal of Sociology* 78: 1360–1380; and "Primates on Facebook," *The Economist* (2009, Feb. 26).

Global Strategy: Competing Around the World

Chapter Outline

Learning Objectives

After studying this chapter, you should be able to:

LO 10-1 Define globalization, multinational enterprise (MNE), foreign direct investment (FDI), and global strategy.

LO 10-2 Explain why companies compete abroad, and evaluate the advantages and disadvantages of going global.

LO 10-3 Apply the CAGE distance framework to guide MNE decisions on which countries to enter.

LO 10-4 Compare and contrast the different options MNEs have to enter foreign markets.

LO 10-5 Apply the integration-responsiveness framework to evaluate the four different strategies MNEs can pursue when competing globally.

LO 10-6 Apply Porter's diamond framework to explain why certain industries are more competitive in specific nations than in others.

IKEA: The World's Most Profitable Retailer

THE WORLD'S MOST profitable global retailer is not Walmart but IKEA, a privately owned home-furnishings company from Sweden. In 2018, IKEA had more than 420 stores across various formats in 50 countries, employed approximately 210,000 people, and earned revenues of more than €38 billion (equivalent to $43 billion). Exhibit 10.1 shows IKEA's growth in the number of stores and revenues worldwide.

Known today for its iconic blue-and-yellow big-box retail stores and its focus on flat-pack furniture boxes with a strong DIY component, IKEA started as a small retail outlet in 1943 by then-17-year-old Ingvar Kamprad. Though IKEA is now known as a global phenomenon, it was initially slow to internationalize. It took 20 years before the company expanded beyond Sweden to neighboring Norway. After honing and refining its core competencies of designing modern functional home furnishings at low cost and offering a unique retail experience in its home market, IKEA pursued an international strategy, expanding first throughout Europe, and then beyond. This international strategy allowed IKEA to leverage its simple, straightforward design in order to sell the same style of home furnishings—with little

Sweden's IKEA is growing quickly in both developed countries, such as the United States and Australia, and emerging economies such as China. Testing/Shutterstock

adaptation—across the globe (although some items have been modified according to country preferences). As its consistent product lines across various countries show, the IKEA aesthetic is popular almost everywhere; this popularity is rising in both developed and growth markets, with new locations opening in India and Latvia in 2018. Exhibit 10.2 shows IKEA's top five countries by sales in 2018.

From day one, IKEA strived to cut costs to keep products as affordable as possible without sacrificing its signature functional designs. Because of its focus on low cost, IKEA shifted from an international strategy to a *global-standardization*

EXHIBIT 10.1   IKEA Stores and Revenues, 1974–2018

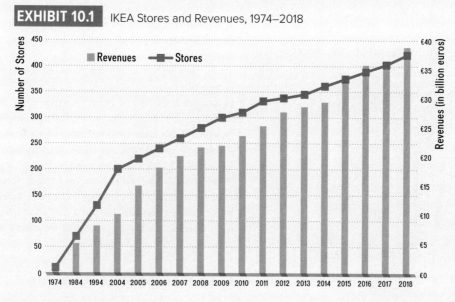

Source: Author's depiction of data from various IKEA yearly summaries (www.ikea.com).

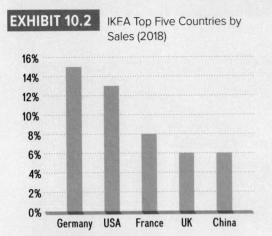

EXHIBIT 10.2 IKFA Top Five Countries by Sales (2018)

Source: Author's depiction of data from IKEA Group Yearly Summary 2018 (www.ikea.com).

strategy, in which it attempts to achieve economies of scale through effectively managing a global supply chain. Globalization has allowed IKEA to gain access to low-cost input factors, such as raw materials and labor. Although Asia currently accounts for only 11 percent of IKEA's sales, this region actually provides 35 percent of IKEA's inputs. To drive costs down further, IKEA has begun to implement production techniques from auto and electronics industries, in which cutting-edge technologies are employed to address complexity while achieving flexibility and lowering cost. IKEA's revenues by geographic region are mainly from Europe (71 percent), with the rest from the Americas (18 percent) and Asia (11 percent), as shown in Exhibit 10.3.

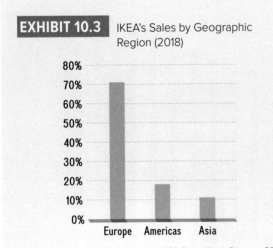

EXHIBIT 10.3 IKEA's Sales by Geographic Region (2018)

Source: Author's depiction of data from IKEA Group Yearly Summary 2018 (www.ikea.com).

With projections that 70 percent of the world's population will live in cities by 2050, and the ensuing changes in consumer demands, IKEA is reinventing itself—and is doing so successfully. It has made a strong push toward newer formats such as placing smaller stores in city centers. For instance, IKEA opened its first store in central Paris in 2019. Despite the new smaller store format, IKEA continues to offer its full range of products. The company has also set up click-and-collect locations (small stores for retrieval of online purchases) and has begun to offer furniture rentals for itinerant city dwellers who move frequently, often across the globe. As an additional effort to meet the needs of a growing urban population, and to encourage more in-store visits, IKEA now also offers customized furniture solutions.

To further reinvent itself, IKEA is investing heavily in its online presence, enabling consumers to make their purchases, schedule delivery, and even request installation services—all online. IKEA's functional website (ikea.com) garners more than 2 billion hits a year. The convenience of doing everything online is especially popular among busy urban professionals who have limited time and are less inclined to travel long distances to an IKEA store, which is traditionally found in an out-of-town setting. In fact, the number of customers who visit these existing brick-and-mortar locations has declined considerably. Yet, despite this stalled growth in the number of in-store visitors, IKEA has remained relatively immune to the recent retail apocalypse; in the last year, close to 1 billion customers visited its big-box stores.

To better adapt to the fast-changing retail landscape, IKEA has opted to undergo major restructuring. In addition to the drop in store visits among busy urban professionals, research also shows that this consumer group is also less inclined to spend the frustrating hours putting IKEA furniture together—rarely do customers enjoy "easy assembly"; moreover, the included tools are low quality and the instructions inferior. To address this customer pain point, IKEA acquired TaskRabbit (a furniture assembly and delivery marketplace) in 2017. It is also currently testing AI and robots to help assemble IKEA furniture. While researchers in Singapore managed to teach robots how to assemble an IKEA chair, these so-called IKEAbots still have a long way to go before they can be considered fully functional. For example, it took these robots close to 20 minutes to accomplish a task that a human being would have accomplished in just a few; nonetheless, these steps represent the first in creating an automated and more cost-efficient style of the future.[1]

Part II of this ChapterCase appears in Section 10.6.

IT IS SOMEWHAT surprising that the world's most profitable retailer is a privately held furniture maker from Sweden and not a behemoth such as the U.S.-based Walmart. IKEA's success in its international markets is critical to its competitive advantage. IKEA succeeds in both rich developed countries such as the United States and Germany, as well as in emerging economies such as China, India, and Russia. Hailing from a small country in Europe, IKEA earns the vast majority of its revenues outside of its borders. Moreover, IKEA's fastest growth is outside Europe.

For more and more U.S. companies, international markets offer the biggest growth opportunities, just as they do for IKEA. Firms from a wide variety of industries—such as Apple, Caterpillar, GE, Intel, and IBM—are global enterprises. They have a global work force and manage global supply chains, and they obtain the majority of their revenues from outside their home market. Once-unassailable U.S. firms now encounter formidable foreign competitors such as Brazil's Embraer (aerospace); China's Tencent (social media and online gaming), Haier (home appliances), Lenovo (PCs), and Huawei (cell phones); India's ArcelorMittal (steel), Infosys (IT services), and Reliance Group (conglomerate); Germany's Siemens (engineering conglomerate), Daimler, BMW, and VW (vehicles); Japan's Toyota, Honda, and Nissan (vehicles); Mexico's Cemex (cement); Russia's Gazprom (energy); South Korea's LG and Samsung (both in electronics and appliances); and Sweden's IKEA (home furnishings) to name just a few. This chapter is about how firms gain and sustain competitive advantage when competing around the world.

In Chapter 8, we looked at the first two dimensions of corporate strategy: managing the degree of vertical integration, and deciding which products and services to offer (the degree of diversification). Now we turn to the third dimension: competing effectively around the world. We begin this chapter by defining globalization and presenting stages of globalization. We then tackle a number of questions that a firm must answer: Why should a company go global? Where and how should it compete? We present the CAGE[2] distance model to answer the question of where the firm should compete globally and the integration-responsiveness framework to link a firm's options of how to compete globally with the different business strategies introduced in Chapter 6 (cost leadership, differentiation, and blue ocean). We then debate the question of why world leadership in specific industries is often concentrated in certain geographic areas. We conclude with the practical *Implications for Strategic Leaders*.

10.1 What Is Globalization?

Globalization is a process of closer integration and exchange between different countries and peoples worldwide, made possible by falling trade and investment barriers, advances in telecommunications, and reductions in transportation costs.[3] Combined, these factors reduce the costs of doing business around the world, opening the doors to a much larger market than any one home country. Globalization also allows companies to source supplies at lower costs, to learn new competencies, and to further differentiate products. Over the last few decades, the world's market economies have become more integrated and interdependent. The world's marketplace—made up of nearly 200 countries—is a staggering $81 trillion in gross domestic product (GDP), of which the U.S. market is roughly $20 trillion, or close to 25 percent.[4]

As the ChapterCase indicates, the competitive playing field is becoming increasingly global. This globalization provides significant opportunities for individuals, companies, and countries. Indeed, you can probably see the increase in globalization on your own campus. The number of students enrolled at universities outside their native countries has risen fivefold between 1980 and 2018 to 5 million.[5] By 2025, the total number is predicted to reach

LO 10-1

Define globalization, multinational enterprise (MNE), foreign direct investment (FDI), and global strategy.

Globalization The process of closer integration and exchange between different countries and peoples worldwide, made possible by falling trade and investment barriers, advances in telecommunications, and reductions in transportation costs.

8 million.[6] The country of choice for foreign students remains the United States, with more than 1 million international students enrolled per year, followed by the United Kingdom. The top five countries (in rank order) sending the most students to study abroad are China, India, South Korea, Germany, and Saudi Arabia.[7]

IKEA, the Swedish home-furnishings retailer featured in the ChapterCase, intends to reach 3 billion people worldwide by 2025. To achieve this stretch goal, IKEA anticipates achieving sales of €50 billion in 2020—doubling its 2011 sales of €25 billion. IKEA also plans to own 500 profitable stores globally by the end of 2020, up from 300 stores in 2010. To accomplish these lofty goals, IKEA must get its global strategy right, especially in growing markets such as China and India. Each country boasts a population of more than 1 billion people and a rapidly expanding middle class, on which IKEA wants to capitalize.

Globalization has led to significant increases in living standards in many economies around the world. Germany and Japan, countries that were largely destroyed during World War II, turned into industrial powerhouses, fueled by export-led growth. The Asian Tigers—Hong Kong, Singapore, South Korea, and Taiwan—turned themselves from underdeveloped countries into advanced economies, enjoying some of the world's highest standards of living. China and India continue to offer significant business opportunities.[8] Indeed, China, with $12 trillion in GDP, has become the second-largest economy worldwide after the United States (with $20 trillion in GDP) and ahead of Japan in third place ($5 trillion GDP), in absolute terms.[9] Adjusting GDP for size of population (per capita) and adjusting for difference in cost of living (purchasing power parity), the United States comes in at 14th place, China at 94th, and Japan at 30th. The three richest countries in the world by income per person are Monaco, Lichtenstein, and Luxembourg, all small and wealthy countries in Europe.

The engine behind globalization is the **multinational enterprise (MNE)**—a company that deploys resources and capabilities in the procurement, production, and distribution of goods and services in at least two countries. MNEs need an effective **global strategy** that enables them to gain and sustain a competitive advantage when competing against other foreign and domestic companies around the world.[10] By making investments in value chain activities abroad, MNEs engage in **foreign direct investment (FDI)**.[11]

For example, the European aircraft manufacturer Airbus invested $600 million in Mobile, Alabama, to build jetliners.[12] The new Mobile Aeroplex is a 53-acre facility where Airbus builds the vast majority of its single-aisle A-320 jetliners. Airbus made a significant strategic commitment to the U.S. market, the destination of the majority of its new jetliners; the A-320 is mainly used in domestic U.S. air travel. Being located in Alabama allows Airbus to be much closer to its customers and thus to receive and incorporate feedback, as individual airlines request specific customizations. It allows Airbus to take advantage of business-friendly conditions such as lower taxes, labor cost, and cost of living, plus other incentives provided by host states in the Southern United States. Making Airbus planes in the United States also prevents the European company from being forced to accept import restrictions or being exposed to tariffs.

U.S. MNEs have a disproportionately positive impact on the U.S. economy.[13] Well-known U.S. multinational enterprises include Boeing, Caterpillar, Coca-Cola Co., GE, John Deere, Exxon Mobil, IBM, Intel, P&G, and Walmart. U.S. MNEs make up less than 1 percent of the number of total U.S. companies, but they

- Account for 11 percent of private-sector employment growth since 1990.
- Employ 19 percent of the work force.
- Pay 25 percent of the wages.
- Provide for 31 percent of the U.S. gross domestic product (GDP).
- Make up 74 percent of private-sector R&D spending.

multinational enterprise (MNE) A company that deploys resources and capabilities in the procurement, production, and distribution of goods and services in at least two countries.

global strategy Part of a firm's corporate strategy to gain and sustain a competitive advantage when competing against other foreign and domestic companies around the world.

foreign direct investment (FDI) A firm's investments in value chain activities abroad.

As a business student, you have several reasons to be interested in MNEs. Not only can these companies provide interesting work assignments in different locations throughout the world, but they also frequently offer the highest-paying jobs for college graduates. Even if you don't want to work for an MNE, chances are that the organization you work for will do business with one, so it's important to understand how they compete around the globe.

STAGES OF GLOBALIZATION

Since the beginning of the 20th century, globalization has proceeded through three notable stages.[14] Each stage presents a different global strategy pursued by MNEs headquartered in the United States.

GLOBALIZATION 1.0: 1900–1941. Globalization 1.0 took place from about 1900 through the early years of World War II. In that period, basically all the important business functions were located in the home country. Typically, only sales and distribution operations took place overseas—essentially exporting goods to other markets. In some instances, firms procured raw materials from overseas. Strategy formulation and implementation, as well as knowledge flows, followed a one-way path—from domestic headquarters to international outposts. This time period saw the blossoming of the idea of MNEs. It ended with the U.S. entry into World War II.

GLOBALIZATION 2.0: 1945–2000. With the end of World War II came a new focus on growing business—not only to meet the needs that went unfulfilled during the war years but also to reconstruct the damage from the war. From 1945 to the end of the 20th century, in the Globalization 2.0 stage, MNEs began to create smaller, self-contained copies of themselves, with all business functions intact, in a few key countries; notably, Western European countries, Japan, and Australia.

This strategy required significant amounts of foreign direct investment. Although it was costly to duplicate business functions in overseas outposts, doing so allowed for greater local responsiveness to country-specific circumstances. While the U.S. corporate headquarters set overarching strategic goals and allocated resources through the capital budgeting process, local mini-MNE replicas had considerable leeway in day-to-day operations. Knowledge flow back to U.S. headquarters, however, remained limited in most instances.

GLOBALIZATION 3.0: 21ST CENTURY. Since 2001, we are in the Globalization 3.0 stage. One watershed event was China's entry into the World Trade Organization in the same year. The World Trade Organization (WTO) is a global organization overseeing and administering the rules of trade between nations.[15] The goal of the WTO is to help companies conduct their business across borders based on multinational treaties that are negotiated and signed by its 164 member nations.

MNEs that had been the vanguard of globalization have since become global collaboration networks (see Exhibit 10.4). Such companies now freely locate business functions anywhere in the world based on an optimal mix of costs, capabilities, and PESTEL factors. Huge investments in fiber-optic cable networks around the world have effectively reduced communication distances, enabling companies to operate 24/7, 365 days a year. When an engineer in Minneapolis, Minnesota, leaves for the evening, an engineer in Mumbai, India, begins her workday.

In the Globalization 3.0 stage, the MNE's strategic objective changes. The MNE reorganizes from a multinational company with self-contained operations in a few selected countries to a more seamless global enterprise with centers of expertise. Each of these centers of expertise is a hub within a global network for delivering products and services. Consulting

EXHIBIT 10.4 Globalization 3.0: 21st Century

Based on an optimal mix of costs, skills, and PESTEL factors, MNEs are organized as global collaboration networks that perform business functions throughout the world.

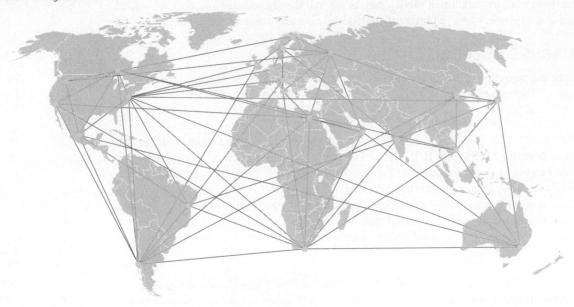

Source: Adapted from "A Decade of Generating Higher Value at IBM," www.ibm.com, 2009.

companies, for example, can now tap into a worldwide network of experts in real time, rather than relying on the limited number of employees in their local offices.

Creating a global network of local expertise is beneficial not only in service industries, but also in the industrial sector. To increase the rate of low-cost innovation that can then be used to disrupt existing markets, GE organizes local growth teams in China, India, Kenya, and many other emerging countries.[16] GE uses the slogan "in country, for country" to describe the local growth teams' autonomy in deciding which products and services to develop, how to make them, and how to shape the business model. Many of these low-cost innovations, first developed to serve local needs, are later introduced in Western markets to become disruptive innovations. Examples include the Vscan, a handheld ultrasound device developed in China; the MAC 400, an ECG device developed in India; and the 9100c, an anesthesia system developed in Kenya.[17]

Some new ventures organize as global collaboration networks from the start. Logitech, the maker of wireless peripherals such as computer mice, presentation "clickers," and video game controllers, started in Switzerland but quickly established offices in Silicon Valley, California.[18] Pursuing a global strategy right from the start allowed Logitech to tap into the innovation expertise contained in Silicon Valley.[19] In 2018, Logitech had sales of $2.6 billion, with offices throughout the Americas, Asia, and Europe. Underlying Logitech's innovation competence is a network of best-in-class skills around the globe. Based on its geographic presence, Logitech can organize work continuously because its teams in different locations around the globe can work 24/7.

Indeed, the trend toward global collaboration networks during the Globalization 3.0 stage raises the interesting question, "What defines a U.S. company?" If it's the address of the headquarters, then IBM, GE, and others are U.S. companies—despite the fact that a majority of their employees work outside the United States. In many instances, the majority of their revenues also come from outside the United States. On the other hand, non-U.S. companies such as carmakers from Japan (Toyota, Honda, and Nissan) and South Korea (Hyundai and Kia) and several engineering companies (Siemens from Germany and ABB, a Swiss-Swedish MNE) all have made significant investments in the United States and created a large number of well-paying jobs.

STATE OF GLOBALIZATION

Before we delve deeper into the question of why and how firms compete for advantage globally, a cautionary note concerning *globalization* is in order. Although many large firms are more than 50 percent globalized—meaning that more than half of their revenues are from outside the home country—the world itself is far less global.[20] If we look at a number of indicators, the level of globalization is no more than 10 to 25 percent. For example, only

- 2 percent of all voice-calling minutes are cross-border.[21]
- 3 percent of the world's population are first-generation immigrants.
- 9 percent of all investments in the economy are foreign direct investments.
- 15 percent of patents list at least one foreign inventor.
- 18 percent of internet traffic crosses national borders.

These data indicate that the world is not quite flat yet,[22] or fully globalized, but at best *semi-globalized.* Pankaj Ghemawat reasons that many more gains in social welfare and living standards can be had through further globalization if future integration is managed effectively through coordinated efforts by governments.[23]

The European Union is an example of coordinated economic and political integration by 28 countries (before Brexit), of which 19 use the euro as a common currency. This coordinated integration took place over several decades following World War II, precisely to prevent future wars in Europe. The EU encompasses 500 million people, which makes it one of the largest economic zones in the world, while the United States remains the largest single-country market in the world. Although the EU has monetary authority administered through the European Central Bank, it does not have fiscal (i.e., budgetary) authority. This important responsibility remains with national governments. This separation between monetary and fiscal authority allowed the sovereign debt crisis during 2009–2015 to emerge.

GLOBAL ECONOMIC DEVELOPMENT: IMPACT ON MNEs. Continued economic development across the globe has two consequences for MNEs. First, rising wages and other costs are likely to negate any benefits of access to low-cost input factors. Second, as the standard of living rises in emerging economies, MNEs are hoping that increased purchasing power will enable workers to purchase the products they used to make for export only.[24] China's labor costs, for example, are steadily rising in tandem with an improved standard of living, especially in the coastal regions, where wages have risen 50 percent since 2005.

Some MNEs have boosted wages following labor unrest in China in recent years. Many now offer bonuses to blue-collar workers and are taking other measures to avoid sweatshop allegations that have plagued companies such as Nike, Apple, and Levi Strauss. Rising wages, fewer workers due to the effects of China's one-child-per-family policy, and appreciation of the Chinese currency now combine to lessen the country's advantage in low-cost manufacturing.[25] This shift is in alignment with the Chinese government's economic policy, which wants to see a move from "Made in China" to "Designed in China," to capture more of the value added.[26] For instance, the value added of manufacturing an iPhone by Foxconn in China is only about 5 percent.[27]

GLOBALIZATION 3.1: RETRENCHMENT? Several *black swan events* (that is, highly improbable, but high-impact events) have buffeted the world economy in recent years. The global financial crisis between 2008 and 2010 led to a deep recession and high unemployment in many parts of the world, including the United States. At the same time, the European sovereign debt crisis unfolded with several countries teetering on the verge of insolvency, leading to high unemployment in some countries. For instance, about 50 percent of the people under 25 were unemployed in Spain and Greece. In the 2010s, the European refugee crisis unfolded with millions of people being displaced. Fleeing civil war zones as well as territory occupied by the Islamic State, over 1.3 million refugees in 2015 alone streamed into the European Union. While the crises in the United States and the EU unfolded, China continued to rise both in economic and political power, establishing itself as a superpower to be reckoned with, and now challenging the supremacy of the United States. Other countries, such as Russia and Turkey, appear to become more autocratic as time unfolds.

All of these macro events contributed to a rise of nationalism in the United States and Western Europe. In 2016, the British voted to leave the EU. Right-wing parties registered strong gains in national elections in many European countries. In general, future viability of entire economic trading blocs such as the EU are being questioned. In the United States, the Trump administration pursues an "America first" policy, which has resulted in a stronger focus on nationalism and a retrenchment of globalization. Bilateral treaties are favored over multinational trade deals negotiated by international bodies such as the World Trade Organization (WTO). In 2018, the North American Free Trade Agreement (NAFTA) was renegotiated.

The United States and China are beginning to view each other more as strategic rivals that are competing for supremacy, rather than deeply intertwined trading partners. As the competition between different political and economic systems and the race toward global supremacy heats up, the United States and China find themselves engaged in a trade war. This trade war will lead to critical consequences worldwide. Any further changes to existing trade rules are likely to affect cross-border trade in a negative fashion, impacting MNEs the most. It remains to be seen whether the trend toward nationalism and the U.S.-Chinese trade war will continue and thus have lasting consequences over the next few years as this process of potential globalization retrenchment unfolds.

10.2 Going Global: Why?

A firm pursues international expansion if, after careful assessment, it determines that doing so can increase its economic value creation and enhance competitive advantage. As detailed in Chapter 5, firms enhance their competitive advantage by increasing a consumer's willingness to pay through higher perceived value. This higher perceived value is based on differentiation and/or lower production and service delivery costs. Expanding beyond the home market, therefore, should reinforce a company's basis of competitive advantage—whether that be differentiation, low cost, or value innovation. Next we consider both the advantages and disadvantages of international expansion (see Exhibit 10.5).

ADVANTAGES OF GOING GLOBAL

Why do firms expand internationally? The main reasons firms expand abroad are to

- Gain access to a larger market.
- Gain access to low-cost input factors.
- Develop new competencies.

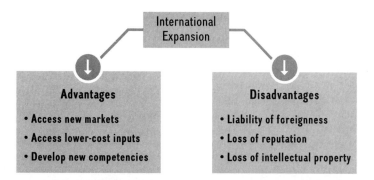

EXHIBIT 10.5

Advantages and
Disadvantages of
International
Expansion

GAIN ACCESS TO A LARGER MARKET. Becoming an MNE provides significant opportunities for companies, given *economies of scale* and *scope* that can be reaped by participating in a much larger market. Companies that base their competitive advantage on *economies of scale* and *economies of scope* have an incentive to gain access to larger markets because this can reinforce the basis of their competitive advantage. This in turn allows MNEs to outcompete local rivals. In Strategy Highlight 6.1, we detailed how Narayana Health, a specialty hospital chain in India, founded and led by Dr. Devi Shetty, obtained a low-cost competitive advantage in complex procedures such as open-heart surgery. Narayana Health is now leveraging its low-cost, high-quality position by opening specialty hospitals in the Cayman Islands (to serve U.S. patients) and Kuala Lumpur, Malaysia.

At the same time, some countries with relatively weak domestic demand, such as China, Germany, South Korea, and Japan, focus on export-led economic growth, which drives many of their domestic businesses to become MNEs. For companies based in smaller economies, becoming an MNE may be necessary to achieve growth or to gain and sustain competitive advantage. Examples include Acer (Taiwan), Casella Wines (Australia), IKEA (featured in the ChapterCase), Nestlé (Switzerland), LEGO (Denmark), Philips (Netherlands), Samsung (South Korea), and Zara (Spain). Unless companies in smaller economies expand internationally, their domestic markets are often too small for them to reach significant economies of scale to compete effectively against other MNEs. Strategy Highlight 10.1 explains how GM is largely betting its future on the Chinese market.

GAIN ACCESS TO LOW-COST INPUT FACTORS. MNEs that base their competitive advantage on a low-cost leadership strategy are particularly attracted to go overseas to gain access to low-cost input factors. Access to low-cost raw *materials* such as lumber, iron ore, oil, and coal was a key driver behind Globalization 1.0 and 2.0. During Globalization 3.0, firms have expanded globally to benefit from lower *labor costs* in manufacturing and services.

India. India carved out a competitive advantage in business process outsourcing (BPO), not only because of low-cost labor but also because of an abundance of well-educated, English-speaking young people. Infosys, TCS, and Wipro are some of the more well-known Indian IT service companies. Together, these companies employ more than 250,000 people and provide services to many of the Global Fortune 500 companies. Many MNEs have close business ties with Indian IT firms. Some, such as IBM, are engaged in foreign direct investment through equity alliances or building their own IT and customer service centers in India. More than a quarter of Accenture's work force, a consultancy specializing in technology and outsourcing, is now in Bangalore, India.[28] Both the CEOs of Google (Sundar Pichai) and Microsoft (Satya Nadella) hail from India.

Strategy Highlight **10.1**

Does GM's Future Lie in China?

Given the sheer size of the U.S. automotive market, the "old" GM focused mainly on its domestic market. GM once held more than 50 percent market share in the United States and was the leader in global car sales (by units) between 1931 and 2007, before filing for bankruptcy in 2009.[29] In its heyday, GM employed 350,000 U.S. workers and was an American icon.

Now, the future for the "new" GM may lie overseas, most notably in China. Close to 60 percent of GM's revenues currently come from outside the United States—quite a high percentage for a company that was once focused more or less on only its domestic market. The Chinese market is becoming increasingly important to GM's performance, already accounting for greater than 40 percent of

Mary Barra, CEO General Motors, is refocusing GM on the U.S. home market and China, among other developing economies, while exiting Europe.
Tomohiro Ohsumi/Bloomberg/Getty Images

total GM revenues. This number has risen steadily in the past few years. In 2018, GM sold more cars in China than it did in the United States. And while Ford's market share in China dropped to less than 3 percent, GM's market share reached a much more successful 14 percent.

Unlike some of its main rivals, GM entered the Chinese market early. In 1997, GM formed a joint venture with Shanghai Automotive Industrial Corp. (SAIC), one of the "big four" Chinese carmakers and one of the largest companies worldwide; it is included in the Fortune Global 100 list (ranked 36th with $130 billion in revenues, just behind the U.S. warehouse club Costco and ahead of Verizon).[30] Over 30 years, GM was able to develop *guanxi*—social networks and relationships that facilitate business dealings—with its Chinese business partners and government officials.

GM's China operation has been cost-competitive from day one. Although GM sells more vehicles in China, it employs only half the number of workers. Moreover, Chinese workers cost a fraction of what U.S. workers do, and GM is not weighed down by additional health care and pension obligations. Although struggling in the United States, GM's Cadillac luxury brand is in high demand in China, where owning a Cadillac is considered a status symbol. In 2018, the sales of Cadillac vehicles increased by 25 percent, while the Buick brand also remains popular in China. Yet, at the premium end of the Chinese market, brands such as Porsche and Audi (both part of Volkswagen Group) remain the most popular choices.

China and other emerging economies in Asia, Latin America, and the Middle East are becoming more critical to GM's future performance as it strives to be a profitable manufacturer of smaller cars compared to the sport utility vehicles (SUVs) and trucks that GM relies on in the United States. To back up its strategic intent, GM has quadrupled its engineering and design personnel in China and is investing a quarter-billion dollars to build a cutting-edge R&D center on its Shanghai campus, home of its international headquarters. Moreover, GM is spending an estimated $14 billion to build five additional manufacturing plants to support anticipated annual sales of 5 million vehicles in China.

At the same time that GM is doubling down on China, it has exited Europe. In 2015, GM stopped manufacturing cars in Russia, citing unstable business conditions as the main reason. After years of losing money and acrimonious parent-subsidiary relationships, GM sold its Opel

(Germany) and Vauxhall (United Kingdom) divisions to Peugeot of France in 2017. That same year, GM CEO Mary Barra also announced that the U.S. automaker would discontinue production of cars in India. This further retrenchment would allow GM to focus more on China. It would also help to fend off such tech startups as Tesla and Uber in the United States, where GM made an equity investment in Lyft, which in turn partnered with Waymo, Alphabet's self-driving car unit. GM also acquired Cruise Automation in 2016, a Silicon Valley tech startup focusing on developing autonomous vehicle technology. GM received additional investments of over $5 billion from Softbank, a Japanese venture fund, as well as Honda Motors, to continue improving GM's autonomous vehicle technology.

Not everything in China is smooth sailing for Barra, however. Given the slowdown in the Chinese economy, the competitive intensity in the world's largest automobile market has grown even more intense. Moreover, several government-supported domestic car manufacturers in China are initiating a cutthroat price war to gain market share and scale. Amid trade tensions with the United States, the slowdown of the Chinese economy was especially pronounced in 2018 when GM's net income fell by one-third. In contrast, low gas prices in the United States in recent years have fueled high demand for SUVs and trucks, where GM (and Ford) hold strong positions. These types of vehicles are also the most profitable for the U.S. automakers to sell.[31]

China. Likewise, China has emerged as a manufacturing powerhouse because of low labor costs and an efficient infrastructure. An American manufacturing worker costs several times more in wages than a similarly skilled worker in China.[32] A cost differential exists not only for low-skilled labor, but for high-skilled labor as well. A Chinese engineer trained at Purdue University, for example, works for only a quarter of the salary in his native country compared with an engineer working in the United States.[33] Wages, however, have been rising much more rapidly in China than in the United States, thus closing the wage gap.

In 2015, China set in motion its "Made in China 2025" plan, an industrial strategic policy meant to move beyond low-cost manufacturing to produce higher-value products and services. In particular, China aspires to be a world leader in high-tech industries such as aerospace and telecommunications and to lead in technologies of the future such as AI and robotics.

DEVELOP NEW COMPETENCIES. Some MNEs pursue a global strategy in order to develop new competencies.[34] This motivation is particularly attractive for firms that base their competitive advantage on a differentiation strategy. These companies are making foreign direct investments to be part of *communities of learning,* which are often contained in specific geographic regions.[35] AstraZeneca, a Swiss-based pharmaceutical company, relocated its research facility to Cambridge, Massachusetts, to be part of the Boston biotech cluster, in hopes of developing new R&D competencies in biotechnology.[36] Cisco invested more than $1.6 billion to create an Asian headquarters in Bangalore and support other locations in India in order to be in the middle of India's top IT location.[37] Likewise, Microsoft, one of the largest tech companies globally, has a key research center in Bangalore, India. Unilever's new-concept center is located in downtown Shanghai, China, attracting hundreds of eager volunteers to test the firm's latest product innovations on-site, while Unilever researchers monitor consumer reactions. In these examples, AstraZeneca, Cisco, Microsoft, and Unilever all reap **location economies**—benefits from locating value chain activities in optimal geographies for a specific activity, wherever that may be.[38]

Many MNEs are now replacing the one-way innovation flow from Western economies to developing markets with a *polycentric innovation strategy*—a strategy in which MNEs draw on multiple, equally important innovation hubs throughout the world characteristic of

location economies Benefits from locating value chain activities in the world's optimal geographies for a specific activity, wherever that may be.

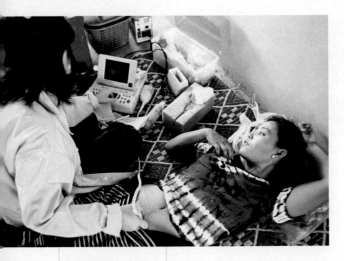

A GE team in China developed the Vscan, an inexpensive, portable ultrasound device, costing some $5,000—rather than the $250,000 cost of a traditional ultrasound machine used in Western hospitals. The Vscan is now widely used in rural areas of developing countries (as shown here in Thailand) and has made its entry as a disruptive innovation in the United States and other rich countries.
Thierry Falise/LightRocket. Getty Images

liability of foreignness
Additional costs of doing business in an unfamiliar cultural and economic environment, and of coordinating across geographic distances.

Globalization 3.0; see Exhibit 10.4. GE Global Research, for example, orchestrates a "network of excellence" with facilities in Niskayuna, New York (United States); Bangalore (India); Shanghai (China); and Munich (Germany). Indeed, emerging economies are becoming hotbeds for low-cost innovations that find their way back to developed markets.[39] In Bangalore, GE researchers developed the MAC 400, a handheld electrocardiogram (ECG).[40] The device is small, portable, and runs on batteries. Although a conventional ECG machine costs $2,000, this handheld version costs $800 and enables doctors to do an ECG test at a cost of only $1 per patient. The MAC 400 is now entering the United States and other Western markets as a disruptive innovation, with anticipated widespread use in the offices of general practitioners and emergency ambulances.

DISADVANTAGES OF GOING GLOBAL

Companies expanding internationally must carefully weigh the benefits and costs of doing so. If the cost of going global as captured by the following disadvantages exceeds the expected benefits in terms of value added ($C > V$), that is, if the economic value creation is negative, then firms are better off by not expanding internationally. Disadvantages to going global include

- Liability of foreignness.
- Loss of reputation.
- Loss of intellectual property.

LIABILITY OF FOREIGNNESS. In international expansion, firms face risks. In particular, MNEs doing business abroad also must overcome the **liability of foreignness**. This liability consists of the additional costs of doing business in an unfamiliar cultural and economic environment, and of coordinating across geographic distances.[41]

For instance, Walmart's problems in several international markets are in large part because of the liability of foreignness. In particular, Walmart failed in Germany and experienced a similar fate in South Korea, where it also exited in 2006. In addition, Walmart has tried for many years to successfully enter the fast-growing markets in Russia and India, but with little or no success. Walmart's success recipe that worked so well domestically didn't work in Germany, South Korea, Russia, or India. Strategy Highlight 10.2 illustrates how Walmart underestimated its liability of foreignness when entering and competing in Germany, and how it is now facing the German grocery industry disruptors, Aldi and Lidl, on its home turf.

LOSS OF REPUTATION. One of the most valuable resources that a firm may possess is its reputation. A firm's reputation can have several dimensions, including a reputation for innovation, customer service, or brand reputation. Apple's brand, for example, stands for innovation and superior customer experience. Apple's reputation is also one of its most important resources. Apple's brand is valued at $300 billion, making it (with Google's) one of the two most valuable brands in the world.[42] We detailed in Chapter 4 that a brand can be the basis for a competitive advantage if it is valuable, rare, and difficult to imitate.

Strategy Highlight **10.2**

Walmart Retreats from Germany, and Lidl Invades the United States

After spending billions of dollars and trying for almost a decade to succeed, Walmart exited Germany in defeat (in 2006). This failure shocked an otherwise successful company, and ghosts from the debacle now haunt Walmart on its native shores. What went wrong?

In 1998, Walmart faced a saturated U.S. market, and Germany, then the third-largest economy in the world, looked appealing. Walmart was already active in six foreign countries, with some 500 stores. Leadership decided the company's superior U.S. strategy—as the low-cost leader—would travel well one more time.

Walmart acquired Germany's 21-store Wertkauf chain and 74 hypermarkets from German retailer Spar Handels AG. And it followed the U.S. playbook: Walmart cheer, a door greeter, associates always available to customers, smiling and offering help, bagging groceries at the checkout, and so on. German employees, however, declined the transfusion of American values. No door greeters. Employees upheld the usual gruff standard of retail customer service found throughout Germany. Worse, the first Walmart boss in Germany—installed directly from the Arkansas headquarters—spoke no German. He decreed that English would be the official in-house language.

Cultural differences aside, Walmart also failed to keep prices down. The retailer lacked its domestic economies of scale and efficient distribution centers. Moreover, German labor laws—more protective than in the United States—drove up costs. The prices at Walmart in Germany were not "always low" despite the company slogan, but fell in the medium range.

Lastly, Walmart faced serious competition. Germany was already home to retail discount powerhouses such as Aldi and Lidl, with thousands of smaller outlets offering higher convenience combined with lower prices. Then it faced Metro, a big-box retailer, which started a price war when Walmart entered Germany. In the end, a defeated Walmart sold its stores to Metro.

One useful definition of strategy is to answer the question of how to deal with competition.[43] Walmart did not find a good strategy for competing with Aldi and Lidl in Germany. Now, Walmart is worried that Aldi and Lidl will

Lidl, a German discounter, entered the United States in 2017. Together with Aldi, Lidl disrupted the grocery market in the United Kingdom. Walmart executives are concerned about a repeat in the United States.
Steve Helber/AP Images

challenge the world's largest retailer on its home turf. Aldi has been competing in the United States since the 1970s with its own Aldi stores as well as the Trader Joe's brand. In 2017, Lidl also entered the United States.

Why does Walmart worry about Lidl's entry into the U.S. grocery business? Aldi has been highly successful with its more than 2,000 stores and another 500 Trader Joe's stores in the United States. Rather than focusing on large big-box outlets, Aldi stores are small, near urban centers with high foot traffic and easy access to public transportation or major roads to suburbia. Trader Joe's, as a neighborhood grocery store, has a loyal fan base. It offers mainly its own brand-name products such as organic, vegetarian, or imported foods at much lower prices than Whole Foods and elsewhere. Trader Joe's generates twice as much revenue per square foot of retail space as Whole Foods.

Lidl is joining the fray. It already has a few dozen stores on the U.S. East Coast, with hundreds more planned. Similarly to Aldi, Lidl also competes on price and offers mainly its own store brands. Another advantage: These competitors typically offer 2,000 products rather than the standard 40,000 or so of large supermarkets. For example, many grocery stores sell 30 types of mustard. These German disruptors carry only two. Products arrive shelf-ready, minimizing stocking and inventory costs, albeit often with a wholesale feel. All products are sold at ultra-low prices. There are no daily or weekly specials.

(Continued)

Indeed, the entry of the German discounters was so successful in the United Kingdom that Tesco, Britain's leading supermarket chain, had to close dozens of stores, with large-scale layoffs. Its market cap fell almost 80 percent, from $80 billion in 2007 to as low as $17 billion in 2017. In 2019, Tesco's market cap had recovered somewhat to reach $30 billion.

Meanwhile, Walmart prepares. With online sales, Walmart leads the German discounters, although it trails Amazon. Walmart's online sales grew by more than 40 percent in 2018. This growth comes in part from a new "order online, pick up in store" concept, with dedicated parking bays for drive-by customers to pick up online purchases. And it successfully improved Walmart.com, offering free, two-day delivery for orders over $35.

Walmart is also working the basics to speed up checkout times and lower some prices even more. And it continues to pressure suppliers so that its cost will be 15 percent lower than the competition's 80 percent of the time. With Amazon on one side (especially after its acquisition of Whole Foods Market) and industry disruptors such as Aldi and Lidl on the other, Walmart is sharpening its strategic position as a low-cost leader. This competitive battle is crucial for Walmart because groceries make up some 60 percent of its annual revenues of over $510 billion, making it the largest grocery chain in the United States.[44]

While cost savings can generally be achieved, globalizing a supply chain can also have unintended side effects. These can lead to a loss of reputation and diminish the MNE's competitiveness. A possible loss in reputation can be a considerable risk and cost for doing business abroad. Because Apple's stellar consumer reputation is critical to its competitive advantage, it should be concerned about any potential negative exposure from its global activities. Problems at Apple's main supplier, Foxconn, brought this concern to the fore.

Low wages, long hours, and poor working and living conditions contributed to a spate of suicides (in 2010) at Foxconn, Apple's main supplier in China.[45] The Taiwanese company, which employs more than a million people, manufactures computers, tablets, smartphones, and other consumer electronics for Apple and other leading consumer electronics companies. The backlash against alleged sweatshop conditions in Foxconn prompted Apple to work with its main supplier to improve working conditions and wages. Tim Cook, Apple's CEO, visited Foxconn in China to personally inspect its manufacturing facility and workers' living conditions. Although conditions at Foxconn have been improving,[46] Apple started to diversify its supplier base by adding Pegatron, another Taiwanese original equipment manufacturer (OEM).[47]

MNEs' search for low-cost labor has had tragic effects where local governments are corrupt and unwilling or unable to enforce a minimum of safety standards. The textile industry is notorious for sweatshop conditions, and many Western companies such as the Gap (United States), H&M (Sweden), and Carrefour (France) have taken a big hit to their reputations in factory accidents in Bangladesh and elsewhere in Southeast Asia. Hundreds of factory workers were killed when a textile factory collapsed in Rana Plaza (in 2013) on the outskirts of Dhaka, Bangladesh.[48] Although much of the blame lies with the often corrupt host governments not enforcing laws, regulations, and building codes, the MNEs that source their textiles in these factories also receive some of the blame with negative consequences for their reputation. The MNEs are accused of exploiting workers and being indifferent to their working conditions and safety, all in an unending quest to drive down costs.

This challenge directly concerns the MNEs' *corporate social responsibility (CSR),* discussed in Chapter 1. Since some host governments are either unwilling or unable to enforce regulation and safety codes, MNEs need to rise to the challenge.[49] Walmart responded by posting a public list of "banned suppliers" on its website. These are suppliers that do not meet adequate safety standards and working conditions. Before the Rana Plaza accident, Walmart had already launched a working and fire-safety academy in Bangladesh to train textile workers.

Given the regulatory and legal void that local governments often leave, several Western MNEs have proposed a concerted action to finance safety efforts and worker training as well as structural upgrades to factory buildings. After earlier revelations about the frequent practice of child labor in many developing countries, Western MNEs in the textile industry worked together to ban their suppliers from using child labor. Ensuring ethical sourcing of raw materials and supplies is becoming ever more important. Besides a moral responsibility, MNEs have a market incentive to protect their reputations given the public backlash in the wake of factory accidents, child labor, worker suicides, and other horrific externalities.

LOSS OF INTELLECTUAL PROPERTY. Finally, the issue of protecting intellectual property in foreign markets also looms large. The software, movie, and music industries have long lamented large-scale copyright infringements in many foreign markets. In addition, when required to partner with a foreign host firm, companies may find their intellectual property being siphoned off and reverse-engineered.

Japanese and European engineering companies entered China to participate in building the world's largest network of high-speed trains worth billions of dollars.[50] Companies such as Kawasaki Heavy Industries (Japan), Siemens (Germany), and Alstom (France) were joint venture partners with domestic Chinese companies. These firms now allege that the Chinese partners built on the Japanese and European partners' advanced technology to create their own, next-generation high-speed trains. To make matters worse, they also claim that the Chinese companies now compete against them in other lucrative markets, such as Saudi Arabia, Brazil, and even California, with trains of equal or better capabilities but offered at much lower prices. This example highlights the *intellectual property exposure* that firms can face when expanding overseas.

10.3 Going Global: Where and How?

After discussing why companies expand internationally, we now turn to the question of how to guide MNE decisions on which countries to enter and how to then enter those countries.

WHERE IN THE WORLD TO COMPETE? THE CAGE DISTANCE FRAMEWORK

The question of where to compete geographically is, following vertical integration and diversification, the third dimension of determining a firm's corporate strategy. The primary driver behind firms expanding beyond their domestic market is to strengthen their competitive position by gaining access to larger markets and low-cost input factors and to develop new competencies. So wouldn't companies choose new markets solely based on measures such as per capita consumption of the product and per capita income?

Yes and no. Consider that several countries and locations can score similarly on such *absolute* metrics of attractiveness. Ireland and Portugal, for example, have similar cost structures, and both provide access to some 500 million customers in the European Union. Both countries use the euro as a common currency, and both have a similarly educated work force and infrastructure. Given these similarities, how does an MNE decide? Rather than looking at absolute measures, MNEs need to consider *relative distance* in the CAGE model.

To aid MNEs in deciding where in the world to compete, Pankaj Ghemawat introduced the **CAGE distance framework**. CAGE is an acronym for different kinds of distance:

- Cultural.
- Administrative and political.
- Geographic.
- Economic.[51]

LO 10-3

Apply the CAGE distance framework to guide MNE decisions on which countries to enter.

CAGE distance framework A decision framework based on the relative distance between home and a foreign target country along four dimensions: cultural distance, administrative and political distance, geographic distance, and economic distance.

Most of the costs and risks involved in expanding beyond the domestic market are created by *distance*. Distance not only denotes geographic distance (in miles or kilometers), but also includes, as the CAGE acronym points out, cultural distance, administrative and political distance, and economic distance. The CAGE distance framework breaks distance into different relative components between any two country pairs that affect the success of FDI.

Although absolute metrics such as country wealth or market size matter to some extent—as we know, for example, that a 1 percent increase in country wealth leads to a 0.8 percent increase in international trade—the relative factors captured by the CAGE distance model matter more. For instance, countries that are 5,000 miles apart trade only 20 percent of the amount traded among countries that are 1,000 miles apart. Cultural distance matters even more. A common language increases trade between two countries by 200 percent over country pairs without one. Thus, in the earlier example regarding which EU country to select for FDI, a U.S. MNE should pick Ireland, while a Brazilian MNE should select Portugal. In the latter case, Brazil and Portugal also share a historic colony–colonizer relationship. This link increases the expected trade intensity between these two countries by yet another 900 percent in comparison to country pairs where absent.

Other CAGE distance factors are significant in predicting the amount of trade between two countries. If the countries belong to the same regional trading bloc, they can expect another 330 percent in trade intensity. Examples include the United States, Canada, and Mexico in the USMCA (update of NAFTA) treaty, or the member states of the European Union. If the two countries use the same currency it increases trade intensity by 340 percent. An example is use of the euro as the common currency in 19 EU countries.[52]

Exhibit 10.6 presents the CAGE distance model. In particular, it details factors that increase the overall distance between the two countries and how distance affects different industries or products along the CAGE dimensions.[53] Next, we briefly discuss each of the CAGE distance dimensions.[54]

EXHIBIT 10.6 The CAGE Distance Framework

Distance	C Cultural	A Administrative and Political	G Geographic	E Economic
Between two countries increases with ...	• Different languages, ethnicities, religions, social norms, and dispositions • Lack of connective ethnic or social networks • Lack of trust and mutual respect	• Absence of trading bloc • Absence of shared currency, monetary or political association • Absence of colonial ties • Political hostilities • Weak legal and financial institutions	• Lack of common border, waterway access, adequate transportation, or communication links • Physical remoteness • Different climates and time zones	• Different consumer incomes • Different costs and quality of natural, financial, and human resources • Different information or knowledge
Most affects industries or products ...	• With high linguistic content (media) • Related to national and/or religious identity (foods) • Carrying country-specific quality associations (wines)	• That a foreign government views as staples (electricity), as building national reputations (aerospace), or as vital to national security (telecommunications)	• With low value-to-weight ratio (cement) • That are fragile or perishable (glass, meats) • In which communications are vital (financial services)	• For which demand varies by income (cars) • In which labor and other cost differences matter (textiles)

Source: Adapted from P. Ghemawat (2001), September, "Distance still matters: The hard reality of global expansion," *Harvard Business Review*: 137-147

CULTURAL DISTANCE. In his seminal research, Geert Hofstede defined and measured **national culture**, the collective mental and emotional "programming of the mind" that differentiates human groups.[55] Culture is made up of a collection of social norms and mores, beliefs, and values. Culture captures the often unwritten and implicitly understood rules of the game.

Although there is no one-size-fits-all culture that accurately describes any nation, Hofstede's work provides a useful tool to proxy cultural distance. Based on data analysis from more than 100,000 individuals from many countries, four main dimensions of culture emerged: *Power distance, individualism, masculinity–femininity,* and *uncertainty avoidance.*[56] Hofstede's data analysis yielded scores for the different countries, for each dimension, on a range of zero to 100, with 100 as the high end. More recently, Hofstede added two additional cultural dimensions: *long-term orientation* and *indulgence.*[57]

Cultural differences find their expression in language, ethnicity, religion, and social norms. They directly affect customer preferences (see Exhibit 10.6). Because of religious beliefs, for example, Hindus do not eat beef, while Muslims do not eat pork. In terms of content-intensive service, cultural and language differences are also the reason global internet companies such as Amazon or Google offer country-specific variations of their sites. Despite these best efforts, they are often outflanked by native providers because of their deeper cultural understanding. For example, in China the leading websites are domestic ones: Alibaba in ecommerce, and Baidu in online search. In Russia, the leading ecommerce site is Ozon, while the leading search engine is Yandex.

Hofstede's national-culture research becomes even more useful for managers by combining the distinct dimensions of culture into an aggregate measure for each country. MNEs then can compare the national-culture measures for any two country pairings to inform their entry decisions.[58] The difference between scores indicates **cultural distance**, the cultural disparity between the internationally expanding firm's home country and its targeted host country. A firm's decision to enter certain international markets is influenced by cultural differences. A greater cultural distance can increase the cost and uncertainty of conducting business abroad. In short, greater cultural distance increases the liability of foreignness.

If we calculate the cultural distance from the United States to various countries, for example, we find that some countries are culturally close to the United States. Australia, for example, has an overall cultural distance score of 0.02. Others are culturally quite distant. Russia has an overall cultural distance score of 4.42. As can be expected, English-speaking countries such as Canada (0.12), Ireland (0.35), New Zealand (0.26), and the United Kingdom (0.09) all exhibit a low cultural distance to the United States. Since culture is embedded in language, it comes as no surprise that cultural and linguistic differences are highly correlated.

Culture even matters in the age of Facebook with its global reach of more than 2 billion users. Most Facebook friends are local rather than across borders. This makes sense when one considers that the online social graph that Facebook users develop in their network of

national culture The collective mental and emotional "programming of the mind" that differentiates human groups.

cultural distance Cultural disparity between an internationally expanding firm's home country and its targeted host country.

When Starbucks entered the Chinese market (in 2000), it moved fast to overcome cultural barriers by handing out key chains to help new customers order. Now it leverages Chinese approaches to social media (WeChat, Weibo, and Jiepang) and fine-tunes its own mobile apps and loyalty programs to lure China's growing middle class. The result? Today China is its second-largest market and growing.[59] Courtesy of Resonance China

friends is mostly a virtual network laid above a (pre)existing social network, rather than forming one anew.[60]

ADMINISTRATIVE AND POLITICAL DISTANCE. Administrative and political distances are captured in factors such as the absence or presence of shared monetary or political associations, political hostilities, and weak or strong legal and financial institutions.[61] The 19 European countries in the eurozone, for example, not only share the same currency but also integrate politically to some extent. It should come as no surprise then that most cross-border trade between European countries takes place within the EU. Germany, one of the world's largest exporters, conducts roughly 75 percent of its cross-border business within the EU.[62] Similarly, Canada and Mexico partner with the United States in the USMCA treaty, facilitating trade in goods and services between the three countries. As a result, United States is the largest trading partner for both Canada and Mexico. After China, Mexico and Canada are the largest trading partners for the United States. Colony–colonizer relationships also have a strong positive effect on bilateral trade between countries. British companies continue to trade heavily with businesses from its former colonies in the commonwealth; Spanish companies trade heavily with Latin American countries; and French businesses trade with the franc zone of West Africa.

Many foreign (target) countries also erect other political and administrative barriers, such as tariffs, trade quotas, FDI restrictions, and so forth, to protect domestic competitors. In many instances, China, for example, requests the sharing of technology in a joint venture when entering the country. This was the case in the high-speed train developments discussed earlier. Other countries, including the United States and EU members, protect national champions such as Boeing or Airbus from foreign competition. Industries that are considered critical to national security—domestic airlines or telecommunications—are often protected. Finally, strong legal and ethical pillars as well as well-functioning economic institutions such as capital markets and an independent central bank reduce distance. Strong institutions, both formal and informal, reduce uncertainty and thus reduce transaction costs.[63]

GEOGRAPHIC DISTANCE. The costs to cross-border trade rise with geographic distance. It is important to note, however, that geographic distance does not simply capture how far two countries are from each other but also includes additional attributes, such as the country's physical size (Canada versus Singapore), the within-country distances to its borders, the country's topography, its time zones, and whether the countries are contiguous to one another or have access to waterways and the ocean. The country's infrastructure, including road, power, and telecommunications networks, also plays a role in determining geographic distance. Geographic distance is particularly relevant when trading products with low value-to-weight ratios, such as steel, cement, or other bulk products, and fragile and perishable products, such as glass or fresh meats and fruits.

ECONOMIC DISTANCE. The wealth and per capita income of consumers is the most important determinant of economic distance. Wealthy countries engage in relatively more cross-border trade than poorer ones. Rich countries tend to trade with other rich countries; in addition, poor countries also trade more frequently with rich countries than with other poor countries. Companies from wealthy countries benefit in cross-border trade with other wealthy countries when their competitive advantage is based on *economies of experience, scale, scope, and standardization.* This is because replication of an existing business model is much easier in a country where the incomes are relatively similar and resources, complements, and infrastructure are of roughly equal quality. Although Walmart in Canada is a virtual carbon copy of the Walmart in the United States, Walmart in China is quite different.[64]

Companies from wealthy countries also trade with companies from poor countries to benefit from *economic arbitrage*. The textile industry (discussed earlier) is a prime example. We also highlighted economic arbitrage as one of the main benefits of going global: access to low-cost input factors.

In conclusion, although the CAGE distance framework helps determine the attractiveness of foreign target markets in a more fine-grained manner based on relative differences, it is necessarily only a first step. A deeper analysis requires looking inside the firm (as done in Chapter 4) to see how a firm's strengths and weaknesses work to increase or reduce distance from specific foreign markets. A company with a large cadre of cosmopolitan managers and a diverse work force will be much less affected by cultural differences, for example, than a company with a more insular and less diverse culture with all managers from the home country. Although technology may make the world seem smaller, the costs of distance along all its dimensions are real. The costs of distance in expanding internationally are often quite high. Ignoring these costs can be expensive (see Walmart's adventure in Germany, discussed in Strategy Highlight 10.2) and can lead to a competitive disadvantage.

HOW DO MNEs ENTER FOREIGN MARKETS?

LO 10-4

Compare and contrast the different options MNEs have to enter foreign markets.

Assuming an MNE has decided why and where to enter a foreign market, the remaining decision is *how* to do so. Exhibit 10.7 displays the different options managers have when entering foreign markets, along with the required investments necessary and the control they can exert. On the left end of the continuum in Exhibit 10.7 are vehicles of foreign expansion that require low investments but also allow for a low level of control. On the right are foreign-entry modes that require a high level of investments in terms of capital and other resources, but also allow for a high level of control. Foreign-entry modes with a high level of control such as foreign acquisitions or greenfield plants reduce the firm's exposure to two particular downsides of global business: loss of reputation and loss of intellectual property.

Exporting—producing goods in one country to sell in another—is one of the oldest forms of internationalization (part of Globalization 1.0). It is often used to test whether a foreign market is ready for a firm's products. When studying vertical integration and diversification (in Chapter 8), we discussed in detail different forms along the make-or-buy continuum. As discussed in Chapter 9, strategic alliances (including licensing, franchising, and joint ventures) and acquisitions are popular vehicles for entry into foreign markets. Since we discussed these organizational arrangements in detail in previous chapters, we therefore keep this section on foreign-entry modes brief.

The framework illustrated in Exhibit 10.7, moving from left to right, has been suggested as a *stage model* of sequential commitment to a foreign market over time.[65] Though it does

EXHIBIT 10.7

Modes of Foreign-Market Entry along the Investment and Control Continuum not apply to globally born companies, it is relevant for manufacturing companies that are just now expanding into global operations. In some instances, companies are required by the host country to form joint ventures in order to conduct business there, while some MNEs prefer *greenfield operations*—building new, fully owned plants and facilities from scratch, as Motorola did when it entered China (in the 1990s).[66]

Apply the integration-responsiveness framework to evaluate the four different strategies MNEs can pursue when competing globally.

10.4 Cost Reductions vs. Local Responsiveness: The Integration-Responsiveness Framework

MNEs face two opposing forces when competing around the globe: *cost reductions* versus *local responsiveness*. Indeed, cost reductions achieved through a global-standardization strategy often reinforce a cost-leadership strategy at the business level. Similarly, local responsiveness increases the differentiation of products and services, reinforcing a differentiation strategy at the business level. Taken together, however, cost reductions and local responsiveness present strategic trade-offs because higher local responsiveness frequently goes along with higher costs. Conversely, a focus on cost reductions does not allow for much local responsiveness. Just like low cost and differentiation at the business strategy level, cost reductions and local responsiveness are trade-offs when competing globally.

One of the core drivers for globalization is to expand a firm's total market in order to achieve economies of scale and drive down costs. For many business executives, the move toward globalization is based on the **globalization hypothesis**, which states that consumer needs and preferences throughout the world are converging and thus becoming increasingly homogenous. Theodore Levitt stated: "Nothing confirms [the globalization hypothesis] as much as the success of McDonald's from [the] Champs-Élysées to Ginza, of Coca-Cola in Bahrain and Pepsi-Cola in Moscow, and of rock music, Greek salad, Hollywood movies, Revlon cosmetics, Sony televisions, and Levi jeans everywhere."[67] In support of the globalization hypothesis, IKEA, as featured in the ChapterCase, sells its home furnishings successfully in 50 countries. Toyota is selling its hybrid Prius vehicle in over 90 countries. Most vehicles today are built on global platforms and modified (sometimes only cosmetically) to meet local tastes and standards.

globalization hypothesis Assumption that consumer needs and preferences throughout the world are converging and thus becoming increasingly homogenous.

The strategic foundations of the globalization hypothesis are based primarily on cost reduction. Lower cost is a key competitive weapon, and MNEs attempt to reap significant cost reductions by leveraging economies of scale and by managing global supply chains to access the lowest-cost input factors.

Although there seems to be some convergence of consumer preferences across the globe, national differences remain, due to distinct institutions and cultures. For example, in the 1990s, Ford Motor Co. followed this one-size-fits-all strategy by offering a more or less identical car throughout the world: the Ford Mondeo, sold as the Ford Contour and the Mercury Mystique in North America. Ford learned the hard way, by lack of sales, that consumers did not subscribe to the globalization hypothesis at the same level as the Ford executives and were not yet prepared to ignore regional differences.[68]

local responsiveness The need to tailor product and service offerings to fit local consumer preferences and host-country requirements.

In some instances, MNEs experience pressure for **local responsiveness**—the need to tailor product and service offerings to fit local consumer preferences and host-country requirements; it generally entails higher costs. Walmart sells live animals (snakes, eels, toads, etc.) for food preparation in China. IKEA sells kimchi refrigerators and metal chopsticks in South Korea. McDonald's uses chicken and fish instead of beef in India and offers a teriyaki burger in Japan, even though its basic business model of offering fast food remains the same the world over. Local responsiveness generally entails higher cost, and sometimes even outweighs cost advantages from economies of scale and lower-cost input factors.

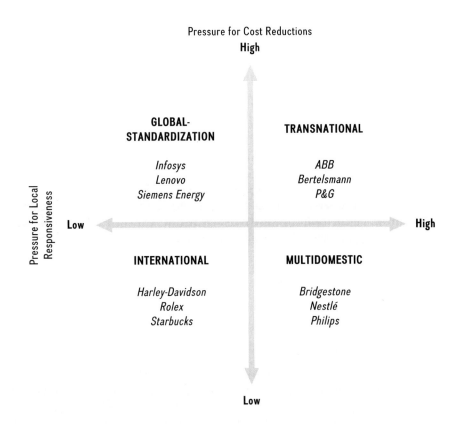

Pressure for Cost Reductions

High

GLOBAL-STANDARDIZATION

Infosys
Lenovo
Siemens Energy

TRANSNATIONAL

ABB
Bertelsmann
P&G

Pressure for Local Responsiveness

Low — **High**

INTERNATIONAL

Harley-Davidson
Rolex
Starbucks

MULTIDOMESTIC

Bridgestone
Nestlé
Philips

Low

EXHIBIT 10.8

The Integration-Responsiveness Framework: Global Strategy Positions and Representative MNEs

Sources: Adapted from C.K. Prahalad and Y.L. Doz (1987), *The Multinational Mission* (New York: Free Press); and K. Roth and A.J. Morrison (1991), "An empirical analysis of the integration-responsiveness framework in global industries," *Journal of International Business Studies* 21: 541–564.

Given the two opposing pressures of cost reductions versus local responsiveness, scholars have advanced the **integration-responsiveness framework**, shown in Exhibit 10.8 .[69] This framework juxtaposes the opposing pressures for cost reductions and local responsiveness to derive four different strategic positions to gain and sustain competitive advantage when competing globally. The four strategic positions, which we will discuss in the following sections, are

- International
- Multidomestic
- Global-standardization
- Transnational[70]

At the end of that discussion, Exhibit 10.10 summarizes each global strategy.

INTERNATIONAL STRATEGY

An **international strategy** is essentially a strategy in which a company sells the same products or services in both domestic and foreign markets. It enables MNEs to leverage their home-based core competencies in foreign markets. An international strategy is one of the oldest types of global strategies (Globalization 1.0) and is frequently the first step companies take when beginning to conduct business abroad. As shown in the integration-responsiveness framework, it is advantageous when the MNE faces low pressures for both local responsiveness and cost reductions.

An international strategy is often used successfully by MNEs with relatively large domestic markets and with strong reputations and brand names. These MNEs, capitalizing on the

integration-responsiveness framework Strategy framework that juxtaposes the pressures an MNE faces for cost reductions and local responsiveness to derive four different strategies to gain and sustain competitive advantage when competing globally.

international strategy Strategy that involves leveraging home-based core competencies by selling the same products or services in both domestic and foreign markets.

fact that foreign customers want to buy the original product, tend to use differentiation as their preferred business strategy. For example, bikers in Shanghai, China, like their Harley-Davidson motorcycles to roar just like the ones ridden by the Hells Angels in the United States. Similarly, a Brazilian entrepreneur importing machine tools from Germany expects superior engineering and quality. Finally, Apple's latest iPhone model is a desired luxury product and status symbol the world over. An international strategy tends to rely on exporting or the licensing of products and franchising of services to reap economies of scale by accessing a larger market.

A strength of the international strategy—its limited local responsiveness—is also a weakness in many industries. For example, when an MNE sells its products in foreign markets with little or no change, it leaves itself open to the expropriation of intellectual property (IP). Looking at the MNE's products and services, pirates can reverse-engineer the products to discover the intellectual property embedded in them. Besides the risk of exposing IP, MNEs following an international strategy are highly affected by exchange-rate fluctuations. Given increasing globalization, however, fewer and fewer markets correspond to this situation—low pressures for local responsiveness *and* cost reductions—that gives rise to the international strategy.

MULTIDOMESTIC STRATEGY

multidomestic strategy Strategy pursued by MNEs that attempts to maximize local responsiveness, with the intent that local consumers will perceive them to be domestic companies.

MNEs pursuing a **multidomestic strategy** attempt to maximize local responsiveness, hoping that local consumers will perceive their products or services as local ones. This strategy arises out of the combination of high pressure for local responsiveness and low pressure for cost reductions. MNEs frequently use a multidomestic strategy when entering host countries with large and/or idiosyncratic domestic markets, such as Japan or Saudi Arabia. This is one of the main strategies MNEs pursued in the Globalization 2.0 stage.

A multidomestic strategy is common in the consumer products and food industries. For example, Swiss-based Nestlé, the largest food company in the world, is known for customizing its product offerings to suit local preferences, tastes, and requirements. Given the strong brand names and core competencies in R&D, and the quality in their consumer products and food industries, it is not surprising that these MNEs generally pursue a differentiation strategy at the business level. An MNE following a multidomestic strategy, in contrast with an international strategy, faces reduced exchange-rate exposure because the majority of the value creation takes place in the host-country business units, which tend to span all functions.

On the downside, a multidomestic strategy is costly and inefficient because it requires the duplication of key business functions across multiple countries. Each country unit tends to be highly autonomous, and the MNE is unable to reap economies of scale or learning across regions. The risk of IP appropriation increases when companies follow a multidomestic strategy. Besides exposing codified knowledge embedded in products, as is the case with an international strategy, a multidomestic strategy also requires exposing tacit knowledge because products are manufactured locally. Tacit knowledge that is at risk of appropriation may include, for example, the process of how to create consumer products of higher perceived quality.

GLOBAL-STANDARDIZATION STRATEGY

global-standardization strategy Strategy attempting to reap significant economies of scale and location economies by pursuing a global division of labor based on wherever best-of-class capabilities reside at the lowest cost.

MNEs following a **global-standardization strategy** attempt to reap significant economies of scale and location economies by pursuing a global division of labor based on wherever best-of-class capabilities reside at the lowest cost. The global-standardization strategy arises out of the combination of high pressure for cost reductions and low pressure for local responsiveness. MNEs using this strategy are often organized as networks (Globalization 3.0).

This lets them strive for the lowest-cost position possible. Their business-level strategy tends to be cost leadership. Because there is little or no differentiation or local responsiveness because products are standardized, price becomes the main competitive weapon. To be cost competitive, the MNE must maintain a minimum efficient scale (see Chapter 6).

MNEs that manufacture commodity products such as computer hardware or offer services such as business process outsourcing generally pursue a global-standardization strategy. Lenovo, the Chinese computer manufacturer, is the maker of the ThinkPad line of laptops, which it acquired from IBM (in 2005). To keep track of the latest developments in computing, Lenovo's research centers are located in Beijing and Shanghai in China, in Raleigh, North Carolina (in the Research Triangle Park), and in Japan.[71] To benefit from low-cost labor and to be close to its main markets to reduce shipping costs, Lenovo's manufacturing facilities are in Mexico, India, and China. The company describes the benefits of its global-standardization strategy insightfully: "Lenovo organizes its worldwide operations with the view that a truly global company must be able to quickly capitalize on new ideas and opportunities from anywhere. By forgoing a traditional headquarters model and focusing on centers of excellence around the world, Lenovo makes the maximum use of its resources to create the best products in the most efficient and effective way possible."[72]

TRANSNATIONAL STRATEGY

MNEs pursuing a **transnational strategy** attempt to combine the benefits of a localization strategy (high local responsiveness) with those of a global-standardization strategy (lowest-cost position attainable). This strategy arises out of the combination of high pressure for local responsiveness and high pressure for cost reductions. A transnational strategy is generally used by MNEs that pursue a blue ocean strategy at the business level by attempting to reconcile product and/or service differentiations at low cost.

Besides harnessing economies of scale and location, a transnational strategy also aims to benefit from global learning. MNEs typically implement a transnational strategy through a global matrix structure. This organizational structure combines economies of scale along specific product divisions with economies of learning attainable in specific geographic regions. The idea is that best practices, ideas, and innovations will be diffused throughout the world, regardless of their origination. The managers' mantra is to *think globally, but act locally*.

Although a transnational strategy is quite appealing, the required matrix structure is rather difficult to implement because of the organizational complexities involved. High local responsiveness typically requires that key business functions are frequently duplicated in each host country, leading to higher costs. Further compounding the organizational complexities is the challenge of finding managers who can dexterously work across cultures in the ways required by a transnational strategy. We'll discuss organizational structure in more depth in the next chapter.

The German multimedia conglomerate Bertelsmann attempts to follow a transnational strategy. Bertelsmann employs over 100,000 people, with two-thirds of that work force outside its home country. Bertelsmann operates in more than 60 countries throughout the world and owns many regional leaders in their specific product categories, including Random House Publishing in the United States and RTL Group, Europe's second-largest TV, radio, and production company (after the BBC). Bertelsmann operates its over 500 regional media divisions as more or less autonomous profit-and-loss centers but attempts to share best practices across units; global learning and human resource strategies for executives are coordinated at the network level.[73]

As a summary, Exhibit 10.9 provides a detailed description of each of the four global strategies in the integration-responsiveness framework.

transnational strategy Strategy that attempts to combine the benefits of a localization strategy (high local responsiveness) with those of a global-standardization strategy (lowest-cost position attainable).

EXHIBIT 10.9 International, Multidomestic, Global-Standardization, and Transnational Strategies: Characteristics, Benefits, and Risks

Strategy	Characteristics	Benefits	Risks
International	Often the first step in internationalizing. Used by MNEs with relatively large domestic markets or strong exporters (e.g., MNEs from the United States, Germany, Japan, South Korea). Well-suited for high-end products with high value-to-weight ratios such as machine tools and luxury goods that can be shipped across the globe. Products and services tend to have strong brands. Main business-level strategy tends to be differentiation because exporting, licensing, and franchising add additional costs.	Leveraging core competencies. Economies of scale. Low-cost implementation through: • Exporting or licensing (for products) • Franchising (for services) • Licensing (for trademarks)	No or limited local responsiveness. Highly affected by exchange-rate fluctuations. IP embedded in product or service could be expropriated.
Multidomestic	Used by MNEs to compete in host countries with large and/or lucrative but idiosyncratic domestic markets (e.g., Germany, Japan, Saudi Arabia). Often used in consumer products and food industries. Main business-level strategy is differentiation. MNE wants to be perceived as local company.	Highest-possible local responsiveness. Increased differentiation. Reduced exchange-rate exposure.	Duplication of key business functions in multiple countries leads to high cost of implementation. Little or no economies of scale. Little or no learning across different regions. Higher risk of IP expropriation.
Global-Standardization	Used by MNEs that are offering standardized products and services (e.g., computer hardware or business process outsourcing). Main business-level strategy is cost leadership.	Location economies: global division of labor based on wherever best-of-class capabilities reside at lowest cost. Economies of scale and standardization.	No local responsiveness. Little or no product differentiation. Some exchange-rate exposure. "Race to the bottom" as wages increase. Some risk of IP expropriation.
Transnational	Used by MNEs that pursue a blue ocean strategy at the business level by simultaneously focusing on product differentiation and low cost. Mantra: Think globally, act locally.	Attempts to combine benefits of localization and standardization strategies simultaneously by creating a global matrix structure. Economies of scale, location, experience, and learning.	Global matrix structure is costly and difficult to implement, leading to high failure rate. Some exchange-rate exposure. Higher risk of IP expropriation.

DYNAMIC STRATEGIC POSITIONING: THE CASE OF YOUTUBE. Keep in mind that effective strategic positions are not constant and are as dynamic as the environment. They can change over time. Consider, for instance, how Google shifted the positioning of its paid YouTube offering. In 2015, it launched YouTube Red, a streaming subscription service that allows users to stream any video and music content via YouTube ad-free and to download videos for viewing offline without an internet connection. Moreover, YouTube Red offers original content on its free YouTube service that is not available on other free services such as Cobra Kai, Step Up: High Water, and Youth & Consequences. What strategic steps did Google take to achieve these repositioning efforts?[74]

First, when Google launched YouTube Red in 2015, it followed an *international strategy*, making the service first available in the United States. In 2016 it was then made available in only a few select other countries that, according to Hofstede's index discussed earlier, exhibited close cultural proximity to the United States—namely, Australia and New Zealand. Across each of these select countries YouTube Red remained the same product offering.

Second, in rebranding YouTube Red as YouTube Premium in 2018 (alongside a relaunch of YouMusic, again as a separate paid streaming service), Google followed a *multidomestic strategy:* It offered YouTube Premium in initially 17 countries, including some, such as Germany, Russia, and South Korea, that are considered culturally distant from the United States. Although the majority of YouTube Premium content is available in most countries, Google's fine-tuned search and recommendation engine serves up country- and culture-specific content to appeal to local audiences. Recommending local content is in line with predictions derived from the CAGE distance framework because cultural distance mostly affects products with high linguistic and artistic content. As of 2019, YouTube Premium was available in 50 countries throughout world.

Third, moving forward, Google aims to refine its search and recommendation engine in order to pursue a *transnational strategy* in the near future. The strategic intent is to allow YouTube Premium subscribers, no matter where they are located, access to some of the same content that appeals to the vast majority of viewers, while also promoting geographic-, language-, and culture-specific content. As YouTube Premium competes more and more with other global video-streaming services such as Netflix, lowering the cost of globally popular content that may come from different regions becomes critical. Keep in mind that neither YouTube Premium nor Netflix rely on advertising as a source of income. Both follow a subscription-based business model and thus must compete for users willing to pay for their services. An ability to collect a large, installed global base of users is essential to creating, curating, and offering quality content.

Exhibit 10.10 tracks how Google changed (and plans to change) the strategic positions for its paid YouTube service in its quest for competitive advantage over time.

10.5 National Competitive Advantage: World Leadership in Specific Industries

Globalization, the prevalence of the internet with other advances in communications technology, and transportation logistics can lead us to believe that firm location is becoming increasingly less important.[75] Because firms can now, more than ever, source inputs globally, many believe that location must be diminishing in importance as an explanation of firm-level competitive advantage. This idea is called the **death-of-distance hypothesis**.[76]

> **death-of-distance hypothesis** Assumption that geographic location alone should not lead to firm-level competitive advantage because firms are now, more than ever, able to source inputs globally.

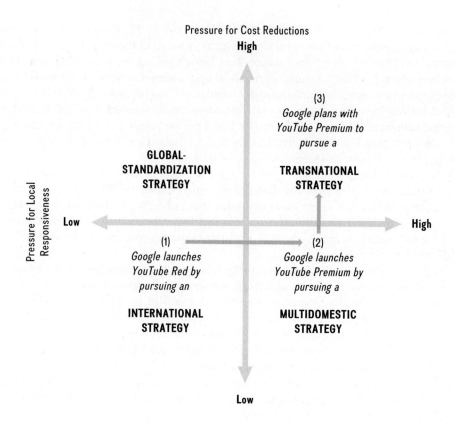

EXHIBIT 10.10

Dynamic Strategic Positioning: Google's YouTube

Despite an increasingly globalized world, however, it turns out that high-performing firms in certain industries *are* concentrated in specific countries.[77] For example, the leading biotechnology, software, and internet companies are headquartered in the United States. Some of the world's best computer manufacturers are in China and Taiwan. Many of the leading consumer electronics companies are in South Korea and Japan. The top mining companies are in Australia. The leading business process outsourcing companies are in India. Some of the best engineering and car companies are in Germany. The world's top fashion designers are in Italy. The best wineries are in France. The list goes on.

Although globalization lowers the barriers to trade and investments and increases human capital mobility, one key question remains: *Why are certain industries more competitive in some countries than in others?* This question goes to the heart of the issue of **national competitive advantage**, a consideration of world leadership in specific industries. That issue, in turn, has a direct effect on firm-level competitive advantage. Companies from home countries that are world leaders in specific industries tend to be the strongest competitors globally.

national competitive advantage World leadership in specific industries.

LO 10-6

Apply Porter's diamond framework to explain why certain industries are more competitive in specific nations than in others.

PORTER'S DIAMOND FRAMEWORK

Michael Porter advanced a framework to explain national competitive advantage—why some nations outperform others in specific industries. This framework is called Porter's diamond

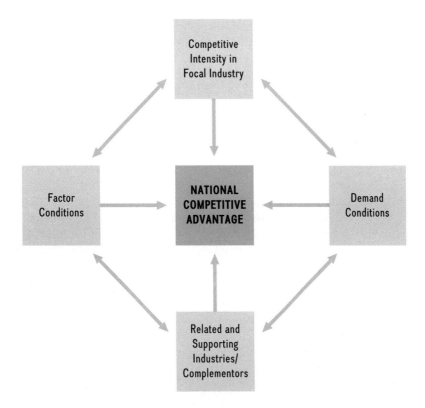

EXHIBIT 10.11

Porter's Diamond of National Competitive Advantage

Source: Adapted from M.E. Porter (1990, March–April), "The competitive advantage of nations," *Harvard Business Review:* 78.

of national competitive advantage. As shown in Exhibit 10.11, it consists of four interrelated factors:

- Factor conditions.
- Demand conditions.
- Competitive intensity in focal industry.
- Related and supporting industries/complementors.

FACTOR CONDITIONS. *Factor conditions* describe a country's endowments in terms of natural, human, and other resources. Other important factors include capital markets, a supportive institutional framework, research universities, and public infrastructure (airports, roads, schools, health care system), among others.

Interestingly, *natural resources* are often not needed to generate world-leading companies because competitive advantage is often based on other factor endowments such as human capital and know-how. Several of the world's most resource-rich countries (such as Afghanistan,[78] Iran, Iraq, Russia, Saudi Arabia, and Venezuela) are not home to any of the world's leading companies, even though some (though not all) do have in place institutional frameworks allowing them to be a productive member of world commerce. In contrast, countries that lack natural resources (e.g., Denmark, Finland, Israel, Japan, Singapore, South Korea, Switzerland, Taiwan, and the Netherlands) often develop world-class human capital to compensate.[79]

DEMAND CONDITIONS. *Demand conditions* are the specific characteristics of demand in a firm's domestic market. A home market made up of sophisticated customers who hold companies to a high standard of value creation and cost containment contributes to national competitive advantage. Moreover, demanding customers may also clue firms into the latest developments in specific fields and may push firms to move research from basic findings to commercial applications for the marketplace.

For example, due to dense urban living conditions, hot and humid summers, and high energy costs, it is not surprising that Japanese customers demand small, quiet, and energy-efficient air conditioners. In contrast to the Japanese, Finns have a sparse population living in a more remote countryside. A lack of landlines for telephone service has resulted in the Finnish demand for high-quality wireless services, combined with reliable handsets (and long-life batteries) that can be operated in remote, often hostile, environments. Cell phones have long been a necessity for survival in rural areas of Finland. This situation enabled Nokia to become an early leader in cell phones.[80]

COMPETITIVE INTENSITY IN A FOCAL INDUSTRY. Companies that face a highly competitive environment at home tend to outperform global competitors that lack such intense domestic competition. Fierce domestic competition in Germany, for example, combined with demanding customers and the no-speed-limit autobahn make a tough environment for any car company. Success requires top-notch engineering of chassis and engines, as well as keeping costs and fuel consumption ($6-per-gallon gas) in check. This extremely tough home environment amply prepared German car companies such as Volkswagen (which also owns Audi and Porsche), BMW, and Daimler for global competition.

RELATED AND SUPPORTING INDUSTRIES/COMPLEMENTORS. Leadership in related and supporting industries can also foster world-class competitors in downstream industries. The availability of top-notch *complementors*—firms that provide a good or service that leads customers to value the focal firm's offering more when the two are combined—further strengthens national competitive advantage. Switzerland, for example, leveraged its early lead in industrial chemicals into pharmaceuticals.[81] A sophisticated health care service industry sprang up alongside as an important complementor, to provide further stimulus for growth and continuous improvement and innovation.

The effects of sophisticated customers and highly competitive industries ripple through the industry value chain to create top-notch suppliers and complementors. Toyota's global success in the 1990s and early 2000s was based to a large extent on a network of world-class suppliers in Japan.[82] This tightly knit network allowed for fast two-way knowledge sharing—this in turn improved Toyota's quality and lowered its cost, which it leveraged into a successful blue ocean strategy at the business level.

It is also interesting to note that by 2010, Toyota's supplier advantage had disappeared.[83] It was unable to solve the trade-off between drastically increasing its volume and maintaining superior quality. Toyota's rapid growth in its quest to become the world's leader in volume required quickly bringing on new suppliers outside Japan. Quality standards, however, could not be maintained. Part of the problem lies in path dependence (discussed in Chapter 4), because Chinese and other suppliers could not be found quickly enough, nor could most foreign suppliers build at the required quality levels fast enough. The cultural distance between Japan and China exacerbated these problems. Combined, these factors explain the quality problems Toyota experienced in recent years, and highlight the importance of related and supporting industries to national competitive advantage.

10.6 Implications for Strategic Leaders

In addition to determining the degree of vertical integration and level of diversification, the strategic leader needs to decide if and how the firm should compete beyond its home market. Decisions along all three dimensions formulate the firm's corporate strategy. Because of increasing global integration in products and services as well as capital markets, the benefits of competing globally outweigh the costs for more and more enterprises. This is true not just for large MNEs, but also for small and medium ones (SMEs). Even small startups are now able to leverage technology such as the internet and AI to compete beyond their home market.

Strategic leaders have a number of frameworks at their disposal to make global strategy decisions. The CAGE framework allows for a detailed analysis of any country pairing. Rather than looking at simple absolute measures such as market size, the strategist can determine the *relative* distance or closeness of a target market to the home market along cultural, administrative/political, geographic, and economic dimensions. Once decided which countries to enter, the *mode* of foreign entry needs to be determined. Considerations of the degree of investment and level of control help in this decision. Higher levels of control, and thus greater protection of IP and a lower likelihood of any loss in reputation, go along with more investment-intensive foreign-entry modes such as acquisitions or greenfield plants (see Exhibit 10.7).

A firm's business-level strategy (discussed in Chapter 6) provides an important clue to possible strategies to be pursued globally. A cost leader, for example, is more likely to have the capabilities to be successful with a global-standardization strategy. In contrast, a differentiator is more likely to be successful in pursuing an international or multidomestic strategy. The same caveats raised concerning a blue ocean strategy at the business level apply at the corporate level: Although attractive on paper, a transnational strategy combining high pressures for cost reductions with high pressures for local responsiveness is difficult to implement because of inherent trade-offs.

Finally, a strategic leader must be aware of the fact that despite globalization and the emergence of the internet, firm geographic location has actually maintained its importance. Critical masses of world-class firms are clearly apparent in *regional geographic clusters.* Think of computer technology firms in Silicon Valley, medical device firms in the Chicago area, and biotechnology firms in and around Boston. This is a worldwide phenomenon. Known for their engineering prowess, car companies such as Daimler, BMW, Audi, and Porsche are clustered in southern Germany. Many fashion-related companies (clothing, shoes, and accessories) are located in northern Italy. Singapore is a well-known cluster for semiconductor materials, and India's leading IT firms are in Bangalore. Porter captures this phenomenon succinctly: "Paradoxically, the enduring competitive advantages in a global economy lie increasingly in local things—knowledge, relationships, and motivation that distant rivals cannot match."[84]

This concludes our discussion of global strategy. We have now completed our study of the first two pillars of the AFI framework—*strategy analysis* (Chapters 1 to 5) and *strategy formulation* (Chapters 6 to 10). Next, we turn to the third and final pillar of the AFI framework—*strategy implementation*. In Chapter 11, we'll study what leaders can do to implement their carefully crafted strategies successfully and how to avoid failure. In Chapter 12, we study corporate governance and business ethics.

Testing/Shutterstock

DESPITE THE Swedish home-furnishing company's tremendous success, IKEA faces significant challenges going forward. Opening new stores is critical to drive future growth (see Exhibit 10.1), as is finding new sources of supply to support more store openings. However, because IKEA's supply chain has become a bottleneck, finding suppliers that are a strategic fit with its highly efficient operations has become a challenge. Related to this issue is the fact that wood remains one of IKEA's main input factors, and the world's consumers are becoming more sensitive to the issue of deforestation and its link to global warming. In the near future, IKEA must find low-cost replacement materials for wood.

Home furnishings is a multibillion-dollar business. Although IKEA is growing in North America, in this particular market, it holds less than 5 percent share relative to the 30 percent share it holds in Europe. Yet, powerful competitors in the United States have taken notice of IKEA's success. IKEA faces strong competition from brick-and-mortar retailers such as Target, Sam's Club, and Costco. To keep IKEA at bay in the United States, Target recruited top designers and launched a wide range of low-priced furnishings.

In the online space, IKEA faces not only the ecommerce giant Amazon, but also Wayfair Inc., an online home-furnishing startup that quickly approached $10 billion in annual sales in 2019. Much like Amazon, Wayfair has also recently announced plans to open its first brick-and-mortar store in an effort to better integrate the online and in-person shopping experience. These strategic initiatives by Amazon and Wayfair are a part of a major push by online retailers to open physical locations to improve customer service and to increase revenue streams.

In addition to these external challenges, IKEA also faces significant internal ones. Since the company's founding in 1943, no strategic decisions had been made without Ingvar Kamprad's involvement and explicit approval until he stepped down in 2013 from chairing Inter IKEA, the foundation that owns the company. (He passed away in 2018 at age 91.) Many observers compare Kamprad's influence on IKEA's culture and organization to that of the legendary Sam Walton at Walmart. Kamprad's three sons have taken on stronger leadership roles at IKEA, including chairing the foundation that controls IKEA. The question remains if they can follow in their father's legendary footsteps.

Under new leadership, IKEA began a major push into online sales. IKEA's store traffic and website visits were indicative of this strategic shift. Unlike its competition, IKEA had been slow to compete online. In fact, its chief executive openly accepted that IKEA failed to recognize what a disruptive role the internet would play in the retailing market.

Recently, IKEA underwent a major restructuring, eliminating thousands of jobs and creating new ones that focus on improving its online presence, delivery offerings, and in-store experience. Since IKEA started building its online presence in greater earnest, website visits have more than doubled; it increased to over 2 billion a year within a five-year period. However, in-person visits have only increased by a mere 2 percent a year (to about 1 billion in 2018). To help drive up in-person visits, IKEA redesigned its new retail spaces to appear more like showrooms rather than large inventory warehouses. This showroom approach allows consumers to see how the images of products they see online actually appear in the physical world.

With so many competitors in the online market, companies must find ways to differentiate themselves from one another—after-market services such as furniture assembly is one of the ways to do this. IKEA acquired TaskRabbit in pursuit of this effort, but it will have to compete with companies such as Wayfair and Walmart, which have both started offering inexpensive furniture assembly services in partnership with the start-up firm Handy.

IKEA also faces some limitations due to its complicated ownership structure. The firm is privately held through a complex network of foundations and holding companies in the Netherlands, Lichtenstein, and Luxembourg. This arrangement provides benefits in terms of reducing tax exposure, but also creates significant constraints in accessing large sums of capital needed for rapid global expansion. In addition, many EU countries as well as the United States have become increasingly more sensitive to the issue of tax avoidance schemes by large multinational enterprises.

IKEA will need to address the slew of internal and external challenges to achieve its strategic intent of doubling its number of yearly openings in an attempt to capture a larger slice of fast-growing markets such as the United States, and to make stronger in-roads in newer markets like China and India. As more and more people are buying furniture online, IKEA now also has to contend with the likes of Wayfair, Amazon, Alibaba, and other online retailers specializing in home furnishings.

Questions

1. List IKEA's external and internal challenges. Looking at IKEA's challenges, which ones do you think pose the greatest threats? Why? How would you address these challenges?

2. Did it surprise you to learn that both wealthy developed countries (e.g., the United States and Australia) as well as emerging economies (e.g., China and India) are the fastest-growing international markets for IKEA? Does this fact pose any challenges to the way IKEA ought to compete across the globe? Why or why not?

3. What can IKEA do to continue to drive growth globally, especially given its strategic intent to double annual store openings?

4. Assume you are hired to consult with IKEA on the topic of *corporate social responsibility* (see also the discussion in Chapter 1). Which areas would you recommend the company be most sensitive to, and how should these be addressed?

mySTRATEGY

How Do You Develop a Global Mind-set?

How can you develop the skills needed to succeed as an international leader? Researchers have developed a personal strategy for building a global mind-set that will facilitate success as an effective manager in a different cultural setting. A global mind-set has three components: *intellectual capital,* the understanding of how business works on a global level; *psychological capital*, openness to new ideas and experiences; and *social capital*, the ability to build connections with people and to influence stakeholders from a different cultural background.[85]

- *Intellectual capital* is considered the easiest to gain if one puts forth the effort. You can gain global business acumen by taking courses, but you can learn a great deal on your own by reading publications with an international scope such as *The Economist*, visiting websites that provide information on different cultures or business operations in foreign countries, or simply watching television programs with an international news or culture focus. Working in global industries with people from diverse cultures is an assignment requiring the ability to manage complexity and uncertainty.

- *Psychological capital* is gained by being receptive to new ideas and experiences and appreciating diversity. It may be the most difficult to develop, because your ability to change your personality has limits. If you are enthusiastic about adventure and are willing to take risks in new environments, then you have the attitudes needed to be energized by a foreign assignment. It takes self-confidence and a sense of humor to adapt successfully to new environments.

- *Social capital* is based on relationships and is gained through experience. You can gain experience with diversity simply by widening your social circle, volunteering to work with international students, or by traveling on vacation or through a study abroad experience.

Now that you have a description of the three components of a global mind-set and a few ideas about how to develop the attributes necessary for global success, consider some ways you can develop a personal strategy that can be implemented during your college career.

1. As a baseline of your current position, list your strengths and weaknesses for each component.

2. Identify your weakest area and make a list of activities that will help you improve your capital in that area.

3. Identify at least three activities you could do this week to get started. For example, you could choose to work with international students on group projects in class. Perhaps invite students with diverse backgrounds to lunch. What questions could you ask that would help you learn about their culture and about doing business in their country? You could go to a museum with an exhibit from another culture, an international movie, or a restaurant with cuisine that is new to you.

If you are interested in more information, go to https://thunderbird.asu.edu/faculty-and-research/najafi-global-mindset-institute, where you can find out about the Global Mindset Inventory (GMI) and other resources.

TAKE-AWAY CONCEPTS

This chapter discussed the roles of MNEs for economic growth; the stages of globalization; why, where, and how companies go global; four strategies MNEs use to navigate between cost reductions and local responsiveness; and national competitive advantage, as summarized by the following learning objectives and related take-away concepts.

LO 10-1 / Define globalization, multinational enterprise (MNE), foreign direct investment (FDI), and global strategy.

- Globalization involves closer integration and exchange between different countries and peoples worldwide, made possible by factors such as falling trade and investment barriers, advances in telecommunications, and reductions in transportation costs.

- A multinational enterprise (MNE) deploys resources and capabilities to procure, produce, and distribute goods and services in at least two countries.

- Many MNEs are more than 50 percent globalized; they receive the majority of their revenues from countries other than their home country.

- Product, service, and capital markets are more globalized than labor markets. The level of everyday activities is roughly 10 to 25 percent integrated, and thus *semi-globalized*.

- Foreign direct investment (FDI) denotes a firm's investments in value chain activities abroad.

LO 10-2 / Explain why companies compete abroad, and evaluate the advantages and disadvantages of going global.

- Firms expand beyond their domestic borders if they can increase their economic value creation and enhance competitive advantage.

- Advantages to competing internationally include gaining access to a larger market, gaining access to low-cost input factors, and developing new competencies.

- Disadvantages to competing internationally include the liability of foreignness, the possible loss of reputation, and the possible loss of intellectual capital.

LO 10-3 / Apply the CAGE distance framework to guide MNE decisions on which countries to enter.

- Most of the costs and risks involved in expanding beyond the domestic market are created by *distance*.

- The CAGE distance framework determines the *relative* distance between home and foreign target country along four dimensions: cultural distance, administrative and political distance, geographic distance, and economic distance.

LO 10-4 / Compare and contrast the different options MNEs have to enter foreign markets.

- The strategist has the following foreign-entry modes available: exporting, strategic alliances (licensing for products, franchising for services), joint venture, and subsidiary (acquisition or greenfield).

- Higher levels of control, and thus a greater protection of IP and a lower likelihood of any loss in reputation, go along with more investment-intensive foreign-entry modes such as acquisitions or greenfield plants.

LO 10-5 / Apply the integration-responsiveness framework to evaluate the four different strategies MNEs can pursue when competing globally.

- To navigate between the competing pressures of cost reductions and local responsiveness, MNEs have four strategy options: international, multidomestic, global-standardization, and transnational.

- An international strategy leverages home-based core competencies into foreign markets, primarily through exports. It is useful when the MNE faces low pressures for both local responsiveness and cost reductions.

- A multidomestic strategy attempts to maximize local responsiveness in the face of low pressure for cost reductions. It is costly and inefficient because it requires the duplication of key business functions in multiple countries.

- A global-standardization strategy seeks to reap economies of scale and location by pursuing a global division of labor based on wherever best-of-class capabilities reside at the lowest cost. It involves little or no local responsiveness.

- A transnational strategy attempts to combine the high local responsiveness of a localization strategy with the lowest-cost position attainable from a global-standardization strategy. It also aims to benefit from global learning. Although appealing, it is difficult to implement due to the organizational complexities involved.

LO 10-6 / **Apply Porter's diamond framework to explain why certain industries are more competitive in specific nations than in others.**

- National competitive advantage, or world leadership in specific industries, is created rather than inherited.

- Four interrelated factors explain national competitive advantage: (1) factor conditions, (2) demand conditions, (3) competitive intensity in a focal industry, and (4) related and supporting industries/complementors.
- Even in a more globalized world, the basis for competitive advantage is often local.

KEY TERMS

CAGE distance framework *(p. 365)*

Cultural distance *(p. 367)*

Death-of-distance hypothesis *(p. 375)*

Foreign direct investment (FDI) *(p. 354)*

Global-standardization strategy *(p. 372)*

Global strategy *(p. 354)*

Globalization *(p. 353)*

Globalization hypothesis *(p. 370)*

Integration-responsiveness framework *(p. 371)*

International strategy *(p. 371)*

Liability of foreignness *(p. 362)*

Local responsiveness *(p. 370)*

Location economies *(p. 361)*

Multidomestic strategy *(p. 372)*

Multinational enterprise (MNE) *(p. 354)*

National competitive advantage *(p. 376)*

National culture *(p. 367)*

Transnational strategy *(p. 373)*

DISCUSSION QUESTIONS

1. Multinational enterprises (MNEs) have an impact far beyond their firm boundaries. Assume you are working for a small firm that supplies a product or service to an MNE. How might your relationship change as the MNE moves from Globalization 2.0 to Globalization 3.0 operations?

2. Strategy Highlight 10.2 discusses the failure of Walmart in Germany. Using the CAGE distance framework, discuss how Lidl should seek to be successful with its move into the US market.

3. The chapter notes that global strategy can change over time for a firm. YouTube is one example in this chapter. Conduct a web search of a firm you know to be operating internationally and determine its current global strategy position. How long has the firm stayed with this approach? Can you find evidence it had a different global strategy earlier?

ENDNOTES

1. This ChapterCase is based on: "Business—this week," *The Economist* (2019, May 9); Chin, K. (2019, Mar. 26), "Wayfair is latest online seller to go bricks and mortar," *The Wall Street Journal;* "As retailers abandon the high street, why is IKEA moving in?" *The Economist* (2019, Jan. 26); Chaudhuri, S. (2018, Nov. 21), "IKEA to slash thousands of jobs in restructuring," *The Wall Street Journal;* Limaye, Y. (2018, Aug. 9), "Will the first IKEA in India succeed?" *BBC News;* "IKEA furniture and the limits of AI," *The Economist* (2018, Apr. 21); "Robots can assemble IKEA furniture," *The Economist* (2018, Apr. 19); "Obituary: Ingvar Kamprad died on January 27th," The Economist (2018, Feb. 8); Chaudhuri, S. (2017, Jan. 29), "IKEA's 'open source' sofa invites customization," *The Wall Street Journal;* Chaudhuri, S. (2016, Dec. 7), "IKEA adapts to growing urban populations," *The Wall Street Journal;* "IKEA experiments with click and collect stores in U.K.," *The Wall Street Journal;* Kowitt, B. (2015, Jun. 9), "It's IKEA's world. We just live in it," *Fortune;* Tabuchi, H. (2015, Jan. 28), "As profit slows, IKEA notes need to move online," *The New York Times*; "IKEA: How the Swedish retailer became a global cult brand," Businessweek (2005, Nov. 14); and IKEA yearly summaries (www.ikea.com), various years.

2. CAGE is an acronym for *c*ultural, *a*dministrative and political, *g*eographic, and *e*conomic distance. The model was introduced by: Ghemawat, P. (2001, September), "Distance still matters: The hard reality of global expansion," *Harvard Business Review.*

3. Stiglitz, J. (2002), *Globalization and Its Discontents* (New York: Norton).

4. World Bank (2019), *World Development Indicators,* https://data.worldbank.org/indicator/ny.gdp.mktp.cd.

5. "Education at a Glance 2018," *OECD Indicators.* www.oecd-ilibrary.org/education/education-at-a-glance_19991487.

6. *International Trends in Higher Education 2015* (Oxford: The University of Oxford), www.ox.ac.uk/sites/files/oxford/International%20Trends%20in%20Higher%20Education%202015.pdf.

7. "Countries with the most students studying abroad," www.worldatlas.com/articles/countries-with-the-most-students-studying-abroad.html.

8. More recent events currently favor India and China; see: "What is the state of the BRIC economies?" *World Economic Forum,* www.weforum.org/agenda/2016/04/what-is-the-state-of-the-brics-economies/.

9. World Bank (2019), *World Development Indicators,* https://data.worldbank.org/indicator/ny.gdp.mktp.cd.

10. We define *global strategy* as a "strategy of firms around the globe—essentially various firms' theories about how to compete successfully." This definition expands on a narrower alternative use of the term *global strategy,* which implies a global cost-leadership strategy in standardized products. This narrower approach we denote as *global-standardization strategy.* In both of these definitions we follow the work of M.W. Peng; see: Peng, M. (2013), *Global Strategy,* 3rd ed. (Mason, OH: South-Western Cengage) and elsewhere.

11. Caves, R. (1996), *Multinational Enterprise and Economic Analysis* (New York: Cambridge University Press); and Dunning, J. (1993), *Multinational Enterprises and the Global Economy* (Reading, MA: Addison-Wesley).

12. www.airbus.com/company/americas/us/alabama/.

13. McKinsey Global Institute (2010), *Growth and Competitiveness in the United States: The Role of Its Multinational Companies* (London: McKinsey Global Institute).

14. IBM (2009), "A decade of generating higher value at IBM," www.ibm.com; and Friedman, T.L. (2005), *The World Is Flat: A Brief History of the Twenty-First Century* (New York: Farrar, Straus, and Giroux).

15. A careful discussion of the WTO is at: www.wto.org/english/thewto_e/whatis_e/whatis_e.htm.

16. Immelt, J.R., V. Govindarajan, and C. Trimble (2009, October), "How GE is disrupting itself," *Harvard Business Review;* author's interviews with Michael Poteran of GE Healthcare (2009, Oct. 30 and Nov. 4); and "Vscan handheld ultrasound: GE unveils 'stethoscope of the 21st century,'" *Huffington Post* (2009, Oct. 20); and Govindarajan, V., and C. Trimble (2012), *Reverse Innovation: Create Far from Home, Win Everywhere* (Boston: Harvard Business Review Press).

17. This process is also referred to as reverse innovation. See: Govindarajan, V., and C. Trimble (2012), *Reverse Innovation: Create Far from Home, Win Everywhere* (Boston: Harvard Business Review Press).

18. Its two founders, one Swiss and the other Italian, each hold master's degrees from Stanford University.

19. Saxenian, A. (1994), *Regional Advantage* (Cambridge: Harvard University Press); and Rothaermel, F.T., and D. Ku (2008),

"Intercluster innovation differentials: The role of research universities," *IEEE Transactions on Engineering Management* 55: 9–22.

20. Ghemawat, P. (2011), *World 3.0: Global Prosperity and How to Achieve It* (Boston: Harvard Business Review Press). The data presented are drawn from Ghemawat (2011) and his TED talk "Actually, the world isn't flat" (2012, June). You can view this excellent talk at www.ted.com/talks/pankaj_ghemawat_actually_the_world_isn_t_flat.

21. The number rises to 6–7 percent if VoIP (such as Skype) is included; Ghemawat, P. (2012, June), "Actually, the world isn't flat," *TED talk,* www.ted.com/talks/pankaj_ghemawat_actually_the_world_isn_t_flat.

22. Friedman, T.L. (2005), *The World Is Flat: A Brief History of the Twenty-First Century* (New York: Farrar, Strauss, and Giroux).

23. Ghemawat, P. (2011), *World 3.0: Global Prosperity and How to Achieve It* (Boston: Harvard Business Review Press).

24. "The rising power of the Chinese worker," *The Economist* (2010, Jul. 29).

25. "Supply chain for iPhone highlights costs in China," *The New York Times* (2010, Jul. 5).

26. This is based on: Friedman, T.L. (2005), *The World Is Flat: A Brief History of the Twenty-First Century* (New York: Farrar, Straus, and Giroux); "Supply chain for iPhone highlights costs in China," *The New York Times* (2010, Jul. 5); and "The rising power of the Chinese worker," *The Economist* (2010, Jul. 29).

27. Ghemawat, P. (2011), *World 3.0: Global Prosperity and How to Achieve It* (Boston: Harvard Business Review Press).

28. "A special report on innovation in emerging markets," *The Economist* (2010, Apr. 15).

29. Keep in mind that selling a large volume of cars doesn't make a company profitable if the cars are sold at a low margin, or even at a loss. In contrast, although Ferrari only sells about 7,500 vehicles a year, it is highly profitable (not surprising given that the sticker price of the entry-level Ferrari is $200,000).

30. Fortune's Global 500 (2018), http://fortune.com/global500/list/filtered?searchByName=SAIC.

31. GM annual reports, various years; and Colias, M. (2019, May 13), "GM looks to jump-start Cadillac—again," *The Wall Street Journal;* Colias, M. (2019, Apr. 30), "GM predicts further pressure from China," *The Wall Street Journal;* Miller, D. (2019, Jan. 27), "Ford is failing in China. What now?" *The*

Motley Fool; Moss, T. (2018, Nov. 27), "Why GM is likely to keep producing in China despite Trump's pleas," *The Wall Street Journal;* Colias, M. (2017, May 18), "General Motors will stop selling cars in India," *The Wall Street Journal;* Bensinger, G. and J. Nicas (2017, May 15), "Alphabet's Waymo, Lyft to collaborate on self-driving cars," *The Wall Street Journal;* Colias, M., and John D. Stoll (2017, Mar. 6), "GM's Opel exit is rare no-confidence vote in European market," *The Wall Street Journal;* and Nagesh, G. (2016, May 13), "GM closes acquisition of Cruise Automation," *The Wall Street Journal.*

32. "The rising power of the Chinese worker," *The Economist* (2010, Jul. 29).

33. Friedman, T.L. (2005), *The World Is Flat: A Brief History of the Twenty-First Century* (New York: Farrar, Straus, and Giroux).

34. Chang, S.J. (1995), "International expansion strategy of Japanese firms: Capability building through sequential entry," *Academy of Management Journal* 38: 383–407; Vermeulen, F., and H.G. Barkema (1998), "International expansion through start-up or acquisition: A learning perspective," *Academy of Management Journal* 41: 7–26; Vermeulen, F., and H.G. Barkema (2002), "Pace, rhythm, and scope: Process dependence in building a profitable multinational corporation," *Strategic Management Journal* 23: 637–653; and Ghemawat, P. (2011), *World 3.0: Global Prosperity and How to Achieve It* (Boston: Harvard Business Review Press).

35. Brown, J.S., and P. Duguid (1991), "Organizational learning and communities-of-practice: Toward a unified view of working, learning, and innovation," *Organization Science* 2: 40–57.

36. Owen-Smith, J., and W.W. Powell (2004), "Knowledge networks as channels and conduits: The effects of spillovers in the Boston biotech community," *Organization Science* 15: 5–21.

37. Examples drawn from: "A special report on innovation in emerging markets," *The Economist* (2010, Apr. 15); and "Cisco globalisation centre east: A hotbed of emerging technologies," www.cisco.com/c/en/us/about/cisco-on-cisco/it-success-stories/111620071.html.

38. Dunning, J.H., and S.M. Lundan (2008), *Multinational Enterprises and the Global Economy,* 2nd ed. (Northampton, MA: Edward Elgar).

39. Govindarajan, V., and C. Trimble (2012), *Reverse Innovation: Create Far from Home, Win Everywhere* (Boston: Harvard Business Review Press).

40. "A special report on innovation in emerging markets," *The Economist* (2010, Apr. 15).

41. Zaheer, S. (1995), "Overcoming the liability of foreignness," *Academy of Management Journal* 38: 341–363.

42. "2018 BrandZ Top 100 Most Valuable Global Brands," report by Millward Brown, WPP.

43. Porter, M.E. (1980), *Competitive Strategy* (New York: Free Press), and Magretta, J. (2011), *Understanding Michael Porter* (Boston: Harvard Business Review Press).

44. Strategy Highlight 10.2 is based on: Knorr, A., and A. Arndt (2003), "Why did Walmart fail in Germany?" in ed. A. Knorr, A. Lemper, A. Sell, and K. Wohlmuth, *Materialien des Wissenschaftsschwerpunktes "Globalisierung der Weltwirtschaft,"* vol. 24 (Bremen, Germany: IWIM—Institute for World Economics and International Management, Universität Bremen); the author's on-site observations at Walmart stores in Germany; and "Hair-shirt economics: Getting Germans to open their wallets is hard," *The Economist* (2010, Jul. 8). For a recent discussion of Walmart's global efforts, see: "After early errors, Walmart thinks locally to act globally," *The Wall Street Journal* (2009, Aug. 14); Sharma, A., and B. Mukherji (2013, Jan. 12), "Bad roads, red tape, burly thugs slow Walmart's passage in India," *The Wall Street Journal*; Berfield, S. (2013, Oct. 10), "Where Walmart isn't: Four countries the retailer can't conquer," *Bloomberg Businessweek.* For reporting regarding the threat posed by the German discounters Lidl and Aldi, see: "Tesco's crisis: A hard rain," *The Economist* (2014, Sep. 27); "Aldi and Lidl: Tomorrow, not quite the world," *The Economist* (2015, Mar. 12); "The decline of established American retailing threatens jobs," *The Economist* (2017, May 13); and Nassauer, S., and H. Haddon (2017, May 16), "Why Walmart is worried about a discount German grocer," *The Wall Street Journal.*

45. "The Foxconn suicides," *The Wall Street Journal* (2010, May 27); Barboza, D. (2016, Dec. 29), "How China built 'iPhone City' with billions in perks for Apple's partner," *The New York Times.*

46. "When workers dream of a life beyond the factory gates," *The Economist* (2012, Dec. 15).

47. "Apple shifts supply chain away from Foxconn to Pegatron," *The Wall Street Journal* (2013, May 29).

48. "Disaster at Rana Plaza," *The Economist* (2013, May 4); "The Bangladesh disaster and corporate social responsibility," *Forbes* (2013, May 2).

49. "Disaster at Rana Plaza," *The Economist* (2013, May 4); "The Bangladesh disaster and corporate social responsibility," *Forbes* (2013, May 2).

50. This example is drawn from: "Train makers rail against China's high-speed designs," *The Wall Street Journal* (2010, Nov. 17).

51. This section is based on: Ghemawat, P. (2001, September), "Distance still matters: The hard reality of global expansion," *Harvard Business Review;* see also Ghemawat, P. (2011), *World 3.0: Global Prosperity and How to Achieve It* (Boston: Harvard Business Review Press).

52. The euro is the official currency of the European Union and is the official currency in the following member countries: Austria, Belgium, Cyprus, Estonia, Finland, France, Germany, Greece, Ireland, Italy, Latvia, Lithuania, Luxembourg, Malta, the Netherlands, Portugal, Slovakia, Slovenia, and Spain.

53. To obtain scores for any two country pairings and to view interactive CAGE distance maps, go to www.ghemawat.com.

54. The discussion of the CAGE distance frameworks and the attributes thereof is based on: Ghemawat, P. (2001, September), "Distance still matters: The hard reality of global expansion," *Harvard Business Review*; see also Ghemawat, P. (2011), *World 3.0: Global Prosperity and How to Achieve It* (Boston: Harvard Business Review Press).

55. Hofstede, G.H. (1984), *Culture's Consequences: International Differences in Work-Related Values* (Beverly Hills, CA: Sage), 21. The description of Hofstede's four cultural dimensions is drawn from Rothaermel, F.T., S. Kotha, and H.K. Steensma (2006), "International market entry by U.S. Internet firms: An empirical analysis of country risk, national culture, and market size," *Journal of Management* 32: 56–82.

56. The *power-distance dimension* of national culture focuses on how a society deals with inequality among people in terms of physical and intellectual capabilities and how those methods translate into power distributions within organizations. High power-distance cultures, like the Philippines (94/100, with 100 = high), tend to allow inequalities among people to translate into inequalities in opportunity, power, status, and wealth. Low power-distance cultures, like Austria (11/100), on the other hand, tend to intervene to create a more equal distribution among people within organizations and society at large.

The *individualism dimension* of national culture focuses on the relationship between individuals in a society, particularly in regard to the relationship between individual and collective pursuits. In highly individualistic cultures, like the United States (91/100), individual freedom and achievements are highly valued. As a result, individuals are only tied loosely to one another within society. In less-individualistic cultures, like Venezuela (12/100), the collective good is emphasized over the individual, and members of society are strongly tied to one another throughout their lifetimes by virtue of birth into groups like extended families.

The *masculinity-femininity dimension* of national culture focuses on the relationship between genders and its relation to an individual's role at work and in society. In more "masculine" cultures, like Japan (95/100), gender roles tend to be clearly defined and sharply differentiated. In "masculine" cultures, values like competitiveness, assertiveness, and exercise of power are considered cultural ideals, and men are expected to behave accordingly. In more "feminine" cultures, like Sweden (5/100), values like cooperation, humility, and harmony are guiding cultural principles. The masculinity–femininity dimension uncovered in Hofstede's research is undoubtedly evolving over time, and values and behaviors are converging to some extent.

The *uncertainty-avoidance dimension* of national culture focuses on societal differences in tolerance toward ambiguity and uncertainty. In particular, it highlights the extent to which members of a certain culture feel anxious when faced with uncertain and unknown situations. Members of high uncertainty-avoidance cultures, like Russia (95/100), value clear rules and regulations as well as clearly structured career patterns, lifetime employment, and retirement benefits. Members of low uncertainty-avoidance cultures, like Singapore (8/100), have greater tolerance toward ambiguity and thus exhibit less emotional resistance to change and a greater willingness to take risks.

57. See: http://geert-hofstede.com/nationalculture.html. The available data, however, on the new dimensions are not, at this point, as comprehensive as for the four original dimensions. Alternatively, see the GLOBE cultural dimensions at www.grovewell.com/pub-GLOBE-intro.html.

58. This is based on: Kogut, B., and H. Singh (1988), "The effect of national culture on the choice of entry mode," *Journal of International Business Studies* 19: 411–432; Rothaermel, F.T., S. Kotha, and H. K. Steensma (2006), "International market entry by U.S. internet firms: An empirical analysis of country risk, national culture, and market size," *Journal of Management 32:* 56–82. Cultural distance from the United States, for example, is calculated as follows:

$$CD_j = \sum_{i=1}^{4} \{(I_{ij} - I_{iu})^2 / V_i\}/4$$

where I_{ij} stands for the index for the ith cultural dimension and jth country, V_i is the variance of the index of ith dimension, u

indicates the United States, and CD_j is the cultural distance difference of the jth country from the United States.

59. "Strong revenue growth in China & Asia-Pacific drives Starbucks' top-line growth in Q2," *Forbes* (2015, Apr. 28); "Starbucks," in Resonance Insights, *China Social Branding Report* (2014, Nov. 24); "Starbucks gets even more social in China, lets fans follow in WeChat app," *Tech in Asia* (2012, Sep. 6).

60. Ghemawat, P. (2012, June), "Actually, the world isn't flat," TED talk, https://www.ted.com/talks/pankaj_ghemawat_actually_the_world_isn_t_flat; and Ghemawat, P. (2011), *World 3.0: Global Prosperity and How to Achieve It* (Boston: Harvard Business Review Press).

61. Ghemawat, P. (2001, September), "Distance still matters: The hard reality of global expansion," *Harvard Business Review.*

62. See statistics provided by Eurostat at: http://epp.eurostat.ec.europa.eu.

63. Williamson, O.E. (1975), *Markets and Hierarchies* (New York: Free Press); Williamson, O.E. (1981), "The economics of organization: The transaction cost approach," *American Journal of Sociology* 87: 548–577; and Williamson, O.E. (1985), *The Economic Institutions of Capitalism* (New York: Free Press).

64. Ghemawat, P. (2001, September), "Distance still matters: The hard reality of global expansion," *Harvard Business Review*; Burkitt, L. (2015, Apr. 29), "Walmart says it will go slow in China," *The Wall Street Journal.*

65. Johanson, J., and J. Vahlne (1977), "The internationalization process of the firm," *Journal of International Business Studies* 4: 20–29.

66. Fuller, A.W., and F.T. Rothaermel (2008), "The interplay between capability development and strategy formation: Motorola's entry into China," *Georgia Institute of Technology Working Paper.*

67. Levitt, T. (1983, May–June), "The globalization of markets," *Harvard Business Review:* 92–102.

68. Mol, M. (2002), "Ford Mondeo: A Model T world car?" in ed. F.B. Tan, *Cases on Global IT Applications and Management: Successes and Pitfalls* (Hershey, PA: Idea Group Publishing), 69–89.

69. Prahalad, C.K., and Y.L. Doz (1987), *The Multinational Mission* (New York: Free Press); and Roth, K., and A.J. Morrison (1990), "An empirical analysis of the integration-responsiveness framework in global industries," *Journal of International Business Studies* 21: 541–564.

70. Bartlett, C.A., S. Ghoshal, and P.W. Beamish (2007), *Transnational Management:*

Text, Cases and Readings in Cross- Border Management, 5th ed. (New York: McGraw-Hill).

71. www.lenovo.com/lenovo/US/en/locations.html.

72. www.lenovo.com/lenovo/US/en/locations.html.

73. Mueller, H.-E. (2001), "Developing global human resource strategies," paper presented at the European International Business Academy, Paris, Dec. 13–15; Mueller, H.-E. (2001), "Wie global player den Kampf um Talente führen," *Harvard Business Manager* 6: 16–25.

74. This example draws from: Popper, B. (2015, Oct. 21), "Red dawn. An inside look at YouTube's new ad-free subscription service," *The Verge,* www.theverge.com/2015/10/21/9566973/youtube-red-ad-free-offline-paid-subscription-service; and Official YouTube Blog (2018, May 16), "Introducing YouTube Premium," https://youtube.googleblog.com/2018/05/introducing-youtube-premium.html.

75. This section draws on: Rothaermel, F.T., and D. Ku (2008), "Intercluster innovation differentials: The role of research universities," *IEEE Transactions on Engineering Management* 55: 9–22.

76. This discussion is based on: Buckley, P.J., and P.N. Ghauri (2004), "Globalisation, economic geography and the strategy of multinational enterprises," *Journal of International Business Studies* 35: 81–98; Cairncross, F. (1997), *The Death of Distance: How the Communications Revolution Will Change Our Lives* (Boston: Harvard Business School Press); and Friedman, T.L. (2005),*The World Is Flat: A Brief History of the Twenty-First Century* (New York: Farrar, Straus, and Giroux). For a counterpoint, see Ghemawat, P. (2001,September), "Distance still matters: The hard reality of global expansion," *Harvard Business Review*; Ghemawat, P. (2007), *Redefining Global Strategy: Crossing Borders in a World Where Differences Still Matter* (Boston: Harvard Business School Press); and Ghemawat, P. (2011), *World 3.0: Global Prosperity and How to Achieve It* (Boston: Harvard Business Review Press).

77. This section is based on: Porter, M.E. (1990, March–April), "The competitive advantage of nations," *Harvard Business Review:* 73–91; and Porter, M.E. (1990), *The Competitive Advantage of Nations* (New York: Free Press).

78. "U.S. identifies vast mineral riches in Afghanistan," *The New York Times* (2010, Jun. 13).

79. For an insightful recent discussion, see: Breznitz, D. (2007), *Innovation and the State: Political Choice and Strategies for Growth in*

Israel, Taiwan, and Ireland (New Haven, CT: Yale University Press).

80. Nokia ceded leadership to RIM (Canada), which subsequently stumbled. Currently, Apple and Samsung (South Korea) are the leaders in the smartphone industry (see discussion in Chapter 7 on the smartphone industry).

81. Murmann, J.P. (2003), *Knowledge and Competitive Advantage* (New York: Cambridge University Press).

82. Dyer, J.H., and K. Nobeoka (2000), "Creating and managing a high-performance knowledge-sharing network: The Toyota case," *Strategic Management Journal* 21: 345–367.

83. This discussion is based on: "Toyota slips up," *The Economist* (2009, Dec. 10,); "Toyota: Losing its shine," *The Economist* (2009, Dec. 10); "Toyota heir faces crises at the wheel," *The Wall Street Journal* (2010, Jan. 27); "Toyota's troubles deepen," *The Economist* (2010, Feb. 4); "The humbling of Toyota,"*Bloomberg Businessweek*

(2010, Mar. 11); and "Inside Toyota, executives trade blame over debacle," *The Wall Street Journal* (2010, Apr. 13).

84. Porter, M. (1998), *The Competitive Advantage of Nations* (New York: Free Press), 77.

85. This myStrategy item is based on: Javidan, M., M. Teagarden, and D. Bowen, (2010, April), "Making it overseas," *Harvard Business Review*: 109–113.

PART

3

Implementation

The AFI Strategy Framework

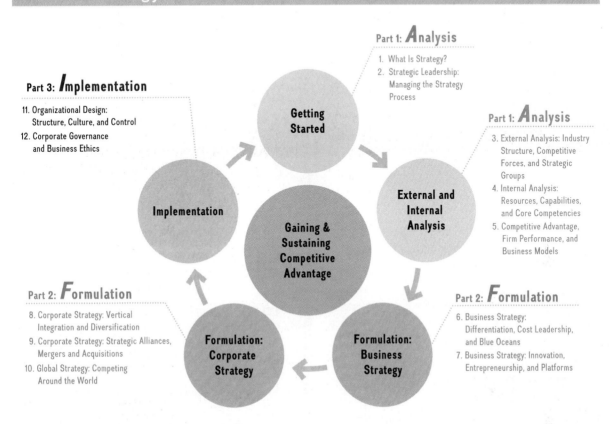

Part 1: **A**nalysis
1. What Is Strategy?
2. Strategic Leadership: Managing the Strategy Process

Part 3: **I**mplementation
11. Organizational Design: Structure, Culture, and Control
12. Corporate Governance and Business Ethics

Part 1: **A**nalysis
3. External Analysis: Industry Structure, Competitive Forces, and Strategic Groups
4. Internal Analysis: Resources, Capabilities, and Core Competencies
5. Competitive Advantage, Firm Performance, and Business Models

Part 2: **F**ormulation
8. Corporate Strategy: Vertical Integration and Diversification
9. Corporate Strategy: Strategic Alliances, Mergers and Acquisitions
10. Global Strategy: Competing Around the World

Part 2: **F**ormulation
6. Business Strategy: Differentiation, Cost Leadership, and Blue Oceans
7. Business Strategy: Innovation, Entrepreneurship, and Platforms

Getting Started

External and Internal Analysis

Gaining & Sustaining Competitive Advantage

Implementation

Formulation: Corporate Strategy

Formulation: Business Strategy

CHAPTER 11

Organizational Design: Structure, Culture, and Control

Chapter Outline

Learning Objectives

After studying this chapter, you should be able to:

LO 11-1 Define organizational design and list its three components.

LO 11-2 Explain how organizational inertia can lead established firms to failure.

LO 11-3 Define organizational structure and describe its four elements.

LO 11-4 Compare and contrast mechanistic versus organic organizations.

LO 11-5 Describe different organizational structures and match them with appropriate strategies.

LO 11-6 Evaluate closed and open innovation, and derive implications for organizational structure.

LO 11-7 Describe the elements of organizational culture, and explain where organizational cultures can come from and how they can be changed.

LO 11-8 Compare and contrast different strategic control-and-reward systems.

"A" Is for Alphabet and "G" Is for Google

"GOOGLE IS NOT A conventional company. We do not intend to become one,"[1] wrote founders Larry Page and Sergey Brin in 2004 for the company's initial public offering (IPO). These computer science graduate students turned entrepreneurs, best known for creating the world's most successful online search engine, also indicated they would make "smaller bets in areas that might seem very speculative or even strange when compared to our current businesses."[2] Some of these smaller bets seemed crazy at the time, but resulted in Google Maps, YouTube, Chrome, and Android—all of which

Pawel Kopczynski/Reuters

have more than 1 billion users today. To say that Google has been hugely successful is an understatement. Since listing on the stock market, this online search and advertising company managed to outperform the tech-heavy NASDAQ-100 index by more than 1,700 percentage points. And in 2019, Google reached a market cap of more than $850 billion, becoming one of the three most valuable companies globally, along with Microsoft and Apple.

Google proved it was not a conventional company yet again when it split itself into several standalone strategic business units (SBUs in 2015). As Google's structure grew increasingly complex and its number of business lines grew increasingly unrelated (think online search and longevity research), it felt the need to transition from a *functional structure* to a *multidivisional structure*. It thus formed Alphabet, a new corporate entity, to act as the parent company in charge of overseeing these varied SBUs, each of which had its own CEO and profit-and-loss responsibilities. Page said he modeled Alphabet's new organizational structure after that of Berkshire Hathaway, a conglomerate led by Warren Buffett. Page had long admired Buffet for effectively managing a set of unrelated businesses. Alphabet's business units, in addition to Google, included Waymo (autonomous vehicles),

Google X (R&D lab), Deep Mind (artificial intelligence), Access (internet service provider), Loon (internet balloons), Calico (longevity research), Wing (delivery drones), Google Ventures (early-stage VC fund), and Google Capital (late-stage VC fund). (See Exhibit 11.1.)

This sweeping restructuring allowed the company to separate its highly profitable search and advertising business from its moon shots, for example, wireless internet connectivity via high-altitude balloons and contact lenses that double as a computer monitor, providing real-time information to the wearer. Furthermore, it created greater financial transparency and accountability.

Perhaps the most notable outcome of Google's restructuring is its pursuit of business opportunities that went far beyond Google's roots in online search—opportunities potentially worth billions of dollars. In his letter to shareholders announcing the restructuring, Larry Page stated that the new structure would prevent Alphabet from becoming complacent and encourage the firm to take a long-term view in pursuing ambitious albeit highly uncertain projects. One of Page's major goals was to ensure that Google would continue to pursue radical innovation, rather than to remain satisfied with incremental innovation only, as is common among other incumbent firms. In keeping with this goal, Alphabet spent over $21 billion in research and development (R&D) in 2018, second only to the $23 billion that Amazon spent.

Alphabet's CEO is Larry Page and its president is Sergey Brin. Alphabet's core business unit, Google, is led by CEO Sundar Pichai. Although slimmer and more focused, Google continues to generate 99 percent of Alphabet's revenues, garnering $140 billion in 2019. Currently, Google's business lines include online search and advertising, YouTube, maps, Android, Chrome, cloud and apps services, and the reintegrated Nest, a smart-home company.

Alphabet houses a number of SBUs that are run by independent CEOs. Besides creating financial transparency and accountability for each SBU, this new organizational structure also allows Alphabet to retain and develop a

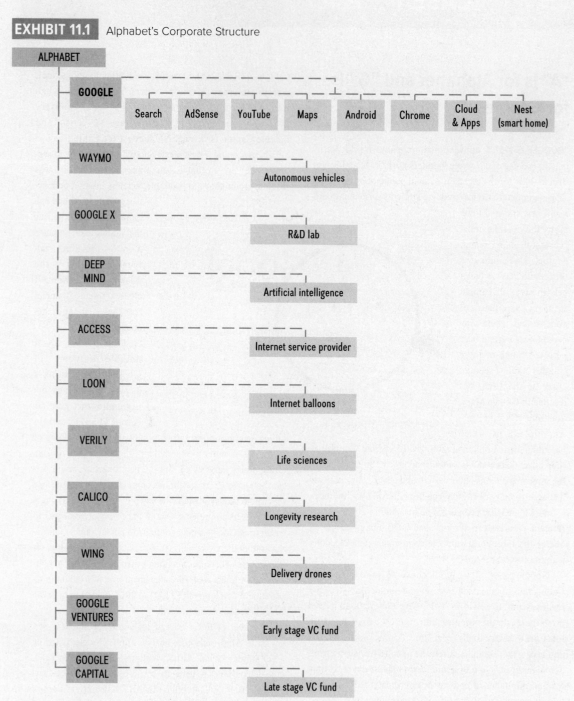

EXHIBIT 11.1 Alphabet's Corporate Structure

- ALPHABET
  - **GOOGLE**
    - Search
    - AdSense
    - YouTube
    - Maps
    - Android
    - Chrome
    - Cloud & Apps
    - Nest (smart home)
  - WAYMO — Autonomous vehicles
  - GOOGLE X — R&D lab
  - DEEP MIND — Artificial intelligence
  - ACCESS — Internet service provider
  - LOON — Internet balloons
  - VERILY — Life sciences
  - CALICO — Longevity research
  - WING — Delivery drones
  - GOOGLE VENTURES — Early stage VC fund
  - GOOGLE CAPITAL — Late stage VC fund

Source: Author's depiction of publicly available data.

cadre of top-notch executives for the various leadership positions within the conglomerate. YouTube, another of Google's successful companies, is run by CEO Susan Wojcicki. To provide resources for each SBU, Alphabet's head office will oversee a rigorous capital allocation process so that each unit can execute its strategy well.[3]

Part II of this ChapterCase appears in Section 11.6.

THE CHAPTERCASE highlights how much weight Alphabet's strategic leaders place on its organizational structure. Co-founders Larry Page and Sergey Brin feel that getting the organizational structure right will allow Alphabet to continue to innovate with more radical technology breakthroughs, while providing financial transparency, accountability, and leadership development opportunities.

This chapter opens the final part of the *AFI framework:* strategy implementation. *Strategy implementation* concerns the organization, coordination, and integration of how work gets done (see the discussion in Chapter 2). Effective strategy implementation is critical to gaining and sustaining competitive advantage. Although the discussion of *strategy formulation* (what to do) is distinct from *strategy implementation* (how to do it), formulation and implementation must be part of an interdependent, reciprocal process to ensure continued success. That need for interdependence explains why the AFI framework is illustrated as a circle, rather than a linear diagram (see Part 3 Opener). The design of an organization, the matching of strategy and structure, and its control-and-reward systems determine whether or not an organization that has chosen an effective strategy will be able to gain and sustain a competitive advantage.

In this chapter, we study the three key levers that managers have at their disposal when designing their organizations for competitive advantage: *structure, culture,* and *control.* Managers employ these three levers to coordinate work and motivate employees across different levels, functions, and geographies. How successful they are in this endeavor determines whether they are able to translate their chosen business, corporate, and global strategy into strategic actions and business models, and ultimately whether the firm is able to gain and sustain a competitive advantage.

We begin our discussion with organizational structure. We discuss different types of organizational structures as well as why and how they need to change over time as successful firms grow in size and complexity. We highlight the critical need to match strategy and structure. We also present different ways to organize for innovation before taking a closer look at corporate culture. An organization's culture can either support or hinder its quest for competitive advantage.[4] We next study strategic control systems, which allow leaders to receive feedback on how well a firm's strategy is being implemented. We conclude our discussion of how to design an organization for competitive advantage with practical *Implications for Strategic Leaders.*

11.1 Organizational Design and Competitive Advantage

Organizational design is the process of creating, implementing, monitoring, and modifying the structure, processes, and procedures of an organization. The key components of organizational design are structure, culture, and control. The goal is to design an organization that allows strategic leaders to effectively translate their chosen strategy into a realized one.

As discussed in the ChapterCase, Google changed its organizational structure from functional (organized according to domain expertise) to multidivisional or M-form (composed of a number of independent strategic business units). Alphabet's strategic leaders hope this new structure will allow them to drive future radical innovation. Moreover, since each SBU has profit and loss responsibility, the new structure allows Alphabet to provide leadership development opportunities for a number of its executives as they are being groomed for larger roles in the future.

Investors are also happy with this new organizational structure because it provides a cleaner picture of Google's profitability. Before the reorganization, Google subsidized all of the loss-making long shots, which in turn depressed its net income. When all businesses

---

LO 11-1

Define organizational design and list its three components.

organizational design
The process of creating, implementing, monitoring, and modifying the structure, processes, and procedures of an organization.

As CEO of Yahoo, Marissa Mayer attempted a turnaround of the struggling internet company by making changes to Yahoo's organizational structure and culture, among other strategic initiatives. In the end, a successful turnaround of the once-leading internet company remained elusive. Once valued at $125 billion (in 2000), Verizon bought Yahoo for a mere $4.5 billion (in 2017) and later wrote off the acquisition.
Julie Jacobson/AP Images

were under Google, it was unclear how much Google invested in R&D to improve its core businesses (online search and advertising) versus how much it spent on moon shots. The new organizational structure freed Google from the huge outlays it had incurred through funding of risky projects over the years, and of which investors had become much less tolerant. Finally, if any of the non-core businesses take off in the same way that Waymo has, then Alphabet could decide to spin Waymo out as an initial public offering (IPO). This would fund future Waymo growth independent of Alphabet, which itself would stand to gain significantly should Waymo go public.

Although Alphabet's strategic leaders have high expectations for their new M-form structure, effective implementation of strategy remains challenging. It is therefore not surprising that the inability to implement strategy effectively is the number-one reason boards of directors fire CEOs.[5] Although Google has been highly successful, Yahoo, once one of Google's main competitors, has struggled, largely due to the lack of an effective organizational design.

Indeed, Yahoo's co-founder and former CEO Jerry Yang was ousted (in 2008) precisely because he failed to implement necessary strategic changes after Yahoo lost its competitive advantage.[6] In the two years leading up to his exit, Yahoo lost more than 75 percent of its market value. Yang was described as someone who preferred consensus among his managers to making tough strategic decisions needed to change Yahoo's structure. That preference, though, led to bickering and infighting. Yang's failure to make the necessary changes to the internet firm's organizational structure led to a destruction of billions of dollars in shareholder value and thousands of layoffs. A number of short-term and interim CEOs followed Yang without much success. Then in 2012, Yahoo hired former Google executive Marissa Mayer as president and CEO. Mayer's turnaround efforts focused on improving the user experience to drive mobile advertising revenues. Such a strategic reorientation required changes in the organizational structure and culture. Despite all these changes, Yahoo was not able to gain significant ground in the online advertising space, which Google and Facebook have dominated, though Amazon is quickly catching up. Eventually, this former leader in online search, which was once valued at $125 billion at the height of the dot-com boom, was acquired by Verizon for $4.5 billion in 2017.[7] In 2018, Verizon wrote off $4.5 billion of the close to $9 billion it spent on acquiring Yahoo and AOL (bought for $4.4 billion in 2015) as Verizon's online search and advertising business faltered.[8]

Because implementation transforms strategy into actions and business models, it often requires changes within the organization. However, strategy implementation often fails because managers are unable to make the necessary changes due to the effects on resource allocation and power distribution within an organization.[9] Strategic leaders are leery about disturbing the status quo. As demonstrated by business historian Alfred Chandler in his seminal book *Strategy and Structure,* organizational structure must follow strategy for firms to achieve superior performance: "Structure can be defined as the design of organization through which the enterprise is administered...*structure follows strategy.*"[10] This tenet implies that to implement a strategy successfully, organizational design must be flexible enough to accommodate the formulated strategy and future growth and expansion.

Zappos (www.zappos.com), the online shoe and clothing retailer (and featured in Strategy Highlight 11.1), exemplifies a company with flexible organizational structure. When establishing customer service as a core competency, one of the hardest decisions CEO Tony Hsieh made early was to pull the plug on drop-shipment orders. These are orders for which Zappos would be the intermediary, relaying them to particular shoe vendors that then ship directly to the customer. Such orders were profitable because Zappos would not have to stock the shoes. They were also appealing because the fledgling startup was still losing money. But the problem was twofold. The vendors were slower than Zappos in filling orders. In addition, they did not accomplish the reliability metric that Zappos wanted for exceptional service: 95 percent accuracy was simply not good enough. Instead, Zappos decided to forgo drop shipments and instead build a large warehouse in Kentucky to stock a full inventory. This move enabled the firm to achieve close to 100 percent accuracy in its shipments, many of which were overnight. Unlike other online retailers, Zappos stocks everything it sells in its own warehouses—this is the only way to get the merchandise as quickly as possible with 100 percent accuracy to the customer. Strategy, therefore, is as much about deciding what to do as it is about deciding what *not* to do.

ORGANIZATIONAL INERTIA: THE FAILURE OF ESTABLISHED FIRMS

LO 11-2

Explain how organizational inertia can lead established firms to failure.

To implement a formulated business strategy successfully, structure must accommodate strategy, not the other way around. In reality, however, a firm's strategy often follows its structure.[11] This reversal implies that some managers consider only strategies that do not change existing organizational structures; they do not want to confront the inertia that often exists in established organizations.[12] **Inertia**, a firm's resistance to change the status quo, can set the stage for the firm's subsequent failure. Successful firms often plant the seed of subsequent failure: They optimize their organizational structure to the current situation. That tightly coupled system can break apart when internal or external pressures occur.

inertia A firm's resistance to change the status quo, which can set the stage for the firm's subsequent failure.

Note that organizational inertia is often the result of success in a particular market during a particular time; it becomes difficult to argue with success. The pattern for successful firms often follows a particular path:

1. Mastery of, and fit with, the current environment.
2. Success, usually measured by financial measurements.
3. Structures, measures, and systems to accommodate and manage size.
4. A resulting organizational inertia that tends to minimize opportunities and accentuate challenges created by shifts in the internal and external environment.

What's missing, of course, is the conscious strategic decision to change the firm's internal environment to fit with the new external environment, turning four steps leading to the endpoint of inertia (Option A) into a virtual circle where the firm essentially reboots and reinvents itself (Option B).

Option A
The Firm Arrives at Inertia

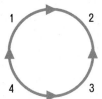

Option B
The Firm Rises above Inertia

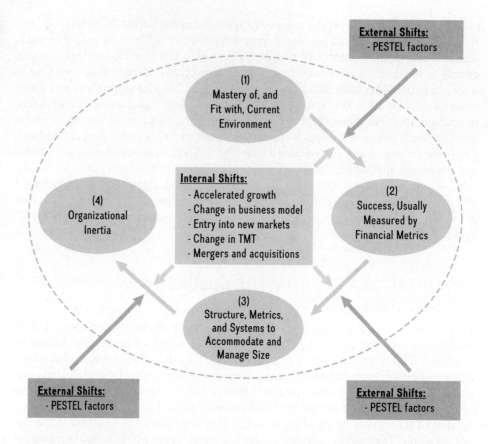

EXHIBIT 11.2

Organizational Inertia and the Failure of Established Firms to Respond to Shifts in the External or Internal Environments

Consider that the need for structural reorganization can be especially intense in many industries where the rate of change is high and potential disruption frequent. Consider also that business leaders find it much easier to create and manage within developed structures than to restructure their organizations to be where they will need to be in future.

Exhibit 11.2 shows how success in the current environment can lead to a firm's downfall in the future, when the tightly coupled system of strategy and structure experiences internal or external shifts.[13] First, the managers achieve a mastery of, and fit with, the firm's current environment. Second, the firm often defines and measures success by financial metrics, with a focus on short-term performance (see discussion in Chapter 5). Third, the firm puts in place structures, metrics, and systems to accommodate and manage increasing firm size and complexity due to continued success. Finally, as a result of a tightly coupled albeit successful system, organizational inertia sets in—and with it, resistance to change.

Such a tightly coupled system is prone to break apart when external and internal shifts put pressure on the system.[14] In Exhibit 11.2, inside the oval, the longer internal arrows show the firm's tightly coupled organizational design over time. The shorter internal arrows indicate pressures radiating from internal shifts such as accelerated growth, a change in the business model, entry into new markets, a change in the top management team (TMT), or mergers and acquisitions. Accelerated growth, for example, was the reason for a decline in employee productivity at Zappos, as discussed in Strategy Highlight 11.1. The longest arrows pointing into and piercing the boundary of the firm indicate external pressures, which can stem from any of the PESTEL forces (political, economic, sociocultural, technological, ecological, and legal, as discussed in Chapter 3). Strong external or internal pressure can break apart the current system, which may lead to firm failure.

To avoid inertia and possible organizational failure, the firm needs a flexible and adaptive structure to effectively translate the formulated strategy into action. Ideally the firm would maintain a virtual cycle of reorganizing, as implied by Option B discussed earlier in this section. As noted in the ChapterCase, the strategic intent of transitioning Google from a functional to M-form structure was to help Google and its other SBUs rise above inertia, to improve its flexibility and responsiveness in order to promote radical innovations rather than mere incremental innovations. As firms grow in size and complexity, they have a tendency and an incentive to focus on incremental innovation (see Chapter 7); however, this can lead to inertia and subsequent failure.

ORGANIZATIONAL STRUCTURE

LO 11-3

Define organizational structure and describe its four elements.

Some of the key decisions strategic leaders must make when designing effective organizations pertain to the firm's **organizational structure**. That structure determines how the work efforts of individuals and teams are orchestrated and how resources are distributed. In particular, an organizational structure defines how jobs and tasks are divided and integrated, delineates the reporting relationships up and down the hierarchy, defines formal communication channels, and prescribes how individuals and teams coordinate their work efforts. The key building blocks of an organizational structure are

- Specialization
- Formalization
- Centralization
- Hierarchy

SPECIALIZATION. **Specialization** describes the degree to which a task is divided into separate jobs—that is, the *division of labor.* Larger firms, such as Fortune 100 companies, tend to have a high degree of specialization; smaller entrepreneurial ventures tend to have a low degree of specialization. For example, an accountant for a large firm may specialize in only one area (e.g., internal audit), whereas an accountant in a small firm needs to be more of a generalist and take on many different things (e.g., internal auditing, plus payroll, accounts receivable, financial planning, and taxes). Specialization requires a trade-off between breadth and depth of knowledge. While a high degree of the division of labor increases productivity, it can also have unintended side-effects such as reduced employee job satisfaction due to repetition of tasks.

organizational structure A key to determining how the work efforts of individuals and teams are orchestrated and how resources are distributed.

specialization An organizational element that describes the degree to which a task is divided into separate jobs (i.e., the division of labor).

FORMALIZATION. **Formalization** captures the extent to which employee behavior is steered by explicit and codified rules and procedures. Formalized structures are characterized by detailed written rules and policies of what to do in specific situations. These are often codified in employee handbooks. McDonald's, for example, uses detailed standard operating procedures throughout the world to ensure consistent quality and service.

Formalization, therefore, is not necessarily negative; often it is necessary to achieve consistent and predictable results. Airlines, for instance, must rely on a high degree of formalization to instruct pilots on how to fly their airplanes to ensure safety and reliability. Yet a high degree of formalization can slow decision making, reduce creativity and innovation, and hinder customer service.[15] Most customer service reps in call centers, for example, follow a detailed script. This is especially true when call centers are outsourced to overseas locations. Zappos deliberately avoided this approach when it made customer service its core competency.

formalization An organizational element that captures the extent to which employee behavior is steered by explicit and codified rules and procedures.

CENTRALIZATION. **Centralization** refers to the degree to which decision making is concentrated at the top of the organization. Centralized decision making often correlates with slow response time and reduced customer satisfaction. In decentralized organizations such as Zappos, decisions are made and problems solved by empowered lower-level employees who are closer to the source of issues.

Different strategic management processes (discussed in Chapter 2) match with different degrees of centralization:

- Top-down strategic planning takes place in highly centralized organizations.
- Planned emergence is found in more decentralized organizations.

Whether centralization or decentralization is more effective depends on the specific situation. During the Gulf of Mexico oil spill in 2010, BP's response was slow and cumbersome because key decisions were initially made in its UK headquarters and not onsite. In this case, centralization reduced response time and led to a prolonged crisis. In contrast, the FBI and the CIA were faulted in the 9/11 Commission report for *not being centralized enough.*[16] The report concluded that although each agency had different types of evidence that a terrorist strike in the United States was imminent, their decentralization made them unable to put together the pieces to prevent the 9/11 attacks.

HIERARCHY. **Hierarchy** determines the formal, position-based reporting lines and thus stipulates *who reports to whom.* Let's assume two firms of roughly equal size: Firm A and Firm B. If many levels of hierarchy exist between the frontline employee and the CEO in Firm A, it has a *tall structure.* In contrast, if there are few levels of hierarchy in Firm B, it has a *flat structure.*

The number of levels of hierarchy, in turn, determines the managers' **span of control**— how many employees directly report to a manager. In tall organizational structures (Firm A), the span of control is narrow. In flat structures (Firm B), the span of control is wide, meaning one manager supervises many employees. In recent years, firms have de-layered by reducing the headcount (often middle managers), making the organizations flatter and more nimble. This, however, puts more pressure on the remaining managers who have to supervise and monitor more direct reports due to an increased span of control.[17] Recent research suggests that managers are most effective at an intermediate point where the span of control is not too narrow or too wide.[18]

LO 11-4

Compare and contrast mechanistic versus organic organizations.

MECHANISTIC VS. ORGANIC ORGANIZATIONS

Several of the building blocks of organizational structure frequently appear together, creating distinct organizational forms—mechanistic or organic organizations.[19]

MECHANISTIC ORGANIZATIONS. **Mechanistic organizations** are characterized by a high degree of specialization and formalization and by a tall hierarchy that relies on centralized decision making. The fast food chain McDonald's fits this description quite well. Each step

---

| **centralization** An organizational element that refers to the degree to which decision making is concentrated at the top of the organization. | **hierarchy** An organizational element that determines the formal, position-based reporting lines and thus stipulates who reports to whom. | **span of control** The number of employees who directly report to a manager. | **mechanistic organization** Characterized by a high degree of specialization and formalization and by a tall hierarchy that relies on centralized decision making. |

of every job such as deep-frying fries is documented in minute detail (e.g., what kind of vat, the quantity of oil, how many fries, what temperature, how long, and so on). Decision power is centralized at the top of the organization: McDonald's headquarters provides detailed instructions to each of its franchisees so that they provide comparable quality and service across the board although with some local menu variations. Communication and authority lines are top-down and well defined. To ensure standardized operating procedures and consistent food quality throughout the world, McDonald's operates Hamburger University, a state-of-the-art teaching facility in a Chicago suburb, where 50 full-time instructors teach courses in chemistry, food preparation, and marketing. In 2010, McDonald's opened a second Hamburger University campus in Shanghai, China. Mechanistic structures allow for standardization and economies of scale, and often are used when the firm pursues a cost-leadership strategy at the business level.

ORGANIC ORGANIZATIONS.   **Organic organizations** have a low degree of specialization and formalization, a flat organizational structure, and decentralized decision making. Organic structures tend to be correlated with the following: a fluid and flexible information flow among employees in both horizontal and vertical directions; faster decision making; and higher employee motivation, retention, satisfaction, and creativity. Organic organizations also typically exhibit a higher rate of entrepreneurial behaviors and innovation. Organic structures allow firms to foster R&D and/or marketing, for example, as a core competency. Firms that pursue a differentiation strategy at the business level frequently have an organic structure.

> **organic organization**
> Characterized by a low degree of specialization and formalization, a flat organizational structure, and decentralized decision making.

For instance, W.L. Gore & Associates, inventors of such path-breaking new products as breathable GORE-TEX fabrics, Glide dental floss, and Elixir guitar strings, use an organic structure to foster continuous innovation.[20] Bill Gore, a former longtime employee of chemical giant DuPont, founded W.L. Gore & Associates (in 1958) with the vision to create an organization "devoted to innovation...where imagination and initiative would flourish, where chronically curious engineers would be free to invent, invest, and succeed."[21] Gore articulated four core values that still guide the company and its associates to this day:

- Fairness to each other and everyone with whom the firm does business.
- Freedom to encourage, help, and allow other associates to grow in knowledge, skill, and scope of responsibility.
- The ability to make one's own commitments and keep them.
- Consultation with other associates before undertaking actions that could cause serious damage to the reputation of the company ("blowing a hole below the waterline").[22]

W.L. Gore & Associates is organized in an informal and decentralized manner: It has no formal job titles, job descriptions, chains of command, formal communication channels, written rules or standard operating procedures. Face-to-face communication is preferred over e-mail. There is no organizational chart. In what is called a *lattice* or *boundaryless* organizational form, everyone is empowered and encouraged to speak to anyone else in the organization. People who work at Gore are called *associates* rather than *employees,* indicating professional expertise and status. Gore associates organize themselves in project-based teams that are led by sponsors, not bosses. Associates invite other team members based on their expertise and interests in a more or less ad hoc fashion. Peer control in these multidisciplinary teams further enhances associate productivity. Group members evaluate each other's performance annually, and these evaluations determine each associate's level of compensation. Moreover, all associates at W.L. Gore are also shareholders of the company, and thus are part owners sharing in profits and losses.

EXHIBIT 11.3 Mechanistic vs. Organic Organizations: Building Blocks of Organizational Structure

	Mechanistic Organizations	Organic Organizations
Specialization	• High degree of specialization • Rigid division of labor • Employees focus on narrowly defined tasks	• Low degree of specialization • Flexible division of labor • Employees focus on "bigger picture"
Formalization	• Intimate familiarity with rules, policies, and processes necessary • Deep expertise in narrowly defined domain required • Task-specific knowledge valued	• Clear understanding of organization's core competencies and strategic intent • Domain expertise in different areas • Generalized knowledge of how to accomplish strategic goals valued
Centralization	• Decision power centralized at top • Vertical (top-down) communication	• Distributed decision making • Vertical (top-down and bottom-up) as well as horizontal communication
Hierarchy	• Tall structures • Low span of control • Clear lines of authority • Command and control	• Flat structures • High span of control • Horizontal as well as two-way vertical communication • Mutual adjustment
Business Strategy	• Cost-leadership strategy • Examples: McDonald's, Walmart	• Differentiation strategy • Examples: W.L. Gore, Zappos

Gore's freewheeling and informal culture has been linked to greater employee satisfaction and retention, higher personal initiative and creativity, and innovation at the firm level. Although W.L. Gore's organizational structure may look like something you might find in a small, high-tech startup, the company has 10,000 employees and over $3 billion in revenues, making Gore one of the largest privately held companies in the United States. W.L. Gore is consistently ranked in *Fortune*'s "100 Best Companies to Work For" list, and has been included in every edition of that prestigious ranking.

Exhibit 11.3 summarizes the key features of mechanistic and organic structures.

Although at first glance organic organizations may appear to be more attractive than mechanistic ones, their relative effectiveness depends on context. McDonald's, with its some 37,000 restaurants across the globe, would not be successful with an organic structure. Similarly, a mechanistic structure would not allow Zappos or W.L. Gore to develop and hone their respective core competencies in customer service and product innovation.

The key point is this: To gain and sustain competitive advantage, *structure must follow strategy.* Moreover, the chosen organizational form must match the firm's business strategy. We will expand further on the required strategy–structure relationship in the next section.

LO 11-5

Describe different organizational structures and match them with appropriate strategies.

11.2 Strategy and Structure

The important and interdependent relationship between strategy and structure directly impacts a firm's performance. Moreover, the relationship is dynamic—changing over time in a somewhat predictable pattern as firms grow in size and complexity. Successful new ventures generally grow first by increasing sales, then by obtaining larger geographic reach, and finally by diversifying through vertical integration and entering into related and unrelated

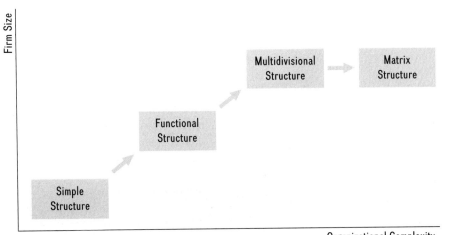

EXHIBIT 11.4

Changing Organizational Structures and Increasing Complexity as Firms Grow

businesses.[23] Different stages in a firm's growth require different organizational structures. This important evolutionary pattern is depicted in Exhibit 11.4. As we discuss next, organizational structures range from simple to functional to multidivisional to matrix.

SIMPLE STRUCTURE

A **simple structure** generally is used by small firms with low organizational complexity. In such firms, the founders tend to make all the important strategic decisions and run the day-to-day operations. Examples include entrepreneurial ventures such as Google in 1998, when the startup operated out of Susan Wojcicki's garage in Menlo Park, California (Ms. Wojcicki is now the CEO of YouTube). Other common examples of firms with simple structures are professional service firms such as smaller advertising, consulting, accounting, and law firms, as well as family-owned businesses. Simple structures are flat hierarchies operated in a decentralized fashion. They exhibit a low degree of formalization and specialization. Typically, neither professional managers nor sophisticated systems are in place, which often leads to an overload for the founder and/or CEO when the firms experience growth.

simple structure Organizational structure in which the founders tend to make all the important strategic decisions as well as run the day-to-day operations.

FUNCTIONAL STRUCTURE

As sales increase, firms generally adopt a **functional structure**, which groups employees into distinct functional areas based on domain expertise. These functional areas often correspond to distinct stages in the value chain such as R&D, engineering and manufacturing, and marketing and sales, as well as supporting areas such as human resources, finance, and accounting. Exhibit 11.5 shows a functional structure, with the lines indicating reporting and authority relationships. The department head of each functional area reports to the CEO, who coordinates and integrates the work of each function. A business school student generally majors in one of these functional areas such as finance, accounting, IT, marketing, operations, or human resources, and is then recruited into a corresponding functional group.

functional structure Organizational structure that groups employees into distinct functional areas based on domain expertise.

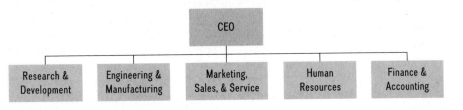

EXHIBIT 11.5

Typical Functional Structure

W.L. Gore & Associates started as a simple structure business operating out of Gore's basement. Two years after its founding, the company received a large manufacturing order for high-tech cable that it could not meet with its ad hoc basement operation. It was at this point when W.L. Gore reorganized into a functional structure. A simple structure would not have provided the effective division, coordination, and integration of work required to accommodate the order, much less future growth.

A functional structure allows for a higher degree of specialization and deeper domain expertise than a simple structure. Higher specialization also allows for a greater division of labor, which is linked to higher productivity.[24] While work in a functional structure tends to be specialized, it is centrally coordinated by the CEO (see Exhibit 11.5). A functional structure allows for an efficient top-down and bottom-up communication chain between the CEO and the functional departments, and thus relies on a relatively flat structure.

FUNCTIONAL STRUCTURE AND BUSINESS STRATEGY. A functional structure is recommended when a firm has a fairly narrow focus in terms of product/service offerings (i.e., low level of diversification) combined with a small geographic footprint. It matches well, therefore, with the different *business* strategies discussed in Chapter 6: cost leadership, differentiation, and blue ocean. Although a functional structure is the preferred method for implementing business strategy, different variations and contexts require careful modifications in each case:

- The goal of a *cost-leadership strategy* is to create a competitive advantage by reducing the firm's cost below that of competitors while offering acceptable value. The cost leader sells a no-frills, standardized product or service to the mainstream customer. To effectively implement a cost-leadership strategy, therefore, managers must create a functional structure that contains the organizational elements of a *mechanistic structure*—one that is centralized, with well-defined lines of authority up and down the hierarchy. Using a functional structure allows the cost leader to nurture and constantly upgrade necessary core competencies in manufacturing and logistics. Moreover, the cost leader needs to create incentives to foster process innovation to drive down cost. Finally, because the firm services the average customer, and thus targets the largest market segment possible, it should focus on leveraging economies of scale to further drive down costs.

- The goal of a *differentiation strategy* is to create a competitive advantage by offering products or services at a higher perceived value, while controlling costs. The differentiator, therefore, sells a non-standardized product or service to specific market segments in which customers are willing to pay a higher price. To effectively implement a differentiation strategy, managers rely on a functional structure that resembles an *organic organization*. In particular, decision making tends to be decentralized to foster and incentivize continuous innovation and creativity as well as flexibility and mutual adjustment across areas. Using a functional structure with an organic organization allows the differentiator to nurture and constantly upgrade necessary core competencies in R&D, innovation, and marketing. Finally, the functional structure should be set up to allow the firm to reap economies of scope from its core competencies, such as by leveraging its brand name across different products or its technology across different devices.

- A successful *blue ocean strategy* requires reconciliation of the trade-offs between differentiation and low cost. To effectively implement a blue ocean strategy, the firm must be both efficient and flexible. It must balance centralization to control costs with decentralization to foster creativity and innovation. Managers must, therefore, attempt to combine the advantages of the functional-structure variations used for cost leadership and differentiation while mitigating their disadvantages. Moreover, the firm pursuing a blue ocean strategy needs to develop several distinct core competencies to both drive up perceived value and lower cost. It must further pursue both product and process innovations in an attempt to reap economies of scale and scope. All of these challenges make it clear that although a blue ocean strategy is attractive at first glance, it is quite difficult to implement given the range of important trade-offs that must be addressed.

A firm's structure is therefore critical when pursuing a blue ocean strategy. The challenge that strategic leaders face is to structure their organizations so that they control cost *and* allow for creativity that can lay the basis for differentiation. Doing both is hard. Achieving a low-cost position requires an organizational structure that relies on strict budget controls, while differentiation requires an organizational structure that allows creativity and customer responsiveness to thrive, which typically necessitates looser organizational structures and controls.

The goal for leaders who want to pursue a blue ocean strategy is to build an **ambidextrous organization**, one that enables managers to balance and harness different activities in trade-off situations.[25] Here the trade-offs to be addressed involve the simultaneous pursuit of low-cost and differentiation strategies. Notable management practices that companies use to resolve this trade-off include flexible and lean manufacturing systems, total quality management, just-in-time inventory management, and Six Sigma.[26] Other management techniques that allow firms to reconcile cost and value pressures are the use of teams in the production process, as well as decentralized decision making at the level of the individual customer.

Ambidexterity describes a firm's ability to address trade-offs not only at one point but also over time. It encourages strategic leaders to balance **exploitation**—applying current knowledge to enhance firm performance in the short term—with **exploration**—searching for new knowledge that may enhance a firm's future performance.[27] For example, while Intel focuses on maximizing sales from its *current* cutting-edge microprocessors, it also has several different teams with different time horizons working on *future* generations of microprocessors.[28] In ambidextrous organizations, strategic leaders must constantly analyze their existing business processes and routines, looking for ways to change them in order to resolve trade-offs across internal value chain activities and time.[29]

Exhibit 11.6 presents a detailed match between different business strategies and their corresponding functional structures.

DISADVANTAGES OF FUNCTIONAL STRUCTURE. While certainly attractive, the functional structure is not without significant drawbacks. Although the functional structure facilitates rich and extensive communication between members of the *same* department, it frequently lacks effective communication channels *across* departments. Notice in Exhibit 11.5 the lack of links between different functions. The lack of linkage between functions is the reason, for example, R&D managers often do not communicate directly with marketing managers. In an ambidextrous organization, a top-level manager such as the CEO must take on the necessary coordination and integration work.

To overcome the lack of cross-departmental collaboration in a functional structure, strategic leaders can set up *cross-functional teams*. In these temporary teams, members come from different functional areas to work together on a specific project or product, usually from start to completion. Each team member reports to two supervisors: the team leader and the respective functional department head. Many companies such as Apple, Nike, or W.L. Gore employ cross-functional (project) teams successfully.

---

ambidextrous organization An organization able to balance and harness different activities in trade-off situations

ambidexterity A firm's ability to address trade-offs not only at one point but also over time. It encourages managers to balance exploitation with exploration.

exploitation Applying current knowledge to enhance firm performance in the short term.

exploration Searching for new knowledge that may enhance a firm's future performance.

Business Strategy	Structure
Cost-leadership	**Functional**
	• Mechanistic organization
	• Centralized
	• Command and control
	• Core competencies in efficient manufacturing and logistics
	• Process innovation to drive down cost
	• Focus on economies of scale
Differentiation	**Functional**
	• Organic organization
	• Decentralized
	• Flexibility and mutual adjustment
	• Core competencies in R&D, innovation, and marketing
	• Product innovation
	• Focus on economies of scope
Blue ocean	**Functional**
	• Ambidextrous organization
	• Balancing centralization with decentralization
	• Multiple core competencies along the value chain required: R&D, manufacturing, logistics, marketing, etc.
	• Process and product innovations
	• Focus on economies of scale and scope

A second critical drawback of the functional structure is that it cannot effectively address a higher level of diversification, which often stems from further growth.[30] This is the stage at which firms find it effective to evolve and adopt a multidivisional or matrix structure, both of which we will discuss next.

MULTIDIVISIONAL STRUCTURE

**multidivisional struc-
ture (M-form)** Organi-
zational structure that
consists of several dis-
tinct strategic business
units (SBUs), each with
its own profit-and-loss
(P&L) responsibility.

Over time, as a firm diversifies into different product lines and geographies, it generally implements a multidivisional or a matrix structure (as shown in Exhibit 11.4 and discussed in the ChapterCase). The **multidivisional structure** (or **M-form**) consists of several distinct strategic business units (SBUs), each with its own profit-and-loss (P&L) responsibility. Each SBU is operated more or less independently from one another, and each is led by a CEO (or equivalent general manager) who is responsible for the unit's business strategy and its day-to-day operations. The CEOs of each division report to the corporate office, which is led by the company's highest-ranking executive (titles vary and include president or CEO for the entire corporation). Because most large firms are diversified to some extent across different product lines and geographies, the M-form is a widely adopted organizational structure.

As featured in the ChapterCase, Google has moved from a functional to an M-form structure by creating the parent company Alphabet. Each unit under Alphabet is an independent SBU, run by a CEO that is responsible for the unit's P&L. The individual CEOs report to Larry Page, who is the CEO of parent company Alphabet, and he oversees capital allocation and strategy execution. As CEO of the holding company, Page also monitors each SBU's performance and adjusts rewards accordingly.

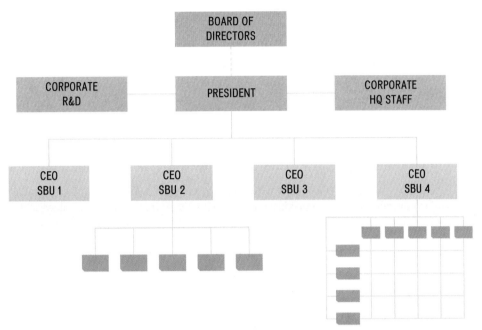

EXHIBIT 11.7

Typical Multidivisional
(M-Form) Structure

Note that SBU 2 uses a
functional structure, and
SBU 4 uses a matrix
structure.

A typical M-form is shown in Exhibit 11.7. In this example, the company has four SBUs, each led by a CEO. Corporations may use SBUs to organize around different businesses and product lines or around different geographic regions. Each SBU represents a self-contained business with its own hierarchy and organizational structure. Note that in Exhibit 11.7, SBU 2 is organized using a functional structure, while SBU 4 is organized using a matrix structure. The CEO of each SBU must determine which organizational structure is most appropriate to implement the SBU's business strategy.

A firm's corporate office (such as Alphabet's) is supported by company-wide staff functions including human resources, finance, and corporate R&D. These staff functions support all of the company's SBUs but are centralized at corporate headquarters to benefit from economies of scale and to avoid duplication within each SBU. Since most of the larger enterprises are publicly held stock companies, the CEO and president report to a board of directors representing the interests of the shareholders, indicated by the dashed line in Exhibit 11.7.

The CEO and/or president of the parent company, with support from corporate headquarters staff, monitors the performance of each SBU and determines how to allocate resources across units.[31] Corporate headquarters adds value by functioning as an internal capital market. The goal is to be more efficient at allocating capital through its budgeting process than what could be achieved in external capital markets. This can be especially effective if the corporation overall can access capital at a lower cost than competitors due to a favorable (AAA) debt rating. Corporate headquarters can also add value through restructuring the company's portfolio of SBUs by selling low-performing businesses and adding promising businesses through acquisitions.

Moreover, corporate executives can also spin off successful strategic business units to grow on their own. For instance, the travel site Expedia was spun out from Microsoft through an initial public offering. In other cases, frustrated employees may leave the parent corporation and start new ventures on their own. Former Fairchild employees started Intel. Likewise, former Xerox employees started Adobe. Ex-Amazon employees started Flipkart, an Indian e-commerce company (in which Walmart in 2018 acquired a majority, valuing the company at $22 billion). All of these spin-offs went on to be largely successful.

M-FORM AND CORPORATE STRATEGY. To achieve an optimal match between strategy and structure, different corporate strategies require different organizational structures. In Chapter 8, we identified four types of corporate diversification (see Exhibit 8.8: *single business, dominant business, related diversification*, and *unrelated diversification*. Each is defined by the percentage of revenues obtained from the firm's primary activity.

▪ Firms that follow a single-business or *dominant-business strategy* at the corporate level gain at least 70 percent of their revenues from their primary activity; they generally employ a *functional structure*.

▪ For firms that pursue either *related* or *unrelated diversification*, the *M-form* is the preferred organizational structure.

▪ Firms using the M-form organizational structure to support a *related-diversification* strategy tend to concentrate decision making at the top of the organization. Doing so allows a high level of integration. It also helps corporate headquarters leverage and transfer across different SBUs the core competencies that form the basis for a related diversification.

▪ Firms using the M-form structure to support an *unrelated-diversification* strategy often decentralize decision making. Doing so allows general managers to respond to specific circumstances, and leads to a low level of integration at corporate headquarters.

Exhibit 11.8 matches different corporate strategies and their corresponding organizational structures.

DISADVANTAGES OF M-FORM. Moving from the functional structure to the M-form results in adding another layer of corporate hierarchy (corporate headquarters). This goes along with all the known problems of increasing bureaucracy, red tape, and sometimes duplication of efforts. It also slows decision making because in many instances a CEO of an SBU must get approval from corporate headquarters when making major decisions that might affect a second SBU or the corporation as a whole.

Also, since each SBU in the M-form is evaluated as a standalone profit-and-loss center, SBUs frequently end up competing with each other. A high-performing SBU might be rewarded with greater capital budgets and strategic freedoms; low-performing businesses might be spun off. SBUs compete with one another for resources such as capital and

EXHIBIT 11.8 Matching Corporate Strategy and Structure	**Corporate Strategy**	**Structure**
	Single business	**Functional structure**
	Dominant business	**Functional structure**
	Related diversification	**Cooperative multidivisional (M-form)**
		• Centralized decision making
		• High level of integration at corporate headquarters
		• Co-opetition among SBUs
		— Competition for resources
		— Cooperation in competency sharing
	Unrelated diversification	**Competitive multidivisional (M-form)**
		• Decentralized decision making
		• Low level of integration at corporate headquarters
		• Competition among SBUs for resources

managerial talent, but they also need to cooperate to share competencies. *Co-opetition*—competition and cooperation at the same time—among the SBUs is both inevitable and necessary. Sometimes, however, it can be detrimental when a corporate process such as resource allocation or transfer pricing between SBUs becomes riddled with corporate politics and turf wars.

In some instances, spinning out SBUs to make them independent companies is beneficial. As discussed in Chapter 8, the BCG growth-share matrix helps corporate executives when making these types of decisions. In the last few years when owned by eBay, PayPal outperformed its parent company. PayPal's executives (and investors) were tired of subsidizing eBay's stagnant business. EBay had bought PayPal in the aftermath of the dot-com stock market crash in 2002 for $1.5 billion. In 2015, eBay and PayPal were de-merged. PayPal was spun off through an initial public offering, and thus became an independent company again. PayPal is now able to fully unlock its value. Investors also liked separating eBay and PayPal, giving PayPal a valuation of more than $130 billion in 2019; eBay's standalone valuation is only about $32 billion.[32]

Strategy Highlight 11.1 discusses how the online retailer Zappos experimented with new organizational forms after realizing the M-form did not yield the expected benefits. Although quite innovative, Zappos' results have been mixed.

Strategy Highlight **11.1**

Zappos: Of Happiness and Holacracy

Zappos (www.zappos.com) made its mark delivering shoes and happiness. When Tony Hsieh, CEO of Zappos, wrote about the company's unique approach in 2010's *Delivering Happiness*, the book joined The *New York Times* bestseller list. Hsieh believes that making customers and employees happy drives success by "delivering WOW through service." The result? The online shoe and clothing store grew from a startup to become a major player in the industry. Service includes easy online shopping with free shipping to and from its customers and a generous 365-day return policy.

Zappos also made its investors happy. In 2008, just 10 years after its founding, Zappos achieved more than $1 billion in annual sales. A year later, Amazon acquired Zappos for $1.2 billion. Although now a subsidiary of Amazon, Zappos continues to operate as an independent business unit, as Amazon maintains a hands-off policy. If anything, new ideas flow up from Zappos to its parent. One example: Zappos weeds out cultural misfits by paying employees to leave after the orientation program. Amazon CEO Jeff Bezos said the "clever people at Zappos" inspired him to offer warehouse workers as much as $5,000 to quit if they were not totally enthusiastic about the importance of their work to Amazon's future.[33]

A flock of birds in flight, immediately shifting direction with self-regulating unity, frequently serves a metaphor of holacracy in action.
Greatonmywall/Alamy Stock Photo

Zappos had grown so much since its founding—receiving over 20 million unique visitors a month to its website—that it sometimes reorganized to ensure it continued to offer the best customer service possible. At one point, to keep the organization flat and responsive to customers, Zappos restructured into 10 separate business units including Zappos.com, Zappos Gift Cards, Zappos IP, and 6pm.com, among others. But to fight the slow bureaucracy that affects larger companies, Hsieh announced (in 2013) an even more radical approach to reorganization—a structure called *holacracy*.

(Continued)

Here is what we know about holacracy. Brian Robertson developed the concept in the 2000s, working from ideas introduced by Arthur Koestler in the 1967 book, *The Ghost in the Machine*, the work in which Koestler coined the term. Forgoing traditional top-down hierarchy, **holacracy** purports to achieve control and coordination by distributing power and authority to self-organizing groups (so-called circles) of employees. Circles of employees are meant to self-organize and self-govern around a specific task, such as confirming online orders or authorizing a customer's credit card. Often compared to a computer's operating system, holacracy constitutes a new organizational structure for governing and running a company. Because it greatly changes how workers interact, proponents hail it as a "social technology."

Hsieh explains holacracy as follows:

> *Research shows that every time the size of a city doubles, innovation or productivity per resident increases by 15 percent. But when companies get bigger, innovation or productivity per employee generally goes down. So we're trying to figure out how to structure Zappos more like a city and less like a bureaucratic corporation. In a city, people and businesses are self-organizing. We're trying to do the same thing by switching from a normal hierarchical structure to a system called holacracy, which enables employees to act more like entrepreneurs and self-direct their work instead of reporting to a manager who tells them what to do.[34]*

Zappos grouped its more than 1,500 employees in some 400 circles, with each employee in two or more circles. Order is supposed to emerge from the bottom up, rather than rely on top-down command and control. The rules are spelled out explicitly in a so-called constitution, which defines the power and authority of each circle. For coordination, the employee circles overlap horizontally, and without vertical hierarchy. The CEO's last act as the highest-ranking person in the organization is to sign the constitution in a symbolic act, relinquishing all executive powers. Thereafter the former leader becomes the "ratifier of the holacracy constitution."

As often happens, a new concept sounds great in theory but proves hard to implement. Zappos' implementation of holacracy is not going well. As a consequence, employee morale has plummeted, and Zappos employees are no longer as happy. In 2011, Zappos was ranked sixth in Fortune's list of "100 Best Companies to Work For" (one of the highest rankings for a relatively young firm). By 2015, after it started implementing holacracy, Zappos fell to 86. In the three years since (2016 to 2018), Zappos failed to place in Fortune's "100 Best Companies to Work For" list. Note that the ranking is determined by what employees say about their own company in anonymous surveys—not some arbitrary external assessment.

Hsieh was frustrated that by 2015 the transition to holacracy was still not yet complete. To accelerate the process, he offered a three-month severance package to employees not willing to adopt the new structure. More than 200 employees, or some 14 percent of Zappos' work force, accepted the offer and resigned. By 2016, Zappos had lost 18 percent of its work force.

Employees that remained with Zappos have complained that holacracy has removed clear paths for career advancement. They have wondered openly how hiring, firing, and promoting would be done. They are also concerned that relying on employee circles for making decisions will not only induce paralysis, but also make the organization more and not less political. In sum, they find that holacracy forces them to waste time in endless meetings rather than allows them to get the actual work done. That Hsieh made a top-down decision for Zappos to implement a holacracy (or decided a few years prior to selling the company to Amazon), in a company that ostensibly celebrated democracy and participation, was an irony that was not lost upon Zappos' employees.[35]

MATRIX STRUCTURE

holacracy An organizational structure in which decision-making authority is distributed through loose collections or circles of self-organizing teams.

To reap the benefits of both the M-form and the functional structure, many firms employ a mix of these two organizational forms, called a **matrix structure**. Exhibit 11.9 shows an example. In it, the firm is organized according to SBUs along a horizontal axis (like in the M-form), but also has a second dimension of organizational structure along a vertical axis. In this case, the second dimension consists of different geographic areas, each of which generally would house a full set of functional activities. The idea behind the matrix structure is to combine the benefits of the M-form (domain expertise, economies of scale, and

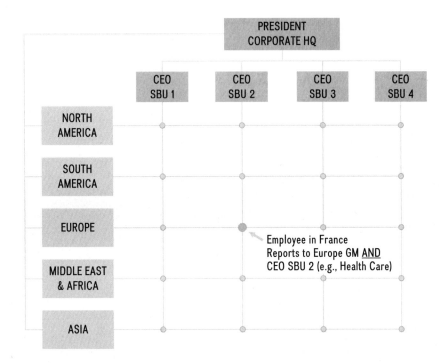

EXHIBIT 11.9

Typical Matrix
Structure with
Geographic and SBU
Divisions

efficient processing of information) with those of the functional structure (responsiveness and decentralized focus).

The horizontal and vertical reporting lines between SBUs and geographic areas intersect, creating nodes in the matrix. Exhibit 11.9 highlights one employee, represented by a large dot and called out by an arrow. This employee works in a group with other employees in SBU 2, the company's health care unit for the Europe division in France. This employee has two bosses—the CEO of the health care SBU and the general manager (GM) for the Europe division. Both supervisors report to corporate headquarters, which is led by the president of the corporation (indicated in Exhibit 11.9 by the reporting lines from the SBUs and geographic units to the president).

Firms tend to use a *global matrix structure* to pursue a *transnational strategy*, in which the firm combines the benefits of a multidomestic strategy (high local responsiveness) with those of a global-standardization strategy (lowest-cost position attainable). In a global matrix structure, the geographic divisions are charged with local responsiveness and learning. At the same time, each SBU is charged with driving down costs through economies of scale and other efficiencies. A global matrix structure also allows the firm to feed local learning back to different SBUs and thus diffuse it throughout the organization. The specific organizational configuration depicted in Exhibit 11.9 is a global matrix structure.

The matrix structure is quite versatile because managers can assign different groupings along the vertical and horizontal axes. A common form of the matrix structure uses different projects or products on the vertical axis and different functional areas on the horizontal axis. In that traditional matrix structure, *cross-functional* teams work together on different projects. The teams in a matrix structure tend to be more permanent rather than project-based with a predetermined time horizon.

Given the advances in online collaboration tools, some firms have replaced the more rigid matrix structure with a *network structure*. A network structure allows the firm to connect centers of excellence, whatever their global location (see Exhibit 10.4).[36] The firm

matrix structure
Organizational structure that combines the functional structure with the M-form.

Global Strategy	Structure
International	**Functional**
Multidomestic	**Multidivisional**
	• Geographic areas
	• Decentralized decision making
Global-standardization	**Multidivisional**
	• Product divisions
	• Centralized decision making
Transnational	**Global matrix**
	• Balance of centralized and decentralized decision making
	• Additional layer of hierarchy to coordinate both:
	— Geographic areas
	— Product divisions

EXHIBIT 11.10

Matching Global Strategy and Structure

benefits from *communities of practice*, which store important organizational learning and expertise. To avoid undue complexity, these network structures need to be supported by corporate-wide procedures and policies to streamline communication, collaboration, and the allocation of resources.[37]

MATRIX STRUCTURE AND GLOBAL STRATEGY. We already noted that a global matrix structure fits well with a transnational strategy. To complete the strategy–structure relationships in the global context, we also need to consider the international, multidomestic, and standardization strategies discussed in Chapter 10. Exhibit 11.10 shows how different global strategies best match different organizational structures.

- In an *international strategy*, the company leverages its home-based core competency by moving into foreign markets. An international strategy is advantageous when the company faces low pressure for both local responsiveness and cost reductions. Companies pursue an international strategy through a differentiation strategy at the business level. The best match for an international strategy is a *functional* organizational structure, which allows the company to leverage its core competency most effectively. This approach is similar to matching a business-level differentiation strategy with a functional structure (discussed in detail earlier).

- When a multinational enterprise (MNE) pursues a *multidomestic strategy*, it attempts to maximize local responsiveness in the face of low pressures for cost reductions. An appropriate match for this type of global strategy is the *multidivisional* organizational structure. That structure would enable the MNE to set up different divisions based on geographic regions (e.g., by continent). The different geographic divisions operate more or less as standalone SBUs to maximize local responsiveness. Decision making is decentralized.

- When following a *global-standardization strategy*, the MNE attempts to reap significant economies of scale as well as location economies by pursuing a global division of labor based on wherever best-of-class capabilities reside at the lowest cost. Since the product offered is more or less an undifferentiated commodity, the MNE pursues a cost-leadership strategy. The optimal organizational structure match is, again, a *multidivisional* structure. Rather than focusing on geographic differences as in the multidomestic strategy, the focus is on driving down costs due to consolidation of activities across different geographic areas.

DISADVANTAGES OF MATRIX STRUCTURE. Though it is appealing in theory, the matrix structure does have shortcomings. It is usually difficult to implement: Implementing two layers of organizational structure creates significant organizational complexity and increases administrative costs. Also, reporting structures in a matrix are often not clear. In particular, employees can have trouble reconciling goals presented by their two (or more) supervisors. Less-clear reporting structures can undermine accountability by creating multiple principal–agent relationships. This can make performance appraisals more difficult. Adding an additional layer of hierarchy can also slow decision making and increase bureaucratic costs.

As just discussed, the development pattern of how organizational structures tend to change in time as firms grow in size and complexity is fairly predictable: Starting with a simple structure, then moving to functional structure, and finally implementing a multidivisional or matrix structure. Exhibit 11.11 summarizes the advantages and disadvantages of different organizational structures.

EXHIBIT 11.11 Advantages and Disadvantages of Different Organizational Structures

	Advantages	Disadvantages
Simple Structure	• Fast decision making • Nimble and responsive organization • Integration of expertise across areas • Given low bandwidth, organizations with simple structures are easily pushed into "crisis mode," requiring "all hands on deck" (i.e., everyone working long hours until project is completed)	• CEO overload • Lack of domain expertise in distinct business functions (e.g., accounting, finance, marketing, etc.) • Unable to accommodate growth • No separation of strategic and day-to-day decision making
Functional Structure	• Clear, top-down lines of authority and decision making • Deeper domain expertise • Higher productivity due to specialization and division of labor • Responsive organization	• Emergence of silos (i.e., no effective communication across different departments) • Growth is limited • Employee alienation, especially in startups that move from simple structure to functional one
Multidivisional Structure (M-Form)	• Accommodates growth (horizontal, vertical, and geographic) • Clear profit & loss responsibilities at SBU level, run by CEO or equivalent • Efficient processing of information • Allows for different competitive strategies at SBU level, while integration takes place at corporate level	• Additional layer of corporate hierarchy (i.e., corporate headquarters) when moving from functional to M-form structure • SBUs stand in competition to one another • Political infighting • Opportunistic behavior by SBUs
Matrix Structure	• Accommodates growth (horizontal, vertical, and geographic) • Combines advantages of functional structure with M-form	• Two layers of organizational structure create multiple principal–agent relationships • Slow in decision making • Potentially inaccurate performance appraisals • Quite difficult to implement

11.3 Organizing for Innovation

After emphasizing throughout this text (and especially in Chapter 7) that continued innovation is critical to gaining and sustaining competitive advantage in today's fast-moving world, the question arises: *How should firms organize for innovation?* During the 20th century, the *closed innovation* approach was the dominant research and development (R&D) approach for most firms: They focused on discovering, developing, and commercializing new products and services internally.[38] Although this approach was costly and time-consuming, it allowed firms to fully capture the returns made from their R&D investments to generate their own innovations.

Several factors, however, led to a shift in the knowledge landscape from closed innovation to open innovation in recent years. They include

- The increasing supply and mobility of skilled workers.
- The exponential growth of venture capital.
- The increasing availability of external options (such as spinning out new ventures) to commercialize ideas that were previously shelved or insource promising ideas and inventions.
- The increasing capability of external suppliers globally.

open innovation A framework for R&D that proposes permeable firm boundaries to allow a firm to benefit not only from internal ideas and inventions, but also from external ones. The sharing goes both ways: Some external ideas and inventions are insourced while others are spun out.

These factors have led more and more companies to adopt an open innovation approach to research and development. **Open innovation** is a framework for R&D that proposes permeable firm boundaries to allow a firm to benefit not only from internal ideas and inventions, but also from ideas and innovation from external sources. External sources of knowledge can be customers, suppliers, universities, start-up companies, and even competitors.[39] The sharing goes both ways: Some external R&D is insourced (and further developed in-house) while the firm may spin out internal R&D that does not fit its strategy to allow others to commercialize it. Even the largest companies, such as AT&T, IBM, Siemens, and Pfizer, are shifting their innovation strategy toward a model that blends internal with external knowledge sourcing via licensing agreements, strategic alliances, joint ventures, and acquisitions.[40]

Exhibit 11.12 depicts the closed and open innovation models. In the closed innovation model (Panel A), the firm is conducting all research and development in-house, using a traditional funnel approach. The boundaries of the firm are impenetrable (indicated by the solid lines in Panel A). Outside ideas and projects cannot enter, nor does the firm allow its own research ideas and development projects to leave the firm. Firms in the closed innovation model are extremely protective of their intellectual property. This not only allows the firm to capture all the benefits from its own R&D, but also prevents competitors from benefiting from it. The mind-set of firms in the closed innovation model is that to profit from R&D, the firm must come up with its own discoveries, develop them on its own, and control the distribution channels. Strength in R&D is equated with a high likelihood of benefiting from first-mover advantages. Firms following the closed innovation model, however, are much more likely to fall prone to the *not-invented-here syndrome:*[41] "If the R&D leading to a discovery and a new development project was not conducted in-house, it cannot be good."

As documented, the pharmaceutical company Merck suffers from the *not-invented-here syndrome.*[42] That is, if a product was not created and developed at Merck, it could not be good enough. Merck's culture and organizational systems perpetuate this logic, which assumes that since the company hired the best people, the smartest people in the industry must work for Merck, and so the best discoveries must be made at Merck. The company leads the industry in terms of R&D spending because Merck believes that if it is the first to

EXHIBIT 11.12 Closed Innovation vs. Open Innovation

Panel A: Closed Innovation

Panel B: Open Innovation

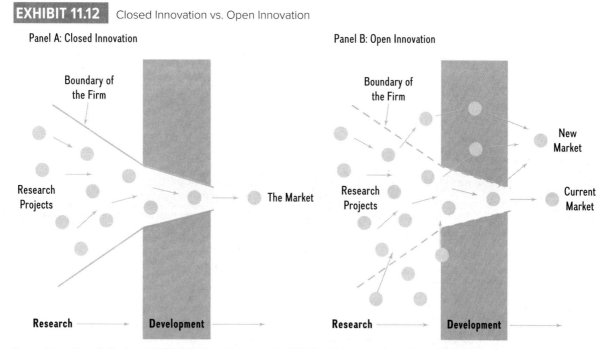

Source: Adapted from H. Chesbrough (2003), ""The Era of Open Innovation," MIT Sloan Management Review, Spring: 35–41.

discover and develop a new drug, it would be the first to market. Merck is one of the most successful companies by total number of active R&D projects. Perhaps even more important, Merck's researchers have been awarded several Nobel Prizes for their breakthrough research, a considerable point of pride for Merck's personnel.

In the open innovation model, in contrast, a company attempts to commercialize both its own ideas and research from other firms. It also finds external alternatives such as spin-off ventures or strategic alliances to commercialize its internally developed R&D. The boundary of the firm has become porous (as represented by the dashed lines in Panel B in Exhibit 11.12), allowing the firm to spin off some R&D projects while insourcing other promising projects. Companies using an open innovation approach realize that great ideas can come from both inside and outside the company. Significant value can be had by commercializing external R&D and letting others commercialize internal R&D that does not fit with the firm's strategy. The focus is on building a more effective *business model* to commercialize both internal *and* external R&D, rather than focusing on being first to market.

One key assumption underlying the open innovation model is that combining the best of internal *and* external R&D will more likely lead to a competitive advantage. This requires that the company must continuously upgrade its internal R&D capabilities to enhance its **absorptive capacity**—its ability to understand external technology developments, evaluate them, and integrate them into current products or create new ones.[43] Exhibit 11.13 compares and contrasts open innovation and closed innovation principles.

Strategy Highlight 11.2 provides a detailed account of how Sony's continued use of a closed innovation system led over time to a sustained competitive disadvantage and inferior performance, while Apple leveraged an open innovation model for decade-long superiority, becoming the first company on the planet to be valued over $1 trillion.

absorptive capacity A firm's ability to understand external technology developments, evaluate them, and integrate them into current products or create new ones.

EXHIBIT 11.13 Contrasting Principles of Closed and Open Innovation

Closed Innovation Principles	Open Innovation Principles
The smart people in our field work for us.	Not all the smart people work for us. We need to work with smart people inside and outside our company.
To profit from R&D, we must discover it, develop it, and ship it ourselves.	External R&D can create significant value; internal R&D is needed to claim (absorb) some portion of that value.
If we discover it ourselves, we will get it to market first.	We don't have to originate the research to profit from it; we can still be first if we successfully commercialize new research.
The company that gets an innovation to market first will win.	Building a better business model is often more important than getting to market first.
If we create the most and best ideas in the industry, we will win.	If we make the best use of internal and external ideas, we will win.
We should control our intellectual property (IP), so that our competitors don't profit from it.	We should profit from others' use of our IP, and we should buy others' IP whenever it advances our own business model.

Source: Adapted from H.W. Chesbrough (2003), *Open Innovation: The New Imperative for Creating and Profiting from Technology* (Boston: Harvard Business School Press).

Strategy Highlight 11.2

Sony vs. Apple: Whatever Happened to Sony?

Apple's market capitalization in 2001 was $7 billion, while Sony's was $55 billion. In other words, Sony was almost eight times larger than Apple. Then, most people would have picked Sony as the company to revolutionize the mobile device industry given its stellar innovation track record. Instead, that honor went to Apple when it introduced the iPod, a portable digital music player, in October 2001 and 18 months later the iTunes Music Store. Through these two strategic moves Apple redefined the music industry, reinventing itself as not only a mobile-device but also a content-delivery company. Many observers wondered what happened to Sony, the company that created the portable music industry by introducing the Walkman in 1979.

Sony's strategy was to differentiate itself through the vertical integration of content and hardware, driven by its 1988 acquisition of CBS Records (later part of Sony Entertainment) and its 1989 acquisition of Columbia Pictures.

This vertical integration strategy contrasted sharply with Sony Music division's desire to protect its lucrative revenue-generating, copyrighted compact discs (CDs). Sony Music's engineers were aggressively combating music piracy by inhibiting the Microsoft Windows media player's ability to rip CDs and by serializing discs (assigning unique ID numbers to discs). The compact disc (CD) became the dominant format for selling music in 1991, replacing analog audiocassettes. The CD had been jointly developed by Sony and European electronics manufacturer Philips.

Media technology, however, soon moved to digital. With the rise of the internet in the 1990s and use of digital music, illegal file sharing on the internet was rampant. Napster allowed peer-to-peer sharing of files, which meant individual users could upload entire albums of music, to be downloaded by anyone, with no payments going to the artists or the record companies. While Sony focused on preventing

Sony created the portable music industry with the Walkman, introduced in 1979.
Chris Willson/Alamy Stock Photo

media players that could rip CDs, Apple was developing a digital rights management (DRM) system to allow for legal downloads of digital music while protecting copyright at the same time. The iTunes Store enabled users to legally download and own individual songs at an attractive 99 cents. Apple's DRM and iTunes succeeded, protecting the music studios' and artists' interests while creating value that enabled consumers to enjoy portable digital music.

Sony had a long history of creating category-defining electronic devices of superior quality and design using a closed innovation approach. It had all the right competencies in-house to launch a successful counterattack to compete with Apple: electronics, software, music, and computer divisions. Sony even supplied the batteries for Apple's iPod. Cooperation among strategic business units had served Sony well in the past, leading to breakthrough innovations such as the Walkman, PlayStation, CD, and VAIO computer line. In digital music, however, the hardware and content divisions each seemed to have its own idea of what needed to be done. Cooperation among the

Sony divisions was also hindered by the fact that their centers of operations were spread across the globe: Music operations were located in New York City and electronics design was in Japan, inhibiting face-to-face communications and making real-time interactions more difficult.

Nobuyuki Idei, then CEO of Sony, learned the hard way that the music division managers were focused on the immediate needs of their recordings competing against the consumer-driven market forces. In 2002, Idei shared his frustrations with the cultural differences between the hardware and content divisions:

> The opposite of soft alliances is hard alliances, which include mergers and acquisitions. Since purchasing the Music and Pictures businesses, more than 10 years have passed, and we have experienced many cultural differences between hardware manufacturing and content businesses.... This experience has taught us that in certain areas where hard alliances would have taken 10 years to succeed, soft alliances can be created more easily. Another advantage of soft alliances is the ability to form partnerships with many different companies. We aim to provide an open and easy-to-access environment where anybody can participate, and we are willing to cooperate with companies that share our vision. Soft alliances offer many possibilities.[44]

In contrast, Apple organized a small, empowered, cross-functional team to produce the iPod in just a few months. Using open innovation, Apple successfully insourced many of its components from external partners (including from Sony and Samsung), and then integrated them. The phenomenal speed and success of the iPod and iTunes development and the seamless integration of hardware and software became a structural approach that Apple applied to its successful development and launches of other category-defining products such as the iPhone, iPad, and Apple Watch.

Apple's market capitalization grew from a paltry $7 billion in 2001 to over $1 trillion in 2018, making it the most valuable company globally (at the time) and the first company globally to cross this threshold. In contrast, in almost 20 years, Sony's market capitalization has barely moved, from $55 billion in 2001 to $65 billion in 2019. The different ways to organize and implement innovation had a great deal to do with this outcome.[45]

LO 11-7

Describe the elements of organizational culture, and explain where organizational cultures can come from and how they can be changed.

11.4 Organizational Culture: Values, Norms, and Artifacts

Organization design consists of formal and informal building blocks, as shown in Exhibit 11.14. The formal component is a firm's organizational structure (discussed in the previous sections), while the informal building block of organizational design is a firm's culture. Organizational culture is the second key building block when designing organizations for competitive advantage. Just as people have distinctive personalities, so too do organizations have unique cultures that capture "how things get done around here." Culture is an informal and thus an intangible building block of organizational design that unlike the formal structure cannot be easily observed or codified.

Organizational culture describes the collectively shared values and norms of an organization's members.[46] *Values* define what is considered important—goals that each organizational member should strive to achieve. As discussed in Chapter 2, an organization's core values are a set of guiding principles to guide employees in achieving an organization's vision and fulfill its mission. **Norms** define appropriate employee attitudes and behaviors in their day-to-day work and interactions.[47]

In a recent survey of almost 2,000 CEOs across the globe, the strategic leaders ranked culture as the most important value driver before operations, marketing, or finance.[48] One clear implication is that a strategic leader must get an organization's culture right. Effective cultures (such as Google's) are credited for being partly responsible for a firm's stellar performance, while ineffective cultures are blamed for corporate failures; consider, for example, Wells Fargo's account fraud scandal and VW's Dieselgate (a more detailed discussion of the latter is found in Strategy Highlight 12.2).

Wells Fargo has been at the center of a number of headline-grabbing scandals over the last few years, with its most recent involving the opening of 3.5 million fake bank accounts by Wells Fargo employees.[49] Other offenses included charging customers for car insurance they did not need or request and overcharging members of the U.S. armed forces when refinancing mortgages. How could this go on at one of the largest banks in the United States? The one common denominator across each of these ethical and legal infractions is Wells Fargo's organizational culture. Known to be hard-driving and demanding, employees faced strict sales quotas around new account openings, insurance sales, mortgage refinancing fees, and so forth. Employees' compensation and bonuses were also directly tied to these super ambitious sales targets. But the problem with these targets was not just that they were overly ambitious, but they also were unrealistic. What do people tend to do when the stakes are high and the pressure is intense? They cut corners. This is precisely what happened in the Wells Fargo case: A culture that valued achieving unrealistic goals took precedence over ethical and legal practice.[50] This slew of scandals has cost the bank dearly. Its stock market valuation fell by 25 percent in 2018, and two CEOs in a row subsequently lost their jobs. Additionally, each of the 5,300 employees involved in opening the fraudulent bank accounts was fired.

organizational culture The collectively shared values and norms of an organization's members; a key building block of organizational design.

Norms Unwritten rules that define appropriate employee attitudes and behaviors in employees' day-to-day work and interactions.

EXHIBIT 11.14   Formal and Informal Building Blocks of Organizational Design

Effective cultures allow for smooth execution of strategy, while ineffective cultures can lead to unintended, unethical, and sometimes even illegal outcomes. Interestingly, the researchers conducting the corporate culture survey also found that only 15 percent of the strategic leaders indicated they have an effective culture in their organization, while a bit more than half of strategic leaders indicated their organizational culture needed some work; about one-third said their cultures needed considerable work or a substantial overhaul. Setting the right values and norms, therefore, allows strategic leaders to create an effective culture, which can lay the foundation for competitive advantage.

Employees learn about an organization's culture through *socialization,* a process whereby employees internalize an organization's values and norms through immersion in its day-to-day operations.[51] Thus, it is critical that strategic leaders must not only set and refine the corporate cultures, but also live them in their day-to-day activities and thus lead by example. Strategic leaders should strive for buy-in of all employees across all levels. *Strong cultures* emerge when the company's core values are widely shared among the firm's employees and when the norms have been internalized. Corporate culture finds its expression in **artifacts**. Artifacts include elements such as the design and layout of physical space (e.g., cubicles or private offices), symbols (e.g., the type of clothing worn by employees), vocabulary, what stories are told, what events are celebrated and highlighted, and how they are celebrated (e.g., a formal dinner versus a casual barbecue when the firm reaches its sales target).

Exhibit 11.15 depicts the elements of organizational culture—values, norms, and artifacts—in concentric circles. The most important yet least visible element—values—is in the center. As we move outward in the figure, from values to norms to artifacts, culture becomes more observable. Understanding what organizational culture is, and how it is created, maintained, and changed, can help you be a more effective strategic leader.

artifacts Elements that allow corporate culture to be expressed, such as via the design and layout of physical space, symbols, vocabulary, what stories are told, what events are celebrated and highlighted, and how they are celebrated.

Google's Culture. From Google's earliest days in 1998, its quirky co-founders Larry Page and Sergey Brin instilled a set of strong core values, which laid the foundation of the online search company's unique culture. In particular, the co-founders created a tech company that is in many respects strikingly similar to their own personalities. Both Page and Brin suggest that their worldview is shaped by early experiences in Montessori schools as well as their engineering training, especially in computer science.

Page and Brin came up with 10 principles they "know to be true," including some of the best-known Google core values today such as *don't be evil, focus on the user first, and profits will follow, you can be serious without a suit,* and *great is just not good enough.*[52] Exhibit 11.16 lists Google's 10 core values.

Eric Schmidt, Google's long-time CEO during its early years (2001–2011), explained how surprised he was that strategic leaders as well as rank-and-file employees believed strongly in their company's core values and made day-to-day decisions based on them. For example, when asked how the core value of not doing evil helped Google, Schmidt recalled:

> When I showed up, I said, "You've got to be kidding." Then one day, very early on, I was in a meeting where an engineer said, "That would be evil." It was as if he'd said there was a murderer in the room. The whole conversation stopped, but then people

**EXHIBIT 11.15** The Elements of Organizational Culture: Values, Norms, and Artifacts

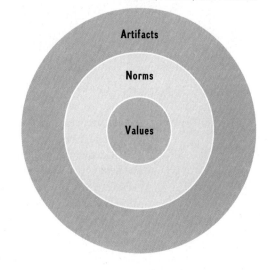

EXHIBIT 11.16 Google's 10 Things the Founders Know to Be True

1. Focus on the user and all else will follow.

2. It's best to do one thing really, really well.

3. Fast is better than slow.

4. Democracy on the web works.

5. You don't need to be at your desk to need an answer.

6. You can make money without doing evil.

7. There's always more information out there.

8. The need for information crosses all borders.

9. You can be serious without a suit.

10. Great just isn't good enough.

Source: Excerpted from "Ten things we know to be true," www.google.com/about/philosophy.html.

In the wake of the #MeToo Movement, Google employees also staged a global walkout over the company's handling of sexual harassment. In particular, the Google employees protested a workplace culture that they allege promotes and protects perpetrators of sexual harassment at the tech giant.

Mason Trinca/Getty Images

challenged his assumptions. This had to do with how we would link our advertising system into search. We ultimately decided not to do what was proposed, because it was evil. That kind of story is repeated every hour now with thousands of people. Think of "Don't be evil" as an organizing principle about values.[53]

Some decisions based on the "Don't be evil" credo concern minor decisions such as not accepting ads for hard liquor or guns. Other decisions are far more wide reaching with significant strategic implications. For instance, in 2006, Google entered the Chinese market with a customized search engine (google.cn) to service the then 400 million online customers.[54] This was a self-censored version of its regular search engine (google.com) to comply with China's restrictions on free speech. At that time, Google felt the good that access to its searches, albeit censored, would bring to the Chinese people would outweigh its discomfort with censorship.

But by 2010, Google felt it could no longer continue to provide self-censored searches; it alleged that the firm was the target of sophisticated hacker attacks, accessing some of its users' Gmail accounts, including those of Chinese human rights activists. Google decided it would no longer censor its searches in China, and thus risked having its search engine shut down by the Chinese government. Google's strong values—such as "Democracy on the web works," "You can make money without doing evil," and "The need for information crosses all borders"—guided this decision, which had potentially far-reaching strategic consequences. From 2010 onward, Google ran its China website on a server in Hong Kong (www.google.com.hk).

Yet, Google's exit from mainland China further strengthened Baidu's lead, a domestic Chinese company that had 70 percent market share in 2019. Today, China has more than 800 million internet users, by far the largest online market globally and the fastest growing. In comparison, the United States has 290 million internet users, which makes the Chinese market almost three times the size of the U.S. market.

The size and growth of the Chinese market appeared too alluring for Google's strategic leaders to ignore. In 2018, it was revealed that a team was secretly working on a search project for China, code named Dragonfly, that would adhere to the Chinese government's censoring requirements.[55] Upset Google employees wrote an open protest letter and staged a walkout brandishing signs saying, "Don't be evil" and "OK Google, Don't contribute to Internet censorship in China," while demanding that the clandestine project be shut down. In 2018, during a congressional hearing, Google CEO Sundar Pichai stated the company has no intention of launching a search engine in China at this point.

This example shows how difficult it is to balance deeply held core values with business opportunities, especially since some of Google's strategic leaders argue that providing search services in China—albeit censored—might do more good than harm, while many employees feel otherwise.

WHERE DO ORGANIZATIONAL CULTURES COME FROM?

Often, company founders define and shape an organization's culture, which can persist for many decades after their departure. This phenomenon is called **founder imprinting**.[56] Founders set the initial strategy, structure, and culture of an organization by transforming their vision into reality. We have already seen how the beliefs of Google founders Page and Brin shaped the culture of the internet company. Other famous founders that have left strong imprints on their organizations include Steve Jobs (Apple), Walt Disney (Disney), Michael Dell (Dell), Oprah Winfrey (Harpo Productions and *OWN,* the Oprah Winfrey Network), Martha Stewart (Martha Stewart Living Omnimedia), Bill Gates (Microsoft), Larry Ellison (Oracle), Ralph Lauren (Polo Ralph Lauren), Herb Kelleher (Southwest Airlines), and Elon Musk (Tesla and SpaceX).

> **founder imprinting** A process by which the founder defines and shapes an organization's culture, which can persist for decades after his or her departure.

Walmart founder Sam Walton personified the retailer's cost-leadership strategy. At one time the richest man in America, Sam Walton drove a beat-up Ford pickup truck, got $5 haircuts, went camping for vacations, and lived in a modest ranch home in Bentonville, Arkansas.[57] Everything Walton did was consistent with the low-cost strategy. Walmart stays true to its founder's tradition. Home to one of the largest companies globally, the company's Arkansas headquarters in Bentonville was described by Thomas Friedman in his book *The World Is Flat* as "crammed into a reconfigured warehouse...a large building made of corrugated metal, I figured it was the maintenance shed."[58]

The culture that founders initially imprint is reinforced by their strong preference to recruit, retain, and promote employees who subscribe to the same values. In turn, more people with similar values are attracted to that organization.[59] As the values and norms held by the employees become more similar, the firm's corporate culture becomes stronger and more distinct. This in turn can have a serious negative side-effect: *groupthink,* a situation in which opinions coalesce around a leader without individuals critically evaluating and challenging that leader's opinions and assumptions. Cohesive, non-diverse groups are highly susceptible to groupthink, which in turn can lead to flawed decision making with potentially disastrous consequences.

In addition to founder imprinting, a firm's culture also flows from its values, especially when they are linked to the company's reward system. For example, Zappos (featured in Strategy Highlight 11.1) established its unique organizational culture through explicitly stated values that are connected to its reward system. To recruit people that fit with the company's values, Hsieh has all new hires go through a four-week training program. It covers such topics as company history, culture, and vision, as well as customer service.[60] New hires also spend two weeks on the phone as customer service reps. What's novel about Zappos' approach is that at the end of the monthlong employee orientation, the company offers an "exit prize": one month's pay plus pay for the time already with Zappos. This allows the company to entice people to leave that are qualified for the job but may not fit with Zappos' culture. Individuals who choose to stay despite the enticing offer tend to fit well with and strengthen Zappos' distinct culture.[61]

HOW DOES ORGANIZATIONAL CULTURE CHANGE?

An organization's culture can be one of its strongest assets, but also its greatest liability. An organization's culture can turn from a core competency into a *core rigidity* if a firm relies too long on the competency without honing, refining, and upgrading as the firm and the environment change.[62] (See the discussion in Chapter 4.) Over time, the original core competency is no longer a good fit and turns from an asset into a liability. This is the time when a culture needs to change.

Mary Barra, General Motors CEO, was appointed with the mandate to fix GM's dysfunctional corporate culture and to make the company competitive again.

Bill Pugliano/Getty Images

GM's bureaucratic culture, combined with its innovative M-form structure, was once hailed as the key to superior efficiency and management.[63] However, that culture became a liability when the external environment changed following the oil-price shocks in the 1970s and the entry of Japanese carmakers into the United States.[64] As a consequence, GM's strong culture led to organizational inertia. This resulted in a failure to adapt to changing customer preferences for more fuel-efficient cars, and it prevented higher quality and more innovative designs. GM lost customers to foreign competitors that offered these features.

More recently, GM's strong culture was again faulted for corporate ineptitude when delaying recalling defective cars.[65] Over 25 million GM cars were recalled for safety defects in 2014, the largest recall ever. In particular, many GM cars were eventually recalled because of a faulty ignition switch, which could turn off the engine while driving and thus disable the airbags. This problem has been linked to more than 120 fatalities in the United States alone.[66] GM is alleged to knowingly have withheld information about the faulty ignition switches and delayed the needed recalls by several years. Indeed, during a U.S. Senate hearing, GM was described as dominated by a "culture of cover-up."[67] In such times of crisis, corporate culture must be changed to avoid such problems in the future and to address a breakdown in the culture-environment fit.

The primary means of cultural change is for the corporate board of directors to bring in new leadership at the top, which is then charged to make changes in strategy and structure. After all, executives shape corporate culture in their decisions on how to structure the organization and its activities, allocate its resources, and develop its system of rewards (see the discussion on strategic leadership in Chapter 2). In 2014, GM's board of directors appointed Mary Barra as CEO with the charge to fix GM's dysfunctional corporate culture and to make the company competitive again.

Similarly, when Marissa Mayer was appointed CEO of Yahoo (in 2012), one of the first things she did was to change the corporate culture and norms. Yahoo had become overly bureaucratic and lost the zeal characteristic of high-tech startups. Many Yahoo employees worked from home. For those who worked in the office, weekends began Thursday afternoons, leaving empty parking garages at Yahoo's campus in Sunnyvale, California. In response, Mayer withdrew the option to work remotely. All of Yahoo's 12,000 employees would have to come to the office. She also instituted weekly town-hall meetings (called FYI) where she and other executives provided updates and fielded questions. All employees were expected to attend and encouraged to participate in the Q&A. Questions were submitted online during the week, and the employees voted which questions executives should respond to. Although Mayer succeeded in reenergizing the once leading internet firm, in the end, a successful turnaround failed and Yahoo was acquired by Verizon for a fire sale price.

ORGANIZATIONAL CULTURE AND COMPETITIVE ADVANTAGE

Can organizational culture be the basis of a firm's competitive advantage? For this to occur, the firm's unique culture must help it in some way to increase its *economic value creation* (*V–C*). That is, it must either help in increasing the perceived value of the product/service and/or lower its cost of production/delivery. Moreover, according to the resource-based view of the firm, the resource—in this case, organizational culture—must be *valuable, rare, difficult to imitate,* and the firm must be *organized* to capture the value created. The VRIO principles (see Chapter 4) must apply even as to organizational culture itself.[68]

Let's look at one well-known example of how culture affects employee behavior and ultimately firm performance. If you have flown with Southwest Airlines (SWA), you may have noticed that things are done a little differently there. Flight attendants might sing a song about the city you're landing in, or they might slide bags of peanuts down the aisle at take-off. Employees celebrate Halloween in a big way by wearing costumes to work. Some argue that SWA's business strategy—being a cost leader in point-to-point air travel—is fairly simple, and that SWA's competitive advantage actually comes from its unique culture.[69] It's not all fun and games, though: Friendly and highly energized employees work across functional and hierarchical levels. Even Southwest's pilots pitch in to help load baggage quickly when needed. As a result, SWA's turn time between flights is only 15 minutes, whereas competitors frequently take two to three times as long. Taken together, SWA's unique culture helps it keep costs low by turning around its planes faster, thus keeping them flying longer hours (among many other activities that lower SWA's cost structure).[70]

Let's consider how an organization's culture can have a strong influence on employee behavior.[71] A positive culture motivates and energizes employees by appealing to their higher ideals. Internalizing the firm's values and norms, employees feel that they are part of a larger, meaningful community attempting to accomplish important things. When employees are intrinsically motivated this way, the firm can rely on fewer levels of hierarchy; thus, close monitoring and supervision are not needed as much. Motivating through inspiring values allows the firms to tap employees' emotions so they use both their heads and their hearts when making business decisions. Strong organizational cultures that are strategically relevant, therefore, align employees' behaviors more fully with the organization's strategic goals. In doing so, they better coordinate work efforts, and they make cooperation more effective. They also strengthen employee commitment, engagement, and effort. Effective alignment in turn allows the organization to develop and refine its core competencies, which can form the basis for competitive advantage.

Applying the VRIO principles to the SWA example, we see that both cultures are *valuable* (lowering costs for SWA), *rare* (none of their competitors has an identical culture), *non-imitable* (despite attempts by competitors), and *organized* to capture some part of the incremental economic value created due to their unique cultures. It appears that at SWA, a unique organizational culture can provide the basis for a competitive advantage. These cultures, of course, need to be in sync with and in support of the respective business strategies pursued: cost leadership in the case for SWA. Moreover, as the firms grow and external economic environments change, these organizational cultures must be flexible enough to adapt.

Once it becomes clear that a firm's culture is a source of competitive advantage, some competitors will attempt to imitate that culture. Therefore, only a culture that cannot be easily copied can provide a competitive advantage. It can be difficult, at best, to imitate the cultures of successful firms, for two reasons: *causal ambiguity* and *social complexity.* While one can observe that a firm has a unique culture, the causal relationships among values, norms, artifacts, and the firm's performance may be hard to establish, even for people who work within the organization. For example, employees may become aware of the effect culture has on performance only after significant organizational changes occur. Moreover, organizational culture is socially complex. It encompasses not only interactions among employees across layers of hierarchy, but also the firm's outside relationships with its customers and suppliers.[72] Such a wide range of factors is difficult for any competing firm to imitate.

It is best to develop a strong and strategically relevant culture in the first few years of a firm's existence. This is precisely what the Google co-founders did. Strategy scholars have documented that the initial structure, culture, and control mechanisms established in a new firm can be a significant predictor of later success.[73] In other empirical research, founder CEOs had a stronger positive imprinting effect than non-founder CEOs.[74] This stronger imprinting effect, in turn, resulted in higher performance of firms led by founder CEOs. In addition, consider that the vehicles of cultural change—changing leadership and M&As—do not have a stellar record of success.[75] Indeed, researchers estimate that only about 20 percent of organizational change attempts are successful.[76] Thus, it is even more important to get the culture right from the beginning and then adapt it as the business evolves.

By combining theory and empirical evidence, we can see that organizational culture can help a firm gain and sustain competitive advantage *if* the culture makes a positive contribution to the firm's economic value creation and obeys the VRIO principles. Organizational culture is an especially effective lever for new ventures due to its malleability. Firm founders, early-stage CEOs, and venture capitalists, therefore, should be proactive in attempting to create a culture that supports a firm's economic value creation.

11.5 Strategic Control-and-Reward Systems

LO 11-8

Compare and contrast different strategic control-and-reward systems.

strategic control-and-reward systems
Internal-governance mechanisms put in place to align the incentives of principals (shareholders) and agents (employees).

Strategic control-and-reward systems are the third and final key building block when designing organizations for competitive advantage. **Strategic control-and-reward systems** are internal governance mechanisms put in place to align the incentives of principals (shareholders) and agents (employees). These formal systems allow managers to specify goals, measure progress, and provide performance feedback. Chapter 5 discussed how firms can use the balanced-scorecard framework as a strategic control system. Here, we discuss additional control-and-reward systems: organizational culture, input controls, and output controls.

As discussed in the preceding section, *organizational culture* can be a powerful motivator. It also can be an effective control system. Norms, informal and tacit in nature, act as a social control mechanism. Peer control, for example, exerts a powerful force on employee conformity and performance.[77] Values and norms also provide control by helping employees address unpredictable and irregular situations and problems (common in service businesses). In contrast, rules and procedures (e.g., codified in an employee handbook) can address only circumstances that can be predicted.

Google relies on data analysis and the latest findings in behavioral economics and psychology research to motivate its employees and to achieve high productivity.[78] The tech industry in general is plagued by problems of employee attrition, turnover, and confidentiality breaches. In addition, highly capable individuals such as star programmers are in short supply and thus have strong bargaining power. Where Google differs from other employers is in its generous on-the-job perks, which include everything from free gourmet food, beverages, and coffee to onsite child care, car detail services, and educational opportunities. Google also provides relaxation opportunities such as complimentary massages and naps using nap pods. Employees are also invited to play table tennis or foosball. In 2019, Google had 103,000 employees and revenues of $142 billion. This implies that each employee on average generates $1.3 million in revenues, justifying the pricey on-the-job perks.

Objectives and Key Results (OKRs) A strategic reward and control system that helps a team and its individual members monitor objectives and outcomes, as well as set ambitious stretch goals.

Less well-known is Google's fine-tuned compensation and reward systems based on pay for performance. Google uses the **Objectives and Key Results (OKRs)** framework as one of its strategic control-and-reward systems; in addition to helping a team and its individual members monitor objectives and outcomes, the OKR framework helps them to set ambitious stretch goals; for example, increase users by 25 percent. The more objective the goal the more easily it can be measured. Google also makes the individual and team OKRs public—doing this puts a degree of peer pressure on those team members who are not carrying their weight. The more public their individual progress, the more likely they will work toward helping their teams achieve their OKRs.

INPUT CONTROLS

Input controls seek to define and direct employee behavior through a set of explicit, codified rules and standard operating procedures. Firms use input controls when the goal is to define the ways and means to reach a strategic goal and to ensure a predictable outcome. They are called input controls because management designs these mechanisms so they are considered *before* employees make any business decisions; thus, they are an input into the value-creating activities.

The use of *budgets* is key to input controls. Managers set budgets before employees define and undertake the actual business activities. For example, strategic leaders decide how much money to allocate to a certain R&D project before the project begins. In diversified companies using the M-form, corporate headquarters determines the budgets for each division. Public institutions, like some universities, also operate on budgets that must be balanced each year. Their funding often depends to a large extent on state appropriations and thus fluctuates depending on the economic cycle. During recessions, budgets tend to be cut, and they expand during boom periods.

Standard operating procedures, or policies and rules, are also a frequently used mechanism when relying on input controls. The discussion on formalization described how McDonald's relies on detailed operating procedures to ensure consistent quality and service worldwide. The goal is to specify the conversion process from beginning to end in great detail to guarantee standardization and minimize deviation. This is important when a company operates in different geographies and with different human capital throughout the globe but needs to deliver a standardized product or service.

> **input controls** Mechanisms in a strategic control-and-reward system that seek to define and direct employee behavior through a set of explicit, codified rules and standard operating procedures that are considered before the value-creating activities.

OUTPUT CONTROLS

Output controls seek to guide employee behavior by defining expected results (outputs), but leave the means to those results open to individual employees, groups, or SBUs. Firms frequently tie employee compensation and rewards to predetermined goals, such as a specific sales target or return on invested capital. When factors internal to the firm determine the relationship between effort and expected performance, outcome controls are especially effective. At the corporate level, outcome controls discourage collaboration among different strategic business units. They are best applied when a firm focuses on a single line of business or pursues unrelated diversification.

These days, more and more work requires creativity and innovation, especially in highly developed economies.[79] As a consequence, so-called *results-only-work-environments (ROWEs)* have attracted significant attention. ROWEs are output controls that attempt to tap intrinsic (rather than extrinsic) employee motivation, which is driven by the employee's interest in and the meaning of the work itself. In contrast, extrinsic motivation is driven by external factors such as awards and higher compensation, or punishments like demotions and layoffs (the *carrot-and-stick approach*). According to a recent synthesis of the strategic human resources literature, intrinsic motivation in a task is highest when an employee has

> **output controls** Mechanisms in a strategic control-and-reward system that seek to guide employee behavior by defining expected results (outputs), but leave the means to those results open to individual employees, groups, or SBUs.

- Autonomy *(about what to do).*
- Mastery *(how to do it).*
- Purpose *(why to do it).*[80]

Today, 3M is best known for its adhesives and other consumer and industrial products.[81] But its full name reflects its origins: 3M stands for Minnesota Mining and Manufacturing Co. Over time, 3M has relied on the ROWE framework and has morphed into a highly science-driven innovation company. At 3M, employees are encouraged to spend 15 percent of their time on projects of their *own choosing.* If any of these projects look promising, 3M provides financing through an internal venture capital fund and other resources to further develop their commercial potential. In fact, several of 3M's flagship products, including Post-it Notes and Scotch Tape, were the results of serendipity. To foster continued innovation, moreover, 3M requires each of its divisions to derive at least 30 percent of their revenues from products introduced in the past four years.

11.6 Implications for Strategic Leaders

This chapter has a clear practical implication for the strategist: Formulating an effective strategy is a necessary but not sufficient condition for gaining and sustaining competitive advantage; strategy *execution* is at least as important for success.

The key levers for strategic leaders to achieve effective strategy implementation are structure, culture, and control. Successful strategy implementation, therefore, requires leaders to design and shape structure, culture, and control mechanisms. In doing so, they execute a firm's strategy as they put its accompanying business model into action. Strategy formulation and strategy implementation, therefore, are iterative and interdependent activities.

Some argue that strategy implementation is more important than strategy formulation.[82] Often, managers do a good job of analyzing the firm's internal and external environments to formulate a promising business, corporate, and global strategy, but then fail to implement the chosen strategy successfully. That is why some scholars refer to implementation as the "graveyard of strategy."[83] In reality, both strategy formulation *and* strategy implementation are necessary to gain and sustain a competitive advantage.

As a company grows and its operations become more complex, it adopts different organizational structures over time following a generally predictable pattern: beginning with a simple structure, then a functional structure, and followed by a multidivisional or matrix structure. Organizing for competitive advantage, therefore, is a dynamic and not a static process. As seen in the Google example discussed in ChapterCase 11 and throughout the chapter, to maintain competitive advantage, companies need to restructure as they grow and the competitive environment changes.

Organizing for innovation is another area that strategic leaders need to pay careful attention to. Many of the more successful companies have either adopted or are moving toward an open innovation model. Strategic leaders must actively manage a firm's internal and external innovation activities. Internally, one can *induce innovation* through a top-down process or motivate innovation through *autonomous actions,* a bottom-up process.[84] In induced innovation, strategic leaders need to put a structure and system in place to foster innovation. Consider 3M: "A core belief of 3M is that creativity needs freedom. That's why...we've encouraged our employees to spend 15 percent of their working time on their own projects. To take our resources, to build up a unique team, and to follow their own insights in pursuit of problem-solving."[85] We discussed *autonomous actions* in detail in Chapter 2. To not only motivate innovations through autonomous behavior, but also ensure their possible success, *internal champions* need to be willing to support promising projects. In Strategy Highlight 2.2 , we detailed how Howard Behar, at that time a senior executive at Starbucks, was willing to support the bottom-up idea of Frappuccino, which turned out to be a multibillion-dollar business. Externally, strategic leaders must manage innovation through cooperative strategies such as licensing, strategic alliances, joint ventures, and acquisitions. These are the vehicles of *corporate strategy* discussed previously.

This concludes our discussion of organizational design. We now move on to our concluding chapter, where we study corporate governance and business ethics.

Pawel Kopczynski/Reuters

AS OF 2019, Alphabet remains a one-trick pony, with Google's online search and advertising business bringing in basically all the profits (99 percent). Yet, competition in the online advertising space is heating up because Facebook has become a viable alternative to Google, and it's growing fast. In addition, Amazon—a newcomer to the digital ad space—is making strong inroads. Alphabet's profit sanctuary may be under threat. With its new organizational structure, Alphabet CEO Larry Page hopes for more radical innovation that will turn into highly profitable businesses like Google.

Before its reorganization from a functional to M-form structure, implemented to manage a set of unrelated businesses, Google had developed many of its most well-known products and services through planned emergence, wherein the impetus for strategic initiatives emerges from the bottom up through autonomous actions by lower-level employees. Google organized the work of its engineers according to a 70-20-10 rule. The majority of the engineers' time (70 percent) focused on its main business—search and ads. One day a week (20 percent) was spent developing ideas of their own choosing, and the remainder (10 percent) on total wild cards such as Project Loon, an envisioned network of high-altitude balloons that travel on the edge of space to provide wireless internet services to the two-thirds of the world's population that do not yet have internet access—primarily those in rural and remote areas. (Loon is now a standalone unit in the new Alphabet structure.) Google has reported that half of its new products came from the 20 percent rule, including Gmail, Google Maps, Google News, Orkut, and AdSense. AdSense started as an experiment by two Google engineers: They attempted to match Gmail content with targeted ads based on that content. Today, AdSense enables creators of content sites in its network, such as Google bloggers, to serve online ads that are targeted to the site's content.

Although Google has a stellar track record for strategy process as planned emergence, it has fumbled its social networking endeavors multiple times. These missteps left the space open to Facebook, now Google's fiercest competitor in the digital ad space. Google's first attempt in social networking goes back to 2002, two years (eons in internet time) before Facebook was founded. Google engineer Orkut Buyukkokten had developed a social network, called Orkut, using his 20 percent discretionary time. Marissa Mayer, then Google's vice president in charge of the project, liked what she saw and provided initial support. More engineers were eventually added to further Orkut's development. Google was astonished at Orkut's early success: Within the first month after its release, hundreds of thousands of people signed up. By 2014, Orkut had 30 million users mostly in Brazil and India. But this paled in comparison to Facebook's more than 1 billion users worldwide at the time.

Why did Google fumble its lead over Facebook? Google had a huge opportunity to become the leader in social networking because Myspace imploded after it was acquired by News Corp. Despite initial support, Google's top executives felt that social networking did not fit its vision *to organize the world's information and make it universally accessible and useful.* Google relied on highly complex and proprietary algorithms to organize the knowledge available on the internet and serve up targeted search ads. Social networking software, in comparison, is fairly pedestrian. Additionally, Page and Brin, both exceptional computer scientists, looked down on social networking. They felt their Page-Rank algorithm that accounts for hundreds of variables and considers all available websites was far superior in providing *objective* recommendations to users' search queries than *subjective* endorsements by someone's online friends. As a consequence, they snubbed social networking. Moreover, given the many different projects Google was pursuing at that time, Orkut was ranked as a low priority by Google's top executives. Starved of further resources, the social networking site withered and was eventually shut down in 2014, making Facebook the undisputed leader.

In yet another effort to catch up with Facebook, Google launched Google Plus in 2011. This social networking site integrated all of Google's services— Gmail, YouTube, Chrome, and others—into one user interface. It required users to sign into its portal, even if they were using just one Google product. After a data breach, Google Plus was shut down unceremoniously in 2019. Meanwhile, Facebook has over 2 billion active users on its platform—and Google is unable to access any of the information tied to these users. Not being able to access Facebook users' activities limits Google's ability to serve targeted ads, which, in turn, cuts directly into its main line of business.[86]

Questions

1. Why did Google restructure itself and create Alphabet? What is it hoping to accomplish? For additional insights, see Larry Page's post announcing the restructuring at https://abc.xyz/.

2. Do you think the reorganization is beneficial for Alphabet's moon shots, now housed in their own business unit with profit-and-loss responsibility? Why, or why not? Explain.

3. Why has Google "failed" to develop other profitable businesses? Is Google's strategy process of planned emergence to blame? Why or why not? Will Alphabet's new structure with independent SBUs enable the company to innovate more and to find the next highly profitable business beyond online search and advertising?

mySTRATEGY

For What Type of Organization Are You Best Suited?

As noted in the chapter, firms can have very distinctive cultures. Recall that Zappos has a standing offer to pay any new hire one month's salary to quit the company after orientation. Zappos makes this offer to help ensure that those who stay with the company are comfortable in its "create fun and a little weirdness" environment. (Parts of this "pay to leave" idea were also picked up by owner Amazon more recently.)

You may have taken a personality test such as Myers-Briggs or the Big Five. These tests may be useful in gauging compatibility of career and personality types. They are often available for both graduate and undergraduate students at university career placement centers. In considering the following questions, think about your next job and your longer-term career plans.

1. Review Exhibit 11.11 and circle the organizational characteristics you find appealing. Cross out those factors you think you would not like.

2. Have you been in school or work situations in which your values did not align with those of your peers or colleagues? How did you handle the situation? Are there certain values or norms important enough for you to consider as you look for a new job?

3. As you consider your career after graduation, which control-and-reward system would you find most motivating? Is this different from the controls used at some jobs you have had in the past? How do you think you would perform in a holacracy such as Zappos?

TAKE-AWAY CONCEPTS

This chapter explored the three key levers that managers have at their disposal when designing their firms for competitive advantage—structure, culture, and control—as summarized by the following learning objectives and related take-away concepts.

LO 11-1 / Define organizational design and list its three components.

- Organizational design is the process of creating, implementing, monitoring, and modifying the structure, processes, and procedures of an organization.

- The key components of organizational design are structure, culture, and control.

- The goal is to design an organization that allows managers to effectively translate their chosen strategy into a realized one.

LO 11-2 / Explain how organizational inertia can lead established firms to failure.

- Organizational inertia can lead to the failure of established firms when a tightly coupled system of strategy and structure experiences internal or external shifts.

- Firm failure happens through a dynamic, four-step process (see Exhibit 11.2).

LO 11-3 / Define organizational structure and describe its four elements.

- An organizational structure determines how firms orchestrate employees' work efforts and distribute resources. It defines how firms divide and integrate tasks, delineates the reporting relationships up and down the hierarchy, defines formal communication channels, and prescribes how employees coordinate work efforts.

- The four building blocks of an organizational structure are specialization, formalization, centralization, and hierarchy (see Exhibit 11.3).

LO 11-4 / Compare and contrast mechanistic versus organic organizations.

- Organic organizations are characterized by a low degree of specialization and formalization, a flat organizational structure, and decentralized decision making.

- Mechanistic organizations are described by a high degree of specialization and formalization, and a tall hierarchy that relies on centralized decision making.

- The comparative effectiveness of mechanistic versus organic organizational forms depends on the context.

LO 11-5 / Describe different organizational structures and match them with appropriate strategies.

- To gain and sustain competitive advantage, not only must structure follow strategy, but also the chosen organizational form must match the firm's business strategy.

- The strategy–structure relationship is dynamic, changing in a predictable pattern—from simple to functional structure, then to multidivisional (M-form) and matrix structure—as firms grow in size and complexity.

- In a simple structure, the founder tends to make all the important strategic decisions as well as run the day-to-day operations.

- A functional structure groups employees into distinct functional areas based on domain expertise. Its different variations are matched with different business strategies: cost leadership, differentiation, and blue ocean (see Exhibit 11.6).

- The multidivisional (M-form) structure consists of several distinct SBUs, each with its own profit-and-loss responsibility. Each SBU operates more or less independently from one another, led by a CEO responsible for the business strategy of the unit and its day-to-day operations (see Exhibit 11.7).

- The matrix structure is a mixture of two organizational forms: the M-form and the functional structure (see Exhibit 11.9).

- Exhibits 11.8 and 11.10 show how best to match different corporate and global strategies with respective organizational structures.

LO 11-6 / Evaluate closed and open innovation, and derive implications for organizational structure.

- Closed innovation is a framework for R&D that proposes impenetrable firm boundaries. Key to

success in the closed innovation model is that the firm discovers, develops, and commercializes new products internally.

- Open innovation is a framework for R&D that proposes permeable firm boundaries to allow a firm to benefit not only from internal ideas and inventions, but also from external ones. The sharing goes both ways: Some external ideas and inventions are insourced while others are spun off.

- Exhibit 11.12 compares and contrasts principles of closed and open innovation.

LO 11-7 / Describe the elements of organizational culture, and explain where organizational cultures can come from and how they can be changed.

- Organizational culture describes the collectively shared values and norms of its members.

- Values define what is considered important, and norms define appropriate employee attitudes and behaviors.

- Corporate culture finds its expression in artifacts, which are observable expressions of an organization's culture.

LO 11-8 / Compare and contrast different strategic control-and-reward systems.

- Strategic control-and-reward systems are internal governance mechanisms put in place to align the incentives of principals (shareholders) and agents (employees).

- Strategic control-and-reward systems allow managers to specify goals, measure progress, and provide performance feedback.

- In addition to the balanced-scorecard framework, managers can use organizational culture, input controls, and output controls as part of the firm's strategic control-and-reward systems.

- Input controls define and direct employee behavior through explicit and codified rules and standard operating procedures.

- Output controls guide employee behavior by defining expected results, but leave the means to those results open to individual employees, groups, or SBUs.

KEY TERMS

Absorptive capacity *(p. 413)*

Ambidexterity *(p. 403)*

Ambidextrous organization *(p. 403)*

Artifacts *(p. 417)*

Centralization *(p. 398)*

Exploitation *(p. 403)*

Exploration *(p. 403)*

Formalization *(p. 397)*

Founder imprinting *(p. 419)*

Functional structure *(p. 401)*

Hierarchy *(p. 398)*

Holacracy *(p. 408)*

Inertia *(p. 395)*

Input controls *(p. 423)*

Matrix structure *(p. 408)*

Mechanistic organization *(p. 398)*

Multidivisional structure (M-form) *(p. 404)*

Norms *(p. 416)*

Objectives and Key Results (OKRs) *(p. 422)*

Open innovation *(p. 412)*

Organic organization *(p. 399)*

Organizational culture *(p. 416)*

Organizational design *(p. 393)*

Organizational structure *(p. 397)*

Output controls *(p. 423)*

Simple structure *(p. 401)*

Span of control *(p. 398)*

Specialization *(p. 397)*

Strategic control-and-reward systems *(p. 422)*

DISCUSSION QUESTIONS

1. Why is it important for an organization to have alignment between its strategy and structure?

2. The chapter describes the role of culture in the successful implementation of strategy. Consider an employment experience of your own or of someone you have observed closely (e.g., a family member). Describe to the best of your ability the values, norms, and artifacts of the organization. What was the socialization process of embedding the culture? Do you consider this to be an example of an effective culture for contributing to the organization's competitive advantage? Why or why not?

3. What makes some strong cultures helpful in gaining and sustaining a competitive advantage, while other strong cultures are a liability to achieving that goal?

ENDNOTES

1. Founders IPO Letter (2004), https://abc.xyz/investor/founders-letters/2004-ipo-letter/.

2. Larry Page Letter (2015) to investors announcing the creation of Alphabet, https://abc.xyz/.

3. This ChapterCase is based on: Alphabet Inc. annual reports (various years); Copeland, R. (2019, Apr. 29), "Alphabet investors search for clues inside tech giant," *The Wall Street Journal*; Vranica, S. (2019, Apr. 4), "Amazon's rise in ad searches dents Google's dominance," *The Wall Street Journal*; Gallagher, D. (2019, Feb. 5), "Google runs up another big tab," *The Wall Street Journal*; Copeland, R. (2019, Feb. 4), "Google parent shows cost of branching out," *The Wall Street Journal*; "The social network shuts down in disgrace," *The Economist*, October 13, 2018; "Harder than ABC. Alphabet's Google is searching for its next hit," *The Economist* (2016, Dec. 15); "What's in a name? The internet giant has announced a new corporate structure," *The Economist* (2015, Aug. 11); "Spelling it out. The internet giant's new corporate structure will provide more clarity for investors," *The Economist* (2015, Apr. 15); Carlson, N. (2015), *Marissa Mayer and the Fight to Save Yahoo!* (New York: Hachette Book Group); Edwards, D. (2012), *I'm Feeling Lucky: The Confessions of Google Employee Number 59* (New York: Houghton Mifflin Harcourt); and Levy, S. (2011), *In the Plex: How Google Thinks, Works, and Shapes Our Lives* (New York: Simon & Schuster).

4. Barney, J.B. (1986), "Organizational culture: Can it be a source of sustained competitive advantage?" *Academy of Management Review* 11: 656–665.

5. Bossidy, L., R. Charan, and C. Burck (2002), *Execution: The Discipline of Getting Things Done;* and Herold, D.M., and D.B. Fedor (2008), *Change the Way You Lead Change: Leadership Strategies That Really Work* (Palo Alto, CA: Stanford University Press).

6. "Yang's exit doesn't fix Yahoo," *The Wall Street Journal* (2008, Nov. 19).

7. Seetharaman, D., and R. McMillan (2017, Mar. 1), "Yahoo CEO Marissa Mayer takes pay cut over security breach," *The Wall Street Journal*.

8. Krouse, S., and M. Maidenberg (2018, Dec. 12), "Verizon takes $4.5 billion charge related to digital media business," *The Wall Street Journal*.

9. Herold, D.M., and D.B. Fedor (2008), *Change the Way You Lead Change: Leadership Strategies That Really Work* (Palo Alto, CA: Stanford University Press).

10. Chandler, A.D. (1962), *Strategy and Structure: Chapters in the History of American Industrial Enterprise* (Cambridge, MA: MIT Press), 14.

11. Hall, D.J., and M.A. Saias (1980), "Strategy follows structure!" *Strategic Management Journal* 1: 149–163.

12. Hill, C.W.L., and F.T. Rothaermel (2003), "The performance of incumbent firms in the face of radical technological innovation," *Academy of Management Review* 28: 257–274.

13. I gratefully acknowledge Professor Luis Martins' input on this exhibit.

14. In his insightful book, Finkelstein identifies several key transition points that put pressure on an organization and thus increase the likelihood of subsequent failure. See: Finkelstein, S. (2003), *Why Smart Executives Fail: And What You Can Learn from Their Mistakes* (New York: Portfolio).

15. Fredrickson, J.W. (1986), "The strategic decision process and organizational structure," *Academy of Management Review* 11: 280–297; Eisenhardt, K.M. (1989), "Making fast strategic decisions in high-velocity environments," *Academy of Management Journal* 32: 543–576; and Wally, S., and R.J. Baum (1994), "Strategic decision speed and firm performance," *Strategic Management Journal* 24: 1107–1129.

16. *The 9/11 Report. The National Commission on Terrorist Attacks upon the United States* (2004), http://govinfo.library.unt.edu/911/report/index.htm.

17. Child, J., and R.G. McGrath (2001), "Organization unfettered: Organizational forms in the information-intensive economy," *Academy of Management Journal* 44: 1135–1148; and Huy, Q.N. (2002), "Emotional balancing of organizational continuity and radical change: The contribution of middle managers," *Administrative Science Quarterly* 47: 31–69.

18. Theobald, N.A., and S. Nicholson-Crotty (2005), "The many faces of span of control: Organizational structure across multiple goals," *Administration and Society* 36: 648–660.

19. This section draws on: Burns, T., and G.M. Stalker (1961), *The Management of Innovation* (London: Tavistock).

20. This example is based on: Hamel, G. (2007) *The Future of Management* (Boston: Harvard Business School Press); Collins, J. (2009), *How the Mighty Fall: And Why Some Companies Never Give In* (New York: Harper-Collins); Collins, J., and M. Hansen (2011), *Great by Choice: Uncertainty, Chaos, and Luck—Why Some Thrive Despite Them All* (New York: HarperCollins); and www.gore.com.

21. Hamel, G. (2007), *The Future of Management* (Boston, MA: Harvard Business School Press), 84.

22. As quoted in: Collins, J. (2009), *How the Mighty Fall: And Why Some Companies Never Give In* (New York: HarperCollins).

23. Chandler, A.D. (1962), *Strategy and Structure: Chapters in the History of American Industrial Enterprise* (Cambridge, MA: MIT Press).

24. Chandler, A.D. (1962), *Strategy and Structure: Chapters in the History of American Industrial Enterprise* (Cambridge, MA: MIT Press). Also, for a more recent treatise across different levels of analysis, see: Ridley, M. (2010), *The Rational Optimist: How Prosperity Evolves* (New York: HarperCollins).

25. This discussion is based on: O'Reilly, C.A., III, and M.L. Tushman (2007), "Ambidexterity as dynamic capability: Resolving the innovator's dilemma," *Research in Organizational Behavior* 28: 1–60; Raisch, S., and J. Birkinshaw (2008), "Organizational ambidexterity: Antecedents, outcomes, and moderators," *Journal of Management* 34: 375–409; and Rothaermel, F.T., and M.T. Alexandre (2009), "Ambidexterity in technology sourcing: The moderating role of absorptive capacity," *Organization Science* 20: 759–780.

26. Hamel, G. (2006, February), "The why, what, and how of management innovation," *Harvard Business Review*.

27. March, J.G. (1991), "Exploration and exploitation in organizational learning," *Organization Science* 2: 319–340; and Levinthal, D.A., and J.G. March (1993), "The myopia of learning," *Strategic Management Journal* 14: 95–112.

28. Author's interviews with Intel managers and engineers.

29. Brown, S.L., and K.M. Eisenhardt (1997), "The art of continuous change: Linking complexity theory and time-paced evolution in relentlessly shifting organizations," *Administrative Science Quarterly* 42: 1–34; and O'Reilly, C.A., B. Harreld, and M. Tushman (2009), "Organizational ambidexterity: IBM and emerging business opportunities," *California Management Review* 51: 75–99.

30. Chandler, A.D. (1962), *Strategy and Structure: Chapters in the History of American Industrial Enterprise* (Cambridge, MA: MIT Press).

31. Williamson, O.E. (1975), *Markets and Hierarchies* (Free Press: New York); and Williamson, O.E. (1985), *The Economic Institutions of Capitalism* (Free Press: New York).

32. Bertoni, S. (2014, Feb. 18), "Elon Musk and David Sacks say PayPal could top $100B away from eBay," *Forbes*; and "EBay's split should make investors happy–and corporate divorces more popular," *The Economist* (2015, Jul. 18); and publicly available stock market valuations (accessed May 20, 2019).

33. Bezos, J. P. (2014, April) "Letter to Shareholders."

34. As quoted at: www.zapposinsights.com/about/holacracy. Also, see video: "What Is Holacracy?" www.youtube.com/watch?v=MUHfVoQUj54 [1:47 min]. Hsieh announced the change to Zappos in March 2013.

35. This Strategy Highlight is based on: Robertson, B. (2015), *Holacracy: The New Management System for a Rapidly Changing World* (New York: Henry Holt); Robertson, B. (2015), "Holacracy: A Radical New Approach to Management," TEDx Grand Rapids talk, www.youtube.com/watch?t=17&v=tJxfJGovkI [18:20 min]; "The holes in holacracy," *The Economist* (2014, Jul. 5); Robertson, B. (2012), "Why not ditch bosses and distribute power," TEDx Drexel University talk, www.youtube.com/watch?v=hR-8AOccyj4 [13:00 min]; and on specific discussions on worker reaction to holacracy at Zappos, including: http://about.zappos.com;www.zapposinsights.com/about/holacracy;www.holacracy.org/; "What is holacracy?"www.youtube.com/watch?v=MUHfVoQUj54 [1:47 min]; Gelles, D. (2016, Jan. 13), "The Zappos exodus continues after a radical experiment," *The New York Times*; Gelles, D. (2015, Jul. 17), "At Zappos, pushing shoes and a vision," *The New York Times*; Greenfield, R. (2015, Jun. 30), "How Zappos converts new hires to its bizarre office culture," *Bloomberg Business*; Silverman, R.E. (2015, May 20), "At Zappos, banishing the bosses brings confusion," *The Wall Street Journal*; Silverman, R.E. (2015, May 7), "At Zappos, some employees find offer to leave too good to refuse," *The Wall Street Journal*; Greenfield, R. (2015, Mar. 30), "Holawhat? Meet the alt-management system invented by a programmer and used by Zappos," *Fast Company*; McGregor, J. (2014, Mar. 31), "Zappos to employees: Get behind our 'no bosses' approach, or leave with severance,"*The Washington Post*; Denning, S. (2014, Jan. 15), "Making sense of Zappos and holacracy," *Forbes*; Sweeney, C., and J. Gosfield (2014, Jan. 6), "No managers required: How Zappos ditched the old corporate structure for something new," *Fast Company*; McGregor, J. (2014, Jan. 3), "Zappos says goodbye to bosses,"*The Washington Post*; and for general background on the Zappos culture: Hsieh, T. (2010), *Delivering Happiness: A Path to Profits, Passion, and Purpose* (New York: Business Plus).

36. Bryan, L.L., and C.I. Joyce (2007), "Better strategy through organizational design," *The McKinsley Quarterly* 2: 21-29; Hagel, J., III, J.S. Brown, and L. Davison (2010), *The Power of Pull: How Small Moves, Smartly Made, Can Set Big Things in Motion* (Philadelphia: Basic Books); Majchrzak, A., A. Malhotra, J. Stamps, and J. Lipnack (2004, May), "Can absence make a team grow stronger?" *Harvard Business Review*; and Malhotra, A., A. Majchrzak, and B. Rosen (2007, March),

"Leading far-flung teams," *Academy of Management Perspectives*.

37. Brown, J.S., and P. Duguid, "Organizational learning and communities-of-practice: Toward a unified view of working, learning, and innovation," *Organization Science* 2: 40-57.

38. The discussion in this section draws mainly on Chesbrough's seminal work, Chesbrough, H.W. (2003), *Open Innovation: The New Imperative for Creating and Profiting from Technology* (Boston: Harvard Business School Press). See also the other insightful sources referenced here: Chesbrough, H. (2003), "The area of open innovation," *MIT Sloan Management Review,* Spring: 35-41; Chesbrough, H. (2007), "Why companies should have open business models," *MIT Sloan Management Review,* Winter: 22-28; Chesbrough, H.W., and M.M. Appleyard (2007), "Open innovation and strategy," *California Management Review* 50: 57-76; Laursen, K., and A. Salter (2006), "Open for innovation: The role of openness in explaining innovation performance among U.K. manufacturing firms,"*Strategic Management Journal* 27: 131-150; and West, J., and S. Gallagher (2006), "Challenges of open innovation: The paradox of firm investment in open-source software," *R&D Management* 36: 319-331.

39. See the recent research, for example, by: Chatterji, A.K., and K.R. Fabrizio (2013), "Using users: When does external knowledge enhance corporate product innovation?" *Strategic Management Journal* 35: 1427-1445. Using a sample of medical device makers and their collaboration with physicians, this research focuses on the conditions under which user knowledge can contribute most effectively to corporate innovation. The underlying literature in this field identifies both the importance of users to corporate innovation (20 to 80 percent of important innovations across a number of fields were user-sourced) and the unique quality of user-driven innovation (users are highly motivated to fulfill unmet needs that they have experienced). Given that cross-boundary interactions increase administrative costs and communication barriers, the study finds that user-driven open innovation has higher benefits in the early stages of technology life cycle and in the development of radical innovations.

40. Rothaermel, F.T., and M.T. Alexandre (2009), "Ambidexterity in technology sourcing: The moderating role of absorptive capacity," *Organization Science* 20: 759-780; and Rothaermel, F.T., and A.M. Hess (2010), "Innovation strategies combined," *MIT Sloan Management Review* 51: 13-15.

41. Katz, R., and T.J. Allen (1982), "Investigating the not invented here (NIH) syndrome: A look at the performance, tenure, and communication patterns of 50 R&D project groups," *R&D Management* 12: 7-20.

42. Horbaczewski, A., and F.T. Rothaermel (2013), "Merck: Open for innovation?" Case Study MH-FTR-009-0077645065, http://create.mcgraw-hill.com.

43. Cohen, W.M., and D.A. Levinthal (1990), "Absorptive capacity: New perspective on learning and innovation," *Administrative Science Quarterly* 35: 128-152; Zahra, S.A., and G. George (2002), "Absorptive capacity: A review, reconceptualization, and extension," *Academy of Management Review* 27: 185-203; and Rothaermel, F.T., and M.T. Alexandre (2009), "Ambidexterity in technology sourcing: The moderating role of absorptive capacity," *Organization Science* 20: 759-780.

44. Sony Annual Report 2002, year ended March 31, 2002, Sony Corp.: 9.

45. This Strategy Highlight is based on: "Sony CEO remains committed to consumer electronics," *The Wall Street Journal* (2015, Jan. 7); "How Sony makes money off Apple's iPhone," *The Wall Street Journal* (2015, Apr. 28); "Sony's blunt finance chief takes spotlight," *The Wall Street Journal* (2014, Nov. 16); "White House deflects doubts on sources of Sony Hack," *The Wall Street Journal* (2014, Dec. 30); "Behind the scenes at Sony as hacking crisis unfolded," *The Wall Street Journal* (2014, Dec. 30); "Japan's electronics under siege," *The Wall Street Journal* (2013, May 15); Hansen, M.T. (2009),*Collaboration: How Leaders Avoid the Traps, Create Unity, and Reap Big Results* (Cambridge, MA: Harvard Business School Press); Sony Corp., www.sony.com; and various Sony annual reports.

46. This section draws on: Barney, J.B. (1986), "Organizational culture: Can it be a source of sustained organizational culture?" *Academy of Management Review* 11(3): 656-665; Chatman, J.A., and S. Eunyoung Cha (2003), "Leading by leveraging culture," *California Management Review* 45: 19-34; Kerr, J., and J.W. Slocum (2005), "Managing corporate culture through reward systems," *Academy of Management Executive* 19: 130-138; O'Reilly, C.A., J. Chatman, and D.L. Caldwell (1991), "People and organizational culture: A profile comparison approach to assessing person-organization fit," *Academy of Management Journal* 34: 487-516; and Schein, E.H. (1992), *Organizational Culture and Leadership* (San Francisco: Jossey-Bass).

47. Chatman, J.A., and S. Eunyoung Cha (2003), "Leading by leveraging culture," *California Management Review* 45: 19-34.

48. Graham, J.R., C.R. Harvey, J. Popadak, and S. Rajgopal (2017). Corporate culture: Evidence from the field, NBER Working Paper 23255, www.nber.org/papers/w23255.

49. This example draws from: "Wells Fargo takes a pasting, from Congress and a regulator," *The Economist* (2019, Mar. 14); and Ensign, R.L. (2019, Mar. 28), "Wells Fargo CEO Tim Sloan steps down," *The Wall Street Journal.*

50. For a detailed discussion of how one can expect people to act in certain high pressure situations, see the excellent work on behavioral economics summarized in books by Dan Ariely, including: Ariely, D. (2009), *Predictably Irrational, Revised and Expanded Edition: The Hidden Forces That Shape Our Decisions* (New York: Harper); and Ariely, D. (2012), *The (Honest) Truth About Dishonesty: How We Lie to Everyone–Especially Ourselves* (New York: Harper).

51. Chao, G.T., A.M. O'Leary-Kelly, S. Wolf, H.J. Klein, and P.D. Gardner (1994), "Organizational socialization: Its content and consequences," *Journal of Applied Psychology* 79: 730-743.

52. Excerpted from: "Ten things we know to be true," www.google.com/about/philosophy.html.

53. As quoted in: Batelle, J. (2005), "Business 2.0: The 70 percent solution," CNN Money, https://money.cnn.com/2005/11/28/news/newsmakers/schmidt_biz20_1205/ (accessed May 21, 2019).

54. The original statement about Google's new approach to China is at http://googleblog.blogspot.com/2010/01/new-approach-to-china.html. Other sources: Chao, L., and A. Bac (2010, Jan. 13), "Google threat jolts China web users," *The Wall Street Journal*; and "Flowers for a funeral," *The Economist* (2010, Jan. 14).

55. MacMillan, D. (2018, Aug. 1), "Google considering censored search engine for return to China," *The Wall Street Journal*; Conger, K., and D. Wakabayashi (2018, Aug. 16), "Google employees protest secret work on censored search engine for China," *The New York Times*.

56. Nelson, T. (2003), "The persistence of founder influence: Management, ownership, and performance effects at initial public offering," *Strategic Management Journal* 24: 707-724.

57. A&E Biography Video (1997), *Sam Walton: Bargain Billionaire.*

58. Friedman, T.L. (2005), *The World Is Flat. A Brief History of the 21st Century* (New York: Farrar, Straus and Giroux), 130- 131.

59. Schneider, B., H.W. Goldstein, and D.B. Smith (1995), "The ASA framework: An update," *Personnel Psychology* 48: 747–773.

60. Hsieh, T. (2010), *Delivering Happiness: A Path to Profits, Passion, and Purpose* (New York: Business Plus), 145.

61. For many years, less than 1 percent of new hires took Zappos up on the $2,000 offer to quit during the training program. In recent years Zappos has not publicized this statistic. If there has been an increase in takers for this offer, it may have to do with the transition of the company from a startup—in which there is an implied reward for stakeholders should the enterprise be purchased—and its post-acquisition phase.

62. Leonard-Barton, D. (1995), *Wellsprings of Knowledge: Building and Sustaining the Sources of Innovation* (Boston: Harvard Business School Press).

63. Chandler, A.D. (1962), *Strategy and Structure: Chapters in the History of American Industrial Enterprise* (Cambridge, MA: MIT Press).

64. Birkinshaw, J. (2010), *Reinventing Management. Smarter Choices for Getting Work Done* (Chichester, West Sussex, UK: Jossey-Bass).

65. Boudette, N.E. (2014, Jun. 17), "GM CEO to testify before House panel," *The Wall Street Journal*.

66. Spector, M., and C.M. Matthews (2015, Jul. 24), "Investigators narrow GM-switch probe," *The Wall Street Journal*.

67. Hughes, S., and J. Bennett (2014, Apr. 2), "Senators challenge GM's Barra, push for faster change," *The Wall Street Journal*.

68. This section is based on: Barney, J.B. (1986), "Organizational culture: Can it be a source of sustained competitive advantage?" *Academy of Management Review* 11: 656–665; Barney, J. (1991), "Firm resources and sustained competitive advantage," *Journal of*

Management 17: 99–120; and Chatman, J.A., and S. Eunyoung Cha (2003), "Leading by leveraging culture," *California Management Review* 45: 19–34.

69. Hoffer Gittel, J. (2003), *The Southwest Airlines Way* (New York: McGraw-Hill); and O'Reilly, C., and J. Pfeffer (1995), "Southwest Airlines: Using human resources for competitive advantage," case study, Graduate School of Business, Stanford University.

70. See discussion in Chapter 4 on SWA's activities supporting its cost-leadership strategy.

71. Chatman, J.A., and S. Eunyoung Cha (2003), "Leading by leveraging culture," *California Management Review* 45: 19–34.

72. Hoffer Gittel, J. (2003), *The Southwest Airlines Way* (New York: McGraw-Hill).

73. Baron, J.N., M.T. Hannan, and M.D. Burton (2001), "Labor pains: Change in organizational models and employee turnover in young, high-tech firms," *American Journal of Sociology* 106: 960–1012; and Hannan, M.T., M.D. Burton, and J.N. Baron (1996), "Inertia and change in the early years: Employment relationships in young, high technology firms," *Industrial and Corporate Change* 5: 503–537.

74. Nelson, T. (2003), "The persistence of founder influence: Management, ownership, and performance effects at initial public offering," *Strategic Management Journal* 24: 707–724.

75. See the section on mergers and acquisitions in Chapter 9.

76. Herold, D.M., and D.B. Fedor (2008), *Change the Way You Lead Change: Leadership Strategies That Really Work* (Palo Alto, CA: Stanford University Press).

77. Hsieh, T. (2010), *Delivering Happiness: A Path to Profits, Passion, and Purpose* (New York: Business Plus).

78. For an in-depth insider perspective of Google's strategic human resource policies,

see: Bock, L. (2015), *Work Rules!: Insights from Inside Google That Will Transform How You Live and Lead* (New York: Twelve). Laszlo Bock leads Google's people function, responsible for attracting, developing, retaining, and delighting "Googlers."

79. Pink, D.H. (2009), *Drive: The Surprising Truth about What Motivates Us* (New York: Riverhead Books).

80. Pink, D.H. (2009), *Drive: The Surprising Truth about What Motivates Us* (New York: Riverhead Books).

81. 3M Co. (2002), *A Century of Innovation: The 3M Story* (Maplewood, MN: The 3M Co.).

82. Bossidy, L., R. Charan, and C. Burck (2002), *Execution: The Discipline of Getting Things Done* (New York: Crown Business); and Hrebiniak, L.G. (2005), *Making Strategy Work: Leading Effective Execution and Change* (Philadelphia: Wharton School Publishing).

83. Grundy, T. (1998), "Strategy implementation and project management," *International Journal of Project Management* 16: 43–50.

84. Burgelman, R.A. (1983), "Corporate entrepreneurship and strategic management: Insights from a process study," *Management Science* 29: 1349–1364; Burgelman, R.A. (1991), "Intraorganizational ecology of strategy making and organizational adaptation: Theory and field research," *Organization Science* 2: 239–262; and Burgelman, R.A., and A. Grove (2007), "Let chaos reign, then rein in chaos—repeatedly: Managing strategic dynamics for corporate longevity," *Strategic Management Journal* 28: 965–979.

85. 3M, http://solutions.3m.com/innovation/en_US/stories/time-to-think.

86. Additional source to those used in Part I of ChapterCase: Carlson, N. (2015), *Marissa Mayer and the Fight to Save Yahoo!* (New York: Hachette Book Group).

Corporate Governance and Business Ethics

Chapter Outline

Learning Objectives

After studying this chapter, you should be able to:

LO 12-1 Describe the shared value creation framework and its relationship to competitive advantage.

LO 12-2 Explain the role of corporate governance.

LO 12-3 Apply agency theory to explain why and how companies use governance mechanisms to align interests of principals and agents.

LO 12-4 Evaluate the board of directors as the central governance mechanism for public stock companies.

LO 12-5 Evaluate other governance mechanisms.

LO 12-6 Explain the relationship between strategy and business ethics.

Theranos: Bad Blood

ELIZABETH HOLMES WAS just 19 years old when she founded Theranos, a medical diagnostic company, in 2003. Although she was a college dropout, she was also ambitious and entrepreneurial and intent on disrupting the health care industry. Holmes' big invention was a miniaturized lab that could run 200 diagnostic tests from a single drop of blood drawn from a painless finger prick—quite the departure from the traditional method of using needles to draw vials of blood from veins. The technology and process of diagnosing blood hadn't changed much since the 1950s. As such, Holmes was convinced that the diagnostic blood testing market was ripe for disruption. She proclaimed she could develop a new technology that could spot everything from cholesterol to cancer within minutes and more accurately than traditional blood-drawing methods—she would do this by merging scientific advances in medical devices with bioengineering.

Elizabeth Holmes, founder of Theranos, pictured here with a "nanotainer," a small container holding a drop of blood to be inserted for testing into the Edison machine, a Theranos invention. Although a promising and appealing idea, Theranos never got the technology to work.
Ethan Pines/Forbes Collection/Corbis/Getty Images

Holmes' strategic intent did not just focus on developing more consumer-friendly blood tests; her intent also focused on providing faster, cheaper, more reliable, and more convenient tests. She wanted consumers to be able to obtain blood tests from their local pharmacy or even from the comfort of their own homes. This added emphasis on convenience would be an important step toward achieving individualized health care, wherein each consumer could obtain important information as they needed it to make their own medical decisions. Since consumers could have an entire suite of blood tests conducted every two weeks or so, and have the resulting data shared with physicians, consumers would find themselves with a much more dynamic view of their overall health profiles. Holmes theorized that repeated testing over short intervals would then allow for early detection and prevention of diseases. With its revolutionary technology, Theranos set out to challenge

incumbent diagnostic companies Quest Diagnostics and LabCorp, both of which were using decades-old technology and charging hundreds of dollars for standard blood tests. Government agencies such as Medicare have sued these firms for overcharging by billions of dollars. Together, Quest Diagnostics and LabCorp had long dominated the U.S. market in a cozy duopoly and owned more than 80 percent share.

At the time Theranos got off the ground, Steve Jobs was dominating Silicon Valley with his larger than life presence. He so inspired Holmes that she duplicated things he did—wearing black turtlenecks every day, hiring former Apple employees who had worked with Jobs, retaining the same advertising firm, and scheduling meetings on the same day as Jobs did (Wednesdays). Jobs was known for his uncanny ability to convince pretty much anyone who encountered him that *his* reality was the true reality, regardless of facts and other constraints—this version of reality has come to be known as Jobs' "reality distortion field." To effect her own reality distortion field, Holmes held constant eye contact with individuals and never blinked (the effect of which was reinforced by her large blue eyes). To sound more assertive and confident, she also trained herself to use a deep baritone voice rather than her natural voice.

So promising was this new Theranos technology that Holmes managed to persuade her adviser, Channing Robertson, then senior associate dean in the School of Engineering at Stanford University, to leave his tenured professorship and join her startup. Robertson's endorsement was enough to convince Tim Draper to provide initial funding. Draper of the famous venture capital firm DFJ was also the first to invest in the now-famous startups Tesla, Skype, and Baidu (China's version of Google). He was convinced that Holmes would "dedicate her life to mak[ing] something extraordinary happen to change the world."[1]

The media hype around the charismatic Holmes and her startup was great; she was featured frequently on the covers of such high-profile business publications as *Fortune, Forbes, Bloomberg Businessweek,* and *Inc.* She also made several TV appearances on *CNBC* and elsewhere. Many investors were gripped by FOMO ("fear of missing out") on the next big thing. As such, other venture capital firms began to invest in Theranos, as did billionaires Rupert Murdoch, Robert Kraft, the Walton family, the DeVos family, and others—each would invest $100 million or more. By 2014, Theranos was valued at $10 billion, making it one of the world's most valuable startups. At that time, Theranos was more valuable than other famous *unicorns* (private startups with valuations of over $1 billion) such as Uber, Airbnb, and Spotify. At its peak, Theranos had more than 800 employees and was considered one of the hottest tech startups in Silicon Valley. With approximately $5 billion in Theranos stock, Elizabeth Holmes had become the world's youngest self-made female billionaire.

Once Theranos went live with its blood testing, however, things began to unravel. Walgreens, in an attempt to preempt rival CVS, began to offer Theranos services to its Arizona-based customers in the fall of 2013. The initial idea was to install Theranos' Edison machines (mini-labs) in each Walgreens wellness center, so blood could be drawn by finger prick and analyzed onsite within minutes, at lower cost and higher accuracy. The problem was the Theranos machines were medical devices that needed FDA approval—which the startup did not obtain. As a work-around, onsite Walgreens technicians collected blood samples by finger prick, stored them in nanotainers, then shipped them to Theranos headquarters in Palo Alto, California, where the blood samples were analyzed. The results then were sent back to the customers.

Given that the Theranos technology failed to work well, if at all, the patients' lab results turned out to be inaccurate. Because the Edison machines couldn't handle the scope of tests Theranos had advertised, Holmes decided to analyze the blood samples collected in Walgreens' Arizona locations using old-line medical devices. Furthermore, because only a drop of blood was drawn from each patient, the samples needed to be diluted to meet the volume required for testing with the older equipment, which further reduced the accuracy of the results. In other instances, Theranos advised patients that larger amounts of blood were needed for testing to be possible, which led patients back to the traditional method of having blood drawn by intravenous needle. So began the gradual unraveling of a $10 billion deception.[2]

Part II of this ChapterCase appears in Section 12.4.

THE THERANOS CHAPTERCASE illustrates how intricate and intertwined business ethics issues and competitive advantage can be. With $10 billion in valuation, Theranos was at one point the most promising startup in Silicon Valley. Elizabeth Holmes, a 19-year-old inventor and CEO of Theranos, had several novel ideas on how to disrupt the medical diagnostic industry using new technology (on which she obtained several patents). As Holmes accumulated more and more funding for her startup, pressures mounted to get the technology to work. With increasing pressure and less and less time, Holmes began to cut corners, and things went from bad to worse. Even though Holmes started as a starry-eyed college dropout with some promising ideas and great potential, cutting corners under high pressure led to a pattern of unethical behavior that turned illegal, including defrauding patients, health care providers, and investors, not to mention the poor treatment of Theranos employees.

In this chapter, we wrap up our discussion of strategy implementation and close the circle in the AFI framework by studying two important areas: corporate governance and business ethics. We begin with the *shared value creation framework* to illuminate the link between strategic management, competitive advantage, and society more fully. We then discuss effective *corporate governance* mechanisms to direct and control the enterprise, which a firm must put in place to ensure pursuit of its intended goals. Next, we study *business ethics,* which enable strategic leaders to think through complex decisions in an increasingly dynamic, interdependent, and global marketplace. The ChapterCase documenting Elizabeth Holmes' controversial decisions and questionable behavior highlights the link between business ethics and sustainable competitive advantage. We conclude with *Implications for Strategic Leaders.*

12.1 The Shared Value Creation Framework

LO 12.1

Describe the shared value creation framework and its relationship to competitive advantage.

The shared value creation framework provides guidance to managers about how to reconcile the economic imperative of gaining and sustaining competitive advantage with corporate social responsibility (introduced in Chapter 1), and thus closing the cycle of the AFI framework.[3] The shared value creation framework helps strategic leaders create a larger pie that benefits both shareholders and other stakeholders. To develop the shared value creation framework, though, we first must understand the role of the public stock company.

PUBLIC STOCK COMPANIES AND SHAREHOLDER CAPITALISM

The public stock company is an important institutional arrangement in modern, free market economies. It provides goods and services as well as employment; it pays taxes and increases the standard of living. An implicit contract based on trust exists between society and the public stock company. Society grants the right to incorporation, but in turn expects companies to be good citizens by adding value to society.

To fund future growth, companies frequently need to go public. Theranos, featured in the ChapterCase, is one of the companies that achieved a high valuation before an initial public offering (IPO). Private start-up companies valued at $1 billion or more are called **unicorns**, because at one time they seemed as rare as the mythical beast. But their elusiveness has changed. The tech sector now has the lion's share: more than 150 unicorns valued at $1 billion or more, for a total of $613 billion.[4] The top five most valuable private startups (as of fall 2019) are Didi Chuxing (Chinese ride-hailing company and mobile logistics network, similar to Uber), JUUL (e-cigarette company offering vaporizers), Stripe (fin-tech), Airbnb (online platform for rental accommodations and tours), and SpaceX (space exploration technologies). These new ventures may eventually go public as did Uber and Lyft (both in 2019), Snap (2017), Twitter (2013), and Facebook (2012). As long as these unicorns remain private, however, they do not have to follow the stringent financial reporting and auditing requirements that public stock companies do. Consider that there may be a connection between firm ownership and the degree to which it integrates ethics. Not needing to expose themselves to as much public scrutiny as a publicly traded company also allows unicorns to push the envelope in their legal and ethical business practices—as happened at Theranos. A potential downside is that a track record of ethics and legal problems may prevent a successful IPO in the future—Theranos was liquidated in 2018.

unicorns Private start-up companies valued at $1 billion or more.

Exhibit 12.1 depicts the levels of hierarchy within a public stock company. The state or society grants a charter of incorporation to the company's shareholders—its legal owners, who own stock in the company. The shareholders appoint a board of directors to govern and oversee the firm's management. The managers hire, supervise, and coordinate employees to manufacture products and provide services. The public stock company enjoys four characteristics that make it an attractive corporate form:[5]

Private companies that achieve a valuation of $1 billion or greater were once rare enough to be called unicorns. In 2019, there were 151 unicorns valued at a combined $613 billion.
Catmando/Shutterstock

1. *Limited liability for investors.* This characteristic means the shareholders who provide the risk capital are liable only for the capital specifically invested, and not for other investments they may have made or for their personal wealth. Limited liability encourages investments by the wider public and entrepreneurial risk-taking.

EXHIBIT 12.1

The Public Stock
Company: Hierarchy
of Authority

2. *Transferability of investor ownership* through the trading of shares of stock on exchanges such as the New York Stock Exchange (NYSE) and NASDAQ,[6] or exchanges in other countries. Each share represents only a minute fraction of ownership in a company, thus easing transferability.

3. *Legal personality*—that is, the law regards a non-living entity such as a for-profit firm as similar to a person, with legal rights and obligations. Legal personality allows a firm's continuation beyond the founder or the founder's family.

4. *Separation of legal ownership and management control.*[7] In publicly traded companies, the stockholders (the principals, represented by the board of directors) are the legal owners of the company, and they delegate decision-making authority to professional managers (the agents).

The public stock company has been a major contributor to value creation since its inception as a new organizational form more than a hundred years ago. Michael Porter and others, however, argue that many public companies have defined value creation too narrowly in terms of financial performance.[8] This in turn has contributed to some of the *black swan events* discussed in Chapter 2, such as large-scale accounting scandals and the global financial crisis. Executives' pursuit of strategies that define value creation too narrowly may have negative consequences for society at large, as evidenced during the global financial crisis. This narrow focus has contributed to the loss of trust in the corporation as a vehicle for value creation, not only for shareholders but also other stakeholders and society.

Nobel laureate Milton Friedman circumscribed a firm's social obligations as follows: "There is one and only one social responsibility of business—to use its resources and engage in activities designed to increase its profits so long as it stays within the rules of the game, which is to say, engages in open and free competition without deception or fraud."[9] This notion is often captured by the term **shareholder capitalism**. According to this perspective, shareholders—the providers of the necessary risk capital and the legal owners of public companies—have the most legitimate claim on profits. When introducing the notion of *corporate social responsibility* (CSR) in Chapter 1, though, we noted that a firm's obligations frequently go beyond the economic responsibility to increase profits, extending to ethical and philanthropic expectations that society has of the business enterprise.[10]

A survey that measured attitudes toward business responsibility in various countries provides more insights into this debate and how opinions may vary across the globe. The survey asked the top 25 percent of income earners holding a university degree in each country surveyed whether they agree with Milton Friedman's philosophy that "the social responsibility of business is to increase its profits."[11] The results, displayed in Exhibit 12.2, revealed intriguing national differences. The United Arab Emirates (UAE), a small and business-friendly federation of seven emirates, had the highest level of agreement, at 84 percent. Roughly two-thirds agreed in the Asian countries of Japan, India, South Korea, and Singapore, which completed the top five in the survey.

The countries where the fewest people agreed with Friedman's philosophy were China, Brazil, Germany, Italy, and Spain; fewer than 40 percent of respondents in those countries supported an exclusive focus on shareholder capitalism. Although they have achieved a high standard of living, European countries such as Germany have tempered the free market system with a strong social element, leading to so-called *social market economies.* The respondents from these countries seemed to be more supportive of a *stakeholder strategy* approach to business. Some critics, however, would argue that too strong a focus on the social dimension contributed to the European debt crisis because sovereign governments such as Greece, Italy, and Spain took on nonsustainable debt levels to fund social programs such as early retirement plans, government-funded health care, and so on. The United States

shareholder capitalism
Shareholders—the providers of the necessary risk capital and the legal owners of public companies—have the most legitimate claim on profits.

EXHIBIT 12.2   Global Survey of Attitudes toward Business Responsibility

The bar chart indicates the percentage of members of the "informed public" who "strongly agree/somewhat agree" with Milton Friedman's philosophy, "the social responsibility of business is to increase its profits."

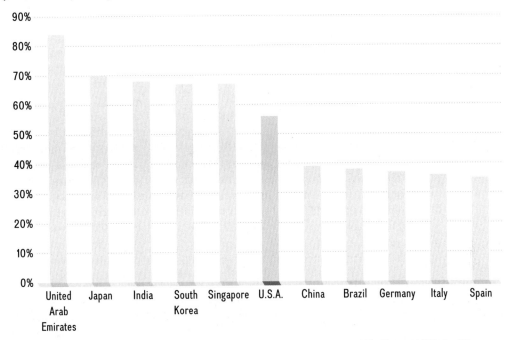

Source: Depiction of data from Edelman's, Trust Barometer, 2011 as included in "Milton Friedman goes on tour," *The Economist* (2011, Jan. 27).

placed roughly in the middle of the continuum—a bit more than half (56 percent) of U.S. respondents subscribed to Friedman's philosophy.

CREATING SHARED VALUE

In contrast to Milton Friedman, Michael Porter argues that executives should not concentrate exclusively on increasing firm profits. Rather, an effective strategic leader should focus on creating *shared value,* a concept that involves creating economic value for shareholders while also creating social value by addressing society's needs and challenges. He argues that managers need to reestablish the important relationship between superior firm performance and societal progress. This dual point of view, Porter argues, will not only allow companies to gain and sustain a competitive advantage but also reshape capitalism and its relationship to society.

The **shared value creation framework** proposes that managers maintain a dual focus on shareholder value creation and value creation for society. It recognizes that markets are defined not only by economic needs but also by societal needs. It also advances the perspective that *externalities* such as pollution, wasted energy, and costly accidents actually create *internal costs,* at least in lost reputation if not directly on the bottom line. Rather than pitting economic and societal needs in a trade-off, Porter suggests the two can be reconciled to create a larger pie. The shared value creation framework seeks to enhance a firm's competitiveness by identifying connections between economic and social needs, and then creating a competitive advantage by addressing these business opportunities.

shared value creation framework A model proposing that managers have a dual focus on shareholder value creation and value creation for society.

GE, for example, has strengthened its competitiveness by creating a profitable business with its "green" Ecomagination initiative. Ecomagination is GE's strategic initiative to provide cleaner and more efficient sources of energy, provide abundant sources of clean water anywhere in the world, and reduce emissions.[12] Jeffrey Immelt, GE's former CEO, would often say, "Green is green,"[13] meaning that addressing ecological needs offers the potential of gaining and sustaining a competitive advantage for GE. Through applying strategic innovation, GE is providing solutions for some tough environmental challenges, while driving company growth at the same time. Ecomagination solutions and products allow GE to increase the perceived value it creates for its customers while lowering costs to produce and deliver the green products and services. Ecomagination allows GE to solve the trade-off between increasing value creation and lowering costs. This in turn enhances GE's contribution to shared value creation.

As such, Ecomagination products and services also create value for society in terms of reducing emissions and lowering energy consumption, among other benefits. By 2016, green energy obtained from renewables (wind, solar, water, etc.) had for the first time surpassed coal in terms of electricity capacity additions. More than half of new energy capacity now comes from renewables and is estimated to be two-thirds within the next five years. In its sustainability report, GE states, "Investing in clean energy has proven good for business, job creation, the economy, and the world."[14] As part of its reorganization, GE has created a standalone division called Renewable Energy, which had $10 billion in revenues in 2018 and was profitable.[15]

To ensure that managers can reconnect economic and societal needs, Porter recommends that managers focus on three things within the shared value creation framework:[16]

1. **Expand the customer base to bring in *nonconsumers*** such as those at the *bottom of the pyramid*—the largest but poorest socioeconomic group of the world's population. The bottom of the pyramid in the global economy can yield significant business opportunities, which—if satisfied—could improve the living standard of the world's poorest. Muhammad Yunus, Nobel Peace Prize winner, founded Grameen Bank in Bangladesh to provide small loans (termed *microcredit)* to impoverished villagers, who used the funding for entrepreneurial ventures that would help them climb out of poverty. Other businesses have also found profitable opportunities at the bottom of the pyramid. In India, Arvind Ltd. offers jeans in a ready-to-make kit that costs only a fraction of the high-end Levi's. The Tata group sells its Nano car for around 150,000 rupees (about $2,500), enabling more Indian families to move from mopeds to cars and potentially adding up to a substantial business.

2. **Expand traditional internal firm value chains to include more nontraditional partners** such as *nongovernmental organizations* (NGOs). NGOs are nonprofit organizations that pursue a particular cause in the public interest and are independent of any governments. Habitat for Humanity and Greenpeace are examples of NGOs.

3. **Focus on creating new** regional clusters such as Silicon Valley in the United States; Electronic City in Bangalore, India; and Chilecon Valley in Santiago, Chile.

In line with *stakeholder theory* (discussed in Chapter 1), Porter argues that these strategic actions will lead to a larger pie of revenues and profits that can be distributed among a company's stakeholders. To ensure that convergence between shareholders and other stakeholders takes place, companies need effective governance mechanisms, which we discuss next.

corporate governance
A system of mechanisms to direct and control an enterprise in order to ensure that it pursues its strategic goals successfully and legally.

LO 12-2

Explain the role of corporate governance.

12.2 Corporate Governance

Corporate governance concerns the mechanisms to direct and control an enterprise in order to ensure that it pursues its strategic goals successfully and legally.[17] Corporate governance is about checks and balances and about asking the tough questions at the right time. The accounting scandals of the early 2000s and the global financial crisis of 2008 and beyond got so out of hand because the enterprises involved did not practice effective corporate governance. As discussed in the ChapterCase, some question whether Theranos had effective corporate governance mechanisms in place, or whether its ethically and legally questionable competitive tactics and decisions were part of a larger scheme to defraud investors (see ChapterCase Part II).

Corporate governance attempts to address the *principal–agent problem* (introduced in Chapter 8), which can occur any time an agent performs activities on behalf of a principal.[18] This problem can arise whenever a principal delegates decision making and control over resources to agents, with the expectation that they will act in the principal's best interest.

We mentioned earlier that the separation of ownership and control is one of the major advantages of the public stock companies. This benefit, however, is also the source of the principal–agent problem. In publicly traded companies, the stockholders are the legal owners of the company, but they delegate decision-making authority to professional managers. The conflict arises if the agents pursue their own personal interests, which can be at odds with the principals' goals. For their part, agents may be more interested in maximizing their total compensation, including benefits, job security, status, and power. Principals desire maximization of total returns to shareholders.

The risk of opportunism on behalf of agents is exacerbated by *information asymmetry:* The agents are generally better informed than the principals. Exhibit 12.3 depicts the principal–agent relationship.

Managers, executives, and board members tend to have access to *private information* concerning important company developments that outsiders, especially investors, are not privy to. Often this informational advantage is based on timing—insiders are the first to learn about important developments before the information is released to the public. Although possessing insider information is not illegal and indeed is part of an executive's job, what *is* illegal is acting upon it through trading stocks or passing on the information to others who might do so.

Insider-trading cases, therefore, provide an example of egregious exploitation of information asymmetry. The hedge fund Galleon Group (holding assets worth $7 billion under management at its peak) was engulfed in an insider-trading scandal involving private information about important developments at companies such as Goldman Sachs, Google, IBM, Intel, and P&G.[19] Galleon Group's founder, Raj Rajaratnam, the mastermind behind a complex network of informants, was sentenced to 11 years in prison and fined more than $150 million. In one instance, an Intel manager had provided Rajaratnam with internal Intel data such as orders for processors and production runs. These data indicated that demand for Intel processors was much higher than analysts had expected. Galleon bought Intel stock well before this information was public to benefit from the anticipated share appreciation.

In another instance, Rajaratnam benefited from insider tips provided by Rajat Gupta, a former McKinsey chief executive who served on Goldman Sachs' board. Often within seconds after the end of a Goldman Sachs board meeting, Gupta

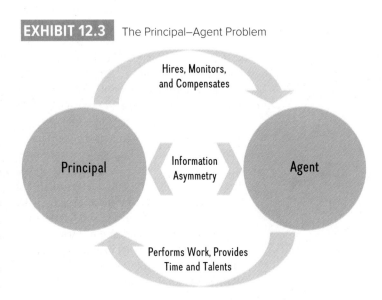

EXHIBIT 12.3 The Principal–Agent Problem

Hires, Monitors, and Compensates

Principal

Information Asymmetry

Agent

Performs Work, Provides Time and Talents

would call Rajaratnam. In one of these phone calls, Gupta revealed the impending multibillion-dollar liquidity injection by Warren Buffett into Goldman Sachs during the midst of the global financial crisis. This information allowed the Galleon Group to buy Goldman Sachs shares before the official announcement about Buffett's investment was made, thus profiting from the subsequent stock appreciation. In another call, Gupta informed Rajaratnam that the investment bank would miss its earnings estimates. Based on this insider information, the Galleon Group was able to sell its holdings in Goldman Sachs stock before the announcement, avoiding a multimillion-dollar loss.[20]

Information asymmetry can also breed *on-the-job consumption,* perquisites, and excessive compensation. Although use of company funds for golf outings, resort retreats, professional sporting events, or elegant dinners and other entertainment is an everyday manifestation of on-the-job consumption, other forms are more extreme. Dennis Kozlowski, former CEO of Tyco, a diversified conglomerate, used company funds for his $30 million New York City apartment (the shower curtain alone was $6,000) and for a $2 million birthday party for his spouse.[21] John Thain, former CEO of Merrill Lynch, spent $1.2 million of company funds on redecorating his office, while he demanded cost cutting and frugality from his employees.[22] Such uses of company funds, in effect, mean that shareholders pay for those items and activities. Thain also allegedly requested a bonus of up to $30 million in 2009, during the height of the global financial crisis, despite Merrill Lynch having lost billions of dollars and being unable to continue as an independent company. Merrill Lynch was later acquired by Bank of America in a fire sale.

LO 12-3

Apply agency theory to explain why and how companies use governance mechanisms to align interests of principals and agents.

agency theory A theory that views the firm as a nexus of legal contracts.

AGENCY THEORY

The principal–agent problem is a core part of **agency theory**, which views the firm as a nexus of legal contracts.[23] In this perspective, corporations are viewed as a set of legal contracts between different parties. Conflicts that may arise are to be addressed in the legal realm. Agency theory finds its everyday application in employment contracts, for example.

Besides dealing with the relationship between shareholders and managers, principal–agent problems also cascade down the organizational hierarchy (shown in Exhibit 12.1). Senior executives, such as the CEO, face agency problems when they delegate authority of strategic business units to general managers.

Employees who perform the actual operational labor are agents who work on behalf of the managers. Such frontline employees often enjoy an informational advantage over management. They may tell their supervisor that it took longer to complete a project or serve a customer than it actually did, for example. Some employees may be tempted to use such informational advantage for their own self-interest (e.g., spending time on Facebook and Instagram during work hours, watching YouTube videos, or using the company's computer and internet connection for personal business).

The lawsuit between Uber and Waymo (mentioned in ChapterCase 9) illustrates the thorny issues that arise out of the inherent principal–agent problem in employment relationships.[24] In this case, Anthony Levandowski, the engineer at the heart of the lawsuit, is alleged to have set up his autonomous-vehicle company, Otto, while still working at Waymo, as a front to siphon off trade secrets and proprietary technology from his employer. Shortly after Levandowski formally left Waymo, Uber acquired his start-up company Otto for close to $700 million in 2016. Waymo alleges that Levandowski set up Otto to steal trade secrets and proprietary designs, and to turn around and use this knowledge to advance self-driving technology at Uber. Waymo alleges that Levandowski and Uber not only acted opportunistically but also illegally. In 2018, the two companies settled the lawsuit, with Uber giving Waymo $245 million worth of equity as well as the promise that Uber wouldn't use any of

Waymo's autonomous-vehicle technology. In 2019, federal authorities charged Anthony Levandowski with 33 counts of trade-secret theft. After his arraignment, Levandowski was released on bail (as the case is ongoing).[25]

The managerial implication of agency theory relates to the management functions of organization and control: The firm needs to design work tasks, incentives, and employment contracts and other control mechanisms in ways that minimize opportunism by agents. Such governance mechanisms are used to align incentives between principals and agents. These mechanisms need to be designed in such a fashion as to overcome two specific agency problems: *adverse selection* and *moral hazard*.

ADVERSE SELECTION. In general, **adverse selection** occurs when information asymmetry increases the likelihood of selecting inferior alternatives. In principal–agent relationships, for example, adverse selection describes a situation in which an agent misrepresents his or her ability to do the job. Such misrepresentation is common during the recruiting process. Once hired, the principal may not be able to accurately assess whether the agent can do the work for which he or she is being paid. The problem is especially pronounced in team production, when the principal often cannot ascertain the contributions of individual team members. This creates an incentive for opportunistic employees to free-ride on the efforts of others.

> **adverse selection** A situation that occurs when information asymmetry increases the likelihood of selecting inferior alternatives.

MORAL HAZARD. In general, **moral hazard** describes a situation in which information asymmetry increases the incentive of one party to take undue risks or shirk other responsibilities because the costs accrue to the other party. For example, bailing out homeowners from their mortgage obligations or bailing out banks from the consequences of undue risk-taking in lending are examples of moral hazard. The costs of default are rolled over to society. Knowing that there is a high probability of being bailed out ("too big to fail") increases moral hazard. In this scenario, any profits remain private, while losses become public.

> **moral hazard** A situation in which information asymmetry increases the incentive of one party to take undue risks or shirk other responsibilities because the costs incur to the other party.

In the principal–agent relationship, moral hazard describes the difficulty of the principal to ascertain whether the agent has really put forth a best effort. In this situation, the agent is *able* to do the work but may decide not to do so. For example, a company scientist at a biotechnology company may decide to work on his own research project, hoping to eventually start his own firm, rather than on the project he was assigned.[26] While working on his own research on company time, he might also use the company's laboratory and technicians. Given the complexities of basic research, it is often challenging, especially for nonscientist principals, to ascertain which problem a scientist is working on.[27] To overcome these principal–agent problems, firms put several governance mechanisms in place. We shall discuss several of them next, beginning with the board of directors.

THE BOARD OF DIRECTORS

The shareholders of public stock companies appoint a **board of directors** to represent their interests (see Exhibit 12.1). The board of directors is the centerpiece of corporate governance in such companies. The shareholders' interests, however, are not uniform. The goals of some shareholders, such as institutional investors (e.g., retirement funds, governmental bodies, and so on), are generally the long-term viability of the enterprise combined with profitable growth. Long-term viability and profitable growth should allow consistent dividend payments and result in stock appreciation over time. The goals of other shareholders, such as hedge funds, are often to profit from short-term movements of stock prices. These more proactive investors often demand changes in a firm's strategy, such as spinning out certain divisions or splitting up companies into parts to enhance overall performance. Votes

> **board of directors** The centerpiece of corporate governance, composed of inside and outside directors who are elected by the shareholders.

LO 12-4

Evaluate the board of directors as the central governance mechanism for public stock companies.

at shareholder meetings, generally in proportion to the amount of ownership, determine whose representatives are appointed to the board of directors.

The day-to-day business operations of a publicly traded stock company are conducted by its managers and employees, under the direction of the chief executive officer (CEO) and the oversight of the board of directors. The board of directors is composed of inside and outside directors who are elected by the shareholders:[28]

inside directors Board members who are generally part of the company's senior management team; appointed by shareholders to provide the board with necessary information pertaining to the company's internal workings and performance.

- **Inside directors** are generally part of the company's senior management team, such as the chief financial officer (CFO) and the chief operating officer (COO). They are appointed by shareholders to provide the board with necessary information pertaining to the company's internal workings and performance. Without this valuable inside information, the board would not be able to effectively monitor the firm. As senior executives, however, inside board members' interests tend to align with management and the CEO rather than the shareholders.

- **Outside directors**, on the other hand, are not employees of the firm. They frequently are senior executives from other firms or full-time professionals, who are appointed to a board and who serve on several boards simultaneously. Given their independence, they are more likely to watch out for the interests of shareholders.

outside directors Board members who are not employees of the firm, but who are frequently senior executives from other firms or full-time professionals.

The board is elected by the shareholders to represent their interests. Each director has a *fiduciary responsibility*—a legal duty to act solely in another party's interests—toward the shareholders because of the trust placed in him or her. Prior to the annual shareholders' meeting, the board proposes a slate of nominees, although shareholders can also directly nominate director candidates. In general, large institutional investors support their favored candidates through their accumulated proxy votes. The board members meet several times a year to review and evaluate the company's performance and to assess its future strategic plans as well as opportunities and threats.

In addition to general strategic oversight and guidance, the board of directors has other, more specific functions, including:

- Selecting, evaluating, and compensating the CEO. The CEO reports to the board. Should the CEO lose the board's confidence, the board may fire him or her.
- Overseeing the company's CEO succession plan.
- Providing guidance to the CEO in the selection, evaluation, and compensation of other senior executives.
- Reviewing, monitoring, evaluating, and approving any significant strategic initiatives and corporate actions such as large acquisitions.
- Conducting a thorough risk assessment and proposing options to mitigate risk. The boards of directors of the financial firms at the center of the global financial crisis were faulted for not noticing or not appreciating the risks the firms were exposed to.
- Ensuring that the firm's audited financial statements represent a true and accurate picture of the firm.
- Ensuring the firm's compliance with laws and regulations. The boards of directors of firms caught up in the large accounting scandals were faulted for being negligent in their company oversight and not adequately performing several of the functions listed here.

Board independence is critical to effectively fulfilling a board's governance responsibilities. Given that board members are directly responsible to shareholders, they have an incentive to ensure that the shareholders' interests are pursued. If not, they can experience a loss in reputation or can be removed outright. More and more directors are also exposed to legal repercussions should they fail in their fiduciary responsibility. To perform their strategic oversight tasks, board members apply the strategic management theories and concepts presented herein, among other more specialized tools such as those originating in finance and accounting.

The functions of the CEO and chairperson of the board roles differ distinctly. A board of directors broadly oversees a company's business activities. The company's CEO reports to the board of directors and acts as a liaison between the company and the board. The CEO maintains high-level responsibilities of strategy and all other management activities of a company while the board's responsibilities include such functions as approving the annual budget and dealing with stakeholders. Moreover, a CEO is the public face of a company or organization and takes the hit or pat on the back if a company fails or succeeds, while the board of directors is there to steer a company on behalf of shareholders.

Arguments can be made both for and against splitting the roles of CEO and chairperson of the board. On the one hand, the CEO has invaluable inside information that can help in chairing the board effectively. The benefit of a combined CEO and chair of the board is the unity streamlines and speeds the decision-making process as well as strategy implementation. On the other hand, the chairperson may influence the board unduly through setting the meeting agendas or suggesting board appointees who are friendly toward the CEO. Because one of the key roles of the board is to monitor and evaluate the CEO's performance, there can be a conflict of interest when the CEO actually chairs the board.

The practice of **CEO/chairperson duality**—holding both the role of CEO and chairperson of the board—has been declining somewhat in recent years.[29] Among the largest 500 publicly traded companies in the United States, about 70 percent of firms had the dual CEO-chair arrangement in 2005 (before the global financial crisis), but this number had declined to some 50 percent of companies in 2018 (post global financial crisis). High-profile examples of the same person serving as CEO and chair of the board include Jeff Bezos (Amazon), Mark Zuckerberg (Facebook), Robert Iger (Disney), Mary Barra (GM), and Virginia Rometty (IBM).

To illustrate how things can go wrong when a board of directors does not fulfill its oversight responsibility, Strategy Highlight 12.1 takes a close look at Hewlett-Packard (HP).

> **CEO/chairperson duality** Situation where the CEO of a publicly traded company is also the chairperson of the board of directors.

OTHER GOVERNANCE MECHANISMS

While the board of directors is the central governance piece for a public stock company, several other corporate mechanisms are also used to align incentives between principals and agents, including

- Executive compensation.
- The market for corporate control.
- Financial statement auditors, government regulators, and industry analysts.

> **LO 12-5**
> Evaluate other governance mechanisms.

EXECUTIVE COMPENSATION. The board of directors determines executive compensation packages. To align incentives between shareholders and management, the board frequently grants **stock options** as part of the compensation package. This mechanism is based on agency theory and gives the recipient the right, but not the obligation, to buy a company's stock at a predetermined price sometime in the future. If the company's share price rises above the negotiated strike price, which is often the price on the day when compensation is negotiated, the executive stands to reap significant gains.

The topic of executive compensation—and CEO pay, in particular—has attracted significant attention in recent years. Two issues are at the forefront:

1. The absolute size of the CEO pay package compared with the pay of the average employee.

2. The relationship between CEO pay and firm performance.

> **stock options** An incentive mechanism to align the interests of shareholders and managers, by giving the recipient the right (but not the obligation) to buy a company's stock at a predetermined price sometime in the future.

Strategy Highlight 12.1

HP's Boardroom Drama and Divorce

Hewlett-Packard (HP) has lost its place among the world's leading technology companies. Within a short 18 months (from spring 2010 to fall 2012), HP's market value dropped by almost 80 percent, wiping out $82 billion in shareholder wealth. A perfect storm of corporate governance problems, combined with repeated ethical shortcomings, had been brewing at HP for a decade. This development is even more astonishing given that, at one point, HP was much admired for its corporate culture—known as the HP Way. The core values of the HP Way include business conducted with "uncompromising integrity," as well as "trust and respect for individuals," among others. HP's board of directors—a group of individuals that is supposed to represent the interests of the firm's shareholders and oversee the CEO—seemed to forget the HP Way as it violated its core values time and time again. In the process, HP's board of directors acted out a drama rivaling *Game of Thrones*.

The first season of the HP drama aired in 2006. The online technology site CNET published an article on HP's strategy. Quoting an anonymous source, the article disclosed sensitive details that could have come only from one of the directors or senior executives at HP. Eager to discover the identity of the leaker, Patricia Dunn, then chair of the board, launched a covert investigation. She hired an outside security firm to conduct surveillance on HP's board members, select employees, and even some journalists. Although it is common for companies to monitor phone and computer use of their employees, HP's investigation went above and beyond. The private investigators used an illegal spying technique called "pretexting" (impersonating the targets) to obtain phone records by contacting telecom service providers. The security firm obtained some 300 telephone records covering mobile, home, and office phones of all directors (including Dunn), nine journalists, and several HP employees. Not to leave anything to chance, the security firm also obtained phone records of the spouses and even the children of HP board members and employees. The firm also conducted physical surveillance of the suspected leaker—board member George Keyworth—and his spouse, as well as two other directors.

In a board meeting, Dunn then presented the evidence gathered, implicating Keyworth as the source of the leak. Dunn's disclosure of the investigation infuriated HP director Thomas Perkins, a prominent venture capitalist, so much that he resigned on the spot. Perkins called the HP-initiated surveillance "illegal, unethical, and a misplaced corporate priority."[30] Perkins also forced HP to disclose the spying campaign to the Securities and Exchange Commission (and thus to the public) as his reason for resigning. Dunn and Keyworth were dismissed from the board along with six senior HP managers. Despite the boardroom drama, HP came out unscathed financially, largely due to the superior performance of then-CEO Mark Hurd.

Hurd was appointed Hewlett-Packard's CEO in 2005. He had begun his business career 25 years earlier as an entry-level salesperson with NCR, a U.S. technology company best known for its bar code scanners in retail outlets and automatic teller machines (ATMs). By the time Hurd worked his way up to the role of CEO at NCR, he had earned a reputation as a low-profile, no-nonsense manager focused on flawless strategy execution. When he was appointed HP's CEO, industry analysts praised its board of directors for its decision. Investors hoped that Hurd would run an efficient and lean operation at HP and return the company to its former greatness and, above all, profitability.

Hurd was highly successful at the helm of HP. The company became number one in desktop computer sales and increased its lead in inkjet and laser printers to more than 50 percent market share. Through significant cost-cutting and streamlining measures, Hurd turned HP into a lean and highly profitable operation. Wall Street rewarded HP shareholders with an almost 90 percent stock price appreciation during Hurd's tenure, outperforming broader stock market indices by a wide margin.

Yet, in 2010, HP aired the second season of its boardroom soap opera. The HP board found itself caught between a rock and a hard place, with no easy options in sight. Jodie Fisher, a former adult-movie actor, filed a lawsuit against Hurd alleging sexual harassment. As an independent contractor, Fisher had worked as a hostess at HP-sponsored events. In this function, she had screened attending HP customers and personally ensured that Hurd spent time with the most important ones. With another ethics scandal looming despite Hurd's stellar financial results for the company, HP's board of directors forced him to resign. He left HP in August 2010 with an exit package worth $35 million.

The third season of HP's boardroom drama began in the fall of 2010 when HP announced Leo Apotheker as its new CEO. Apotheker, who came to HP after being let go from the German enterprise software company SAP, proposed a new corporate strategy for HP. He suggested the company focus on enterprise software solutions and spin off its low-margin consumer hardware business. Under Apotheker, HP also exited the mobile device industry, most notably tablet computers. Many viewed this move as capitulating to Apple's dominance.

As part of his new corporate strategy, Apotheker was eager to make a high-impact acquisition to put his strategic vision of HP as a software and service company into action. He ended up acquiring the British software company Autonomy for $11 billion, which analysts saw as grossly overvalued. Shortly thereafter, HP took an almost $9 billion write-down due to alleged "accounting inaccuracies" at Autonomy. HP's stock went into free fall. During Apotheker's short 11 months at the helm of HP, the share price dropped by almost 50 percent. HP's due diligence process by the board was clearly flawed when acquiring Autonomy. The process itself had been truncated. Moreover, the HP board did not heed the red flags thrown up by Deloitte, Autonomy's auditor. Indeed, a few days before the Autonomy acquisition was finalized, Deloitte auditors asked to meet with the board to inform them about a former Autonomy executive who accused the company of accounting irregularities.

Perhaps most problematic, the board fell victim to groupthink, rallying around Apotheker as CEO and Ray Lane, the board chair, who strongly supported him. In the wake of the Hurd ethics scandal, an outside recruiting firm had proposed Apotheker as CEO and Lane as the new chair of HP's board of directors. The full board never met either of the men before hiring them into key strategic positions! The HP board of directors experienced a major shakeup after the Hurd ethics scandal and then again after the departure of Apotheker. Lane stepped down as chair of HP's board in the spring of 2013 but remains a director (at Hewlett Packard Enterprise).

After Apotheker was let go, HP did not conduct a search for its next CEO. Instead, in the fall of 2011, the board appointed one of its directors, Meg Whitman, as CEO because the board members were too exhausted by the fighting. Whitman had been the CEO at eBay, was appointed to HP's board of directors in 2011, and was a director when the Autonomy acquisition was approved. In an effort to regain competitiveness Whitman cut 55,000 jobs.

In 2015 HP split into two firms: HP Inc., which focused on consumer hardware (PCs and printers) and earned some $60 billion in 2019 revenues, and Hewlett Packard Enterprise, which focused on business equipment and services and earned $30 billion in 2019 revenues.[31]

Absolute Size of Pay Package. The ratio of CEO to average employee pay in the United States is about 300 to 1, up from roughly 30 to 1 in 1980.[32] In 2018, the median compensation of CEOs in the S&P 500 was $12.4 million.[33] Note: Annual compensation is broadly defined to include salary, stock options, equity grants, bonuses, and pension payments. Many of the CEOs with the highest compensation in 2018 ran health care, media, and financial companies (18 out of the top 25).

In 2018, the three highest paid CEOs were David Zaslav of Discovery, a media company ($129.4 million); Stephen Angel of Linde, an industrial gases and engineering company ($66.1 million); and Robert Iger of Disney ($65.6 million). Noteworthy are also some of lowest paid CEOs in the S&P 500: both Jack Dorsey of Twitter and Larry Page of Alphabet receive just *$1* in annual compensation, the minimum payment required by law.

CEO Pay and Firm Performance. Overall, survey results also show that two-thirds of CEO pay is linked to firm performance.[34] The relationship between pay and performance is positive, but the link is weak at best. Although agency theory would predict a positive link between pay and performance as this aligns incentives, some recent experiments in *behavioral economics* caution that incentives that are too high-powered (e.g., outsized bonuses) may have a negative effect on job performance.[35] That is, when the incentive level is very high, an individual may get distracted from strategic activities because too much attention is devoted to the outsized bonus to be enjoyed in the near future. This can further increase job stress and negatively impact job performance.

THE MARKET FOR CORPORATE CONTROL. Whereas the board of directors and executive compensation are *internal* corporate governance mechanisms, the *market for corporate control* is an important *external* corporate governance mechanism. It consists of activist investors who seek to gain control of an underperforming corporation by buying shares of its stock in the open market. To avoid such attempts, corporate managers strive to protect shareholder value by delivering strong share-price performance or putting in place poison pills (discussed later).

Here's how the market for corporate control works: If a company is poorly managed, its performance suffers and its stock price falls as more and more investors sell their shares. Once shares fall to a low enough level, the firm may become the target of a *hostile takeover* (as discussed in Chapter 9) when new bidders believe they can fix the internal problems that are causing the performance decline. Besides competitors, so-called *corporate raiders* (e.g., Carl Icahn and Daniel Loeb) or *private-equity firms* and *hedge funds* (e.g., The Blackstone Group and Pershing Square Capital Management) may buy enough shares to exert control over a company.

In a **leveraged buyout (LBO)**, a single investor or group of investors buys, with the help of borrowed money (leveraged against the company's assets), the outstanding shares of a publicly traded company to take it private. In short, an LBO changes the ownership structure of a company from public to private. The expectation is often that the private owners will restructure the company and eventually take it public again through an initial public offering (IPO).

Private companies enjoy certain benefits that public companies do not. Private companies are not required to disclose financial statements. They experience less scrutiny from analysts and can often focus more on long-term viability. These are also some of the reasons some unicorns delay going public in the first place.

Dell's LBO, Transformation, and Re-Listing as Public Company. In 2013, after years of consistently poor performance, computer maker Dell Inc. became a takeover target of famed corporate raider Carl Icahn.[36] Icahn jumped into action after Dell's founder and largest shareholder, Michael Dell, announced he was intending a *leveraged buyout* with the help of Silverlake Partners, a private-equity firm, to take the company private. In the Dell buyout battle, many observers, including Icahn who was then the second-largest shareholder of Dell Inc., saw the attempt by Dell to take the company private as the "ultimate insider trade."

This view implied that Dell, who is also CEO and chairman, had private information about the future value of the company and that his offer was too low. Dell Inc., which had $57 billion in revenues in its fiscal year 2013, had been struggling in the ongoing transition from personal computers to mobile devices and services. Between December 2004 and February 2009, Dell (which until just a few years earlier was the number-one computer maker) lost more than 80 percent of its market capitalization, dropping from $76 billion to a mere $14 billion. In late 2013, Dell's shareholders approved the founder's $25 billion offer to take the company private, thus avoiding a hostile takeover.

To continue with its makeover and the transformation of a company that Michael Dell founded in 1984 in a dorm room at the University of Texas at Austin, Dell acquired EMC, a cloud computing company, for $60 billion in 2016. Just two years later, Dell engineered a *reverse takeover,* in which Dell and VMware, a virtualization-software unit, swapped equity shares. A *reverse takeover* is the acquisition of a larger private company by a smaller, but

leveraged buyout (LBO) A single investor or group of investors buys, with the help of borrowed money (leveraged against the company's assets), the outstanding shares of a publicly traded company in order to take it private.

public company. This special case of an acquisition allows the larger private firm to list on the public stock market, without having to go through a lengthy, complex, and frequently costly process of an initial public offering. The reverse takeover of VMware allowed Michael Dell to re-list his company on a public stock exchange. Since December 2018, the new Dell Technologies Inc. is again a publicly traded company (NYSE ticker: Dell) and had a market valuation of $40 billion in fall 2019. This completed the turnaround cycle of the company that Michael Dell took private through a leveraged buyout in 2013.

Hostile Takeovers and Poison Pills. If a hostile takeover attempt is successful, however, the new owner frequently replaces the old management and board of directors to manage the company in a way that creates more value for shareholders. In some instances, the new owner will break up the company and sell its pieces. In either case, since a firm's existing executives face the threat of losing their jobs and their reputations if the firm sustains a competitive disadvantage, the market for corporate control is a credible governance mechanism.

To avoid being taken over against their consent, some firms put in place a **poison pill**. These are defensive provisions that kick in should a buyer reach a certain level of share ownership without top management approval. For example, a poison pill could allow existing shareholders to buy additional shares at a steep discount. Those additional shares would make any takeover attempt much more expensive and function as a deterrent. With the rise of actively involved institutional investors, poison pills have become rare because they retard an effective function of equity markets.

Although poison pills are becoming rarer, the market for corporate control is alive and well, as shown in the battle over control of Dell Inc. or the hostile takeover of Cadbury by Kraft (featured in Strategy Highlight 9.2). However, the market for corporate control is a last resort because it comes with significant transaction costs. To succeed in its hostile takeover bid, buyers generally pay a significant premium over the given share price. This often leads to overpaying for the acquisition and subsequent shareholder value destruction—the so-called *winner's curse.* The market for corporate control is useful, however, when internal corporate-governance mechanisms have not functioned effectively and the company is underperforming.

> **poison pill** Defensive provisions to deter hostile takeovers by making the target firm less attractive.

AUDITORS, GOVERNMENT REGULATORS, AND INDUSTRY ANALYSTS. Auditors, government regulators, and industry analysts serve as additional external governance mechanisms. All public companies listed on the U.S. stock exchanges must file a number of financial statements with the *Securities and Exchange Commission (SEC),* a federal regulatory agency whose task it is to oversee stock trading and enforce federal securities laws. To avoid the misrepresentation of financial results, all public financial statements must follow *generally accepted accounting principles (GAAP)*[37] and be audited by certified public accountants.

As part of its disclosure policy, the SEC makes all financial reports filed by public companies available electronically via the EDGAR database.[38] This database contains more than 7 million financial statements, going back several years. Industry analysts scrutinize these reports in great detail, trying to identify any financial irregularities and assess firm performance. Given recent high-profile accounting scandals and fraud cases, the SEC has come under pressure to step up its monitoring and enforcement.

Industry analysts often base their buy, hold, or sell recommendations on financial statements filed with the SEC and business news published in *The Wall Street Journal, Bloomberg Businessweek, Fortune, Forbes,* and other business media such as CNBC. Researchers have questioned the independence of industry analysts and credit-rating agencies that evaluate companies (such as Fitch Ratings, Moody's, and Standard & Poor's),[39] because the investment banks and rating agencies frequently have lucrative business relationships with

s they are supposed to evaluate, creating conflicts of interest. A study of over
' ratings of corporate equity securities, for example, revealed that investment
heir own clients more favorably.[40]

ın industry has sprung up around assessing the effectiveness of corporate gov-
idual firms. Research outfits, such as GMI Ratings,[41] provide independent
ance ratings. The ratings from these external watchdog organizations inform
akeholders, including investors, insurers, auditors, regulators, and others.

ernance mechanisms play an important part in aligning the interests of
nts. They enable closer monitoring and controlling, as well as provide
to align interests of principals and agents. Perhaps even more important are the
"most internal of control mechanisms": *business ethics*—a topic we discuss next.

12.3 Strategy and Business Ethics

LO 12-6

Explain the relationship
between strategy and
business ethics.

business ethics An
agreed-upon code of
conduct in business,
based on societal
norms.

Corporate scandals (such as Theranos featured in the ChapterCase or VW's Dieselgate,
discussed below in Strategy Highlight 12.2), high-profile accounting frauds, and the global
financial crisis have placed business ethics center stage in the public eye. **Business ethics** are
an agreed-upon code of conduct in business, based on societal norms. Business ethics lay
the foundation and provide training for "behavior that is consistent with the principles,
norms, and standards of business practice that have been agreed upon by society."[42] These
principles, norms, and standards of business practice differ to some degree in different cultures around the globe. But a large number of research studies have found that some
notions—such as fairness, honesty, and reciprocity—are universal norms.[43] As such, many of
these values have been codified into law.

Law and ethics, however, are not synonymous. This distinction is important and not
always understood by the general public. Staying within the law is a *minimum acceptable
standard.* A note of caution is therefore in order: A manager's actions can be completely
legal, but ethically questionable. For example, consider the actions of mortgage-loan officers
who—being incentivized by commissions—persuaded unsuspecting consumers to sign up for
exotic mortgages, such as option ARMs (adjustable rate mortgages). These mortgages offer
borrowers the choice to pay less than the required interest, which is then added to the principal while the interest rate can adjust upward. Such actions may be legal, but they are
unethical, especially if there are indications that the borrower might be unable to repay the
mortgage once the interest rate moves up.[44]

To go beyond the minimum acceptable standard codified in law, many organizations
have explicit *codes of conduct.* These codes go above and beyond the law in detailing how the
organization expects an employee to behave and to represent the company in business dealings. Codes of conduct allow an organization to overcome moral hazards and adverse selec-
tions as they attempt to resonate with employees' deeper values of justice, fairness, honesty,
integrity, and reciprocity. Since business decisions are not made in a vacuum but are embedded within a societal context that expects ethical behavior, managers can improve their decision making by also considering the following:

- When facing an ethical dilemma, a manager can ask whether the intended course of
  action falls within the *acceptable norms of professional behavior* as outlined in the organization's code of conduct and defined by the profession at large.
- The manager should imagine whether he or she would feel *comfortable explaining and
  defending the decision in public.* How would the media report the business decision if it
  were to become public? How would the company's stakeholders feel about it?

Strategy Highlight 12.2 takes a close look a the Volkswagen emissions scandal.

Strategy Highlight **12.2**

VW's Dieselgate: School of Hard NOx

Volkswagen (VW) used to have a reputation as one of the most reliable car manufacturers in the world.[45] VW cars were known for highly reliable engines with superior performance, a class above other competitors in the mass market. The iconic Volkswagen beetle, designed by Ferdinand Porsche in the 1930s, became the symbol of the counterculture in the United States during the 1960s and 1970s. During that time, VW sold 500,000 cars per year in the U.S. market. But VW didn't keep up with the times because it failed to innovate. By the early 1990s, sales and profits had dropped as fast as its vehicles' quality. In 1993, VW's U.S. sales had fallen to a low of 38,000 vehicles in a market that sold 17 million vehicles that year; that is, VW market share had declined to 0.2 percent. Given the poor product lineup at the time, VW's losses were mounting, and the mighty company faced bankruptcy.

Ferdinand Piëch, who was leading the much smaller Audi brand at the time, was brought in to turn around the struggling VW. Audi was one of VW's luxury brands and had just gained market share against BMW and Mercedes thanks to Piëch's innovation and rebranding. Piëch is the grandson of VW founder Ferdinand Porsche (who also designed the famous Porsche sports car). Piëch himself is known to be a world-class automotive engineer as well as super competitive. In his first press conference as newly appointed head of the VW Group, Piëch made his marching orders clear: "Whenever there is war, fewer remain at the end. There are always winners and losers. And I intend … to emerge victorious!"[46]

In the early years of his reign, however, Piëch was caught up in an internal power struggle. In the early 2000s, the Porsche company was attempting a hostile takeover of the much larger Volkswagen Group. In terms of size, VW was more than 15 times larger than Porsche at that time. Part of the hostile takeover attempt of the teetering VW Group was motivated by a bitter family feud resulting from estranged members of the Porsche and Piëch families, each holding leading executive positions in both companies. Both families are directly related to one another as they share Ferdinand Porsche as their grandfather. As the global financial crisis took hold, the Porsche company collapsed under a heavy debt burden caused by the hostile takeover attempt. Piëch turned the tables and took over Porsche in 2012, fired the existing Porsche executive team, and sidelined his cousins.

Meanwhile Piëch, as chairman of the board of the VW Group, installed his protégé Martin Winterkorn as CEO of VW in 2007. Winterkorn had already worked closely with Piëch at Audi, and he viewed his role as implementer of Piëch's grand ideas. At Audi, Piëch had developed a smaller diesel engine for use in passenger cars with superior performance and higher fuel efficiency due to turbocharging and fuel-injection technology. This was a revolutionary concept at the time, because diesel engines were used only in larger commercial trucks, not in passenger cars. It also laid the foundation for the "clean diesel" initiative upon which VW would embark.

In the mid-1990s, Piëch decreed that the clean diesel engine (called "TDI" for turbocharged direct injection) would be key to conquering the U.S. market—the only market globally where VW was not a leader. In 1996, VW introduced the new clean diesel concept in the United States with great fanfare and provocative TV ads. VW's clean diesel cars seemed like a dream come true for the environmentally conscious drivers. They drove like sports cars, got 800 miles to a tank, and lasted forever (diesel engines can run over 1 million miles).

However, the problem with diesel engines is that there is an engineering trade-off between performance, fuel

Ads like these promoted the benefits of TDI Clean Diesel technology (i.e., environmentally friendly, fuel efficient, and high performing). The VW Group had huge success in the United States between 2009 and 2015. But it turns out the cars with TDI engines were all equipped with defeat devices to produce fraudulent results during mandatory and stringent emissions test in the United States.
VW Group

(Continued)

efficiency, and emissions. You can achieve two of the three goals, but not all three at the same time. This was not a problem until the Bush (in 2007) and Obama (in 2009) administrations raised the U.S. emissions standards to a much more stringent level than what Europe deems acceptable. This was done to combat air pollution: Smog was becoming a serious problem, especially in larger cities such as Los Angeles, and the link to global warming was becoming more clear.

At the same time, VW's strategy was to become the world's largest car manufacturer, and success in North America was key. VW CEO Winterkorn decided the company would continue to bet on the new TDI engine, which customers in Europe loved. However, diesel engines disgorge nasty pollutants such as nitrogen oxides (NOx) that endanger human health. To meet the stricter U.S. environmental standards, VW engineers created NOx traps to burn and catch these pollutants. But this specialized equipment had a threefold problem: It was expensive, it needed to be replaced frequently, and it lowered engine performance and fuel efficiency. Given the inherent trade-offs of TDI engines between performance, fuel efficiency, and emissions, VW engineers could not meet the U.S. environmental regulations.

When stakes are high and the pressure to deliver results is intense, people tend to cut corners. Beginning with the 2009 model year, VW engineers installed so-called defeat devices in all its smaller (2.0 liter) TDI engines. These defeat devices were software codes contained in the car's onboard computer. The computer was programmed to detect when the car was being tested for emissions by assessing a host of variables, including whether the car was moving or stationary, whether the steering wheel was being touched, what the speed and duration of the engine run was, and so forth. This sophisticated defeat device allowed the vehicles to pass the required and rigid U.S. emissions tests. In reality, however, the vehicles equipped with TDI engines actually exceeded the limits for pollutants by up to 40 times during use. Between 2009 and 2015, VW sold 500,000 TDI vehicles equipped with defeat devices in the United States and a total of 11 million worldwide. Dieselgate turned out to be the greatest corporate fraud in history.

When the Dieselgate scandal broke in the fall of 2015, VW's share price dropped by more than 30 percent. Senior executives at the VW Group were replaced, and some were prosecuted and jailed. VW had to repurchase all the vehicles sold in the United States or retrofit them with proper emissions software and technology. Some former, long-term VW employees insist the orders for the defeat devices must have been top-down (or at least approved by the top), because rules at VW are so strict that "you can't even get a pen without three signatures on the proper request form."[47] In contrast, VW's top executives insist the defeat devices were created and installed by some rogue, midlevel engineers without their knowledge. In the end, Dieselgate cost VW $25 billion in fines and legal settlements, not to mention the loss of reputation.[48]

BAD APPLES VS. BAD BARRELS

Some people believe that unethical behavior is limited to a few "bad apples" in organizations.[49] The assumption is that the vast majority of the population—and by extension, organizations—are good, and that we need only safeguard against abuses by a few bad actors. According to agency theory, it's the "bad agents" who act opportunistically, and principals need to be on guard against bad actors.

However, research indicates it is not just the few "bad apples" but entire organizations that can create a climate in which unethical, even illegal behavior is tolerated.[50] While there clearly are some people with unethical or even criminal inclinations, in general one's ethical decision-making capacity depends very much on the organizational context. Research shows that if people work in organizations that expect and value ethical behavior, they are more likely to act ethically.[51] The opposite is also true. Enron's *stated* key values included respect and integrity, and its mission statement proclaimed that all business dealings should be open and fair.[52] Yet, the ethos at Enron was all about creating an inflated share price at any cost, and its employees observed and followed the behavior set by their leaders.

Sometimes, it's the bad barrel that can spoil the apples! This is precisely what some of the former VW employees claim happened with Dieselgate, featured in Strategy Highlight 12.2. Although many participants are attempting to shift the blame, what is clear is that strategic leaders are ultimately responsible for what happens in their organization. If they did know or condone any wrongdoing, they are directly implicated. If they didn't know what was going on, they should have known.

Employees take cues from their environment on how to act. Therefore, ethical leadership is critical, and strategic leaders set the tone for the ethical climate within an organization. This is one of the reasons the HP board removed then-CEO Mark Hurd in 2010 even without proof of illegal behavior or violation of the company's sexual-harassment policy. The forced resignation was prompted by a lawsuit alleging sexual harassment against Hurd by a former adult movie actress who worked for HP as an independent contractor. This action shows that CEOs of Fortune 500 companies are under constant public scrutiny and ought to adhere to the highest ethical standards. If they do not, they cannot rationally expect their employees to behave ethically. Unethical behavior can quickly destroy the reputation of a CEO, one of the most important assets he or she possesses.

To foster ethical behavior in employees, boards must be clear in their ethical expectations, and top management must create an organizational structure, culture, and control system that values and encourages desired behavior. Furthermore, a company's formal and informal cultures must be aligned, and executive behavior must be in sync with the formally stated vision and values. Employees will quickly see through any duplicity. Actions by executives speak louder than words in vision statements. Strategic goals must be achievable with legal means. As shown in Strategy Highlight 12.2, when the stakes are high and top-down pressure is intense to meet goals, employees are more likely to cut corners and act unethically and sometimes even illegally.

Other leading professions have accepted codes of conduct (e.g., the bar association in the practice of law and the Hippocratic oath in medicine); management has not.[53] Some argue that management needs an accepted code of conduct,[54] holding members to a high professional standard and imposing consequences for misconduct. Misconduct by an attorney, for example, can result in being disbarred and losing the right to practice law. Likewise, medical doctors can lose their professional accreditations if they engage in misconduct.

To anchor future managers in professional values and to move management closer to a truly professional status, a group of Harvard Business School students developed an MBA oath (see Exhibit 12.4).[55] Since 2009, over 6,000 MBA students from more than 300 institutions around the world have taken this voluntary pledge. The oath explicitly recognizes the role of business in society and its responsibilities beyond shareholders. It also holds managers to a high ethical standard based on more or less universally accepted principles in order to "create value responsibly and ethically."[56] Having the highest personal integrity is of utmost importance to one's career. It takes decades to build a career, but sometimes just a few moments to destroy one. The voluntary MBA oath sets professional standards, but its effect on behavior is unknown, and it does not impose any consequences for misconduct.

12.4 Implications for Strategic Leaders

An important implication for the strategic leader is the recognition that effective corporate governance and solid business ethics are critical to sustaining competitive advantage over time. Governance and ethics are closely intertwined in an intersection of setting the right organizational core values and then ensuring compliance.

A variety of corporate governance mechanisms can be effective in addressing the principal–agent problem. These mechanisms tend to focus on monitoring, controlling, and providing incentives, and they must be complemented by a strong code of conduct and strategic leaders who act with integrity. The effective strategic leader must help employees to "walk the talk"; leading by ethical example often has a stronger effect on employee behavior than words alone.

EXHIBIT 12.4

The MBA Oath

Source: MBA Oath and Max
Anderson.

As a business leader I recognize my role in society.

- *My purpose is to lead people and manage resources to create value that no single individual can create alone.*
- *My decisions affect the well-being of individuals inside and outside my enterprise, today and tomorrow.*

Therefore, I promise that:

- *I will manage my enterprise with loyalty and care, and will not advance my personal interests at the expense of my enterprise or society.*
- *I will understand and uphold, in letter and spirit, the laws and contracts governing my conduct and that of my enterprise.*
- *I will refrain from corruption, unfair competition, or business practices harmful to society.*
- *I will protect the human rights and dignity of all people affected by my enterprise, and I will oppose discrimination and exploitation.*
- *I will protect the right of future generations to advance their standard of living and enjoy a healthy planet.*
- *I will report the performance and risks of my enterprise accurately and honestly.*
- *I will invest in developing myself and others, helping the management profession continue to advance and create sustainable and inclusive prosperity.*

In exercising my professional duties according to these principles, I recognize that my behavior must set an example of integrity, eliciting trust and esteem from those I serve. I will remain accountable to my peers and to society for my actions and for upholding these standards.

This oath I make freely, and upon my honor.

The strategist needs to look beyond shareholders and apply a stakeholder perspective to ensure long-term survival and success of the firm. A firm that does not respond to stakeholders beyond stockholders in a way that keeps them committed to its vision will not be successful. Stakeholders want fair treatment even if not all of their demands can be met. Fairness and transparency are critical to maintaining good relationships within the network of stakeholders the firm is embedded in. Finally, the large number of glaring ethical lapses in recent decades makes it clear that organizational core values and a code of conduct are key to the continued professionalization of management. Strategic leaders need to live organizational core values by example.

CHAPTER**CASE 12**   Part II

IN 2004, SHORTLY after founding Theranos, securing initial funding, and receiving high-powered venture capitalist and scientist endorsements, Elizabeth Holmes set out to build a hand-selected board of directors. Assembling Theranos' board of directors was not done with the goal of providing strategic guidance and to oversee corporate governance, but to provide a seal of approval and legitimacy. A powerful board of directors would allow Theranos, so Holmes reasoned, to intimidate government agencies such as regulatory bodies to not challenge Theranos'

assertion that its technology worked as proclaimed. Holmes put on the charm and convinced elder statesman George Schultz, Henry Kissinger (former secretary of state), James Matthis (future secretary of defense), and William Perry (former secretary of defense), among other high-powered individuals, to join Theranos' board of

Ethan Pines/Forbes
Collection/Corbis/Getty Images

directors. Holmes was also close to the Clinton Global Initiative and former President Bill Clinton; she even threw a fund-raiser for then presidential candidate Hillary Clinton. Holmes cozied up to the Obama administration as well, touring the Theranos facility in the Bay Area with then Vice President Joe Biden and explaining that he just witnessed the lab of the future—Theranos was going to provide higher-quality services at lower costs.

Shortly after Theranos went live with its blood testing in the fall of 2013, however, medical doctors began questioning the lab results their patients had obtained from the high-flying startup. Some actually had their patients retested at traditional labs. After comparing Theranos' results with those obtained from Quest or LabCorp for the same patients, physicians found discrepancies, proving that Theranos technology was faulty and not working. Recognizing the inherent risks of providing patients with faulty lab results (which can result, for instance, in the start of aggressive treatments for combating cancer or not undertaking a treatment when needed), one Theranos employee filed a whistle-blower complaint with a government agency, while another employee shared information with an investigative reporter at *The Wall Street Journal (WSJ)*. The *WSJ* published a series of articles in the fall of 2015 exposing the Theranos fraud, which resulted in several unannounced inspections at Theranos by regulatory agencies.

In 2018, federal prosecutors filed criminal charges against Elizabeth Holmes and her enforcer and second in command at Theranos, Ramesh "Sunny" Balwani, alleging they defrauded investors, doctors, and patients. The case is scheduled to begin in the summer of 2020, with both facing up to 20 years in prison if convicted. The story of college dropout wunderkind Elizabeth Holmes is so compelling that Hollywood is producing a movie about it, with Jennifer Lawrence cast in the leading role.

Questions

1. What was the original mission and vision of Theranos founder Elizabeth Holmes? How did Holmes set out to fulfill her mission?

2. What is the designated role of a board of directors? Did the Theranos board of directors fulfill this role? Why, or why not? If not, what was the motivation behind stacking the board the way Holmes did? Explain.

3. Theranos was valued at some $10 billion at its peak. Did the investors overlook any red flags? Or was it simply FOMO ("fear of missing out") that made them hurry to jump on the Theranos bandwagon? Why were so many people caught up in the hype around Theranos and Elizabeth Holmes, its charismatic leader?

4. Why and how did Theranos get in trouble?

5. What lessons can be learned from the Theranos case?

mySTRATEGY

Are You Part of Gen Z, or Will You Manage Gen-Z Workers?

Generation Z (born between 1997 and 2012) is just starting to enter the college-aged work force and beginning their careers now, as the Baby Boomers (born between 1946 and 1964) retire in large numbers, and Millennials (1981–1996) and Gen X (1965–1980) workers reach leadership roles. About 67 million people make up Gen Z (compared to 72 million Millennials). This generation is also the most racially diverse in U.S. history. Nearly half of Gen Zers are non-Caucasian, including 24 percent Hispanic. Gen Zers have been described as the most well-educated, well-behaved generation in several cycles. However, they are also the highest stressed and depressed generation—perhaps ever in the United States.

The financial crisis of 2008, September 11th attacks, and ongoing global and societal conflicts seem to have scarred this generation more than any since their great-great grandparents, who survived the Great Depression of the 1930s and World War II. This seems to have instilled a desire for personal financial stability and a more cautious approach to life than the prior three generations. For example, many Gen Zers are delaying driver's licenses and using their finely honed smartphone skills to navigate with ride hailing services, e-scooters, and public transit, rather than driving a personal car.

The early trends are that this generation may shy away from starting their own firms (due to the financial uncertainty of such new ventures). Gen Z also desires the flexible schedules of "gig jobs" even in more traditional work settings. Classic beginning jobs in retailing and hospitality are having trouble finding young workers to fill traditional work shifts used to cover the store or restaurant hours, for example. Additionally, this generation is comfortable trusting adults, and many large firms are creating small work groups so that older workers can assist with broadly needed training and mentoring. Firms such as EY are now using video technology in the recruiting and interview process to attract more Gen Z workers. Intuit has added all its job openings on the internal Slack messaging system so current employees, who may not follow their emails closely, will not miss out on new job opportunities within the firm. Intuit hopes to improve retention rates with such methods.

1. As this cohort expands in the work force, do you expect to see different sets of business ethics and workplace culture take hold? Please explain.

2. Are efforts such as the MBA oath (discussed in this chapter) reflections of a different approach that Gen Z will bring to the business environment, compared with prior generations?

TAKE-AWAY CONCEPTS

In this final chapter, we looked at stakeholder strategy, corporate governance, business ethics, and strategic leadership, as summarized by the following learning objectives and related take-away concepts.

LO 12-1 / Describe the shared value creation framework and its relationship to competitive advantage.

- By focusing on financial performance, many companies have defined value creation too narrowly.
- Companies should instead focus on creating *shared value,* a concept that includes value creation for both shareholders and society.
- The shared value creation framework seeks to identify connections between economic and social needs, and then leverage them into competitive advantage.

LO 12-2 / Explain the role of corporate governance.

- Corporate governance involves mechanisms used to direct and control an enterprise to ensure that it pursues its strategic goals successfully and legally.
- Corporate governance attempts to address the principal–agent problem, which describes any situation in which an agent performs activities on behalf of a principal.

LO 12-3 / Apply agency theory to explain why and how companies use governance mechanisms to align interests of principals and agents.

- Agency theory views the firm as a nexus of legal contracts.

- The principal–agent problem concerns the relationship between owners (shareholders) and managers and also cascades down the organizational hierarchy.
- The risk of opportunism on behalf of agents is exacerbated by information asymmetry: Agents are generally better informed than the principals.
- Governance mechanisms are used to align incentives between principals and agents.
- Governance mechanisms need to be designed in such a fashion as to overcome two specific agency problems: adverse selection and moral hazard.

LO 12-4 / Evaluate the board of directors as the central governance mechanism for public stock companies.

- The shareholders are the legal owners of a publicly traded company and appoint a board of directors to represent their interests.
- The day-to-day business operations of a publicly traded stock company are conducted by its managers and employees, under the direction of the chief executive officer (CEO) and the oversight of the board of directors. The board of directors is composed of inside and outside directors, who are elected by the shareholders.
- Inside directors are generally part of the company's senior management team, such as the chief financial officer (CFO) and the chief operating officer (COO).
- Outside directors are not employees of the firm. They frequently are senior executives from other firms or full-time professionals who are appointed to a board and who serve on several boards simultaneously.

LO 12-5 / Evaluate other governance mechanisms.

- Other important corporate mechanisms are executive compensation, the market for corporate control, and financial statement auditors, government regulators, and industry analysts.
- Executive compensation has attracted significant attention in recent years. Two issues are at the forefront: (1) the absolute size of the CEO pay package compared with the pay of the average employee and (2) the relationship between firm performance and CEO pay.
- The board of directors and executive compensation are internal corporate governance mechanisms. The market for corporate control is an important external corporate governance mechanism. It consists of activist investors who seek to gain control of an underperforming corporation by buying shares of its stock in the open market.
- All public companies listed on the U.S. stock exchanges must file a number of financial statements with the Securities and Exchange

Commission (SEC), a federal regulatory agency whose task it is to oversee stock trading and enforce federal securities laws. Auditors and industry analysts study these public financial statements carefully for clues of a firm's future valuations, financial irregularities, and strategy.

LO 12-6 / Explain the relationship between strategy and business ethics.

- The ethical pursuit of competitive advantage lays the foundation for long-term superior performance.
- Law and ethics are not synonymous; obeying the law is the minimum that society expects of a corporation and its managers.
- A manager's actions can be completely legal, but ethically questionable.
- Some argue that management needs an accepted code of conduct that holds members to a high professional standard and imposes consequences for misconduct.

KEY TERMS

Adverse selection *(p. 441)*

Agency theory *(p. 440)*

Board of directors *(p. 441)*

Business ethics *(p. 448)*

CEO/chairperson duality *(p. 443)*

Corporate governance *(p. 438)*

Inside directors *(p. 442)*

Leveraged buyout (LBO) *(p. 446)*

Moral hazard *(p. 441)*

Outside directors *(p. 442)*

Poison pill *(p. 447)*

Shared value creation framework *(p. 437)*

Shareholder capitalism *(p. 436)*

Stock options *(p. 443)*

Unicorns *(p. 435)*

DISCUSSION QUESTIONS

1. The shared value creation framework provides help in making connections between economic and societal needs in a way that transforms a business opportunity. Taking the role of a consultant to Uber (ride-hailing service), discuss how Uber might move into fields serving more of a societal need. Provide some suggestions or concrete actions the firm can take that would connect its economic and social needs.

2. How can a top management team lower the chances that key managers will pursue their own

self-interests at the expense of stockholders? At the expense of the employees? At the expense of other key stakeholders?

3. The Business Roundtable has recommended that the CEO should not also serve as the chairman of the board. Discuss the disadvantages for building a sustainable competitive advantage if the two positions are held by one person. What are the disadvantages for stakeholder management? Are there situations where it would be advantageous to have one person in both positions?

ENDNOTES

1. As quoted in: *The Inventor: Out for Blood in Silicon Valley*, HBO documentary (2019), www.hbo.com/documentaries/the-inventor-out-for-blood-in-silicon-valley.

2. This ChapterCase is based on the work of John Carreyrou, investigative reporter of *The Wall Street Journal* who revealed the Theranos' fraud in a set of articles beginning the fall of 2015. In 2018, he published an excellent and in-depth book about Theranos; see: Carreyrou, J. (2018), *Bad Blood: Secrets and Lies in a Silicon Valley Startup* (New York: Knopf Doubleday Publishing Group). In 2019, HBO ran an excellent documentary about the rise and fall of Theranos, titled *The Inventor: Out for Blood in Silicon Valley.*

3. Porter, M.E., and M.R. Kramer (2006, December), "Strategy and society: The link between competitive advantage and corporate social responsibility,"*Harvard Business Review*, 80–92; and Porter, M.E., and M.R. Kramer (2011, January–February), "Creating shared value: How to reinvent capitalism—and unleash innovation and growth," *Harvard Business Review.*

4. "The billion dollar startup club," *The Wall Street Journal* (2019, April), http://graphics.wsj.com/billion-dollar-club/.

5. "The endangered public company," *The Economist* (2012, Mar. 19); the classic work by Berle, A., and G. Means (1932), *The Modern Corporation & Private Property* (New York: Macmillan); and Monks, R.A.G., and N. Minow (2008), *Corporate Governance,* 4th ed. (West Sussex, UK: John Wiley & Sons).

6. NASDAQ was originally an acronym for National Association of Securities Dealers Automated Quotations, but it is now a standalone term.

7. Berle, A., and G. Means (1932), *The Modern Corporation & Private Property* (New York: Macmillan); and Monks, R.A.G., and N. Minow (2008), *Corporate Governance,* 4th ed. (West Sussex, UK: John Wiley & Sons).

8. This section is based on: Porter, M.E., and M.R. Kramer (2006, December), "Strategy and society: The link between competitive advantage and corporate social responsibility," *Harvard Business Review:* 80–92; and Porter, M.E., and M.R. Kramer (2011, January–February), "Creating shared value: How to reinvent capitalism—and unleash innovation and growth," *Harvard Business Review.*

9. Friedman, M. (1962), *Capitalism and Freedom* (Chicago, IL: University of Chicago Press), quoted in: Friedman, M. (1970, Sep. 13), "The social responsibility of business is to increase its profits," *The New York Times Magazine.*

10. Carroll, A.B., and A.K. Buchholtz (2012), *Business & Society. Ethics, Sustainability, and Stakeholder Management* (Mason, OH: South-Western Cengage).

11. "Milton Friedman goes on tour," *The Economist* (2011, Jan. 27).

12. For detailed data and descriptions on the GE Ecomagination initiative, see: www.ge.com/about-us/ecomagination.

13. "GE to invest more in 'green' technology," *The New York Times* (2005, May 10).

14. GE Sustainability Report, www.gesustainability.com/performance-data/ecomagination/, and GE Annual Report 2018, www.ge.com/investor-relations/annual-report.

15. GE Sustainability Report, www.gesustainability.com/performance-data/ecomagination/; and GE Annual Report 2018, www.ge.com/investor-relations/annual-report.

16. Porter, M.E., and M.R. Kramer (2011, January–February), "Creating shared value: How to reinvent capitalism—and unleash innovation and growth," *Harvard Business Review.*

17. Monks, R.A.G., and N. Minow (2008), *Corporate Governance,* 4th ed. (West Sussex, UK: John Wiley & Sons).

18. Berle, A., and G. Means (1932), *The Modern Corporation & Private Property* (New York: Macmillan); Jensen, M., and W. Meckling (1976), "Theory of the firm: Managerial behavior, agency costs and ownership structure," *Journal of Financial Economics* 3: 305–360; and Fama, E. (1980), "Agency problems and the theory of the firm," *Journal of Political Economy* 88: 375–390.

19. "Fund titan found guilty," *The Wall Street Journal* (2011, May 12).

20. "Fund titan found guilty," *The Wall Street Journal* (2011, May 12).

21. "Top 10 crooked CEOs," *Time* (2009, Jun. 9).

22. "Thain ousted in clash at Bank of America," *The Wall Street Journal* (2009, Jan. 23).

23. Agency theory originated in finance; see: Jensen, M., and W. Meckling (1976), "Theory of the firm: Managerial behavior, agency costs and ownership structure," *Journal of Financial Economics* 3: 305–360; and Fama, E. (1980), "Agency problems and the theory of the firm," *Journal of Political Economy* 88: 375–390. For an application to strategic management, see Eisenhardt, K.M. (1989), "Agency theory: An assessment and review," *Academy of Management Review* 14: 57–74; and Mahoney, J.T. (2005), *Economic Foundations of Strategy* (Thousand Oaks, CA: Sage).

24. Detailed coverage of the ongoing Waymo-Uber lawsuit can be found in: Isaac, M. (2017, May 17), "How Uber and Waymo ended up rivals in the race for driverless cars," *The New York Times.*

25. Bensinger, G. (2018, Feb. 9), "Uber agrees bot to use Waymo technology in self-driving cars," *The Wall Street Journal;* and Somerville, H. and R. McMillan (2019, Aug. 29), "Former Google engineer charged with stealing trade secrets," *The Wall Street Journal.*

26. Fuller, A.W., and F.T. Rothaermel (2012), "When stars shine: The effects of faculty founders on new technology ventures," *Strategic Entrepreneurship Journal* 6: 220–235.

27. Eisenhardt, K.M. (1989), "Agency theory: An assessment and review," *Academy of Management Review* 14: 57–74.

28. This section draws on: Monks, R.A.G., and N. Minow (2008), *Corporate Governance,* 4th ed. (West Sussex, UK: John Wiley & Sons); Williamson, O.E. (1984), "Corporate governance," *Yale Law Journal* 93: 1197–1230; and Williamson, O.E. (1985), *The Economic Institutions of Capitalism* (New York: Free Press).

29. For a research update on the topic of CEO/chairperson duality, see: Larcker, D.F., and B. Tayan (2016, Jun. 24), "Chairman and CEO. The controversy of board leadership structure," *Stanford Closer Look Series*; Krause, R., and M. Semadeni (2014), "Last dance or second chance? Firm performance, CEO career horizon, and the separation of board leadership roles," *Strategic Management Journal* 35: 808–825. This research looks at the three forms of splitting the CEO/chairman roles: apprentice, departure, and demotion. They look at several determinants of the type of split. They find that poor firm performance is more likely to result in a demotion split. The strength of this relationship increases when the board is more independent. The career horizon of the executive is also a determinant. Apprentice shifts involve executives with the shortest career horizons, while demotion shifts are associated with executives with longer career horizons. When performance is poor and boards are independent, the strength of the relationship with career horizon is magnified; see also: Flickinger, M., M. Wrage, A. Tuschke, and R. Bresser (2015, Mar.18), "How CEOs protect themselves against dismissal: A social status perspective," *Strategic Management Journal.*

30. "Suspicions and spies in Silicon Valley," *Newsweek* (2006, Sep. 17).

31. This Strategy Highlight is based on: Thomas, P. (2019, May 23), "Hewlett Packard Enterprise boosts outlook despite falling revenue," *The Wall Street Journal;* Maidenberg, M. (2019, May 23), "HP reports flat revenue but beats Wall Street targets," *The Wall Street Journal;* King, R. (2017, Feb. 22), "HP revenue grows again on PC rebound," The Wall Street Journal; King, R. (2016, Jul. 24), "Dell, HP take opposite tacks amid roiling tech market," *The Wall Street Journal;* "As H-P split nears, bosses tick off a surgery checklist," *The Wall Street Journal* (2015, Jun. 30); "Split today, merge tomorrow," *The Economist* (2014, Oct. 7); "Inside HP's missed chance to avoid a disastrous deal," *The Wall Street Journal* (2013, Jan. 21); "The HP Way out," *The Economist* (2013, Apr. 5); "How Hewlett-Packard lost its way," CNN Money (2012, May 8); "HP shakes up board in scandal's wake," *The Wall Street Journal* (2011, Jan. 21); "HP CEO Mark Hurd resigns after sexual harassment probe," *The Huffington Post* (2010, Aug. 6); "The curse of HP," *The Economist* (2010, Aug. 12); "Corporate governance: Spying and leaking are wrong," *The Economist* (2006, Sep. 14); "Corporate governance: Pretext in context," *The Economist* (2006, Sep. 14); Packard, D. (1995), *HP Way: How Bill Hewlett and I Built Our Company* (New York: Collins); and Collins, J.C., and J.I. Porras (1994), *Built to Last: Successful Habits of Visionary Companies* (New York: HarperCollins).

32. Mohan, B. and M. I. Norton (2018, May 20), "Consumers care about CEO-employee pay ratios," *The Wall Street Journal.*

33. The data presented here are drawn from: Francis, T., and L. Ketineni (2019, May 16), "The WSJ CEO pay ranking," *The Wall Street Journal.*

34. Lublin, J. (2015, Jun. 25), "How much the best-performing and worst-performing CEOs got paid," *The Wall Street Journal.*

35. Ariely, D. (2010), *The Upside of Irrationality: The Unexpected Benefits of Defying Logic at Work and at Home* (New York: HarperCollins).

36. The Dell LBO battle is described in: "Dell buyout pushed to brink," *The Wall Street Journal (2013,* Jul. 18); and "Monarchs versus managers. The battle over Dell raises the question of whether tech firms' founders make the best long-term leaders of their creations," *The Economist* (2013, Jul. 27).

37. www.fasb.org: "The term 'generally accepted accounting principles' has a specific meaning for accountants and auditors. The AICPA Code of Professional Conduct prohibits members from expressing an opinion or stating affirmatively that financial statements or other financial data 'present fairly . . . in conformity with generally accepted accounting principles,' if such information contains any departures from accounting principles promulgated by a body designated by the AICPA Council to establish such principles. The AICPA Council designated FASAB as the body that establishes generally accepted accounting principles (GAAP) for federal reporting entities."

38. www.secfilings.com.

39. Lowenstein, R. (2010), *The End of Wall Street* (New York: Penguin Press).

40. Hayward, M.L.A., and W. Boeker (1998), "Power and conflicts of interest in professional firms: Evidence from investment banking," *Administrative Science Quarterly* 43: 1–22.

41. www2.gmiratings.com/.

42. Trevino, L.K., and K.A. Nelson (2011), *Managing Business Ethics: Straight Talk About How to Do It Right,* 5th ed. (Hoboken, NJ: John Wiley & Sons).

43. Several such studies, such as the "ultimatum game," are described in: Ariely, D. (2008), *Predictably Irrational: The Hidden Forces That Shape Our Decisions* (New York: HarperCollins); and Ariely, D. (2010), *The Upside of Irrationality: The Unexpected Benefits of Defying Logic at Work and at Home* (New York: HarperCollins).

44. Lowenstein, R. (2010), *The End of Wall Street* (New York: Penguin Press).

45. Volkswagen (VW) is a stock company owned by the holding company Porsche SE (50.73%), Porsche GmbH (2.37%), Federal State of Lower Saxony (20%), State of Qatar (17%), and the rest is widely distributed (9.90%). Besides its own VW brand, it owns the following brands: Audi, Bentley, Bugatti, Ducati, Giugiaro, Lamborghini, MAN, Porsche, Scania, Seat, and Skoda.

46. Translated from German into English. Source: "Die Volkswagen-Story–wie ein Konzern seinen guten Ruf verspielte," ARD-Dokumentation, Nov. 16, 2015 www.youtube.com/watch?v=7OTqsQLihE8.

47. Quote from: *Dirty Money: Hard NOx,* Netflix documentary (2018).

48. This Strategy Highlight is based on: *Dirty Money: Hard NOx,* Netflix documentary (2018); Ewing, J. (2017, May 6), "Inside VW's campaign of trickery," *The New York Times*; Ewing, J. (2017), *Faster, Higher, Farther: The Volkswagen Scandal* (New York: Norton); "Die Volkswagen-Story – wie ein Konzern seinen guten Ruf verspielte," ARD-Dokumentation (2015, Nov. 16), www.youtube.com/watch?v=7OTqsQLihE8 ; "The Volkswagen scandal. A mucky business," *The Economist* (2015, Sep. 15).

49. Treviño, L.K., and K.A. Nelson (2011), *Managing Business Ethics: Straight Talk About How to Do It Right,* 5th ed. (Hoboken, NJ: John Wiley & Sons).

50. Treviño, L., and A. Youngblood (1990), "Bad apples in bad barrels: A causal analysis of ethical-decision behavior," *Journal of Applied Psychology* 75: 378–385.

51. Treviño, L., and A. Youngblood (1990), "Bad apples in bad barrels: A causal analysis of ethical-decision behavior," *Journal of Applied Psychology* 75: 378–385. Also, for a superb review and discussion of this issue, see: Treviño, L.K., and K.A. Nelson (2011), *Managing Business Ethics: Straight Talk About How to Do It Right,* 5th ed. (Hoboken, NJ: John Wiley & Sons).

52. McLean, B., and P. Elkind (2004), *The Smartest Guys in the Room: The Amazing Rise and Scandalous Fall of Enron* (New York: Portfolio).

53. Khurana, R. (2007), *From Higher Aims to Hired Hands: The Social Transformation of American Business Schools and the Unfulfilled Promise of Management as a Profession* (Princeton, NJ: Princeton University Press).

54. Khurana, R., and N. Nohria (2008, October), "It's time to make management a true profession," *Harvard Business Review*: 70–77.

55. For a history of the MBA oath and other information, see: www.mbaoath.org. See also: Anderson, M. (2010), *The MBA Oath: Setting a Higher Standard for Business Leaders* (New York: Portfolio).

56. www.mbaoath.org.

How to Conduct a Case Analysis

THE CASE STUDY is a fundamental learning tool in strategic management. The cases that accompany this text are carefully written to ensure tight integration with the strategic management concepts and frameworks presented. The goal is to ensure that the student learner is exposed to a wide variety of key concepts, industries, protagonists, and strategic problems.

In simple terms, cases tell the story of a company facing a strategic dilemma. Each case has a protagonist who has to make one or a set of strategic decisions to address the situation presented. The idea is that you put yourself in the situation of the protagonist and view the case from his or her perspective. The firms may be real or fictitious, and the problem may be current or past. Although the details of the cases vary, in general they start with a description of the challenge(s) to be addressed, followed by the history of the firm up until the decision point, and then additional information to help you with your analysis. To address the strategic dilemma, you will use the AFI Strategy Framework to conduct a case analysis as well as the strategic management tools and concepts provided in this text. After careful analysis, you will be able to formulate a strategic response and make recommendations about how to implement it.

Why Do We Use Cases?

Strategy is something that people learn by doing; it cannot be learned simply by reading a text or listening carefully in class. While those activities will help you become more familiar with the concepts and models used in strategic management, the only way to improve your skills in analyzing, formulating, and implementing strategy is to *practice.*

We encourage you to take advantage of the cases in this text as a "laboratory" in which to experiment with the strategic management tools you have been given, so you can learn more about how, when, and where they might work in the real world. Cases are valuable because they expose you to a number and variety of situations in which you can refine your strategic management skills without worrying about making mistakes (that may end up costing millions of dollars and/or result in the loss of jobs). The companies in these cases will not lose profits or fire you if you miscalculate a financial ratio, misinterpret someone's intentions, or make an incorrect prediction about environmental trends.

Cases also invite you to "walk in" and explore many more kinds of companies in a wider array of industries than you will ever be able to work at in your lifetime. With this strategy content, you will find MiniCases (i.e., shorter cases) about coffee chains (Starbucks), mass media and entertainment (Disney), technology (Apple), and innovative business models (Dollar Shave Club), among others. Some of these featured companies have enjoyed success (e.g., Apple and Disney), while others have struggled or failed (e.g., GE, Yahoo, BlackBerry, and JCPenney). Longer cases with complete financial data about companies such as Airbnb, Vanguard, Facebook, Tesla, McDonald's, and Uber are available in Connect and on Create.

Your personal organizational experiences are usually somewhat limited, defined by the jobs held by your family members or by your own forays into the working world. Learning about companies that are involved in so many different types of products and services may open up new employment possibilities for you. Diversity also forces us to think about the ways in which industries (as well as people) are both similar, yet distinct, and to critically examine the degree to which lessons learned in one forum transfer to other settings (i.e., to what degree are they generalizable). In short, cases are a great training tool, and they are fun to study.

Many of our cases are written from the perspective of the CEO or general manager responsible for strategic decision making in the organization. While you do not need to be a member of a top management team to utilize the strategic management process, these senior leaders are usually responsible for determining strategy in most of the organizations we study. Importantly, cases allow us to put ourselves "in the shoes" of strategic leaders and invite us to view the issues from their perspective. Having responsibility for the performance of an entire organization is quite different from managing a single project team, department, or functional area. Cases can help you see the *big picture* in a way that most of us are not accustomed to in our daily organizational lives. We recognize that most undergraduate students and even MBAs do not land immediately in the corporate boardroom. Yet having a basic understanding of the types of conversations going on in the boardroom not only increases your current value as an employee, but also improves your chances of getting there someday, should you so desire. Perhaps even more important, it allows you to find a company that aligns with your values and aspirations, and to develop a career with significant future upside.

Finally, cases help give us a *long-term* view of the firms they depict. Corporate history is immensely helpful in understanding how a firm got to its present position and why people within that organization think the way they do. Case authors spent many hours poring over historical documents and news reports in order to re-create each company's heritage for you, a luxury that most of us do not have when we are bombarded on a daily basis with homework, tests, and papers or project team meetings, deadlines, and reports. We invite you not just to learn from but also to savor reading each company's story.

Strategic Case Analysis

The first step in analyzing a case is to *skim it for the basic facts.* As you read, jot down your notes regarding the following basic questions:

- What company or companies is the case about?
- Who are the principal actors?
- What are the key events? When and where do they happen (in other words, what is the timeline)?

Second, go back and reread the case in greater detail, this time with a focus on *defining the problem.* Which facts are relevant and why? Just as a doctor begins by interviewing the patient ("What are the symptoms?"), you likewise gather information and then piece the clues together to figure out what is wrong. Your goal at this stage is to identify the *symptoms* in order to figure out which *tests* to run in order to make a definitive *diagnosis* of the main *disease.* Only then can you prescribe a *treatment* with confidence that it will

actually help the situation. Rushing too quickly through this stage often results in *malpractice* (that is, giving a patient with an upset stomach an antacid when she really has the flu), with effects that range from unhelpful to downright dangerous. The best way to ensure that you *do no harm* is to analyze the facts carefully, fighting the temptation to jump right to proposing a solution.

The third step, continuing the medical analogy, is to determine which analytical tools will help you to most accurately diagnose the problem(s). Doctors may choose to run blood tests or take an X-ray. In doing case analysis, we follow the steps of the *strategic management process.* You have any and all of the following models and frameworks at your disposal:

1. Perform an **external environmental analysis** of the:
   - Macro-level environment (PESTEL analysis).
   - Industry environment (e.g., Porter's five forces).
   - Competitive environment.
   - Strategic group analysis.

2. Perform an **internal analysis** of the firm using the resource-based view:
   - What are the firm's resources, capabilities, and competencies?
   - Does the firm possess valuable, rare, costly to imitate resources, and is it organized to capture value from those resources (VRIO analysis)?
   - What is the firm's value chain?

3. Analyze the firm's current **business-level** and **corporate-level** strategies:
   - Business-level strategy (product market positioning).
   - Corporate-level strategy (diversification).
   - International strategy (geographic scope and mode of entry).
   - How are these strategies being implemented?

4. Analyze the firm's **performance**:
   - Use both financial and market-based measures.
   - How does the firm compare to its competitors as well as the industry average?
   - What trends are evident over the past three to five years?
   - Consider the perspectives of multiple stakeholders (internal and external).
   - Does the firm possess a competitive advantage? If so, can it be sustained?

CALCULATING FINANCIAL RATIOS. Financial ratio analysis is an important tool for assessing the outcomes of a firm's strategy. Although financial performance is not the only relevant outcome measure, long-term profitability is a necessary precondition for firms to remain in business and to be able to serve the needs of all their stakeholders. Accordingly, at the end of this introductory module, we have provided a table of financial measures that can be used to assess firm performance (see Exhibit CA.2 at the end of this module).

All of the following aspects of performance should be considered, because each provides a different type of information about the financial health of the firm:

- **Profitability ratios**—how efficiently a company utilizes its resources.
- **Activity ratios**—how effectively a firm manages its assets.
- **Leverage ratios**—the degree to which a firm relies on debt versus equity (capital structure).
- **Liquidity ratios**—a firm's ability to pay off its short-term obligations.
- **Market ratios**—returns earned by shareholders who hold company stock.

MAKING THE DIAGNOSIS. With all of this information in hand, you are finally ready to *make a diagnosis.* Describe the problem(s) or opportunity(ies) facing the firm at this time and/or in the near future. How are they interrelated? By staying with the medical example, for instance, a runny nose, fever, stomach upset, and body aches are all indicative of the flu. Support your conclusions with data generated from your analyses.

The following general themes may be helpful to consider as you try to pull all the pieces together into a cohesive summary:

- Are the firm's value chain (primary and support) activities mutually reinforcing?
- Do the firm's resources and capabilities fit with the demands of the external environment?
- Does the firm have a clearly defined strategy that will create a competitive advantage?
- Is the firm making good use of its strengths and taking full advantage of its opportunities?
- Does the firm have serious weaknesses or face significant threats that need to be mitigated?

Keep in mind that "problems" can be positive (how to manage increased demand) as well as negative (declining stock price) in nature. Even firms that are currently performing well need to figure out how to maintain their success in an ever-changing and highly competitive global business environment.

Formulation: Proposing Feasible Solutions

When you have the problem figured out (your diagnosis), the next step is to *propose a treatment plan* or solution. There are two parts to the treatment plan: the *what* and the *why.* Using our medical analogy: The *what* for a patient with the flu might be antiviral medication, rest, and lots of fluids. The *why*: antivirals attack the virus directly, shortening the duration of illness; rest enables the body to recuperate naturally; and fluids are necessary to help the body fight fever and dehydration. *The ultimate goal is to restore the patient to wellness.* Similarly, when you are doing case analysis, your task is to figure out *what* the leaders of the company should do and *why* this is an appropriate course of action. Each part of your proposal should be justifiable based on your analyses.

The purpose of doing case analysis is to *look past* the easy answers and to help figure out not just what works but what might be *a better* answer. In other words, do not just take the first idea that comes to your mind and run with it. Instead, write down that idea for subsequent consideration but then think about what other solutions might achieve the same (or even better) results. Some of the most successful companies engage in scenario planning, in which they develop several possible outcomes and estimate the likelihood that each will happen. If their first prediction turns out to be incorrect, then they have a Plan B ready and waiting to be executed.

Plan for Implementation

The final step in the AFI framework is to develop a plan for implementation. Under formulation, you came up with a proposal, tested it against alternatives, and used your research to support why it provides the best solution to the problem at hand. To demonstrate its feasibility, however, you must be able to explain *how to put it into action.* Consider the following questions:

1. *What activities need to be performed?* The value chain is a very useful tool when you need to figure out how different parts of the company are likely to

be affected. What are the implications of your plan with respect to both primary activities (e.g., operations and sales/marketing/service) and support activities (e.g., human resources and infrastructure)?

2. *What is the timeline?* What steps must be taken first and why? Which ones are most critical? Which activities can proceed simultaneously, and which ones are sequential in nature? How long is your plan going to take?

3. *How are you going to finance your proposal?* Does the company have adequate cash on hand, or does it need to consider debt and/or equity financing? How long until your proposal breaks even and pays for itself?

4. *What outcomes is your plan likely to achieve?* Provide goals that are "SMART": specific, measurable, achievable, realistic, and timely in nature. Make a case for how your plan will help the firm to achieve a strategic competitive advantage.

Exhibit CA.1 aids you in assessing the implementation proposals you come up with along time and resource intensity.

In-Class Discussion

Discussing your ideas in class is often the most valuable part of a case study. The instructor will moderate the class discussion, guiding the AFI process and asking probing questions when necessary. Case discussion classes are most effective and interesting when everybody comes prepared and participates in the exchange.

Actively listen to your fellow students; mutual respect is necessary to create an open and inviting environment in which people feel comfortable sharing their thoughts with one another. This does not mean you need to agree with what everyone else is saying, however. Everyone has unique perspectives and biases based on differences in life experiences, education and training, values, and goals. As a result, no two people will interpret the same information in exactly the same way. Be prepared to be challenged, as well as to challenge others, to consider the case from another vantage point. Conflict is natural and even beneficial as long as it is managed in constructive ways.

Throughout the discussion, you should be prepared to support your ideas based on the analyses you conducted. Even students who agree with you on the general steps to be taken may disagree on the order of importance. Alternatively, they may like your plan in principle but argue that it is not feasible for the company to accomplish. You should not be surprised if others come up with an altogether different diagnosis and prescription. For better or worse, a good idea does not stand on its own merit—you must be able to convince your peers of its value by backing it up with sound logic and support.

Things to Keep in Mind While Doing Case Analysis

While some solutions are clearly better than others, it is important to remember that there is no single correct answer to any case. Unlike an optimization equation or accounting spreadsheet, cases cannot be reduced to a mathematical formula. Formulating and implementing strategy involves people, and working with people is inherently messy. Thus, the best way to get the maximum value from case analysis is to maintain an open mind and carefully consider the strengths and weaknesses of all the options. Strategy is an iterative process, and it is important not to rush to a premature conclusion.

For some cases, your instructor may be able to share with you what the company actually did, but that does not necessarily mean it was the best course of action. Too often students find out what happened in the *real world* and their creative juices stop flowing. Whether due to lack of information, experience, or time, companies quite often make the most expedient decision.

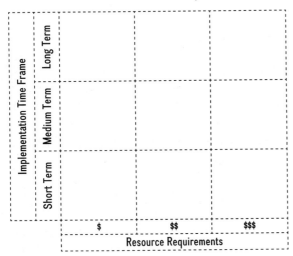

EXHIBIT CA.1 Assessing Implementation Proposals along Time and Resource Intensity

Source: Author's own creation.

With your access to additional data and time to conduct more detailed analyses, you may very well arrive at a different and better conclusion. Stand by your findings as long as you can support them with solid research data. Even Fortune 500 companies make mistakes.

Unfortunately, to their own detriment, students sometimes discount the value of cases based on fictional scenarios or set some time in the past. One significant advantage of fictional cases is that everybody has access to the same information. Not only does this level the playing field, but it also prevents you from being unduly biased by actual events, thus cutting short your own learning process. Similarly, just because a case occurred in the past does not mean it is no longer relevant. The players and technology may change over time, but many questions that businesses face are timeless in nature: how to adapt to a changing environment, the best way to compete against other firms, how to expand, or how to best implement needed changes.

Case Limitations

As powerful a learning tool as case analysis can be, it does come with some limitations. One of the most important for you to be aware of is that case analysis relies on a process known as *inductive reasoning,* in which you study specific business cases to derive general principles of management. Intuitively, we rely on inductive reasoning across almost every aspect of our lives. We know that we need oxygen to survive, so we assume that all living organisms need oxygen. Similarly, if all the swans we have ever seen are white, we extrapolate this to mean that all swans are white. While such relationships are often built upon a high degree of probability, it is important to remember that they are not empirically proven. We have in fact discovered life forms (microorganisms) that rely on sulfur instead of oxygen. Likewise, just because all the swans you have seen have been white, black swans do exist.

What does this caution mean with respect to case analysis? First and foremost, do not assume that just because one company utilized a joint venture to commercialize a new innovation, another company will be successful employing the same strategy. The first company's success may not be due to the particular organizational form it selected; it might instead be a function of its competencies in managing interfirm relationships or the particularities of the external environment. Practically speaking, this is why the analysis

step is so fundamental to good strategic management. Careful research helps us to figure out all of the potential contributing factors and to formulate hypotheses about which ones are most likely critical to success. Put another way, what happens at one firm does not necessarily generalize to others. However, solid analytical skills go a long way toward enabling you to make informed, educated guesses about when and where insights gained from one company have broader applications.

In addition, we have a business culture that tends to put high-performance firms and their leaders on a pedestal. Critical analysis is absolutely essential in order to discern the reasons for such firms' success. Upon closer inspection, we have sometimes found that their image is more a mirage than a direct reflection of sound business practices. For example, many business analysts have been taken in by the likes of Enron, Theranos, and Volkswagen only to humbly retract their praise when their shaky foundations began to crumble. We selected many of the firms in these cases because of their unique stories and positive performance, but we would be remiss if we let students interpret their presence in this book as a wholehearted endorsement of all their business activities.

Finally, our business culture also places a high premium on benchmarking and best practices. Although we present you with a sample of firms that we believe are worthy of in-depth study, we would again caution you against uncritical adoption of their activities in the hope of emulating their achievements. Even when a management practice has broad applications, strategy involves far more than merely copying the industry leader. The company that invents a best practice is already far ahead of its competitors on the learning curve, and even if other firms do catch up, the best they can usually hope for is to match (but not exceed) the original firm's success. By all means, learn as much as you can from whomever you can, but use that information to strengthen your organization's *own* strategic identity.

Frequently Asked Questions about Case Analysis

1. *Is it OK to use outside materials?*

   Ask your instructor. Some use cases as a springboard for analysis and will want you to look up more recent financial and other data. Others may want you to base your analysis on the information from the case only, so that you are not influenced by the actions actually taken by the company.

2. *Can I talk about the case with other students?*

   Again, you should check with your instructor, but many will strongly encourage you to meet and talk about the case with other students as part of your preparation process. The goal is not to come to a group consensus, but to test your ideas in a small group setting and revise them based on the feedback you receive.

3. *Is it OK to contact the company for more information?*

   If your instructor permits you to gather outside information, you may want to consider contacting the company directly. If you do so, it is imperative that you represent yourself and your school in the most professional and ethical manner possible. Explain to them that you are a student studying the firm and that you are seeking additional information, with your instructor's permission. Our experience is that some companies are quite receptive to student inquiries; others are not. You cannot know how a particular company will respond unless you try.

4. *What should I include in my case analysis report?*

   Instructors generally provide their own guidelines regarding content and format, but a general outline for a case analysis report is as follows: (1) analysis of the problem; (2) proposal of one or more alternative solutions; and (3) justification for which solution you believe is best and why. The most important thing to remember is not to waste precious space repeating facts from the case. You can assume that your professor has read the case carefully. What he or she is most interested in is your analysis of the situation and your rationale for choosing a particular solution.

EXHIBIT CA.2 When and How to Use Financial Measures to Assess Firm Performance

Overview: We have grouped the financial performance measures into five main categories:

Table 1a: Profitability: How profitable is the company?

Table 1b: Activity: How efficient are the operations of the company?

Table 1c: Leverage: How effectively is the company financed in terms of debt and equity?

Table 1d: Liquidity: How capable is the business of meeting its short-term obligations as they fall due?

Table 1e: Market: How does the company's performance compare to other companies in the market?

Table 1a: Profitability Ratios

	Formula	Characteristics
Gross margin (or EBITDA, EBIT, etc.)	(Sales – COGS) / Sales	Measures the relationship between sales and the costs to support those sales (e.g., manufacturing, procurement, advertising, payroll, etc.)
Return on assets (ROA)	Net income / Total assets	Measures the firm's efficiency in using assets to generate earnings
Return on equity (ROE)	Net income / Total stockholders' equity	Measures earnings to owners as measured by net assets
Return on invested capital (ROIC)	Net income / Invested capital	Measures how effectively a company uses its total invested capital, which consists of two components: (1) shareholders' equity through the selling of shares to the public, and (2) interest-bearing debt through borrowing from financial institutions and bondholders
Return on revenue (ROR)	Net income / Revenue	Measures the profit earned per dollar of revenue
Dividend payout	Common dividends / Net income	Measures the percent of earnings paid out to common stockholders

Limitations

1. Static snapshot of balance sheet.
2. Many important intangibles not accounted for.
3. Affected by accounting rules on accruals and timing. Onetime nonoperating income/expense.
4. Does not take into account cost of capital.
5. Affected by timing and accounting treatment of operating results.

EXHIBIT CA.2   When and How to Use Financial Measures to Assess Firm Performance (*continued*)

Table 1b: Activity Ratios

Activity Ratios	Formula	Characteristics
Inventory turnover	COGS / Inventory	Measures inventory management
Receivables turnover	Revenue / Accounts receivable	Measures the effectiveness of credit policies and the needed level of receivables investment for sales
Payables turnover	Revenue / Accounts payable	Measures the rate at which a firm pays its suppliers
Working capital turnover	Revenue / Working capital	Measures how much working (operating) capital is needed for sales
Fixed asset turnover	Revenue / Fixed assets	Measures the efficiency of investments in net fixed assets (property, plant, and equipment after accumulated depreciation)
Total asset turnover	Revenue / Total assets	Represents the overall (comprehensive) efficiency of assets to sales
Cash turnover	Revenue / Cash (which usually includes marketable securities)	Measures a firm's efficiency in its use of cash to generate sales
Limitations	Good measures of cash flow efficiency, but with the following limitations:	
	1. Limited by accounting treatment and timing (e.g., monthly/quarterly close)	
	2. Limitations of accrual vs. cash accounting	

EXHIBIT CA.2 When and How to Use Financial Measures to Assess Firm Performance (continued)

Table 1c: Leverage Ratios

Leverage Ratios	Formula	Characteristics
Debt to equity	Total liabilities/Total stockholders' equity	Direct comparison of debt to equity stakeholders and the most common measure of capital structure
Debt to assets	Total liabilities/Total assets	Debt as a percent of assets
Interest coverage (times interest earned)	(Net income + Interest expense + Tax expense) / Interest expense	Direct measure of the firm's ability to meet interest payments, indicating the protection provided from current operations
Long-term debt to equity	Long-term liabilities/Total stockholders' equity	A long-term perspective of debt and equity positions of stakeholders
Debt to market equity	Total liabilities at book value / Total equity at market value	Market valuation may represent a better measure of equity than book value; most firms have a market premium relative to book value.
Bonded debt to equity	Bonded debt/Stockholders' equity	Measures a firm's leverage in terms of stockholders' equity
Debt to tangible net worth	Total liabilities/(Common equity – Intangible assets)	Measures a firm's leverage in terms of tangible (hard) assets captured in book value
Financial leverage index	Return on equity/Return on assets	Measures how well a company is using its debt
Limitations	Overall good measures of a firm's financing strategy; needs to be looked at in concert with operating results because 1. These measures can be misleading if looked at in isolation. 2. They can also be misleading if using book values as opposed to market values of debt and equity.	

EXHIBIT CA.2 When and How to Use Financial Measures to Assess Firm Performance *(continued)*

Table 1d: Liquidity Ratios

Table 1d: Liquidity Ratios	Formula	Characteristics
Current	Current assets / Current liabilities	Measures short-term liquidity. Current assets are all assets that a firm can readily convert to cash to pay outstanding debts and cover liabilities without having to sell hard assets. Current liabilities are a firm's debt and other obligations that are due within a year.
Quick (acid-test)	(Cash + Marketable securities + Net receivables) / Current liabilities	Eliminates inventory from the numerator, focusing on cash, marketable securities, and receivables
Cash	(Cash + Marketable securities) / Current liabilities	Considers only cash and marketable securities for payment of current liabilities
Operating cash flow	Cash flow from operations / Current liabilities	Evaluates cash-related performance (as measured from the statement of cash flows) relative to current liabilities
Cash to current assets	(Cash + Marketable securities) / Current assets	Indicates the part of current assets that are among the most fungible (i.e., cash and marketable securities)
Cash position	(Cash + Marketable securities) / Total assets	Indicates the percent of total assets that are most fungible (i.e., cash)
Current liability position	Current liabilities / Total assets	Indicates what percent of total assets the firm's current liabilities represent
Limitations	Liquidity measures are important, especially in times of economic instability, but they also need to be looked at holistically along with financing and operating measures of a firm's performance. 1. Accounting processes (e.g., monthly close) limit efficacy of these measures when you want to understand daily cash position. 2. No account taken of risk and exposure on the liability side.	

EXHIBIT CA.2 When and How to Use Financial Measures to Assess Firm Performance (*continued*)

Table 1e: Market Ratios

	Formula	Characteristics
Book value per share	Total stockholders' equity / Number of shares outstanding	Equity or net assets, as measured on the balance sheet
Earnings-based growth models	$P = kE/(r - g)$, where E = earnings, k = dividend payout rate, r = discount rate, and g = earnings growth rate	Valuation models that discount earnings and dividends by a discount rate adjusted for future earnings growth
Market-to-book	(Stock price × Number of shares outstanding) / Total stockholders' equity	Measures accounting-based equity
Price-earnings (PE) ratio	Stock price / EPS	Measures market premium paid for earnings and future expectations
Price-earnings growth (PEG) ratio	PE / Earnings growth rate	PE compared to earnings growth rates, a measure of PE "reasonableness"
Sales-to-market value	Sales / (Stock price × Number of shares outstanding)	A sales activity ratio based on market price
Dividend yield	Dividends per share / Stock price	Direct cash return on stock investment
Total return to shareholders	Stock price appreciation + Dividends	
Limitations	Market measures tend to be more volatile than accounting measures but also provide a good perspective on the overall health of a company when used holistically with the other measures of financial performance. 1. Market volatility/noise is the biggest challenge with these measures. 2. Understanding what is a result of a firm strategy/decision vs. the broader market is challenging.	

Apple: What's Next?

APPLE IS THE first company whose stock market valuation crossed the $1 trillion threshold (in 2018). Some 20 years earlier, however, Apple would likely have gone bankrupt if archrival Microsoft (which enjoyed a valuation of $615 billion in December 1999)[1] had not invested $150 million in Apple. Under investigation by the Department of Justice at the time for alleged abuse of monopoly power, Microsoft was eager to not have another competitor go out of business.

The Apple Ecosystem

Apple achieved its success over two decades by implementing a potent competitive strategy. That strategy, conceptualized by co-founder Steve Jobs, combined innovation in products, services, and business models. In 1997, Apple was near bankruptcy. But in 2001, its revitalization took off with the introduction of the iPod, a portable digital music player; this was the same year Apple opened its first retail stores (see Exhibit MC1.1). Today, Apple's stores earn some of the highest sales per square foot of any retail outlets, including Tiffany & Co., a luxury jeweler, and LVMH, a purveyor of fine handbags and other high-end goods.

In 2003, Apple soared even higher when it launched its digital store iTunes. And it didn't stop there. In 2007, the California tech company revolutionized the smartphone market with the introduction of the iPhone. Just three years later, Apple re-created the tablet segment by introducing the iPad. For each of its iPod, iPhone, and iPad lines of businesses, Apple followed up with incremental product innovations that extended each product category. In 2017, Apple launched the 10th anniversary edition of the iPhone 10 and in 2018 it introduced the iPhone XS Max. Globally, Apple has also sold more than 1 billion

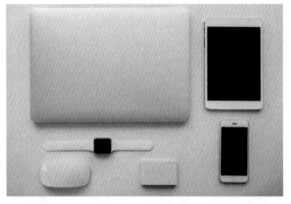

Apple's category-defining products (iPhone, iPad, iMac, and Apple Watch) are critical building blocks for its ecosystem anchored around its proprietary iOS operating system.
Studio Monkey/Shutterstock

iPhones. (The classic iPod was discontinued in 2014; the intent was always that the iPhone would subsume the MP3 capability. In 2019, Apple phased out iTunes and replaced it with three apps: Apple Music, Podcasts, and Apple TV.) Also, in 2019, Apple introduced the iPhone 11 and Apple TV+, its new streaming service.

By combining tremendous brainpower, intellectual property, and iconic brand value, Apple has enjoyed dramatic increases in revenues, profits, and stock market valuation. By 2019, it was one of the most profitable companies ever, with $225 billion in cash holdings alone.

A Good Strategy

Why was Apple so successful? Why did Apple's competitors, such as Sony, Dell, Hewlett-Packard (HP), Nokia, and BlackBerry, struggle or go out of business? The short answer is: Apple had a better strategy. But this raises the question: What is a good strategy? A good strategy is more than a mere goal or a company slogan. A good strategy defines the competitive challenges facing an organization through a critical and

EXHIBIT MC1.1 Apple's Stock Market Valuation ($ bn) and Key Events, 1976–2019

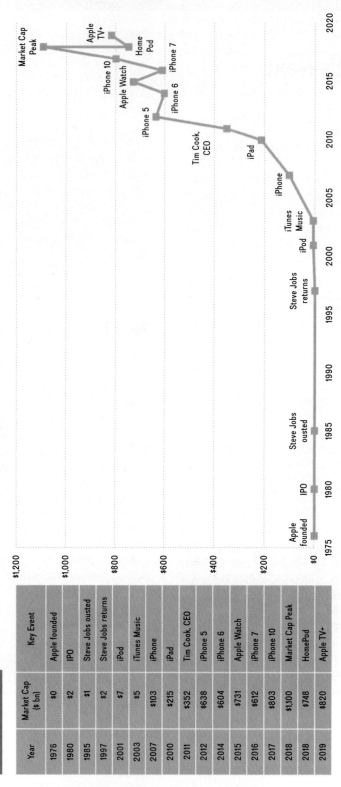

Year	Market Cap ($ bn)	Key Event
1976	$0	Apple founded
1980	$2	IPO
1985	$1	Steve Jobs ousted
1997	$2	Steve Jobs returns
2001	$7	iPod
2003	$5	iTunes Music
2007	$103	iPhone
2010	$215	iPad
2011	$352	Tim Cook, CEO
2012	$638	iPhone 5
2014	$604	iPhone 6
2015	$731	Apple Watch
2016	$612	iPhone 7
2017	$803	iPhone 10
2018	$1,100	Market Cap Peak
2018	$748	HomePod
2019	$820	Apple TV+

Source: Author's depiction of publicly available data.

honest assessment of the status quo. A good strategy also provides an overarching approach (policy) on how to deal with the competitive challenges identified. Last, a good strategy requires effective implementation through a coherent set of actions. A good strategy, therefore, consists of three elements:[2]

1. A *diagnosis* of the competitive challenge.
2. A *guiding policy* to address the competitive challenge.
3. A *set of coherent actions* to implement the firm's guiding policy.

THE COMPETITIVE CHALLENGE. First, consider the diagnosis of the competitive challenge. Above, we briefly traced Apple's renewal from the year 2001, when it hit upon the product and business-model innovations of the iPod/iTunes combination. Before that, Apple was merely a niche player in the desktop-computing industry and struggling financially. Steve Jobs turned the sinking company around by focusing on only two computer models (one laptop and one desktop) in each of two market segments (the professional market and the consumer market) as opposed to dozens of non-differentiated products within each segment. This streamlining of its product lineup enhanced Apple's strategic focus. Even so, the outlook for Apple was grim. Jobs believed that Apple, with less than 5 percent market share, could not win in the personal computer industry where desktops and laptops had become commoditized gray boxes. In that world, Microsoft, Intel, and Dell were the star performers. Jobs knew that he needed to create the "next big thing."[3]

A GUIDING POLICY. Second, Apple shifted its competitive focus away from personal computers to mobile devices. In doing so, Apple disrupted several industries through its product and business-model innovations. Combining hardware (i.e., the iPod) with a complementary service product (i.e., the iTunes Store) enabled Apple to devise a new business model. Users could download individual songs legally (at 99 cents) rather than buying an entire CD or downloading the songs illegally using Napster and other file-sharing services. The availability of the iTunes Store drove sales of iPods. Along with rising sales for the new iPod and iTunes products, demand rose for iMacs. The new products helped disrupt the existing personal computer market because people wanted to manage their music

and photos on a computer that worked seamlessly with their mobile device. Apple then leveraged the success of the iPod/iTunes business-model innovation, following up with product-category-defining innovations when launching the iPhone (in 2007) and the iPad (in 2010).

COHERENT ACTIONS. Third, Apple implemented its guiding policy with a set of coherent actions. Apple's coherent actions took a two-pronged approach: It drastically streamlined its product lineup through a simple rule—"we will make only one laptop and one desktop model for each of the two markets we serve, professional and consumer."[4] It also disrupted the industry status quo through a potent combination of product and business-model innovations, executed at planned intervals. These actions allowed Apple to create a string of temporary competitive advantages (see Exhibit MC1.1). Taken together, this enabled Apple to sustain its superior performance for over a decade.

Peak iPhone: What's Next?

Past performance, however, is no guarantee of future performance. Although Microsoft struggled to keep up with Apple, by spring 2019 it surpassed Apple to become the world's most valuable company once again with its renewed focus on cloud and mobile computing. In the same fashion, Amazon has also surpassed Apple in stock market valuation, while Alphabet is closing in. At the same time, Apple continues to face stiff competition from such non-U.S. rivals as Samsung (a South Korean firm) and Huawei, Xiaomi, and Oppo (all Chinese firms).

The trillion-dollar question today is whether Apple can continue to maintain a competitive advantage in the face of increasingly strong competition and rapidly changing industry environments. One big issue that Apple faces is "what's next?" after the iPhone. The situation in 2019 is akin to that of 2005 when Apple faced peak sales with the iPod, and competitors were starting to offer flip phones with MP3 player capabilities. As a response Apple launched the iPhone in 2007. The iPhone was a complete game changer. Although it made the iPod as a product category obsolete, Apple dominated the smartphone market for the decade to come.

The problem is that the global smartphone market has peaked. After reaching double-digit growth rates in 2013 and 2014, in 2017 and 2018 growth in sales of new phones contracted. This implies that most purchases are replacements of existing phones, while consumers hold on to their phones for longer as the cost of the phones has increased. Moreover, subsequent models offer mere incremental improvements over current models, often not worth the price differential. For instance, the introductory price of Apple's iPhone XS Max was $1,349 in the United States and nearly $1,800 in China! The "peak iPhone" situation is a huge problem for Apple because two-thirds of Apple's revenues in 2015 came directly from iPhone sales. By 2018, iPhone sales made up 50 percent of total revenues ($265 billion). With declining sales of iPhone units, Apple's revenues fell in 2016 and 2017, but rebounded in 2018, in part due to higher-priced iPhones. In other words, fewer units were sold, but the price increase made up for the unit fall in sales. In early 2019, Apple's market cap dropped again by 40 percent from its peak of $1.1 trillion in the fall of 2018 to $672 billion, but recovered to stand at $900 billion in summer 2019.

In recent years, sales in China made up 20 percent of Apple's revenues. However, Apple's popularity in China is declining rapidly in the face of local competition and trade tensions. The Chinese smartphone makers Huawei, Xiaomi, and Oppo offer phones of similar capabilities and user-friendliness for one-half the price or less. Moreover, given the trade tensions between the United States and China, Apple can expect more headwinds in China. For example, a consumer boycott could be instigated, or a stiff tax could be levied on Apple products by the Chinese authorities. In 2019, Huawei was facing several U.S. charges, among them misleading the U.S. government about its business dealings with Iran (while it was under U.S. economic sanctions) and allegations of bank fraud and technology theft (Huawei has denied both claims).

Will Apple introduce another game changer like the iPhone? In 2015, it introduced the Apple Watch, the first new product category launched since the iPad in 2010. Despite the unfulfilled potential of AirPower, which would have disrupted the charging industry and redefined the way consumers charge their Apple products, the Apple Watch is gaining more traction and has become the most popular smartwatch. In mobile payment systems (Apple Pay launched in 2014), music streaming (Apple Music launched in 2015), smart speaker systems (Apple's HomePod launched in 2018), and streaming services (Apple TV+ launched in 2019), Apple was a late mover.

Going forward, Apple CEO Tim Cook has explained that Apple will focus on services to make up for losses resulting from declining iPhone sales. In 2019, Apple had more than 1 billion users in its ecosystem, which comprises mobile devices (iPhone, iPad, iMac, or Apple Watch) combined with services such as iTunes, iCloud, and ApplePay. The Apple ecosystem is centered around its proprietary iOS operating system, which anchors a family of Apple products with its accompanying, co-dependent services. This allows the firm to benefit from customer lock-in and network effects. In other words, if a user is embedded in the Apple ecosystem, that makes it much harder for that user to switch to a mobile phone that relies on Google's Android operating system.

DISCUSSION QUESTIONS

1. How did Apple's introduction of the iPhone in 2007 lead to its success over its main competitors? Think about which industries it has disrupted and how.

2. What are some of the challenges facing Apple today? What should Apple do to address them? Be specific.

3. Apply the three-step process for developing a *good strategy* (diagnose the competitive challenge, derive a guiding policy, and implement a set of coherent actions) to Apple's current situation. What recommendations would you offer Apple to outperform its competitors in the future? Be specific.

Endnotes

1. Inflation adjusted, Microsoft's 1999 stock market valuation of $615 billion is about $940 billion in today's dollars.

2. This discussion is based on Rumelt, R. (2011), *Good Strategy, Bad Strategy* (New York: Crown Business).

3. Rumelt, R. (2011), *Good Strategy, Bad Strategy* (New York: Crown Business).

4. Ibid.

Sources: Apple Inc. annual reports (various years); Sull, D., and K.E. Eisenhardt (2015), *Simple Rules: How to Thrive in a Complex World* (New York: Houghton Mifflin Harcourt); Sull, D., and K.E. Eisenhardt (2012, September), "Simple rules for a complex world," *Harvard Business Review;* Isaacson, W. (2011), *Steve Jobs* (New York: Simon & Schuster); and Rumelt, R. (2011), *Good Strategy, Bad Strategy* (New York: Crown Business).

Starbucks CEO Kevin Johnson: "I'm not Howard Schultz"

STARBUCKS HAS MORE than 30,000 stores and $26 billion in annual revenues, making it the largest coffeehouse chain in the world. Starbucks has also experienced a sustained competitive advantage. Exhibit MC2.1 shows that since its IPO in 1992, Starbucks has outperformed the wider stock market by a huge margin—23,500 percentage points!—with an especially pronounced performance increase since 2008, when former CEO Howard Schultz came out of retirement.

How did all this start, especially since the United States is not known for its coffee culture? Inspired by Italian coffee bars, Schultz set out to provide a completely new consumer experience. The trademark of any Starbucks location is its ambience—the music and comfortable chairs and sofas draw customers in to sit and visit with friends while enjoying their beverages (and in some locations wine), food (a more recent addition), and complimentary WiFi. The menu boasts an array of offerings: Caffé Misto, Caramel Macchiato, Cinnamon Dolce Latte, Espresso Con Panna, and Mint Mocha Chip Frappuccino, as well as nearly 30 different coffee blends. Impressed customers then pay up to $4.50 for a Venti-sized drink. Starbucks has been so successful at creating its Starbucks experience that customers keep going back for more.

Starbucks' Core Competency

Starbucks' core competency is to create a unique consumer experience the world over. When buying out the original owners of Starbucks (a coffee bean roaster initially) in 1987, Schultz's strategic intent was to create a "third place," between home and work, where people would want to visit, ideally daily, and enjoy a sophisticated cup of coffee. Customers would pay for the unique experience and ambience, not just for the

coffee. The consumer experience that Starbucks created is a valuable, rare, and costly to imitate intangible resource. This allowed Starbucks to gain a competitive advantage. Since 2000, Starbucks' revenues have grown 13-fold, from less than $2 billion to nearly $26 billion in 2019.

While core competencies are often built through learning from experience, they can atrophy through forgetting. This is what happened to Starbucks between 2004 and 2008, when it rapidly expanded operations by doubling its stores from 8,500 to almost 17,000 (see Exhibit MC2.2). It also branched out into ice cream, desserts, sandwiches, books, music, and other retail merchandise, straying from its core business.

In trying to keep up with its explosive growth in both stores and diverse product offerings, Starbucks began to forget its core competency. It lost the appeal that made it special and its unique culture became diluted. For example, it used to be that baristas would grind coffee beans each time a new pot of coffee needed to be brewed (which was at least every eight minutes, so basically throughout the day). The sound of coffee beans grinding and the fresh aroma of coffee filling the air were ubiquitous across all Starbucks stores. But to accommodate the brand's rapid growth, many baristas began to take shortcuts: They would grind all the coffee beans in the morning and then store the ground beans for use throughout the day. The new espresso machines that were great for efficiency were not so great for customer service; they were so tall, they blocked interaction between baristas and customers. Although these and other operational changes allowed Starbucks to reduce costs and improve efficiency, they undercut Starbucks' primary reason for success—going to Starbucks not simply for the quick cup of coffee, but for the whole Starbucks coffee experience.

Losing a blind taste-test to fast food giant McDonald's further underscored the negative impact of cost-reduction measures. As one of among six coffees tested, Starbucks came in last. Even run-of-the-mill supermarket brands rated higher. Customers that were

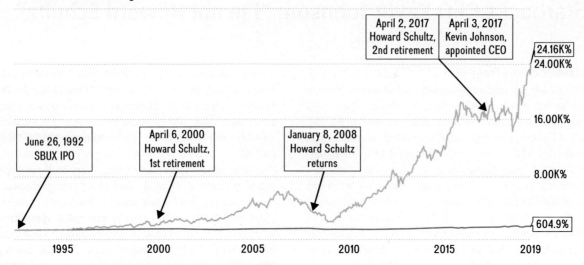

—— Starbucks Corp. Price % Change

—— S&P 500 Level % Change

Source: Author's depiction of publicly available data.

not fans of the Starbucks flavor had nicknamed the chain "Charbucks" to reflect what some critics claimed to be an apt description: overly roasted, dark, and bitter.

To make matters worse, the 2008 global financial crisis hit Starbucks hard. As is usually the case during a recession, the first items consumers tend to sacrifice are luxury items—people were no longer ordering $4.50 Venti cups of Starbucks coffee (see revenue drop in Exhibit MC2.2).

Howard Schultz's Return

In January 2008, Howard Schultz came out of an eight-year retirement to once again take the reins as CEO of

EXHIBIT MC2.2 Total Number of Starbucks Stores and Revenues ($ bn), 1971–2019*

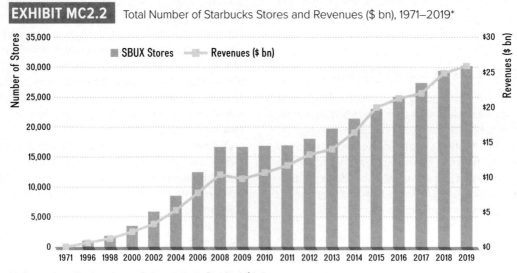

* Left vertical axis: Number of stores. Right vertical axis: Revenues ($ bn).

Source: Author's depiction of publicly available data drawn from various Starbucks annual reports.

Starbucks. His mission was to re-create what had made Starbucks so special from the start. Upon his return, he immediately launched several strategic initiatives to turn the company around. Just a month after coming back, Schultz ordered more than 7,000 Starbucks stores across the United States to close for one day, so baristas could relearn the perfect way to prepare coffee. The company lost over $6 million in revenue that day, which heightened investor jitters. The financial hit and investor anxiety notwithstanding, Schultz knew it was critical for Starbucks employees to relearn what made the Starbucks experience so unique—he saw this as the key to restoring its corporate culture.

NEW STRATEGIC INITIATIVES. In 2009, Starbucks introduced Via, its new instant coffee, a move that some worried might further dilute the brand. In 2010, Schultz rolled out new customer service guidelines: Baristas would no longer make multiple drinks at the same time, but, rather, concentrate on no more than two drinks at a time, starting a second one while finishing the first. Schultz also focused on readjusting store managers' goals. Before Schultz's return, managers had been mandated to focus on sales growth. Schultz, however, knowing that Starbucks' main differentiator was its special customer experience, instructed managers to shift their attention and efforts accordingly.

Although its earlier attempt to diversify away from its core business in the mid-2000s failed, it succeeded under Schultz. Late afternoons and early evenings were traditionally always the slowest times for Starbucks, so it became Schultz's goal to increase store traffic beyond the regular morning hours, when customers typically visited for their daily shots of caffeine. Schultz started by adding baked goods, sandwiches, and other small food items to the menu. To invite an even later crowd, he then introduced fresh vegetable plates, flatbread pizza, cheese plates, and desserts. Eventually, he added alcoholic beverages such as wine and beer (to be served after 4 p.m. only) as part of Starbucks' "Evenings" program.

Starbucks continued in these efforts by introducing new luxury items, catering to the wealthier customers within its existing customer base. It introduced limited-run, exclusive batches of varietal coffees for home use and sold them at high price points online and in stores. Some stores also included these same higher-priced roasts on their menus.

By 2014, Starbucks had launched its new Starbucks Reserve Roastery and Tasting Room. The first of these super high-end stores—with more on the horizon—was opened in Starbucks' home city, Seattle. Indeed, Schultz's plan was to open as many as 1,000 of these large-format, high-end roasteries in both national and international locations with the hopes they would improve declining sales and refresh the brand. Schultz believed that customers would enjoy the experience of watching baristas brew speciality coffees using the latest techniques (and thus willing to pay $12 a cup), mixing cocktails, and serving artisanal baked goods and other food items. Schultz wanted these roasteries to be a new "third place" for people to visit between work and home.

MODIFIED STRATEGIC INITIATIVES. Many of the new initiatives just discussed have since been modified. For example, Starbucks has retooled its Evenings program, announcing in 2017 that it would serve alcohol only at its roastery locations. These modification have not dampened its ambitions. Over the next few years, Starbucks aims to double its food revenues and be recognized as an evening food-and-wine destination. To symbolize its transition from a traditional coffeehouse, Starbucks dropped the word *coffee* from its logo.

Schultz also pushed the adoption of new technology to engage with customers more intimately and effectively. It now uses Facebook and Twitter to communicate with customers more or less in real time. In 2019, Starbucks had 26 million mobile payment users, more than that of Apple Pay (25 million), Google Pay (13 million), and Samsung Pay (12 million). Experts predict that by 2022, Starbucks will have 30 million users on its mobile ordering and payment app, and will continue to lead Apple, Google, and Samsung. Some 30 percent of all transactions in U.S. stores are now made using mobile devices. The Starbucks app allows customers to order and pay for drinks and food ahead of time, so that they can bypass standing in line and simply pick up their order when they arrive at a location.

With more than 14,000 stores in the U.S. market, Schultz started looking overseas for growth opportunities. Although traditionally a tea-drinking nation, coffee is catching on with urban professionals in China. In 2019, Starbucks had more than 3,500 stores in China, up from 1,500 in 2015. Starbucks plans to continue its rapid penetration of the Chinese market, aiming to operate 6,000 stores by 2022. Over the next few years, Starbucks also plans to double its presence in other areas of Asia (opening more than 4,000 cafés).

Kevin Johnson Is Not Howard Schultz

In 2017, nine years after coming out of retirement to initiate a successful turnaround, Howard Schultz once again stepped down as Starbucks CEO in a second attempt at retirement (see Exhibit MC2.1).[1] After his return, Starbucks' market valuation had appreciated approximately five-fold.

Schultz's strategic leadership was clearly critical in turning Starbucks around. Some worry that Starbucks' success is uniquely dependent on Schultz, suggesting that Schultz (and Starbucks) may have a strategic weakness in executive leadership succession planning. The primary evidence of this is that Starbucks stagnated and even went into decline during Schultz's absence. Some argue that Starbucks' struggle after Schultz's first departure is similar to Microsoft's challenges after Bill Gates stepped down from day-to-day business, Dell Computer after the first retirement of Michael Dell (now back), Walmart after the retirement of Sam Walton, and Apple after Steve Jobs was forced out in 1985. Although technically speaking, Howard Schultz is not a founder of Starbucks, he is the one who created the company as we know it today.

Schultz hopes that this second retirement from the company that he built from the ground up will be his last. In the meantime, new CEO Kevin Johnson, who transitioned from Microsoft, faces several challenges—

China represents a significant future growth opportunity for Starbucks, assuming it can transfer its core competency successfully. By 2022, the Seattle-based coffee chain plans on operating more than 6,000 stores in China, up from a mere 1,500 in 2015.
Stephen Shaver/Zumapress.com/Alamy Stock Photo

in particular, how to maintain Starbucks' core competencies and how to achieve future growth—both domestically and internationally. The maturing sales of the more than 14,000 U.S.-based stores is one of the biggest challenges facing Johnson today. Exhibit MC2.3 displays the growth of *same-store sales* (same-store sales is an important performance metric in the retail industry; it applies to stores that have been in

EXHIBIT MC2.3   Starbucks Same-Store Sales (change from prior year, in %), 2011–2019*

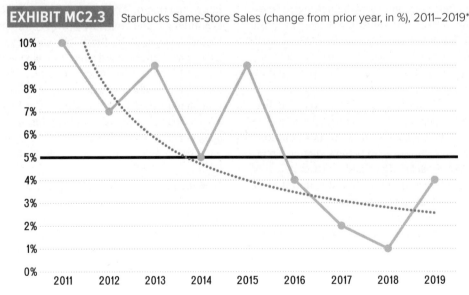

* Trend line added (dotted). Black, solid line shows the historic and target growth rate for same-store sales of 5% per year.

Source: Author's depiction of data from Jargon, J. (2019, Jan. 7), "Starbucks CEO Kevin Johnson reins in predecessor's ambitions: 'I'm not Howard,'" *The Wall Street Journal.*

existence for at least one year). Such sales have not only declined over the past decade, but have also fallen under its historic 5-percent growth threshold—a number that Starbucks has achieved for most of the past three decades.

To address the issue of declining same-store-sales growth, Johnson is taking a more rational and data-driven approach than did Schultz, who led by intuition and emotion. First, Johnson drastically scaled back on Schultz's vision to open 1,000 new high-end roasteries and tasting rooms, capping this number to a mere 10. He wants to see whether they provide an appropriate return on investment before expanding further and has laid out a stringent and disciplined approach to test the new store concept. By terminating this strategic initiative, Johnson freed up capital to refresh its existing stores, and to return cash to shareholders, one of Johnson's stated goals. Johnson also plans to grow revenue by 10 percent and open an additional 12,000 traditional stores around the world by 2021. In addition, he plans to expand Starbucks' coffee delivery business, even though some observers are skeptical, claiming this runs counter to the entire "third place" idea on which Starbucks was created.

During his first year as CEO, Kevin Johnson would often open meetings with Starbucks executives and employees by saying "I'm not Howard, I'm Kevin."[2] One of Johnson's overarching goals is to bring more financial discipline to Starbucks, to run it based on hard data analysis, cutting-edge management and operational practices. Whether Kevin Johnson will be as successful as Howard Schultz remains to be seen.

DISCUSSION QUESTIONS

1. How did Starbucks create its uniqueness in the first place? Why was this uniqueness so successful?

2. To be a source of competitive advantage over time, core competencies need to be continuously honed and upgraded. Why and how did Starbucks lose its uniqueness and struggle in the mid-2000s? What

strategic initiatives did Howard Schultz, following his return as CEO in 2008, put in place to re-create Starbucks' uniqueness?

3. What is your assessment of Howard Schultz as a strategic leader? Where on the Level-5 pyramid of strategic leadership (see Exhibit 2.2) would you place Schultz? Why? Explain.

4. Howard Schultz, as the creator of the Starbucks brand that we know today, is a larger than life figure in the company and business community. Do you think it is difficult to follow such an iconic leader? Why, or why not?

5. How is Kevin Johnson as CEO different from Howard Schultz? What leadership style is Johnson pursuing? Do you think he will be successful? Why, or why not?

Endnotes

1. Schultz's struggles are well chronicled in his *New York Times* bestseller (written with Joanne Gordon): *Onward: How Starbucks Fought for Its Life without Losing Its Soul* (New York: Rodale, 2012).

2. As quoted in: Jargon, J. (2019, Jan. 7), "Starbucks CEO Kevin Johnson reins in predecessor's ambitions: 'I'm not Howard,'" *The Wall Street Journal*.

Sources: Jargon, J. (2019, Jan. 7), "Starbucks CEO Kevin Johnson reins in predecessor's ambitions: 'I'm not Howard,'" *The Wall Street Journal*; Dignan, L. (2018, May 22), "Why Starbucks remains the mobile payment app leader ahead of Apple, Google, Samsung," *ZDnet*; Jargon, J. (2017, Apr. 3), "New Starbucks CEO sees growth in suburbs, Midwest and lunch," *The Wall Street Journal*; Trefis Team (2017, Jan. 13), "Starbucks is ending its 'Evenings' beer and wine program," *Forbes*; Lublin, J.S., and J. Jargon (2016, Dec. 7), "At Starbucks, CEO transition plan includes vow not to hover," *The Wall Street Journal*"; Jargon, J. (2015, Jul. 6), "Starbucks raises prices despite declining coffee costs," *The Wall Street Journal*; Jargon, J. (2013, Jul. 23), "Starbucks profit jumps, as revenue surges 18%," *The Wall Street Journal*; "Forty years young: A history of Starbucks," *The Telegraph* (2011, May 11); Schultz, H. (2011), *Onward: How Starbucks Fought for Its Life without Losing Its Soul* (New York: Rodale Books); Jargon, J. (2010, Oct. 13), "At Starbucks, baristas told no more than two drinks," *The Wall Street Journal*; Jargon, J. (2009, Aug. 4), "Latest Starbucks buzzword: 'Lean' Japanese techniques," *The Wall Street Journal*; Behar, H. (2007), *It's Not About the Coffee: Leadership Principles from a Life at Starbucks* (New York: Portfolio); Clark, T. (2007), *Starbucked: A Double Tall Tale of Caffeine, Commerce, and Culture*. (New York: Little, Brown, 2007); Schultz, H., and D.J. Yang (1999), *Pour Your Heart Into It: How Starbucks Built a Company One Cup at a Time* (New York: Hyperion). See also "The Roastery experience: An unofficial guide to the Starbucks Roastery," www.thestarbucksroastery.com/(accessed August 3, 2017); and Starbucks annual reports (various years).

BlackBerry's Rise and Fall

A PIONEER IN smartphones, BlackBerry (formerly known as Research in Motion, or RIM) was the undisputed industry leader in the early 2000s. Corporate IT managers preferred BlackBerry. Its devices allowed users to receive e-mail and other data in real time globally, with enhanced security features. For executives, a BlackBerry was not just a tool to increase productivity—and to free them from their laptops—but also an important status symbol. As a consequence, by 2008 BlackBerry's market cap had peaked at $75 billion. Yet within a short four years, by 2012, this lofty valuation had fallen to just $7 billion; and, by 2019, it stood at a mere $4 billion. Since its peak, BlackBerry's market cap had fallen by almost 95 percent. What happened?

Jim Balsillie, a Canadian and BlackBerry's longtime co-CEO, unsurprisingly calls ice hockey his favorite sport. He likes to quote Wayne Gretzky, whom many consider to be the best ice hockey player ever: "Skate to where the puck is going to be, not to where it is." Alas, BlackBerry did not follow that advice and failed to consider the impact of two important factors in its external environment: technological and sociocultural.

Let's start with a discussion of the technological factor that led to BlackBerry's decline. The introduction of the Apple iPhone in 2007 changed the game in the mobile device industry. Equipped with a camera, the iPhone's slick design offered a touchscreen user interface and virtual keyboard. The iPhone connected seamlessly to cellular networks and Wi-Fi. Combined with thousands of apps via the Apple iTunes store, the iPhone provided a powerful user experience, or as the late Steve Jobs said, "the internet in your pocket."

BlackBerry engineers and executives initially dismissed the iPhone as a mere toy with poor security features. Everyday users thought differently. They were less concerned about making sure the device's software was

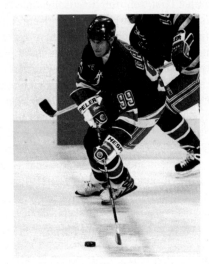

NHL great Wayne Gretzky, shown here in 1999, his final season with the New York Rangers, holds the record for most career regular-season goals.
Jim Rogash/AP Images

encrypted for security than they were about the user experience, which was fun and diverse. The iPhone allowed users to text, surf the web, take pictures, play games, and write and send e-mails. Although BlackBerry devices were great in productivity applications, such as receiving and responding to e-mail via typing on its iconic physical keyboard, they provided a poor mobile web browsing experience.

The second external development that helped erode BlackBerry's dominance was sociocultural. Initially, mobile devices were issued top-down by corporate IT departments. The only available device for executives was a company-issued BlackBerry. This made it easy for IT departments to ensure network security. Consumers, however, began to bring their personal iPhones (and other mobile devices with an Apple-like user experience) to work and used them for corporate communication and productivity applications. This bottom-up groundswell known as BYOT ("bring your own technology") forced corporate IT departments to open up their services beyond the BlackBerry.

Frank T. Rothaermel prepared this MiniCase from public sources. This MiniCase is developed for the purpose of class discussion. It is not intended to be used for any kind of endorsement, source of data, or depiction of efficient or inefficient management. All opinions expressed, all errors and omissions are entirely the author's. Revised and updated: May 28, 2019. ©Frank T. Rothaermel.

The two PESTEL factors—technological and socio-cultural—set BlackBerry back in the smartphone market. Unlike Gretzky, it failed to skate in the direction that the puck was headed and remained instead in its current position, that is, focused on its existing customer base of corporate IT departments and government. Although it attempted to promote some product modifications later, they were too little, too late. By then Apple was the innovation driver in the smartphone industry, bringing out more advanced iPhone models and enhancing the usefulness of its business and productivity apps.

Ten years after the iPhone was introduced, Apple has sold more than 1 billion iPhones globally, directly driving more than two-thirds of its annual revenues, which stood at a whopping $265 billion in 2018. Meanwhile, BlackBerry sold its iconic line of smartphones, including its BlackBerry brand name, to TCL Communication, a Chinese electronics company. The original BlackBerry company pivoted away from consumer electronics to enterprise software and the internet of things.

Let's think about the rapid progress in mobile computing. BlackBerry, once an undisputed leader in the smartphone industry, did not recognize or act upon the changes in the external environment early enough.

Consumer preferences changed quickly once the iPhone and later the iPad were introduced. Professionals brought their own Apple or other devices to work instead of using company-issued BlackBerries. Although the Canadian technology company made a valiant effort to make up lost ground with its new BlackBerry 10 operating system and several new models, it was too late.

DISCUSSION QUESTIONS

1. What made BlackBerry so successful initially in the smartphone industry?

2. What role did external factors play in BlackBerry's demise? Which external factors were most potent, and why?

3. What could BlackBerry's strategic leaders have done differently to address the external factors you identified in Question 2? Be specific.

Sources: For an in-depth discussion of BlackBerry and the smartphone industry, see Burr, J.F., F.T. Rothaermel, and J. Urbina (2015), Case MHE-FTR-020 (0077645065), "Make or break at RIM: Launching BlackBerry 10," http://create.mheducation.com; McNish, J., and S. Silcoff (2016), *Losing the Signal: The Untold Story Behind the Extraordinary Rise and Spectacular Fall of BlackBerry* (New York: Flatiron Books); Dvorak, P. (2011, Sep. 30), "BlackBerry maker's issue: Gadgets for work or play?" *The Wall Street Journal*; Dyer, J., H. Gregersen, C.M. Christensen (2011), *The Innovator's DNA: Mastering the Five Skills of Disruptive Innovators* (Boston: Harvard Business Review Press); and publicly available data.

Nike's Core Competency: The Risky Business of Creating Heroes

NIKE IS A globally recognized brand and the undisputed leader in the athletic shoe and apparel industry. The number-two leader, Adidas, has achieved $26 billion in sales, while recent entrant Under Armour reported $5 billion in revenues. Nike is tremendously successful, holding close to a 60 percent market share in running shoes and nearly a 90 percent market share in basketball shoes and apparel. As an indicator of Nike's sustained competitive advantage, the brand has outperformed the S&P 500 index, a common benchmark to proxy the broader stock market, by a wide margin over the past decade (see Exhibit MC4.1), wherein its annual revenues doubled. These revenues are expected to reach $40 billion by 2020.

Yet one of its greatest strengths can also be seen as one of its greatest vulnerabilities. To understand that strength, it helps to know how Nike started.

Nike Co-founders: Bill Bowerman and Phil Knight

The Beaverton, Oregon, company has come a long way from its humble beginnings. It was founded by University of Oregon track and field coach Bill Bowerman and middle-distance runner Phil Knight in 1964 and was first called Blue Ribbon Sports. In 1971, the company changed its name to Nike (after the goddess of victory in Greek mythology) and called upon a Portland State University graphic design student to design its now iconic "swoosh." Knight, who was teaching at the university at the time, paid the student $35 for it. By the summer of

that year, Nike's swoosh logo was registered at the U.S. Patent and Trademark office.

BOWERMAN'S INNOVATION. Coach Bowerman was a true innovator because he was constantly seeking ways to give his athletes a competitive edge. He experimented with many factors affecting running performance, from different track surfaces to rehydration drinks. Bowerman's biggest focus, however, was on designing a better running shoe. While sitting at the breakfast table one Sunday morning and absentmindedly looking at his waffle iron, Bowerman had an epiphany. He poured hot, liquid urethane into the waffle iron—ruining it, of course. But through this process, Bowerman came up with the now-famous waffle sole that provided better traction than and weighed a lot less than traditional running shoes.

KNIGHT'S DISRUPTION. After completing his undergraduate degree at the University of Oregon and serving in the U.S. Army, Phil Knight entered Stanford University's MBA program. One entrepreneurship class required him to come up with a business idea, so he focused on how to disrupt the leading athletic shoemaker, Adidas. The research question he came up with was, "Can Japanese sports shoes do to German sports shoes what Japanese cameras have done to German cameras?"[1]

At the time, Adidas athletic shoes were the gold standard. They were also expensive and hard to find in the United States. After several failed attempts to interest Japanese sneaker makers, Knight managed to strike a distribution agreement with Tiger Shoes (a forerunner of today's ASICS footwear company, which is known for high-quality athletic shoes that fall in the higher price range). After Knight's first shipment of running shoes arrived, he sent some to Coach Bowerman, his running coach during his track-and-field days at University of Portland, hoping

EXHIBIT MC4.1   Nike's Stock Market Performance vis-à-vis S&P 500 Index, 2010–2019

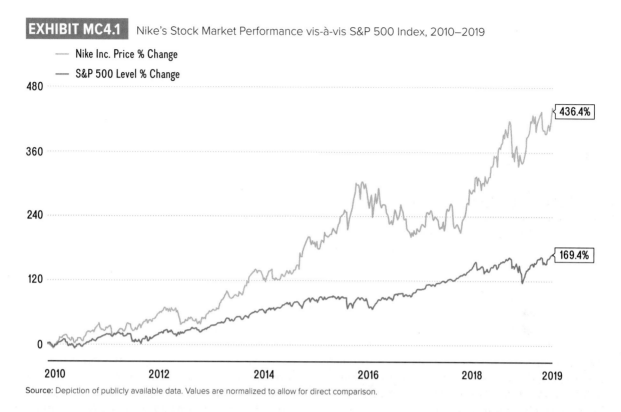

Source: Depiction of publicly available data. Values are normalized to allow for direct comparison.

to make a sale. To Knight's surprise, Bowerman expressed interest in becoming business partners and contributing his innovative ideas on how to improve running shoes, including his original waffle design. With an investment of $500 each and a handshake, the venture commenced.

Creating Heroes

By the late 1970s, because of a highly successful string of innovations, including the Nike Air, Nike had reached a considerable level of success. By 1979, the company had captured more than a 50 percent of the U.S. market share for running shoes. A year later, Nike went public but had yet to establish one of its most effective marketing tactics.

In 1984, Nike signed Michael Jordan—still early in his career, before he was hailed by many as the greatest basketball player of all time—with an unprecedented multimillion-dollar endorsement deal. Rather than spreading its marketing budget more widely as was common in the sports industry at that time, Nike made the unorthodox move to spend basically its entire budget for a specific sport on a single star athlete. Nike sought to sponsor future superstars that embodied an

unlikely success story. Michael Jordan did not make the varsity team as a junior in high school, and yet he became (one of) the greatest basketball player ever. Nike's Air Jordan basketball shoes are all-time classics that remain popular to this day.

In the 1990s and 2000s, Nike continued to sponsor track and field stars such as Marion Jones as well as basketball stars such as Kobe Bryant. Eventually, it expanded its scope to include golf prodigy Tiger Woods, tennis champion Serena Williams, cycling celebrity Lance Armstrong, soccer star Wayne Rooney, and football legend Michael Vick. Some of these names likely evoke associations with scandal as much as they do athletic achievement—therein lay both the power and the risks of sports celebrity endorsements.

The company continues to make mega-deals with athletes such as LeBron James, Kevin Durant, Megan Rapinoe, Naomi Osaka, and Christiano Ronaldo. In 2017, football wide receiver Odell Beckham, Jr. made headlines with an estimated $25 million endorsement deal with Nike, the highest endorsement contract in the National Football League. Nike's largest endorsement agreement, however, is with NBA all-star LeBron James. The company extended its endorsement and entered a lifetime deal with James in 2015. The specifics have not been disclosed, but the total value of the deal is estimated near $1 billion. In 2019 alone, Nike paid some $1.5 billion in endorsement contracts, with a net income of $4 billion.

Nike's message is about unlocking human potential, which is captured in its mission *to bring inspiration and innovation to every athlete in the world* (and *if you have a body, you are an athlete*).[2] Nike uses its heroes to tell the story that through sheer will, tenacity, and hard work, *anyone* can unlock the hero within and achieve amazing things if they would only *Just Do It!* Ultimately, Nike is all about making heroes. This type of mythical branding has allowed Nike to enter, and often dominate, one sport after another—from running to ice hockey. It spends more than $1 billion a year sponsoring athletes and will sponsor only those known for succeeding despite and against all odds, for example, cancer survivor and cyclist Lance Armstrong, double amputee "blade runner" sprinter Oscar Pistorius, and other athletes hailing from disadvantaged backgrounds.

Nike astutely focuses on its core competency in athlete sponsorship as well as shoe and apparel design, while it outsources noncore activities such as manufacturing and much of retailing. To create heroes, Nike has to engage in a number of activities:

- Find athletes that succeed against the odds.
- Identify them before they are well-known superstars.
- Sign the athletes.
- Create products that are closely linked with the athlete.
- Promote the athletes or teams and Nike products through TV ads and social media to create the desired image.

Each activity contributes to the relative value of the product and service offering in the eyes of potential customers and the firm's relative cost position vis-à-vis its rivals. Over time, Nike developed a deep expertise in creating heroes. More importantly, having consistently better expectations of the future value of resources allows Nike not only to shape the desired image of the athlete, but also to capture some of the value these athletes create.

WHEN HEROES FALL. Although the hero core competency has contributed to Nike's sustained success, it has also raised some scandals, putting the brand at risk. Over the years, some of Nike's "heroes" were unmasked as cheaters, frauds, and criminals;

others have been convicted of felonies. But as long-time CEO and Chairman Phil Knight declared long ago, scandals are "part of the game."[3] With that statement, it appears that Nike is tolerant of such risks—at least in some cases. In others, it simply is not.

When NBA star Kobe Bryant was accused of rape, Nike continued to sponsor him (Bryant was later cleared of all charges). When Tiger Woods found himself engulfed in an infidelity and sex scandal in 2009, Nike also continued to sponsor him—a decision for which Nike felt vindicated after his Masters victory in 2019 (his first major championship since 2008). But when NFL quarterback Michael Vick was convicted of running a dog-fighting ring and engaging in animal cruelty in 2007, which caused a public outcry, Nike ended his endorsement contract. However, in 2011, after serving a prison sentence and restarting his career at the Philadelphia Eagles, Nike signed a new endorsement deal with Vick. In 2012, Nike terminated its long-term relationship with disgraced cyclist Lance Armstrong. Just before Armstrong's public admission to doping during an interview with Oprah Winfrey, Knight was asked whether Nike would ever sponsor Armstrong again, to which Knight replied, "Never say never."[4] In 2013, Nike removed its ads showing Oscar Pistorius and the unfortunate tagline, "I am the bullet in the chamber," after the South African track and field athlete was charged with homicide; he was later convicted.

In 2014, Nike got entangled in the FIFA (the world governing body of soccer) bribery scandal, which began 20 years earlier; after the United States hosted the 1994 World Cup, Nike decided it wanted to gain a stronger presence in soccer. In 1996, it signed a long-term sponsorship agreement worth hundreds of millions of dollars with the Brazilian national team. This was a huge win for Nike because soccer has been the basis of Adidas' success, much like running and basketball have been for Nike. At the time, Brazil had already won the tournament five times (more than any other nation) and was the only team to have played in every tournament thus far, which is only held every four years.

Nike is alleged to have paid some $30 million to a middleman, who used that money for bribing soccer officials and politicians in Brazil. This middleman—Jose Hawilla—has admitted to a number of crimes including fraud, money laundering, and extortion related to the FIFA soccer investigation by U.S. prosecutors.

Nike may be at a point where it is facing the Icarus paradox—that is, its greatest strengths are becoming its greatest weakness. The Icarus paradox describes the phenomenon of abrupt failure after a period of tremendous success. It is named after Icarus, a figure in Greek mythology. As the story goes, Icarus was able to escape prison with the help of a pair wings made out of a wood frame, beeswax, and feathers. Not only did Icarus fly out of jail, but he also found that he loved flying so much that he soared higher and higher, despite warnings not to get too close to the sun. Alas, Icarus failed to heed this warning. He got too close to the sun and his wings melted, causing him to plunge to his death.

Time and time again Nike's heroes have fallen from grace, causing the company itself to also fall under suspicion of wrongdoing. Clearly, Nike's approach in building its core competency of creating heroes is not without risks. Too many of these public relations flops combined with too severe shortcomings of some of Nike's most celebrated heroes could damage the company's reputation and lead to a loss of competitive advantage. Disappointment with the brand and its promise may eventually set in, causing customers to go elsewhere.

Nike Endorser Colin Kaepernick: Inspirational or Controversial?

In the fall of 2018, Nike ran a U.S.-based ad featuring Colin Kaepernick with the tagline "Believe in something, even if it means sacrificing everything. Just do it."[5] Some considered the ad inspirational and others controversial. Why?

In 2016, NFL quarterback Colin Kaepernick (a free agent then playing for the San Francisco 49ers) knelt on one knee instead of standing during the national anthem as an act of protest against police brutality and racism in the United States. The anthem, which is always played before the start of any live professional sporting event, was televised and thus visible to millions of people. The action was supported by many, inspiring other athletes to take the knee during the playing of the national anthem; it also catalyzed the Black Lives Matter movement. Yet it enraged others, inciting accusations that Kaepernick was unpatriotic. Many demanded that he be blacklisted by NFL teams.

After the 2016 season, Kaepernick was not signed by any NFL team, despite having been the starting quarterback for the 49ers and having favorable performance statistics relative to other players that were signed. In 2017, Kaepernick filed a grievance, alleging that all 32 NFL teams colluded in not signing him,

Nike ran the Colin Kaepernick ad in the fall of 2018. Opinions varied from "inspirational" to "controversial." Regardless, the marketing opportunity was tailor-made for Nike, which likes to interest the younger generation of consumers and convey that it stands for something meaningful.
Image of Sport/Newscom

thus preventing him from working, because of his protest action. In 2019, the NFL settled the matter by paying Kaepernick $10 million, even though Kaepernick's market value as a NFL quarterback is estimated to be about $15 million a season; by the time of the settlement, he had not played for two seasons.

The marketing opportunity surrounding Kaepernick was tailor-made for Nike, which has been trying to appeal to younger consumers with people and campaigns that promote doing or standing for something meaningful. Adidas, which recently has become more popular with the under-18 crowd, now poses a significant threat to Nike. Thus, winning over this next generation of customers has become even more critical for the firm. Moreover, Adidas boasts major endorsements itself from such pop superstars as Kanye West and Pharrell Williams.

In the wake of the Kaepernick ad, Nike and Kaepernick gained tremendous visibility. Kaepernick became the most mentioned athlete on Twitter, way ahead of sport greats such as Lionel Messi, Cristiano Ronaldo, Serena Williams, and LeBron James. Likewise, Nike also became the most mentioned company on Twitter, four times more than Apple, the next most mentioned company. At the same time, the hashtag #NikeBoycott started trending. Whether the new ad will result in increased sales for Nike, or whether the boycott will hurt sales, remains to be seen.

Nike and Colin Kaepernick took the spotlight again in the summer of 2019. Nike had planned to release a limited edition of U.S.A.-themed sneaker (a version of the Air Max 1), featuring an early American flag that was flown during the Revolutionary War, with 13 white stars in a circle symbolizing the original colonies, commonly known as the Betsy Ross flag after its designer. Nike did not consult Colin Kaepernick about the design of the shoe commemorating Independence Day. Kaepernick saw photos of the shoe on Twitter shortly after its release. The former football quarterback turned social activist and celebrity endorser for Nike vehemently objected to the sneaker design as he was concerned about associations of the Betsy Ross flag with an era of slavery and its adoption by some extremist groups. Following Colin Kaepernick's intervention, Nike decided to pull the shoe from all U.S. retailers.

DISCUSSION QUESTIONS

1. The MiniCase indicates that Nike's core competency is to create heroes. What does this mean? How did Nike build its core competency? Does this core competency obey the criteria resulting from a VRIO analysis in a resource-based view of the firm? In other words, is the core competency *v*aluable, *r*are, and *i*nimitable, and is Nike *o*rganized to capture the value created?

2. Is Nike facing the Icarus paradox? What would it take for Nike's approach to turn from a strength into a weakness? Did this tipping point already occur? Why or why not?

3. What recommendations would you offer Nike? Can you identify a way to reframe the core competency of "creating heroes"? Or a new way to build the Nike brand through other, similar concepts?

4. If you are a competitor of Nike (such as Adidas or Under Armour), how could you exploit Nike's vulnerability? Define that vulnerability and provide a set of concrete recommendations.

Endnotes

1. As quoted in: "Knight the king: The founding of Nike," *Harvard Business School Case Study,* 9-810-077, 2.

2. Nike.com.

3. According to Reuters, cited in: www.sportbusiness.com (2009, Dec 15).

4. Nike tagline.

5. The full Nike ad "Dream Crazy" can be seen at www.youtube.com/watch?v=Fq2CvmgoO7I [2:05 min]; Nike, Inc.

Sources: Safdar, K., Beaton, A., and C. McWhirter (2019, Jul. 2), "Nike defends pulling 'Betsy Ross' shoe and sparks a national debate," *The Wall Street Journal;* Beaton, A. (2019, Mar. 21), "NFL paid under $10 million to settle Colin Kaepernick grievance," *The Wall Street Journal;* Powell, M. (2019, Feb. 15), "A timeline of Colin Kaepernick vs. the N.F.L.," *The New York Times;* Wolken, D. (2018, Sep. 7), "Just watch it: Nike's Colin Kaepernick TV ad is inspirational, not controversial," *USA Today;* Gay, J. (2018, Sep. 5), "Colin Kaepernick and Nike, starring you and me," *The Wall Street Journal;* Beaton, A. (2018, Sep. 4), "Nike shares slide on plans to use Colin Kaepernick in ads," *The Wall Street Journal;* Beaton, A., and K. Safdar (2018, Sep. 4), "Nike risks backlash with Colin Kaepernick deal," *The Wall Street Journal;* Stevens, L., and S. Germano (2017, Jun. 28), "Nike thought it didn't need Amazon—then the ground shifted," *The Wall Street Journal;* Germano, S. (2017, Jun. 15), "Nike to cut jobs as it combats sneaker slump," *The Wall Street Journal;* Knight, P. (2016), *Shoe Dog: A Memoir by the Creator of Nike* (New York: Scribner); Germano, S., and P. Kowsmann (2015, Jun. 4), "Nike's bold push into soccer entangled it in FIFA probe," *The Wall Street Journal;* Baer, D. (2015, Jul. 25), "How Nike got an insane deal on the 'swoosh' logo," *Business Insider;* Futterman, M. (2014, Feb. 14), "The big business of fairy tales," *The Wall Street Journal;* Sachs, J. (2012), *Winning the Story Wars* (Boston: Harvard Business School Press); *Nike, Inc.,* History and Heritage, http://nikeinc.com/pages/history-heritage; Vermeulen, F. (2009, March), "Businesses and the Icarus paradox," *Harvard Business Review;* Halberstam, D. (2000), *Playing for Keeps: Michael Jordan and the World* (New York: Broadway Books); Miller, D. (1990). *The Icarus Paradox* (New York: HarperBusiness), and Nike, Inc., annual reports (various years).

Business Model Innovation: How Dollar Shave Club Disrupted Gillette

ALTHOUGH MOST OF our attention is captured by fancy high-tech innovations such as the iPhone or Tesla's sleek electric vehicles, innovations do not need to be high-tech or radical to be successful. Until recently, Gillette, a company that invented the safety razor and the razor–razor-blade business model, dominated the $3 billion U.S. market for wet shaving with some 75 percent market share. Yet Dollar Shave Club, a young, fledgling startup with an initial budget of $8,000, disrupted the powerful Gillette with a low-tech innovation and is gaining market share rapidly. How can the powerful Gillette, a unit of Procter & Gamble with annual revenues of $67 billion, be beaten by a brash startup? Gillette's pattern of incremental innovation over time led to overshooting in the market, resulting in a product that was overengineered and too expensive.

King Gillette invented the safety razor about 115 years ago. The company also came up with the highly profitable business model of selling the razor for a low price and charging a premium for replacement razor blades. This business model is now widely adopted (think printers and cartridges, for example), and is called the razor–razor-blade business model commemorating its origins. When introduced, the new safety razor was a radical innovation, allowing Gillette a temporary competitive advantage. To sustain this advantage over time, Gillette followed up with incremental innovations, mainly by adding additional razor blades to the razor, all the way from one blade to six. As a result of this innovation pattern over time, one of Gillette's newest razors, the Fusion ProGlide with Flexball technology, a razor handle that features a swiveling ball hinge, costs $11.49 (and $12.59 for a battery-operated one) *per razor*.

Entrepreneur Michael Dubin founded Dollar Shave Club using a business model innovation by providing an online subscription-based mail-order alternative to in-store retail purchases of razor blades. Many customers were not only turned off by Gillette's premium prices, but also by the inconveniences that in-store purchases entail. Given that packs of razor blades are a prime target for shoplifters, many stores lock them in glass vitrines, much to the dismay of customers who have to hunt down an employee with a key to access razor blades.
Dan Krauss

This created a situation where Gillette exposed itself to low-cost disruption. One key is that the high-end, highly priced offering of the market leader is not only overshooting what the market demands, but also often priced too high. One wonders if a person really does need six blades on one razor, or wants to pay over $10 for one cartridge.

Seeing this opening provided by Gillette's focus on the high-end, high-margin business of the market, Dollar Shave Club established a low-cost alternative to invade Gillette's market from the bottom up. With an $8,000 budget and the help of a hilarious promotional video that went viral with over 25 million views, the entrepreneur Michael Dubin launched Dollar Shave Club, an ecommerce startup that delivers razors by mail. After the promotional video was uploaded on YouTube in March 2012, some 12,000 people signed up for Dollar Shave membership within the first 48 hours. It also raised more than $20 million in venture capital funding from prominent firms such as Kleiner Perkins Caufield & Byers and Andreessen Horowitz, among others. Dollar Shave Club followed up with advertising on regular television in addition to its online campaigns and has expanded its product lines with the introduction of additional personal grooming products.

Dollar Shave Club is an ecommerce company that uses a subscription-based business model. As the company's name suggests, its entry-level membership plan delivers a razor and five cartridges a month for just $1 (plus $2 shipping). The member selects an appropriate plan, pays a monthly fee, and will receive razors every month in the mail. Dollar Shave Club is using a business model innovation to disrupt an existing market. Technology is defined as the methods and materials used to achieve a commercial objective. The technology or method here is the business model innovation, a potent competitive weapon. The entrepreneur identified the need in the market for serving those who don't like to go shopping for razors and certainly don't like to pay the high prices commanded by market leaders such as Gillette.

Procter & Gamble's competition also took notice. Unilever, P&G's European rival, has long stayed away from the U.S. wet shaving market because Gillette was so dominant. But seeing how Dollar Shave Club disrupted Gillette, resulting in a rapid market share decline, Unilever saw its opening. The Anglo-Dutch multinational consumer products company, with some $60 billion in annual revenues and thus roughly the same size as P&G, offered a whopping $1 billion in cash in 2016 to buy Dollar Shave Club. Not a bad offer for a five-year-old startup. Michael Dubin happily accepted the offer and sold Dollar Shave Club to Unilever.

With sales of razors and razor blades moving rapidly online, Unilever is hoping to leverage this business model innovation to unseat Gillette's dominance in the U.S. market. But Gillette responded swiftly by offering its own subscription-based service (Gillette Shave Club) and by lowering prices up to 20 percent, an unimaginable move in recent history. Successful innovations also led to imitations. A mere two years after

Dollar Shave Club started, two entrepreneurs founded Harry's, also an online, subscription-based mail order business for shaving equipment. After Target invited Harry's to put displays in all its stores in 2016, its business took off. This was a smart move on Target's part because it allowed Target to put pressure on Gillette, which held more or less a monopoly position as a supplier with 75 percent market share. Similar to Dollar Shave Club, Harry's business is growing rapidly. As a consequence of increased competition, Gillette's market share in the $3 billion market for razors and razor blades has declined from some 75 percent in 2010 to about 50 percent by 2019, and continues to slide.

DISCUSSION QUESTIONS

1. If you buy shaving equipment, do you purchase it in a retail store or online? Explain your choice.

2. How was Gillette initially able to gain a competitive advantage? How was Gillette able to sustain its competitive advantage for so long, leading to a near monopoly position of 75 percent market share at its peak?

3. What led to the opening in the market that entrepreneurs such as Michael Dubin with Dollar Shave Club used to enter the industry? How did they enter the industry? What type of business model did they use, and why were they successful?

4. Why did Unilever offer $1 billion (in cash!) for Dollar Shave Club?

5. Do you think online startups such as Dollar Shave Club and Harry's will continue to steal market share from Gillette? Why or why not?

Sources: Dan, A. (2019, Jan. 16), "For men, Gillette is no longer the best a brand can get," *Forbes*; Terlap, S. (2017, Apr. 4), "Gillette, bleeding market share, cuts prices of razors," *The Wall Street Journal*; Terlep, S., and K. Safdar (2016, Nov. 9), "Online upstart Harry's razor jumps into Gillette's turf," *The Wall Street Journal*; Terlep, S. (2016, Jul. 20), "Unilever buys Dollar Shave Club," *The Wall Street Journal*; Ng, S., and P. Ziobro (2015, Jun. 23), "Razor sales move online, away from Gillette," *The Wall Street Journal*; Luna, T. (2014, Apr. 29), "The new Gillette Fusion Pro-Glide Flexball razor, to be available in stores June 9," *The Boston Globe*; Glazer, E. (2012, Apr. 12), "A David and Gillette story," *The Wall Street Journal*; and Dollar Shave Club promotional video, www.youtube.com/dollarshaveclub.

How JCPenney Sailed into a Red Ocean

JCPENNEY WAS once one of the top department stores in the United States, with more than 2,000 locations at its peak. Indeed, the retailer was so common in the suburbs that one could not imagine a shopping mall without a JCPenney. Generations of America's children were mesmerized by its annual holiday catalog. As recent as 2007, JCPenney had enjoyed a market valuation of $18 billion. In a bit over a decade, JCPenney's market cap had fallen to a mere $269 million. Thus, the retailer lost 98.5 percent of its valuation or $17.7 billion in a bit over decade. Many observers expect JCPenney to follow Sears—once the leading American retailer—to also file for bankruptcy, which Sears did in 2018. What went wrong?

Of course, all retailers are exposed to the same threat, Amazon, which has become synonymous with online shopping. Although Walmart, Target, and Best Buy all have become more competitive in recent years, JCPenney sped up its own demise with a bad business strategy. In particular, JCPenney under former CEO Ron Johnson learned the hard way how difficult it is to change a strategic position. When hired as JCPenney's CEO in 2011, Johnson was hailed as a star executive. Johnson was poached from Apple, where he had created and led Apple's retail stores since 2000. Apple's stores are the most successful retail outlets globally in terms of sales per square foot. No other retail outlet, not even luxury jewelers, achieves more. This poaching didn't come cheap: JCPenney paid Ron Johnson close to $53 million in total compensation in 2011, even though he didn't start until November of that year.

Once on board with JCPenney, Johnson immediately began to change the company's strategic position

from a cost-leadership to a *blue ocean strategy,* attempting to combine its traditional cost-leadership position with a differentiation position. In particular, he tried to reposition the department store more toward the high end by providing an improved customer experience and more exclusive merchandise through in-store boutiques. Johnson ordered all clearance racks with steeply discounted merchandise, common in JCPenney stores, to be removed. He also did away with JCPenney's long-standing practice of mailing discount coupons to its customers. Rather than following industry best practice by testing the more drastic strategic moves in a small number of selected stores, Johnson implemented them in all of the then 1,800 stores at once. When one executive raised the issue of pretesting, Johnson bristled and responded: "We didn't test at Apple."[1] Under his leadership, JCPenney also got embroiled in a legal battle with Macy's because of Johnson's attempt to lure away homemaking maven Martha Stewart and her exclusive merchandise collection.

The envisioned blue ocean strategy failed badly, and JCPenney ended up being stuck in the middle. Within 12 months with Johnson at the helm, JCPenney's sales dropped by 25 percent. In a hypercompetitive industry such as retailing where every single percent of market share counts, this was a landslide. Things went from bad to worse. In 2013, JCPenney's stock performed so poorly it was dropped from the S&P 500 index. Less than 18 months into his new job, Johnson was fired. JCPenney had lost over two-thirds of its market valuation (or $6 billion) under Johnson's leadership. The attempted overhaul of JCPenney under Johnson also left the company burdened with more than $4 billion in debt. Myron Ullman, his predecessor, was brought out of retirement as a temporary replacement. Exhibit MC6.1 shows JCPenney's stock market valuation and CEO appointments over time.

Under Johnson's leadership, JCPenney failed at its attempted blue ocean strategy and instead sailed deeper into the *red ocean* of bloody competition. This highlights

Frank T. Rothaermel prepared this MiniCase from public sources. This Mini-Case is developed for the purpose of class discussion. It is not intended to be used for any kind of endorsement, source of data, or depiction of efficient or inefficient management. All opinions expressed, all errors and omissions are entirely the author's. Revised and updated: June 3, 2019. © Frank T. Rothaermel.

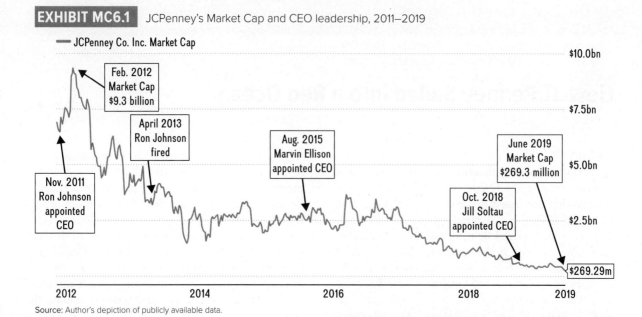

EXHIBIT MC6.1 JCPenney's Market Cap and CEO leadership, 2011–2019

— JCPenney Co. Inc. Market Cap

Feb. 2012
Market Cap
$9.3 billion

April 2013
Ron Johnson
fired

Aug. 2015
Marvin Ellison
appointed CEO

June 2019
Market Cap
$269.3 million

Nov. 2011
Ron Johnson
appointed
CEO

Oct. 2018
Jill Soltau
appointed CEO

$10.0bn

$7.5bn

$5.0bn

$2.5bn

$269.29m

2012 2014 2016 2018 2019

Source: Author's depiction of publicly available data.

the perils of attempting a blue ocean strategy because of the inherent trade-offs in the underlying generic business strategies of cost leadership and differentiation. As a result, JCPenney continues to experience a sustained competitive disadvantage and may go out of business.

To turn around the 120-year-old icon, the board appointed Marvin Ellison as CEO in 2015. With a strong background in operations management and leadership skills honed at The Home Depot, he focused on lowering JCPenney's cost structure while increasing perceived value offered to its customers. In an attempt to stem losses, in 2017 JCPenney closed some 140 retail stores across the United States out of a total of 1,000 remaining outlets. Marvin Ellison was lured back into the home improvement industry when he was appointed CEO of Lowe's in 2018.

In October 2018, Jill Soltau was appointed CEO of JCPenney. She was previously the CEO of Jo-Ann Stores, a fabric-and-craft retailer. Her new business strategy is not yet clear, and several top executive positions were still vacant as of spring 2019. Soltau retained McKinsey, a strategy consulting firm, to help with the turnaround. One question she faces is whether to continue selling appliances, which her predecessor brought back in 2016 to take away sales from failing Sears. JCPenney had discontinued sales of appliances in 1983 to focus on apparel, and the majority of JCPenney's sales still come from apparel, an area the retailer has neglected in recent years, even though

Jill Soltau was appointed CEO of JCPenney in October 2018. She is tasked with turning the ailing retailer around.
Paul Bruinooge/Patrick McMullan/Getty Images

JCPenney was once the go-to apparel retailer for American middle-class families. Whether Soltau will successfully sharpen JCPenney's strategic position and thus make the American icon competitive again remains to be seen.

DISCUSSION QUESTIONS

1. While all brick-and-mortar retailers face the threat of Amazon and online shopping in general, why did JCPenney perform so poorly while other retailers such as Walmart, Best Buy, or Target fared better?

2. Ron Johnson was hailed as a star executive at Apple, where he led the company's highly successful retail arm. As CEO of JCPenney he applied the "Apple playbook," for example, moving JCPenney toward the higher end of the market or going with hunches ("we didn't test at Apple"), rather than applying more traditional decision making. Why did his attempt to change JCPenney's strategic position from cost-leadership to a blue ocean strategy fail so spectacularly? What are some of the lessons?

3. You are part of the McKinsey strategy consulting team that the new CEO, Jill Soltau, retained to help in turning around JCPenney. What recommendations would you give her? In particular, what type of business strategy would you want JCPenney to pursue, and how would you make the changes necessary? Be specific.

Endnote

1. As quoted in Mattioli, D. (2013, Feb. 24), "For Penney's heralded boss, the shine is off the apple," *The Wall Street Journal*.

Sources: Kapner, S. (2019, Mar. 15), "How Sears lost the American shopper," *The Wall Street Journal;* Kapner, S. (2019, Jan. 21), "J.C. Penney struggles to avoid same fate as Sears," *The Wall Street Journal;* La Monica, P.R. (2018, May 17), "JCPenney is running out of time," *CNN Business;* Lublin, S., and D. Mattioli (2013, Apr. 8), "Penney CEO out, old boss back in," *The Wall Street Journal;* Bray, C. (2013, Feb. 25), "Macy's CEO: Penney, Martha Stewart deal made me 'sick,'" *The Wall Street Journal;* Mattioli, D. (2013, Feb. 24), "For Penney's heralded boss, the shine is off the apple," *The Wall Street Journal*; and Talley, K. (2012, Apr. 2), "Penney CEO paid $53 million," *The Wall Street Journal*.

Platform Strategy: How PayPal Solved the Chicken-or-Egg Problem

PAYPAL IS A leader in online payment systems and services with more than 200 million active customer accounts and a growing number of transactions per active account. The platform leverages digital technology to connect buyers with sellers, creating a more frictionless way of transferring money from one person to the next. One of the biggest impediments PayPal had to overcome while launching its platform was the infamous chicken-or-egg debate. When building a platform business that serves two equally important sides of the market, which side comes first?

When it comes to new payment systems, the chicken-or-egg problem is especially prominent. Without sellers of products and services that are willing to accept the new form of payment, buyers won't use the new service. At the same time, buyers have no incentive to sign up for the new digital payment service if sellers won't invest the necessary time and resources to join the platform. This leads to the question of how do you successfully launch a new payments platform when you have no starting base and each side is dependent on the other to join? In short, how do initiate positive network effects?

At first glance, this might seem like an insolvable conundrum, but through a series of smart strategic moves, PayPal not only solved this problem but also leveraged network effects to stimulate more demand and become increasingly successful. The first step was to make the sign-up process easier. The simplicity of using just an email address and a credit card to sign up was a major differentiator between PayPal and previous online payment systems, which often required several rounds of verification and a tedious setup process. By making the initial process of joining almost frictionless,

PayPal was able to attract a good number of buyers, but not quite enough to start attracting sellers.

PayPal's next big challenge was finding ways to get new customers. Company leaders attempted a variety of methods, including advertising and business development deals with banks, but to no avail. They finally realized the most effective method for their platform was organic, viral growth. To accomplish this, they started giving away "free" money. New customers received $10 for signing up and existing ones received $10 for referrals. This new incentives-driven approach led to exponential growth, significantly increasing its customer base by 7 to 10 percent daily. Furthermore, the ingenuity of this tactic lies in not only incentivizing sign-ups but also retaining users. This move effectively guaranteed user participation on the platform—if only to spend the $10 they had been gifted. This was a key take-away from the PayPal team: Simply getting people to sign up was not enough. The importance of customer retention far exceeded that of customer acquisition.

The explosive growth from this tactic led to the creation of numerous positive feedback loops. The more users experienced the convenience of online payment methods and cashless transactions, the more they expected sellers to have this payment method available when shopping online. This resulted in more sellers signing up for PayPal and displaying the PayPal logo on their websites, which helped to further spread the word about PayPal and led to more user sign-ups. PayPal also rolled out a referral fee for sellers to attract even more buyers and sellers.

PayPal's success thus far comes in part due to its ability to leverage network effects to drive demand, helping it spawn the organic, viral growth needed to jump-start the platform; however, this was far from the last step in PayPal's journey to initiate network effects. It then refocused its efforts toward eBay, a natural niche for the online payments platform since most sellers on eBay are ordinary people who don't have the

This MiniCase was prepared by Frank T. Rothaermel with Laura Zhang, who provided superb research assistance. This MiniCase is developed for the purpose of class discussion. It is not intended to be used for any kind of endorsement, source of data, or depiction of efficient or inefficient management. All opinions expressed, all errors and omissions are entirely the author's. Revised and updated: May 29, 2019. © Frank T. Rothaermel.

setup to accept credit cards or other forms of online payment.

PayPal proceeded to simulate consumer demand on eBay by creating a bot to buy goods and then insist on using PayPal to pay. This apparent growth in demand led more eBay sellers to sign up for PayPal's service, which then led to more people using PayPal to pay for goods (hence initiating yet another positive feedback loop). This method was so effective that within three months, PayPal's user base grew from 100,000 to one million. Additionally, it led to eBay's acquisition of PayPal in 2002 for $1.4 billion.

PayPal is a business that facilitates value-creating interactions between its vendors and customers. Since it started, it has enabled millions of frictionless transactions between small merchants and consumers, allowing these merchants to conduct business online more seamlessly than ever before. PayPal's ability to evince and manage positive network effects has been critical to producing value for each participant and has allowed it to gain and sustain a competitive advantage over other online payments platforms.

Even today, PayPal is still looking for more ways to initiate positive feedback loops. Venmo, which is a mobile payment service with an emphasis on the social sharing aspect and one of PayPal's newer products, has become a ubiquitous payment method and is particularly popular with millennials. About 90 percent of Venmo transactions are shared within a social context, which is a coveted feature from a merchant's point of view. As millennials use Venmo to pay, and by identifying the merchant in the subject line of their payment, it becomes free advertising for that merchant. With ever-present social media, word-of-mouth advertising is not only free advertising but also one of the most powerful ways of getting a brand out there. This in turn triggers another positive feedback loop as more merchants begin providing "Pay with Venmo" as an option on their website, which leads to more users signing up for Venmo.

In 2019, just four years after eBay had spun off PayPal to again make it a standalone company, PayPal's revenues were over $15 billion and its market cap stood at over $125 billion. In comparison, at the same time, the market cap of the famous investment bank Goldman Sachs was $75 billion and that of Wells Fargo, one of the largest American banks, was $215 billion. As an online-only financial institution, PayPal has been a

EXHIBIT MC7.1 PayPal's Stock Performance versus Dow Jones U.S. Bank Index, 2015–2019

Source: Depiction of publicly available data. Note: All data are normalized.

huge success, in no small part due to the fact that its strategic leaders, including co-founders Peter Thiel and Elon Musk, figured out how to initiate positive network effects.

DISCUSSION QUESTIONS

1. Why are positive network effects so crucial to the success of platform strategy?

2. Why is it so difficult to initiate positive network effects?

3. How did PayPal overcome the thorny chicken-or-egg problem?

Sources: Paul, K. (2018, Feb. 19), "PayPal's vision for the future of mobile payments," *The Wall Street Journal*; Parker, G.G., M.W. Van Alstyne, and S.P. Choudary, S.P. (2016), *Platform Revolution: How Networked Markets Are Transforming the Economy—and How to Make Them Work for You* (New York: W.W. Norton & Co.).

GE: Corporate Strategy Gone Wrong

IN 2000, General Electric (GE) was the most valuable company globally with a market capitalization of almost $600 billion (see Exhibit MC8.1). An investment of a mere $100 in GE in April 1981, when Jack Welch took over as chairman and CEO, would have been worth $10,679 in August 2000 when GE's market value peaked. Given his success in making GE the most valuable company globally, Welch was hailed as the best CEO of the century by business media.

Jack Welch was known as a super-hard-charging CEO who felt that GE was hampered by inefficient bureaucracy. To address this problem, Welch eliminated 100,000 jobs during his tenure, which earned him the nickname "Neutron Jack." Welch also required each of GE's businesses to be either number one or number two in their respective markets; if they failed to achieve this goal, he would tell his leaders to "fix it, close it, or sell it."[1] He also required each GE manager to provide a stacked ranking of all its employees, and each year the bottom 10 percent would be fired. Exhibit MC8.2 depicts GE's product and geographic scope from 2001, the last year of Welch's 20-year tenure, to 2018.

Fast-forward to spring 2019, the year GE's market valuation dropped to $87 billion. GE had lost a whopping $507 billion (more than 85 percent) of its market valuation. What happened? Answer: A bad corporate strategy.

To decide how to compete as a multi-business enterprise, strategic leaders formulate corporate strategy along the three dimensions:

1. *Vertical integration*—in what stages of the industry value chain should the company participate?
2. *Diversification*—what range of products and services should the company offer?

Frank T. Rothaermel prepared this MiniCase from public sources. This MiniCase is developed for the purpose of class discussion. It is not intended to be used for any kind of endorsement, source of data, or depiction of efficient or inefficient management. All opinions expressed, all errors and omissions are entirely the author's. Revised and updated: June 10, 2019. ©Frank T. Rothaermel.

3. *Geographic scope*—where should the company compete in terms of regional, national, and international markets?

For this discussion, we will focus on diversification (product scope) and geographic scope (where to compete).

GE, founded in 1892, was known as a maker of home appliances, power turbines, locomotive engines, jet engines, and MRI machines, but also TV shows (such as *Seinfeld*), making it an unrelatedly diversified business. For most, it is not readily apparent what nuclear power plants, light bulbs, and TV shows have in common. By 2001, the year Welch stepped down as CEO, almost half of GE's $130 billion revenues and more than half of its profits came from one business unit: GE Capital (see Exhibit MC8.2 for GE's product scope). Under Welch, the hugely profitable GE Capital, which provided discounted capital to each of GE's business units, was considered the main driver behind GE's success. GE's AAA credit rating also allowed it to access capital more inexpensively than its rivals could. Albeit profitable for many years, GE Capital would eventually become the conglomerate's prime weakness because it created huge exposure to macroeconomic forces for a company that, at its core, was an industrial company.

Moreover, under Welch, GE basically was a domestic U.S. company with two-thirds of its revenues coming from its home market (see Exhibit MC8.3 for GE's geographic scope). This prevented GE from taking advantage of significant global growth opportunities in the emerging BRIC economies (Brazil, Russia, India, and China), where growth was rising rapidly during the 2000s.

On September 7, 2001, Jeffrey Immelt was appointed the new GE chairman and CEO (see Exhibit MC8.1). Since then, the external environment experienced the social and economic effects of the 9/11 terrorist attacks followed later by the 2008–2009 global financial crisis. Although GE is a diversified conglomerate that spans

EXHIBIT MC8.1 General Electric's Market Cap and Key Events, 2000–2019

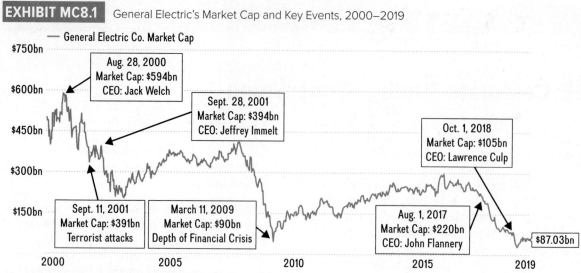

Source: Author's depiction of publicly available data.

many industries and markets, the recession of 2001 and the even deeper recession of 2008 hit the company especially hard, with GE Capital taking an especially hard financial blow (recall that more than half of GE's profits were coming from that unit at the time). During the critical 17 months that followed, GE's share price fell 84 percent, from $42.12 (on October 2, 2007) to a low of $6.66 (on March 5, 2009), equating to a loss in shareholder value of $378 billion (see Exhibit MC8.1).

To compound matters, GE also lost its AAA credit rating. As a result, the company had to ask for a $15 billion liquidity injection from famed investor Warren Buffett. In addition, the U.S. government had to bail out GE when the Federal Reserve stepped in to

EXHIBIT MC8.2 GE's Changing Product Scope, 2001 and 2018*

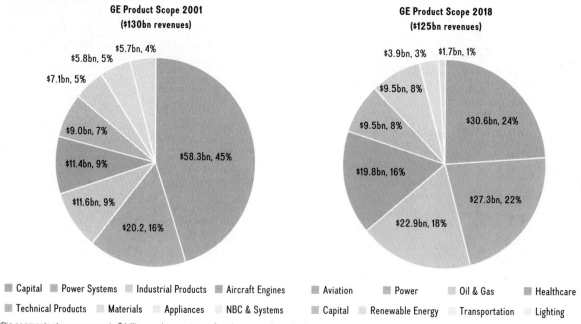

*Pie segments show revenues in $ billion, and percentage of total revenues (rounding).

Source: Author's depiction of publicly available data.

EXHIBIT MC8.3   GE's Changing Geographic Scope, 2001 and 2018

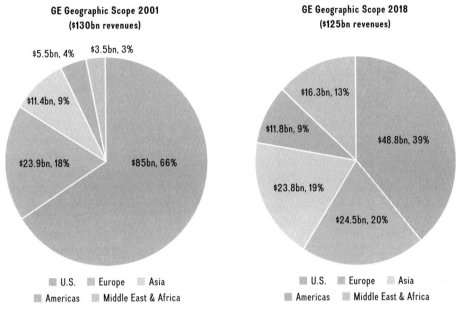

GE Geographic Scope 2001
($130bn revenues)

$5.5bn, 4% $3.5bn, 3%

$11.4bn, 9%

$23.9bn, 18%

$85bn, 66%

◼ U.S.   ◼ Europe   ◼ Asia
◼ Americas   ◼ Middle East & Africa

GE Geographic Scope 2018
($125bn revenues)

$16.3bn, 13%

$11.8bn, 9%

$48.8bn, 39%

$23.8bn, 19%

$24.5bn, 20%

◼ U.S.   ◼ Europe   ◼ Asia
◼ Americas   ◼ Middle East & Africa

Source: Author's depiction of publicly available data.

ensure continued liquidity for what was viewed as one of the largest banks in the United States, which GE had by de facto become. Indeed, during the global financial crisis, the Federal Reserve had designated GE a "systemically important financial institution (SIFI)," which meant that its failure could trigger a financial crisis (too big to fail). This SIFI designation submitted GE to additional federal regulation and oversight, which would limit executives' decision-making freedom. When GE lost its AAA credit rating, it also lost favorable access to debt funding, which had provided a competitive edge over other engineering companies such as Siemens. The 2008 financial crisis demonstrated clearly the risk of both selling and financing its products, a practice that was at the core of the way GE did business. For example, GE would build power plants in emerging economies and provide discounted financing through GE Capital to its customers at the same time.

Conglomerates such as GE that pursue unrelated diversification tend to experience a diversification discount: The stock price of such highly diversified firms is valued at less than the sum of their individual business units. GE experienced a significant diversification discount, as its capital unit contributed 50 percent of profits for many years. The presence of the diversification

discount in GE's depressed stock price was a major reason GE's then CEO, Jeffrey Immelt, decided to spin out GE Capital in 2015. On the day of the announcement, GE's stock price jumped 11 percent, adding $28 billion to GE's market capitalization (see Exhibit MC8.1).

The need for corporate restructuring was clear to Immelt. By 2009, GE's five business units (Technology Infrastructure, Energy Infrastructure, Capital Finance, Consumer and Industrial, and NBC Universal) brought in $157 billion in annual revenues. More than 50 percent of those revenues came from outside the United States, and GE employed more than 300,000 people in over 100 countries. Immelt decided to refocus GE's portfolio of businesses to reduce its exposure to capital markets and to achieve reliable and sustainable future growth; he attempted to achieve this by leveraging its core competency in industrial engineering. GE sold NBC Universal to Comcast, the largest U.S. cable operator; it also sold its century-old appliance unit to Haier, a Chinese manufacturer.

Immelt then used the cash injection from the sale of GE Capital to double down on the power business: He acquired the ailing French engineering group Alstom in 2015 for a deal valued at $17 billion. Under Immelt's restructuring, GE shifted its product focus to industrial products and engineering, making aviation, power, oil and gas, and health care its four largest units (see Exhibit MC8.2). By 2018, GE's geographic scope was more diversified, with the U.S. now accounting for less than 40 percent of annual sales, and Europe and Asia each accounting for about 20 percent of revenues (see Exhibit MC8.3).

Yet, GE continued to lose money. By 2018, GE's Alstom acquisition was its power unit and designated the second-largest strategic business. However, by the end of the year, its revenues fell by over 20 percent. Overall, in the third quarter of 2018 alone, GE posted a loss of $34 billion. The firm had amassed too much debt and had too little cash flow. The diagnosis was that Immelt overpaid on several high-profile acquisitions (Alstom, being one, and the oil-field services company Baker Hughes, which it acquired for $32 billion, being another). In addition to overpaying for these firms, it also sold or spun off other GE units for too little.

On August 1, 2017, the board of GE replaced the haphazard Immelt with John Flannery, a 30-year GE insider who had led the health care unit (see Exhibit MC8.1). After only one year on the job, the board decided to let Flannery go because it felt he was too indecisive, spending too much time in endless meetings focusing on analysis and consensus building rather than on taking the drastic actions they felt were needed to right the firm. In June 2018, when morale among GE employees was already low, GE reached its lowest point: It was dropped from the Dow Jones Industrial Average (DJIA) and replaced by Walgreens. GE had continuously been listed on the DJIA (the most widely cited stock index representing the 30 most prestigious U.S. companies) since 1907. Its replacement by Walgreens was the final blow for the firm.

In 2019 the board appointed Lawrence "Larry" Culp as the new CEO; he had previously led Danaher Corp., another globally diversified conglomerate, albeit much smaller than GE. Culp is the first outsider to be appointed CEO in GE's 126-year history. To GE-lifers such as Welch, Immelt, and Flannery, the appointment of an outsider came as a complete shock; in their minds the best managers in the world that could run any business better than anyone else were all produced at GE. Executives that did not ascend to the CEO job left and became CEOs elsewhere, for example, 3M, Boeing, and The Home Depot, among many others. Each of these firms is considered among the greatest U.S. enterprises. GE's current board of directors, which now includes a seat held by the activist investor Trian Fund (run by billionaire Nelson Peltz), is clearly wanting to shake things up.

DISCUSSION QUESTIONS

1. What kind of diversification is GE pursuing? What are the sources of value creation with this type of diversification?

2. How did GE lose $507 billion (more than 85 percent) of its market valuation since its peak? What went wrong?

3. After leaving GE, Jeffrey Immelt stated in 2018: "The notion of plugging financial services and industrial companies together, maybe it was a good idea at a point in time, but it is a uniquely bad idea now."[2] To what is Immelt referring? Why does he think this is a bad idea? Do you agree? Why, or why not?

4. In the bestseller *Good to Great,* Jim Collins advances the hypothesis that the greatness of a leader is known only after the leader has departed. The business press has celebrated Jack Welch as the greatest CEO of the last century. After reading this MiniCase, do you agree with Collins' strategic leadership hypothesis? Why, or why not? Note: When interviewed in 2018 about the GE situation, Jack Welch had this to say: "I give myself an A for the operation of GE, but an F for my choice of successor."[3]

Endnotes

1. As quoted in: Gryta, T., and T. Mann (2018, Dec. 15), "GE powered the American century—Then it burned out," *The Wall Street Journal.*

2. Gryta, T., and T. Mann (2018, Dec. 15), "GE powered the American century—Then it burned out," *The Wall Street Journal.*

3. As quoted in: Gryta, T., and T. Mann (2018, Dec. 15), "GE powered the American century—Then it burned out," *The Wall Street Journal.*

Sources: Gryta, T., and T. Mann (2018, Dec. 15), "GE powered the American century—Then it burned out," *The Wall Street Journal;* "General Electric powers downwards," *The Economist* (2018, Nov. 3); Gryta, T., J.S. Lublin, and D. Benoit (2018, Feb. 21), "How Jeffrey Immelt's 'success theater' masked the rot at GE," *The Wall Street Journal;* Collins, J. (2001). *Good to Great. Why Some Companies Make the Leap and Others Don't* (New York: Harper Business); and GE annual reports (various years).

Disney: Building Billion-Dollar Franchises

DISNEY IS the world's largest media company and is world-renowned for its Walt Disney Studios and the popular Walt Disney Parks and Resorts. In 2019 it achieved $60 billion in annual revenues. As a diversified media company, Disney is active in a wide array of business activities—movies, amusement parks, cable and broadcast television networks (ABC, ESPN, and others), as well as cruises, retailing, and streaming. It became the world's leading media company by pursuing a corporate strategy of diversification and vertical integration, executed through a series of high-profile acquisitions, which included Pixar (2006), Marvel (2009), Lucasfilm (2012) (the creator of *Star Wars*), and 21st Century Fox (2019).

Disney's Corporate Strategy

Disney's main goal in pursuing its corporate strategy is to build billion-dollar franchises based on movie sequels, park rides, and merchandise. CEO Robert Iger leads a group of about 20 executives whose sole responsibility is to hunt for new billion-dollar franchises. This group of senior leaders decides top-down which projects are a go and which are not. They also allocate resources to particular projects. Disney even organizes its employees into consumer product groups built around franchises such as *Frozen*, *Toy Story*, *Star Wars*, and other cash cows. Disney's corporate strategy around building billion-dollar franchises is certainly paying off: It has seen steady growth, earning $14 billion in profits in 2019—up from a mere $3 billion a decade earlier. Disney has been the most profitable movie studio for years and thus has enjoyed a sustained competitive advantage.

Star Wars: The Last Jedi is part of the global Star Wars franchise. This sequel alone grossed over $1.3 billion in the box office.
Matthew Leane/Alamy Stock Photo

DISNEY AND PIXAR: "TRY BEFORE YOU BUY." To understand how Disney's corporate strategy of growth through acquisition came about, let's look at one of its most successful deals: Disney's acquisition of Pixar, around which it then built a number of billion-dollar franchises. It all began with a strategic alliance. Pixar started as a computer hardware company that produced high-end graphic display systems. One of its customers was Disney. To demonstrate the capabilities of the graphic display systems, Pixar produced short,

This MiniCase was prepared by Frank T. Rothaermel with Laura Zhang, who provided superb research assistance. This MiniCase is developed for the purpose of class discussion. It is not intended to be used for any kind of endorsement, source of data, or depiction of efficient or inefficient management. All opinions expressed, all errors and omissions are entirely the author's. Revised and updated: June 7, 2019. © Frank T. Rothaermel.

computer-animated movies. Although sophisticated, Pixar's computer hardware was not selling well, and the new venture was hemorrhaging money. To the rescue rode not Buzz Lightyear, but Steve Jobs. Shortly after being ousted from Apple in 1986, Jobs bought the struggling hardware company for $5 million and founded Pixar Animation Studios, investing another $5 million into the company. The Pixar team led by Edwin Catmull and John Lasseter then transformed the company into a computer-animation film studio.

To finance and distribute its newly created computer-animated movies, Pixar entered a strategic alliance with Disney. Disney's distribution network and its stellar reputation in animated movies were critical complementary assets that Pixar needed to commercialize its new genre of films. In turn, Pixar's assets gave Disney what it it needed to rejuvenate its floundering product lineup. (Disney retained the rights to all Pixar films and their sequels.)

Pixar's success exceeded expectations. It rolled out one blockbuster after another: *Toy Story (*1, 2, and 3*), A Bug's Life, Monsters, Inc.,* and *The Incredibles,* collectively grossing several billion dollars. Given Pixar's huge success and Disney's abysmal performance with its own releases during this time, the bargaining power in the alliance shifted dramatically. Renegotiations of the Pixar–Disney alliance broke down in 2004, reportedly because of personality conflicts between Steve Jobs and then-Disney Chairman and CEO Michael Eisner.

Enter Robert Iger, who was appointed the new CEO in 2005. Under his leadership, Disney acquired Pixar for $7.4 billion a year later. The success of the alliance demonstrates the power of complementary assets and shared core competencies. It gave Disney an inside perspective on Pixar's core competencies (computer animation) and allowed Disney to transfer and apply some of its unique competencies, for example, marketing, brand building, and product extensions.

ACQUISITIONS EVER AFTER & INTEGRATING TO INFINITY AND BEYOND. In 2009, Disney turned to acquisitions again. The acquisition of Marvel Entertainment for $4 billion added Spider-Man, Iron Man, The Incredible Hulk, and Captain America to its lineup of characters. Marvel's superheroes grossed a cumulative $15 billion at the box office, with *The Avengers* bringing in $2 billion. In 2012, when Disney acquired Lucasfilm for more than $4 billion, Mickey's extended family was joined by Darth Vader, Obi-Wan Kenobi, Princess Leia, and Luke Skywalker.

In 2014, Disney acquired Maker Studios, a YouTube-based multi-channel network, for $675 million. Under Disney, Maker Studies no longer had to support 60,000 YouTube creators through channel promotions and ad sales. Instead, it had to focus on no more than the top 250 YouTube content creators with large followings—the goal: Build billion-dollar franchises in the new on-demand TV space.

In 2019, Disney acquired 21st Century Fox for $71 billion, adding the *Simpsons, Deadpool,* and the Fox-owned Marvel heroes, the X-Men and the Fantastic Four, to its character lineup. The acquisition also added Fox television networks (FX cable network, National Geographic properties, and Fox Searchlight). In addition, Disney took over Fox's 30 percent ownership of Hulu, a streaming service that competes directly with Netflix, the streaming giant in family programming (an already hypercompetitive market). With it, Disney now owns two-thirds of Hulu, but has full control over the streaming service. (The remaining third ownership stake in Hulu is owned by Comcast). Fox is by far the largest acquisition in Disney's nearly 100-year history, and the company is placing major bets on Fox becoming a core element of Disney's corporate strategy. This move represents a new effort from Disney to compete in the online streaming space, already the preferred way for most people to consume media. Hulu allows Disney to compete more effectively with Netflix, the success of which has forced traditional studios to rethink how to modify their business models to more directly engage with consumers through forward integration.

Disney did not stop there; it went on to develop a streaming service of its own. In late 2019 it plans to launch Disney+, a direct-to-consumer streaming service built around some of Disney's most popular franchises, such as *Star Wars* and *High School Musical.* Subscriptions will be offered at half the price of Netflix's monthly fee. Thus, in addition to creating its own content, Disney will also distribute its own content through its streaming services. Disney's foray into the streaming space is not new, however; in 2018, it launched ESPN+, a sports streaming service that currently has more than 2 million subscribers, a number achieved in less than a year.

Fox's extensive library of entertainment hits, in conjunction with Disney's well-known characters and franchises, should give Disney a major play-to-win advantage. However, whether this forward integration strategy will pay off in the long run, and make up for revenue losses resulting from lucrative Netflix licensing ties, cable fees, and even movie ticket sales, cannot yet be determined. If this strategy does succeed, it would result in a steady stream of recurring revenue from tens of millions of Americans and potentially even hundreds of millions of international subscribers. To succeed in this industry, Disney needs to transform itself into a fully integrated, but agile technology company capable of adapting quickly to a rapidly changing environment.

BUILDING BILLION-DOLLAR FRANCHISES. After taking the reins in 2005, CEO Iger transformed Disney from a lackluster firm of inferior performance into one refocused around *franchises,* which generally begin with a big movie hit and subsequently follow up with derivative TV shows, theme park rides, video games, toys, and apparel. Rather than churn out 30 movies per year as it did prior to Iger, Disney now produces about 10 movies per year, concentrating on box office hits. Disney's annual movie lineup is now dominated by franchises (*Star Wars*), superheroes, and live-action versions of animated classics such as *Aladdin, Cinderella,* and *Beauty and the Beast.* The biggest Disney franchises include *Pirates of the Caribbean* (grossing more than $4 billion), *Toy Story* (over $2 billion), *Monsters, Inc.* (close to $2 billion), *Cars* (over $1 billion), and *Frozen* (over $1.5 billion).

Most recently, Disney's Marvel franchise released *Avengers: Endgame,* which was a smash hit in the box office. It surpassed $2 billion in sales in record time and is currently the second-highest grossing movie of all time. It is the last installment in a series of 22 films, which has grossed over $8 billion in the domestic box office and is the highest grossing franchise series in the United States.

The *Star Wars* franchise, however, remains Disney's crown jewel. Aswath Damodaran, a finance professor at New York University, estimates the *Star Wars* franchise to be worth over $10 billion.[1] Product extensions beyond box office receipts (over $2.5 billion) include streaming revenues from Netflix, AmazonPrime, and other providers ($2.5 billion), toys and merchandise ($3 billion), gaming ($1.5 billion), as well as books and e-books ($500 million). Again, this astonishing valuation is explained by Disney's ability to build billion-dollar franchises through product extensions. Damodaran shows that the Star Wars empire has a far reach in many corners of commerce.

Clouds on Disney's Horizon

While things seem to be sunny right now in Southern California, there are some clouds on the horizon. First, relying on a few big franchises is risky. What if the pipeline dries up? Many of Disney's greatest franchises such as *Star Wars* joined the family through an acquisition. An acquisition-led growth strategy, however, may not be sustainable because of the limited number of media companies that Disney can acquire. Indeed, a number of recent tech acquisitions such as online video producer Maker Studios (2014) and social-gaming company Playdom Inc. (2010) have not yielded the desired results. So far, success with these recent acquisitions is eluding Disney.

Second, some critics assert that focusing too much on billion-dollar franchises reduces originality and bores consumers more quickly. Disney has been dubbed a one-trick pony by some critics for its formulaic recipe of success: a blockbuster hit followed by derivative shows, merchandise, and other spin-offs. Moreover, all of Disney's recent blockbuster successes were remakes or sequels. This may not be a sustainable strategy in the long run as the number of sagas worth remaking begins to dwindle.

Third, and perhaps most important, roughly half of Disney profits come from its TV networks ESPN, ABC, and others. The media industry, however, is being disrupted: People spend much less time and money watching movies on the big screen and spend more time consuming content online via YouTube, Netflix, Hulu, and Amazon Prime. While ESPN is certainly very successful, the cost of rights to show the big sporting events live has escalated dramatically in recent years. In addition, more and more subscribers have cut their cable cord to get their media including sports and entertainment online. As a response, cable providers are more likely to unbundle their service offerings, which may pose challenges for ESPN, often the most expensive part of the cable bundle (some estimate $10). The resulting narrow focus may not appeal to everyone. Although Disney has already launched ESPN+ and will soon launch Disney+, there appears to be room for only a few, if not just one or two winners, in the highly competitive streaming landscape where Apple, Netflix, Comcast, AT&T, and Amazon are all chasing after the same end goal. This fierce competition has shifted the conversation in the direction of who has the most valuable and high-quality content, which will ultimately attract the greatest number of subscribers.

Finally, Disney's corporate strategy of building billion-dollar franchises was masterminded and executed smoothly by CEO Robert Iger. Although he was scheduled to step down in 2015, he decided to extend his tenure until 2021. No heir apparent is in sight, thus no one knows for certain who will fill the void created when Iger steps down. This void may dampen the growth prospects of the world's biggest media company, and its star may shine less brightly in the future.

DISCUSSION QUESTIONS

1. What type of corporate strategy is Disney pursuing? Which core competencies are shared across its activities and how?

2. Why do you think Disney acquisitions of Pixar, Marvel, and Lucasfilm were so successful, while others such as Sony's acquisition of Columbia Pictures or News Corp.'s acquisition of Myspace were much less successful?

3. Given the build-borrow-or-buy framework, do you think Disney should pursue alternatives to acquisitions? Why or why not? Explain.

4. Do you think focusing on billion-dollar franchises is a good corporate strategy for Disney? What are pros and cons of this strategy?

Endnote

1. Damodaran, A. (2016, Jan. 6), "Intergalactic finance: Why the Star Wars franchise is worth nearly $10 billion to Disney," *Forbes*.

Sources: Watson, R. (2019, May 5), "'Avengers: Endgame' surpasses $2 billion in record time," *The Wall Street Journal;* Eastwood, J., Moriarty, D., and Aaronson, S. (2019, May 1), "Marvel's mightiest zeros: How the Avengers broke box office records," *The Wall Street Journal;* Schwartzel, E. (2019, Apr. 10), "Disney's next big remake: Itself," *The Wall Street Journal;* "Disney, AT&T and Comcast v Netflix, Amazon, and Apple," *The Economist* (2019, Mar. 30); Schwartz, M. (2019, Mar. 20), "Disney officially owns 21st Century Fox," *NPR;* Schwartzel, E., and Flint, J. (2019, Mar. 20), "Disney closes $71.3 billion deal for 21st Century Fox assets," *The Wall Street Journal;* "Disney goes back to the future," *The Economist* (2019, Jan. 3); Fritz, B. (2017, May 16), "Disney's Iger isn't about to let go as CEO," *The Wall Street Journal;* "ESPN is losing subscribers but it is still Disney's cash machine," *The Economist* (2017, May 6); Fritz, B. (2017, Mar. 23), "Disney extends CEO Robert Iger's tenure to 2019," *The Wall Street Journal;* Fritz, B. (2017, Feb. 7), "Walt Disney pressured by sagging ESPN performance," *The Wall Street Journal;* Damodaran, A. (2016, Jan. 6), "Intergalactic finance: Why the Star Wars franchise is worth nearly $10 billion to Disney," *Forbes;* Fitz, B. (2015, Jun. 8), "How Disney milks its hits for profits ever after," *The Wall Street Journal;* Catmull, E., and A. Wallace (2014), *Creativity, Inc.: Overcoming the Unseen Forces That Stand in the Way of True Inspiration* (New York: Random House); "Superman v Spider-Man," *The Economist* (2013, Jan. 15); "Disney buys out George Lucas, the creator of 'Star Wars,'" *The Economist* (2012, Nov. 3); Isaacson, W. (2011), *Steve Jobs* (New York: Simon & Schuster); "Marvel superheroes join the Disney family," *The Wall Street Journal* (2009, Aug. 31); Paik, K. (2007), *To Infinity and Beyond!: The Story of Pixar Animation Studios* (New York: Chronicle Books); and Disney annual reports (various years).

Hollywood Goes Global

HOLLYWOOD MOVIES HAVE always been a quintessentially American product, but globalization has changed the economics of the industry. By 2020, more than 70 percent of total ticket sales for Hollywood blockbusters will come from foreign ticket sales—up from 50 percent in 2000. Some movies (e.g., *Transformers: Age of Extinction* [2014] and *The Fate of the Furious* [2017]) grossed 80 percent of total box-office receipts overseas. Of the total $42 billion that Hollywood movies grossed in 2018, more than $30 billion (71 percent) came from outside the United States. Today, Hollywood would be unable to continue producing big-budget movies without foreign revenues. Foreign sales now make or break the success of newly released big-budget movies. In particular, big-budget movies must do well in China, which has become the largest market globally.

The Avengers: Endgame (the Marvel movie that was released in 2019 and grossed over $2.5 billion by that summer) is on track to being the highest-grossing movie of all time. The movie's international performance, which brought in $1.75 billion of total sales (70 percent), testifies to the power of foreign revenue. In India, *Endgame* has been shown in English and translated to three other Indian languages. In China, it is currently the highest-grossing import movie.

Avatar (2009) remains the highest-grossing movie to date, earning almost $3 billion since its release. Non-U.S. box-office sales account for close to 75 percent of that number. *Avatar* was hugely popular in Asia, especially in China, where the government gave permission to increase the number of movie theaters showing the film from 5,000 to 35,000. Another of James Cameron's popular films, *Titanic* (1997), grossed close to $2 billion, with almost 70 percent of that total coming from overseas box-office sales. Exhibit MC10.1 depicts the lifetime

This MiniCase was prepared by Frank T. Rothaermel with Laura Zhang, who provided superb research assistance. This MiniCase is developed for the purpose of class discussion. It is not intended to be used for any kind of endorsement, source of data, or depiction of efficient or inefficient management. All opinions expressed, all errors and omissions are entirely the author's. Revised and updated: June 1, 2019. ©Frank T. Rothaermel.

The Marvel movie *Avengers: The Endgame* broke all records in its release year. It is set to become the highest-grossing movie ever. Over 70 percent of its box-office revenues are from outside the United States.
Imaginechina/AP Images

revenues of Hollywood's all-time blockbuster movies, broken down into U.S. and foreign sales by dollars.

Among the Hollywood studios, Disney-owned Marvel Studios has been the most successful studio in recent years. Exhibit MC10.2 shows the breakdown between U.S. and foreign sales for movies produced by Marvel Studios. This exhibit shows that basically for all of the studio's megahits, the majority of revenues are from foreign sources, with the biggest hit of all—*Endgame*—grossing more than 70 percent of total revenues overseas.

"We Need Movies That Break Out Internationally"

Given the increasing importance of non-U.S. box-office sales, Hollywood studios are changing their business models. Rob Moore, vice chairman of Paramount Pictures, explains: "We need to make movies that have the ability to break out internationally. That's the only way to make the economic puzzle of film production work today."[1] For instance, in 2014, only one film grossed more than $300 million in the U.S. market (*Guardians*

EXHIBIT MC10.1 Lifetime Revenues of Top 20 Hollywood Blockbuster Movies by U.S. and Non-U.S. Sales, in $ millions (release year in parentheses)

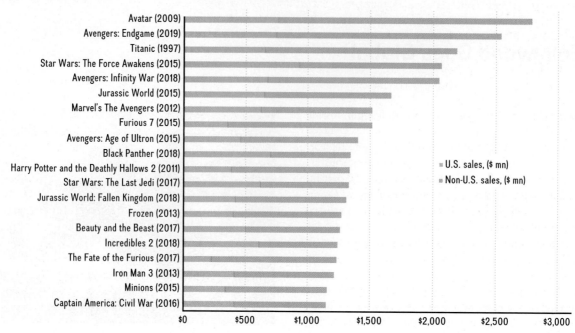

Source: Author's depiction of data from Box Office Mojo (http://boxofficemojo.com), 2009–2019.

EXHIBIT MC10.2 Marvel Cinematic Films: Percentage of U.S. Sales vs. Non-U.S. Sales

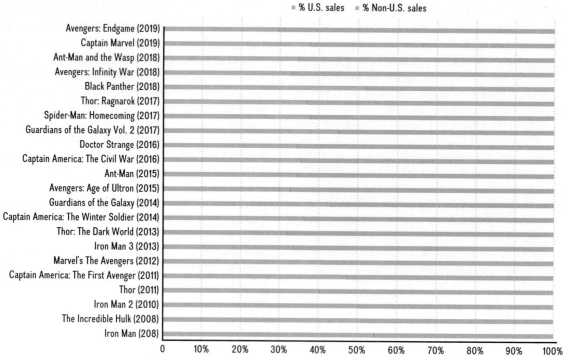

Source: Author's depiction of data from Box Office Mojo (http://boxofficemojo.com), 2008–2019.

of the Galaxy). Thanks to international releases, however, 2014 ended up being one of the most profitable years for Hollywood. This led movie studios to modify their release tactics. For example, some opted to release installments from their most popular movie franchises to their foreign markets first and then to the U.S. market. Disney followed this strategy with its initial release of *Monsters University* (2013), the prequel to *Monsters, Inc.* (2001). *Avengers: Age of Ultron* (2015) set the record for the biggest overseas opening, surpassing a record set weeks earlier by *Furious 7* (2015), from *The Fast and the Furious* series. This record was later surpassed by the foreign premiere of the eighth installment of the series, *The Fate of the Furious* (2017), which brought in $44.3 million during its opening weekend—a whopping 80 percent of which came from foreign box-office sales.

Although Hollywood has long been editing films to satisfy government censors, more recently, it has been dropping in unique scenes to cater specifically to the non-U.S. audiences it is targeting. Studios are also adapting their scripts to better appeal to global audiences. For example, although the remake of the movie *Red Dawn* (2012) was a box-office flop, with proceeds of a mere $51 million on a budget of $65 million, producers revised the script to avoid alienating Chinese moviegoers (and to satisfy Chinese censors). Instead of a Chinese army invading the West Coast of the United States, audiences now saw a North Korean army. Moreover, Hollywood has begun casting foreign actors in leading roles. For example, the film *G.I. Joe: The Rise of Cobra* prominently featured South Korean movie star Byung-hun Lee and South African actor Arnold Vosloo. Lastly, Hollywood has been known to pull the plug on projects that seem too U.S.-centric. For instance, Disney's *Wedding Banned,* a romantic comedy about a divorced couple trying to prevent their daughter from getting married, was axed in the advanced production stage despite several marquee stars (Robin Williams, Anna Faris, and Diane Keaton) because of perceptions that it would not succeed outside the American market.

Hollywood's Global Challenges

The fact that roughly $7 out of $10 of Hollywood's revenues come from international ticket sales is a bit surprising given the challenges Hollywood faces in some international markets. One challenge is potential government interference with content. For example, in China, before a film import gets seen by the public, it must undergo screening by government censors. The Chinese release of the Oscar-award winning film *Django Unchained* was temporarily canceled due to "technical reasons," which were interpreted to mean excessive violence and sexual content. By the time the film was recut and released, it performed poorly, in part because many Chinese filmgoers had already seen the unedited version of the film on pirated DVDs.

This brings us to another challenge that Hollywood studios face in their effort to go global: *piracy.* Responses to piracy can vary, as in the case of the European Union (EU), where, for instance, Britain and France impose fines on producers and buyers of pirated content, but Spain does not—in fact, Spain has long been a safe haven for the distribution of illegal movies (and music). Although Spain did pass a law in 2011 to provide better protection of copyrighted material, when nearly 50 percent of the country's internet users admit to illegally downloading copyrighted content (twice the EU average rate), that makes enforcement of the law notoriously difficult. Piracy results in lost revenue, which is one reason movie studios are moving toward simultaneous, worldwide release of anticipated blockbusters—the hope is that this tactic will cut down on those revenues losses.

China is also infamous for rampant infringement of copyright, resulting in a flourishing market for bootleg content. A Chinese government report in 2010 found that the market for pirated DVDs was $6 billion. As a comparison, the total box-office revenues in China in the same year were a mere $1.5 billion. One reason is that ticket prices for movies in China are steep and movies are considered luxury entertainment that few can afford. Another reason that black-market sales in China are so high is that legitimate sales often are not allowed. China allows only a few dozen new non-Chinese movies into its theaters each year. Additionally, it has strict licensing rules on the sale of home-entertainment goods. As a result, there is often no legitimate product competing with the bootleg offerings available via DVD and the internet in China.

With the move from physical media such as DVDs and Blu-ray discs to online streaming, Chinese streaming and video-on-demand services are also growing rapidly. In 2016, PPTV, a Chinese online streaming website, secured the post-theater rights to *Warcraft* for $24 million, indicating a potentially new source of revenues for Hollywood.

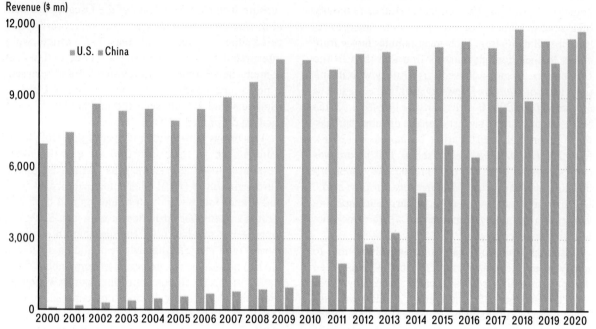

EXHIBIT MC10.3 Box Office Revenue in the United States and China, 2000–2020

Revenue ($ mn)

Source: Author's depiction data from IHS Markit (with projections for 2019 and 2020).

China: Now the Largest Movie Market

That the economics of the movie industry have fundamentally changed is further bolstered by the fact that in 2018 China became the second-largest contributor to Hollywood's top line, comprising close to $9 billion in annual revenues. China's overall box office revenues tripled between 2013 and 2018. China is poised to exceed the United States in terms of total box-office sales by 2020, making it the largest movie market globally. China has already exceeded the United States in terms of the number of movie screens in the country. However, growth in movie attendance is not as profitable in China as traditional releases in the United States. Film distributors typically earn 50 to 55 percent of box-office revenues in the United States. The average in many other countries is closer to 40 percent (the rest goes to the cinema owner). But in China, a typical Hollywood film distributor gets only 15 percent of the box-office ticket revenue. Exhibit MC10.3 depicts overall box office revenues for the United States and China.

Given China's importance as a movie market, it is no wonder that Hollywood executives are willing to do what they can to enter that market, which is difficult, given the Chinese government's stringent screening regulations. Only a select few Hollywood movies actually make it into China's theaters. As of 2018, the number of foreign movie imports allowed per year was 41. During national holidays, the state-backed distributor China Film Group restricts most Chinese theaters to Chinese films, further impacting revenue for Hollywood studios.

To get on that list of 41 film imports, studios will produce multiple versions of the same film. For instance, Disney's Marvel Studios produced two versions of the box-office hit *Iron Man 3*. One version of the film was produced for general release, and the other version was produced specifically for the Chinese market. This version included bonus footage of scenes shot in Beijing and guest appearances by Chinese movie stars. Producers edited *Mission Impossible III* and *Skyfall* for the Chinese market as well, cutting scenes that Chinese censors believed portrayed China in a negative light.

Some critics assert that Hollywood's accommodating of Chinese preferences amounts to pandering. For instance, in *The Martian*, NASA is depicted as seemingly pleading with its counterpart, the China National Space Administration, to supply a classified booster rocket that would carry payload to Mars and thus allow NASA (which did not have such an advanced rocket at its disposal) to rescue one of its stranded astronauts. Although this pleading scene is included in the namesake book by Andy Weir, on which the movie is based, critics still saw it as pandering.

The Great Wall (released in China in 2016 and the United States in 2017) marked a new level of U.S.-China collaboration in movie production. *The Great Wall* marked a distinct change in strategy for Hollywood studies as the movie was co-produced by both Hollywood and Chinese studios. The movie is directed by Zhang Yimou, a well-known Chinese filmmaker who garnered international recognition for choreographing the opening and closing ceremonies of the 2008 Beijing Summer Olympic Games. *The Great Wall* co-stars Matt Damon and Jing Tian. Damon plays a European mercenary who joins forces with a Chinese commander (played by Jing Tian) to fight mysterious invaders at the Great Wall. With a mega-budget of $150 million, *The Great Wall* is the most ambitious co-production between Hollywood and Chinese film studios to date. It is also the most expensive movie ever shot exclusively in China.

The hope was that *The Great Wall* as a transnational movie would be a blockbuster in both China and the United States. Although the movie grossed $335 million, it flopped in the United States where it made only $35 million. But in the Chinese market, it grossed $300 million. While not *Avatar* or *Avengers* territory, the movie achieved respectable commercial success, further underscoring the importance of the Chinese market for big-budget movies. In the meantime, Hollywood movie executives continue to highlight the huge market opportunities in China and emphasize that they will soon find the right formula to make movies that are attractive to both American and Chinese audiences alike.

DISCUSSION QUESTIONS

1. How has the global environment changed for U.S. (Hollywood) movie studios since 2000? Explain.

2. Apply the *integration-responsiveness framework* (see Exhibit 10.8) to describe which global strategy Hollywood studios followed originally, and how their strategic positioning has changed over time. Explain how and why.

3. Given the economics of the now global movie industry, what are the strategic implications for Hollywood studios? What are some opportunities, and what are some threats? How should Hollywood movie studies take advantage of these opportunities, while mitigating the threats?

4. When commenting on the disappointing performance of *The Great Wall,* movie executives continue to highlight the huge market opportunities in China and emphasize that they will soon find the right formula to make movies that are attractive to both American and Chinese audiences alike. Do you agree with this assessment? Why or why not?

   a. Assuming that movie studies will be able to create breakthrough hits that are attractive for both Eastern and Western audiences, what type of global strategy would that entail? What are some benefits of this type of global positioning? What are some of its risks? Why is this type of global positioning so hard to achieve?

   b. What can movie producers do to ensure that future Chinese-American co-productions are more successful? Explain.

Endnote

1. Schuker, L. (2010, Aug. 2), "Plot change: Foreign forces transform Hollywood films," *The Wall Street Journal.*

Sources: "'Avengers: Endgame' has been an unusual hit in China," *The Economist* (2019, May 2); "'Avengers: Endgame' is already the year's highest-grossing film," *The Economist* (2019, Apr. 29); Schwartzel, E. (2019, Apr. 28), "Avengers: Endgame pulverizes box-office records with $1.2 billion debut," *The Wall Street Journal;* McNary, D. (2019, Jan. 2), "2018 worldwide box office hits record as Disney dominates," *Variety;* Hong, W. (2018, Dec. 31), "China's box office revenue growth slowed in 2018," *CNBC;* Shaw, L. (2018, Dec. 13), "China approves release of more U.S. films to meet goal," *Bloomberg;* Faughnder, R. (2017, Apr. 25), "Netflix finds a path into China through Baidu streaming service," *The Los Angeles Times;* McClintock, P., and S. Galloway (2017, Mar. 2), "Matt Damon's 'The Great Wall' to lose $75 million; future U.S.-China productions in doubt," *The Hollywood Reporter,* www.hollywoodreporter.com/news/what-great-walls-box-office-flop-will-cost-studios-981602; Schwartzel, E. (2016, Aug. 18), "'Warcraft' deal sets record for streaming video in China," *The Wall Street Journal;* Lin, L., and W. Ma (2017, Jul. 1), "Hollywood seeks better deal as China's box office growth slows," *The Wall Street Journal;* Langfitt, F. (2015, May 18), "How China's censors influence Hollywood," *NPR,* www.npr.org/sections/parallels/2015/05/18/407619652/how-chinas-censors-influence-hollywood; Lin, L. (2015, May 15), "Netflix in talks to take content to China," *The Wall Street Journal;* Editorial Board (2015, Jan. 31), "China's losing battle with Internet censorship," *Chicago Tribune;* Brook, T. (2014, Oct. 21), "How the global box office is changing Hollywood," *BBC;* Kuo, L. (2014, Mar. 27), "China's film market is going gangbusters, but it may not help Hollywood much," *Quartz;* Miller, D. (2014, Jun. 14), "After the controversy, 'Django Unchained' flops in China," *The Los Angeles Times;* McCarthy, N. (2014, Sep. 3), "Bollywood: India's film industry by the numbers," infographic, *Forbes;* Takada, K. (2013, Apr. 11), "China debut of Django Unchained suddenly cancelled for technical reasons," *Reuters;* MacSlarrow, J. (2013, Jun. 7), "Is Bollywood India's next greatest export?" *Global Intellectual Property Center;* "'Hobbit' to break $1 billion," *Daily Variety* (2013, Jan. 22); "China gets its own version of Iron Man 3 after Disney allows the country's film censors onto the set," *MailOnline* (2012, Apr. 14); Levin, D., and J. Horn (2011, Mar. 22), "DVD pirates running rampant in China," *The Los Angeles Times;* "Ending the open season on artists," *The Economist* (2011, Feb. 17); "Bigger abroad," *The Economist* (2011, Feb. 17); Schuker, L. (2010, Aug. 2) "Plot change: Foreign forces transform Hollywood films," *The Wall Street Journal;* Schuker, L. (2009, Apr. 2), "Hollywood squeezes stars' pay in slump," *The Wall Street Journal;* "News Corporation," *The Economist* (2009, Feb. 26); and Cieply, M., and D. Carr (2009, Feb. 23), "A 'Slumdog' kind of the night at the Oscar ceremony," *The New York Times.*

Yahoo: From Internet Darling to Fire Sale

WHEN SHE WAS appointed CEO of yahoo in 2012, Marissa Mayer had just one job: Turn the company around. Yahoo was once the go-to internet leader, a web portal with e-mail and finance, sports, social media, and video sharing services. Advertisers loved it. At the height of the dot-com bubble in the spring of 2000, Yahoo was valued at more than $125 billion. In 2017, Yahoo's core internet business was sold to Verizon for a mere $4.5 billion. What had happened?

By the time Marissa Mayer got the CEO job, Yahoo's market cap stood at $19 billion. The once-leading internet company had lost some 85 percent of its market value. Yahoo was in deep trouble as indicated by a high CEO turnover: Mayer was the seventh CEO in less than five years. By the time she sold Yahoo to Verizon five years later, Yahoo's market cap stood at $53 billion. How did she almost triple the firm's market cap? And what explains the difference between the over $50 billion market cap in 2017 and the sale price of less than $5 billion to Verizon? Let's answer these questions one at a time. We begin by looking at Marissa Mayer's background and how she attempted to turn Yahoo around.

Pre-Yahoo

Mayer grew up in Wausau, Wisconsin, but took her higher education and built her career in California's Silicon Valley. She entered Stanford University in 1993, majoring in symbolic systems, a discipline that combines cognitive sciences, artificial intelligence, and human–computer interaction. Still at Stanford, Mayer earned a master's degree in computer science. On graduation in 1999, she declined over a dozen job offers, ranging from prestigious consulting firms to top-tier universities. Instead she went to a garage that housed a

Marissa Mayer, CEO Yahoo, 2012–2017.
Robyn Beck/AFP/Getty Images

handful of employees for a small startup just a few months old. It was called Google.

Google's 20th hire and its first female engineer, Mayer became a star. With a superior skill set and strong work ethic, she rose quickly to the rank of vice president. She helped develop many of Google's best known features: Gmail, images, news, and maps. In particular, she designed the functionality and uncluttered look and feel of Google's iconic search site. Mayer is known for her attention to detail, her commitment of time, and her desire to provide the very best user experience possible, putting products before profits. She maintains that if you build the best products possible, profits will come. No doubt Mayer's pedigree at Google appealed to the Yahoo board. She was deeply involved in everything that Google had done right. And she was ready.

At Yahoo

Mayer's first acts at Yahoo revolved around mission, culture, and cash. She developed a new mission for Yahoo—*to make the world's daily habits more inspiring and entertaining*—to help reinvigorate Yahoo's employees and get its customers excited again. Mayer's mission attempted to inspire Yahoo's employees to resume

Frank T. Rothaermel prepared this MiniCase from public sources. This MiniCase is developed for the purpose of class discussion. It is not intended to be used for any kind of endorsement, source of data, or depiction of efficient or inefficient management. All opinions expressed, all errors and omissions are entirely the author's. Revised and updated: May 31, 2019. ©Frank T. Rothaermel.

leadership in online advertising. To retain existing talent and restore morale, she also had to sell her workers on the new mission. She did so by sharing this mantra with them via tweets and other means: *People then products then traffic then revenue.* Employees understood they were the start of the transformation. To put Yahoo's new mission into action, she also worked to rejuvenate Yahoo's bureaucratic culture and engaged in more open and frequent communication, with weekly FYI town-hall meetings where she and other executives provided updates and fielded questions. All employees were expected to attend and encouraged to participate in the Q&A. Questions were submitted online during the week, and the employees voted for which questions executives should address.

Mayer also took on Yahoo's organizational culture. Yahoo had become overly bureaucratic and lost the zeal characteristic of high-tech startups. Many Yahoo employees worked from home. For those who worked in the office, weekends began Thursday afternoons, leaving empty parking garages at Yahoo's campus in Sunnyvale, California. In response, Mayer withdrew the option to work remotely. All of Yahoo's 12,000 employees would have to come to the office. Her rationale was that working in the same shared space encourages collaboration, teamwork, and the creative spark to foster innovation. She moved out of her corner office and instead worked in a cubicle among other Yahoo rank-and-file employees. To ease the transition into now being required to work on the Yahoo campus in Sunnyvale, California, Mayer ordered a renovation and upgrade to Yahoo's cafeteria, making gourmet meals—breakfast, lunch, and dinner—available free for all Yahoos.

Mayer also implemented other less-than-popular changes. Where before Yahoos enjoyed a casual work culture, now they faced a stacked ranking system of employee performance. Managers had to grade their direct reports along a bell curve, with a fixed percentage as "underperforming." Team leaders were now to rank their employees in defined groups: 10 percent in "greatly exceeds," 25 percent in "exceeds," 50 percent in "achieves," 10 percent in "occasionally misses," and 5 percent in "misses." Unintended consequences ensued. High performers refused to work with one another in the same team. Managers cynically traded team members to fill their quotas. Political infighting increased.

To raise cash, Mayer sold part of Yahoo's ownership stake in Alibaba, the Chinese ecommerce company, for more than $6 billion. She then spent about $2 billion acquiring more than three dozen tech ventures, including paying a bit over $1 billion for microblogging and social networking site Tumblr and $640 million for video ad company BrightRoll. The acquisitions filled gaps in product line and brought in new engineering talent (so-called "aqui-hires").

To turn around Yahoo, Mayer identified four strategic growth areas for investing significant resources and attention: mobile advertising, video, native advertising, and social media.[1] Mayer came up with the catchy phrase for the four areas: *MaVeNS* (= mobile advertising, video, native advertising, and social media), which she enjoyed using during investor presentations and earnings calls.

Failed Turnaround at Yahoo

After five years on the job, it became apparent that Yahoo would no longer be able to compete against Google and Facebook in online advertising. Once a leader in online advertising in the Web 1.0 portal world, Yahoo had fallen to third place well before Mayer took charge. Yahoo once owned the user experience in the early days of the internet for desktop users. But much has changed. In the early days, the internet was somewhat cumbersome to use. Yahoo provided a web portal that solved this problem for millions of users worldwide. It was their first stop once they logged in. With successful Yahoo products like Yahoo Mail, Yahoo Finance, and Yahoo Sports, many users spent their entire time online at Yahoo. In the first decade of the internet, this made Yahoo extremely attractive for online advertisers.

By 2012, however, the internet had undergone a dramatic shift from the Web 1.0 on personal computers to a Web 2.0 on mobile devices. The mobile experience, and with it mobile advertising, had become the new frontier. The difficulty that Mayer encountered as the new Yahoo CEO was that Google and Facebook had moved much faster and more successfully into the mobile space and thus captured the lion share of advertising. Google had long been the undisputed leader in online search due to its superior page rank algorithm technology over Yahoo's older and less effective keyword-based searches. Since 2009, Yahoo's searches were powered by Microsoft's Bing. In addition, newer social media platforms such as Facebook captured online users' attention and activities. With these changes, Google and Facebook started to dominate digital advertising. By 2016, Google captured 43 percent of all ad dollars spent, and Facebook captured 15 percent.

In online advertising, Yahoo only had 3 percent market share, which had been declining consistently over time.

To complicate matters for CEO Mayer, Yahoo experienced two major data hacks under her watch. In 2013, data for more than 1 billion accounts were stolen, the largest corporate hack on record. A year later, Yahoo disclosed a second hack, this time affecting some 500 million users. As a result, Yahoo required all of its users to reset their passwords; many did not return. In the end, Verizon acquired Yahoo's core internet business for $4.5 billion. After the sale of Yahoo's core business to Verizon, Yahoo's shareholders continue to own the investments made earlier by Yahoo in the Chinese ecommerce company Alibaba as well as in Yahoo Japan, valued jointly at more than $40 billion. Verizon retained the name Yahoo for its web properties, while the "original Yahoo" renamed itself Altaba (a portmanteau of "Alternate" and "Alibaba").

Why did Verizon acquire Yahoo's core internet business? Verizon's core business as a wireless service provider is maturing, and the company has ambitious plans to compete with Google and Facebook in online advertising. Verizon is adding the Yahoo acquisition to its prior purchase of the online media company AOL in 2015 for $4.4 billion. Verizon has more than 110 million wireless subscribers. It hopes to build a portfolio of internet properties by merging AOL and Yahoo to offer news, sports, and finance against which to sell better targeted digital advertising.

Verizon's strategy of acquiring internet assets that had fallen on hard times and to combine them to create an online search and advertising business to compete with Google and Facebook did not work out either. In 2018, Verizon wrote off $4.5 billion of the close to $9 billion it spent on acquiring Yahoo and AOL (bought for $4.4 billion in 2015) as Verizon's online search and advertising business faltered.

Although Marissa Mayer failed to turn Yahoo around, she did create shareholder value when compared to the dire situation Yahoo was in when she took the helm. Indeed, by the time Yahoo sold its core business to Verizon, the internet company's market value had almost tripled. Mayer also did well for herself: She departed Yahoo with some $230 million in total compensation for the five years as CEO.

DISCUSSION QUESTIONS

1. In an attempt to turn around Yahoo, Marissa Mayer defined a new mission for the internet company. How do strategic leaders such as Mayer develop and implement a mission for their company to achieve strategic goals? Why is an inspiring mission important?

2. What were some of the major changes Mayer implemented to turn Yahoo around? How do you evaluate them? In hindsight, what should Mayer have done differently, if anything? Explain.

3. What grade would you give Mayer for her job performance as strategic leader? What were her strengths and her weaknesses? Explain.

4. Do you believe the $230 million in total compensation was justified for Mayer's efforts? Why or why not? Explain.

Endnote

1. Native advertising is online advertising that attempts to present itself as naturally occurring editorial content rather than a search-driven paid placement.

Sources: Detailed background on Yahoo, Marissa Mayer, Google, and the online advertising and search industry is presented in the following books: Carlson, N. (2015), *Marissa Mayer and the Fight to Save Yahoo!* (New York: Hachette Book Group); Thiel, P. (2014), *Zero to One. Notes on Startups or How to Build the Future* (New York: Crown Business); Edwards, D. (2012), *I'm Feeling Lucky: The Confessions of Google Employee Number 59* (New York: Houghton Mifflin Harcourt); and Levy, S. (2011), *In the Plex: How Google Thinks, Works, and Shapes Our Lives* (New York: Simon & Schuster). Other sources include: Krouse, S., and M. Maidenberg (2018, Dec. 12), "Verizon takes $4.5 billion charge related to digital media business," *The Wall Street Journal;* Seetharaman, D. (2017, Apr. 25), "Yahoo's Marissa Mayer to reap $187 million after Verizon deal," *The Wall Street Journal;* Knutson, R. (2017, Feb. 21), "Why Verizon decided to stick with Yahoo deal after big data breaches," *The Wall Street Journal;* Goel, V., and M.J. de la Merced (2016, Jul. 24), "Yahoo's sale to Verizon ends an era for a web pioneer," *The New York Times;* "Yahoo to spin off remaining Alibaba stake," *The Wall Street Journal* (2015, Jan. 28); "Yahoo sales, profit gains may allay Mayer critics," *The Wall Street Journal* (2014, Oct. 22); Jackson, E. (2014, Oct. 19), "Yahoo CEO set to refresh turnaround plan," *The Wall Street Journal;* "Alibaba IPO to give Yahoo windfall," *The Wall Street Journal* (2014, Sep. 19); "How do you solve a problem like Marissa?" *Forbes* (2014, Jul. 29); "Is Alibaba or SoftBank about to buy Yahoo?" *Forbes* (2014, Jul. 23); "Mayer culpa," *The Economist* (2013, Mar. 2); "A makeover made in Google's image," *The Wall Street Journal* (2012, Aug. 9); "Google's Marissa Mayer," *Vogue* (2012, Mar. 28); and Yahoo annual reports (various years), www.sec.gov.

Uber: Ethically Most Challenged Tech Company?

UBER'S pre-initial public offering (IPO) valuation was as high as $120 billion, making it the most valuable privately held company ever. Yet when Uber had its IPO on May 10, 2019, it was valued at $76 billion at the end of its first trading day. What happened to the difference in valuations? Where did the $44 billion or some 37 percent of its valuation go? Answer: It evaporated—and many argue that the pattern of unethical behavior over the years was a major contributing factor.

Unicorns (private startups with a valuation of $1 billion or higher) such as Uber are not subject to the same public scrutiny as publicly traded companies are, which allows them to push the envelope in their legal and ethical business practices. A potential downside, however, is that a track record of ethics and legal problems may prevent a successful IPO in the future. In the process of achieving such success, Uber's unethical, if not illegal, activity generated controversy after controversy. Before we look more closely at those ethical issues, we need to understand the business success that could have tempted Uber to engage in ethical shortcuts.

Record-Breaking Growth

Facebook took seven years to reach a valuation of $50 billion for a private, venture-capital-backed firm; Uber only took five. If we compare Uber with the car-rental giant Hertz—which has 150 locations, a fleet of 500,000 cars, and about 30,000 employees—it's astounding to learn that Hertz reaches less than 1 percent of Uber's valuation. Uber reached its astronomical valuation because it successfully expanded both in the

Travis Kalanick, Uber's co-founder and former CEO, came to be seen as too much of a liability for the comfort of major Uber investors and was pressured to resign the key post. The relentlessly ambitious and combative entrepreneur was well aware of his reputation, which he described during a speech celebrating Uber's fifth anniversary: "I realize that I can come off as a somewhat fierce advocate for Uber. I also realize that some have used a different 'a'-word to describe me."[1]
Danish Siddiqui/Reuters

United States and globally. Today this ride-hailing company serves approximately 600 cities in more than 60 countries worldwide and with 100 million monthly users.

As a powerful platform business, Uber's popularity grew exponentially; it currently transports millions of riders daily and continues to expand rapidly in the United States and abroad. Revenues grew almost 30-fold, from $400 million in 2014 to more than $11 billion in 2018—yet Uber is not profitable. Why? The answer is that Uber continues to subsidize its rides to build a strong position in this winner-take-all market. In 2018, it lost a whopping $3 billion, more than any other startup in the year before its IPO.

Ethically Challenged?

Trailing Uber's meteoric rise were multiple lawsuits and accusations, often tied directly to decisions and actions made by its co-founder and now former CEO,

Frank T. Rothaermel prepared this MiniCase from public sources. This Mini-Case is developed for the purpose of class discussion. It is not intended to be used for any kind of endorsement, source of data, or depiction of efficient or inefficient management. All opinions expressed, all errors and omissions are entirely the author's. Revised and updated: June 3, 2019. ©Frank T. Rothaermel.

Travis Kalanick. Consider just some of the incidents and issues in the company's short history:

- **Early disregard for laws, rules, and regulations.** Within months of its San Francisco launch, the local Metro Transit Authority and the state Public Utilities Commission ordered Uber to cease and desist. They called out Uber as an unlicensed and illegal taxi service. Similar injunctions followed in major markets, including New York City, Los Angeles, Toronto, Paris, London, Berlin, and Delhi. Uber's response? Ignore all such warnings.

- **Dynamic pricing.** Unlike the taxi industry, in which pricing is fixed by regulation, Uber uses dynamic pricing, following the model of airlines, hotels, and other industries. Uber's fares go up or down based on real-time supply and demand. During a snowstorm or on New Year's Eve, short Uber rides can cost hundreds of dollars. Kalanick argued that surge pricing efficiently matches supply and demand. But many Uber users rant online against the practice and call it price gouging.

- **Punking the competition as well as its own drivers.** Lyft, the main competing ride-share company, accused Uber of ordering over 5,000 rides from Lyft and then canceling, so Lyft drivers lost business from legitimate rides. Uber also reportedly told its New York drivers that they could not work for both Uber and Lyft because of city regulations. No such regulations exist.

- **Poaching drivers.** Uber brand ambassadors have been accused of actively targeting successful drivers from Lyft and other competitors and pressuring them to defect—allegedly all part of Uber's secret Operation SLOG (Supplying Long-term Operations Growth).

- **Poisoning competitor's well.** Given their significant burn rate, startups live or die based on access to capital. Kalanick reportedly poisoned Lyft's efforts to raise venture capital, telling investors, "Before you decide whether you want to invest in [Lyft], just make sure you know that we are going to be fund-raising immediately after."[2]

- **Attacking critics.** Uber senior executive Emil Michael suggested spending $1 million to hire private investigators to dig up dirt on journalists who wrote damaging pieces on Uber, with particular focus on Sarah Lacy, of tech blog PandoDaily. When the remarks became public in 2014, Michael apologized and Kalanick decried the attempt, but Michael was not disciplined. In the wake of Kalanick's forced resignation in June 2017, Michael also resigned.

- **Tech transfer by stealth.** Uber opened its Advanced Tech Center in Pittsburgh in 2015 to develop autonomous cars and sophisticated mapping services. Funding research at Carnegie Mellon University's National Robotics Engineering Center (NREC) brought Uber access to the university's scientists. A few months later, Uber poached the entire NREC research team with signing bonuses, twice the salaries, and stock options. The NREC was left a shell, with its entire future in question.

- **Allegations of sexual harassment and gender discrimination.** A blog post by a former Uber engineer went viral. It alleged rampant sexual harassment, persistent mistreatment of female employees, and the company's failure to respond to complaints. The former employee said that women engineers in her work group dropped from 25 percent to as low as 3 percent within a year because of the hostile work environment. She also claimed managers downgraded her performance review for reporting a supervising manager for harassment.

- **Slow response.** Public outcry forced Kalanick to act on the allegations of sexual harassment, and once he acted, he went big. He hired former U.S. Attorney General Eric Holder to lead an internal investigation with Arianna Huffington, then Uber's only female board member.

- **Operation Greyball.** *The New York Times* exposed Uber's use of stealth technology for a number of years to foil law enforcement and regulators investigating Uber and its drivers.[3] In a secret operation code-named Greyball, Uber programmed its software to set up GPS rings around government offices and track low-cost phones and credit cards linked to government accounts. Thus, when law enforcement officers posed as Uber customers, Uber showed them dummy screens with fake Uber cars moving, none of which would stop and pick them up. Greyball was deployed worldwide, especially in cities where Uber was outlawed.

- **Kalanick caught on video.** When an Uber driver complained to Kalanick about recent fare cuts, he told the driver upon leaving the vehicle, "You know what, some people don't like to take responsibility for their own sh**,"[4] and slammed the door. Kalanick did not realize he was being filmed by the driver's dashboard cam. The driver uploaded the video to social media, where it went viral.

- **Waymo lawsuit.** Waymo, a unit of Alphabet (Google's parent company), sued Uber for stealing Waymo's proprietary self-driving technology. When Uber acquired the autonomous-vehicle startup Otto, its founder, Anthony Levandowski, was working for Waymo at the same time on its autonomous-vehicle program. Waymo accused Levandowski of stealing more than 14,000 proprietary files from the firm. Uber settled the lawsuit with Waymo in the spring of 2018, giving it $245 million in equity and making the promise that it would not use Waymo's technology in its self-driving cars. For Waymo, the stakes were just too high. According to expert predictions, only one or two technology standards will prevail for self-driving technology. Waymo wants to become the default operating system for self-driving cars with its proprietary technology.

Forced to Resign

Many of the issues described came to a head in mid-2017. In May, the results of the Holder investigation, along with 50 recommendations, were delivered to the Uber board. In June, responding to pressure from key investors, Kalanick formally resigned as CEO. The investors had expressed no confidence in Kalanick's ability to continue to lead the company that he co-founded.

You could say the company developed a reputation to live down. Uber's ethical challenges were called out publicly throughout its rise, and as early as 2014, venture capitalist Peter Thiel called Uber the "most ethically challenged company in Silicon Valley."[5] Of course, Thiel, the billionaire co-founder of PayPal and Palantir (a data analytics company), is also an investor in Lyft. Lyft (featured in ChapterCase 9) also went public in the spring of 2019 (before Uber) and ended up with a valuation of $26 billion at the end of its first trading day, roughly one-third that of Uber.

Echoing Thiel's assessment, *The Wall Street Journal* argued that Uber itself—rather than Lyft or old-line taxi and limo services—is its biggest threat, thereby functioning as its own biggest rival. The competitive tactics and comments by Uber executives and constant scandals surrounding Kalanick were harming the company's reputation and becoming a liability.

Disaster Averted?

Will Travis Kalanick's departure as CEO allow Uber to develop a more grounded and ethical corporate culture? It may take several years to answer that question confidently. Here are some observations about Uber's future.

A CYNIC'S VIEW. Critics may see the resignation of Kalanick as just one more stunt to reduce heat and scrutiny, and unlikely to result in meaningful change. Corporate culture is never easy to change, this line of reasoning goes, and Kalanick, as co-founder, remains a strong presence in two ways. First, he has contributed too much to the company's DNA (through the imprinting process discussed in Chapter 11), so the company is prone to lapses by nature. And second, Kalanick has not cut his ties; he still remains intimately involved in the company. Although no longer CEO and chairman, Kalanick remains a member of Uber's board of directors. Given this situation, some observers question whether Uber has in place effective corporate governance mechanisms, or whether its ethically and legally questionable competitive tactics and decisions are simply part of its larger intended strategy: to dominate the mobile, on-demand logistics business first and to address any remaining stakeholder grievances next.

BEYOND CYNICISM. On the other hand, business as usual for Uber is becoming increasingly problematic. For years, Uber seemed willing to flout rules, laws, and regulations because the service was liked by users who didn't want to see it be removed. Uber's customers were happy because they could hail rides conveniently and cheaply, often in areas that were underserved by regular taxis; drivers were happy because they could choose when and how long to work. Local politicians were cautious about throwing a monkey wrench in the works. Why make your voters unhappy?

Such tactics may work fine at the local level, but not beyond. Uber's challenges are growing increasingly broader, both nationally and internationally. Uber now fights well-funded lawsuits instead of hamstrung municipal bureaucrats. Uber can no longer fly under the radar. The company is so big and established that the CEO's boorish behavior or an employee's complaints about sexual harassment quickly go viral on a global basis.

EYE ON THE PRIZE. Uber may be at a point in its trajectory where investors simply won't allow it to continue its self-destructive tendency to cut ethical corners. Too much is at stake. In this line of thought, the biggest opportunity with Uber is not its current business. Uber's goal remains centered around self-driving cars, supported by high-powered mobile logistics networks and online mapping systems. In this view, its current business is secondary.

Which takes us back to Uber's inherent disruptive nature. With a fleet of autonomous vehicles offering cheap rides, people don't need to own cars anymore. When car ownership is no longer needed, it will impact the old-line car manufacturers. From there Uber might expand into the "delivery of everything," taking over last-mile deliveries for Amazon and other online retailers. Uber might even work in concert with shippers such as UPS and FedEx.

ONE POSSIBLE FUTURE. In this version of the future, Uber is the primary player and provider of self-driving car technology. It controls the platform under which customers might summon a car to their door, and some of Uber's current challenges would disappear. According to Kalanick, "The reason Uber could be expensive is because you're not just paying for the car—you're paying for the other dude in the car. When there's no other dude in the car, the cost of taking an Uber anywhere becomes cheaper than owning a vehicle."[6] Kalanick is pitching benefits of self-driving technology for both the firm and the consumer. Paying for the driver is currently the largest single cost of an Uber ride. Not having to deal with drivers thus becomes an attractive option not only because it saves on costs for customer and firm, but also because it eliminates a contentious relationship once shared between the firm and its work force (as evidenced by driver walkouts).

Globally, courts are still considering whether Uber drivers should be considered freelancers or actual employees, given the rules by which they must abide. If drivers are to be classified as employees, Uber must pay benefits and so forth; the cost per ride would further increase. Moreover, Uber loses money on each ride and continues to subsidize both the consumer and driver to build an installed base of as many users as possible. On the regulatory front it's reasonable to assume that states will continue to remove obstacles to self-driving cars and the companies that manage them. So in this future, many of its compliance failures go away.

CURRENT CHALLENGES. But Uber has to get through current challenges to reach its future goals. Before Kalanick resigned, the firm engaged in perception management to deal with all the scandals and controversies. In 2015 Uber hired David Plouffe as senior vice president of policy and strategy, explicitly to improve public relations and to lobby politicians. Previously, Plouffe had been the manager for the 2008 Obama presidential campaign and then a senior adviser in the administration. At Uber he pitched the social benefit of Uber's contribution to the transportation ecosystem and its ability to fix traffic congestion, cut down on drunk driving, and provide reliable and safe services to underserved city and suburban areas—even helping to end poverty by increasing access to reliable transportation. He also minimized the criticisms, calling them misguided.[7]

EXODUS OF TALENT. Plouffe walked away in early 2017. He was followed by Rachel Whetstone, who headed policy and communications globally; she was hired in 2015 and left in April 2017. The number of senior executives and lead engineers that have left Uber in the wake of continuous scandals has been a steady stream. They include Uber's head of autonomous-car technology, head of online mapping, and an artificial intelligence (AI) expert. Some cited issues with the company's values as the reason for their departure. When resigning after only six months on the job in spring 2017, Uber President Jeff Jones stated, "The beliefs and approach to leadership that have guided my career are inconsistent with what I saw and experienced at Uber."[8] As these executives departed before Uber's IPO, they left behind promised stock options estimated to be worth millions.

HOPE FOR THE FUTURE? If Uber is able to mend its ways—and much depends on how the full board responds to major investors—Uber has a much better chance of realizing the future it hopes will unfold.

DISCUSSION QUESTIONS

1. Would you like to work for Uber? Why or why not?

2. Do you agree with Peter Thiel's assessment that Uber is the "most ethically challenged company in Silicon Valley"? Why or why not? Explain.

3. Some observers had argued that Uber's greatest problem was not any of its scandals, but CEO Travis Kalanick. Now that Kalanick no longer serves that role, how much better off is Uber? Do you think Kalanick's reduced profile will turn the tide for Uber? Or are Kalanick's drive and competitiveness necessary to Uber's continued success, regardless of the title he holds? If you were on the

board of directors, what would you recommend? And why? Note: Due to his shareholdings in the company and how ownership is structured, Kalanick is an Uber board member. See www.uber.com/en-DE/newsroom/leadership/.

4. What should Uber CEO Dara Khosrowshahi do to address the company's poor reputation? How can he instill an ethical culture in this hard-charging startup?

Endnotes

1. Travis Kalanick quoted in: Huet, E. (2015, Jun. 3), "Uber is adding 'hundreds of thousands' of new drivers every month" *Forbes*.

2. As quoted in: Austin, S., and D. MacMillan (2014, Nov. 18), "Is Uber's biggest rival itself? A collection of controversy," *The Wall Street Journal*.

3. Isaac, M. (2017, Mar. 3), "How Uber deceives the authorities worldwide," *The New York Times*.

4. The Kalanick quote appeared in a number of news sources, including: "Uber CEO apologizes after being caught in argument with Uber driver," *CBS News* (2017, Feb. 28).

5. Thiel, P. (2014, Nov. 18), "Uber is most ethically challenged company in Silicon Valley," *CNN Money*, http://money.cnn.com/2014/11/18/technology/uber-unethicalpeter-thiel.

6. As quoted in Austin, S., and D. MacMillan (2014, Nov. 18), "Is Uber's biggest rival itself? A collection of controversy," *The Wall Street Journal*.

7. "I don't subscribe to the idea that the company has an image problem," Plouffe said. "I actually think when you are a disrupter you are going to have a lot of people throwing arrows." As quoted in: Swisher, K. (2014, December), "Man and Uber man," *Vanity Fair*: 1–11.

8. As quoted in: "Uber is facing the biggest crisis in its short history," *The Economist* (2017, Mar. 25).

Sources: Driebusch, C., and M. Farrell (2019, May 10), "Uber's high-profile IPO upsets with weak debut," *The Wall Street Journal;* Hoffman, L., G. Bensinger, and M. Farrell (2018, Oct. 16), "Uber proposals value company at $120 billion in a possible IPO," *The Wall Street Journal;* Stone, B. (2017), *The Upstarts: Uber, Airbnb, and the Battle for the New Silicon Valley* (New York: Little, Brown and Co.); Bensinger, G. (2017, Jun. 21), "Uber CEO Travis Kalanick quits as investors revolt," *The Wall Street Journal;* "What's behind the conflict between Google and Uber," *The Economist* (2017, May 8); "Here's how much Uber made in revenue in 2016," *Reuters* (2017, Apr. 14); "Uber is facing the biggest crisis in its short history," *The Economist* (2017, Mar. 25); "Travis Kalanick's uber-apology," *The Economist* (2017, Mar. 4); Isaac, M. (2017, Mar. 3), "How Uber deceives the authorities worldwide," *The New York Times;* Bensinger, G. (2017, Feb. 20), "Uber to investigate sexism, harassment claims," *The Wall Street Journal;* Fowler, S.J. (2017, Feb. 19), "Reflecting on one very, very strange year at Uber," www.susanjfowler.com/blog/2017/2/19/reflecting-on-one-very-strange-year-at-uber; "Potholes ahead," *The Economist* (2015, Jun. 17); "Driving hard," *The Economist* (2015, Jun. 13); Ramsey, M., and D. MacMillan (2015, May 31), "Carnegie Mellon reels after Uber lures away researchers," *The Wall Street Journal;* Austin, S., and D. MacMillan (2014, Nov. 18), "Is Uber's biggest rival itself? A collection of controversy," *The Wall Street Journal;* Thiel, P. (2014, Nov. 18), "Uber is most ethically challenged company in Silicon Valley," *CNN Money*, http://money.cnn.com/2014/11/18/technology/uber-unethical-peter-thiel/; "Uber-competitive," *The Economist* (2014, Nov. 22); "Pricing the surge," *The Economist* (2014, Mar. 29); and "Tap to hail," *The Economist* (2013, Oct. 19).

COMPANY INDEX

NAME INDEX

SUBJECT INDEX

FINANCIAL RATIOS USED IN CASE ANALYSIS

	Formula
Profitability Ratios: "How profitable is the company?"	
Gross Margin (or EBITDA, EBIT, etc.)	(Sales − COGS) / Sales
Return on Assets (ROA)	Net Income / Total Assets
Return on Equity (ROE)	Net Income / Total Stockholders' Equity
Return on Invested Capital (ROIC)	Net Operating Profit After Taxes / (Total Stockholders' Equity + Total Debt − Value of Preferred Stock)
Return on Revenue (ROR)	Net Profits / Revenue
Dividend Payout	Common Dividends / Net Income
Activity Ratios: "How efficient are the operations of the company?"	
Inventory Turnover	COGS / Inventory
Receivables Turnover	Revenue / Accounts Receivable
Payables Turnover	Revenue / Accounts Payable
Working Capital Turnover	Revenue / Working Capital
Fixed Asset Turnover	Revenue / Fixed Assets
Total Asset Turnover	Revenue / Total Assets
Cash Turnover	Revenue / Cash (which usually includes marketable securities)
Leverage Ratios: "How effectively is the company financed in terms of debt and equity?"	
Debt to Equity	Total Liabilities / Total Stockholders' Equity
Financial Leverage Index	Return on Equity / Return on Assets
Debt Ratio	Total Liabilities / Total Assets
Interest Coverage (Times Interest Earned)	(Net Income + Interest Expense + Tax Expense) / Interest Expense
Long-Term Debt to Equity	Long-Term Liabilities / Total Stockholders' Equity
Debt to Market Equity	Total Liabilities at Book Value / Total Equity at Market Value
Bonded Debt to Equity	Bonded Debt / Stockholders' Equity
Debt to Tangible Net Worth	Total Liabilities / (Common Equity − Intangible Assets)
Liquidity Ratios: "How capable is the company of meeting its short-term obligations?"	
Current	Current Assets / Current Liabilities
Quick (Acid-Test)	(Cash + Marketable Securities + Net Receivables) / Current Liabilities
Cash	(Cash + Marketable Securities) / Current Liabilities
Operating Cash Flow	Cash Flow from Operations / Current Liabilities
Cash to Current Assets	(Cash + Marketable Securities) / Current Assets
Cash Position	Cash / Total Assets
Current Liability Position	Current Liabilities / Total Assets
Market Ratios: "How does the company's performance compare to other companies?"	
Book Value per Share	Total Stockholders' Equity / Number of Shares Outstanding
Earnings-Based Growth Models	$P = kE / (r - g)$, where k = Dividend Payout Rate, E = Earnings, r = Discount Rate, and g = Earnings Growth Rate
Market-to-Book	(Stock Price × Number of Shares Outstanding) / Total Stockholders' Equity
Price-Earnings (PE) Ratio	Stock Price / EPS
Price-Earnings Growth (PEG) Ratio	PE / Earnings Growth Rate
Sales-to-Market Value	Sales / (Stock Price × Number of Shares Outstanding)
Dividend Yield	Dividends per Share / Stock Price
Total Return to Shareholders	Stock Price Appreciation + Dividends